Business
Plans
Handbook

FOR REFERENCE ONLY
DO NOT REMOVE FROM THIS ROOM

Business Plans Handbook

A COMPILATION OF BUSINESS PLANS DEVELOPED BY INDIVIDUALS THROUGHOUT NORTH AMERICA

WITHDRAWN

VOLUME

32

Kristin B. Mallegg, Project Editor

HD
62
.7
.B865
v32

GALE
CENGAGE Learning

Farmington Hills, Mich • San Francisco • New York • Waterville, Maine
Meriden, Conn • Mason, Ohio • Chicago

LIBRARY

COLLEGE OF SOUTHERN MARYLAND
LA PLATA CAMPUS

Business Plans Handbook, Volume 32

Project Editor: Kristin B. Mallegg

Content Developer: Michele P. LaMeau

Product Design: Jennifer Wahi

Composition and Electronic Prepress: Evi Seoud

Manufacturing: Rita Wimberley

© 2015 Gale, Cengage Learning

WCN: 01-100-101

ALL RIGHTS RESERVED. No part of this work covered by the copyright herein may be reproduced, transmitted, stored, or used in any form or by any means graphic, electronic, or mechanical, including but not limited to photocopying, recording, scanning, digitizing, taping, Web distribution, information networks, or information storage and retrieval systems, except as permitted under Section 107 or 108 of the 1976 United States Copyright Act, without the prior written permission of the publisher.

This publication is a creative work fully protected by all applicable copyright laws, as well as by misappropriation, trade secret, unfair competition, and other applicable laws. The authors and editors of this work have added value to the underlying factual material herein through one or more of the following: unique and original selection, coordination, expression, arrangement, and classification of the information.

For product information and technology assistance, contact us at
Gale Customer Support, 1-800-877-4253.
For permission to use material from this text or product,
submit all requests online at **www.cengage.com/permissions.**
Further permissions questions can be emailed to
permissionrequest@cengage.com

While every effort has been made to ensure the reliability of the information presented in this publication, Gale, a part of Cengage Learning, does not guarantee the accuracy of the data contained herein. Gale accepts no payment for listing; and inclusion in the publication of any organization, agency, institution, publication, service, or individual does not imply endorsement of the editors or publisher. Errors brought to the attention of the publisher and verified to the satisfaction of the publisher will be corrected in future editions.

Gale, a part of Cengage Learning
27500 Drake Rd.
Farmington Hills, MI 48331-3535

ISBN-13: 978-1-56995-843-8
1084-4473

Printed in Mexico
1 2 3 4 5 6 7 19 18 17 16 15

Contents

BUSINESS PLANS

CONTENTS

Highlights

Business Plans Handbook, Volume 32 (BPH-32) is a collection of business plans compiled by entrepreneurs seeking funding for small businesses throughout North America. For those looking for examples of how to approach, structure, and compose their own business plans, *BPH-32* presents 20 sample plans, including plans for the following businesses:

- 3D Archery Range
- ATM Sales and Service Company
- Bail Bonding
- Concealed Carry Training Business
- Country Club
- Credit Monitoring Service
- Electronic Waste Collection Service
- Food Truck
- General Contractor
- Gluten-Free Bakery
- Home Energy Auditor
- Interactive Testing Service
- Multilevel Marketing Company
- Nonprofit Organization
- Organic Grower and Supplier
- Pet Boarding
- Pet Services Coordination Business
- Shooting Range
- Sports Tournament Organizer
- Tour Company

FEATURES AND BENEFITS

BPH-32 offers many features not provided by other business planning references including:

- Twenty business plans, each of which represent an attempt at clarifying (for themselves and others) the reasons that the business should exist or expand and why a lender should fund the enterprise.
- Two fictional plans that are used by business counselors at a prominent small business development organization as examples for their clients. (You will find these in the Business Plan Template Appendix.)

- A directory section that includes listings for venture capital and finance companies, which specialize in funding start-up and second-stage small business ventures, and a comprehensive listing of Service Corps of Retired Executives (SCORE) offices. In addition, the Appendix also contains updated listings of all Small Business Development Centers (SBDCs); associations of interest to entrepreneurs; Small Business Administration (SBA) Regional Offices; and consultants specializing in small business planning and advice. It is strongly advised that you consult supporting organizations while planning your business, as they can provide a wealth of useful information.

- A Small Business Term Glossary to help you decipher the sometimes confusing terminology used by lenders and others in the financial and small business communities.

- A cumulative index, outlining each plan profiled in the complete Business Plans Handbook series.

- A Business Plan Template which serves as a model to help you construct your own business plan. This generic outline lists all the essential elements of a complete business plan and their components, including the Summary, Business History and Industry Outlook, Market Examination, Competition, Marketing, Administration and Management, Financial Information, and other key sections. Use this guide as a starting point for compiling your plan.

- Extensive financial documentation required to solicit funding from small business lenders. You will find examples of Cash Flows, Balance Sheets, Income Projections, and other financial information included with the textual portions of the plan.

Introduction

Perhaps the most important aspect of business planning is simply doing it. More and more business owners are beginning to compile business plans even if they don't need a bank loan. Others discover the value of planning when they must provide a business plan for the bank. The sheer act of putting thoughts on paper seems to clarify priorities and provide focus. Sometimes business owners completely change strategies when compiling their plan, deciding on a different product mix or advertising scheme after finding that their assumptions were incorrect. This kind of healthy thinking and re-thinking via business planning is becoming the norm. The editors of *Business Plans Handbook, Volume 32 (BPH-32)* sincerely hope that this latest addition to the series is a helpful tool in the successful completion of your business plan, no matter what the reason for creating it.

This thirty-second volume, like each volume in the series, offers business plans created by real people. *BPH-32* provides 20 business plans. The business and personal names and addresses and general locations have been changed to protect the privacy of the plan authors.

NEW BUSINESS OPPORTUNITIES

As in other volumes in the series, *BPH-32* finds entrepreneurs engaged in a wide variety of creative endeavors. Examples include a gluten-free bakery, a general contractor, and a credit monitoring service. In addition, several other plans are provided, including a country club, a home energy auditor, and a food truck, among others.

Comprehensive financial documentation has become increasingly important as today's entrepreneurs compete for the finite resources of business lenders. Our plans illustrate the financial data generally required of loan applicants, including Income Statements, Financial Projections, Cash Flows, and Balance Sheets.

ENHANCED APPENDIXES

In an effort to provide the most relevant and valuable information for our readers, we have updated the coverage of small business resources. For instance, you will find a directory section, which includes listings of all of the Service Corps of Retired Executives (SCORE) offices; an informative glossary, which includes small business terms; and a cumulative index, outlining each plan profiled in the complete *Business Plans Handbook* series. In addition we have updated the list of Small Business Development Centers (SBDCs); Small Business Administration Regional Offices; venture capital and finance companies, which specialize in funding start-up and second-stage small business enterprises; associations of interest to entrepreneurs; and consultants, specializing in small business advice and planning. For your reference, we have also reprinted the business plan template, which provides a comprehensive overview of the essential components of a business plan and two fictional plans used by small business counselors.

SERIES INFORMATION

If you already have the first thirty-one volumes of *BPH*, with this thirty-second volume, you will now have a collection of over 600 business plans (not including the updated plans); contact information for hundreds of organizations and agencies offering business expertise; a helpful business plan template; more than 1,500 citations to valuable small business development material; and a comprehensive glossary of terms to help the business planner navigate the sometimes confusing language of entrepreneurship.

ACKNOWLEDGEMENTS

The Editors wish to sincerely thank the contributors to *BPH-32*, including:

- BizPlanDB.com
- Fran Fletcher
- Paul Greenland
- Claire Moore
- Zuzu Enterprises

COMMENTS WELCOME

Your comments on *Business Plans Handbook* are appreciated. Please direct all correspondence, suggestions for future volumes of *BPH*, and other recommendations to the following:

Managing Editor, Business Product
Business Plans Handbook
Gale, a part of Cengage Learning
27500 Drake Rd.
Farmington Hills, MI 48331-3535
Phone: (248)699-4253
Fax: (248)699-8052
Toll-Free: 800-347-GALE
E-mail: BusinessProducts@gale.com

3D Archery Range
ALL-AMERICAN ARCHERY, LLC

1674 Seminole Wind Hwy.
Jesup, Georgia 31546

Fran Fletcher

All-American Archery, LLC is a 3D archery range located in the heart of Georgia deer country. Owners John Moss and Hunter Helms envision an outdoor archery range made up of 25 shooting lanes, each with a 3D life-like animal mannequin.

BUSINESS SUMMARY

All-American Archery, LLC is a 3D archery range located in the heart of Georgia deer country. Owners John Moss and Hunter Helms envision an outdoor archery range made up of 25 shooting lanes, each with a 3D life-like animal mannequin.

Just minutes from Jesup, Georgia, All-American Archery is a place where hunters of all ages and abilities can shoot for fun or enjoy friendly competition.

All-American Archery will stock a selection of archery accessories and offer bow and arrow rental. Hunter Helms will provide archery instruction and arrow fletching services.

According to the Bureau of Labor Statistics, the job outlook for recreation industries is expected to increase by 18% from 2010 to 2020. Additionally, the National Hunting Association reports that there are currently more than 400,000 hunters in Georgia. The number of bow hunters is expected to increase by 10 percent each year for the next five years. This increase is contributed to an ever-growing number of hunters who want to take advantage of an extended hunting season and who want to make hunting more challenging.

All-American Archery will target Southeast Georgia hunters of all ages and abilities who want to practice archery on life-sized mannequins to improve their hunting skills.

There are no other comparable archery ranges in the immediate area. All-American Archery plans to set itself apart from the competition with the number and variety of targets that it offers.

The growth strategy of All-American Archery is simply to provide superior customer service in a safe but fun atmosphere. The archery range will be modified each year to update and improve the course. This will encourage current members to renew their memberships year after year and to refer the archery range to friends and family.

All-American Archery, LLC is currently seeking financing in the form of a business line of credit in the amount of $67,000. This will cover start-up and operating expenses for the first three months. The owners plan to apply one third of its annual profits to make a lump sum payment at the end of each year. This should enable the company to repay the line of credit in two years.

COMPANY DESCRIPTION

All-American Archery, LLC is an outdoor archery range consisting of 25 shooting lanes, each with a 3D life-like animal mannequin. Archers can shoot for fun or enjoy friendly competition using the club's point system. All-American Archery will offer club memberships but will also have limited hours that are open to the public. The range will regularly host tournaments for archers of all ages and abilities.

Location

All-American Archery is located on ten acres in rural Wayne County, Georgia. The 3D archery range is located approximately five miles outside of Jesup and is located on a main highway, which will provide easy access to patrons from the Fort Savannah military base and other nearby areas.

Hours of Operation

All-American Archery will operate as follows:

Members Only Hours

Monday—Friday, 10 AM—2 PM

Saturday, 8 AM—dark

Sunday, 10 AM—dark

Public Access Hours

Monday—Friday, 3 PM—dark

Personnel

John Moss

Mr. Moss is currently the owner of Jesup Insurance Agency and holds a B.S. in Business. He has been an avid hunter for twenty years. Ten years ago, he became interested in archery, and has been bow hunting ever since. Mr. Moss will serve as the Finance Manager for All-American Archery.

Hunter Helms

Mr. Helms has competed in various archery tournaments for the last ten years, starting with 4H. He most recently was a member of the Georgia Southern College archery team and traveled all over the United States competing against the top teams in the nation. He earned the "Top Shot" award for American Colleges and Universities two years in a row. Mr. Helms will serve as the Operations Manager and will oversee the daily activities of the archery range.

Range Workers

Two part-time range workers will assist with business operations. Additional workers will be hired as needed.

Products and Services

Products

All American Archery will stock various archery accessories for purchase. Products include:

- Arrows
- Quivers
- Arm guards
- Bow sights
- Releases
- Arrow rests

Services

All-American Archery will provide a 3D archery range with a variety of life-like mannequins.

Mannequins include:

Elk	Strutting turkey	Big horn sheep	Red fox	African lion
Large deer	Gobbling turkey	Mountain goat	Coyote	Leopard
Grazing deer	Medium black bear	Mule deer	Bobcat	Antelope
Alert deer	Standing black bear	Bison	Cougar	Warthog
Bedded deer	Climbing bear	Wolf	Alligator	Hyena

In addition to use of the archery range, services provided by All-American Archery include:

- Equipment rental

- Archery instruction

- Arrow fletching

- Arrow straightening

- Parties/Group events

MARKET ANALYSIS

Industry Overview

According to the Bureau of Labor Statistics, the job outlook for recreation industries is expected to increase by 18% from 2010 to 2020. *American Hunter* magazine reports that $22.9 billion dollars is spent annually on hunting expenditures in the U.S., or approximately $2,000 per hunter.

According to the National Hunting Association, there are more than 400,000 hunters in Georgia. The number of bow hunters is expected to increase by 10 percent each year for the next five years. This increase is attributed to an ever-growing number of hunters who want to take advantage of an extended hunting season and who want to make hunting more challenging.

Target Market

All-American Archery will target area hunters of all ages and abilities who want to practice archery on life-sized mannequins to improve their hunting skills.

According to demographic data, Jesup and surrounding counties had a male population of approximately 175,936 in 2010. If 10% of those males are hunters, there are 17,000 potential clients in the area surrounding Wayne County.

Competition

All-American Archery wants to give its customers the opportunity to experience practicing on life-like wildlife mannequins to improve their archery skills. Some of these mannequins will also move to make the experience mimic a true hunting scenario. There are two other businesses that offer archery targets within a 100-mile radius.

1. Deer Pro Store, Savannah, Georgia—Offers a variety of hunting merchandise, including bows, arrows, and targets. Store has a small indoor archery range mainly for trying out archery accessories before purchasing. Targets include one deer and one turkey.

2. Top Targets, Brunswick, Georgia—Offers ten traditional round targets and two animal targets.

All-American Archery plans to set itself apart from the competition with the number and variety of targets that it offers.

GROWTH STRATEGY

The company's growth strategy is to simply provide superior customer service in a safe but fun atmosphere. Each year, the range will be modified and improved in order to keep the archery range interesting. This strategy should encourage current members to renew their memberships year after year and to refer the archery range to friends and family.

The owners hope to achieve financial independence during the first two years of operation and will hire additional personnel as needed. The owners will also consider building an indoor range or opening an additional location as dictated by customer interest after it reaches financial independence.

Sales and Marketing

The company has identified key sales and marketing strategies to support the company's growth. The owners will start advertising two months before opening to create anticipation and excitement. They will also begin selling memberships one month before opening. Anyone who buys a membership during the presale will be invited to attend an exclusive preview party with refreshments and giveaways. The owners will also participate in area hunting expos to reach potential clients.

Advertising will include:

- Partnering/advertising with local hunting retailers

- Advertising in area newspapers

- Using social media

Ongoing marketing strategies include:

- Hosting a booth at hunting tradeshows

- Special events i.e. tournaments, military appreciation

- Offering a military/veterans discount

FINANCIAL ANALYSIS

Start-up Costs

The owners have purchased ten acres for the archery range and a small clubhouse. The land was cleared to suit their purpose before they purchased it. They will initially purchase twenty-five 3D targets. These targets have a middle insert that will need replacing in approximately six months. The cost of replacement will be built into the monthly expenses. Additionally, five bows for kids, five adult compound bows, five long bows, and numerous arrows will be bought that will be used for rentals.

Estimated start-up costs

Land (10 acres)	$20,000
Clubhouse	$20,000
Legal fees	$ 3,000
Business license	$ 250
Initial advertising	$ 500
Insurance	$ 500
Animal mannequins	$ 7,000
Fletching machine	$ 250
Arrow straighteners	$ 400
Moving targets	$ 1,000
Bow hangers	$ 500
Bows and arrows (for rental)	$ 4,000
Inventory (archery accessories)	$ 1,800
Membership cards	$ 200
Total	**$59,400**

Estimated Monthly Expenses

Monthly expenses are expected to remain constant. The owners will purchase two mannequin inserts each month to spread out the cost of replacement.

Monthly expenses

Loan payment, including land	$1,000
Mannequin inserts	$ 600
Phone/internet	$ 150
Advertising	$ 100
Insurance	$ 250
Wages owners	$2,680
Wages employees	$ 768
Club house supplies	$ 250
Drink/snack machine rental	$ 200
Total	**$5,998**

Estimated Monthly Income

The number of memberships sold each month will determine income. All-American Archery will begin selling memberships one month before opening. Members will be required to sign a one-year contract and must pay in full or sign up for monthly bank drafts. This will ensure a steady monthly income.

Membership

All-American Archery will offer three membership levels. Memberships will include:

	Individual	Kids (under 16)	Family**
Price (per month)*	$80	$25	$150
Safety/training session	yes	yes	yes
Guest pass	1 per month	no	1 per month
Arrow fletching	10 free/year	5 free/year	15 free/year
Bow rental	yes	yes	yes
Special days/times	yes	yes	yes
Discounted parties	yes	no	yes
Discounted merchandise	10%	no	10%
Discounted instruction	$10 off each lesson	$10 off each lesson	$10 off each lesson

*Monthly installments are only available when using an automatic bank draft.
**Family memberships are for families of four. Each additional family member is $50 per year.

Non-members will be charged $30 for one round and $40 for two rounds.

Archery Instruction

Mr. Helms will offer archery instruction in both private and group settings. Members will receive a $10 discount per lesson.

Instruction	Price (Per ½ hour)
Individual	$40
Group (5+)	$20
Non member	$40

Safety

Safety will be extremely important to business sustainability. Anyone found breaking safety rules will be asked to leave and their membership revoked. Rules will be posted on the range and will be included on the release waiver. All customers must adhere to the following safety rules:

1. Everyone must sign in before using the range

2. Members must sign a release waiver annually and nonmembers must sign a release waiver before using the range

3. No alcohol allowed on the range

4. Shoot only from established shooting lanes

5. Make sure the group in front of you is clear before advancing and shooting

6. Do not move or modify lanes or targets

7. Prop your bow in front of target in plain view while looking for arrows

8. Only shoot the designated target

9. Persons under age 16 must be accompanied by an adult age 25 or older

Additional rules that will ensure a more enjoyable experience for all customers include:

1. Allow smaller groups of hunters to play through if your group is larger or moving more slowly

2. Only one shot is allowed per target per round

3. Dispose of trash in receptacles

Profit/Loss

The owners hope to sell a minimum of 50 individual, 12 family, and 10 kid memberships during its presale event. If this goal is met, the business will break even. The owners hope to gain additional customers through referrals once the range is open. Conservative estimates show that the number of new memberships during the first three months of business will be approximately 15 individual, 3 family, and 3 kid memberships. This will increase the monthly income as shown in the "Monthly Profit/Loss" table. The first month's income includes memberships that were sold prior to opening as well as the memberships sold during the first month of operation.

New memberships will most likely show a decline during the summer months and during bow hunting season. Profit estimates used in this plan include memberships sold during the first three months only. Income generated through instruction, merchandise sales, and group events are not considered when generating monthly profit/loss data. Estimated profits are demonstrated in the "Annual Profit/Loss" chart. Profits should remain steady during the second year of operation.

Monthly profit/loss

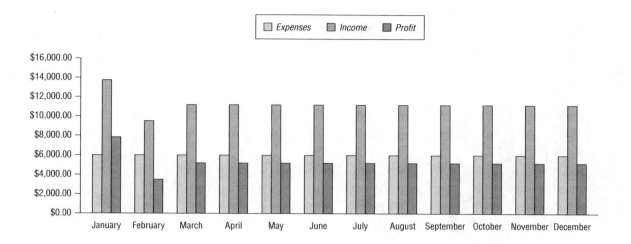

Annual profit/loss

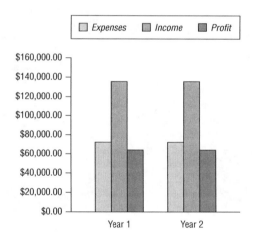

Financing

All-American Archery, LLC is currently seeking financing in the form of a business line of credit in the amount of $67,000. This will cover start-up and operating expenses for the first three months. The owners plan to apply one third of its annual profits to make a lump sum payment at the end of each year. The "Repayment Plan" chart illustrates that the line of credit will be repaid in two years.

Repayment plan

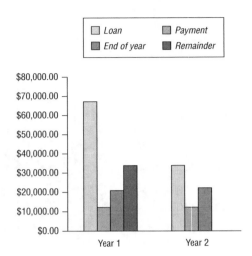

ATM Sales and Service Company

American ATM Sales and Service Company, Inc.

4533 Capitol Blvd.
Staten Island, NY 10301

BizPlanDB.com

American ATM Sales and Service Company, Inc.is a New York-based corporation that will manage several stand-alone ATM machines in grocery stores and malls throughout the state. The Company was founded by Michael Barrows.

1.0 EXECUTIVE SUMMARY

The purpose of this business plan is to raise $100,000 for the development of a business that manages a network of ATM machines while showcasing the expected financials and operations over the next three years. American ATM Sales and Service Company, Inc. ("the Company") is a New York-based corporation that will manage several stand-alone ATM machines in grocery stores and malls throughout the state. The Company was founded by Michael Barrows.

1.1 The Services

As stated above, the Company's state-of-the-art ATM machines will provide customers with access to cash. The Company will provide location partners with a 30% revenue share for all income derived from each ATM machine.

The Founder, prior to the onset of operations, will develop relationships with malls, grocery stores, and property managers for the distribution of the Company's ATM machines.

The third section of the business plan will further describe the services offered by American ATM Sales and Service Company, Inc.

1.2 Financing

Mr. Barrows is seeking to raise $100,000 from a bank loan. The interest rate and loan agreement are to be further discussed during negotiation. This business plan assumes that the business will receive a 10-year loan with a 9% fixed interest rate. The financing will be used for the following:

- Acquisition and distribution of at least 8 ATM machines.

- Financing for the first six months of operation.

- Capital to purchase the inventory of monies.

Mr. Barrows will contribute $10,000 to the venture.

1.3 Mission Statement

Mr. Barrows' mission is to provide quick access to cash to customers while concurrently ensuring that businesses and organizations that allow the Company's machines on-site are compensated for the use of their space.

1.4 Management Team

The Company was founded by Michael Barrows. Mr. Barrows has more than 10 years of experience in the retail industry. Through his expertise, he will be able to bring the operations of the business to profitability within its first year of operations.

1.5 Sales Forecasts

Mr. Barrows expects a strong rate of growth at the start of operations. Below are the expected financials over the next three years.

Proforma profit and loss (yearly)

Year	1	2	3
Sales	$378,600	$454,320	$531,554
Operating costs	$188,688	$196,351	$204,301
EBITDA	$ 76,332	$121,673	$167,787
Taxes, interest, and depreciation	$ 43,815	$ 57,348	$ 74,461
Net profit	$ 32,517	$ 64,324	$ 93,326

Sales, operating costs, and profit forecast

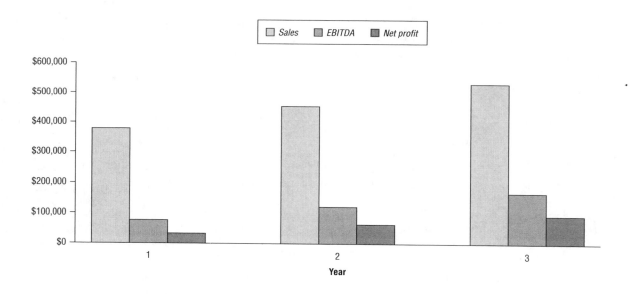

1.6 Expansion Plan

Over the next three years, Mr. Barrows intends to reinvest the after-tax cash flow of the business into the purchase of new ATM machines which will substantially increase the revenues of the business. The Company will continually source new high-traffic locations where the business can place additional ATM machines.

2.0 COMPANY AND FINANCING SUMMARY

2.1 Registered Name and Corporate Structure

American ATM Sales and Service Company, Inc. is registered as a corporation in the State of New York.

2.2 Required Funds

At this time, American ATM Sales and Service Company, Inc. requires $100,000 of debt funds. Below is a breakdown of how these funds will be used:

Projected startup costs

Working capital	$ 35,000
General FF&E	$ 10,000
ATM machines	$ 45,000
Inventory	$ 5,000
Insurance	$ 2,500
Distribution budget	$ 7,500
Miscellaneous and unforeseen costs	$ 5,000
Total startup costs	**$110,000**

Use of funds

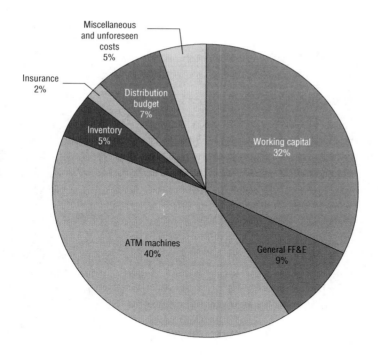

2.3 Investor Equity

Mr. Barrows is not seeking an investment from a third party at this time.

2.4 Management Equity

Michael Barrows owns 100% of American ATM Sales and Service Company, Inc.

2.5 Exit Strategy

If the business is very successful, Mr. Barrows may seek to sell the business to a third party for a significant earnings multiple. Most likely, the Company will hire a qualified business broker to sell the business on behalf of American ATM Sales and Service Company, Inc. Based on historical numbers, the business could fetch a sales premium of up to 4 times earnings.

3.0 PRODUCTS AND SERVICES

As stated in the executive summary, the Company will be actively engaged in the business of developing a network of Automated Teller Machines (ATMs) that will be placed among several locations within the New York metropolitan region. These machines will provide customers with the ability to make financial transactions from their debit or credit cards including cash withdrawals and transfers of money to separate accounts.

Management has already sourced a distributor that will provide ATM machines that will be used in conjunction with the business.

In exchange for placing an ATM machine on a property or within a store, the Company will provide a share of the revenues generated from ATM transactions.

3.1 ATM Servicing

The Company will maintain service contracts with a nationally recognized ATM machine service business that renders these services.

4.0 STRATEGIC AND MARKET ANALYSIS

4.1 Economic Outlook

The business of ATM machine management is a relatively simple business. This section of analysis will detail the overall economic climate, the interest rate environment, and the industry.

Currently, the economic market condition in the United States is moderate. The economy has improved substantially over the past three years. The number of new businesses has increased significantly, asset class prices have risen, and unemployment rates have dropped. It should be noted that the low pricing point of the Company's ATM usage services will ensure that the Company can remain profitable despite any current issues with the economy.

4.2 Industry Analysis

Within the United States, there are more than 7,000 companies that are actively engaged in the sale, management, and servicing of ATM machines. In each of the last five years, these companies have aggregately generated more than $14.4 billion of revenues while providing jobs to more than 125,000 people. Total payrolls in each of the last five years have exceeded $5 billion.

This is a mature industry, and the expected growth rate during the next five to ten years is expected to mirror that of the general economy.

4.3 Customer Profile

Among the retailers that will serve as locations for the Company's ATMs, Management has outlined the general characteristics of this user base:

- Operates in a retail capacity.

- Is located within the New York metropolitan area.

- Has annual revenues of $200,000 to $1,000,000+.

- Is seeking to expand revenue base through ancillary onsite services via the use of ATM machines.

4.4 Competition

At this time it is difficult to determine the competition that the Company will face as it progresses through its operations. There are a number of companies that maintain ATM machines within grocery stores, apartment buildings, and malls.

5.0 MARKETING PLAN

Below is a description of the marketing plan that American ATM Sales and Service Company, Inc. will use to establish its locations throughout the State of New York.

5.1 Marketing Objectives

- Establish relationships with property management firms, grocery stores, and malls.

- Maintain strong relationships with ATM machine equipment wholesalers throughout the State of New York.

5.2 Marketing Strategies

Marketing for the business' ATM machines will be very limited. The Company's marketing campaigns will be limited to developing relationships with property management firms. Prior to the onset of operations, Mr. Barrows will approach these businesses for placing ATM machines on their properties.

The Company intends to also develop a website that will showcase the operations of the business, how a potential location can work with ATM Sales and Service Company, Inc., and relevant contact information. As the economy is currently recovering, many property management firms and related organizations are looking for ways to establish secondary lines of revenue; namely through the rental of space to ATM machine businesses.

Management will also directly approach newly developed properties that are looking to expand their secondary revenue streams as well.

5.3 Pricing

The business will receive approximately 70 cents of operating income per dollar for each transaction carried out through ATM machines owned and operated by the Company.

6.0 ORGANIZATIONAL PLAN AND PERSONNEL SUMMARY

6.1 Corporate Organization

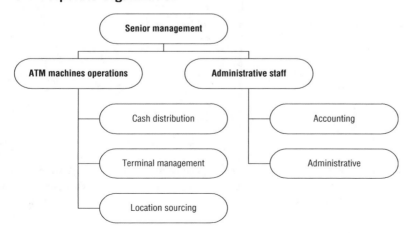

6.2 Organizational Budget

Personnel plan—yearly

Year	1	2	3
Owner	$ 40,000	$ 41,200	$ 42,436
Owner's assistant	$ 35,000	$ 36,050	$ 37,132
ATM machine manager	$ 32,500	$ 33,475	$ 34,479
Accountant (P/T)	$ 12,500	$ 12,875	$ 13,261
Total	**$120,000**	**$123,600**	**$127,308**

Numbers of personnel

Owner	1	1	1
Owner's assistant	1	1	1
ATM machine manager	1	1	1
Accountant (P/T)	1	1	1
Totals	**4**	**4**	**4**

Personnel expense breakdown

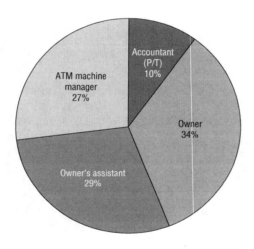

7.0 FINANCIAL PLAN

7.1 Underlying Assumptions

The Company has based its proforma financial statements on the following:

- American ATM Sales and Service Company, Inc. will have an annual revenue growth rate of 16% per year.

- The Owner will acquire $100,000 of debt funds to develop the business.

- The loan will have a 10-year term with a 9% interest rate.

7.2 Sensitivity Analysis

The Company's revenues are not sensitive to changes in the general economy. The demand for people to have access to physical cash does not fluctuate. As such, Management will be able to continually grow the business despite the external business climate.

7.3 Source of Funds

Financing

Equity contributions

Management investment	$ 10,000.00
Total equity financing	**$ 10,000.00**
Banks and lenders	
Banks and lenders	$ 100,000.00
Total debt financing	**$100,000.00**
Total financing	**$110,000.00**

7.4 General Assumptions

General assumptions

Year	1	2	3
Short term interest rate	9.5%	9.5%	9.5%
Long term interest rate	10.0%	10.0%	10.0%
Federal tax rate	33.0%	33.0%	33.0%
State tax rate	5.0%	5.0%	5.0%
Personnel taxes	15.0%	15.0%	15.0%

7.5 Profit and Loss Statements

Proforma profit and loss (yearly)

Year	1	2	3
Sales	**$378,600**	**$454,320**	**$531,554**
Cost of goods sold	$113,580	$136,296	$159,466
Gross margin	70.00%	70.00%	70.00%
Operating income	**$265,020**	**$318,024**	**$372,088**
Expenses			
Payroll	$120,000	$123,600	$127,308
General and administrative	$ 25,200	$ 26,208	$ 27,256
Marketing expenses	$ 1,893	$ 2,272	$ 2,658
Professional fees and licensure	$ 5,219	$ 5,376	$ 5,537
Insurance costs	$ 1,987	$ 2,086	$ 2,191
Travel and vehicle costs	$ 7,596	$ 8,356	$ 9,191
Rent and utilities	$ 4,250	$ 4,463	$ 4,686
Miscellaneous costs	$ 4,543	$ 5,452	$ 6,379
Payroll taxes	$ 18,000	$ 18,540	$ 19,096
Total operating costs	**$188,688**	**$196,351**	**$204,301**
EBITDA	**$ 76,332**	**$121,673**	**$167,787**
Federal income tax	$ 25,189	$ 37,469	$ 52,905
State income tax	$ 3,817	$ 5,677	$ 8,016
Interest expense	$ 8,738	$ 8,131	$ 7,468
Depreciation expenses	$ 6,071	$ 6,071	$ 6,071
Net profit	**$ 32,517**	**$ 64,324**	**$ 93,326**
Profit margin	**8.59%**	**14.16%**	**17.56%**

Sales, operating costs, and profit forecast

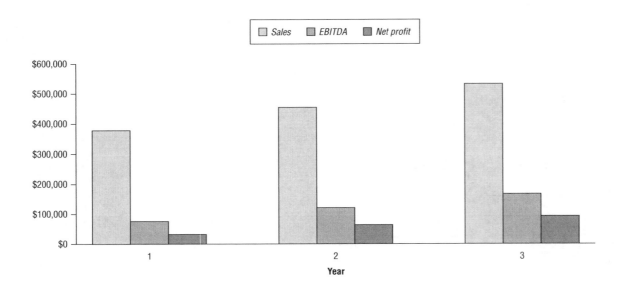

7.6 Cash Flow Analysis

Proforma cash flow analysis—yearly

Year	1	2	3
Cash from operations	$ 38,588	$ 70,396	$ 99,398
Cash from receivables	$ 0	$ 0	$0
Operating cash inflow	**$ 38,588**	**$ 70,396**	**$ 99,398**
Other cash inflows			
Equity investment	$ 10,000	$ 0	$ 0
Increased borrowings	$100,000	$ 0	$ 0
Sales of business assets	$ 0	$ 0	$ 0
A/P increases	$ 37,902	$ 43,587	$ 50,125
Total other cash inflows	**$147,902**	**$ 43,587**	**$ 50,125**
Total cash inflow	**$186,490**	**$113,983**	**$149,523**
Cash outflows			
Repayment of principal	$ 6,463	$ 7,070	$ 7,733
A/P decreases	$ 24,897	$ 29,876	$ 35,852
A/R increases	$ 0	$ 0	$ 0
Asset purchases	$ 85,000	$ 17,599	$ 24,849
Dividends	$ 27,012	$ 49,277	$ 69,578
Total cash outflows	**$143,372**	**$103,822**	**$138,012**
Net cash flow	**$ 43,118**	**$ 10,161**	**$ 11,511**
Cash balance	**$ 43,118**	**$ 53,279**	**$ 64,790**

Proforma cash flow (yearly)

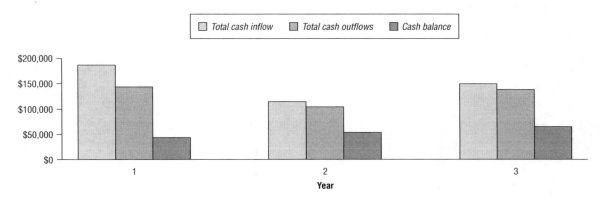

7.7 Balance Sheet

Proforma balance sheet—yearly

Year	1	2	3
Assets			
Cash	$ 43,118	$ 53,279	$ 64,790
Amortized development/expansion costs	$ 30,000	$ 34,400	$ 40,612
FF&E	$ 10,000	$ 10,000	$ 10,000
ATM machines	$ 45,000	$ 58,199	$ 76,836
Accumulated depreciation	($ 6,071)	($ 12,143)	($ 18,214)
Total assets	**$122,047**	**$143,735**	**$174,024**
Liabilities and equity			
Accounts payable	$ 13,005	$ 26,716	$ 40,990
Long term liabilities	$ 93,537	$ 86,467	$ 79,397
Other liabilities	$ 0	$ 0	$ 0
Total liabilities	**$106,542**	**$113,183**	**$120,387**
Net worth	**$ 15,505**	**$ 30,552**	**$ 53,637**
Total liabilities and equity	**$122,047**	**$143,735**	**$174,024**

Proforma balance sheet

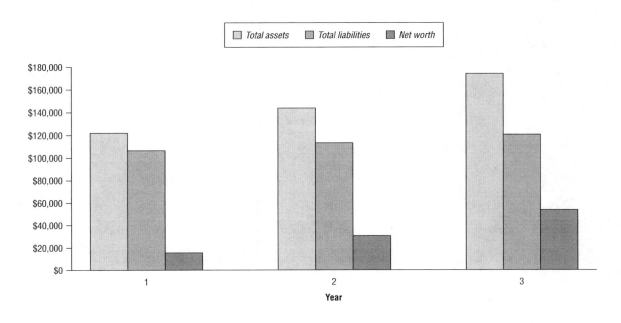

7.8 Breakeven Analysis

Monthly break even analysis

Year	1	2	3
Monthly revenue	$ 22,463	$ 23,375	$ 24,322
Yearly revenue	$269,555	$280,502	$291,859

Break even analysis

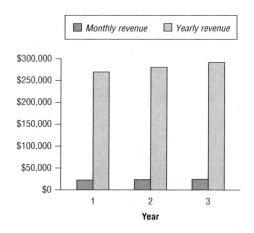

7.9 Business Ratios

Business ratios—yearly

Year	1	2	3
Sales			
Sales growth	0.0%	20.0%	17.0%
Gross margin	70.0%	70.0%	70.0%
Financials			
Profit margin	8.59%	14.16%	17.56%
Assets to liabilities	1.15	1.27	1.45
Equity to liabilities	0.15	0.27	0.45
Assets to equity	7.87	4.70	3.24
Liquidity			
Acid test	0.40	0.47	0.54
Cash to assets	0.35	0.37	0.37

7.10 Three Year Profit and Loss Statement

Profit and loss statement (first year)

Months	1	2	3	4	5	6	7
Sales	**$31,000**	**$31,100**	**$31,200**	**$31,300**	**$31,400**	**$31,500**	**$31,600**
Cost of goods sold	$ 9,300	$ 9,330	$ 9,360	$ 9,390	$ 9,420	$ 9,450	$ 9,480
Gross margin	70.0%	70.0%	70.0%	70.0%	70.0%	70.0%	70.0%
Operating income	**$21,700**	**$21,770**	**$21,840**	**$21,910**	**$21,980**	**$22,050**	**$22,120**
Expenses							
Payroll	$10,000	$10,000	$10,000	$10,000	$10,000	$10,000	$10,000
General and administrative	$ 2,100	$ 2,100	$ 2,100	$ 2,100	$ 2,100	$ 2,100	$ 2,100
Marketing expenses	$ 158	$ 158	$ 158	$ 158	$ 158	$ 158	$ 158
Professional fees and licensure	$ 435	$ 435	$ 435	$ 435	$ 435	$ 435	$ 435
Insurance costs	$ 166	$ 166	$ 166	$ 166	$ 166	$ 166	$ 166
Travel and vehicle costs	$ 633	$ 633	$ 633	$ 633	$ 633	$ 633	$ 633
Rent and utilities	$ 354	$ 354	$ 354	$ 354	$ 354	$ 354	$ 354
Miscellaneous costs	$ 379	$ 379	$ 379	$ 379	$ 379	$ 379	$ 379
Payroll taxes	$ 1,500	$ 1,500	$ 1,500	$ 1,500	$ 1,500	$ 1,500	$ 1,500
Total operating costs	**$15,724**	**$15,724**	**$15,724**	**$15,724**	**$15,724**	**$15,724**	**$15,724**
EBITDA	**$ 5,976**	**$ 6,046**	**$ 6,116**	**$ 6,186**	**$ 6,256**	**$ 6,326**	**$ 6,396**
Federal income tax	$ 2,063	$ 2,069	$ 2,076	$ 2,082	$ 2,089	$ 2,096	$ 2,102
State income tax	$ 313	$ 314	$ 315	$ 316	$ 317	$ 318	$ 319
Interest expense	$ 750	$ 746	$ 742	$ 738	$ 734	$ 730	$ 726
Depreciation expense	$ 506	$ 506	$ 506	$ 506	$ 506	$ 506	$ 506
Net profit	**$ 2,345**	**$ 2,411**	**$ 2,477**	**$ 2,544**	**$ 2,610**	**$ 2,676**	**$ 2,743**

Profit and loss statement (first year cont.)

Month	8	9	10	11	12	1
Sales	**$31,700**	**$31,800**	**$31,900**	**$32,000**	**$32,100**	**$378,600**
Cost of goods sold	$ 9,510	$ 9,540	$ 9,570	$ 9,600	$ 9,630	$113,580
Gross margin	70.0%	70.0%	70.0%	70.0%	70.0%	70.0%
Operating income	**$22,190**	**$22,260**	**$22,330**	**$22,400**	**$22,470**	**$265,020**
Expenses						
Payroll	$10,000	$10,000	$10,000	$10,000	$10,000	$120,000
General and administrative	$ 2,100	$ 2,100	$ 2,100	$ 2,100	$ 2,100	$ 25,200
Marketing expenses	$ 158	$ 158	$ 158	$ 158	$ 158	$ 1,893
Professional fees and licensure	$ 435	$ 435	$ 435	$ 435	$ 435	$ 5,219
Insurance costs	$ 166	$ 166	$ 166	$ 166	$ 166	$ 1,987
Travel and vehicle costs	$ 633	$ 633	$ 633	$ 633	$ 633	$ 7,596
Rent and utilities	$ 354	$ 354	$ 354	$ 354	$ 354	$ 4,250
Miscellaneous costs	$ 379	$ 379	$ 379	$ 379	$ 379	$ 4,543
Payroll taxes	$ 1,500	$ 1,500	$ 1,500	$ 1,500	$ 1,500	$ 18,000
Total operating costs	**$15,724**	**$15,724**	**$15,724**	**$15,724**	**$15,724**	**$188,688**
EBITDA	**$ 6,466**	**$ 6,536**	**$ 6,606**	**$ 6,676**	**$ 6,746**	**$ 76,332**
Federal income tax	$ 2,109	$ 2,116	$ 2,122	$ 2,129	$ 2,136	$ 25,189
State income tax	$ 320	$ 321	$ 322	$ 323	$ 324	$ 3,817
Interest expense	$ 722	$ 718	$ 714	$ 710	$ 706	$ 8,738
Depreciation expense	$ 506	$ 506	$ 506	$ 506	$ 506	$ 6,071
Net profit	**$ 2,809**	**$ 2,876**	**$ 2,942**	**$ 3,008**	**$ 3,075**	**$ 32,517**

ATM SALES AND SERVICE COMPANY

Profit and loss statement (second year)

Quarter	Q1	2 Q2	Q3	Q4	2
Sales	$90,864	$113,580	$122,666	$127,210	$454,320
Cost of goods sold	$27,259	$ 34,074	$ 36,800	$ 38,163	$136,296
Gross margin	70.0%	70.0%	70.0%	70.0%	70.0%
Operating income	**$63,605**	**$ 79,506**	**$ 85,866**	**$ 89,047**	**$318,024**
Expenses					
Payroll	$24,720	$ 30,900	$ 33,372	$ 34,608	$123,600
General and administrative	$ 5,242	$ 6,552	$ 7,076	$ 7,338	$ 26,208
Marketing expenses	$ 454	$ 568	$ 613	$ 636	$ 2,272
Professional fees and licensure	$ 1,075	$ 1,344	$ 1,451	$ 1,505	$ 5,376
Insurance costs	$ 417	$ 522	$ 563	$ 584	$ 2,086
Travel and vehicle costs	$ 1,671	$ 2,089	$ 2,256	$ 2,340	$ 8,356
Rent and utilities	$ 893	$ 1,116	$ 1,205	$ 1,250	$ 4,463
Miscellaneous costs	$ 1,090	$ 1,363	$ 1,472	$ 1,527	$ 5,452
Payroll taxes	$ 3,708	$ 4,635	$ 5,006	$ 5,191	$ 18,540
Total operating costs	**$39,270**	**$ 49,088**	**$ 53,015**	**$ 54,978**	**$196,351**
EBITDA	**$24,335**	**$ 30,418**	**$ 32,852**	**$ 34,068**	**$121,673**
Federal income tax	$ 7,494	$ 9,367	$ 10,117	$ 10,491	$ 37,469
State income tax	$ 1,135	$ 1,419	$ 1,533	$ 1,590	$ 5,677
Interest expense	$ 2,092	$ 2,053	$ 2,013	$ 1,973	$ 8,131
Depreciation expense	$ 1,518	$ 1,518	$ 1,518	$ 1,518	$ 6,071
Net profit	**$12,096**	**$ 16,061**	**$ 17,671**	**$ 18,497**	**$ 64,324**

Profit and loss statement (third year)

Quarter	Q1	3 Q2	Q3	Q4	3
Sales	$106,311	$132,889	$143,520	$148,835	$531,554
Cost of goods sold	$ 31,893	$ 39,867	$ 43,056	$ 44,651	$159,466
Gross margin	70.0%	70.0%	70.0%	70.0%	70.0%
Operating income	**$ 74,418**	**$ 93,022**	**$100,464**	**$104,185**	**$372,088**
Expenses					
Payroll	$ 25,462	$ 31,827	$ 34,373	$ 35,646	$127,308
General and administrative	$ 5,451	$ 6,814	$ 7,359	$ 7,632	$ 27,256
Marketing expenses	$ 532	$ 664	$ 718	$ 744	$ 2,658
Professional fees and licensure	$ 1,107	$ 1,384	$ 1,495	$ 1,550	$ 5,537
Insurance costs	$ 438	$ 548	$ 591	$ 613	$ 2,191
Travel and vehicle costs	$ 1,838	$ 2,298	$ 2,482	$ 2,574	$ 9,191
Rent and utilities	$ 937	$ 1,171	$ 1,265	$ 1,312	$ 4,686
Miscellaneous costs	$ 1,276	$ 1,595	$ 1,722	$ 1,786	$ 6,379
Payroll taxes	$ 3,819	$ 4,774	$ 5,156	$ 5,347	$ 19,096
Total operating costs	**$ 40,860**	**$ 51,075**	**$ 55,161**	**$ 57,204**	**$204,301**
EBITDA	**$ 33,557**	**$ 41,947**	**$ 45,302**	**$ 46,980**	**$167,787**
Federal income tax	$ 10,581	$ 13,226	$ 14,284	$ 14,813	$ 52,905
State income tax	$ 1,603	$ 2,004	$ 2,164	$ 2,244	$ 8,016
Interest expense	$ 1,932	$ 1,889	$ 1,846	$ 1,802	$ 7,468
Depreciation expense	$ 1,518	$ 1,518	$ 1,518	$ 1,518	$ 6,071
Net profit	**$ 17,924**	**$ 23,309**	**$ 25,490**	**$ 26,603**	**$ 93,326**

7.11 Three Year Cash Flow Analysis

Cash flow analysis (first year)

Month	1	2	3	4	5	6	7
Cash from operations	$ 2,851	$ 2,917	$ 2,983	$ 3,050	$ 3,116	$ 3,182	$ 3,249
Cash from receivables	$ 0	$ 0	$ 0	$ 0	$ 0	$ 0	$ 0
Operating cash inflow	**$ 2,851**	**$ 2,917**	**$ 2,983**	**$ 3,050**	**$ 3,116**	**$ 3,182**	**$ 3,249**
Other cash inflows							
Equity investment	$ 10,000	$ 0	$ 0	$ 0	$ 0	$ 0	$ 0
Increased borrowings	$100,000	$ 0	$ 0	$ 0	$ 0	$ 0	$ 0
Sales of business assets	$ 0	$ 0	$ 0	$ 0	$ 0	$ 0	$ 0
A/P increases	$ 3,159	$ 3,159	$ 3,159	$ 3,159	$ 3,159	$ 3,159	$ 3,159
Total other cash inflows	**$113,159**	**$ 3,159**	**$ 3,159**	**$ 3,159**	**$ 3,159**	**$ 3,159**	**$ 3,159**
Total cash inflow	**$116,009**	**$ 6,076**	**$ 6,142**	**$ 6,208**	**$ 6,274**	**$ 6,341**	**$ 6,407**
Cash outflows							
Repayment of principal	$ 517	$ 521	$ 525	$ 528	$ 532	$ 536	$ 540
A/P decreases	$ 2,075	$ 2,075	$ 2,075	$ 2,075	$ 2,075	$ 2,075	$ 2,075
A/R increases	$ 0	$ 0	$ 0	$ 0	$ 0	$ 0	$ 0
Asset purchases	$ 85,000	$ 0	$ 0	$ 0	$ 0	$ 0	$ 0
Dividends	$ 0	$ 0	$ 0	$ 0	$ 0	$ 0	$ 0
Total cash outflows	**$ 87,592**	**$ 2,595**	**$ 2,599**	**$ 2,603**	**$ 2,607**	**$ 2,611**	**$ 2,615**
Net cash flow	**$ 28,418**	**$ 3,480**	**$ 3,543**	**$ 3,605**	**$ 3,667**	**$ 3,730**	**$ 3,792**
Cash balance	**$ 28,418**	**$31,898**	**$35,441**	**$39,046**	**$42,713**	**$46,443**	**$50,235**

Cash flow analysis (first year cont.)

Month	8	9	10	11	12	1
Cash from operations	$ 3,315	$ 3,381	$ 3,448	$ 3,514	$ 3,581	$ 38,588
Cash from receivables	$ 0	$ 0	$ 0	$ 0	$ 0	$ 0
Operating cash inflow	**$ 3,315**	**$ 3,381**	**$ 3,448**	**$ 3,514**	**$ 3,581**	**$ 38,588**
Other cash inflows						
Equity investment	$ 0	$ 0	$ 0	$ 0	$ 0	$ 10,000
Increased borrowings	$ 0	$ 0	$ 0	$ 0	$ 0	$100,000
Sales of business assets	$ 0	$ 0	$ 0	$ 0	$ 0	$ 0
A/P increases	$ 3,159	$ 3,159	$ 3,159	$ 3,159	$ 3,159	$ 37,902
Total other cash inflows	**$ 3,159**	**$ 3,159**	**$ 3,159**	**$ 3,159**	**$ 3,159**	**$147,902**
Total cash inflow	**$ 6,474**	**$ 6,540**	**$ 6,606**	**$ 6,673**	**$ 6,739**	**$186,490**
Cash outflows						
Repayment of principal	$ 545	$ 549	$ 553	$ 557	$ 561	$ 6,463
A/P decreases	$ 2,075	$ 2,075	$ 2,075	$ 2,075	$ 2,075	$ 24,897
A/R increases	$ 0	$ 0	$ 0	$ 0	$ 0	$ 0
Asset purchases	$ 0	$ 0	$ 0	$ 0	$ 0	$ 85,000
Dividends	$ 0	$ 0	$ 0	$ 0	$27,012	$ 27,012
Total cash outflows	**$ 2,619**	**$ 2,623**	**$ 2,627**	**$ 2,632**	**$29,648**	**$143,372**
Net cash flow	**$ 3,854**	**$ 3,917**	**$ 3,979**	**$ 4,041**	**−$22,908**	**$ 43,118**
Cash balance	**$54,089**	**$58,006**	**$61,985**	**$66,026**	**$43,118**	**$ 43,118**

Cash flow analysis (second year)

| | | 2 | | | |
Quarter	Q1	Q2	Q3	Q4	2
Cash from operations	$14,079	$17,599	$19,007	$19,711	$ 70,396
Cash from receivables	$ 0	$ 0	$ 0	$ 0	$ 0
Operating cash inflow	**$14,079**	**$17,599**	**$19,007**	**$19,711**	**$ 70,396**
Other cash inflows					
Equity investment	$ 0	$ 0	$ 0	$ 0	$ 0
Increased borrowings	$ 0	$ 0	$ 0	$ 0	$ 0
Sales of business assets	$ 0	$ 0	$ 0	$ 0	$ 0
A/P increases	$ 8,717	$10,897	$11,769	$12,204	$ 43,587
Total other cash inflows	**$ 8,717**	**$10,897**	**$11,769**	**$12,204**	**$ 43,587**
Total cash inflow	**$22,797**	**$28,496**	**$30,775**	**$31,915**	**$113,983**
Cash outflows					
Repayment of principal	$ 1,708	$ 1,747	$ 1,787	$ 1,827	$ 7,070
A/P decreases	$ 5,975	$ 7,469	$ 8,067	$ 8,365	$ 29,876
A/R increases	$ 0	$ 0	$ 0	$ 0	$ 0
Asset purchases	$ 3,520	$ 4,400	$ 4,752	$ 4,928	$ 17,599
Dividends	$ 9,855	$12,319	$13,305	$13,798	$ 49,277
Total cash outflows	**$21,059**	**$25,935**	**$27,910**	**$28,918**	**$103,822**
Net cash flow	**$ 1,738**	**$ 2,560**	**$ 2,865**	**$ 2,997**	**$ 10,161**
Cash balance	**$44,856**	**$47,416**	**$50,282**	**$53,279**	**$ 53,279**

Cash flow analysis (third year)

| | | 3 | | | |
Quarter	Q1	Q2	Q3	Q4	3
Cash from operations	$19,880	$24,849	$26,837	$27,831	$ 99,398
Cash from receivables	$ 0	$ 0	$ 0	$ 0	$ 0
Operating cash inflow	**$19,880**	**$24,849**	**$26,837**	**$27,831**	**$ 99,398**
Other cash inflows					
Equity investment	$ 0	$ 0	$ 0	$ 0	$ 0
Increased borrowings	$ 0	$ 0	$ 0	$ 0	$ 0
Sales of business assets	$ 0	$ 0	$ 0	$ 0	$ 0
A/P increases	$10,025	$12,531	$13,534	$14,035	$ 50,125
Total other cash inflows	**$10,025**	**$12,531**	**$13,534**	**$14,035**	**$ 50,125**
Total cash inflow	**$29,905**	**$37,381**	**$40,371**	**$41,866**	**$149,523**
Cash outflows					
Repayment of principal	$ 1,869	$ 1,911	$ 1,954	$ 1,999	$ 7,733
A/P decreases	$ 7,170	$ 8,963	$ 9,680	$10,038	$ 35,852
A/R increases	$ 0	$ 0	$ 0	$ 0	$ 0
Asset purchases	$ 4,970	$ 6,212	$ 6,709	$ 6,958	$ 24,849
Dividends	$13,916	$17,395	$18,786	$19,482	$ 69,578
Total cash outflows	**$27,925**	**$34,481**	**$37,130**	**$38,477**	**$138,012**
Net cash flow	**$ 1,980**	**$ 2,900**	**$ 3,241**	**$ 3,390**	**$ 11,511**
Cash balance	**$55,259**	**$58,159**	**$61,400**	**$64,790**	**$ 64,790**

Bail Bonding

Lyons Bail Bonds

87791 Middleton Ave.
Brooklyn, NY 11201

BizPlaDB.com

Lyons Bail Bonds, Inc. ("the Company") is a New York-based corporation that will provide bail bonding services and bounty hunting within the Company's targeted market of New York. The Company was founded by Joe Lyons.

1.0 EXECUTIVE SUMMARY

The purpose of this business plan is to raise $100,000 for the development of a bail bonding company while showcasing the expected financials and operations over the next three years. Lyons Bail Bonds, Inc. ("the Company") is a New York-based corporation that will provide bail bonding services and bounty hunting within the Company's targeted market of New York. The Company was founded by Joe Lyons.

1.1 The Services

The primary revenue center for the business will come from the ongoing bail bonding services rendered to people that have been arrested and must put up bond in order to be released on bail. On each transaction, the Company will earn a fee equal to 10%–12% of the aggregate bond set forth by the court.

The business will also generate secondary streams of revenue by acting in a licensed bounty hunter capacity among individuals that have fled after Lyons Bail Bonds, Inc. put up the appropriate collateral for an individuals bail bond.

The third section of the business plan will further describe the services offered by Lyons Bail Bonds, Inc.

1.2 Financing

Mr. Lyons is seeking to raise $100,000 as a private investment. The business is seeking to sell a 45% interest in the business in exchange for the requisite capital sought in this business plan. The investor will also receive a seat on the board of directors and a regular stream of dividends. The financing will be used for the following:

- Development of the Company's location.

- Financing for the first six months of operation.

- Capital to purchase a company vehicle.

1.3 Mission Statement

Lyons Bail Bonds' mission is to develop a business that provides outstanding bail bonding services to people within the New York metropolitan area.

1.4 Management Team

The Company was founded by Joe Lyons. Mr. Lyons has more than 10 years of experience in the law enforcement industry. Through his expertise, he will be able to bring the operations of the business to profitability within its first year of operations.

1.5 Sales Forecasts

Mr. Lyons expects a strong rate of growth at the start of operations. Below are the expected financials over the next three years.

Proforma profit and loss (yearly)

Year	1	2	3
Sales	$833,250	$899,910	$971,903
Operating costs	$504,842	$536,725	$570,151
EBITDA	$245,083	$273,194	$304,561
Taxes, interest, and depreciation	$ 97,239	$107,921	$119,840
Net profit	$147,844	$165,273	$184,721

Sales, operating costs, and profit forecast

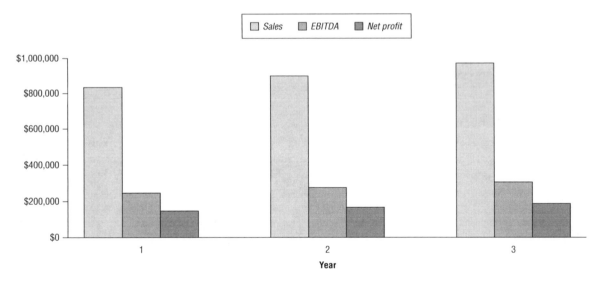

1.6 Expansion Plan

The Founder expects that the business will aggressively expand during the first three years of operation. Mr. Lyons intends to implement marketing campaigns that will effectively target individuals that are in need of bail bonds after they have been arrested and need to post bail.

2.0 COMPANY AND FINANCING SUMMARY

2.1 Registered Name and Corporate Structure

Lyons Bail Bonds, Inc. is registered as a corporation in the State of New York.

2.2 Required Funds

At this time, Lyons Bail Bonds, Inc. requires $100,000 of equity funds. Below is a breakdown of how these funds will be used:

Projected startup costs

Business startup year	1
Bail bond licensing	$ 10,000
Working capital	$ 35,000
FF&E	$ 23,000
Leasehold improvements	$ 5,000
Security deposits	$ 5,000
Insurance	$ 2,500
Vehicle	$ 17,000
Marketing budget	$ 7,500
Miscellaneous and unforeseen costs	$ 5,000
Total startup costs	**$110,000**

Use of funds

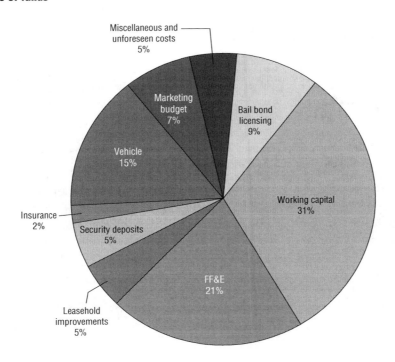

2.3 Investor Equity

Mr. Lyons is seeking to sell a 45% equity interest in the business in exchange for the capital required in order to launch the operations of Lyons Bail Bonds.

2.4 Management Equity

Joe Lyons owns 100% of Lyons Bail Bonds, Inc. This capital structure will change once the requisite capital has been raised.

2.5 Exit Strategy

If the business is very successful, Mr. Lyons may seek to sell the business to a third party for a significant earnings multiple. Most likely, the Company will hire a qualified investment bank to sell the business on behalf of Lyons Bail Bonds. Based on historical numbers, the business could fetch a sales premium of up to 4 times earnings.

3.0 PRODUCTS AND SERVICES

Below is a description of the bail bonding services offered by Lyons Bail Bonds.

3.1 Bail Bonding Services

As discussed in the executive summary, the primary revenue center for the business will come from the ongoing bail bonding services provided to people that have been arrested and are in need of bail funding. The business will charge an amount equal to 10% to 12% of the face value of the bail amount set by the court. The Company, in all instances, will ensure that proper contracts are in place in the event that an individual flees. This will ensure that the business of Lyons Bail Bonds, Inc. can recover the funds that were provided to secure the release of someone who has been arrested. At all times, Lyons Bail Bonds will maintain the appropriate licensure in order to act in a bail bonding capacity.

3.2 Bounty Hunter Services

Lyons Bail Bonds' secondary revenue center will come from bounty hunting for other businesses that are engaged in the bail bonding industry, but do not have a licensed bounty hunter on staff in the event that a client flees from their obligations to court. Fees received from this service will be based on the amount recovered when the person is found and taken back into custody.

4.0 STRATEGIC AND MARKET ANALYSIS

4.1 Economic Outlook

This section of the analysis will detail the economic climate, the bail bonding industry, the customer profile, and the competition that the business will face as it progresses through its business operations.

At this time, the economy has rebounded significantly. The job market has improved, and businesses are beginning to make investments into expansion. As such, the demand among companies that are seeking capital to expand is immense. Since people are arrested in any economic climate (and usually more so during times of economic recession), the business will be able to remain profitable and cash flow positive at all times.

4.2 Industry Analysis

Within the United States, there are 3,500 companies that are actively engaged in the business of providing bail bonding services. The industry generates approximately $1.2 billion of revenue per year while concurrently providing jobs to more than 15,000 people. Annual payrolls in each of the last five years have exceeded $250,000,000.

The industry growth rate is expected to remain in lockstep with that of the general economy. With the exceptions of four states (Illinois, Kentucky, Oregon, and Wisconsin), all states currently allow for some level of bail bonding or bounty hunting. At this time, no pending legislation appears to limit the scope of practice in any other state.

4.3 Customer Profile

Lyons Bail Bonds' average client will be someone that does not have the proper capital to secure their release from jail. Below is an overview of the demographics anticipated by the Company:

- Is based in the New York metropolitan area.

- Has been arrested for a misdemeanor or felony offense.

- Will spend $1,000 to $10,000 on Lyons Bail Bonds Services.

4.4 Competition

Within the greater New York area, there are currently 100 companies operating as licensed bail bonding firms. However, these firms have not kept up with the demand among indicted individuals as it relates to posting bond. As such, Lyons Bail Bonds, Inc. can easily enter this market with the bail bonding and bounty hunter services outlined in the third section of the business plan.

5.0 MARKETING PLAN

Lyons Bail Bonds, Inc. intends to maintain an extensive marketing campaign that will ensure maximum visibility for the business in its targeted market. Below is an overview of the marketing strategies and objectives of Lyons Bail Bonds.

5.1 Marketing Objectives

- Establish relationships with area criminal defense attorneys.

- Develop a broad-range website that showcases the licensure and bail bonding services rendered by the business.

- Maintain a strong database of bounty hunters that can assist the business with exponential growth over the next three years of operation.

5.2 Marketing Strategies

Mr. Lyons intends on using a number of strategies that will aggressively showcase the services available through Lyons Bail Bonds, Inc. These advertisements will focus on the local New York metropolitan market. The marketing messages to be used by the business will focus on the experience of the Company's bail bonding services while concurrently ensuring quick releases for people that have been arrested.

The business will also develop a highly informative website that shows the operations of the business, its bail bonding services, and how an individual can become a customer of Lyons Bail Bonds, Inc.

5.3 Pricing

The Company will charge a fee equal to 10%–12% of the bonded amount requested by a court.

6.0 ORGANIZATIONAL PLAN AND PERSONNEL SUMMARY

6.1 Corporate Organization

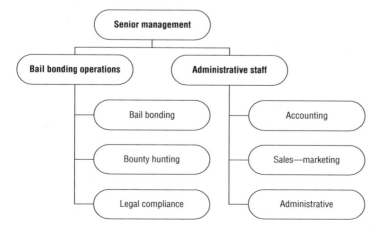

6.2 Organizational Budget

Personnel plan—yearly

Year	1	2	3
Senior management	$ 80,000	$ 82,400	$ 84,872
Bounty hunter	$105,000	$108,150	$111,395
Owner's assistant	$130,000	$133,900	$137,917
Accountant	$ 37,500	$ 51,500	$ 66,306
Administrative	$ 22,000	$ 22,660	$ 23,340
Total	**$374,500**	**$398,610**	**$423,830**

Numbers of personnel

Senior management	2	2	2
Bounty hunter	3	3	3
Owner's assistant	4	4	4
Accountant	3	4	5
Administrative	1	1	1
Totals	**13**	**14**	**15**

Personnel expense breakdown

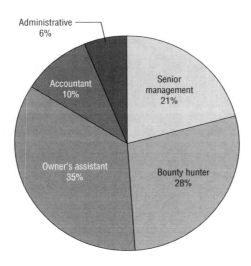

7.0 FINANCIAL PLAN

7.1 Underlying Assumptions

The Company has based its proforma financial statements on the following:

- Lyons Bail Bonds, Inc. will have an annual revenue growth rate of 16% per year.

- Management will acquire $100,000 of investor funds to launch the operations of Lyons Bail Bonds.

- Management will settle most short-term payables on a monthly basis.

7.2 Sensitivity Analysis

In the event of an economic downturn, the business may have a decline in its revenues. However, bail bonding businesses tend to thrive in times of economic difficulty as more people tend to commit crimes during recessions. As such, Lyons Bail Bonds, Inc. will be able to remain profitable and cash flow positive at all times.

7.3 Source of Funds

Financing

Equity contributions

Investor(s)	$ 100,000.00
Management	$ 10,000.00
Total equity financing	**$110,000.00**
Banks and lenders	
Total debt financing	**$ 0.00**
Total financing	**$110,000.00**

7.4 General Assumptions

General assumptions

Year	1	2	3
Short term interest rate	9.5%	9.5%	9.5%
Long term interest rate	10.0%	10.0%	10.0%
Federal tax rate	33.0%	33.0%	33.0%
State tax rate	5.0%	5.0%	5.0%
Personnel taxes	15.0%	15.0%	15.0%

7.5 Profit and Loss Statements

Proforma profit and loss (yearly)

Year	1	2	3
Sales	**$833,250**	**$899,910**	**$971,903**
Cost of goods sold	$ 83,325	$ 89,991	$ 97,190
Gross margin	90.00%	90.00%	90.00%
Operating income	**$749,925**	**$809,919**	**$874,713**
Expenses			
Payroll	$374,500	$398,610	$423,830
General and administrative	$ 25,200	$ 26,208	$ 27,256
Marketing expenses	$ 4,166	$ 4,500	$ 4,860
Professional fees and licensure	$ 5,219	$ 5,376	$ 5,537
Insurance costs	$ 1,987	$ 2,086	$ 2,191
Travel and vehicle costs	$ 7,596	$ 8,356	$ 9,191
Rent and utilities	$ 20,000	$ 21,000	$ 22,050
Miscellaneous costs	$ 9,999	$ 10,799	$ 11,663
Payroll taxes	$ 56,175	$ 59,792	$ 63,574
Total operating costs	**$504,842**	**$536,725**	**$570,151**
EBITDA	**$245,083**	**$273,194**	**$304,561**
Federal income tax	$ 80,877	$ 90,154	$100,505
State income tax	$ 12,254	$ 13,660	$ 15,228
Interest expense	$ 0	$ 0	$ 0
Depreciation expenses	$ 4,107	$ 4,107	$ 4,107
Net profit	**$147,844**	**$165,273**	**$184,721**
Profit margin	**17.74%**	**18.37%**	**19.01%**

Sales, operating costs, and profit forecast

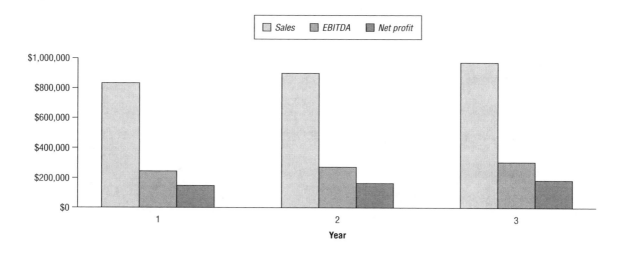

7.6 Cash Flow Analysis

Proforma cash flow analysis—yearly

Year	1	2	3
Cash from operations	$151,951	$169,380	$188,828
Cash from receivables	$ 0	$ 0	$ 0
Operating cash inflow	**$151,951**	**$169,380**	**$188,828**
Other cash inflows			
Equity investment	$110,000	$ 0	$ 0
Increased borrowings	$ 0	$ 0	$ 0
Sales of business assets	$ 0	$ 0	$ 0
A/P increases	$ 37,902	$ 43,587	$ 50,125
Total other cash inflows	**$147,902**	**$ 43,587**	**$ 50,125**
Total cash inflow	**$299,853**	**$212,967**	**$238,953**
Cash outflows			
Repayment of principal	$ 0	$ 0	$ 0
A/P decreases	$ 24,897	$ 29,876	$ 35,852
A/R increases	$ 0	$ 0	$ 0
Asset purchases	$ 57,500	$ 25,407	$ 28,324
Dividends	$121,561	$135,504	$151,062
Total cash outflows	**$203,958**	**$190,787**	**$215,238**
Net cash flow	**$ 95,895**	**$ 22,180**	**$ 23,715**
Cash balance	**$ 95,895**	**$118,075**	**$141,790**

Proforma cash flow (yearly)

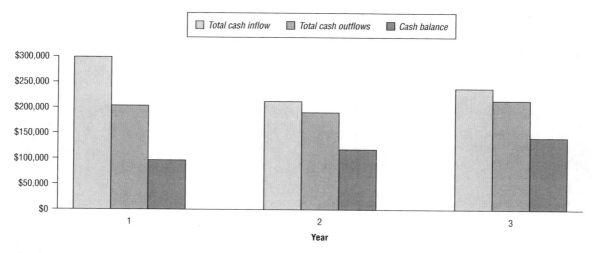

7.7 Balance Sheet

Proforma balance sheet—yearly

Year	1	2	3
Assets			
Cash	$ 95,895	$118,075	$141,790
Amortized development/expansion costs	$ 17,500	$ 39,096	$ 63,172
Company vehicle	$ 17,000	$ 17,000	$ 17,000
FF&E	$ 23,000	$ 26,811	$ 31,060
Accumulated depreciation	($ 4,107)	($ 8,214)	($ 12,321)
Total assets	**$149,288**	**$192,768**	**$240,700**
Liabilities and equity			
Accounts payable	$ 13,005	$ 26,716	$ 40,990
Long term liabilities	$ 0	$ 0	$ 0
Other liabilities	$ 0	$ 0	$ 0
Total liabilities	**$ 13,005**	**$ 26,716**	**$ 40,990**
Net worth	**$136,283**	**$166,052**	**$199,710**
Total liabilities and equity	**$149,288**	**$192,768**	**$240,700**

Proforma balance sheet

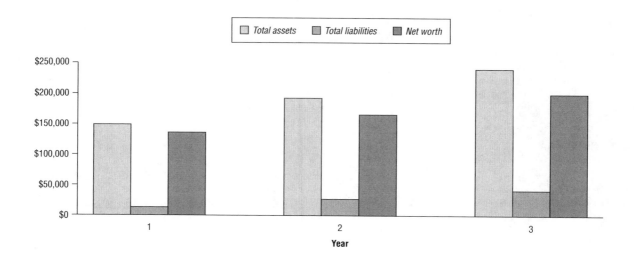

7.8 Breakeven Analysis

Monthly break even analysis

Year	1	2	3
Monthly revenue	$ 46,745	$ 49,697	$ 52,792
Yearly revenue	$560,936	$596,362	$633,501

Break even analysis

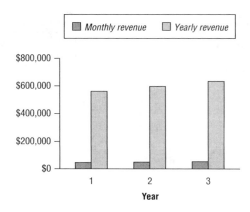

7.9 Business Ratios

Business ratios—yearly

Year	1	2	3
Sales			
Sales growth	0.0%	8.0%	8.0%
Gross margin	90.0%	90.0%	90.0%
Financials			
Profit margin	17.74%	18.37%	19.01%
Assets to liabilities	11.48	7.22	5.87
Equity to liabilities	10.48	6.22	4.87
Assets to equity	1.10	1.16	1.21
Liquidity			
Acid test	7.37	4.42	3.46
Cash to assets	0.64	0.61	0.59

7.10 Three Year Profit and Loss Statement

Profit and loss statement (first year)

Months	1	2	3	4	5	6	7
Sales	$68,750	$68,875	$69,000	$69,125	$69,250	$69,375	$69,500
Cost of goods sold	$ 6,875	$ 6,888	$ 6,900	$ 6,913	$ 6,925	$ 6,938	$ 6,950
Gross margin	90.0%	90.0%	90.0%	90.0%	90.0%	90.0%	90.0%
Operating income	**$61,875**	**$61,988**	**$62,100**	**$62,213**	**$62,325**	**$62,438**	**$62,550**
Expenses							
Payroll	$31,208	$31,208	$31,208	$31,208	$31,208	$31,208	$31,208
General and administrative	$ 2,100	$ 2,100	$ 2,100	$ 2,100	$ 2,100	$ 2,100	$ 2,100
Marketing expenses	$ 347	$ 347	$ 347	$ 347	$ 347	$ 347	$ 347
Professional fees and licensure	$ 435	$ 435	$ 435	$ 435	$ 435	$ 435	$ 435
Insurance costs	$ 166	$ 166	$ 166	$ 166	$ 166	$ 166	$ 166
Travel and vehicle costs	$ 633	$ 633	$ 633	$ 633	$ 633	$ 633	$ 633
Rent and utilities	$ 1,667	$ 1,667	$ 1,667	$ 1,667	$ 1,667	$ 1,667	$ 1,667
Miscellaneous costs	$ 833	$ 833	$ 833	$ 833	$ 833	$ 833	$ 833
Payroll taxes	$ 4,681	$ 4,681	$ 4,681	$ 4,681	$ 4,681	$ 4,681	$ 4,681
Total operating costs	**$42,070**	**$42,070**	**$42,070**	**$42,070**	**$42,070**	**$42,070**	**$42,070**
EBITDA	**$19,805**	**$19,917**	**$20,030**	**$20,142**	**$20,255**	**$20,367**	**$20,480**
Federal income tax	$ 6,673	$ 6,685	$ 6,697	$ 6,709	$ 6,722	$ 6,734	$ 6,746
State income tax	$ 1,011	$ 1,013	$ 1,015	$ 1,017	$ 1,018	$ 1,020	$ 1,022
Interest expense	$ 0	$ 0	$ 0	$ 0	$ 0	$0	$ 0
Depreciation expense	$ 342	$ 342	$ 342	$ 342	$ 342	$ 342	$ 342
Net profit	**$11,778**	**$11,877**	**$11,975**	**$12,074**	**$12,173**	**$12,271**	**$12,370**

Profit and loss statement (first year cont.)

Month	8	9	10	11	12	1
Sales	$69,625	$69,750	$69,875	$70,000	$70,125	$833,250
Cost of goods sold	$ 6,963	$ 6,975	$ 6,988	$ 7,000	$ 7,013	$ 83,325
Gross margin	90.0%	90.0%	90.0%	90.0%	90.0%	90.0%
Operating income	**$62,663**	**$62,775**	**$62,888**	**$63,000**	**$63,113**	**$749,925**
Expenses						
Payroll	$31,208	$31,208	$31,208	$31,208	$31,208	$374,500
General and administrative	$ 2,100	$ 2,100	$ 2,100	$ 2,100	$ 2,100	$ 25,200
Marketing expenses	$ 347	$ 347	$ 347	$ 347	$ 347	$ 4,166
Professional fees and licensure	$ 435	$ 435	$ 435	$ 435	$ 435	$ 5,219
Insurance costs	$ 166	$ 166	$ 166	$ 166	$ 166	$ 1,987
Travel and vehicle costs	$ 633	$ 633	$ 633	$ 633	$ 633	$ 7,596
Rent and utilities	$ 1,667	$ 1,667	$ 1,667	$ 1,667	$ 1,667	$ 20,000
Miscellaneous costs	$ 833	$ 833	$ 833	$ 833	$ 833	$ 9,999
Payroll taxes	$ 4,681	$ 4,681	$ 4,681	$ 4,681	$ 4,681	$ 56,175
Total operating costs	**$42,070**	**$42,070**	**$42,070**	**$42,070**	**$42,070**	**$504,842**
EBITDA	**$20,592**	**$20,705**	**$20,817**	**$20,930**	**$21,042**	**$245,083**
Federal income tax	$ 6,758	$ 6,770	$ 6,782	$ 6,794	$ 6,807	$ 80,877
State income tax	$ 1,024	$ 1,026	$ 1,028	$ 1,029	$ 1,031	$ 12,254
Interest expense	$ 0	$ 0	$ 0	$ 0	$ 0	$ 0
Depreciation expense	$ 342	$ 342	$ 342	$ 342	$ 342	$ 4,107
Net profit	**$12,468**	**$12,567**	**$12,665**	**$12,764**	**$12,862**	**$147,844**

Profit and loss statement (second year)

| | | 2 | | | |
Quarter	Q1	Q2	Q3	Q4	2
Sales	$179,982	$224,978	$242,976	$251,975	$899,910
Cost of goods sold	$ 17,998	$ 22,498	$ 24,298	$ 25,197	$ 89,991
Gross margin	90.0%	90.0%	90.0%	90.0%	90.0%
Operating income	$161,984	$202,480	$218,678	$226,777	$809,919
Expenses					
Payroll	$ 79,722	$ 99,653	$107,625	$111,611	$398,610
General and administrative	$ 5,242	$ 6,552	$ 7,076	$ 7,338	$ 26,208
Marketing expenses	$ 900	$ 1,125	$ 1,215	$ 1,260	$ 4,500
Professional fees and licensure	$ 1,075	$ 1,344	$ 1,451	$ 1,505	$ 5,376
Insurance costs	$ 417	$ 522	$ 563	$ 584	$ 2,086
Travel and vehicle costs	$ 1,671	$ 2,089	$ 2,256	$ 2,340	$ 8,356
Rent and utilities	$ 4,200	$ 5,250	$ 5,670	$ 5,880	$ 21,000
Miscellaneous costs	$ 2,160	$ 2,700	$ 2,916	$ 3,024	$ 10,799
Payroll taxes	$ 11,958	$ 14,948	$ 16,144	$ 16,742	$ 59,792
Total operating costs	$107,345	$134,181	$144,916	$150,283	$536,725
EBITDA	$ 54,639	$ 68,298	$ 73,762	$ 76,494	$273,194
Federal income tax	$ 18,031	$ 22,538	$ 24,342	$ 25,243	$ 90,154
State income tax	$ 2,732	$ 3,415	$ 3,688	$ 3,825	$ 13,660
Interest expense	$ 0	$ 0	$ 0	$ 0	$ 0
Depreciation expense	$ 1,027	$ 1,027	$ 1,027	$ 1,027	$ 4,107
Net profit	$ 32,849	$ 41,318	$ 44,706	$ 46,400	$165,273

Profit and loss statement (third year)

| | | 3 | | | |
Quarter	Q1	Q2	Q3	Q4	3
Sales	$194,381	$242,976	$262,414	$272,133	$971,903
Cost of goods sold	$ 19,438	$ 24,298	$ 26,241	$ 27,213	$ 97,190
Gross margin	90.0%	90.0%	90.0%	90.0%	90.0%
Operating income	$174,943	$218,678	$236,172	$244,920	$874,713
Expenses					
Payroll	$ 84,766	$105,957	$114,434	$118,672	$423,830
General and administrative	$ 5,451	$ 6,814	$ 7,359	$ 7,632	$ 27,256
Marketing expenses	$ 972	$ 1,215	$ 1,312	$ 1,361	$ 4,860
Professional fees and licensure	$ 1,107	$ 1,384	$ 1,495	$ 1,550	$ 5,537
Insurance costs	$ 438	$ 548	$ 591	$ 613	$ 2,191
Travel and vehicle costs	$ 1,838	$ 2,298	$ 2,482	$ 2,574	$ 9,191
Rent and utilities	$ 4,410	$ 5,513	$ 5,954	$ 6,174	$ 22,050
Miscellaneous costs	$ 2,333	$ 2,916	$ 3,149	$ 3,266	$ 11,663
Payroll taxes	$ 12,715	$ 15,894	$ 17,165	$ 17,801	$ 63,574
Total operating costs	$114,030	$142,538	$153,941	$159,642	$570,151
EBITDA	$ 60,912	$ 76,140	$ 82,232	$ 85,277	$304,561
Federal income tax	$ 20,101	$ 25,126	$ 27,136	$ 28,141	$100,505
State income tax	$ 3,046	$ 3,807	$ 4,112	$ 4,264	$ 15,228
Interest expense	$ 0	$ 0	$ 0	$ 0	$ 0
Depreciation expense	$ 1,027	$ 1,027	$ 1,027	$ 1,027	$ 4,107
Net profit	$ 36,739	$ 46,180	$ 49,957	$ 51,845	$184,721

7.11 Three Year Cash Flow Analysis

Cash flow analysis (first year)

Month	1	2	3	4	5	6	7
Cash from operations	$ 12,121	$12,219	$12,318	$ 12,416	$ 12,515	$ 12,613	$ 12,712
Cash from receivables	$ 0	$ 0	$ 0	$ 0	$ 0	$ 0	$ 0
Operating cash inflow	**$ 12,121**	**$12,219**	**$12,318**	**$ 12,416**	**$ 12,515**	**$ 12,613**	**$ 12,712**
Other cash inflows							
Equity investment	$110,000	$ 0	$ 0	$ 0	$ 0	$ 0	$ 0
Increased borrowings	$ 0	$ 0	$ 0	$ 0	$ 0	$ 0	$ 0
Sales of business assets	$ 0	$ 0	$ 0	$ 0	$ 0	$ 0	$ 0
A/P increases	$ 3,159	$ 3,159	$ 3,159	$ 3,159	$ 3,159	$ 3,159	$ 3,159
Total other cash inflows	**$113,159**	**$ 3,159**	**$ 3,159**	**$ 3,159**	**$ 3,159**	**$ 3,159**	**$ 3,159**
Total cash inflow	**$125,279**	**$15,378**	**$15,476**	**$ 15,575**	**$ 15,673**	**$ 15,772**	**$ 15,870**
Cash outflows							
Repayment of principal	$ 0	$ 0	$ 0	$ 0	$ 0	$ 0	$ 0
A/P decreases	$ 2,075	$ 2,075	$ 2,075	$ 2,075	$ 2,075	$ 2,075	$ 2,075
A/R increases	$ 0	$ 0	$ 0	$ 0	$ 0	$ 0	$ 0
Asset purchases	$ 57,500	$ 0	$ 0	$ 0	$ 0	$ 0	$ 0
Dividends	$ 0	$ 0	$ 0	$ 0	$ 0	$ 0	$ 0
Total cash outflows	**$ 59,575**	**$ 2,075**	**$ 2,075**	**$ 2,075**	**$ 2,075**	**$ 2,075**	**$ 2,075**
Net cash flow	**$ 65,704**	**$13,303**	**$13,402**	**$ 13,500**	**$ 13,599**	**$ 13,697**	**$ 13,796**
Cash balance	**$ 65,704**	**$79,007**	**$92,409**	**$105,909**	**$119,508**	**$133,205**	**$147,000**

Cash flow analysis (first year cont.)

Month	8	9	10	11	12	1
Cash from operations	$ 12,810	$ 12,909	$ 13,007	$ 13,106	$ 13,205	$151,951
Cash from receivables	$ 0	$ 0	$ 0	$ 0	$ 0	$ 0
Operating cash inflow	**$ 12,810**	**$ 12,909**	**$ 13,007**	**$ 13,106**	**$ 13,205**	**$151,951**
Other cash inflows						
Equity investment	$ 0	$ 0	$ 0	$ 0	$ 0	$110,000
Increased borrowings	$ 0	$ 0	$ 0	$ 0	$ 0	$ 0
Sales of business assets	$ 0	$ 0	$ 0	$ 0	$ 0	$ 0
A/P increases	$ 3,159	$ 3,159	$ 3,159	$ 3,159	$ 3,159	$ 37,902
Total other cash inflows	**$ 3,159**	**$ 3,159**	**$ 3,159**	**$ 3,159**	**$ 3,159**	**$147,902**
Total cash inflow	**$ 15,969**	**$ 16,067**	**$ 16,166**	**$ 16,264**	**$ 16,363**	**$299,853**
Cash outflows						
Repayment of principal	$ 0	$ 0	$ 0	$ 0	$ 0	$ 0
A/P decreases	$ 2,075	$ 2,075	$ 2,075	$ 2,075	$ 2,075	$ 24,897
A/R increases	$ 0	$ 0	$ 0	$ 0	$ 0	$ 0
Asset purchases	$ 0	$ 0	$ 0	$ 0	$ 0	$ 57,500
Dividends	$ 0	$ 0	$ 0	$ 0	$121,561	$121,561
Total cash outflows	**$ 2,075**	**$ 2,075**	**$ 2,075**	**$ 2,075**	**$123,636**	**$203,958**
Net cash flow	**$ 13,894**	**$ 13,993**	**$ 14,091**	**$ 14,190**	**−$107,273**	**$ 95,895**
Cash balance	**$160,894**	**$174,887**	**$188,978**	**$203,168**	**$ 95,895**	**$ 95,895**

Cash flow analysis (second year)

Quarter	Q1	2 Q2	Q3	Q4	2
Cash from operations	$ 33,876	$ 42,345	$ 45,733	$ 47,426	$169,380
Cash from receivables	$ 0	$ 0	$ 0	$ 0	$ 0
Operating cash inflow	**$ 33,876**	**$ 42,345**	**$ 45,733**	**$ 47,426**	**$169,380**
Other cash inflows					
Equity investment	$ 0	$ 0	$ 0	$ 0	$ 0
Increased borrowings	$ 0	$ 0	$ 0	$ 0	$ 0
Sales of business assets	$ 0	$ 0	$ 0	$ 0	$ 0
A/P increases	$ 8,717	$ 10,897	$ 11,769	$ 12,204	$ 43,587
Total other cash inflows	**$ 8,717**	**$ 10,897**	**$ 11,769**	**$ 12,204**	**$ 43,587**
Total cash inflow	**$ 42,593**	**$ 53,242**	**$ 57,501**	**$ 59,631**	**$212,967**
Cash outflows					
Repayment of principal	$ 0	$ 0	$ 0	$ 0	$ 0
A/P decreases	$ 5,975	$ 7,469	$ 8,067	$ 8,365	$ 29,876
A/R increases	$ 0	$ 0	$ 0	$ 0	$ 0
Asset purchases	$ 5,081	$ 6,352	$ 6,860	$ 7,114	$ 25,407
Dividends	$ 27,101	$ 33,876	$ 36,586	$ 37,941	$135,504
Total cash outflows	**$ 38,157**	**$ 47,697**	**$ 51,513**	**$ 53,420**	**$190,787**
Net cash flow	**$ 4,436**	**$ 5,545**	**$ 5,989**	**$ 6,210**	**$ 22,180**
Cash balance	**$100,331**	**$105,876**	**$111,865**	**$118,075**	**$118,075**

Cash flow analysis (third year)

Quarter	Q1	3 Q2	Q3	Q4	3
Cash from operations	$ 37,766	$ 47,207	$ 50,984	$ 52,872	$188,828
Cash from receivables	$ 0	$ 0	$ 0	$ 0	$ 0
Operating cash inflow	**$ 37,766**	**$ 47,207**	**$ 50,984**	**$ 52,872**	**$188,828**
Other cash inflows					
Equity investment	$ 0	$ 0	$ 0	$ 0	$ 0
Increased borrowings	$ 0	$ 0	$ 0	$ 0	$ 0
Sales of business assets	$ 0	$ 0	$ 0	$ 0	$ 0
A/P increases	$ 10,025	$ 12,531	$ 13,534	$ 14,035	$ 50,125
Total other cash inflows	**$ 10,025**	**$ 12,531**	**$ 13,534**	**$ 14,035**	**$ 50,125**
Total cash inflow	**$ 47,791**	**$ 59,738**	**$ 64,517**	**$ 66,907**	**$238,953**
Cash outflows					
Repayment of principal	$ 0	$ 0	$ 0	$ 0	$ 0
A/P decreases	$ 7,170	$ 8,963	$ 9,680	$ 10,038	$ 35,852
A/R increases	$ 0	$ 0	$ 0	$ 0	$ 0
Asset purchases	$ 5,665	$ 7,081	$ 7,648	$ 7,931	$ 28,324
Dividends	$ 30,212	$ 37,766	$ 40,787	$ 42,297	$151,062
Total cash outflows	**$ 43,048**	**$ 53,810**	**$ 58,114**	**$ 60,267**	**$215,238**
Net cash flow	**$ 4,743**	**$ 5,929**	**$ 6,403**	**$ 6,640**	**$ 23,715**
Cash balance	**$122,818**	**$128,747**	**$135,150**	**$141,790**	**$141,790**

Concealed Carry Training Business

ProtectionStar Inc.

98765 Country Rd. E
Ridgefield, IL 63505

Paul Greenland

ProtectionStar Inc. provides "concealed carry" training classes, which equip individuals with the knowledge and skills needed to safely and legally carry a concealed weapon, as well as other types of handgun training.

EXECUTIVE SUMMARY

ProtectionStar Inc. provides "concealed carry" training classes, which equip individuals with the knowledge and skills needed to safely and legally carry a concealed weapon. The company is being established by successful entrepreneur and business owner Roy Fisher, Tim Stevens (owner of the local shooting range where ProtectionStar will be based), and instructors Ron Johnson and Patrick Sharp, who have extensive law enforcement and military backgrounds.

ProtectionStar is based in Illinois, which was the very last state in the union to allow concealed carry following a federal court order in 2013. Illinois is unique because its permit requirements are the most stringent of any state, requiring 16 hours of training. Although more than 20 states honored Illinois' concealed carry permit in 2014, Illinois did not recognize permits from other states, requiring residents to undergo specific training. In addition, according to an August 2014 report issued by Fenton & Associates, Illinois was home to six of the 25 most dangerous U.S. neighborhoods, two of which were located in Ridgefield. Based on these factors, the owners believe that ProtectionStar has tremendous growth potential.

ProtectionStar's operations will be based on the grounds of Tim Stevens' shooting range, Ridgefield Range. Classroom training will be provided in a modular classroom building, while live fire exercises with concealable firearms, which are required as part of Illinois training, are provided at Ridgefield Range's facilities.

INDUSTRY ANALYSIS

By 2014, laws allowing concealed carry had been passed in all 50 states. Although requirements and restrictions varied, many states had "reciprocity agreements" in place to recognize one another's permits. For example, permits from Florida and Utah (which required only four hours of training) were honored in more than 30 different states.

Significant opportunities exist for providers of concealed carry training, and according to a July 4, 2013, *Wall Street Journal* article, the number of new concealed carry permits has been increasing in many states. The publication reported that, over the previous 12 months, Florida had experienced a 17 percent increase in new permits (173,000). Ohio was on-pace to double the number of new permits issued, and states such as Wyoming, Nebraska, Tennessee, and Oklahoma had either met or exceeded totals achieved for all of 2012 by the middle of 2013.

MARKET ANALYSIS

Illinois was the very last state in the union to allow concealed carry, following a federal court order in 2013. Illinois is unique because its permit requirements are the most stringent of any state, requiring 16 hours of training. Although more than 20 states honored Illinois' concealed carry permit in 2014, Illinois did not recognize permits from other states, requiring residents to undergo specific training and effectively creating strong demand for training companies like ProtectionStar.

According to NBCChicago.com, by August of 2014 a total of 84,000 concealed carry applications had been filed in Illinois during the first seven months of the year alone. Although demand is strong statewide, it arguably is even stronger in ProtectionStar's primary market of Ridgefield, Illinois. An August 2014 report issued by Fenton & Associates, based on national law-enforcement data, attempted to predict the U.S. neighborhoods with the highest rates of violent crime. The report indicated that Illinois was home to five of the 25 most dangerous U.S. neighborhoods, two of which were located in Ridgefield.

Beyond neighborhoods impacted by frequent violent crime, so-called "good neighborhoods" throughout the city of Ridgefield and surrounding communities also have experienced violent crimes, including home invasions. Conditions such as these have created concern among community members, along with a heightened interest in security and self-protection methods.

Insight regarding the target market for individuals seeking concealed carry training can be gained by reviewing reports from states that share demographic data. A report issued on July 31, 2014, by the Florida Department of Agriculture and Consumer Services Division of Licensing provided a profile of concealed weapon or firearm license holders 'in that state. According to the report, license holders typically are males (78%). In terms of age, the 51-65 category had the highest percentage (31.72%) of active licensees, followed by those aged 36-50 (26.33%), 66+ (23.59%), and 18-35 (18.37%).

Although ProtectionStar will provide concealed carry training to all individuals over the age of 21 (the minimum age allowable by Illinois state law), and all genders, the business' marketing and promotional efforts mainly will concentrate on middle-aged and older males (e.g., those aged 45-74) with higher household income levels (more than $50,000) in the Ridgefield, Illinois metropolitan area. The company also will employ a highly targeted strategy to reach women who have limited or no shooting experience.

Working in partnership with a market research firm, the owners have obtained demographic data on the Ridgefield metropolitan area. In 2014 the area included nearly 345,000 people, 49 percent of which (approximately 169,000) were males. An estimated 60,500 males (35.8% of the total male population) fall within the business' target age range of 45-74. This universe of prospects is further refined to 31,000 after a household income filter of $50,000+ is applied.

Although the state does not release gun registration records for marketing purposes, the owners believe that approximately 20 percent of Illinois residents are gun owners. Based on this percentage, it is plausible to believe that about 6,000 of ProtectionStar's prospects fall within this category, some of whom already may have obtained concealed carry permits.

PERSONNEL

ProtectionStar is being established by four professionals, who each bring unique skill sets to the business.

Roy Fisher, President

Entrepreneur Roy Fisher knows what it takes to run a successful business. Before rising crime rates inspired him to establish ProtectionStar, Roy began his business career by developing Fisher's Deli in 1994. Since then, the fast, casual restaurant concept has grown to include 13 locations throughout northern Illinois and southern Wisconsin. Roy learned many successful business management principles from his father, Pete, who operated a thriving family-owned hardware store for nearly 40 years. In addition, he holds an undergraduate business administration degree from Northern Illinois University. As president, Roy will be responsible for ProtectionStar's growth strategy. He holds a 51 percent ownership stake in the company.

Tim Stevens, Vice President of Operations

After retiring as the chief operating officer of a large manufacturing company, Tim Stevens decided to go into business for himself and recently acquired Thompson's Shooting Range. Renamed Ridgefield Range, Tim is significantly improving the shooting range business, and welcomed the opportunity to also become a partner in ProtectionStar, which is a complementary operation. In addition to providing a portion of the capital needed to establish the business, Tim also will lease ProtectionStar the land needed for classroom space (on the grounds of Ridgefield Range). He holds a 19 percent ownership stake in the company.

Ron Johnson, Instructor

Ron recently retired from a 30-year career in law enforcement, having served as a firearms instructor, police officer, and detective. A long-time gun enthusiast, Ron has received numerous awards in area shooting competitions. He is an NRA Certified Pistol Instructor, an Illinois State Certified Firearms Instructor, and an Illinois State Police Certified Concealed Carry Instructor. Ron holds a 15 percent ownership stake in the business, and will serve as a primary instructor.

Patrick Sharp, Instructor

A Vietnam veteran with 31 years of career military experience, Patrick's background includes working as a military policeman and a sniper instructor. Like Ron Johnson, he also is an NRA Certified Pistol Instructor, as well as a DOD Certified Law-Enforcement Firearms Instructor. In addition to being an Illinois State Police Certified Concealed Carry Instructor, Patrick also is licensed as a Utah Concealed Carry Instructor. Patrick holds a 15 percent ownership interest in ProtectionStar, where he will serve as a primary instructor.

Professional & Advisory Support

ProtectionStar has established a business banking account with Midwestern Regional Bank, including a merchant account for accepting credit card payments. Tax advisement is provided by Leonard Smith Partners LP. The owners worked in partnership with the local law firm, Healy & Brooks, to establish their corporation. The law firm will continue to provide the business with legal counsel on an as-needed basis.

Independent Contractors

ProtectionStar has identified eight independent contractors who are Illinois State Police Certified Concealed Carry Instructors. These individuals will work under the guidance and supervision of, and in partnership with, Ron Johnson and Patrick Sharp to provide class instruction on an as-needed basis, based on registration volumes.

GROWTH STRATEGY

Year one: Establish ProtectionStar as a trusted local resource for quality concealed carry training. Achieve gross revenues of $875,880, and net income of $132,235. Recoup the owners' initial startup investment of $110,000.

Year two: Begin offering concealed carry training for additional states for residents who wish to relocate or carry firearms while traveling. Increase gross revenues 15 percent, to $1,007,262, and generate net income of $183,013.

Year three: Achieve gross revenues of $1.16 million and net income of $245,595. Develop a new business plan for doubling the business' training capacity in year four by building a new (permanent construction) training facility.

The following table provides information regarding projected individual class registrations and services, on a per-unit basis:

Volume projections (units per year)	2015	2016	2017
8-hour course	324	373	428
12-hour course	648	745	857
16-hour course	1,080	1,242	1,428
Private instruction (16 hrs)	216	248	286
Permit application assistance	1,080	1,242	1,428

The following graph illustrates the business' projected growth in gross annual revenues (by category) during its first three years of operations:

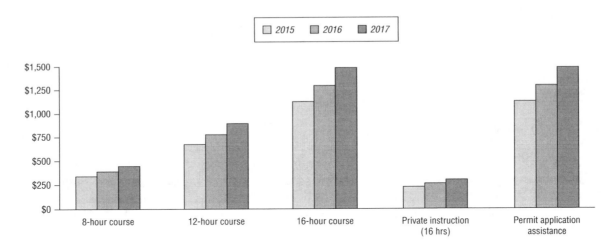

SERVICES

Training Courses

ProtectionStar will offer training in six distinct modules, which collectively provide the 16 hours of training required by the State of Illinois. Specifically, ProtectionStar's curriculum will satisfy the requirements of Illinois Public Act 098-0063 (https://ccl4illinois.com/ccw/Public/098-0063.pdf), which are listed below, as excerpted directly from Section 75 of the act:

1. firearm safety;

2. the basic principles of marksmanship;

3. care, cleaning, loading, and unloading of a concealable firearm;

4. all applicable State and federal laws relating to the ownership, storage, carry, and transportation of a firearm; and

5. instruction on the appropriate and lawful interaction with law enforcement while transporting or carrying a concealed firearm.

Students may qualify for as many as eight hours of credit toward the 16-hour requirement. Credit is awarded in specific cases, such as for training completed in other states, completion of specific courses offered by the National Rifle Association, completion of the Illinois Hunter Safety Course, and prior military experience. A complete list is available to customers upon request. When credit is given, students may not need to complete every module. For this reason, ProtectionStar will package course modules into 8-, 12-, and 16-hour training courses.

Students with no prior experience will first complete the 8-hour NRA Basic Pistol Shooting Course. Through a combination of classroom and range training, this course provides basic skills training for pistol ownership and operation. It covers topics such as shooting fundamentals, range rules, gun safety, pistol parts/operation, cleaning, and more. This course also is taken by individuals with no interest in concealed carry training.

Beyond the NRA Basic Pistol Shooting Course, the remainder of ProtectionStar's curriculum will satisfy the other requirements of Illinois Public Act 098-0063.

In addition to training, ProtectionStar's staff also will provide course graduates with assistance (for a fee) filing their application with the state of Illinois, if desired.

Fees

ProtectionStar has established the following fee structure for its training courses and other offerings:

- 8-hour training course ($200)

- 12-hour training course ($325)

- 16-hour training course ($360)

- Private one-on-one training (16 hours total; $800)

- Application assistance ($50)

MARKETING & SALES

In order to reach key prospects, ProtectionStar will run a highly-targeted direct marketing initiative, involving the purchase of a mailing list from a reputable list broker. This will enable the business to send quarterly mailings to approximately 7,500 households (to reach the total prospect universe of 31,000 identified in the Market Analysis section of this plan). In addition, the business will purchase highly-specialized, niche mailing lists from gun shows and gun magazines to ensure that key prospects (e.g., gun enthusiasts and prospective gun owners) are being reached with information about concealed carry training opportunities.

The centerpiece of ProtectionStar's direct mail campaign will be a glossy, four-color postcard, developed in partnership with a local advertising agency. The marketing collateral will feature a "protect yourself from violent crime" thematic, and will include a call to action with a special incentive (e.g., register to win a free training course) for contacting ProtectionStar for more information about its services. Respondents will receive a four-color brochure (also developed by the aforementioned advertising agency) containing specific details regarding ProtectionStar's program, along with a thank-you letter from the owners.

ProtectionStar also will maintain its own customer/prospect database, based on responses to its direct mailings, class registrations, referrals, drawings at special events, and information requests received via mail and interactive channels.

In addition to direct marketing, ProtectionStar's marketing strategy also will include several other key tactics, including a Web site (created by a local independent Web developer) with online registration capabilities, a Facebook page, and exhibition at regional gun shows, fishing and hunting shows, county fairs, home shows, and related events. The owners also will attempt to sponsor a handgun-themed radio show on a local AM talk station (this tactic has been successful in other markets nationwide) and will pursue the development of a guest column in an independent local newspaper, which is distributed freely throughout the community.

OPERATIONS

Location

ProtectionStar's operations will be based on the grounds of Tim Stevens' shooting range, Ridgefield Range, in a modular classroom building (28' x 60'). The pre-owned structure, which was relocated from a nearby location, includes two classrooms, two offices, men's and women's bathrooms, and a small meeting space. It contains two entrances/exits and is equipped with both air conditioning and heat. Live fire exercises with concealable firearms, which are required as part of Illinois training, are provided at Ridgefield Range's facilities. ProtectionStar and Ridgefield Range are easily accessible to the public from several major roadways, and offer ample, convenient parking. As a separate and distinct business, ProtectionStar will maintain its own phone number and registration activities.

Start-up Equipment

It will be necessary for ProtectionStar's owners to make several capital purchases prior to establishing the business. Totaling $59,533, these include:

- 30 Pistols/.22 Caliber (for rental) ($8,370)
- Ammunition (initial inventory) ($1,500)
- 4 Ramps for Portable Classroom Building Access (18' long, 4' wide): ($2,000)
- 2010 Modular Classroom Building (28' x 60'): ($26,000)
- Site Preparation Costs ($15,000)
- 2 Proxima Projectors ($1,250)
- 2 Projection screens ($375)
- 2 Laptop Computers ($1,000)
- 2 MS Office Software Licenses ($825)
- HP Laser Printer ($275)
- 2 Instructor Desks ($450)
- 2 Office Chairs ($300)
- 60 Student Desk/Chairs (with Tablet Arms) ($1,688)
- Assorted Office Supplies/Equipment ($500)

LEGAL

ProtectionStar has developed very specific policies, rules, and regulations (available for review upon request) in connection with its training courses. These ensure adherence to all applicable local, state, and federal laws. For example, training is only offered to individuals aged 21 and over with a valid Firearm Owners Identification card and no criminal record. Class participants are not allowed to bring live ammunition into the classroom (a designated, secure storage area is provided adjacent to the shooting range). At their sole discretion, instructors may disqualify any student from class participation for any reason, including concerns regarding safety and behavior. ProtectionStar's owners have purchased appropriate liability insurance coverage.

FINANCIAL ANALYSIS

The owners anticipate first-year gross revenues of nearly $900,000, which are projected to grow at a compound rate of 15 percent during years two and three. The business is expected to be profitable from the very beginning, with net revenue of approximately $132,000 anticipated during year one.

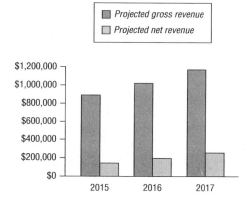

ProtectionStar has prepared a complete set of pro forma financial statements, which are available upon request. The following table provides an overview of key projections during the first three years of operations:

Revenue	2014	2015	2016
8-hour course	$ 64,800	$ 74,520	$ 85,698
12-hour course	$233,280	$ 268,272	$ 308,513
16-hour course	$351,000	$ 403,650	$ 464,198
Private instruction (16 hrs)	$172,800	$ 198,720	$ 228,528
Permit application assistance	$ 54,000	$ 62,100	$ 71,415
Total revenue	**$875,880**	**$1,007,262**	**$1,158,351**
Expenses			
Salaries	$380,000	$ 418,000	$ 458,000
Payroll taxes	$ 57,000	$ 62,700	$ 68,700
Independent contractors	$200,000	$ 230,000	$ 264,500
Utilities	$ 2,500	$ 2,750	$ 3,000
Rent	$ 8,970	$ 8,970	$ 8,970
Insurance	$ 4,225	$ 4,436	$ 4,879
Course materials	$ 38,750	$ 44,563	$ 51,247
Office supplies	$ 1,950	$ 2,080	$ 2,210
Equipment	$ 3,500	$ 3,500	$ 3,500
Marketing & advertising	$ 40,000	$ 40,000	$ 40,000
Telecommunications & internet	$ 1,500	$ 1,500	$ 1,500
Professional development	$ 2,500	$ 2,500	$ 2,500
Travel & entertainment	$ 250	$ 250	$ 250
Taxes & fees	$ 2,500	$ 3,000	$ 3,500
Total expenses	**$743,645**	**$ 824,249**	**$ 912,756**
Net income/loss	**$132,235**	**$ 183,013**	**$ 245,595**

Startup Costs

In addition to approximately $60,000 in start-up costs, the owners require an additional $50,000 to fund initial operations, for a total of $110,000. With a 51 percent ownership stake in the business, Roy Fisher will provide $56,100 in funding, with $20,900 provided by Tim Stevens, and $16,500 provided by both Ron Johnson and Patrick Sharp.

Country Club

Leaning Tree Country Club

3423 Jefferson Ave.
Woodbury, NY 11797

BizPlaDB.com

Leaning Tree Country Club, Inc. is a New York-based corporation that will provide customers with a massive 36 hole golf course, a private membership restaurant, and a day spa that will be operated on-site. The Company was founded by George Hempster.

1.0 EXECUTIVE SUMMARY

The purpose of this business plan is to raise $20,000,000 for the development of a country club while showcasing the expected financials and operations over the next three years. Leaning Tree Country Club, Inc. ("the Company") is a New York-based corporation that will provide customers with a massive 36 hole golf course, a private membership restaurant, and a day spa that will be operated on-site. The Company was founded by George Hempster.

1.1 The Services

As stated above, the business intends to develop an expansive country club facility that will feature a 36 hole golf course, private membership restaurants services, an on-site day spa, and many other ancillary services that are in demand among people that frequent country clubs.

The business intends to solicit membership fees (including initiation fees) as the Leaning Tree Country Club facility nears its completion. The business will also generate very high gross margins generated from the services mentioned above.

The third section of the business plan will further describe the services offered by Leaning Tree Country Club.

1.2 Financing

Mr. Hempster is seeking to raise $20,000,000 from an investor(s). Mr. Hempster expects to sell a 50% equity interest in the business in exchange for the requisite capital. The tentative terms of this agreement can be found in the second section of the business plan. The financing will be used for the following:

- Development of the Company's location.

- Financing for the first six months of operation.

- Capital to purchase FF and E for Leaning Tree Country Club.

1.3 Mission Statement

Leaning Tree Country Club, Inc.'s mission is to become a well known golf course facility and family entertainment destination for wealthier residents living within the Company's targeted market.

1.4 Management Team

The Company was founded by George Hempster. Mr. Hempster has more than 10 years of experience in the hospitality industry. Through his expertise, he will be able to bring the operations of the business to profitability within its first year of operations.

1.5 Sales Forecasts

Mr. Hempster expects a strong rate of growth at the start of operations. Below are the expected financials over the next three years.

Proforma profit and loss (yearly)

Year	1	2	3
Sales	$13,836,672	$16,604,006	$19,426,687
Operating costs	$ 6,626,540	$ 7,000,660	$ 7,385,689
EBITDA	$ 3,758,171	$ 5,460,993	$ 7,194,445
Taxes, interest, and depreciation	$ 1,923,361	$ 2,570,434	$ 3,229,145
Net profit	$ 1,834,810	$ 2,890,559	$ 3,965,299

Sales, operating costs, and profit forecast

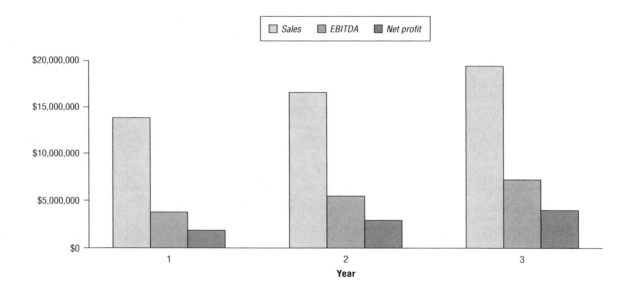

1.6 Expansion Plan

The Founder expects that the business will aggressively expand during the first three years of operation. Mr. Hempster intends to implement marketing campaigns that will effectively target individuals that are interested in becoming members of a country club.

The Company may seek to develop additional country club properties after the third to fifth year of operation.

2.0 COMPANY AND FINANCING SUMMARY

2.1 Registered Name and Corporate Structure
Leaning Tree Country Club, Inc. is registered as a corporation in the State of New York.

2.2 Required Funds
At this time, Leaning Tree Country Club requires $20,000,000 of equity funds. Below is a breakdown of how these funds will be used:

Projected startup costs

Golf course development	$ 13,000,000
Working capital	$ 1,300,000
FF&E	$ 1,250,000
Property improvements	$ 500,000
Security deposits	$ 75,000
Insurance	$ 100,000
Facility	$ 3,000,000
Marketing budget	$ 750,000
Miscellaneous and unforeseen costs	$ 25,000
Total startup costs	**$20,000,000**

2.3 Investor Equity
At this time, the Company is seeking to sell a 50% equity interest in the business for the requisite capital sought in this business plan. The investor(s) will also receive a seat on the board of directors and a regular stream of dividends starting in the first year of operation. Please reference the Company's private placement memorandum for more information regarding the specifics of this investment.

2.4 Management Equity
After the requisite capital is raised, Mr. Hempster will retain a 50% ownership in the business.

2.5 Exit Strategies
The Management has planned for three possible exit strategies. The first strategy would be to sell the Company to a larger entity at a significant premium. Since the country club industry maintains a moderate risk profile once the business is established, the Management feels that the Company could be sold for ten to fifteen times earnings.

The second exit scenario would entail selling a portion of the Company via an initial public offering (or "IPO"). After a detailed analysis, it was found that the Company could sell for twenty times earnings on the open market depending on the business's annual growth rate and strength of earnings. However, taking a company public involves significant legal red tape. Leaning Tree Country Club, Inc. would be bound by the significant legal framework of the Sarbanes-Oxley Act in addition to the legal requirements set forth in form S1 of the Securities and Exchange Commission. The Company would also have to comply with the Securities Act of 1933 and the Exchange Act of 1934.

The last exit scenario would involve the use of a private placement memorandum to raise capital from private sources. This is also a significantly expensive process that requires the assistance of both an experienced securities law firm and an investment bank. Funds would be raised from private equity and merchant banking sources in exchange for a percentage of the Company's stock.

2.6 Investor Divesture
This will be discussed during negotiations.

3.0 COUNTRY CLUB SERVICES

Below is a description of the services offered by Leaning Tree Country Club.

3.1 Golf Course

As stated in the executive summary, Leaning Tree Country Club will feature a full 36 hole golf course (two different 18 hole courses) that will be of PGA championship quality.

Currently, Management is reviewing applications from a number of professional golfers and professional golf course designers that will assist the business in developing a layout of a golf course that will be of moderate difficulty for country club members.

3.2 Country Club Restaurant

As part of the members' enrollment, they will have access to a highly developed club house that will feature a high-end restaurant. No cash will change hands when members use the Company's country club facility. All accounts will be billed on a monthly basis to members. At this time, Management is seeking to hire an outstanding chef to develop the menu, restaurant layout, and general operations of Leaning Tree Country Club Restaurant.

3.3 Day Spa

Leaning Tree Country Club, Inc. will also have a full service day spa that will provide massage therapy services, manicures/pedicures, as well as other spa services including, but not limited to:

- Facials

- Body Waxing

- Anti-Aging Treatments

- Aromatherapy

Each of these services will render a significant amount of revenue for the business.

4.0 STRATEGIC AND MARKET ANALYSIS

4.1 Economic Outlook

This section of the analysis will detail the economic climate, the country club industry, the customer profile, and the competition that the business will face as it progresses through its business operations.

Currently, the economic market condition in the United States is moderate. Unemployment rates have declined while asset prices have risen substantially. However, in the event of an economic recession, there may be a negative impact on Leaning Tree Country Club's ability to secure new membership on an ongoing basis.

4.2 Industry Analysis

Within the United States, there are approximately 12,261 country clubs that operate on a for-profit basis or a not-for-profit basis. Each year, these businesses generate approximately $20 billion of revenues while providing jobs to more than 312,000 people. Annual payrolls in each of the last five years have exceeded $8 billion.

This is a mature industry, and the expected future growth rate is expected to wane as the demand for country club lifestyles have declined sharply given the current economic climate. Additionally, as many younger people now travel more frequently, the demand for new members is expected to decline over the next ten years. However, country clubs may be able to recruit new members from the baby boomer population.

4.3 Customer Profile

Leaning Tree Country Club's average client will be an upper-middle class man or woman that frequently enjoys playing golf, tennis, and belonging to a membership club. Common traits among clients will include:

- Annual household income exceeding $250,000

- Will spend $20,000 on membership fees and usage of Leaning Tree Country Club's facilities.

- Lives within 10 miles of the Company's country club facility.

4.4 Competition

Within the greater New York metropolitan area, there are approximately 30 private country clubs in operation. As such, and from the onset of operations, it is imperative that the business develop a strong brand name for the luxurious quality of Leaning Tree Country Club's golf course and amenities (as outlined the previous section of the business plan). Additionally, Leaning Tree Country Club intends to target younger members of the golfing community so that the will become lifelong members of the club. This will ensure profitability at all times.

5.0 MARKETING PLAN

Leaning Tree Country Club intends to maintain an extensive marketing campaign that will ensure maximum visibility for the business in its targeted market. Below is an overview of the marketing strategies and objectives of the business.

5.1 Marketing Objectives

- Establish relationships with the local community of the target market.

- Engage a broad-based public relations firm targeted towards wealthy people living within the target market.

- Develop relationships with trade associations, legal associations, medical associations, and related entities in order to drive individuals to Leaning Tree Country Club for membership enrollment.

5.2 Marketing Strategies

Management intends to use a qualified advertising and marketing firm to help Leaning Tree Country Club reach its intended audience of wealthy people living in the Company's targeted market. This campaign will include the use of traditional print and media advertising as well as the Internet. Direct advertising campaigns will be of significant importance to the Company as the business is offering its services to a specified group of upper-middle and upper income people.

Timely coverage of the Company and its facilities will be further directed through ongoing press relations, news releases and feature stories targeted at key professional communities and other media outlets. Publicity activities will be designed to generate ongoing coverage about Leaning Tree Country Club in targeted media by providing writers and editors with newsworthy releases, features, stories, briefs, and visual material for their columns and stories. In-depth coverage may also be obtained about the Company by hosting in-house interviews to be conducted by our company spokesperson, George Hempster.

The Company may also use a number of TV and radio personalities to visit and experience Leaning Tree Country Club so that they may "plug" the facility in lifestyle and travel columns during their respective interviews.

5.3 Pricing

It is expected that a Club member will pay approximately $20,000 per year in fees and dues to become and remain a member of the facility.

6.0 ORGANIZATIONAL PLAN AND PERSONNEL SUMMARY

6.1 Corporate Organization

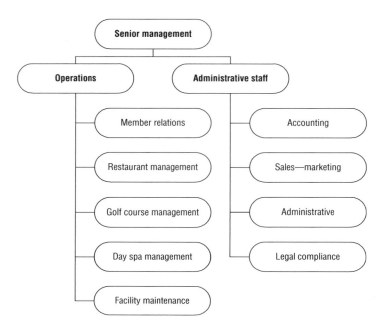

6.2 Organizational Budget

Personnel plan—yearly

Year	1	2	3
Senior management	$ 750,000	$ 772,500	$ 795,675
Customer service staff	$1,050,000	$1,081,500	$1,113,945
Restaurant and day spa staff	$ 825,000	$ 849,750	$ 875,243
Golf course staff	$ 700,000	$ 721,000	$ 742,630
Accounting and administrative	$ 675,000	$ 695,250	$ 716,108
Total	**$4,000,000**	**$4,120,000**	**$4,243,600**
Numbers of personnel			
Senior management	6	6	6
Customer service staff	35	35	35
Restaurant and day spa staff	30	30	30
Golf course staff	20	20	20
Accounting and administrative	15	15	15
Totals	**106**	**106**	**106**

Personnel expense breakdown

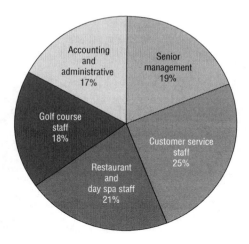

7.0 FINANCIAL PLAN

7.1 Underlying Assumptions

The Company has based its proforma financial statements on the following:

• Leaning Tree Country Club will have an annual revenue growth rate of 16% per year.

• The Founder will acquire $20,000,000 of equity funds to develop the facility.

• Leaning Tree Country Club property will have an annual appreciation rate of 6% per annum.

7.2 Sensitivity Analysis

In the event of an economic downturn, the business may have a decline in its revenues. Enrolling as a member in a country club is a luxury and during times of deleterious economic conditions, the business may have issues with its top line income. However, the Company is targeting its services towards wealthy people who are less swayed by difficult economic climates. Additionally, the high margins generated by the business will ensure its continued profitability despite moderate decreases in revenue.

7.3 Source of Funds

Financing

Equity contributions	
Investor(s)	$ 20,000,000.00
Total equity financing	**$20,000,000.00**
Banks and lenders	
Total debt financing	**$ 0.00**
Total financing	**$20,000,000.00**

7.4 General Assumptions

General assumptions

Year	1	2	3
Short term interest rate	9.5%	9.5%	9.5%
Long term interest rate	10.0%	10.0%	10.0%
Federal tax rate	33.0%	33.0%	33.0%
State tax rate	5.0%	5.0%	5.0%
Personnel taxes	15.0%	15.0%	15.0%

7.5 Profit and Loss Statements

Proforma profit and loss (yearly)

Year	1	2	3
Sales	**$13,836,672**	**$16,604,006**	**$19,426,687**
Cost of goods sold	$ 3,451,961	$ 4,142,354	$ 4,846,554
Gross margin	75.05%	75.05%	75.05%
Operating income	**$10,384,711**	**$12,461,653**	**$14,580,134**
Expenses			
Payroll	$ 4,000,000	$ 4,120,000	$ 4,243,600
General and administrative	$ 495,000	$ 514,800	$ 535,392
Marketing expenses	$ 830,200	$ 996,240	$ 1,165,601
Professional fees and licensure	$ 52,190	$ 53,756	$ 55,368
Insurance costs	$ 219,870	$ 230,864	$ 242,407
Travel and vehicle costs	$ 117,596	$ 129,356	$ 142,291
Facility maintenance	$ 242,500	$ 254,625	$ 267,356
Miscellaneous costs	$ 69,183	$ 83,020	$ 97,133
Payroll taxes	$ 600,000	$ 618,000	$ 636,540
Total operating costs	**$ 6,626,540**	**$ 7,000,660**	**$ 7,385,689**
EBITDA	**$ 3,758,171**	**$ 5,460,993**	**$ 7,194,445**
Federal income tax	$ 1,240,196	$ 1,802,128	$ 2,374,167
State income tax	$ 187,909	$ 273,050	$ 359,722
Interest expense	$ 0	$ 0	$ 0
Depreciation expenses	$ 495,256	$ 495,256	$ 495,256
Net profit	**$ 1,834,810**	**$ 2,890,559**	**$ 3,965,299**
Profit margin	**13.26%**	**17.41%**	**20.41%**

Sales, operating costs, and profit forecast

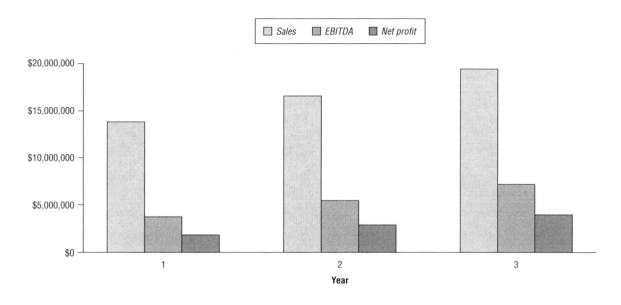

7.6 Cash Flow Analysis

Proforma cash flow analysis—yearly

Year	1	2	3
Cash from operations	$ 2,330,066	$3,385,815	$4,460,556
Cash from receivables	$ 0	$ 0	$ 0
Operating cash inflow	**$ 2,330,066**	**$3,385,815**	**$4,460,556**
Other cash inflows			
Equity investment	$20,000,000	$ 0	$ 0
Increased borrowings	$ 0	$ 0	$ 0
Sales of business assets	$ 0	$ 0	$ 0
A/P increases	$ 37,902	$ 43,587	$ 50,125
Total other cash inflows	**$20,037,902**	**$ 43,587**	**$ 50,125**
Total cash inflow	**$22,367,968**	**$3,429,403**	**$4,510,681**
Cash outflows			
Repayment of principal	$ 0	$ 0	$ 0
A/P decreases	$ 24,897	$ 29,876	$ 35,852
A/R increases	$ 0	$ 0	$ 0
Asset purchases	$17,950,000	$ 338,582	$ 446,056
Dividends	$ 1,864,053	$2,708,652	$3,568,444
Total cash outflows	**$19,838,950**	**$3,077,110**	**$4,050,352**
Net cash flow	**$ 2,529,018**	**$ 352,292**	**$ 460,329**
Cash balance	**$ 2,529,018**	**$2,881,311**	**$3,341,640**

Proforma cash flow (yearly)

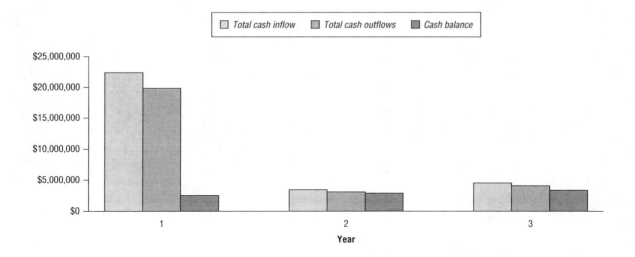

7.7 Balance Sheet

Proforma balance sheet—yearly

Year	1	2	3
Assets			
Cash	$ 2,529,018	$ 2,881,311	$ 3,341,640
Amortized development/expansion costs	$ 700,000	$ 733,858	$ 778,464
Golf course and facilities	$ 17,490,000	$ 18,539,400	$ 19,651,764
FF&E	$ 1,125,000	$ 1,429,723	$ 1,831,173
Accumulated depreciation	($ 495,256)	($ 990,513)	($ 1,485,769)
Total assets	**$21,348,762**	**$22,593,779**	**$24,117,272**
Liabilities and equity			
Accounts payable	$ 13,005	$ 26,716	$ 40,990
Long term liabilities	$ 0	$ 0	$ 0
Other liabilities	$ 0	$ 0	$ 0
Total liabilities	**$ 13,005**	**$ 26,716**	**$ 40,990**
Net worth	**$21,335,757**	**$22,567,063**	**$24,076,282**
Total liabilities and equity	**$21,348,762**	**$22,593,779**	**$24,117,272**

Proforma balance sheet

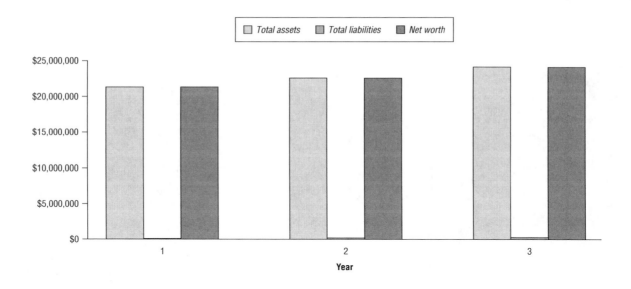

7.8 Breakeven Analysis

Monthly break even analysis

Year	1	2	3
Monthly revenue	$ 735,771	$ 777,311	$ 820,063
Yearly revenue	$8,829,255	$9,327,736	$9,840,752

Break even analysis

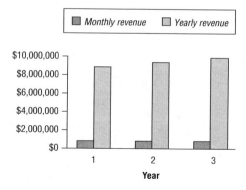

7.9 Business Ratios

Business ratios—yearly

Year	1	2	3
Sales			
Sales growth	0.00%	20.00%	17.00%
Gross margin	75.10%	75.10%	75.10%
Financials			
Profit margin	13.26%	17.41%	20.41%
Assets to liabilities	1,641.58	845.71	588.38
Equity to liabilities	1,640.58	844.71	587.38
Assets to equity	1.00	1.00	1.00
Liquidity			
Acid test	194.47	107.85	81.52
Cash to assets	0.12	0.13	0.14

7.10 Three Year Profit and Loss Statement

Profit and loss statement (first year)

Months	1	2	3	4	5	6	7
Sales	$1,152,000	$1,152,192	$1,152,384	$1,152,576	$1,152,768	$1,152,960	$1,153,152
Cost of goods sold	$ 287,400	$287,448	$ 287,496	$ 287,544	$ 287,592	$ 287,640	$ 287,687
Gross margin	75.1%	75.1%	75.1%	75.1%	75.1%	75.1%	75.1%
Operating income	$ 864,600	$ 864,744	$ 864,888	$ 865,032	$ 865,176	$ 865,321	$ 865,465
Expenses							
Payroll	$ 333,333	$ 333,333	$ 333,333	$ 333,333	$ 333,333	$ 333,333	$ 333,333
General and administrative	$ 41,250	$ 41,250	$ 41,250	$ 41,250	$ 41,250	$ 41,250	$ 41,250
Marketing expenses	$ 69,183	$ 69,183	$ 69,183	$ 69,183	$ 69,183	$ 69,183	$ 69,183
Professional fees and licensure	$ 4,349	$ 4,349	$ 4,349	$ 4,349	$ 4,349	$ 4,349	$ 4,349
Insurance costs	$ 18,323	$ 18,323	$ 18,323	$ 18,323	$ 18,323	$ 18,323	$ 18,323
Travel and vehicle costs	$ 9,800	$ 9,800	$ 9,800	$ 9,800	$ 9,800	$ 9,800	$ 9,800
Facility maintenance	$ 20,208	$ 20,208	$ 20,208	$ 20,208	$ 20,208	$ 20,208	$ 20,208
Miscellaneous costs	$ 5,765	$ 5,765	$ 5,765	$ 5,765	$ 5,765	$ 5,765	$ 5,765
Payroll taxes	$ 50,000	$ 50,000	$ 50,000	$ 50,000	$ 50,000	$ 50,000	$ 50,000
Total operating costs	$ 552,212	$ 552,212	$ 552,212	$ 552,212	$ 552,212	$ 552,212	$ 552,212
EBITDA	$ 312,388	$ 312,532	$ 312,677	$ 312,821	$ 312,965	$ 313,109	$ 313,253
Federal income tax	$ 103,255	$ 103,272	$ 103,289	$ 103,307	$ 103,324	$ 103,341	$ 103,358
State income tax	$ 15,645	$ 15,647	$ 15,650	$ 15,653	$ 15,655	$ 15,658	$ 15,660
Interest expense	$ 0	$ 0	$ 0	$ 0	$ 0	$ 0	$ 0
Depreciation expense	$ 41,271	$ 41,271	$ 41,271	$ 41,271	$ 41,271	$ 41,271	$ 41,271
Net profit	$ 152,217	$ 152,342	$ 152,466	$ 152,590	$ 152,714	$ 152,839	$ 152,963

Profit and loss statement (first year cont.)

Month	8	9	10	11	12	1
Sales	$1,153,344	$1,153,536	$1,153,728	$1,153,920	$1,154,112	$13,836,672
Cost of goods sold	$ 287,735	$ 287,783	$ 287,831	$ 287,879	$ 287,927	$ 3,451,961
Gross margin	75.1%	75.1%	75.1%	75.1%	75.1%	75.1%
Operating income	$ 865,609	$ 865,753	$ 865,897	$ 866,041	$ 866,185	$10,384,711
Expenses						
Payroll	$ 333,333	$ 333,333	$ 333,333	$ 333,333	$ 333,333	$ 4,000,000
General and administrative	$ 41,250	$ 41,250	$ 41,250	$ 41,250	$ 41,250	$ 495,000
Marketing expenses	$ 69,183	$ 69,183	$ 69,183	$ 69,183	$ 69,183	$ 830,200
Professional fees and licensure	$ 4,349	$ 4,349	$ 4,349	$ 4,349	$ 4,349	$ 52,190
Insurance costs	$ 18,323	$ 18,323	$ 18,323	$ 18,323	$ 18,323	$ 219,870
Travel and vehicle costs	$ 9,800	$ 9,800	$ 9,800	$ 9,800	$ 9,800	$ 117,596
Facility maintenance	$ 20,208	$ 20,208	$ 20,208	$ 20,208	$ 20,208	$ 242,500
Miscellaneous costs	$ 5,765	$ 5,765	$ 5,765	$ 5,765	$ 5,765	$ 69,183
Payroll taxes	$ 50,000	$ 50,000	$ 50,000	$ 50,000	$ 50,000	$ 600,000
Total operating costs	$ 552,212	$ 552,212	$ 552,212	$ 552,212	$ 552,212	$ 6,626,540
EBITDA	$ 313,397	$ 313,541	$ 313,685	$ 313,829	$ 313,973	$ 3,758,171
Federal income tax	$ 103,376	$ 103,393	$ 103,410	$ 103,427	$ 103,444	$ 1,240,196
State income tax	$ 15,663	$ 15,666	$ 15,668	$ 15,671	$ 15,673	$ 187,909
Interest expense	$ 0	$ 0	$ 0	$ 0	$ 0	$ 0
Depreciation expense	$ 41,271	$ 41,271	$ 41,271	$ 41,271	$ 41,271	$ 495,256
Net profit	$ 153,087	$ 153,212	$ 153,336	$ 153,460	$ 153,584	$ 1,834,810

Profit and loss statement (second year)

Quarter	Q1	2 Q2	Q3	Q4	2
Sales	$3,320,801	$4,151,002	$4,483,082	$4,649,122	$16,604,006
Cost of goods sold	$ 828,471	$1,035,588	$1,118,435	$1,159,859	$ 4,142,354
Gross margin	75.1%	75.1%	75.1%	75.1%	75.1%
Operating income	$2,492,331	$3,115,413	$3,364,646	$3,489,263	$12,461,653
Expenses					
Payroll	$ 824,000	$1,030,000	$1,112,400	$1,153,600	$ 4,120,000
General and administrative	$ 102,960	$ 128,700	$ 138,996	$ 144,144	$ 514,800
Marketing expenses	$ 199,248	$ 249,060	$ 268,985	$ 278,947	$ 996,240
Professional fees and licensure	$ 10,751	$ 13,439	$ 14,514	$ 15,052	$ 53,756
Insurance costs	$ 46,173	$ 57,716	$ 62,333	$ 64,642	$ 230,864
Travel and vehicle costs	$ 25,871	$ 32,339	$ 34,926	$ 36,220	$ 129,356
Facility maintenance	$ 50,925	$ 63,656	$ 68,749	$ 71,295	$ 254,625
Miscellaneous costs	$ 16,604	$ 20,755	$ 22,415	$ 23,246	$ 83,020
Payroll taxes	$ 123,600	$ 154,500	$ 166,860	$ 173,040	$ 618,000
Total operating costs	$1,400,132	$1,750,165	$1,890,178	$1,960,185	$ 7,000,660
EBITDA	$1,092,199	$1,365,248	$1,474,468	$1,529,078	$ 5,460,993
Federal income tax	$ 360,426	$ 450,532	$ 486,574	$ 504,596	$ 1,802,128
State income tax	$ 54,610	$ 68,262	$ 73,723	$ 76,454	$ 273,050
Interest expense	$ 0	$ 0	$ 0	$ 0	$ 0
Depreciation expense	$ 123,814	$ 123,814	$ 123,814	$ 123,814	$ 495,256
Net profit	$ 553,349	$ 722,640	$ 790,356	$ 824,214	$ 2,890,559

Profit and loss statement (third year)

Quarter	Q1	3 Q2	Q3	Q4	3
Sales	$3,885,337	$4,856,672	$5,245,206	$5,439,472	$19,426,687
Cost of goods sold	$ 969,311	$1,211,638	$1,308,570	$1,357,035	$ 4,846,554
Gross margin	75.1%	75.1%	75.1%	75.1%	75.1%
Operating income	$2,916,027	$3,645,033	$3,936,636	$4,082,437	$14,580,134
Expenses					
Payroll	$ 848,720	$1,060,900	$1,145,772	$1,188,208	$ 4,243,600
General and administrative	$ 107,078	$ 133,848	$ 144,556	$ 149,910	$ 535,392
Marketing expenses	$ 233,120	$ 291,400	$ 314,712	$ 326,368	$ 1,165,601
Professional fees and licensure	$ 11,074	$ 13,842	$ 14,949	$ 15,503	$ 55,368
Insurance costs	$ 48,481	$ 60,602	$ 65,450	$ 67,874	$ 242,407
Travel and vehicle costs	$ 28,458	$ 35,573	$ 38,419	$ 39,842	$ 142,291
Facility maintenance	$ 53,471	$ 66,839	$ 72,186	$ 74,860	$ 267,356
Miscellaneous costs	$ 19,427	$ 24,283	$ 26,226	$ 27,197	$ 97,133
Payroll taxes	$ 127,308	$ 159,135	$ 171,866	$ 178,231	$ 636,540
Total operating costs	$1,477,138	$1,846,422	$1,994,136	$2,067,993	$ 7,385,689
EBITDA	$1,438,889	$1,798,611	$1,942,500	$2,014,444	$ 7,194,445
Federal income tax	$ 474,833	$ 593,542	$ 641,025	$ 664,767	$ 2,374,167
State income tax	$ 71,944	$ 89,931	$ 97,125	$ 100,722	$ 359,722
Interest expense	$ 0	$ 0	$ 0	$ 0	$ 0
Depreciation expense	$ 123,814	$ 123,814	$ 123,814	$ 123,814	$ 495,256
Net profit	$ 768,297	$ 991,325	$1,080,536	$1,125,141	$ 3,965,299

7.11 Three Year Cash Flow Analysis

Cash flow analysis (first year)

Month	1	2	3	4	5	6	7
Cash from operations	$ 193,489	$ 193,613	$ 193,737	$ 193,861	$ 193,986	$ 194,110	$ 194,234
Cash from receivables	$ 0	$ 0	$ 0	$ 0	$ 0	$ 0	$ 0
Operating cash inflow	$ 193,489	$ 193,613	$ 193,737	$ 193,861	$ 193,986	$ 194,110	$ 194,234
Other cash inflows							
Equity investment	$20,000,000	$ 0	$ 0	$ 0	$ 0	$ 0	$ 0
Increased borrowings	$ 0	$ 0	$ 0	$ 0	$ 0	$ 0	$ 0
Sales of business assets	$ 0	$ 0	$ 0	$ 0	$ 0	$ 0	$ 0
A/P increases	$ 3,159	$ 3,159	$ 3,159	$ 3,159	$ 3,159	$ 3,159	$ 3,159
Total other cash inflows	$20,003,159	$ 3,159	$ 3,159	$ 3,159	$ 3,159	$ 3,159	$ 3,159
Total cash inflow	$20,196,647	$ 196,771	$ 196,896	$ 197,020	$ 197,144	$ 197,269	$ 197,393
Cash outflows							
Repayment of principal	$ 0	$ 0	$ 0	$ 0	$ 0	$ 0	$ 0
A/P decreases	$ 2,075	$ 2,075	$ 2,075	$ 2,075	$ 2,075	$ 2,075	$ 2,075
A/R increases	$ 0	$ 0	$ 0	$ 0	$ 0	$ 0	$ 0
Asset purchases	$17,950,000	$ 0	$ 0	$ 0	$ 0	$ 0	$ 0
Dividends	$ 0	$ 0	$ 0	$ 0	$ 0	$ 0	$ 0
Total cash outflows	$17,952,075	$ 2,075	$ 2,075	$ 2,075	$ 2,075	$ 2,075	$ 2,075
Net cash flow	$ 2,244,572	$ 194,697	$ 194,821	$ 194,945	$ 195,069	$ 195,194	$ 195,318
Cash balance	$ 2,244,572	$2,439,269	$2,634,090	$2,829,035	$3,024,105	$3,219,298	$3,414,616

Cash flow analysis (first year cont.)

Month	8	9	10	11	12	1
Cash from operations	$ 194,359	$ 194,483	$ 194,607	$ 194,731	$ 194,856	$ 2,330,066
Cash from receivables	$ 0	$ 0	$ 0	$ 0	$ 0	$ 0
Operating cash inflow	**$ 194,359**	**$ 194,483**	**$ 194,607**	**$ 194,731**	**$ 194,856**	**$ 2,330,066**
Other cash inflows						
Equity investment	$ 0	$ 0	$ 0	$ 0	$ 0	$20,000,000
Increased borrowings	$ 0	$ 0	$ 0	$ 0	$ 0	$ 0
Sales of business assets	$ 0	$ 0	$ 0	$ 0	$ 0	$ 0
A/P increases	$ 3,159	$ 3,159	$ 3,159	$ 3,159	$ 3,159	$ 37,902
Total other cash inflows	**$ 3,159**	**$ 3,159**	**$ 3,159**	**$ 3,159**	**$ 3,159**	**$20,037,902**
Total cash inflow	**$ 197,517**	**$ 197,641**	**$ 197,766**	**$ 197,890**	**$ 198,014**	**$22,367,968**
Cash outflows						
Repayment of principal	$ 0	$ 0	$ 0	$ 0	$ 0	$ 0
A/P decreases	$ 2,075	$ 2,075	$ 2,075	$ 2,075	$ 2,075	$ 24,897
A/R increases	$ 0	$ 0	$ 0	$ 0	$ 0	$ 0
Asset purchases	$ 0	$ 0	$ 0	$ 0	$ 0	$17,950,000
Dividends	$ 0	$ 0	$ 0	$ 0	$1,864,053	$ 1,864,053
Total cash outflows	**$ 2,075**	**$ 2,075**	**$ 2,075**	**$ 2,075**	**$1,866,128**	**$19,838,950**
Net cash flow	**$ 195,442**	**$ 195,567**	**$ 195,691**	**$ 195,815**	**−$1,668,114**	**$ 2,529,018**
Cash balance	**$3,610,059**	**$3,805,625**	**$4,001,316**	**$4,197,131**	**$2,529,018**	**$ 2,529,018**

Cash flow analysis (second year)

Quarter	Q1	2 Q2	Q3	Q4	2
Cash from operations	$ 677,163	$ 846,454	$ 914,170	$ 948,028	$3,385,815
Cash from receivables	$ 0	$ 0	$ 0	$ 0	$ 0
Operating cash inflow	**$ 677,163**	**$ 846,454**	**$ 914,170**	**$ 948,028**	**$3,385,815**
Other cash inflows					
Equity investment	$ 0	$ 0	$ 0	$ 0	$ 0
Increased borrowings	$ 0	$ 0	$ 0	$ 0	$ 0
Sales of business assets	$ 0	$ 0	$ 0	$ 0	$ 0
A/P increases	$ 8,717	$ 10,897	$ 11,769	$ 12,204	$ 43,587
Total other cash inflows	**$ 8,717**	**$ 10,897**	**$ 11,769**	**$ 12,204**	**$ 43,587**
Total cash inflow	**$ 685,881**	**$ 857,351**	**$ 925,939**	**$ 960,233**	**$3,429,403**
Cash outflows					
Repayment of principal	$ 0	$ 0	$ 0	$ 0	$ 0
A/P decreases	$ 5,975	$ 7,469	$ 8,067	$ 8,365	$ 29,876
A/R increases	$ 0	$ 0	$ 0	$ 0	$ 0
Asset purchases	$ 67,716	$ 84,645	$ 91,417	$ 94,803	$ 338,582
Dividends	$ 541,730	$ 677,163	$ 731,336	$ 758,423	$2,708,652
Total cash outflows	**$ 615,422**	**$ 769,278**	**$ 830,820**	**$ 861,591**	**$3,077,110**
Net cash flow	**$ 70,458**	**$ 88,073**	**$ 95,119**	**$ 98,642**	**$ 352,292**
Cash balance	**$2,599,477**	**$2,687,550**	**$2,782,669**	**$2,881,311**	**$2,881,311**

Cash flow analysis (third year)

Quarter	Q1	3 Q2	Q3	Q4	3
Cash from operations	$ 892,111	$1,115,139	$1,204,350	$1,248,956	$4,460,556
Cash from receivables	$ 0	$ 0	$ 0	$ 0	$ 0
Operating cash inflow	**$ 892,111**	**$1,115,139**	**$1,204,350**	**$1,248,956**	**$4,460,556**
Other cash inflows					
Equity investment	$ 0	$ 0	$ 0	$ 0	$ 0
Increased borrowings	$ 0	$ 0	$ 0	$ 0	$ 0
Sales of business assets	$ 0	$ 0	$ 0	$ 0	$ 0
A/P increases	$ 10,025	$ 12,531	$ 13,534	$ 14,035	$ 50,125
Total other cash inflows	**$ 10,025**	**$ 12,531**	**$ 13,534**	**$ 14,035**	**$ 50,125**
Total cash inflow	**$ 902,136**	**$1,127,670**	**$1,217,884**	**$1,262,991**	**$4,510,681**
Cash outflows					
Repayment of principal	$ 0	$ 0	$ 0	$ 0	$ 0
A/P decreases	$ 7,170	$ 8,963	$ 9,680	$ 10,038	$ 35,852
A/R increases	$ 0	$ 0	$ 0	$ 0	$ 0
Asset purchases	$ 89,211	$ 111,514	$ 120,435	$ 124,896	$ 446,056
Dividends	$ 713,689	$ 892,111	$ 963,480	$ 999,164	$3,568,444
Total cash outflows	**$ 810,070**	**$1,012,588**	**$1,093,595**	**$1,134,098**	**$4,050,352**
Net cash flow	**$ 92,066**	**$ 115,082**	**$ 124,289**	**$ 128,892**	**$ 460,329**
Cash balance	**$2,973,376**	**$3,088,459**	**$3,212,748**	**$3,341,640**	**$3,341,640**

Credit Monitoring Service

First Check Credit Monitoring Service, Inc.

PO Box 23112
New York, NY 10012

BizPlaDB.com

First Check Credit Monitoring Service, Inc. is a New York-based corporation that will provide credit monitoring services and, when necessary, credit repair services to customers in its targeted market. The Company was founded by Charles E. Smythe.

1.0 EXECUTIVE SUMMARY

The purpose of this business plan is to raise $100,000 for the development of a credit monitoring business while showcasing the expected financials and operations over the next three years. First Check Credit Monitoring Service, Inc. ("the Company") is a New York-based corporation that will provide credit monitoring services and, when necessary, credit repair services to customers in its targeted market. The Company was founded by Charles E. Smythe.

1.1 The Services

First Check Credit Monitoring Service, Inc. will provide customers with a high level of credit repair services that seek to alert customers to blemishes on a client's credit report among the three major credit bureaus. Approximately 40% of the U.S. population has issues with their credit profiles and, as such, the market for knowing a credit score is very strong. The Company will charge approximately $30 per month for these services. It will provide customers with the knowledge and help they need to monitor and correct their scores while at the same time providing the company with a highly recurring stream of revenue.

The business also will hire licensed debt advisory and credit counselors that will work directly with both clients and lenders in regards to a client's credit profile or debt issues if they are detected by First Check Credit Monitoring. The business will receive fixed fees for these services.

The third section of the business plan will further describe the services offered by First Check Credit Monitoring Service, Inc.

1.2 Financing

Mr. Smythe is seeking to raise $100,000 as a bank loan. The interest rate and loan agreement are to be further discussed during negotiation. This business plan assumes that the business will receive a 10-year loan with a 9% fixed interest rate. The financing will be used for the following:

- Development of the Company's office location.
- Financing for the first six months of operation.
- Capital to purchase FF and E and computers.

Mr. Smythe will contribute $10,000 to the venture.

1.3 Mission Statement

First Check Credit Monitoring's mission is to assist people with understanding and protecting their credit through continual monitoring.

1.4 Management Team

The Company was founded by Charles E. Smythe. Mr. Smythe has more than 10 years of experience in the credit and lending industry. Through his expertise, he will be able to bring the operations of the business to profitability within its first year of operations.

1.5 Sales Forecasts

Mr. Smythe expects a strong rate of growth at the start of operations. Below are the expected financials over the next three years.

Proforma profit and loss (yearly)

Year	1	2	3
Sales	$867,438	$1,040,926	$1,217,883
Operating costs	$576,785	$ 639,983	$ 666,682
EBITDA	$191,777	$ 282,291	$ 412,379
Taxes, interest, and depreciation	$ 85,006	$ 115,705	$ 164,727
Net profit	$106,771	$ 166,586	$ 247,65

Sales, operating costs, and profit forecast

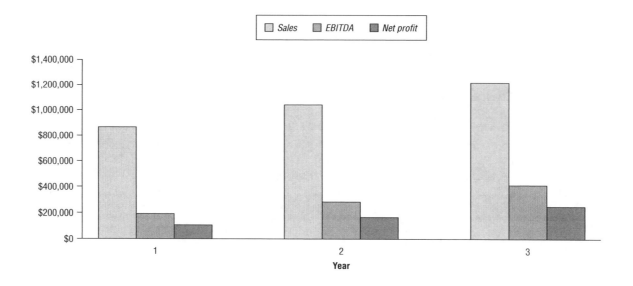

1.6 Expansion Plan

The Founder expects that the business will aggressively expand during the first three years of operation. Mr. Smythe intends to implement marketing campaigns that will effectively target individuals within the target market.

2.0 COMPANY AND FINANCING SUMMARY

2.1 Registered Name and Corporate Structure

First Check Credit Monitoring Service, Inc. is registered as a corporation in the State of New York.

2.2 Required Funds

At this time, First Check Credit Monitoring Service, Inc. requires $100,000 of debt funds. Below is a breakdown of how these funds will be used:

Projected startup costs

Initial lease payments and deposits	$ 10,000
Working capital	$ 35,000
FF&E	$ 20,000
Leasehold improvements	$ 5,000
Security deposits	$ 5,000
Insurance	$ 2,500
Computer equipment	$ 10,000
Marketing budget	$ 17,500
Miscellaneous and unforeseen costs	$ 5,000
Total startup costs	**$110,000**

Use of funds

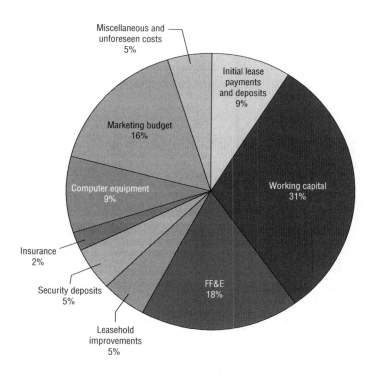

2.3 Investor Equity

Mr. Smythe is not seeking an investment from a third party at this time.

2.4 Management Equity

Charles E. Smythe owns 100% of First Check Credit Monitoring Service, Inc.

2.5 Exit Strategy

If the business is very successful, Mr. Smythe may seek to sell the business to a third party for a significant earnings multiple. Most likely, the Company will hire a qualified business broker to sell the business on behalf of First Check Credit Monitoring. Based on historical numbers, the business could fetch a sales premium of up to 4 times earnings.

3.0 SERVICES

Below is a description of the credit repair and advisory services offered by the company.

3.1 Credit Monitoring Services

The primary revenue center for the business will come from the ongoing monitoring of credit reports among people that are enrolled in the Company's services. As stated in the executive summary, the business will charge approximately $30 per month for these services. The business will have access to any new alerts from all three major credit bureaus (Experian, TransUnion, and Equifax). The business will have a website where individuals can login to see their credit report and read any new notifications regarding their accounts.

This service will provide a recurring income stream for the business, which will substantially increase the Company's valuation.

3.2 Credit Repair Services

The secondary source of revenue for the business will come from the direct consultation to clients that have minor or substantial credit issues that are detected by the Company through its monitoring services. The Company's counselors will properly advise and work with clients to effectively mitigate negative remarks on an individual's credit reports.

The Company will also offer advice to clients regarding how to properly maintain their credit scores.

4.0 STRATEGIC AND MARKET ANALYSIS

4.1 Economic Outlook

This section of the analysis will detail the economic climate, the credit monitoring and counseling industry, the customer profile, and the competition that the business will face as it progresses through its business operations.

Currently, the economic market condition in the United States is moderate. Unemployment rates have declined while asset prices have increased substantially. However, it should be noted that credit counseling and credit repair businesses typically operate with a great degree of economic immunity as people will continue to require these services on an ongoing basis. As such, Management feels that the current economic climate is actually an excellent time to launch this type of business.

4.2 Industry Analysis

The credit management industry (which includes credit monitoring) represents over 5,000 established businesses that employ more than 15,000. Each year, these businesses aggregately generate more than $2 billion dollars a year of revenue and provide gross annual payrolls of $600 million dollars. The growth rate for this industry has been tremendous over the last five years as the growth of financial transactions over the Internet has increased significantly. Over the last five years, the number of agents operating within this market more than doubled, with income received by these firms increasing more than 300%.

As lending has become much more scientific over the last fifteen years with the implementation of electronic credit reporting, FICO scores, and electronic employment records, the need for consumers to maintain strong credit profiles is tremendous.

4.3 Customer Profile

Management expects that a diverse group of people will use the Company's credit monitoring (and, from time to time, credit repair) services. The business, after obtaining licensure to operate in multiple states, will be able to effectively assist thousands of people with their credit monitoring needs. Approximately 40% of adult Americans have some form of issue with the credit profile. As such, the potential market for this type of service exceeds 70 million people. Mr. Smythe expects that the average income of a customer will be $28,000 to $45,000 per year.

4.4 Competition

All three primary credit bureaus currently offer services that are significantly similar to that of First Check Credit Monitoring Service, Inc. However, the business will create a specific differentiating factor in that it can alert an individual to any change among all of their credit reports (rather than one specific credit report). Additionally, the business will allow customers to have direct access to specialized lenders in regards to their large purchases that require financing. These lenders will be prescreened so that consumers can get the best interest rates on mortgages, vehicle loans/leases, credit cards, and other credit facilities.

5.0 MARKETING PLAN

First Check Credit Monitoring Service, Inc. intends to maintain an extensive marketing campaign that will ensure maximum visibility for the business in its targeted market. Below is an overview of the marketing strategies and objectives of the Company.

5.1 Marketing Objectives
- Establish relationships with accountants within the targeted market.

- Showcase a number of free services offered by the Company so that the business can generate a large customer base from the onset of operations.

5.2 Marketing Strategies

The Company will maintain a sizable amount of print and traditional advertising methods within regional markets to promote the credit monitoring and ancillary services that the Company is offering. Mr. Smythe will also develop ongoing referral relationships with accountants within the Company's local market who will refer clients with significant credit issues and need to have their credit reports continually monitored. In time, this will become an invaluable source of new business for First Check Credit Monitoring Service, Inc.

From the launch of operations, the business will retain a specialized marketing firm that has substantial experience in marketing financial related products to the general public. Concurrently, the business will also hire a search engine optimization firm that will ensure that the Company's website is prominently featured among search engines when individuals seek credit monitoring services. Ideally, the business will work with a third party marketing firm that can provide both of these services in-house.

Finally, the Company will use pay-per-click marketing strategies (among all major search engines) in order to appropriately generate traffic to the Company's website. Initially, this will be an expensive strategy for marketing the business as competition is fierce within this industry. However, if it is properly executed, the financial results can be tremendous for the business.

5.3 Pricing

The business will charge approximately $30 per month for ongoing credit monitoring.

The Company will also receive large streams of revenue by providing ancillary credit repair and advisory services to the general public. This secondary revenue center could potentially yield thousands of dollars per customer.

6.0 ORGANIZATIONAL PLAN AND PERSONNEL SUMMARY

6.1 Corporate Organization

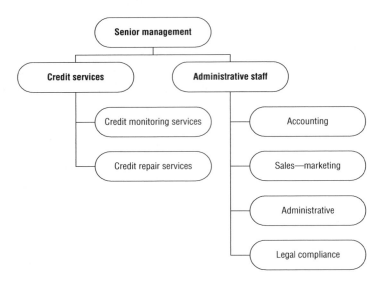

6.2 Organizational Budget

Personnel plan—yearly

Year	1	2	3
Owner	$ 75,000	$ 77,250	$ 79,568
General manager	$ 55,000	$ 56,650	$ 58,350
Credit monitors	$162,500	$200,850	$206,876
Bookkeeper	$ 25,000	$ 25,750	$ 26,523
Administrative	$ 69,000	$ 71,070	$ 73,202
Total	**$386,500**	**$431,570**	**$444,517**

Numbers of personnel

Owner	1	1	1
General manager	1	1	1
Credit monitors	5	6	6
Bookkeeper	1	1	1
Administrative	3	3	3
Totals	**11**	**12**	**12**

Personnel expense breakdown

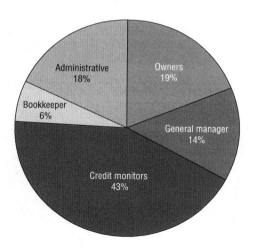

7.0 FINANCIAL PLAN

7.1 Underlying Assumptions

The Company has based its proforma financial statements on the following:

- First Check Credit Monitoring Service, Inc. will have an annual revenue growth rate of 16% per year.

- The Owner will acquire $100,000 of debt funds to develop the business.

- The loan will have a 10-year term with a 9% interest rate.

7.2 Sensitivity Analysis

The Company's revenues are not sensitive to changes in the general economy. In fact, during deleterious economic conditions (like the current economy), Mr. Smythe expects an increase in revenue as more people turn to credit monitoring services to make sure that they do not have any credit issues. Additionally, the Company generates high margin income from its services, which will allow First Check Credit Monitoring Service, Inc. to thrive in any economic climate.

7.3 Source of Funds

Financing

Equity contributions

Management investment	$ 10,000.00
Total equity financing	**$ 10,000.00**
Banks and lenders	
Banks and lenders	$ 100,000.00
Total debt financing	**$100,000.00**
Total financing	**$110,000.00**

7.4 General Assumptions

General assumptions

Year	1	2	3
Short term interest rate	9.5%	9.5%	9.5%
Long term interest rate	10.0%	10.0%	10.0%
Federal tax rate	33.0%	33.0%	33.0%
State tax rate	5.0%	5.0%	5.0%
Personnel taxes	15.0%	15.0%	15.0%

7.5 Profit and Loss Statements

Proforma profit and loss (yearly)

Year	1	2	3
Sales	**$867,438**	**$1,040,926**	**$1,217,883**
Cost of goods sold	$ 98,876	$ 118,651	$ 138,822
Gross margin	88.60%	88.60%	88.60%
Operating income	**$768,562**	**$ 922,275**	**$1,079,061**
Expenses			
Payroll	$386,500	$ 431,570	$ 444,517
General and administrative	$ 25,200	$ 26,208	$ 27,256
Marketing expenses	$ 26,023	$ 31,228	$ 36,536
Professional fees and licensure	$ 15,000	$ 15,450	$ 15,914
Insurance costs	$ 12,500	$ 13,125	$ 13,781
Travel and vehicle costs	$ 15,000	$ 16,500	$ 18,150
Rent and utilities	$ 34,250	$ 35,963	$ 37,761
Miscellaneous costs	$ 4,337	$ 5,205	$ 6,089
Payroll taxes	$ 57,975	$ 64,736	$ 66,678
Total operating costs	**$576,785**	**$ 639,983**	**$ 666,682**
EBITDA	**$191,777**	**$ 282,291**	**$ 412,379**
Federal income tax	$ 63,286	$ 90,473	$ 133,621
State income tax	$ 9,589	$ 13,708	$ 20,246
Interest expense	$ 8,738	$ 8,131	$ 7,468
Depreciation expenses	$ 3,393	$ 3,393	$ 3,393
Net profit	**$106,771**	**$ 166,586**	**$ 247,652**
Profit margin	**12.31%**	**16.00%**	**20.33%**

Sales, operating costs, and profit forecast

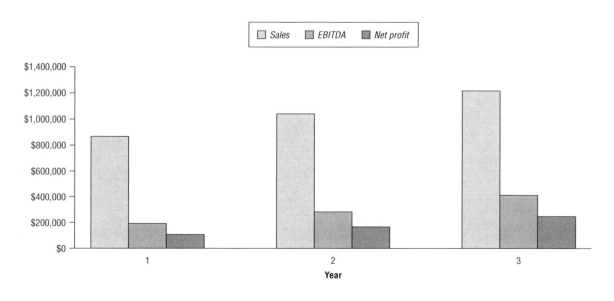

7.6 Cash Flow Analysis

Proforma cash flow analysis—yearly

Year	1	2	3
Cash from operations	$110,164	$169,979	$251,045
Cash from receivables	$ 0	$ 0	$ 0
Operating cash inflow	**$110,164**	**$169,979**	**$251,045**
Other cash inflows			
Equity investment	$ 10,000	$ 0	$ 0
Increased borrowings	$100,000	$ 0	$ 0
Sales of business assets	$ 0	$ 0	$ 0
A/P increases	$ 37,902	$ 43,587	$ 50,125
Total other cash inflows	**$147,902**	**$ 43,587**	**$ 50,125**
Total cash inflow	**$258,066**	**$213,566**	**$301,170**
Cash outflows			
Repayment of principal	$ 6,463	$ 7,070	$ 7,733
A/P decreases	$ 24,897	$ 29,876	$ 35,852
A/R increases	$ 0	$ 0	$ 0
Asset purchases	$ 57,500	$ 16,998	$ 25,104
Dividends	$ 77,115	$144,482	$213,388
Total cash outflows	**$165,975**	**$198,426**	**$282,077**
Net cash flow	**$ 92,091**	**$ 15,140**	**$ 19,093**
Cash balance	**$ 92,091**	**$107,231**	**$126,324**

Proforma cash flow (yearly)

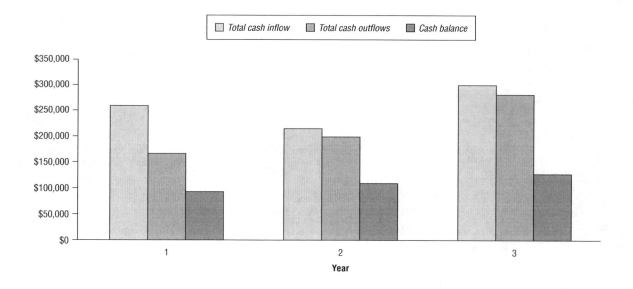

7.7 Balance Sheet

Proforma balance sheet—yearly

Year	1	2	3
Assets			
Cash	$ 92,091	$ 107,231	$126,324
Amortized development/expansion costs	$ 17,500	$ 19,200	$ 21,710
Computer equipment	$ 10,000	$ 18,499	$ 31,051
FF&E	$ 20,000	$ 26,799	$ 36,841
Accumulated depreciation	($ 3,393)	($ 6,786)	($ 10,179)
Total assets	**$136,198**	**$164,943**	**$205,748**
Liabilities and equity			
Accounts payable	$ 13,005	$ 26,716	$ 40,990
Long term liabilities	$ 93,537	$ 86,467	$ 79,397
Other liabilities	$ 0	$ 0	$ 0
Total liabilities	**$106,542**	**$113,183**	**$120,387**
Net worth	**$ 29,656**	**$ 51,760**	**$ 85,361**
Total liabilities and equity	**$136,198**	**$164,943**	**$205,748**

Proforma balance sheet

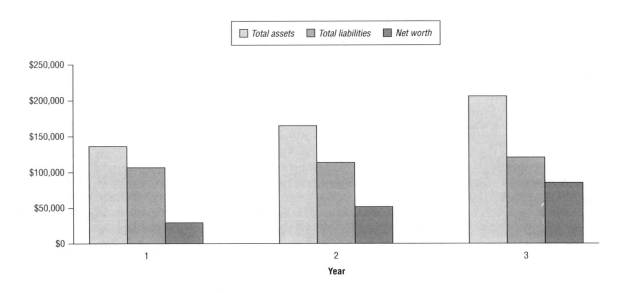

7.8 Breakeven Analysis

Monthly break even analysis

Year	1	2	3
Monthly revenue	$ 54,249	$ 60,193	$ 62,704
Yearly revenue	$650,989	$722,317	$752,451

Break even analysis

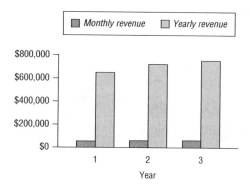

7.9 Business Ratios

Business ratios—yearly

Year	1	2	3
Sales			
Sales growth	0.0%	20.0%	17.0%
Gross margin	88.6%	88.6%	88.6%
Financials			
Profit margin	12.31%	16.00%	20.33%
Assets to liabilities	1.28	1.46	1.71
Equity to liabilities	0.28	0.46	0.71
Assets to equity	4.59	3.19	2.41
Liquidity			
Acid test	0.86	0.95	1.05
Cash to assets	0.68	0.65	0.61

7.10 Three Year Profit and Loss Statement

Profit and loss statement (first year)

Months	1	2	3	4	5	6	7
Sales	$71,500	$71,643	$71,786	$71,929	$72,072	$72,215	$72,358
Cost of goods sold	$ 8,150	$ 8,166	$ 8,183	$ 8,199	$ 8,215	$ 8,232	$ 8,248
Gross margin	88.6%	88.6%	88.6%	88.6%	88.6%	88.6%	88.6%
Operating income	$63,350	$63,477	$63,603	$63,730	$63,857	$63,984	$64,110
Expenses							
Payroll	$32,208	$32,208	$32,208	$32,208	$32,208	$32,208	$32,208
General and administrative	$ 2,100	$ 2,100	$ 2,100	$ 2,100	$ 2,100	$ 2,100	$ 2,100
Marketing expenses	$ 2,169	$ 2,169	$ 2,169	$ 2,169	$ 2,169	$ 2,169	$ 2,169
Professional fees and licensure	$ 1,250	$ 1,250	$ 1,250	$ 1,250	$ 1,250	$ 1,250	$ 1,250
Insurance costs	$ 1,042	$ 1,042	$ 1,042	$ 1,042	$ 1,042	$ 1,042	$ 1,042
Travel and vehicle costs	$ 1,250	$ 1,250	$ 1,250	$ 1,250	$ 1,250	$ 1,250	$ 1,250
Rent and utilities	$ 2,854	$ 2,854	$ 2,854	$ 2,854	$ 2,854	$ 2,854	$ 2,854
Miscellaneous costs	$ 361	$ 361	$ 361	$ 361	$ 361	$ 361	$ 361
Payroll taxes	$ 4,831	$ 4,831	$ 4,831	$ 4,831	$ 4,831	$ 4,831	$ 4,831
Total operating costs	$48,065	$48,065	$48,065	$48,065	$48,065	$48,065	$48,065
EBITDA	$15,285	$15,411	$15,538	$15,665	$15,791	$15,918	$16,045
Federal income tax	$ 5,216	$ 5,227	$ 5,237	$ 5,248	$ 5,258	$ 5,269	$ 5,279
State income tax	$ 790	$ 792	$ 794	$ 795	$ 797	$ 798	$ 800
Interest expense	$ 750	$ 746	$ 742	$ 738	$ 734	$ 730	$ 726
Depreciation expense	$ 283	$ 283	$ 283	$ 283	$ 283	$ 283	$ 283
Net profit	$ 8,245	$ 8,364	$ 8,482	$ 8,601	$ 8,719	$ 8,838	$ 8,957

Profit and loss statement (first year cont.)

Month	8	9	10	11	12	1
Sales	$72,501	$72,644	$72,787	$72,930	$73,073	$867,438
Cost of goods sold	$ 8,264	$ 8,280	$ 8,297	$ 8,313	$ 8,329	$ 98,876
Gross margin	88.6%	88.6%	88.6%	88.6%	88.6%	88.6%
Operating income	$64,237	$64,364	$64,490	$64,617	$64,744	$768,562
Expenses						
Payroll	$32,208	$32,208	$32,208	$32,208	$32,208	$386,500
General and administrative	$ 2,100	$ 2,100	$ 2,100	$ 2,100	$ 2,100	$ 25,200
Marketing expenses	$ 2,169	$ 2,169	$ 2,169	$ 2,169	$ 2,169	$ 26,023
Professional fees and licensure	$ 1,250	$ 1,250	$ 1,250	$ 1,250	$ 1,250	$ 15,000
Insurance costs	$ 1,042	$ 1,042	$ 1,042	$ 1,042	$ 1,042	$ 12,500
Travel and vehicle costs	$ 1,250	$ 1,250	$ 1,250	$ 1,250	$ 1,250	$ 15,000
Rent and utilities	$ 2,854	$ 2,854	$ 2,854	$ 2,854	$ 2,854	$ 34,250
Miscellaneous costs	$ 361	$ 361	$ 361	$ 361	$ 361	$ 4,337
Payroll taxes	$ 4,831	$ 4,831	$ 4,831	$ 4,831	$ 4,831	$ 57,975
Total operating costs	$48,065	$48,065	$48,065	$48,065	$48,065	$576,785
EBITDA	$16,171	$16,298	$16,425	$16,552	$16,678	$191,777
Federal income tax	$ 5,290	$ 5,300	$ 5,310	$ 5,321	$ 5,331	$ 63,286
State income tax	$ 801	$ 803	$ 805	$ 806	$ 808	$ 9,589
Interest expense	$ 722	$ 718	$ 714	$ 710	$ 706	$ 8,738
Depreciation expense	$ 283	$ 283	$ 283	$ 283	$ 283	$ 3,393
Net profit	$ 9,076	$ 9,194	$ 9,313	$ 9,432	$ 9,551	$106,771

Profit and loss statement (second year)

Quarter	Q1	2 Q2	Q3	Q4	2
Sales	$208,185	$260,231	$281,050	$291,459	$1,040,926
Cost of goods sold	$ 23,730	$ 29,663	$ 32,036	$ 33,222	$ 118,651
Gross margin	88.6%	88.6%	88.6%	88.6%	88.6%
Operating income	$184,455	$230,569	$249,014	$258,237	$ 922,275
Expenses					
Payroll	$ 86,314	$107,893	$116,524	$120,840	$ 431,570
General and administrative	$ 5,242	$ 6,552	$ 7,076	$ 7,338	$ 26,208
Marketing expenses	$ 6,246	$ 7,807	$ 8,431	$ 8,744	$ 31,228
Professional fees and licensure	$ 3,090	$ 3,863	$ 4,172	$ 4,326	$ 15,450
Insurance costs	$ 2,625	$ 3,281	$ 3,544	$ 3,675	$ 13,125
Travel and vehicle costs	$ 3,300	$ 4,125	$ 4,455	$ 4,620	$ 16,500
Rent and utilities	$ 7,193	$ 8,991	$ 9,710	$ 10,070	$ 35,963
Miscellaneous costs	$ 1,041	$ 1,301	$ 1,405	$ 1,457	$ 5,205
Payroll taxes	$ 12,947	$ 16,184	$ 17,479	$ 18,126	$ 64,736
Total operating costs	$127,997	$159,996	$172,796	$179,195	$ 639,983
EBITDA	$ 56,458	$ 70,573	$ 76,219	$ 79,042	$ 282,291
Federal income tax	$ 18,095	$ 22,618	$ 24,428	$ 25,332	$ 90,473
State income tax	$ 2,742	$ 3,427	$ 3,701	$ 3,838	$ 13,708
Interest expense	$ 2,092	$ 2,053	$ 2,013	$ 1,973	$ 8,131
Depreciation expense	$ 848	$ 848	$ 848	$ 848	$ 3,393
Net profit	$ 32,682	$ 41,626	$ 45,228	$ 47,050	$ 166,586

Profit and loss statement (third year)

Quarter	Q1	3 Q2	Q3	Q4	3
Sales	**$243,577**	**$304,471**	**$328,828**	**$341,007**	**$1,217,883**
Cost of goods sold	$ 27,764	$ 34,705	$ 37,482	$ 38,870	$ 138,822
Gross margin	88.6%	88.6%	88.6%	88.6%	88.6%
Operating income	**$215,812**	**$269,765**	**$291,347**	**$302,137**	**$1,079,061**
Expenses					
Payroll	$ 88,903	$111,129	$120,020	$124,465	$ 444,517
General and administrative	$ 5,451	$ 6,814	$ 7,359	$ 7,632	$ 27,256
Marketing expenses	$ 7,307	$ 9,134	$ 9,865	$ 10,230	$ 36,536
Professional fees and licensure	$ 3,183	$ 3,978	$ 4,297	$ 4,456	$ 15,914
Insurance costs	$ 2,756	$ 3,445	$ 3,721	$ 3,859	$ 13,781
Travel and vehicle costs	$ 3,630	$ 4,538	$ 4,901	$ 5,082	$ 18,150
Rent and utilities	$ 7,552	$ 9,440	$ 10,195	$ 10,573	$ 37,761
Miscellaneous costs	$ 1,218	$ 1,522	$ 1,644	$ 1,705	$ 6,089
Payroll taxes	$ 13,336	$ 16,669	$ 18,003	$ 18,670	$ 66,678
Total operating costs	**$133,336**	**$166,671**	**$180,004**	**$186,671**	**$ 666,682**
EBITDA	**$ 82,476**	**$103,095**	**$111,342**	**$115,466**	**$ 412,379**
Federal income tax	$ 26,724	$ 33,405	$ 36,078	$ 37,414	$ 133,621
State income tax	$ 4,049	$ 5,061	$ 5,466	$ 5,669	$ 20,246
Interest expense	$ 1,932	$ 1,889	$ 1,846	$ 1,802	$ 7,468
Depreciation expense	$ 848	$ 848	$ 848	$ 848	$ 3,393
Net profit	**$ 48,923**	**$ 61,891**	**$ 67,104**	**$ 69,734**	**$ 247,652**

7.11 Three Year Cash Flow Analysis

Cash flow analysis (first year)

Month	1	2	3	4	5	6	7
Cash from operations	$ 8,528	$ 8,646	$ 8,765	$ 8,883	$ 9,002	$ 9,121	$ 9,240
Cash from receivables	$ 0	$ 0	$ 0	$ 0	$ 0	$ 0	$ 0
Operating cash inflow	**$ 8,528**	**$ 8,646**	**$ 8,765**	**$ 8,883**	**$ 9,002**	**$ 9,121**	**$ 9,240**
Other cash inflows							
Equity investment	$ 10,000	$ 0	$ 0	$ 0	$ 0	$ 0	$ 0
Increased borrowings	$100,000	$ 0	$ 0	$ 0	$ 0	$ 0	$ 0
Sales of business assets	$ 0	$ 0	$ 0	$ 0	$ 0	$ 0	$ 0
A/P increases	$ 3,159	$ 3,159	$ 3,159	$ 3,159	$ 3,159	$ 3,159	$ 3,159
Total other cash inflows	**$113,159**	**$ 3,159**	**$ 3,159**	**$ 3,159**	**$ 3,159**	**$ 3,159**	**$ 3,159**
Total cash inflow	**$121,686**	**$11,805**	**$11,923**	**$12,042**	**$12,161**	**$ 12,279**	**$ 12,398**
Cash outflows							
Repayment of principal	$ 517	$ 521	$ 525	$ 528	$ 532	$ 536	$ 540
A/P decreases	$ 2,075	$ 2,075	$ 2,075	$ 2,075	$ 2,075	$ 2,075	$ 2,075
A/R increases	$ 0	$ 0	$ 0	$ 0	$ 0	$ 0	$ 0
Asset purchases	$ 57,500	$ 0	$ 0	$ 0	$ 0	$ 0	$ 0
Dividends	$ 0	$ 0	$ 0	$ 0	$ 0	$ 0	$ 0
Total cash outflows	**$ 60,092**	**$ 2,595**	**$ 2,599**	**$ 2,603**	**$ 2,607**	**$ 2,611**	**$ 2,615**
Net cash flow	**$ 61,595**	**$ 9,209**	**$ 9,324**	**$ 9,439**	**$ 9,553**	**$ 9,668**	**$ 9,783**
Cash balance	**$ 61,595**	**$70,804**	**$80,128**	**$89,567**	**$99,120**	**$108,788**	**$118,571**

Cash flow analysis (first year cont.)

Month	8	9	10	11	12	1
Cash from operations	$ 9,358	$ 9,477	$ 9,596	$ 9,715	$ 9,834	$110,164
Cash from receivables	$ 0	$ 0	$ 0	$ 0	$ 0	$ 0
Operating cash inflow	**$ 9,358**	**$ 9,477**	**$ 9,596**	**$ 9,715**	**$ 9,834**	**$110,164**
Other cash inflows						
Equity investment	$ 0	$ 0	$ 0	$ 0	$ 0	$ 10,000
Increased borrowings	$ 0	$ 0	$ 0	$ 0	$ 0	$100,000
Sales of business assets	$ 0	$ 0	$ 0	$ 0	$ 0	$ 0
A/P increases	$ 3,159	$ 3,159	$ 3,159	$ 3,159	$ 3,159	$ 37,902
Total other cash inflows	**$ 3,159**	**$ 3,159**	**$ 3,159**	**$ 3,159**	**$ 3,159**	**$147,902**
Total cash inflow	**$ 12,517**	**$ 12,636**	**$ 12,754**	**$ 12,873**	**$12,992**	**$258,066**
Cash outflows						
Repayment of principal	$ 545	$ 549	$ 553	$ 557	$ 561	$ 6,463
A/P decreases	$ 2,075	$ 2,075	$ 2,075	$ 2,075	$ 2,075	$ 24,897
A/R increases	$ 0	$ 0	$ 0	$ 0	$ 0	$ 0
Asset purchases	$ 0	$ 0	$ 0	$ 0	$ 0	$ 57,500
Dividends	$ 0	$ 0	$ 0	$ 0	$77,115	$ 77,115
Total cash outflows	**$ 2,619**	**$ 2,623**	**$ 2,627**	**$ 2,632**	**$79,751**	**$165,975**
Net cash flow	**$ 9,897**	**$ 10,012**	**$ 10,127**	**$ 10,242**	**−$66,759**	**$ 92,091**
Cash balance	**$128,469**	**$138,481**	**$148,608**	**$158,849**	**$92,091**	**$ 92,091**

Cash flow analysis (second year)

Quarter	Q1	2 Q2	Q3	Q4	2
Cash from operations	$33,996	$42,495	$ 45,894	$ 47,594	$169,979
Cash from receivables	$ 0	$ 0	$ 0	$ 0	$ 0
Operating cash inflow	**$33,996**	**$42,495**	**$ 45,894**	**$ 47,594**	**$169,979**
Other cash inflows					
Equity investment	$ 0	$ 0	$ 0	$ 0	$ 0
Increased borrowings	$ 0	$ 0	$ 0	$ 0	$ 0
Sales of business assets	$ 0	$ 0	$ 0	$ 0	$ 0
A/P increases	$ 8,717	$10,897	$ 11,769	$ 12,204	$ 43,587
Total other cash inflows	**$ 8,717**	**$10,897**	**$ 11,769**	**$ 12,204**	**$ 43,587**
Total cash inflow	**$42,713**	**$53,392**	**$ 57,663**	**$ 59,799**	**$213,566**
Cash outflows					
Repayment of principal	$ 1,708	$ 1,747	$ 1,787	$ 1,827	$ 7,070
A/P decreases	$ 5,975	$ 7,469	$ 8,067	$ 8,365	$ 29,876
A/R increases	$ 0	$ 0	$ 0	$ 0	$ 0
Asset purchases	$ 3,400	$ 4,249	$ 4,589	$ 4,759	$ 16,998
Dividends	$28,896	$36,121	$ 39,010	$ 40,455	$144,482
Total cash outflows	**$39,980**	**$49,586**	**$ 53,453**	**$ 55,407**	**$198,426**
Net cash flow	**$ 2,734**	**$ 3,805**	**$ 4,210**	**$ 4,391**	**$ 15,140**
Cash balance	**$94,824**	**$98,630**	**$102,839**	**$107,231**	**$107,231**

Cash flow analysis (third year)

Quarter	Q1	3 Q2	Q3	Q4	3
Cash from operations	$ 50,209	$ 62,761	$ 67,782	$ 70,293	$251,045
Cash from receivables	$ 0	$ 0	$ 0	$ 0	$ 0
Operating cash inflow	**$ 50,209**	**$ 62,761**	**$ 67,782**	**$ 70,293**	**$251,045**
Other cash inflows					
Equity investment	$ 0	$ 0	$ 0	$ 0	$ 0
Increased borrowings	$ 0	$ 0	$ 0	$ 0	$ 0
Sales of business assets	$ 0	$ 0	$ 0	$ 0	$ 0
A/P increases	$ 10,025	$ 12,531	$ 13,534	$ 14,035	$ 50,125
Total other cash inflows	**$ 10,025**	**$ 12,531**	**$ 13,534**	**$ 14,035**	**$ 50,125**
Total cash inflow	**$ 60,234**	**$ 75,293**	**$ 81,316**	**$ 84,328**	**$301,170**
Cash outflows					
Repayment of principal	$ 1,869	$ 1,911	$ 1,954	$ 1,999	$ 7,733
A/P decreases	$ 7,170	$ 8,963	$ 9,680	$ 10,038	$ 35,852
A/R increases	$ 0	$ 0	$ 0	$ 0	$ 0
Asset purchases	$ 5,021	$ 6,276	$ 6,778	$ 7,029	$ 25,104
Dividends	$ 42,678	$ 53,347	$ 57,615	$ 59,749	$213,388
Total cash outflows	**$ 56,738**	**$ 70,497**	**$ 76,027**	**$ 78,815**	**$282,077**
Net cash flow	**$ 3,496**	**$ 4,795**	**$ 5,289**	**$ 5,513**	**$ 19,093**
Cash balance	**$110,727**	**$115,523**	**$120,811**	**$126,324**	**$126,324**

Electronic Waste Collection Service

e-WasteExpress LLC

2759 Mountain View Ave.
Pennington Industrial Park
Pennington, IL 62215

Paul Greenland

e-WasteExpress LLC specializes in the collection and transportation of electronic waste, including items such as computers, cell phones, and televisions.

EXECUTIVE SUMMARY

e-WasteExpress LLC specializes in the collection and transportation of electronic waste, including items such as computers, cell phones, and televisions. The business follows an "intermediary" model, in that it does not directly recycle the items it collects. Instead, e-WasteExpress has an exclusive transportation services arrangement with Pennington Recyclers Inc., which pays the company a 10 percent commission on all revenues generated from the reuse, recovery, and/or recycling of electronics collected by e-WasteExpress.

Pennington Recyclers is a traditional scrap metal recycling business that has experienced strong growth in the electronics recycling category. Because electronics pickup, decommissioning, and transportation is not a core competency of Pennington Recyclers, the company has chosen to outsource this "front-end" function to e-WasteExpress, a newly established business owned by Nathan Smith, who in addition to an entrepreneurial spirit has exceptional skills and experience in the areas of logistics and project management.

In addition to electronics pickup and disposal, one critical service provided by e-WasteExpress is media degaussing (demagnetizing) and sanitizing. This process ensures the on-site removal of sensitive information (e.g., health records, financial information, trade secrets, customer records, etc.) from items such as computers, hard drives, and servers. The company's degaussing and destruction equipment ensures that it meets government standards pertaining to a number of different regulations, including DOD 5220.22-M, Health Information Portability and Accountability Act (HIPAA), and PCI DSS (Payment Card Industry) Data Security Standard.

In 2014 the electronic recycling industry generated annual revenues of approximately $8.4 billion, according to the August 2014 market research report, *Electronic Goods Recycling*, published by IBIS World. Compared to projected annual gross domestic product growth of 2.5 percent through the year 2019, the report indicated that the e-recycling industry would experience annual growth of 10 percent during the same time period.

INDUSTRY ANALYSIS

As technology becomes more pervasive, the number of electronic devices on the market is increasing rapidly. Manufacturers constantly produce newer and better versions of devices such as mobile phones, tablet computers, DVD players, and televisions. Although older electronic devices may be used for a time, they eventually are discarded. However, improper disposal can be harmful to the environment. For example, the glass from old computer monitors and televisions contains lead compounds and cadmium. By 2014 roughly half of all states had laws pertaining to the proper disposal of electronic waste. Globally, electronic waste is a major problem in developing countries, including Africa, which are the recipients of waste from developed countries such as the United States.

In 2014 the electronic recycling industry generated annual revenues of approximately $8.4 billion, according to the August 2014 market research report, *Electronic Goods Recycling*, published by IBIS World. Compared to projected annual gross domestic product growth of 2.5 percent through the year 2019, the report indicated that the e-recycling industry would experience annual growth of 10 percent during the same time period.

According to *IEEE Spectrum*, a publication of the Institute of Electrical and Electronics Engineers, a 2013 study by the Solving the E-Waste Problem (StEP) Initiative revealed that China and the United States produced approximately 50 percent of the world's electronic waste in 2012. The United States generated 29.8 kilograms of waste per person, while China produced 5.4 kilograms per person. By 2017 StEP projected a 33 percent increase in the amount of electronic waste produced on a global basis, which was expected to reach 72 million tons.

In addition to being good for the environment, electronic waste disposal offers a variety of lucrative business opportunities. There literally is gold in electronic waste, with circuit boards containing gold-plated components. Other recoverable metals include brass. Roughly 80 percent of the components found in an electronic device either can be reused or recycled.

In conjunction with the disposal of electronic waste, data security often is a concern among individual consumers, as well as organizations and government agencies. Sensitive information (e.g., health records, financial information, trade secrets, customer records, etc.) must be permanently and securely removed from computers, hard drives, and servers. This is dictated by a variety of government regulations and standards, such as DOD 5220.22-M, Health Information Portability and Accountability Act (HIPAA), and PCI DSS (Payment Card Industry) Data Security Standard.

The recycling of electronic waste is supported by leading organizations such as the Consumer Electronics Association (CEA). In 2014 CEA was participating in the eCycling Leadership Initiative via its "billion pound challenge," which had a goal of pushing the amount of electronics recycled annually to 1 billion pounds by 2016. In support of this strategy, the organization established greenergadgets.org, a consumer Web site that provided information about recycling locations and tips regarding responsible disposal.

MARKET ANALYSIS

Regulatory Climate

e-WasteExpress is based in the State of Illinois, where the legal disposal of electronic waste is done in accordance with Illinois Public Act 97-0287 (The Electronic Products Recycling & Reuse Act). Effective in 2012, the act made it illegal to dispose of a variety of electronic devices, including televisions, computers, DVD players, and cable receivers, in landfills.

Consumer Market

The community of Pennington is located in Plainfield County. Covering 90 square miles, the city's population included 198,776 residents and 79,625 households in 2014, according to a community study conducted by the City of Pennington.

Based on the aforementioned study conducted by the Solving the E-Waste Problem (StEP) Initiative, the United States generates approximately 29.8 kilograms (65.7 pounds) of electronic waste per person. Using this figure as a rough guideline, the community of Pennington generates nearly 6 million kilograms (13.2 million pounds) of electronic waste per year.

Although individual residential pickups produce a regular stream of electronic waste, special disposal drives and events provide opportunities for large-scale collections. According to information from Pennington Recyclers, previous community pickup drives have yielded an average of 850 televisions, 400 computer monitors, 250 printers and copiers, as well as 74,000 pounds of CRT screens.

Commercial Market

Commercial customers represent a very important market, due to the amount of electronic waste they produce. Organizations produce electronic waste for a variety of reasons, including outsourcing, downsizing, and routine technology upgrades. In 2014 the community of Pennington was home to 10,445 businesses. Pennington Recyclers already has a customer base of 550 businesses, including several government agencies and large corporations, from which it collects electronic waste. These will now become customers of e-WasteExpress.

Competition

e-WasteExpress currently faces limited competition. Its principal competitor is Electronic Recyclers International, which claims to be North America's largest electronics recycler and provide services to every U.S. ZIP code via a network of eight facilities. In partnership with Pennington Recyclers, e-WasteExpress is the only local transporter of electronic waste.

PERSONNEL

Nathan Smith, Owner

e-WasteExpress is owned and operated by Nathan Smith, who in addition to an entrepreneurial spirit has exceptional skills and experience in the areas of logistics and project management. Prior to establishing the company, Smith was in charge of logistics and route management for ABC Alliance Co., a regional supplier of parts and equipment for manufacturing companies. When long-time friend Robert Mulford, owner of Pennington Recyclers, decided to expand the electronic waste segment of his business, but did not wish to manage the associated front-end activities, Smith identified a business opportunity with strong growth potential.

Support Staff

e-WasteExpress will commence operations with a staff that includes owner Nathan Smith, as well as one full-time associate and four part-time associates. Additional staff will be hired as the business expands, as outlined in the Growth Strategy section of this plan.

Professional & Advisory Support

e-WasteExpress has established a commercial checking account with Pennington Community Bank. Nathan Smith will rely upon Citizen Tax Service for accounting and tax preparation.

GROWTH STRATEGY

Pennington Recyclers Inc. pays a 10 percent commission on all revenues generated from the reuse, recovery, and recycling of electronics collected by e-WasteExpress. During its initial years of operation, e-WasteExpress will work exclusively with Pennington Recyclers, handling all of the electronic waste that the company recycles. For this reason, e-WasteExpress' growth strategy is interconnected with that of Pennington Recyclers.

According to an analysis of the local market, and previous recycling activity, the two organizations estimate that Pennington Recyclers' revenues pertaining to electronic waste recycling and reuse will total $5 million in 2015, $7 million in 2016, and $9 million in 2017. Based on these projections, e-WasteExpress is anticipating revenues of $500,000 in year one, $700,000 in year two, and $900,000 in year three. e-WasteExpress will focus on gradually increasing the commercial side of its business, as well as the number of electronic waste drives it holds in the community. This will allow for more streamlined and consolidated collection efforts. By reducing residential pickups slightly each year, e-WasteExpress will be able to improve its operational costs by saving time, lowering fuel costs, and reducing vehicle usage.

The following goals have been established in support of the company's financial growth targets:

Year One: Begin operations with one box truck and a staff that includes owner Nathan Smith, one full-time associate, and four part-time associates. In addition to residential and commercial pickups, host six community electronic waste drives. During the business' first year of operations, Nathan Smith anticipates that 30 percent of revenues will be attributed to commercial accounts. Of the 70 percent of revenues generated within the consumer segment, 25 percent are projected to be residential pickups, followed by 45 percent from recycling drives.

Year Two: Expand operations to include two box trucks. Hire one additional full-time associate and two additional part-time associates. In addition to residential and commercial pickups, host nine community electronic waste drives. Increase revenues attributed to commercial accounts to 35 percent, with 15 percent attributed to consumer/residential pickups and 50 percent attributed to recycling drives.

Year Three: Expand operations to include three box trucks. Hire one additional full-time associate and two additional part-time associates. In addition to residential and commercial pickups, host 12 community electronic waste drives. Increase revenues attributed to commercial accounts to 40 percent, with 5 percent attributed to residential pickups and 55 percent attributed to recycling drives.

SERVICES

e-WasteExpress collects, transports, and disposes of a wide range of electronic devices. These include, but are not limited to:

- Cable Receivers
- Cell Phones
- Computer Cable
- Computers
- Digital Converter Boxes
- DVD Players
- Electronic Keyboards

- Electronic Mice

- Fax Machines

- Monitors

- Portable Digital Assistants

- Portable Music Players

- Printers

- Satellite Receivers

- Scanners

- Servers

- Televisions

- VCRs

- Videogame Systems

- Zip Drives

Collection Arrangements

e-WasteExpress collects electronic waste from individual consumers and the commercial market via two different methods: public collection drives/events and individual pickups. Individual pickups must be scheduled in advance. Although lead times vary depending upon e-WasteExpress' workload, the company strives to complete all consumer pickups within five business days. A two-week lead time is required for large commercial pickups, which may require e-WasteExpress to be on-location for several days.

Data Destruction

In addition to electronics pickup and disposal, one critical service provided by e-WasteExpress is media degaussing (demagnetizing) and sanitizing. This process ensures the on-site removal of sensitive information (e.g., health records, financial information, trade secrets, customer records, etc.) from computers, hard drives, and servers. The company's equipment ensures that it meets government standards pertaining to a number of different regulations, including DOD 5220.22-M, Health Information Portability and Accountability Act (HIPAA), and PCI DSS (Payment Card Industry) Data Security Standard.

Fees

e-WasteExpress collects electronic waste from customers at no charge.

MARKETING & SALES

A marketing plan has been developed for e-WasteExpress that includes these main tactics:

1. **Social Media:** Guests will be able to follow e-WasteExpress on Facebook, Twitter, YouTube, and LinkedIn. These channels will provide the business with several platforms for connecting with both consumer and business audiences.

2. **Blog:** Nathan Smith will blog about electronics recycling, focusing on environmental topics, as well as security issues related to proper data destruction.

3. **Guest Column:** In addition to his blog, Nathan Smith also will attempt to write a regular monthly guest column for the *Pennington Gazette*, a free weekly newspaper that is distributed throughout the community at various businesses.

4. **Web Site:** e-WasteExpress will develop a Web site with useful customer features. These include a tool for scheduling online pickups, which allows consumers and businesses to specify the type and number of items they are disposing of. (Does not apply to large commercial pickups). Additionally, the site will include information about the business; our certifications and liability coverage (to alleviate concerns about the proper disposal of data on hard drives and other devices with storage capabilities); and the fact that e-WasteExpress does not collect fees directly from consumers.

5. **Direct Marketing:** e-WasteExpress will produce two four-color direct-mailers (one for individual consumers and one for the business market). Working in partnership with a local mailing list broker/mail house, these postcards will be sent to every home and business in Pennington throughout the course of each year, with mail drops scheduled on an ongoing/weekly basis.

6. **Print & Online Advertising:** e-WasteExpress will run a regular print and online advertisement in the *Pennington Gazette*. Additionally, the business also will advertise in *Pennington Business Today*, a monthly publication produced by the local Chamber of Commerce.

7. **Event Marketing:** Based on the schedule in the Growth Strategy section of this plan, e-WasteExpress will sponsor public recycling drives, usually in partnership with a local retailer. In connection with this tactic, the business has established an arrangement with a local radio station, which will attempt to sell an optional "live remote" package to the host business, providing dual exposure for both the business and the electronics drive/e-WasteExpress.

8. **Advertising Specialties:** e-WasteExpress will distribute premium items such as pens, notepads, and magnetic business cards at community recycling drives, in order to remain visible with consumers throughout the year, in the event that they have additional disposal needs.

OPERATIONS

Location

e-WasteExpress will conduct operations in leased space within Pennington Recyclers' facility at 2759 Mountain View Ave. This facility is situated within the Pennington Industrial Park, which provides easy access to major roadways and a major interstate. The facility includes a small office for operations, designated space for parking e-WasteExpress' trucks, and a dock/enclosed area for unloading used electronic items. After unloading, all electronic waste is sorted and processed by Pennington Recyclers.

Fleet

The company will begin operations with one new box truck, and will expand its fleet based upon demand, as outlined in the Growth Strategy section of this plan. e-WasteExpress has agreed to purchase a new, 2015 ISUZ NPR C15045 box truck from a local dealer for $47,000. In the event of large commercial electronic waste disposal projects, the company will rent additional vehicles as needed from a local U-Haul dealer.

Hours of Operations

e-WasteExpress typically will maintain regular business hours from 8 AM to 5 PM, Monday through Friday. Exceptions will be made for recycling drives, which may be held on Saturdays. In addition, the business will make staff available to meet the needs of commercial customers with large projects (e.g., when a large volume of electronic waste must be removed from their facility).

Certification

e-WasteExpress has met the e-Stewards and Responsible Recycling Practices (R2) accreditation certification standards, demonstrating that the company meets specific criteria pertaining to the safe and legal recycling of electronics. As the U.S. Environmental Protection Agency explains, "Certified electronics recyclers have demonstrated through audits and other means that they continually meet specific high environmental standards and safely manage used electronics."

Liability

e-WasteExpress has secured an appropriate level of liability insurance coverage. This policy is available for review upon request.

FINANCIAL ANALYSIS

e-WasteExpress has prepared a complete set of pro forma financial statements, which are available upon request. The following table provides an overview of key projections during the first three years of operations:

Electronic waste collection service business: e-wasteexpress llc—images

Revenue	2014	2015	2016
Commercial pickups	$150,000	$245,000	$360,000
Residential pickups	$125,000	$105,000	$ 45,000
Recycling drives	$225,000	$350,000	$495,000
Total revenue	**$500,000**	**$700,000**	**$900,000**
Expenses			
Salaries	$ 22,000	$300,000	$380,000
Payroll taxes	$ 33,000	$ 45,000	$ 57,000
Diesel fuel	$ 8,820	$ 17,640	$ 26,460
Lease	$ 7,500	$ 7,500	$ 7,500
Insurance	$ 2,850	$ 2,993	$ 3,142
Vehicle purchases	$ 47,000	$ 50,000	$ 50,000
Office supplies	$ 500	$ 500	$ 500
Equipment	$ 500	$ 1,000	$ 1,000
Marketing & advertising	$ 50,000	$ 50,000	$ 50,000
Telecommunications	$ 1,200	$ 1,200	$ 1,200
Professional development	$ 1,500	$ 1,500	$ 1,500
Fees/certifications	$ 750	$ 750	$ 750
Total expenses	**$373,620**	**$478,083**	**$579,052**
Net income/loss	**$126,380**	**$221,917**	**$320,948**

Startup Costs

Pennington Recyclers has agreed to purchase the initial box truck that e-WasteExpress will need to begin operations. Nathan Smith will reimburse Pennington Recyclers for the truck purchase at the end of year one. Other nominal startup costs, including items such as media degaussing (demagnetizing) equipment, safety braces, uniforms, dollies, gloves, route management software, office furniture, and radios, will total approximately $25,000, which Nathan Smith will provide from his personal savings.

Food Truck
Thai Fusion

421 High Street
Modesto, CA 95350

Claire Moore

Thai Fusion is an Asian fusion restaurant that combines traditional Thai and Lao dishes such as Pad Thai and Lop with exotic Northern Indian dishes such as Dahi Gosht, Butter Chicken and Samosas. Thai Fusion will be a small business limited liability company organized in the state of California and operating out of a custom-built food truck. Head chef Marco Villareal and Velma Villareal are the owner-operators and will share in the responsibilities of day-to-day operations.

EXECUTIVE SUMMARY

Thai Fusion is an Asian fusion restaurant that combines traditional Thai and Lao dishes such as Pad Thai and Lop with exotic Northern Indian dishes such as Dahi Gosht, Butter Chicken and Samosas.

Mission Statement

Thai Fusion will provide our clientele an extraordinary dining experience that combines healthy, exotic cuisine with exceptional customer service. We will use local ingredients and make healthy, low-fat modifications to our recipes without compromising taste and satiety. We will ensure that customers are informed about key ingredients in our foods so that they can make healthy and informed choices to meet their dietary needs.

Management Plan

Thai Fusion will be a small business limited liability company organized in the state of California and operating out of a custom-built food truck. Head chef Marco Villareal and Velma Villareal are the owner-operators and will share in the responsibilities of day-to-day operations.

Operations Plan

Thai Fusion will operate six days a week serving lunch and dinner each day. We will also offer special event catering services.

Marketing Plan

Thai Fusion will use social media such as Twitter and Facebook to reach current and potential customers. Our Facebook page will be a meeting space for our fans where they can see menus, new items and print coupons. Crowdfunding will help us to raise capital and spread the word about our fantastic menus.

Financial

Thai Fusion requires $53,400 in startup funding. The owners have contributed cash and equipment comprising a 43.8% investment. The remaining 56.2% to be obtained through a 5-year loan from a local bank at 5% interest. In order to secure our loan, we will receive the assistance of the Valley Small Business Development Corporation.

COMPANY SUMMARY

Thai Fusion will be a food truck operation in the downtown Modesto area. We will serve traditional Thai and Lao dishes such as Pad Thai and Lop with exotic Northern Indian dishes such as Dahi Gosht, Butter Chicken and Samosas.

We will use local ingredients and make healthy, low-fat modifications to our recipes without compromising taste and satiety. We will ensure that customers are informed about key ingredients in our foods so that they can make healthy and informed choices to meet their dietary needs.

Our menu will change four times a year and will include options for those customers who prefer to avoid gluten, nuts, and nut oils.

Competition

Thai Fusion's goal is to serve the people of Modesto the best in fresh Thai and Northern Indian cuisine. Other food providers in the Modesto area are our direct competitors. While there are currently no other food trucks with an Asian theme, there are several brick and mortar competitors including: JP Asian Fusion, Surla's, and OndiJo Asian Fusian Family Restaurant. None of these restaurants incorporates Northern Indian dishes on their menus.

MARKET ANALYSIS

Industry Profile

According to the 2013 report from Los Angeles-based industry research group IBISWorld, the street-food business is a $1 billion industry. From 2007 to 2012 this industry, which includes mobile food trucks and nonmechanized carts, experienced a growth rate of 8.4 percent.

Food trucks have lower overhead than a restaurant and it can be moved from one location to another. This makes it possible for the food truck to go where it can take advantage of the most business. For customers, food trucks offer variety and convenience.

As of 2013, Modesto had 35 mobile food carts and food trucks. Over 90 percent of these venues specialize in tacos and Mexican-themed food.

Competitive Advantage

Our competitive advantage is our unique menu which includes traditional Thai recipes and the unique flavors of Northern India. Dishes such as Biryani, Daal Makhani and Dahi Gosht are prepared with spices that include coriander, cumin, cardamon, cinnamon and cloves. These herbs are not only known for their ability to add flavor, they also have health benefits.

For example, according to an article for WebMD, "Spices and Herbs: Their Health Benefits" by Elizabeth M. Ward, MS, RD, "Certain herbs and spices curb inflammation in the body, which may give rise to heart disease and cancer. For example, antioxidants in cinnamon have been linked to lower inflammation, as well as reductions in blood glucose concentrations in people with diabetes."

Our preparation time for dishes averages less than five minutes which places us either on par or better than our competitors.

Our menus are an exotic alternative to the usual tacos and similar fare that are typically offered on food trucks in Modesto. Customers will be able to order healthy, low-fat, gluten-free dishes prepared with locally-grown fresh ingredients. No other food truck in Modesto specifically offers gluten-free choices.

Target Market

Thai Fusion focuses on the middle- and upper- income markets. This group, to a large extent, includes working adults and students who are interested in the convenience of food truck fare.

Our food truck locations are within easy reach of workers, students, and shoppers in the greater Modesto area.

We also provide food services at special events attended by the public which will comprise about 30 percent of our revenues. The high visibility achieved by attendance at these events ads to the building of our brand and spreading the word about us.

Critical Risk

Threats to the success of Thai Fusion include:

- truck performance issues

- weather conditions

- limitations related to locations (cannot locate too close to brick and mortar competitors)

- customer preferences

- customer knowledge of our locations

- customer knowledge of our menus and ingredients

In order to increase customer awareness of our menus we intend to schedule tasting events at public venues where we will set up and give out free samples of key menu items along with printed menus emblazoned with our Facebook page address.

Location limitations arise due to zoning regulations within the city of Modesto. In the past two years the number of food trucks in Modesto has increased to the point where brick and mortar vendors have requested that food truck locations be regulated. This situation is still under review by the City Council and we expect that there will be some formal regulations set in the future.

MARKETING PLAN

Marketing Objective

To establish ourselves as an affordable and healthy alternative to the usual food truck fare. Secondarily, we want to establish our brand as a trusted space where customers who require gluten-free options can find tasty and healthy choices.

Marketing Mix

Product: Thai Fusion will specialize in creating dishes based on the traditional recipes of both Thai and Northern Indian cuisine. The menu will include classic dishes created with locally-grown, fresh ingredients. We will emphasize that our dishes are naturally gluten-free and are low-fat as well.

While many Thai dishes include peanuts or peanut oil, our preparation technique allows the customers to choose a non-peanut option. When dishes are to include peanuts, they will only be added at the end of the assembly process, if at all. Many dishes will offer crushed peanuts on the side. At no time will peanut products contact any of the cooking surfaces and therefore there will be no danger of contamination.

Many of our Indian breads, Thai soups, vegetable rolls and curry sauces will be made in advance. Stir-fry dishes and salads will be assembled and cooked to order in the truck using fresh vegetables obtained from local growers and sellers.

Place: Our dishes will only be available for purchase via the truck. Our truck will be decorated with a graphic wrap that displays our name, website, Facebook and contact information. This wrapping will turn our truck into a traveling advertisement that will add to our brand recognition as we travel throughout Modesto.

By our fifth year in business, we hope to establish a brick and mortar location by which time we will have developed a loyal following that will frequent our establishment and spread the word about our menus and service.

Price: After conducting a review of other food trucks in Modesto, we have found that our prices are slightly lower than our competitors for lunch and dinner entrees. Compared to brick and mortar restaurants serving Asian food, our prices are two to three dollars lower. Maintaining low prices will help us to remain competitive, especially with brick and mortar restaurants. Unless our costs increase, we expect to keep our prices stable.

Promotion

We plan to promote our business through the following methods:

Social media will allow us to connect with our followers and provide updated menus, coupons and location information. We can run campaigns and contests that encourage and reward participation. Social media platforms will include: Twitter, Foursquare and Facebook.

Crowdfunding campaign will help us to raise capital in small amounts ranging from $50 to $250. In exchange our backers will receive rewards in the form of food discounts.

Press publicity through the *Modesto Bee* and its online site will spread the word about our brand and our activities.

Opening Day Menu

Pad Thai: Fresh stir-fried rice noodles with original homemade pad thai sauce, tofu, egg, bean sprouts, green onion, cilantro and your choice of chicken, beef, prawns (+$2), or vegetarian.

Som Tum Salad: Shredded green papaya tossed with cherry tomatoes, carrots, Thai chilies, lime juice, and topped with a side of crushed peanuts.

Side Cucumber Salad: Sliced cucumber with shredded carrots and red onions drizzled with vinegar dressing.

Ka Pow: Stir fried chicken with Thai basil, bell peppers, and Thai chilies served over rice.

Thai Iced Tea

Red Curry: A milder curry with kabocha squash, green beans, bell peppers, Thai basil and chicken or vegetarian.

Green Curry: Spiciest of the curries, this includes green beans, Thai basil, bell peppers, and beef or vegetarian.

Homemade Coconut Ice Cream

Bottled water

MANAGEMENT

Legal Form of Business

The business is formed as a limited liability company within the state of California. Member ownership rests with Marco Villareal (50%) and Velma Villareal (50%).

Management Team

Marco Villareal is a graduate of the culinary program at the Art Institute of Sacramento. Marco has seven years experience in the restaurant industry where he started as a sous chef and rose to manager for a major chain restaurant in Sacramento. Marco served as the head chef of Parasteve's Restaurant for four years. He managed a staff of three. His duties included inventory management, employee scheduling, and ensuring safety and health code compliance. Marco will serve as head chef for Thai Fusion.

Velma is in her final semester in the business program at West Coast College where she will earn her associate's degree in the fall of 2014. Velma is currently working as the bookkeeper for a local sandwich shop. Before returning to school for her degree, Velma worked as an assistant for a marketing firm in Sacramento where her duties included graphic design, social media branding, and ad placement. Velma will split her duties between marketing, bookkeeping and scheduling.

Advisory Board

An advisory board comprised of experts in the field of culinary, marketing, and food trucks will help management to achieve its business goals. Members have agreed to be available for consultation as needed.

Advisory team members include:

- Chef Potter—instructor at the Art Institute Sacramento

- Dotty Gardner—retired attorney

- Jim Gladwyn—Counselor at the Valley Small Business Development Corporation

- Jason Villareal—retired owner of the Mexicali Food Truck

OPERATIONS PLAN

Customers will love our fresh, local ingredients but what makes Thai Fusion unique is our recipes and dishes. In addition to traditional Thai fare such as Pad Thai, we offer fresh, low-calorie offerings such as cucumber salad and Som Tum Salad with green papaya, tossed cherry tomatoes, carrots and Thai chilies. Customers can specify that dishes come without peanuts.

Fresh produce will be purchased and prepped daily. Inventory management will ensure that sufficient quantities are prepared and that there is little excess. Some dishes such as spring rolls will be prepared twice a week and stored for the week's sales. Sea food, beef, and poultry will be purchased weekly based on estimated sales projections for the week.

Our office and supply storage are located at our facility at 421 High Street in Modesto. Prepping the truck for lunch will begin at 10 am, and prep for dinner will begin at 3:30. Cleaning will be done at the end of the evening shift, about 8 pm. The food truck will be stored each night at HighGarden Maintenance which will also provide truck maintenance.

Hours of food truck operation will be:

	Mon	Tues	Wed	Ths	Fri	Sat	Sun
Lunch	—	11 pm–2 pm	11 pm–2 pm	11 pm–2 pm	11 pm–2 pm	11 pm–2 pm	11 pm–2 pm
Dinner	—	5 pm–8 pm	5 pm–8 pm	5 pm–8 pm	5 pm–8 pm	5 pm–8 pm	5 pm–8 pm

Truck locations include:

- Kansas-Woodland Business Park
- Modesto Farmers Market
- 10 St. Plaza
- University of the Pacific Campus

Special events in the area where we serve include:

- Cesar E. Chavez Celebration
- Earth Day in the Park
- Night at the Bowl
- American Graffiti

Company Milestones

Present—December: Complete establishment of LLC and obtain all required licenses. Establish a social media presence, acquire food truck, and open for business.

Years 1—2: Hire a part-time employee to assist with prep and work on the food truck. Gradually increase the hours so that Velma can reduce her hours on the truck in favor of marketing, bookkeeping and scheduling.

Years 3—4: Hire an additional part-time employee and reduce Marco's hours on the truck so that he can devote more time to marketing for catering events.

Year 5: Evaluate the options for opening a brick-and-mortar location.

FINANCIAL PROJECTIONS

This plan makes the following assumptions:

- The owners will provide 43.8% equity investment in the business in cash and assets.
- The business will secure a loan with the assistance of the Valley Small Business Development Corporation for five years at 5% to acquire and equip a custom-built, furnished truck including a custom wrap and a three year warranty.
- The food will cost an average of 30% of the product pricing.
- One of the owners will be working on the truck full time in Year 1, the other owner will work 75% of the time on the truck and 25% of the time in the office in Year 1. In Year Two hiring of additional staff to work on the truck will begin.
- Ingredients will be supplied by local growers and from Costco.
- We will use professional services for legal, accounting and insurance advice.

Sources and uses of cash

November 2014

Current assets	Total	Owner	Loan
Cash	4,500	4,500	
Food inventory	1,500	1,500	
Total current	**6,000**	**6,000**	
Fixed assets			
Office equipment	800	800	
Kitchen equipment	400	400	
POS system	1,200	1,200	
Vehicles	45,000	15,000	30,000
Total fixed	**47,400**	**17,400**	**30,000**
Total assets	**53,400**	**23,400**	**30,000**
Percent	100.0%	43.8%	56.2%

Cash flow

	2015	2016	2017
Begin cash	4,500	13,661	23,392
Net profit after tax	8,278	9,125	21,119
Plus: depr	6,400	6,400	6,400
Inv decr (incr)	(100)	(100)	(100)
LT debt incr (decr)	(5,417)	(5,694)	(6,291)
End cash	13,661	23,392	44,520

Income statement

	2015	2016	2017
Sales	**$144,000**	**$172,800**	**$190,080**
Cost of sales	$ 43,200	$ 51,840	$ 57,024
Gross profit	$100,800	$120,960	$133,056
Expenses			
Licenses & permits	$ 425	$ 425	$ 425
Parking fees	$ 1,400	$ 1,600	$ 1,600
Insurance: liability & business interruption	$ 2,500	$ 2,500	$ 2,500
Insurance: commercial auto	$ 2,000	$ 2,000	$ 2,000
Salaries: managerial	$ 40,000	$ 40,000	$ 40,000
Wages	$ 15,000	$ 30,000	$ 30,000
Payroll taxes	$ 5,500	$ 7,000	$ 7,000
Workers comp ins	$ 550	$ 700	$ 700
Employee benefits	$ 2,500	$ 3,000	$ 3,000
Accounting	$ 2,400	$ 2,400	$ 2,400
Truck fuel	$ 4,400	$ 5,000	$ 5,500
Truck repairs & maint	$ 2,400	$ 3,500	$ 3,500
Truck storage	$ 1,600	$ 1,600	$ 1,600
Electricity	$ 800	$ 1,100	$ 1,300
Water	$ 500	$ 700	$ 700
Truck supplies	$ 460	$ 500	$ 500
Office supplies	$ 350	$ 350	$ 350
Internet	$ 700	$ 700	$ 700
Web site	$ 360	$ 360	$ 360
Telephone	$ 900	$ 900	$ 900
Depreciation	$ 6,400	$ 6,400	$ 6,400
Total expenses	**$ 91,145**	**$110,735**	**$111,435**
Interest expense	$ 1,377	$ 1,100	$ 502
Profit before taxes	$ 8,278	$ 9,125	$ 21,119
Taxes	$ 0	$ 0	$ 0
Net income	**$ 8,278**	**$ 9,125**	**$ 21,119**

Balance sheet

Assets	Starting	12/31/2015	12/31/2016	12/31/2017
Cash in bank	$ 4,500	$13,661	$ 23,392	$ 44,520
Food inventory	$ 1,500	$ 1,600	$ 1,700	$ 1,800
Total current assets	**$ 6,000**	**$15,261**	**$ 25,092**	**$ 46,320**
Fixed assets				
Office equipment	$ 800	$ 800	$ 800	$ 800
Kitchen equipment	$ 400	$ 400	$ 400	$ 400
POS system	$ 1,200	$ 1,200	$ 1,200	$ 1,200
Food truck	$45,000	$45,000	$ 45,000	$ 45,000
Less: depreciation		$ (6,400)	$(12,800)	$(19,200)
Total assets	**$53,400**	**$56,261**	**$ 59,692**	**$ 74,520**
Liabilities				
Accounts payable	$ —	$ —	$ —	$ —
Current maturities truck loan	$ 6,793	$ 6,793	$ 6,793	$ 6,793
Total current liabilities	**$ 6,793**	**$ 6,793**	**$ 6,793**	**$ 6,793**
Long term liabilities truck loan	$23,207	$17,790	$ 12,096	$ 6,111
Total liabilities	**$30,000**	**$24,583**	**$ 18,889**	**$ 12,904**
Member investment	$23,400	$23,400	$ 23,400	$ 23,400
Retained earnings		$ 8,278	$ 17,403	$ 38,216
Total owner's equity	**$23,400**	**$31,678**	**$ 40,803**	**$ 61,616**
Total liabilities & equity	**$53,400**	**$56,261**	**$ 59,692**	**$ 74,520**

General Contractor

Teltow Construction

2231 Northern Blvd.
Queens, NY 11368

BizPlaDB.com

Teltow Construction, Inc. is a New York-based corporation that will provide home building and remodeling services to customers in its targeted market. The Company was founded by Aaron Teltow.

1.0 EXECUTIVE SUMMARY

The purpose of this business plan is to raise $200,000 for the development of a general contracting business while showcasing the expected financials and operations over the next three years. Teltow Construction, Inc. ("the Company") is a New York-based corporation that will provide home building and remodeling services to customers in its targeted market. The Company was founded by Aaron Teltow.

1.1 The Services

Teltow Construction is in the business of providing general contractor services. The Company is able to provide home owners and real estate investors with a multitude of services including kitchen/bathroom remodeling, room additions, drywall repair, and other repair/upgrade services for a reasonable price and within a reasonable timeframe.

The Company will also develop a program that will allow the business to develop new housing with specificity towards single family homes. This is an important profit center for the business as the Company will be able to generate profits from the outsourcing of work to subcontracted development businesses.

The third section of the business plan will further describe the services offered by Teltow Construction.

1.2 Financing

Mr. Teltow is seeking to raise $200,000 from a bank loan. The interest rate and loan agreement are to be further discussed during negotiation. This business plan assumes that the business will receive a 10-year loan with a 9% fixed interest rate. The financing will be used for the following:

- Acquisition of tools and other equipment pieces commonly used in contracting.

- Financing for the first six months of operation.

- Capital to purchase a company vehicle.

Mr. Teltow will contribute $10,000 to the venture.

1.3 Mission Statement

It is the goal of the Company to create a business that provides customers with high quality construction services that include kitchens and bathroom remodeling, drywall repairs, room additions, and development of new homes.

1.4 Management Team

The Company was founded by Aaron Teltow. Mr. Teltow has more than 10 years of experience in the construction industry. Through his expertise, he will be able to bring the operations of the business to profitability within its first year of operations.

1.5 Sales Forecasts

Mr. Teltow expects a strong rate of growth at the start of operations. Below are the expected financials over the next three years.

Proforma profit and loss (yearly)

Year	1	2	3
Sales	$1,290,000	$1,548,000	$1,811,160
Operating costs	$ 384,157	$ 400,318	$ 449,931
EBITDA	$ 320,843	$ 445,682	$ 539,889
Taxes, interest, and depreciation	$ 151,181	$ 191,228	$ 226,204
Net profit	$ 169,662	$ 254,454	$ 313,685

Sales, operating costs, and profit forecast

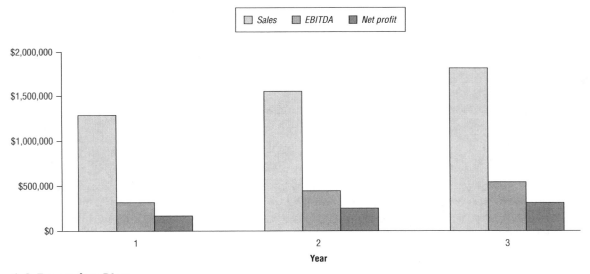

1.6 Expansion Plan

The Founder expects that the business will aggressively expand during the first three years of operation. Mr. Teltow intends to implement marketing campaigns that will effectively target individual home-owners, real estate investors, and real estate developers within the target market.

2.0 COMPANY AND FINANCING SUMMARY

2.1 Registered Name and Corporate Structure

Teltow Construction, Inc. is registered as a corporation in the State of New York.

2.2 Required Funds

At this time, Teltow Construction requires $200,000 of debt funds. Below is a breakdown of how these funds will be used:

Projected startup costs

Initial lease payments and deposits	$ 10,000
Working capital	$ 35,000
Construction equipment	$ 65,000
Leasehold improvements	$ 5,000
Security deposits	$ 5,000
Insurance	$ 2,500
Construction vehicles	$ 75,000
Marketing budget	$ 7,500
Miscellaneous and unforeseen costs	$ 5,000
Total startup costs	**$210,000**

Use of funds

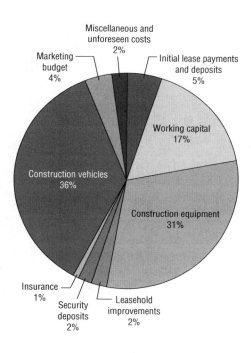

2.3 Investor Equity

Mr. Teltow is not seeking an investment from a third party at this time.

2.4 Management Equity

Aaron Teltow owns 100% of Teltow Construction, Inc.

2.5 Exit Strategy

If the business is very successful, Mr. Teltow may seek to sell the business to a third party for a significant earnings multiple. Most likely, the Company will hire a qualified business broker to sell the business on behalf of Teltow Construction. Based on historical numbers, the business could fetch a sales premium of up to 6 to 8 times the previous year's earnings.

3.0 PRODUCTS AND SERVICES

Below is a description of the general contracting and home development services offered by Teltow Construction.

3.1 General Contracting Services

The business will provide the design and implementation of constructions that include complete kitchen remodeling (including cabinetry, appliance installation, countertop installation, and flooring), bathroom remodeling, drywall repairs and installations, and room additions.

The Company will maintain its own staff of construction workers and project managers that oversee all interior home remodeling and contracting services. The business also has the ability to provide these services on a subcontracted basis to general contractors operating within the targeted market.

The Company's owner, Mr. Teltow, will also maintain all licenses required by the State of New York to operate this business legally. Additionally, the Company will have extensive workman's compensation, legal liability, and general insurance policies that insure that in the event of a serious injury or construction failure, the Company will be able to maintain business operations.

3.2 New Housing Development

The Company will also have the ability to develop new housing projects on behalf of its clients. This is an important revenue and profit center for the business as the Company will be able to use subcontractors to complete a majority of the interior work. The Company will maintain a small construction crew to assist subcontractors in the development of new housing projects.

Management anticipates that each new housing construction will yield $100,000 to $150,000 of revenue for each completed project. The Company will have the ability to complete five of these projects within the first year of operation.

4.0 STRATEGIC AND MARKET ANALYSIS

4.1 Economic Outlook

This section of the analysis will detail the economic climate, the general contracting industry, the customer profile, and the competition that the business will face as it progresses through its business operations.

Currently, the US economy is doing very well. The correction from the housing fallout over the past six years is complete. New constructions have increased substantially while interest rates have remained near historical lows. As such, general contractors are in a strong market to operate.

4.2 Industry Analysis

The construction industry is an extremely large group of contractors that generate over $490 billion dollars a year of gross management fees for the construction and management of real estate (including new home developments). This business has grown tremendously with the increase in the value of American real estate. There are over 710,000 businesses that specialize in managing specific construction projects. Additionally, the industry employs more than 1,110,000 people and generates gross annual payrolls in excess of $62 billion dollars.

This trend is expected to continue as the demand for real estate has continually increased. With this increase in demand comes the need for more specialty construction works in developments and neighborhoods. While interest rates are rising, and the general construction market is expected to slow over the next two years, Management feels that by providing specialty construction services, the business will be able to reap significant contracting profits regardless of the general direction of the economic markets.

4.3 Customer Profile

Management expects that the primary client base for its services will be residential homeowner or real estate investors that are seeking to have their homes remodeled for increasing the livability and value. However, the Company has outlined several demographics of the targeted client of the business:

- Is seeking to increase livability and value of home

- Household income of $65,000 or more

- Median home value of $300,000

- Will spend $1,000 to $20,000 on each contracting job.

4.4 Competition

The New York metropolitan area has more than 10,000 licensed general contractors that are able to render a variety of construction services (including the development of new properties). As such, Teltow Construction, Inc. will need to develop a strong brand name as it relates to the quality of the craftsmanship offered by the business. Initially, the business will also need to keep its fees under fair market value in order to obtain business from the onset of operations.

5.0 MARKETING PLAN

Teltow Construction intends to maintain an extensive marketing campaign that will ensure maximum visibility for the business in its targeted market. Below is an overview of the marketing strategies and objectives of Teltow Construction.

5.1 Marketing Objectives

- Establish relationships with other contractors and real estate developers/investors within the target market.

- Develop an expansive presence online that showcases the work previous completed by Teltow Construction, Inc.

5.2 Marketing Strategies

Mr. Teltow intends on using a number of marketing strategies that will allow Teltow Construction to easily target homeowners, real estate investors, and real estate developers within the target market. Initially, Mr. Teltow intends to call on his expansive list of contracts that will allow him to have referrals in place among other contractors and real estate developers within the New York metropolitan area. This will ensure that the business is able to immediately generate revenues from the onset of operations.

The business will also continue to develop relationships among general contractors, electricians, interior decorators, and other associated trade business' and practitioners that will continually outsource work to Teltow Construction and provide a regular stream of referrals for additional work.

Teltow Construction, Inc. will also frequently advertise in trade publications focused on the contracting and real estate development community within the New York metropolitan area. This will further assist the business in developing referral relationships among other contractors that will work with the business as time progresses.

Finally, Teltow Construction, Inc. will develop an interactive website that continually showcases newly completed projects. The business, over time, will hire a search engine optimization firm so that this website is prominently featured among major search engines. The business will also develop a large presence among social media platforms including FaceBook, Twitter, and Google+. On social media, the business will showcase images of recently completed projects and information regarding how to contact the Company.

5.3 Pricing

As each project will render a different revenue result for the Company, it is difficult to quantify the amount of revenue that the business will receive per contract. However, Management anticipates that the average contract will generate $4,000 to $5,000 for the business.

6.0 ORGANIZATIONAL PLAN AND PERSONNEL SUMMARY

6.1 Corporate Organization

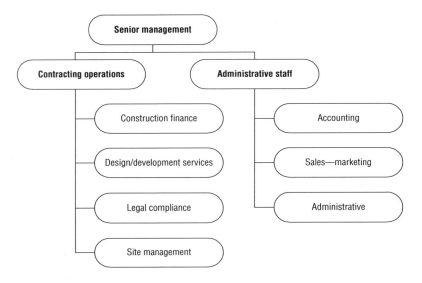

6.2 Organizational Budget

Personnel plan—yearly

Year	1	2	3
Owner	$ 45,000	$ 46,350	$ 47,741
Foreman—site manager	$ 40,000	$ 41,200	$ 42,436
Construction crew	$135,000	$139,050	$171,866
Bookkeeper (P/T)	$ 12,500	$ 12,875	$ 13,261
Administrative	$ 44,000	$ 45,320	$ 46,680
Total	$276,500	$284,795	$321,983

Numbers of personnel

Owner	1	1	1
Foreman—site manager	1	1	1
Construction crew	5	5	6
Bookkeeper (P/T)	1	1	1
Administrative	2	2	2
Totals	10	10	11

Personnel expense breakdown

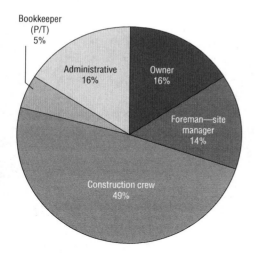

7.0 FINANCIAL PLAN

7.1 Underlying Assumptions

The Company has based its proforma financial statements on the following:

- Teltow Construction will have an annual revenue growth rate of 16% per year.

- The Owner will acquire $200,000 of debt funds to develop the business.

- The loan will have a 10-year term with a 9% interest rate.

7.2 Sensitivity Analysis

The Company's revenues are moderately sensitive to the overall condition of the economic markets. In times of economic recession, Management anticipates that the demand for new constructions will decrease moderately. However, the Company will be able to control its rate of build, and in times of economic recession, Teltow Construction can scale down its operations very quickly.

7.3 Source of Funds

Financing

Equity contributions	
Investor(s)	$ 10,000.00
Total equity financing	**$ 10,000.00**
Banks and lenders	
Banks and lenders	$ 200,000.00
Total debt financing	**$200,000.00**
Total financing	**$210,000.00**

7.4 General Assumptions

General assumptions

Year	1	2	3
Short term interest rate	9.5%	9.5%	9.5%
Long term interest rate	10.0%	10.0%	10.0%
Federal tax rate	33.0%	33.0%	33.0%
State tax rate	5.0%	5.0%	5.0%
Personnel taxes	15.0%	15.0%	15.0%

7.5 Profit and Loss Statements

Proforma profit and loss (yearly)

Year	1	2	3
Sales	**$1,290,000**	**$1,548,000**	**$1,811,160**
Cost of goods sold	$ 585,000	$ 702,000	$ 821,340
Gross margin	54.65%	54.65%	54.65%
Operating income	**$ 705,000**	**$ 846,000**	**$ 989,820**
Expenses			
Payroll	$ 276,500	$ 284,795	$ 321,983
General and administrative	$ 25,200	$ 26,208	$ 27,256
Marketing expenses	$ 6,450	$ 7,740	$ 9,056
Professional fees and licensure	$ 5,219	$ 5,376	$ 5,537
Insurance costs	$ 1,987	$ 2,086	$ 2,191
Travel and vehicle costs	$ 7,596	$ 8,356	$ 9,191
Rent and utilities	$ 4,250	$ 4,463	$ 4,686
Miscellaneous costs	$ 15,480	$ 18,576	$ 21,734
Payroll taxes	$ 41,475	$ 42,719	$ 48,297
Total operating costs	**$ 384,157**	**$ 400,318**	**$ 449,931**
EBITDA	**$ 320,843**	**$ 445,682**	**$ 539,889**
Federal income tax	$ 105,878	$ 141,708	$ 173,234
State income tax	$ 16,042	$ 21,471	$ 26,248
Interest expense	$ 17,475	$ 16,263	$ 14,936
Depreciation expenses	$ 11,786	$ 11,786	$ 11,786
Net profit	**$ 169,662**	**$ 254,454**	**$ 313,685**
Profit margin	**13.15%**	**16.44%**	**17.32%**

Sales, operating costs, and profit forecast

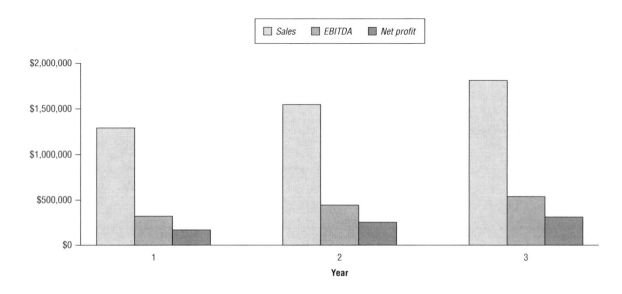

7.6 Cash Flow Analysis

Proforma cash flow analysis—yearly

Year	1	2	3
Cash from operations	$181,447	$266,240	$325,471
Cash from receivables	$ 0	$ 0	$ 0
Operating cash inflow	**$181,447**	**$266,240**	**$325,471**
Other cash inflows			
Equity investment	$ 10,000	$ 0	$ 0
Increased borrowings	$200,000	$ 0	$ 0
Sales of business assets	$ 0	$ 0	$ 0
A/P increases	$ 37,902	$ 43,587	$ 50,125
Total other cash inflows	**$247,902**	**$ 43,587**	**$ 50,125**
Total cash inflow	**$429,349**	**$309,827**	**$375,596**
Cash outflows			
Repayment of principal	$ 12,927	$ 14,139	$ 15,466
A/P decreases	$ 24,897	$ 29,876	$ 35,852
A/R increases	$ 0	$ 0	$ 0
Asset purchases	$165,000	$ 66,560	$ 81,368
Dividends	$127,013	$186,368	$227,829
Total cash outflows	**$329,837**	**$296,944**	**$360,515**
Net cash flow	**$ 99,512**	**$ 12,883**	**$ 15,081**
Cash balance	**$ 99,512**	**$112,396**	**$127,477**

Proforma cash flow (yearly)

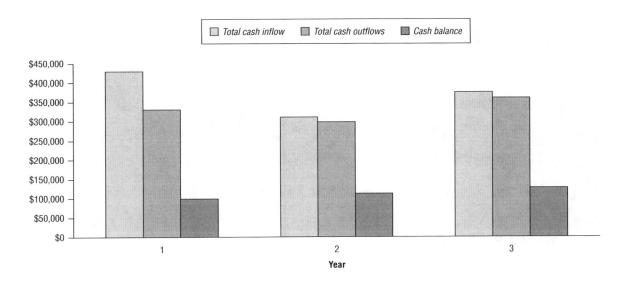

7.7 Balance Sheet

Proforma balance sheet—yearly

Year	1	2	3
Assets			
Cash	$ 99,512	$112,396	$127,477
Amortized expansion costs	$ 25,000	$ 31,656	$ 39,793
Company vehicle	$ 75,000	$124,920	$185,946
Construction equipment	$ 65,000	$ 74,984	$ 87,189
Accumulated depreciation	($ 11,786)	($ 23,571)	($ 35,357)
Total assets	**$252,727**	**$320,384**	**$405,048**
Liabilities and equity			
Accounts payable	$ 13,005	$ 26,716	$ 40,990
Long term liabilities	$187,073	$172,934	$158,794
Other liabilities	$ 0	$ 0	$ 0
Total liabilities	**$200,078**	**$199,650**	**$199,784**
Net worth	**$ 52,648**	**$120,735**	**$205,264**
Total liabilities and equity	**$252,727**	**$320,384**	**$405,048**

Proforma balance sheet

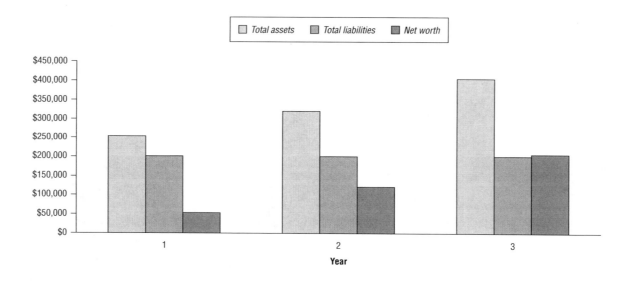

7.8 Breakeven Analysis

Monthly break even analysis

Year	1	2	3
Monthly revenue	$ 58,577	$ 61,041	$ 68,606
Yearly revenue	$702,926	$732,497	$823,278

Break even analysis

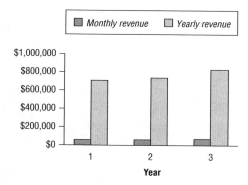

7.9 Business Ratios

Business ratios—yearly

Year	1	2	3
Sales			
Sales growth	0.0%	20.0%	17.0%
Gross margin	54.7%	54.7%	54.7%
Financials			
Profit margin	13.15%	16.44%	17.32%
Assets to liabilities	1.26	1.60	2.03
Equity to liabilities	0.26	0.60	1.03
Assets to equity	4.80	2.65	1.97
Liquidity			
Acid test	0.50	0.56	0.64
Cash to assets	0.39	0.35	0.31

7.10 Three Year Profit and Loss Statement

Profit and loss statement (first year)

Months	1	2	3	4	5	6	7
Sales	$130,000	$35,000	$140,000	$45,000	$150,000	$55,000	$160,000
Cost of goods sold	$ 55,000	$17,500	$ 60,000	$22,500	$ 65,000	$27,500	$ 70,000
Gross margin	57.7%	50.0%	57.1%	50.0%	56.7%	50.0%	56.3%
Operating income	$ 75,000	$17,500	$ 80,000	$22,500	$ 85,000	$27,500	$ 90,000
Expenses							
Payroll	$ 23,042	$23,042	$ 23,042	$23,042	$ 23,042	$23,042	$ 23,042
General and administrative	$ 2,100	$ 2,100	$ 2,100	$ 2,100	$ 2,100	$ 2,100	$ 2,100
Marketing expenses	$ 538	$ 538	$ 538	$ 538	$ 538	$ 538	$ 538
Professional fees and licensure	$ 435	$ 435	$ 435	$ 435	$ 435	$ 435	$ 435
Insurance costs	$ 166	$ 166	$ 166	$ 166	$ 166	$ 166	$ 166
Travel and vehicle costs	$ 633	$ 633	$ 633	$ 633	$ 633	$ 633	$ 633
Rent and utilities	$ 354	$ 354	$ 354	$ 354	$ 354	$ 354	$ 354
Miscellaneous costs	$ 1,290	$ 1,290	$ 1,290	$ 1,290	$ 1,290	$ 1,290	$ 1,290
Payroll taxes	$ 3,456	$ 3,456	$ 3,456	$ 3,456	$ 3,456	$ 3,456	$ 3,456
Total operating costs	$ 32,013	$32,013	$ 32,013	$32,013	$ 32,013	$32,013	$ 32,013
EBITDA	$ 42,987	−$14,513	$ 47,987	−$ 9,513	$ 52,987	−$ 4,513	$ 57,987
Federal income tax	$ 10,670	$ 2,873	$ 11,491	$ 3,693	$ 12,311	$ 4,514	$ 13,132
State income tax	$ 1,617	$ 435	$ 1,741	$ 560	$ 1,865	$ 684	$ 1,990
Interest expense	$ 1,500	$ 1,492	$ 1,484	$ 1,477	$ 1,469	$ 1,461	$ 1,453
Depreciation expense	$ 982	$ 982	$ 982	$ 982	$ 982	$ 982	$ 982
Net profit	$ 28,218	−$20,295	$ 32,289	−$16,225	$ 36,359	−$12,154	$ 40,430

Profit and loss statement (first year cont.)

Month	8	9	10	11	12	1
Sales	$65,000	$170,000	$75,000	$180,000	$85,000	$1,290,000
Cost of goods sold	$32,500	$ 75,000	$37,500	$ 80,000	$42,500	$ 585,500
Gross margin	50.0%	55.9%	50.0%	55.6%	50.0%	54.7%
Operating income	$32,500	$ 95,000	$37,500	$100,000	$42,500	$ 705,000
Expenses						
Payroll	$23,042	$ 23,042	$23,042	$ 23,042	$23,042	$ 276,500
General and administrative	$ 2,100	$ 2,100	$ 2,100	$ 2,100	$ 2,100	$ 25,200
Marketing expenses	$ 538	$ 538	$ 538	$ 538	$ 538	$ 6,450
Professional fees and licensure	$ 435	$ 435	$ 435	$ 435	$ 435	$ 5,219
Insurance costs	$ 166	$ 166	$ 166	$ 166	$ 166	$ 1,987
Travel and vehicle costs	$ 633	$ 633	$ 633	$ 633	$ 633	$ 7,596
Rent and utilities	$ 354	$ 354	$ 354	$ 354	$ 354	$ 4,250
Miscellaneous costs	$ 1,290	$ 1,290	$ 1,290	$ 1,290	$ 1,290	$ 15,480
Payroll taxes	$ 3,456	$ 3,456	$ 3,456	$ 3,456	$ 3,456	$ 41,475
Total operating costs	$32,013	$ 32,013	$32,013	$ 32,013	$32,013	$ 384,157
EBITDA	$ 487	$ 62,987	$ 5,487	$ 67,987	$10,487	$ 320,843
Federal income tax	$ 5,335	$ 13,953	$ 6,156	$ 14,774	$ 6,976	$ 105,878
State income tax	$ 808	$ 2,114	$ 933	$ 2,238	$ 1,057	$ 16,042
Interest expense	$ 1,445	$ 1,436	$ 1,428	$ 1,420	$ 1,411	$ 17,475
Depreciation expense	$ 982	$ 982	$ 982	$ 982	$ 982	$ 11,786
Net profit	−$ 8,083	$ 44,501	−$ 4,012	$ 48,573	$ 60	$ 169,662

Profit and loss statement (second year)

Quarter	Q1	2 Q2	Q3	Q4	2
Sales	$309,600	$387,000	$417,960	$433,440	$1,548,000
Cost of goods sold	$140,400	$175,500	$189,540	$196,560	$ 702,000
Gross margin	54.7%	54.7%	54.7%	54.7%	54.7%
Operating income	$169,200	$211,500	$228,420	$236,880	$ 846,000
Expenses					
Payroll	$ 56,959	$ 71,199	$ 76,895	$ 79,743	$ 284,795
General and administrative	$ 5,242	$ 6,552	$ 7,076	$ 7,338	$ 26,208
Marketing expenses	$ 1,548	$ 1,935	$ 2,090	$ 2,167	$ 7,740
Professional fees and licensure	$ 1,075	$ 1,344	$ 1,451	$ 1,505	$ 5,376
Insurance costs	$ 417	$ 522	$ 563	$ 584	$ 2,086
Travel and vehicle costs	$ 1,671	$ 2,089	$ 2,256	$ 2,340	$ 8,356
Rent and utilities	$ 893	$ 1,116	$ 1,205	$ 1,250	$ 4,463
Miscellaneous costs	$ 3,715	$ 4,644	$ 5,016	$ 5,201	$ 18,576
Payroll taxes	$ 8,544	$ 10,680	$ 11,534	$ 11,961	$ 42,719
Total operating costs	$ 80,064	$100,080	$108,086	$112,089	$ 400,318
EBITDA	$ 89,136	$111,420	$120,334	$124,791	$ 445,682
Federal income tax	$ 28,342	$ 35,427	$ 38,261	$ 39,678	$ 141,708
State income tax	$ 4,294	$ 5,368	$ 5,797	$ 6,012	$ 21,471
Interest expense	$ 4,184	$ 4,106	$ 4,027	$ 3,946	$ 16,263
Depreciation expense	$ 2,946	$ 2,946	$ 2,946	$ 2,946	$ 11,786
Net profit	$ 49,370	$ 63,573	$ 69,302	$ 72,208	$ 254,454

Profit and loss statement (third year)

Quarter	Q1	Q2	Q3	Q4	3
Sales	$362,232	$452,790	$489,013	$507,125	$1,811,160
Cost of goods sold	$164,268	$205,335	$221,762	$229,975	$ 821,340
Gross margin	54.7%	54.7%	54.7%	54.7%	54.7%
Operating income	$197,964	$247,455	$267,251	$277,150	$ 989,820
Expenses					
Payroll	$ 64,397	$ 80,496	$ 86,935	$ 90,155	$ 321,983
General and administrative	$ 5,451	$ 6,814	$ 7,359	$ 7,632	$ 27,256
Marketing expenses	$ 1,811	$ 2,264	$ 2,445	$ 2,536	$ 9,056
Professional fees and licensure	$ 1,107	$ 1,384	$ 1,495	$ 1,550	$ 5,537
Insurance costs	$ 438	$ 548	$ 591	$ 613	$ 2,191
Travel and vehicle costs	$ 1,838	$ 2,298	$ 2,482	$ 2,574	$ 9,191
Rent and utilities	$ 937	$ 1,171	$ 1,265	$ 1,312	$ 4,686
Miscellaneous costs	$ 4,347	$ 5,433	$ 5,868	$ 6,085	$ 21,734
Payroll taxes	$ 9,659	$ 12,074	$ 13,040	$ 13,523	$ 48,297
Total operating costs	$ 89,986	$112,483	$121,481	$125,981	$ 449,931
EBITDA	$107,978	$134,972	$145,770	$151,169	$ 539,889
Federal income tax	$ 34,647	$ 43,309	$ 46,773	$ 48,506	$ 173,234
State income tax	$ 5,250	$ 6,562	$ 7,087	$ 7,349	$ 26,248
Interest expense	$ 3,863	$ 3,778	$ 3,692	$ 3,603	$ 14,936
Depreciation expense	$ 2,946	$ 2,946	$ 2,946	$ 2,946	$ 11,786
Net profit	$ 61,272	$ 78,377	$ 85,272	$ 88,764	$ 313,685

7.11 Three Year Cash Flow Analysis

Cash flow analysis (first year)

Month	1	2	3	4	5	6	7
Cash from operations	$ 29,200	−$19,313	$ 33,271	−$15,243	$ 37,341	−$11,172	$ 41,412
Cash from receivables	$ 0	$ 0	$ 0	$ 0	$ 0	$ 0	$ 0
Operating cash inflow	$ 29,200	−$19,313	$33,271	−$15,243	$ 37,341	−$11,172	$ 41,412
Other cash inflows							
Equity investment	$ 10,000	$ 0	$ 0	$ 0	$ 0	$ 0	$ 0
Increased borrowings	$200,000	$ 0	$ 0	$ 0	$ 0	$ 0	$ 0
Sales of business assets	$ 0	$ 0	$ 0	$ 0	$ 0	$ 0	$ 0
A/P increases	$ 3,159	$ 3,159	$ 3,159	$ 3,159	$ 3,159	$ 3,159	$ 3,159
Total other cash inflows	$213,159	$ 3,159	$ 3,159	$ 3,159	$ 3,159	$ 3,159	$ 3,159
Total cash inflow	$242,359	−$16,155	$36,429	−$12,084	$ 40,500	−$ 8,013	$ 44,571
Cash outflows							
Repayment of principal	$ 1,034	$ 1,041	$ 1,049	$ 1,057	$ 1,065	$ 1,073	$ 1,081
A/P decreases	$ 2,075	$ 2,075	$ 2,075	$ 2,075	$ 2,075	$ 2,075	$ 2,075
A/R increases	$ 0	$ 0	$ 0	$ 0	$ 0	$ 0	$ 0
Asset purchases	$165,000	$ 0	$ 0	$ 0	$ 0	$ 0	$ 0
Dividends	$ 0	$ 0	$ 0	$ 0	$ 0	$ 0	$ 0
Total cash outflows	$168,108	$ 3,116	$ 3,124	$ 3,132	$ 3,140	$ 3,148	$ 3,156
Net cash flow	$ 74,251	−$19,271	$33,305	−$15,216	$ 37,360	−$11,161	$ 41,415
Cash balance	$ 74,251	$54,980	$88,285	$73,069	$110,430	$99,269	$140,684

Cash flow analysis (first year cont.)

Month	8	9	10	11	12	1
Cash from operations	−$ 7,101	$ 45,484	−$ 3,030	$ 49,555	$ 1,042	$181,447
Cash from receivables	$ 0	$ 0	$ 0	$ 0	$ 0	$ 0
Operating cash inflow	**−$ 7,101**	**$ 45,484**	**−$ 3,030**	**$ 49,555**	**$ 1,042**	**$181,447**
Other cash inflows						
Equity investment	$ 0	$ 0	$ 0	$ 0	$ 0	$ 10,000
Increased borrowings	$ 0	$ 0	$ 0	$ 0	$ 0	$200,000
Sales of business assets	$ 0	$ 0	$ 0	$ 0	$ 0	$ 0
A/P increases	$ 3,159	$ 3,159	$ 3,159	$ 3,159	$ 3,159	$ 37,902
Total other cash inflows	**$ 3,159**	**$ 3,159**	**$ 3,159**	**$ 3,159**	**$ 3,159**	**$247,902**
Total cash inflow	**−$ 3,942**	**$ 48,642**	**$ 129**	**$ 52,713**	**$ 4,200**	**$429,349**
Cash outflows						
Repayment of principal	$ 1,089	$ 1,097	$ 1,105	$ 1,114	$ 1,122	$ 12,927
A/P decreases	$ 2,075	$ 2,075	$ 2,075	$ 2,075	$ 2,075	$ 24,897
A/R increases	$ 0	$ 0	$ 0	$ 0	$ 0	$ 0
Asset purchases	$ 0	$ 0	$ 0	$ 0	$ 0	$165,000
Dividends	$ 0	$ 0	$ 0	$ 0	$127,013	$127,013
Total cash outflows	**$ 3,164**	**$ 3,172**	**$ 3,180**	**$ 3,188**	**$130,210**	**$329,837**
Net cash flow	**−$ 7,106**	**$ 45,470**	**−$ 3,051**	**$ 49,525**	**−$126,009**	**$ 99,512**
Cash balance	**$133,578**	**$179,048**	**$175,997**	**$225,522**	**$ 99,512**	**$ 99,512**

Cash flow analysis (second year)

Quarter	Q1	2 Q2	Q3	Q4	2
Cash from operations	$ 53,248	$ 66,560	$ 71,885	$ 74,547	$266,240
Cash from receivables	$ 0	$ 0	$ 0	$ 0	$ 0
Operating cash inflow	**$ 53,248**	**$ 66,560**	**$ 71,885**	**$ 74,547**	**$266,240**
Other cash inflows					
Equity investment	$ 0	$ 0	$ 0	$ 0	$ 0
Increased borrowings	$ 0	$ 0	$ 0	$ 0	$ 0
Sales of business assets	$ 0	$ 0	$ 0	$ 0	$ 0
A/P increases	$ 8,717	$ 10,897	$ 11,769	$ 12,204	$ 43,587
Total other cash inflows	**$ 8,717**	**$ 10,897**	**$ 11,769**	**$ 12,204**	**$ 43,587**
Total cash inflow	**$ 61,965**	**$ 77,457**	**$ 83,653**	**$ 86,752**	**$309,827**
Cash outflows					
Repayment of principal	$ 3,417	$ 3,494	$ 3,574	$ 3,655	$ 14,139
A/P decreases	$ 5,975	$ 7,469	$ 8,067	$ 8,365	$ 29,876
A/R increases	$ 0	$ 0	$ 0	$ 0	$ 0
Asset purchases	$ 13,312	$ 16,640	$ 17,971	$ 18,637	$ 66,560
Dividends	$ 37,274	$ 46,592	$ 50,319	$ 52,183	$186,368
Total cash outflows	**$ 59,978**	**$ 74,195**	**$ 79,931**	**$ 82,840**	**$296,944**
Net cash flow	**$ 1,988**	**$ 3,261**	**$ 3,723**	**$ 3,912**	**$ 12,883**
Cash balance	**$101,500**	**$104,761**	**$108,484**	**$112,396**	**$112,396**

Cash flow analysis (third year)

Quarter	Q1	3 Q2	Q3	Q4	3
Cash from operations	$ 65,094	$ 81,368	$ 87,877	$ 91,132	$325,471
Cash from receivables	$ 0	$ 0	$ 0	$ 0	$ 0
Operating cash inflow	**$ 65,094**	**$ 81,368**	**$ 87,877**	**$ 91,132**	**$325,471**
Other cash inflows					
Equity investment	$ 0	$ 0	$ 0	$ 0	$ 0
Increased borrowings	$ 0	$ 0	$ 0	$ 0	$ 0
Sales of business assets	$ 0	$ 0	$ 0	$ 0	$ 0
A/P increases	$ 10,025	$ 12,531	$ 13,534	$ 14,035	$ 50,125
Total other cash inflows	**$ 10,025**	**$ 12,531**	**$ 13,534**	**$ 14,035**	**$ 50,125**
Total cash inflow	**$ 75,119**	**$ 93,899**	**$101,411**	**$105,167**	**$375,596**
Cash outflows					
Repayment of principal	$ 3,737	$ 3,822	$ 3,909	$ 3,997	$ 15,466
A/P decreases	$ 7,170	$ 8,963	$ 9,680	$ 10,038	$ 35,852
A/R increases	$ 0	$ 0	$ 0	$ 0	$ 0
Asset purchases	$ 16,274	$ 20,342	$ 21,969	$ 22,783	$ 81,368
Dividends	$ 45,566	$ 56,957	$ 61,514	$ 63,792	$227,829
Total cash outflows	**$ 72,747**	**$ 90,084**	**$ 97,072**	**$100,611**	**$360,515**
Net cash flow	**$ 2,372**	**$ 3,815**	**$ 4,339**	**$ 4,556**	**$ 15,081**
Cash balance	**$114,768**	**$118,583**	**$122,922**	**$127,477**	**$127,477**

Gluten-Free Bakery

Comstock Loaf

7060 Greenback Lane
Carmichael, CA 95622

Claire Moore

Comstock Loaf is a gluten-free bakery serving the people of the California with imminent plans to expand to grocery and specialty stores throughout the U.S.

EXECUTIVE SUMMARY

Comstock Loaf is a gluten-free bakery serving the people of the California with imminent plans to expand to grocery and specialty stores throughout the U.S. The business has operated out of the kitchen of owner Karin Carter since June 2012 but will expand its operation by moving into a 2,400 square-foot commercial space that includes a commercial bakery and storefront.

Comstock has established contracts with two grocery chain stores in California. We project that additional contracts will be possible once our move to larger facilities is complete. We will also pursue distribution through hotels and restaurants.

Operation of a storefront will allow for sales to the public in addition to special orders and catering sales.

The gluten-free lifestyle is a choice for some and a necessity for others. Gluten is a mixture of proteins that occur naturally in wheat, rye, barley and crossbreeds of these grains. Celiac disease is condition that occurs when the body's natural defense system reacts to gluten by attacking the lining of the small intestine, thus preventing the absorption of nutrients from food. Sufferers of the disease experience nutritional deficiencies that may lead to conditions that include anemia and osteoporosis. According to the FDA, as many as 3 million people in the U.S. suffer from its effects.

In August 2013 the FDA set the gluten limit to no more than 20 ppm (parts per million) for products that claim to be gluten-free. This is the lowest level that can be consistently detected in foods using valid scientific analytical tools. Because people with celiac disease can tolerate very small amounts of gluten, this level is considered by the FDA to be a valid safety standard.

Although the current trend toward gluten-free foods may subside in future years, we know that there will always be a market for our product with those who must follow the gluten-free diet for health reasons.

Mission Statement

Comstock Loaf provides the highest quality gluten-free goods to those who seek gluten-free foods either from preference or from medical necessity. Our signature recipes and flour mixtures ensure that our products replicate the taste and consistency of wheat products while meeting FDA guidelines for gluten-free labeling.

Management

Comstock Loaf is organized as a limited liability company within the state of California. The management team is comprised of member owners Karin Carter, Tim Carter, and Don Carter.

Operations

Comstock Loaf will operate six days a week creating products to fill its orders to retail outlets and local sales.

Marketing

Comstock will use a combination of web-based and print channels to market its products. Our website and social media presence on Twitter and Facebook will allow us to build a community of followers who will frequent our establishment and spread the word about our healthy offerings.

We will concentrate the bulk of our marketing efforts on gaining the attention of chain stores and food distributors nationwide that are looking to add health-oriented products to their inventories. In this effort we will rely on the contacts and experience of Tim Carter who has six years experience as a sales representative in the food industry.

Financial

Comstock Loaf requires $56,070 in startup funding. The owners have contributed cash and equipment comprising a 25.1% investment. The remaining 74.9% to be obtained through a 7-year loan from a local bank at 6% interest. In order to secure our loan, we will receive the assistance of the Sacramento Small Business Development Center.

COMPANY SUMMARY

Comstock Loaf is a California Limited Liability company managed by its owner partners Karin Carter, Tim Carter, and Don Carter. We create and sell gluten-free products such as breads, rolls, pastries, cookies and pizza dough. Our customers will include both commercial and retail audiences. Our ingredients will meet the FDA standard of less than 20 ppm (parts per million) gluten, therefore our customers can buy with confidence.

Competition

Many grocery stores sell gluten-free products and many restaurants offer them on their menus. However, our research shows that there are only two bakeries in the Sacramento area that specifically advertise that they make and sell gluten-free items. Both are located in the heart of the city and neither houses a seating area for customers.

The grocery stores purchase their GF products from such providers as:

- Miglet's in Danville, CA
- Mariposa Bakery, Oakland, CA
- New Grains, Provo, UT
- Canyon Bakehouse, Loveland, CO

Comstock Loaf currently has contracts to provide product to two chain grocery stores in the state of California. We are confident that our new facility will enable us to expand our commercial client base by stressing our ability to deliver a fresh product in a timely fashion.

As far as national exposure is concerned, our greatest competitor may be Udi's Healthy Foods, LLC which was recently acquired by Smart Balance. Begun in Colorado in 1994, Udi's grew from a small bakery and cafe to a national brand. The company gained its largest growth in 2010 when it partnered with E&A Industries. The guidance and contacts that E&A provided made it possible for Udi's to move into more than 16,000 locations across the country within the next year.

We seek to follow in the footsteps of Udi's and we believe that there is room in this growing market for other companies that can produce healthy gluten-free products that have the taste and appeal of their wheat-based counterparts.

We are especially proud of our sweet treats menu that includes cakes, coffee cakes and cookies. Udi's only offers a few dessert items and they are priced very high. We found that in their online store one brownie alone is $5. While it's hard to match the per item price, we are confident in our ability to offer a more affordable product when packaged in containers of 25 units or more.

Clearly the market for gluten-free products is growing. Consumers typically appreciate having more than one choice in products. While Udi's makes healthy and appealing products, the growth in this market indicates that there is room for more than one producer of gluten-free foods.

MARKET ANALYSIS

Competitive Advantage

Comstock Loaf's competitive advantage is in our proprietary flour mixtures which can be used in place of wheat flour cup-for-cup in any recipe. Chef Karin Carter has created several flour mixes that create gluten-free products with the same taste and feel as wheat-based products. They don't crumble and fall apart like most gluten-free fare. Unlike the typical gluten-free product, they produce a moist texture and appealing taste.

Our secret recipes offer a tasty alternative for the thousands of people who either prefer or require a gluten-free diet.

We have created a line of gluten-free sweet treats that includes: cupcakes, cake (chocolate and carrot), coffee cake, and biscotti. At this time there are few options on the market shelves for sweet baked goods that are moist, delicious and healthy. Our products are the exception.

Moreover, we can deliver our product to local customers faster than our competition because we are located closer to them. Stores and restaurants within Sacramento, Placer, Yolo and El Dorado counties will receive their product faster than they would if they dealt with other suppliers.

Target Market

Our target market includes anyone who has chosen to avoid gluten in their diet. This includes those who are health conscious as well as those who must avoid gluten due to celiac disease and other food allergies.

According to the University of Chicago Celiac Disease Center, celiac disease affects about 3 million Americans. Recent research indicates that as many as 83 percent of them are not diagnosed. In contrast it may be interesting to note that in the U.S. epilepsy affects 2.7 million people and that 2.1 million people are living with rheumatoid arthritis.

In October 2012 the market research company Packaged Facts stated that the gluten-free market had reached $4.2 billion for a compound annual growth rate of 28 percent over the 2008-2012 period. An August 2012 survey showed that 18 percent of adults were buying or consuming food products labeled as gluten-free, up from 15 percent in October 2010.

The Gluten-Free Agency is a consulting group dedicated to helping advertisers improve the market results within the gluten-free community. In 2012 The Gluten-Free Agency reported that the market for gluten-free products had grown to about 40 million consumers. Of this group about 4 million suffer from celiac disease. An additional 18 to 22 million choose the gluten-free lifestyle in order to manage gluten sensitivity.

The Agency stated that about three million consumers purchase gluten-free products for fad or non-medical reasons.

According to the *2008 Understanding Gluten-Free Shoppers' Survey* conducted by The Agency, 55 percent of consumers spend 30 percent or more of their grocery budget for gluten-free foods. Moreover, 68 percent shop at three or more stores per month in their search for gluten-free foods. When it comes to finding gluten-free foods, 71 percent of survey respondents said that they prefer to shop at the grocery store.

MARKETING PLAN

Our marketing strategy is to concentrate on selling our products through chain grocery stores. We already have contracts with two local chain stores and we are working to develop more. We will attend trade shows related to food and health in order to build our brand awareness and gain visibility with possible equity partners.

One such trade show is the Natural Products Expo West which will be held in Anaheim, California in March 2015. In a press release that described the conclusion of the 2014 Expo, it was stated that the event had brought together over 67,000 industry members.

We will also utilize Tim Carter's experience as a food sales representative to cultivate accounts with chain grocery stores in California and nationwide.

MANAGEMENT

Management Team

Co-owner and head pastry chef: Karin Carter was trained as a pastry chef and has worked in that field for the past ten years. She also studied chocolate sculpting in France.

Co-owner and business manager: Tim Carter has a bachelor's degree in business. Tim has also taken classes in business development through the Northern California Small Business Development Center (SBDC). Tim has six years experience as an outside sales representative for a large food and beverage manufacturer in California. His experience includes: acquiring and maintaining customers such as restaurants and hotels, providing product demonstrations, monitoring inventory, and producing sales reports.

Co-owner and operations manager: Don Carter has five years experience in the food service industry working as a pastry chef and front-of-house manager.

OPERATIONS PLAN

Our customers will appreciate the ability to receive fresh, tasty, gluten-free products on a regular basis. Our commercial customers will always have a sufficient inventory on hand.

Company Milestones

Present—December: Complete establishment of LLC and obtain all required licenses. Establish a social media presence, move into new facility, acquire equipment and furnishings, and open for business.

Year 1: Hire two employees to assist with baking and serving customers in the cafe. Acquire additional contracts with store chains.

Year2: Hire at least two additional employees to help with baking. Acquire a larger facility in which to fulfill orders. Maintain a small cafe for sales to the public. Develop web sales through website. Attend trade shows to build brand recognition and connect with possible grocery accounts.

Year 3-4: Hire additional employees as needed. Continue to expand distribution channels.

Year 4-5: Explore the option of joining forces with a private equity partner to create long-term appreciation through sales growth.

FINANCIAL PROJECTIONS

This plan makes the following assumptions:

- The owners will provide 25.1% equity investment in the business in cash and assets.

- The business will secure a loan with the assistance of the Sacramento Small Business Development Center for seven years at 6% to acquire and renovate a new facility and purchase kitchen equipment.

- Direct costs of production will average of 35% of the product pricing.

- All owners will work full-time in the business. In year one, hiring of additional help will begin.

- Ingredients will be supplied by local growers and from Costco.

- We will use professional services for legal, accounting and insurance advice.

Sources and uses of cash

December 31, 2014

Current assets	Total	Owner	Loan
Cash	5,200	5,200	
Food inv	1,500	1,500	
Total current	**6,700**	**6,700**	
Fixed assets	—		
Office equipment	1,320	1,320	
Kitchen equipment	26,850	4,850	22,000
POS system	1,200	1,200	
Leasehold improvements	20,000		20,000
Total fixed	—		
Total assets	**56,070**	**14,070**	**42,000**
Percent	100.0%	25.1%	74.9%

Equipment list

Equipment	Cost
Convection oven	2,500
Deck oven	3,000
Proof box	1,500
Dishwasher	3,200
Small wares	1,500
Refrigerator–2 door	1,500
Range	800
Utensils	400
Scale	300
Coffee maker	1,000
Work tables stainless	800
Food processor	300
Racks	1,300
Dishes	500
Planetary mixer–30qt	3,700
Display case 4–6 ft	2,700
Tables/chairs	1,000
POS system	1,200
Music system	400
Computer/software	700
Desk/chair	220
Filing cabinet	100
Shelving	300
Total	**28,920**

Pro forma profit and loss

	2015	2016	2017
Sales	$230,000	$320,000	$395,000
Direct cost of goods	$ 80,500	$112,000	$138,250
Gross margin	$149,500	$208,000	$256,750
Gross margin %	65.00%	65.00%	65.00%
Expenses			
Payroll	$ 85,000	$115,000	$125,000
Sales and marketing	$ 12,000	$ 14,000	$ 16,000
Depreciation	$ 5,200	$ 5,200	$ 5,200
Utilities	$ 1,275	$ 1,680	$ 1,880
Insurance	$ 2,200	$ 2,500	$ 2,900
Travel	$ 2,000	$ 2,500	$ 2,700
Payroll taxes	$ 13,050	$ 15,750	$ 16,650
Automobile expense	$ 3,000	$ 3,400	$ 3,800
Supplies	$ 2,800	$ 3,100	$ 3,600
Repairs & maintenance	$ 1,800	$ 1,600	$ 1,800
Telephone/internet	$ 2,800	$ 3,000	$ 3,300
Professional fees	$ 2,400	$ 2,400	$ 2,400
Other			
Total operating expenses	**$133,525**	**$170,130**	**$185,230**
Profit before interest and taxes	$ 15,975	$ 37,870	$ 71,520
Interest expense	$ 2,350	$ 1,990	$ 1,595
Taxes incurred	$ 3,406	$ 8,970	$ 17,481
Net profit	**$ 10,219**	**$ 26,910**	**$ 52,444**
Net profit/sales	**4.4%**	**8.4%**	**13.3%**

Projected balance sheet

Assets	2014	2015	2016	2017
Current assets				
Cash	$ 5,200	$15,419	$42,329	$ 94,773
Other current assets	$ 1,500	$ 1,800	$ 2,000	$ 2,300
Total current assets	**$ 6,700**	**$17,219**	**$44,329**	**$ 97,073**
Long-term assets	$ 7,370	$49,370	$49,370	$ 49,370
Accumulated depreciation	$ 2,950	$ 8,150	$13,350	$ 18,550
Total long-term assets	**$ 4,420**	**$41,220**	**$36,020**	**$ 30,820**
Total assets	**$11,120**	**$58,439**	**$80,349**	**$127,893**
Liabilities and capital				
Current liabilities				
Accounts payable	$ 285	$ 1,381	$ 747	$ 2,605
Current maturities		$ 8,353	$ 8,353	$ 8,353
Other current liabilities				
Subtotal current liabilities	$ 285	$ 9,734	$ 9,100	$ 10,958
Long-term liabilities		$27,651	$21,285	$ 14,527
Total liabilities	**$ 285**	**$37,385**	**$30,385**	**$ 25,485**
Paid-in capital	$ 5,000	$ 5,000	$ 7,000	$ 7,000
Retained earnings	$ 5,835	$16,054	$42,964	$ 95,408
Earnings				
Total capital	**$10,835**	**$21,054**	**$49,964**	**$102,408**
Total liabilities and capital	**$11,120**	**$58,439**	**$80,349**	**$127,893**
Net worth		**$21,054**	**$49,964**	**$102,408**

Break Even Analysis

This break-even analysis includes direct costs of production which include:

- ingredients for baking products

- direct payroll

- rent

- direct utilities

Average price	$ 6.00
Variable cost	$ 2.10
Average percent variable cost	35%
Estimated monthly fixed cost	$13,833
Units BE	3,547
Monthly $BE	$21,282

RESOURCES

http://articles.bplans.com/the-bakers-guide-to-opening-a-successful-bakery/

http://www.bplans.com/bakery_business_plan/executive_summary_fc.php

http://www.timesdispatch.com/business/local/columnists-blogs/randy-hallman/biz-buzz-gluten-free-bakery-rising-fast/article_0acc0aee-c46f-5987-a3c6-8d20808b4582.html

http://www.buffalonews.com/city-region/lockport/mom-of-3-turns-gluten-free-baking-into-a-business-20140405

http://www.bakingbusiness.com/Features/Company%20Profiles/Rudis%20Organic%20Bakery%20solves%20the%20gluten-free%20puzzle.aspx?cck=1

http://www.timescall.com/business/ci_25412636/aimes-love-new-longmont-bakery-only-gluten-free

http://www.webstaurantstore.com/article/52/how-to-write-a-bakery-business-plan.html

http://www.sugarplumvegan.com/

http://www.pushkinsbakery.com/

http://www.findmeglutenfree.com/us/ca/sacramento/dessert

http://www.urbanspoon.com/t/36/1/Sacramento/Gluten-Free-Friendly-restaurants

http://www.fda.gov/forconsumers/consumerupdates/ucm363069.htm

http://www.referenceforbusiness.com/business-plans/Business-Plans-Volume-05/Bread-Bakery-Business-Plan.html

http://nymag.com/guides/changeyourlife/16046/

http://www.cureceliacdisease.org/

http://udisglutenfree.com/about-us/story/

http://thegluten-freeagency.com/gluten-free-market-trends/

Home Energy Auditor

A 1 E n e r g y A u d i t i n g L L C

23409 Center Ave.
Edwards Ridge, IN 46124

Paul Greenland

A1 Energy Auditing is a new home energy auditing business. The company was established by Peter Gambino.

EXECUTIVE SUMMARY

Business Overview

A1 Energy Auditing is a new home energy auditing service being established by Peter Gambino. Typical energy efficiency problems result from poorly installed insulation, inadequate insulation, inefficient appliances, and old windows. As more consumers have become interested in improving the energy efficiency of their homes, Peter Gambino is capitalizing on his knowledge of home construction and insulation by establishing a service that provides an objective evaluation, along with specific recommendations for making improvements. Regardless of the service provided, the ultimate outcome will be to help homeowners reduce energy demand by increasing energy efficiency.

In addition to completing a small business ownership certificate program at Central Community College, Peter Gambino also has received certification as a Home Energy Professional from the Business Performance Institute Inc., providing him with the credentials he needs to ensure homeowners that they will receive the very best service.

MARKET ANALYSIS

A1 Energy Auditing is located in the city of Edwards Ridge, Indiana, in Noble County. The business will serve a geographic area that includes the counties of Noble, Whiteside, Henry, and Scoville. This primary service area includes many older houses that are not energy efficient, many of which are located in clusters of older subdivisions, providing ample opportunity for new business.

According to U.S. Census Bureau data issued in July of 2013, among all occupied U.S. housing units in 2011, the median age of owner-occupied homes was 35. In addition, data from the 2009 Census Housing Survey found that Indiana ranked 10th among the states with the largest number of homes constructed before 1939.

Edwards Ridge Regional Housing Analysis

According to demographic data for the Edwards Ridge market, the community is comprised of approximately 128,500 housing units, 94 percent of which are occupied. Of these, 68 percent are owner-occupied properties. A1 Energy Auditing will focus on marketing to homes with a value of $200,000 or higher. About 66 percent of area homes had a value of more than $200,000 in 2014:

- $200,000-$249,000 (34.8%)
- $250,000-$299,999 (16.9%)
- $300,000-$399,999 (7.2%)
- $400,000-$499,999 (4.5%)
- $500,000-$749,999 (2.8%)

Competition

A1 Energy Auditing will face limited competition in this emerging field, mainly from the following businesses:

- Cohen Heating & Air Conditioning Inc.
- Starwood Energy Consulting Inc.

Cohen Heating & Air Conditioning is considered to be a secondary competitor, because energy auditing is not a primary focus. In addition, Starwood Energy Consulting limits its service area to Henry and Scoville Counties.

INDUSTRY ANALYSIS

By 2014 there was a strong global focus on improving energy efficiency. According to a conservative estimate from the International Energy Agency (IEA), market-related investments in this area totaled approximately $300 billion by 2011. One key driver is the need for energy efficiency in buildings and homes. According to an IEA report, in 2012 Germany's government-developed bank, KfW, supported energy-efficient investments in residential buildings by offering $12.7 billion in related loans, leading to an estimated $35 billion in home efficiency improvements. Other countries have initiated programs as well, including a home insulation program in New Zealand that generated $243 million in investment over the course of four years.

Energy auditing is considered to be a "green job" according to the U.S. Bureau of Labor Statistics, because it focuses on the conservation of natural resources and providing services that are beneficial to the environment. Although the bureau discontinued employment data collection pertaining to green goods and services in 2013, due to government spending cuts, in 2011 this emerging category represented more than 3.4 million jobs, about 2.5 million of which were within the private sector. Professional, scientific, and technical services were the third-leading employment category within the industry, behind manufacturing and construction.

Although there is not a single national training and education requirement for energy auditors, some states do have minimum certification and education requirements. The Building Performance Institute, Association of Energy Engineers, and the Residential Energy Services Network are organizations that provide education and certification programs.

PERSONNEL

Peter Gambino (Owner)

Peter Gambino began his career as a general laborer in the construction trade. After one year, he joined Midcity Insulation as an insulation installer. Within one year Gambino was promoted to the position of crew leader. He soon advanced to a supervisory position after the business owners recognized his exceptional customer service and employee relations skills. As more consumers have become interested in improving the energy efficiency of their homes, Gambino saw an opportunity to combine his knowledge of home insulation with a service that provides an objective evaluation of customers' dwellings, along with specific recommendations for making improvements.

In addition to completing a small business ownership certificate program at Central Community College, Gambino also has received certification as a Home Energy Professional from the Business Performance Institute Inc., providing him with the credentials he needs to ensure homeowners that they will receive the very best service.

Professional & Advisory Support

A1 Energy Auditing has established a business banking account with Edwards Ridge Community Bank, including a merchant account for accepting credit card payments. Tax advisement is provided by Lewiston & Associates LLC. In addition, legal services are provided by the law offices of Ander Johnson LP.

GROWTH STRATEGY

With low overhead costs, minimal competition, and strong demand projections, A1 Energy Auditing is anticipating that the business will experience strong growth during its first three years of operations. Peter Gambino has outlined the following growth strategy for the business:

Year One: Focus on generating awareness about A1 Energy Auditing within the community, building trust with area homeowners, and generating word-of-mouth referrals. Perform a total of 525 energy audits (detailed breakdown provided below). Generate gross revenues of $93,375.

Year Two: Continue to concentrate on building awareness and trust within the local market. Perform a total of 650 energy audits. Generate gross revenues of $123,000.

Year Three: Perform a total of 800 energy audits. Begin preparations to hire a part-time auditor to accommodate additional business volume and develop a strategy to expand into the neighboring counties of Webster and Lincoln. Generate gross revenues of $164,500.

The following table provides a snapshot of A1 Energy Auditing's projected service packages for the business' first three years of operations:

	Bronze	Sales	Silver	Sales	Gold	Sales
2014	300	$ 9,000	150	$48,750	75	$35,625
2015	350	$10,500	200	$65,000	100	$47,500
2016	400	$12,000	250	$81,250	150	$71,250

Although the most affordable packages will represent the majority of energy audits by volume, steady growth is anticipated within each auditing package:

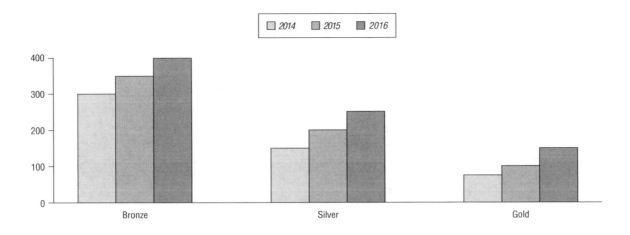

SERVICES

A1 Energy Auditing will offer a wide range of services to assess the energy efficiency of customers' homes, including:

- Insulation Checks

- Homeowner Education

- Blower Door Tests

- Furnace Evaluations

- Thermal Imaging

- Appliance Combustion Zone Safety Testing

- Visual Inspections (Internal & External)

- Energy Bill Analysis

- Detailed Audit Reporting

Services will be provided in three different packages, including:

Bronze (Basic Energy Assessment) ($30; one hour)

This service package focuses on general education, providing homeowners with steps they can take right away to improve energy efficiency and lower their bills. Peter Gambino will show the customer how to access free online tools they can use to compare their energy utilization to nearby homes. In addition, he will show customers how to perform a comprehensive review of their utility bills, providing them with a baseline of their current energy utilization. Finally, he will provide general tips for improving efficiency and will do a basic home walk-through to identify potential problem spots.

Silver (Standard Energy Assessment) ($325; three hours)

This package includes a visual inspection within and outside of the customer's home. Peter Gambino will utilize objective tools, including a blower door test, pressure room test, thermal scan, and appliance combustion zone safety testing. Combined with information from the customer's energy bills, a detailed energy audit report will be provided, equipping the customer with specific recommendations for improvement.

Gold (Premium Energy Assessment) ($475; four hours)

This service package includes everything provided at the Bronze and Silver levels, along with a scan of the customer's home utilizing thermal imaging technology (e.g., an infrared camera). Energy loss is documented in color photographs (e.g., cooler temperatures appearing as dark colors and warmer temperatures appearing as light colors), which are included with the energy audit report.

Peter Gambino anticipates that, on a percentage basis, service packages for his business will break down as follows:

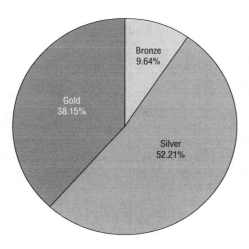

MARKETING & SALES

A1 Energy Auditing has developed a marketing plan that includes the following primary tactics:

1. A Web site with a complete list of services provided, helpful information about home energy efficiency, background information about Peter Gambino, links to the business' Facebook page, details about A1 Energy Auditing's Better Business Bureau membership, insurance coverage, certifications, and online appointment request and contact forms.

2. Promotional graphics for the company's van, providing mobile marketing exposure.

3. Magnetic business cards (e.g., refrigerator magnets) that can be left behind with customers, and also distributed at home shows and other events.

4. A bi-fold brochure that includes information about A1 Energy Auditing's energy auditing services/packages, certifications, insurance coverage, and licenses. This can be used for distribution at home shows, special events, and also for promotional mailings.

5. Regular direct mailings to homeowners in Noble, Whiteside, Henry, and Scoville Counties with properties that are at least 25 years old and have a value of $200,000 or more. A local mail house has been identified to assist with mailings to key prospects four times per year. In addition to preparing the actual mailings, the mail house also will provide targeted mailing lists for each campaign.

6. Membership in the Edwards Ridge Chamber of Commerce.

7. Participation in home shows and other special events.

8. A social media strategy involving Angie's List and Facebook, with a goal of generating new business and building/maintaining positive word-of-mouth.

9. A customer referral program, providing former clients with a $25 gift card for referrals that result in either a silver or gold energy auditing package.

10. Regional print advertising in Noble, Whiteside, Henry, and Scoville Counties.

11. Submission of press releases/guest columns to regional media with information about home energy efficiency tips and savings opportunities.

12. Placemat advertising at local family restaurants.

OPERATIONS

Facility & Location
A1 Energy Auditing will operate from a home office within Peter Gambino's residence, which also includes enclosed garage space for a business vehicle.

Equipment
A1 Energy Auditing will require the following equipment (total cost $14,579) at start-up, which Peter Gambino will cover from personal savings. In addition, a vehicle loan has been obtained to purchase a used cargo van.

- Infrared Camera ($2,600)
- Portable Combustible Gas Leak Detector ($163)
- Air Flow Indicator with Pencil Stream Adaptor ($50)
- Blower Door Equipment ($2,550)
- Touchscreen Laptop Computer ($650)
- Portable Color Printer ($466)
- Flashlights ($50)
- Ladders ($300)
- Home Energy Assessment Software ($7,500)
- Carbon Monoxide Monitor ($250)

Hours of Operation
A1 Energy Auditing will provide services between the hours of 8 AM and 5 PM, Monday through Saturday. The business will be closed on Sundays and holidays.

LEGAL

A1 Energy Auditing will maintain appropriate liability and automotive insurance policies (available upon request).

FINANCIAL ANALYSIS

After generating nearly $95,000 in gross sales during the business' first year of operations, A1 Energy Auditing is projecting that sales will increase more than 30 percent during both years two and three.

Annual sales

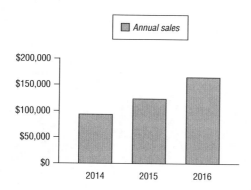

Peter Gambino will provide the financial capital required to cover the $14,579 needed for initial startup costs, as well as an additional $15,000 to cover initial operations.

A complete set of pro forma financial statements has been prepared for A1 Energy Auditing and are available from our accountants upon request. The following table provides an overview of key projections during the first three years of operations:

	2014	2015	2016
Sales	$93,375	$123,000	$164,500
Expenses			
Marketing & advertising	$15,000	$ 20,000	$ 25,000
General/administrative	$ 500	$ 500	$ 500
Accounting/legal	$ 1,500	$ 1,000	$ 1,000
Office supplies	$ 850	$ 850	$ 850
Vehicle loan	$ 3,600	$ 3,600	$ 3,600
Equipment	$ 1,000	$ 1,000	$ 1,000
Business insurance	$ 875	$ 900	$ 925
Payroll	$50,000	$ 60,000	$ 70,000
Payroll taxes	$ 6,000	$ 7,200	$ 8,400
Health insurance	$ 1,750	$ 2,000	$ 2,250
Postage	$ 2,500	$ 3,000	$ 3,500
Fuel	$ 2,000	$ 2,500	$ 3,000
Maintenance & repairs	$ 300	$ 400	$ 500
Telecommunications	$ 1,000	$ 1,000	$ 1,000
Total expenses	**$86,875**	**$103,950**	**$121,525**
Net income	**$ 6,500**	**$ 19,050**	**$ 42,975**

Interactive Testing Service

Greenbrier Technology Testing LLC

705 Viewpoint Ave., Suite 7
Landsberg , MO 62215

Paul Greenland

Greenbrier Technology Testing is an interactive testing service focused on usability testing for computer software, mobile applications, and Web sites.

EXECUTIVE SUMMARY

Landsberg, Missouri-based Greenbrier Technology Testing is a newly established interactive testing service. Specifically, the business concentrates on usability testing, helping a global client base to ensure that computer software, mobile applications, and Web sites function properly and are well received by end-users.

Greenbrier Technology Testing is led by Melissa Greenbrier, who prior to establishing her own business worked as an interactive marketing specialist for Landsberg Community Health System. In that position she played a key role in managing the Web site and intranet site for a leading network of hospitals and clinics in the Kansas City area. Additionally, her responsibilities included managing the organization's presence on various social media outlets and overseeing the development of custom mobile applications used by healthcare practitioners, physicians, and patients.

Melissa Greenbrier will personally evaluate technology platforms on behalf of her clients, including technology companies, Web developers, advertising agencies, and corporations. Additionally, she will utilize a network of consumer test subjects who fit the target market profile for the application being tested. Ultimately, customers will be provided with a detailed usability analysis that includes objective assessments in several key areas, samplings of subjective user comments/feedback, and recommendations for improvement.

MARKET ANALYSIS

Greenbrier Technology Testing's customer base will include technology companies, Web developers, advertising agencies, and corporations throughout the world. By operating in Missouri and keeping overhead low, the company will be able to gain a competitive edge over larger firms in more expensive markets, such as Seattle or Silicon Valley. Mid-sized advertising agencies represent a key target market for Greenbrier Technology Testing, which can function as a scalable extension of traditional agencies that wish to expand their offerings in the interactive arena.

In addition to Web sites, social media channels, and a plethora of traditional computer software applications, by 2014 consumers had what seemed to be an unlimited number of mobile applications to choose from. These fell into broad categories such as:

- Communication
- Culture
- Education
- Enterprise
- Entertainment
- Environment
- Games
- Health
- Law
- Lifestyle
- Music
- Navigation
- News
- Object Recognition
- Payment
- Photos & Video
- Productivity
- Search
- Shopping/Retail
- Social Networking
- Sports
- Tools
- Travel
- Utilities
- Weather

Within each category were virtually unlimited numbers of sub-categories, providing an application for almost every need, interest, or situation. Additionally, available options became even more staggering when one considered the number of available platforms, such as Android, iPhone, Windows, and Blackberry, and the various versions of those platforms.

Mobile applications, in particular, represented an exploding market for providers of usability testing. According to a report from ABI Research, by 2012 the mobile application testing market already was generating revenues of $200 million. Data from the University of Alabama at Birmingham Collat School of Business revealed that, by 2014, more than 91 percent of individuals in the United States owned a cell phone, according to *CMS Wire*. Additionally, by 2016 the number of mobile Internet devices was projected to reach the 10 billion mark. Compared to $11.4 billion in 2014, revenue from mobile apps was projected to reach $24.5 billion by 2016.

PERSONNEL

Greenbrier Technology Testing is led by Melissa Greenbrier, who prior to establishing her own business worked as interactive marketing specialist for Landsberg Community Health System. In that position she played a key role in managing the Web site and intranet site for a leading network of hospitals and clinics in the Kansas City area. Additionally, her responsibilities included managing the organization's presence on various social media outlets and overseeing the development of custom mobile applications used by healthcare practitioners, physicians, and patients.

Support Staff

Melissa Greenbrier will begin operations with one full-time assistant. The need for additional staff will be evaluated annually.

Independent Contractors

In order to offer scalable testing options for clients, Greenbrier Technology Testing will recruit test candidates from a variety of demographic backgrounds and situations. These individuals will be compensated as independent contractors. Melissa Greenbrier anticipates that approximately 25 percent of her business' revenues will be needed for independent contract labor.

Professional & Advisory Support

Greenbrier Technology Testing has established a Business Advantage checking account with Bank of America, and will utilize Forreston Financial Services for accounting and tax preparation.

GROWTH STRATEGY

Greenbrier Technology Testing has established the following growth targets for its first three years of operations:

Year One: Secure a $50,000 business loan, with a term of 36 months at 6% interest. Average 25 billable hours per week, resulting in gross revenue of $292,500. Generate net income of $27,372.

Year Two: Increase billable hours to an average of 30 per week, resulting in gross revenue of $357,750. Generate net income of $30,466. Recoup Melissa Greenbrier's $35,000 personal investment in the business during the first half of the year.

Year Three: Achieve an average of 35 billable hours per week, resulting in gross revenue of $411,320. Generate net income of $37,297. Repay three-year business loan.

The following graph provides a visual snapshot of Greenbrier Technology Testing's revenue and net income targets for the first three years of operations:

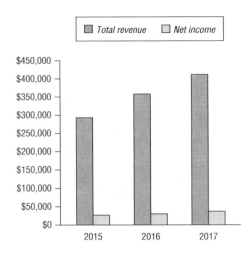

Melissa Greenbrier understands that her firm will need to devote additional (e.g., non-billable) time to administrative and operational tasks, such as invoicing, marketing, and project estimation.

SERVICES

Interactive Testing Process

Greenbrier Technology Testing has developed a formal approach to working with clients in need of testing services. This involves five essential phases, including:

Discovery

During this phase, Melissa will learn about the prospective customer's business, as well as the application that must be tested. This will include an initial review of the application, as well as related information provided by the customer regarding its functionality. Melissa will gain a solid understanding of the user, business, and functional requirements related to the application. Additionally, she will identify specific goals and objectives that the customer wishes to achieve during the testing process, as well as other important information such as a profile of the typical application user (e.g., the target market).

Project Planning

Based on the information obtained during the discovery phase, Greenbrier Technology Testing will develop a detailed plan. This will outline the scope of the project, stated objectives, required resources, project timelines/milestones, and a detailed time and cost estimate. The project plan also will include a very detailed "test plan" that will outline the scope of the testing, as well as details such as the location, time, number of sessions, test subjects, metrics, equipment involved, and desired technology platforms/operating systems.

Participant Recruitment

Once the ideal user/target market has been identified, Greenbrier Technology Testing will begin the process of recruiting the desired number of test participants who meet the appropriate criteria. Typically, five participants are adequate for usability testing/discovering usability problems. Melissa Greenbrier will compensate participants for their time as independent contractors. All testing will take place at Greenbrier Technology Testing's offices.

Testing

This phase will involve the actual process of usability testing. Depending on the goals of the testing, different moderating techniques will be employed. For example, moderators may ask participants probing questions during the testing process, or once the session is complete. Alternatively, participants may be asked to provide vocal feedback concurrently, while interacting with technology, or retrospectively (perhaps watching a video replay of their interaction with the technology being tested).

A variety of techniques and scenarios may be utilized for conducting the actual testing. For example, when testing a mobile application the moderator and participant may sit together in a well lit room. The participant might be provided with a comfortable chair and a "cafe-style" table. A small camera could be mounted directly onto the mobile device, providing footage of both the screen and the user's fingers as they manipulate the application. In addition to being captured, the footage could be displayed on a large monitor in the room, or in an adjacent room if the session needs to be reviewed live. Other software applications capture footage of an application being used in real time. However, they don't capture the user's fingers, as is the case with a mountable camera. Based on the needs of the client, a variety of techniques and methods can be used to capture necessary aspects of the user experience.

Results Reporting
The final phase of the usability testing process will result in a detailed report for the client, which includes both quantitative and qualitative findings. Specifically, the report will include sections summarizing the project itself, including the date and location of the testing, equipment used, etc.; the specific methodology used; the results; and detailed recommendations for improvement.

Fees
Greenbrier Technology Testing typically will bill clients at a rate of $225 per hour. Clients will be provided with a flat figure estimate, calculated using the aforementioned hourly rate, and factoring in any equipment acquisition (e.g., leasing, purchasing, etc.) and participant recruitment costs. Melissa Greenbrier will require clients to pay 50 percent of the estimate in advance.

MARKETING & SALES

Greenbrier Technology Testing will use its Web site as a prime example of the firm's capabilities. In addition to ranking highly in the area of usability, the site will feature case studies that highlight successful testing projects, as well as video clips of Greenbrier Technology Testing in action (e.g., showing footage of actual testing sessions).

Additionally, Melissa Greenbrier will write a technology blog and publish regular interviews on the company's YouTube channel regarding usability testing and related topics. Social media channels such as LinkedIn and Twitter also will play a critical role in the company's marketing strategy.

Other tactics include:

1. Promotional premiums: Greenbrier Technology Testing will order 20 GB flash drives, imprinted with the company's logo, which will be given away to prospective clients in exchange for agreeing to a 15-minute telephone sales consultation.

2. Printed collateral, which can be used for direct mail purposes, distribution at trade shows and conferences, and also as a leave-behind following sales calls.

3. A monthly e-mail newsletter for target prospects that provides case studies, tips, and insight from experiences with past usability testing projects.

4. Direct mailings to key prospects, such as technology companies, Web developers, advertising agencies, and corporations.

5. A media relations strategy that involves the submission of case studies/success stories to appropriate business and trade magazines.

6. Presentations and networking at industry conferences attended by software, Web, and app developers.

OPERATIONS

Facilities

Greenbrier Technology Testing will conduct operations in leased space at 705 Viewpoint Ave., Suite 7, in Landsberg, Missouri. The space is approximately 30 minutes north of the Kansas City International Airport, with easy access off Interstate 39. Formerly home to a recording and video production studio, the office includes several rooms and adjacent observation areas that are ideal for conducting testing sessions. In addition, the space includes conference room space, a small kitchenette, restaurants, four offices, and ample parking. Importantly, Greenbrier Technology Testing's location is equipped with business-class broadband service, which will support high-quality videoconferencing and Internet telephony (VoIP).

Equipment

Melissa Greenbrier will attempt to establish relationships with leading consumer electronics manufacturers and obtain equipment and devices that can be used for testing purposes. When necessary, Greenbrier Technology Testing will purchase equipment based on specific customer needs. Any device/equipment acquisition costs will be factored into project estimates.

In order to outfit Greenbrier Technology Testing's facilities, Melissa Greenbrier estimates that approximately $35,000 in capital purchases will be needed for equipment (video cameras, VoIP telephone system, computers, microphones, lights, flat-screen monitors, cabling, etc.), computer software (applications for monitoring/recording user experiences on various technology platforms), office equipment, and furniture. An itemized breakdown of these items is available upon request.

Hours of Operation

Greenbrier Technology Testing will keep regular office hours of 9 AM to 5 PM, Monday through Friday. However, because the business will serve customers throughout the world, Melissa Greenbrier will make herself available at irregular hours when necessary (e.g., for conference calls, meetings, etc.).

FINANCIAL ANALYSIS

Greenbrier Technology Testing has prepared a complete set of pro forma financial statements, which are available upon request. The following table provides an overview of key projections during the first three years of operations:

	2015	2016	2017
Total revenue	**$292,500**	**$357,750**	**$411,320**
Expenses			
Salaries	$ 90,000	$115,000	$130,000
Payroll taxes	$ 13,500	$ 17,250	$ 19,500
Independent contractors	$ 73,125	$ 89,438	$102,830
Business loan	$ 18,253	$ 18,253	$ 18,253
Utilities	$ 2,500	$ 2,750	$ 3,000
Facility lease	$ 7,800	$ 7,800	$ 7,800
Insurance	$ 1,850	$ 1,943	$ 2,040
Office supplies	$ 1,500	$ 1,750	$ 2,000
Equipment	$ 20,000	$ 25,000	$ 30,000
Marketing & advertising	$ 30,000	$ 40,000	$ 50,000
Telecommunications & internet	$ 2,600	$ 2,600	$ 2,600
Professional development	$ 1,500	$ 2,500	$ 2,500
Travel & entertainment	$ 2,000	$ 2,500	$ 3,000
Subscriptions & dues	$ 500	$ 500	$ 500
Total expenses	**$265,128**	**$327,284**	**$374,023**
Net income	**$ 27,372**	**$ 30,466**	**$ 37,297**

Multilevel Marketing Company

Dunn Multilevel Marketing, Inc.

23433 W. 151st St.
New York, NY 10012

BizPlanDB.com

Dunn Multilevel Marketing, Inc. is a New York-based corporation that will provide distribution of products to customers and associated agents in its targeted market. The Company was founded by Alex Dunn.

1.0 EXECUTIVE SUMMARY

The purpose of this business plan is to raise $100,000 for the development of a multilevel marketing company while showcasing the expected financials and operations over the next three years. Dunn Multilevel Marketing, Inc. ("the Company") is a New York-based corporation that will provide distribution of products to customers and associated agents in its targeted market. The Company was founded by Alex Dunn.

1.1 The Services

Management intends to develop a large network of independent sales people that will distribute products on behalf of Dunn Multilevel Marketing, Inc. Each independent distributor will be free to hire additional distributors that will work under them to make sales within their selected territories. The business will specialize in the ongoing distribution of daily household goods with a focus on cleaning equipment. The business will generate secondary revenues from enrollment fees among people that become members of Dunn Multilevel Marketing.

The third section of the business plan will further describe the services offered by Dunn Multilevel Marketing, Inc.

1.2 Financing

Mr. Dunn is seeking to raise $100,000 from a bank loan. The interest rate and loan agreement are to be further discussed during negotiation. This business plan assumes that the business will receive a 10-year loan with a 9% fixed interest rate. The financing will be used for the following:

- Development of the Company's office location.

- Financing for the first six months of operation.

- Capital to purchase the initial inventory of products to be distributed.

Mr. Dunn will contribute $10,000 to the venture.

1.3 Mission Statement

The mission of Dunn Multilevel Marketing is to become the recognized leader in its targeted market for product distribution and marketing services among its licensed distributors.

1.4 Management Team

The Company was founded by Alex Dunn. Mr. Dunn has more than 10 years of experience in the sales and marketing industry. Through his expertise, he will be able to bring the operations of the business to profitability within its first year of operations.

1.5 Sales Forecasts

Mr. Dunn expects a strong rate of growth at the start of operations. Below are the expected financials over the next three years.

Proforma profit and loss (yearly)

Year	1	2	3
Sales	$806,778	$871,320	$941,026
Operating costs	$291,067	$316,515	$343,310
EBITDA	$253,053	$271,135	$291,352
Taxes, interest, and depreciation	$109,005	$112,180	$119,451
Net profit	$144,048	$158,955	$171,901

Sales, operating costs, and profit forecast

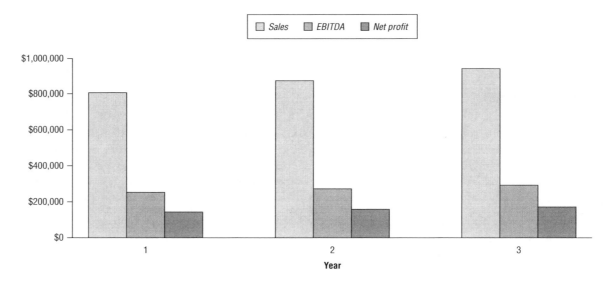

1.6 Expansion Plan

The Founder expects that the business will aggressively expand during the first three years of operation. Mr. Dunn intends to implement marketing campaigns that will effectively target individuals within the target market.

2.0 COMPANY AND FINANCING SUMMARY

2.1 Registered Name and Corporate Structure

Dunn Multilevel Marketing is registered as a corporation in the State of New York.

2.2 Required Funds

At this time, Dunn Multilevel Marketing, Inc. requires $100,000 of debt funds. Below is a breakdown of how these funds will be used:

Projected startup costs

Initial lease payments and deposits	$ 10,000
Working capital	$ 35,000
FF&E	$ 23,000
Leasehold improvements	$ 5,000
Security deposits	$ 5,000
Insurance	$ 2,500
Initial inventory	$ 17,000
Marketing budget	$ 7,500
Miscellaneous and unforeseen costs	$ 5,000
Total startup costs	**$110,000**

Use of funds

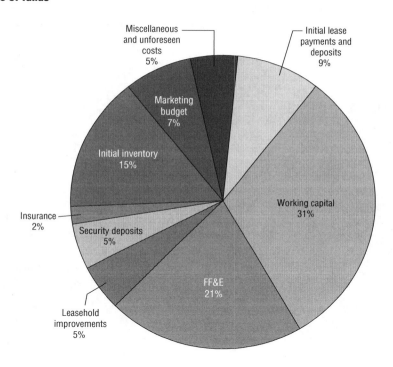

2.3 Investor Equity

Mr. Dunn is not seeking an investment from a third party at this time.

2.4 Management Equity

Alex Dunn owns 100% of Dunn Multilevel Marketing, Inc.

2.5 Exit Strategy

If the business is very successful, Mr. Dunn may seek to sell the business to a third party for a significant earnings multiple. Most likely, the Company will hire a qualified business broker to sell the business on behalf of Dunn Multilevel Marketing, Inc. Based on historical numbers, the business could fetch a sales premium of up to 7 times earnings.

3.0 PRODUCTS AND SERVICES

Below is a description of the products and services offered by Dunn Multilevel Marketing, Inc.

3.1 Distribution of Products

The primary revenue for the business will come from the ongoing distribution of products that are used during the course of the day among households within the New York metropolitan area. The business will directly sell these products via the Company's internal sales staff coupled with individuals that have become affiliated distributors of the business. As stated in the executive summary, the business intends to build a large network of independent sales distributors that will work on behalf of the business for the distribution of household products.

3.2 Enrollment Fees

Dunn Multilevel Marketing, Inc. will also generate high-margin secondary revenues from the ongoing enrollment fees that will be charged among distributors that want to enroll in the Company's sales programs. These fees will be used to defray costs related to providing distributors with handbooks and sales materials as it relates to the Company's multilevel marketing product distribution operations.

4.0 STRATEGIC AND MARKET ANALYSIS

4.1 Economic Outlook

This section of the analysis will detail the economic climate, the multilevel marketing industry, the customer profile, and the competition that the business will face as it progresses through its business operations.

Currently, the economic market condition in the United States is moderate. The unemployment rate of the country has declined while asset prices have increased substantially (among nearly all asset classes including stocks and real estate). Dunn Multilevel Marketing, Inc. will be able to remain profitable in any economic climate as the business intends to focus its operations on useful household goods. Additionally, the fees generated from establishing new partnerships with third party sellers will ensure that the business is able to remain profitable and cash flow positive at all times.

4.2 Industry Analysis

Within the United States, general wholesalers and marketers of merchandise generate more than $2 trillion per year. The industry employs more than 5 million people and provides annual payrolls in excess of $300 billion. This is a highly mature industry, and the continued wholesale distribution (including through multilevel marketing channels) is anticipated to have a growth rate equivalent to that of the general economy.

4.3 Customer Profile

Dunn Multilevel Marketing, Inc.'s average client will be a middle- to upper-middle class man or woman living in the Company's target market. Common traits among clients will include:

- Annual household income exceeding $50,000

- Lives or works no more than 15 miles from the Company's location.

- Will spend $20 per month on products distributed by Dunn Multilevel Marketing, Inc.

Among people that will enroll in the Company's independent sales programs, Management has outlined the following demographics:

- Household income of $30,000 to $50,000 per year.

- Will make sales of approximately $50,000 to $100,000 per year.

- Between the ages of 25 to 50.

- Will spend up to $1,000 on initial enrollment fees.

4.4 Competition

Due to the unique nature of multilevel marketing businesses, there are only a handful of companies that are engaged in this business. Foremost, there are high barriers to entry to do the extensive legal filings that must be completed for this type of company to operate within the letter of the law. The primary competitor to Dunn Multilevel Marketing, Inc. is Amway. This business has been established for almost 55 years. However, by maintaining a strong marketing infrastructure and lucrative commission schedule, the business will be able to effectively enter this market and expand.

5.0 MARKETING PLAN

Dunn Multilevel Marketing, Inc. intends to maintain an extensive marketing campaign that will ensure maximum visibility for the business in its targeted market. Below is an overview of the marketing strategies and objectives of Dunn Multilevel Marketing, Inc.

5.1 Marketing Objectives

- Develop an online presence by developing a website and placing the Company's name and contact information with online directories.

- Establish relationships with local independent sales agents that will enroll in the Company's distribution programs.

5.2 Marketing Strategies

In regards to the Company's general product distribution operations, Management intends to use its sales force (hired internally) to generate initial revenues through the sale of the products discussed throughout this business plan. This will ensure that the business can generate a positive cash flow while soliciting additional independent sales people and distributors.

On a regular basis, the Company will reach out to independent sales organizations that would be interested in having their members enroll in the Company's multilevel marketing operations. The business will hold functions and meetings that showcase the products distributed by the business coupled with how an individual can become a member of the Dunn Multilevel Marketing organization.

The Company will frequently host large-scale events that showcase the products (as well as the potential to become a selling partner with the business) to the general public. These events will be held at major venues in order to attract as many people as possible.

5.3 Pricing

As the business will carry thousands of items in its inventory, it is hard to quantify pricing. However, Management anticipates that the Company will achieve gross margins of at least 60% on each item sold directly by the business.

For each new enrollee into the Company's sales program, Management expects that the business will receive $1,000 to $2,000 of income.

6.0 ORGANIZATIONAL PLAN AND PERSONNEL SUMMARY

6.1 Corporate Organization

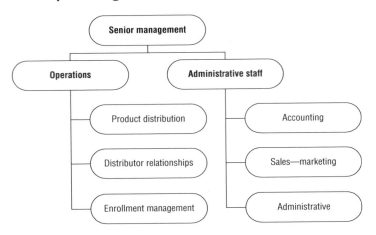

6.2 Organizational Budget

Personnel plan—yearly

Year	1	2	3
Senior management	$ 40,000	$ 41,200	$ 42,436
Sales manager	$ 35,000	$ 36,050	$ 37,132
Distribution managers	$ 32,500	$ 33,475	$ 34,479
Sales staff	$ 37,500	$ 51,500	$ 66,306
Customer services	$ 44,000	$ 45,320	$ 46,680
Total	**$189,000**	**$207,545**	**$227,033**

Numbers of personnel

Senior management	1	1	1
Sales manager	1	1	1
Distribution managers	1	1	1
Sales staff	3	4	5
Customer services	2	2	2
Totals	**8**	**9**	**10**

Personnel expense breakdown

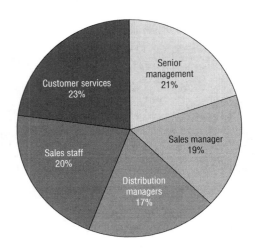

7.O FINANCIAL PLAN

7.1 Underlying Assumptions

The Company has based its proforma financial statements on the following:

- Dunn Multilevel Marketing, Inc. will have an annual revenue growth rate of 16% per year.

- The Owner will acquire $100,000 of debt funds to develop the business.

- The loan will have a 10-year term with a 9% interest rate.

7.2 Sensitivity Analysis

In the event of an economic downturn, the business may have a decline in its revenues. However, the pricing point for the Company's products is relatively low and the products are in continued demand among households. Additionally, the business will generate highly predictable streams of revenue from its independent distributors and sales force.

7.3 Source of Funds

Financing

Equity contributions	
Management investment	$ 10,000.00
Total equity financing	**$ 10,000.00**
Banks and lenders	
Banks and lenders	$ 100,000.00
Total debt financing	**$100,000.00**
Total financing	**$110,000.00**

7.4 General Assumptions

General assumptions

Year	1	2	3
Short term interest rate	9.5%	9.5%	9.5%
Long term interest rate	10.0%	10.0%	10.0%
Federal tax rate	33.0%	33.0%	33.0%
State tax rate	5.0%	5.0%	5.0%
Personnel taxes	15.0%	15.0%	15.0%

7.5 Profit and Loss Statements

Proforma profit and loss (yearly)

Year	1	2	3
Sales	**$806,778**	**$871,320**	**$941,026**
Cost of goods sold	$262,658	$283,670	$306,364
Gross margin	67.44%	67.44%	67.44%
Operating income	**$544,120**	**$587,650**	**$634,662**
Expenses			
Payroll	$189,000	$207,545	$227,033
General and administrative	$ 25,200	$ 26,208	$ 27,256
Marketing expenses	$ 4,034	$ 4,357	$ 4,705
Professional fees and licensure	$ 5,219	$ 5,376	$ 5,537
Insurance costs	$ 1,987	$ 2,086	$ 2,191
Travel and vehicle costs	$ 7,596	$ 8,356	$ 9,191
Rent and utilities	$ 20,000	$ 21,000	$ 22,050
Miscellaneous costs	$ 9,681	$ 10,456	$ 11,292
Payroll taxes	$ 28,350	$ 31,132	$ 34,055
Total operating costs	**$291,067**	**$316,515**	**$343,310**
EBITDA	**$253,053**	**$271,135**	**$291,352**
Federal income tax	$ 83,507	$ 86,791	$ 93,682
State income tax	$ 12,653	$ 13,150	$ 14,194
Interest expense	$ 8,738	$ 8,131	$ 7,468
Depreciation expenses	$ 4,107	$ 4,107	$ 4,107
Net profit	**$144,048**	**$158,955**	**$171,901**
Profit margin	**17.85%**	**18.24%**	**18.27%**

Sales, operating costs, and profit forecast

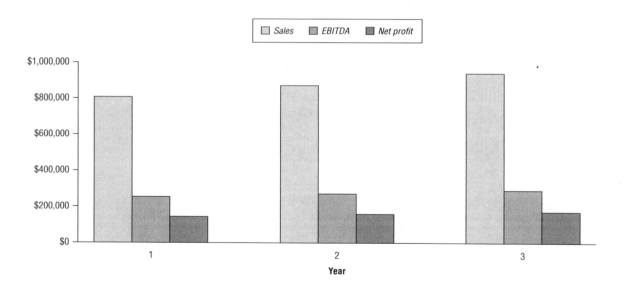

7.6 Cash Flow Analysis

Proforma cash flow analysis—yearly

Year	1	2	3
Cash from operations	$148,155	$163,062	$176,008
Cash from receivables	$ 0	$ 0	$ 0
Operating cash inflow	**$148,155**	**$163,062**	**$176,008**
Other cash inflows			
Equity investment	$ 10,000	$ 0	$ 0
Increased borrowings	$100,000	$ 0	$ 0
Sales of business assets	$ 0	$ 0	$ 0
A/P increases	$ 37,902	$ 43,587	$ 50,125
Total other cash inflows	**$147,902**	**$ 43,587**	**$ 50,125**
Total cash inflow	**$296,057**	**$206,650**	**$226,133**
Cash outflows			
Repayment of principal	$ 6,463	$ 7,070	$ 7,733
A/P decreases	$ 24,897	$ 29,876	$ 35,852
A/R increases	$ 0	$ 0	$ 0
Asset purchases	$ 57,500	$ 24,459	$ 26,401
Dividends	$118,524	$130,450	$140,806
Total cash outflows	**$207,385**	**$191,855**	**$210,792**
Net cash flow	**$ 88,673**	**$ 14,794**	**$ 15,341**
Cash balance	**$ 88,673**	**$103,467**	**$118,808**

Proforma cash flow (yearly)

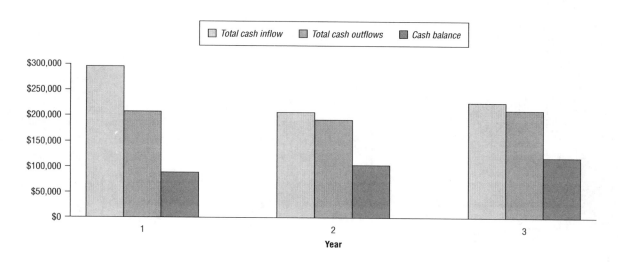

7.7 Balance Sheet

Proforma balance sheet—yearly

Year	1	2	3
Assets			
Cash	$ 88,673	$103,467	$118,808
Amortized development/expansion costs	$ 17,500	$ 19,946	$ 22,586
Initial inventory	$ 17,000	$ 35,345	$ 55,145
FF&E	$ 23,000	$ 26,669	$ 30,629
Accumulated depreciation	($ 4,107)	($ 8,214)	($ 12,321)
Total assets	**$142,065**	**$177,212**	**$214,847**
Liabilities and equity			
Accounts payable	$ 13,005	$ 26,716	$ 40,990
Long term liabilities	$ 93,537	$ 86,467	$ 79,397
Other liabilities	$ 0	$ 0	$ 0
Total liabilities	**$106,542**	**$113,183**	**$120,387**
Net worth	**$ 35,524**	**$ 64,029**	**$ 94,460**
Total liabilities and equity	**$142,065**	**$177,212**	**$214,847**

Proforma balance sheet

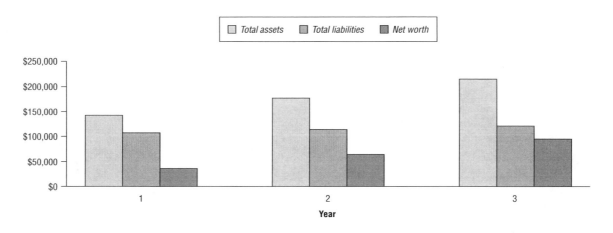

7.8 Breakeven Analysis

Monthly break even analysis

Year	1	2	3
Monthly revenue	$ 35,964	$ 39,109	$ 42,419
Yearly revenue	$431,571	$469,303	$509,033

Break even analysis

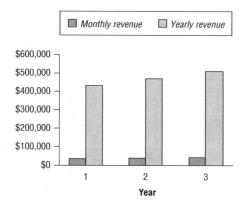

7.9 Business Ratios

Business ratios—yearly

Year	1	2	3
Sales			
Sales growth	0.0%	8.0%	8.0%
Gross margin	67.4%	67.4%	67.4%
Financials			
Profit margin	17.85%	18.24%	18.27%
Assets to liabilities	1.33	1.57	1.78
Equity to liabilities	0.33	0.57	0.78
Assets to equity	4.00	2.77	2.27
Liquidity			
Acid test	0.83	0.91	0.99
Cash to assets	0.62	0.58	0.55

7.10 Three Year Profit and Loss Statement

Profit and loss statement (first year)

Months	1	2	3	4	5	6	7
Sales	**$66,500**	**$66,633**	**$66,766**	**$66,899**	**$67,032**	**$67,165**	**$67,298**
Cost of goods sold	$21,650	$21,693	$21,737	$21,780	$21,823	$21,867	$21,910
Gross margin	67.4%	67.4%	67.4%	67.4%	67.4%	67.4%	67.4%
Operating income	**$44,850**	**$44,940**	**$45,029**	**$45,119**	**$45,209**	**$45,299**	**$45,388**
Expenses							
Payroll	$15,750	$15,750	$15,750	$15,750	$15,750	$15,750	$15,750
General and administrative	$ 2,100	$ 2,100	$ 2,100	$ 2,100	$ 2,100	$ 2,100	$ 2,100
Marketing expenses	$ 336	$ 336	$ 336	$ 336	$ 336	$ 336	$ 336
Professional fees and licensure	$ 435	$ 435	$ 435	$ 435	$ 435	$ 435	$ 435
Insurance costs	$ 166	$ 166	$ 166	$ 166	$ 166	$ 166	$ 166
Travel and vehicle costs	$ 633	$ 633	$ 633	$ 633	$ 633	$ 633	$ 633
Rent and utilities	$ 1,667	$ 1,667	$ 1,667	$ 1,667	$ 1,667	$ 1,667	$ 1,667
Miscellaneous costs	$ 807	$ 807	$ 807	$ 807	$ 807	$ 807	$ 807
Payroll taxes	$ 2,363	$ 2,363	$ 2,363	$ 2,363	$ 2,363	$ 2,363	$ 2,363
Total operating costs	**$24,256**	**$24,256**	**$24,256**	**$24,256**	**$24,256**	**$24,256**	**$24,256**
EBITDA	**$20,594**	**$20,684**	**$20,774**	**$20,863**	**$20,953**	**$21,043**	**$21,133**
Federal income tax	$ 6,883	$ 6,897	$ 6,911	$ 6,925	$ 6,938	$ 6,952	$ 6,966
State income tax	$ 1,043	$ 1,045	$ 1,047	$ 1,049	$ 1,051	$ 1,053	$ 1,055
Interest expense	$ 750	$ 746	$ 742	$ 738	$ 734	$ 730	$ 726
Depreciation expense	$ 342	$ 342	$ 342	$ 342	$ 342	$ 342	$ 342
Net profit	**$11,576**	**$11,654**	**$11,731**	**$11,809**	**$11,887**	**$11,965**	**$12,043**

Profit and loss statement (first year cont.)

Month	8	9	10	11	12	1
Sales	$67,431	$67,564	$67,697	$67,830	$67,963	$806,778
Cost of goods sold	$21,953	$21,996	$22,040	$22,083	$22,126	$262,658
Gross margin	67.4%	67.4%	67.4%	67.4%	67.4%	67.4%
Operating income	$45,478	$45,568	$45,657	$45,747	$45,837	$544,120
Expenses						
Payroll	$15,750	$15,750	$15,750	$15,750	$15,750	$189,000
General and administrative	$ 2,100	$ 2,100	$ 2,100	$ 2,100	$ 2,100	$ 25,200
Marketing expenses	$ 336	$ 336	$ 336	$ 336	$ 336	$ 4,034
Professional fees and licensure	$ 435	$ 435	$ 435	$ 435	$ 435	$ 5,219
Insurance costs	$ 166	$ 166	$ 166	$ 166	$ 166	$ 1,987
Travel and vehicle costs	$ 633	$ 633	$ 633	$ 633	$ 633	$ 7,596
Rent and utilities	$ 1,667	$ 1,667	$ 1,667	$ 1,667	$ 1,667	$ 20,000
Miscellaneous costs	$ 807	$ 807	$ 807	$ 807	$ 807	$ 9,681
Payroll taxes	$ 2,363	$ 2,363	$ 2,363	$ 2,363	$ 2,363	$ 28,350
Total operating costs	$24,256	$24,256	$24,256	$24,256	$24,256	$291,067
EBITDA	$21,222	$21,312	$21,402	$21,491	$21,581	$253,053
Federal income tax	$ 6,980	$ 6,993	$ 7,007	$ 7,021	$ 7,035	$ 83,507
State income tax	$ 1,058	$ 1,060	$ 1,062	$ 1,064	$ 1,066	$ 12,653
Interest expense	$ 722	$ 718	$ 714	$ 710	$ 706	$ 8,738
Depreciation expense	$ 342	$ 342	$ 342	$ 342	$ 342	$ 4,107
Net profit	$12,121	$12,199	$12,277	$12,355	$12,433	$144,048

Profit and loss statement (second year)

Quarter	Q1	2 Q2	Q3	Q4	2
Sales	$174,264	$217,830	$235,256	$243,970	$871,320
Cost of goods sold	$ 56,734	$ 70,918	$ 76,591	$ 79,428	$283,670
Gross margin	67.4%	67.4%	67.4%	67.4%	67.4%
Operating income	$117,530	$146,912	$158,665	$164,542	$587,650
Expenses					
Payroll	$ 41,509	$ 51,886	$ 56,037	$ 58,113	$207,545
General and administrative	$ 5,242	$ 6,552	$ 7,076	$ 7,338	$ 26,208
Marketing expenses	$ 871	$ 1,089	$ 1,176	$ 1,220	$ 4,357
Professional fees and licensure	$ 1,075	$ 1,344	$ 1,451	$ 1,505	$ 5,376
Insurance costs	$ 417	$ 522	$ 563	$ 584	$ 2,086
Travel and vehicle costs	$ 1,671	$ 2,089	$ 2,256	$ 2,340	$ 8,356
Rent and utilities	$ 4,200	$ 5,250	$ 5,670	$ 5,880	$ 21,000
Miscellaneous costs	$ 2,091	$ 2,614	$ 2,823	$ 2,928	$ 10,456
Payroll taxes	$ 6,226	$ 7,783	$ 8,406	$ 8,717	$ 31,132
Total operating costs	$ 63,303	$ 79,129	$ 85,459	$ 88,624	$316,515
EBITDA	$ 54,227	$ 67,784	$ 73,206	$ 75,918	$271,135
Federal income tax	$ 17,358	$ 21,698	$ 23,434	$ 24,302	$ 86,791
State income tax	$ 2,630	$ 3,288	$ 3,551	$ 3,682	$ 13,150
Interest expense	$ 2,092	$ 2,053	$ 2,013	$ 1,973	$ 8,131
Depreciation expense	$ 1,027	$ 1,027	$ 1,027	$ 1,027	$ 4,107
Net profit	$ 31,120	$ 39,719	$ 43,182	$ 44,934	$158,955

Profit and loss statement (third year)

Quarter	Q1	Q2	Q3	Q4	3
Sales	$188,205	$235,256	$254,077	$263,487	$941,026
Cost of goods sold	$ 61,273	$ 76,591	$ 82,718	$ 85,782	$306,364
Gross margin	67.4%	67.4%	67.4%	67.4%	67.4%
Operating income	$126,932	$158,665	$171,359	$177,705	$634,662
Expenses					
Payroll	$ 45,407	$ 56,758	$ 61,299	$ 63,569	$227,033
General and administrative	$ 5,451	$ 6,814	$ 7,359	$ 7,632	$ 27,256
Marketing expenses	$ 941	$ 1,176	$ 1,270	$ 1,317	$ 4,705
Professional fees and licensure	$ 1,107	$ 1,384	$ 1,495	$ 1,550	$ 5,537
Insurance costs	$ 438	$ 548	$ 591	$ 613	$ 2,191
Travel and vehicle costs	$ 1,838	$ 2,298	$ 2,482	$ 2,574	$ 9,191
Rent and utilities	$ 4,410	$ 5,513	$ 5,954	$ 6,174	$ 22,050
Miscellaneous costs	$ 2,258	$ 2,823	$ 3,049	$ 3,162	$ 11,292
Payroll taxes	$ 6,811	$ 8,514	$ 9,195	$ 9,535	$ 34,055
Total operating costs	$ 68,662	$ 85,827	$ 92,694	$ 96,127	$343,310
EBITDA	$ 58,270	$ 72,838	$ 78,665	$ 81,579	$291,352
Federal income tax	$ 18,736	$ 23,420	$ 25,294	$ 26,231	$ 93,682
State income tax	$ 2,839	$ 3,549	$ 3,832	$ 3,974	$ 14,194
Interest expense	$ 1,932	$ 1,889	$ 1,846	$ 1,802	$ 7,468
Depreciation expense	$ 1,027	$ 1,027	$ 1,027	$ 1,027	$ 4,107
Net profit	$ 33,737	$ 42,953	$ 46,666	$ 48,545	$171,901

7.11 Three Year Cash Flow Analysis

Cash flow analysis (first year)

Month	1	2	3	4	5	6	7
Cash from operations	$ 11,918	$11,996	$12,074	$ 12,151	$ 12,229	$ 12,307	$ 12,385
Cash from receivables	$ 0	$ 0	$ 0	$ 0	$ 0	$ 0	$ 0
Operating cash inflow	$ 11,918	$11,996	$12,074	$ 12,151	$ 12,229	$ 12,307	$ 12,385
Other cash inflows							
Equity investment	$ 10,000	$ 0	$ 0	$ 0	$ 0	$ 0	$ 0
Increased borrowings	$100,000	$ 0	$ 0	$ 0	$ 0	$ 0	$ 0
Sales of business assets	$ 0	$ 0	$ 0	$ 0	$ 0	$ 0	$ 0
A/P increases	$ 3,159	$ 3,159	$ 3,159	$ 3,159	$ 3,159	$ 3,159	$ 3,159
Total other cash inflows	$113,159	$ 3,159	$ 3,159	$ 3,159	$ 3,159	$ 3,159	$ 3,159
Total cash inflow	$125,077	$15,154	$15,232	$ 15,310	$ 15,388	$ 15,466	$ 15,544
Cash outflows							
Repayment of principal	$ 517	$ 521	$ 525	$ 528	$ 532	$ 536	$ 540
A/P decreases	$ 2,075	$ 2,075	$ 2,075	$ 2,075	$ 2,075	$ 2,075	$ 2,075
A/R increases	$ 0	$ 0	$ 0	$ 0	$ 0	$ 0	$ 0
Asset purchases	$ 57,500	$ 0	$ 0	$ 0	$ 0	$ 0	$ 0
Dividends	$ 0	$ 0	$ 0	$ 0	$ 0	$ 0	$ 0
Total cash outflows	$ 60,092	$ 2,595	$ 2,599	$ 2,603	$ 2,607	$ 2,611	$ 2,615
Net cash flow	$ 64,985	$12,559	$12,633	$ 12,707	$ 12,781	$ 12,854	$ 12,928
Cash balance	$ 64,985	$77,544	$90,177	$102,884	$115,665	$128,519	$141,447

Cash flow analysis (first year cont.)

Month	8	9	10	11	12	1
Cash from operations	$ 12,463	$ 12,541	$ 12,619	$ 12,697	$ 12,775	$148,155
Cash from receivables	$ 0	$ 0	$ 0	$ 0	$ 0	$ 0
Operating cash inflow	**$ 12,463**	**$ 12,541**	**$ 12,619**	**$ 12,697**	**$ 12,775**	**$148,155**
Other cash inflows						
Equity investment	$ 0	$ 0	$ 0	$ 0	$ 0	$ 10,000
Increased borrowings	$ 0	$ 0	$ 0	$ 0	$ 0	$100,000
Sales of business assets	$ 0	$ 0	$ 0	$ 0	$ 0	$ 0
A/P increases	$ 3,159	$ 3,159	$ 3,159	$ 3,159	$ 3,159	$ 37,902
Total other cash inflows	**$ 3,159**	**$ 3,159**	**$ 3,159**	**$ 3,159**	**$ 3,159**	**$147,902**
Total cash inflow	**$ 15,621**	**$ 15,699**	**$ 15,777**	**$ 15,855**	**$ 15,933**	**$296,057**
Cash outflows						
Repayment of principal	$ 545	$ 549	$ 553	$ 557	$ 561	$ 6,463
A/P decreases	$ 2,075	$ 2,075	$ 2,075	$ 2,075	$ 2,075	$ 24,897
A/R increases	$ 0	$ 0	$ 0	$ 0	$ 0	$ 0
Asset purchases	$ 0	$ 0	$ 0	$ 0	$ 0	$ 57,500
Dividends	$ 0	$ 0	$ 0	$ 0	$118,524	$118,524
Total cash outflows	**$ 2,619**	**$ 2,623**	**$ 2,627**	**$ 2,632**	**$121,160**	**$207,385**
Net cash flow	**$ 13,002**	**$ 13,076**	**$ 13,150**	**$ 13,224**	**−$105,226**	**$ 88,673**
Cash balance	**$154,450**	**$167,526**	**$180,675**	**$193,899**	**$ 88,673**	**$ 88,673**

Cash flow analysis (second year)

Quarter	Q1	2 Q2	Q3	Q4	2
Cash from operations	$32,612	$40,766	$44,027	$ 45,657	$163,062
Cash from receivables	$ 0	$ 0	$ 0	$ 0	$ 0
Operating cash inflow	**$32,612**	**$40,766**	**$44,027**	**$ 45,657**	**$163,062**
Other cash inflows					
Equity investment	$ 0	$ 0	$ 0	$ 0	$ 0
Increased borrowings	$ 0	$ 0	$ 0	$ 0	$ 0
Sales of business assets	$ 0	$ 0	$ 0	$ 0	$ 0
A/P increases	$ 8,717	$10,897	$11,769	$ 12,204	$ 43,587
Total other cash inflows	**$ 8,717**	**$10,897**	**$11,769**	**$ 12,204**	**$ 43,587**
Total cash inflow	**$41,330**	**$51,662**	**$55,795**	**$ 57,862**	**$206,650**
Cash outflows					
Repayment of principal	$ 1,708	$ 1,747	$ 1,787	$ 1,827	$ 7,070
A/P decreases	$ 5,975	$ 7,469	$ 8,067	$ 8,365	$ 29,876
A/R increases	$ 0	$ 0	$ 0	$ 0	$ 0
Asset purchases	$ 4,892	$ 6,115	$ 6,604	$ 6,849	$ 24,459
Dividends	$26,090	$32,612	$35,221	$ 36,526	$130,450
Total cash outflows	**$38,666**	**$47,944**	**$51,679**	**$ 53,567**	**$191,855**
Net cash flow	**$ 2,664**	**$ 3,719**	**$ 4,116**	**$ 4,295**	**$ 14,794**
Cash balance	**$91,337**	**$95,056**	**$99,172**	**$103,467**	**$103,467**

Cash flow analysis (third year)

Quarter	Q1	3 Q2	Q3	Q4	3
Cash from operations	$ 35,202	$ 44,002	$ 47,522	$ 49,282	$176,008
Cash from receivables	$ 0	$ 0	$ 0	$ 0	$ 0
Operating cash inflow	**$ 35,202**	**$ 44,002**	**$ 47,522**	**$ 49,282**	**$176,008**
Other cash inflows					
Equity investment	$ 0	$ 0	$ 0	$ 0	$ 0
Increased borrowings	$ 0	$ 0	$ 0	$ 0	$ 0
Sales of business assets	$ 0	$ 0	$ 0	$ 0	$ 0
A/P increases	$ 10,025	$ 12,531	$ 13,534	$ 14,035	$ 50,125
Total other cash inflows	**$ 10,025**	**$ 12,531**	**$ 13,534**	**$ 14,035**	**$ 50,125**
Total cash inflow	**$ 45,227**	**$ 56,533**	**$ 61,056**	**$ 63,317**	**$226,133**
Cash outflows					
Repayment of principal	$ 1,869	$ 1,911	$ 1,954	$ 1,999	$ 7,733
A/P decreases	$ 7,170	$ 8,963	$ 9,680	$ 10,038	$ 35,852
A/R increases	$ 0	$ 0	$ 0	$ 0	$ 0
Asset purchases	$ 5,280	$ 6,600	$ 7,128	$ 7,392	$ 26,401
Dividends	$ 28,161	$ 35,202	$ 38,018	$ 39,426	$140,806
Total cash outflows	**$ 42,481**	**$ 52,676**	**$ 56,780**	**$ 58,855**	**$210,792**
Net cash flow	**$ 2,746**	**$ 3,857**	**$ 4,276**	**$ 4,462**	**$ 15,341**
Cash balance	**$106,213**	**$110,071**	**$114,346**	**$118,808**	**$118,808**

Nonprofit Organization

United Charities, Inc.

PO Box 45564
New York, NY 10013

BizPlanDB.com

Unified Charities, Inc. is a New York-based 501(c)(3) corporation that will provide charitable donations to a number of charities throughout the United States and abroad. The Foundation was founded by Jeremy Meadows.

1.0 EXECUTIVE SUMMARY

The purpose of this business plan is to raise $250,000 for the development of a not-for-profit organization while showcasing the expected financials and operations over the next three years. Unified Charities, Inc. ("the Foundation") is a New York-based 501(c)(3) corporation that will provide charitable donations to a number of charities throughout the United States and abroad. The Foundation was founded by Jeremy Meadows.

1.1 The Charitable Operations

As mentioned above, Unified Charities will collect funds from individual donors and corporate sponsors with the intent to collect and distribute funds to other charities, hospitals, and other groups that have a charitable mission.

The Foundation will generate revenues from donations, sponsorships, and enrollment in ongoing donation programs that the Company will market to the general public. From time to time, the Company will host gala events to raise additional capital for its charitable causes, which will primary focus on the needs of children.

The third section of the business plan will further describe the operations offered by Unified Charities.

1.2 Financing

Management intends that the first round of capital will come as a sponsorship grant for $250,000, which will be used to launch the charitable operations of the Foundation. As the organization is a non-stock corporation, no equity position or distribution of EBITDA income will be distributed to any party that provides capital for the Foundation. After immediately receiving the capital infusion, the Foundation will establish its office and begin to make grants to other not-for-profit organizations and causes as discussed above. The initial funds will be used for the following:

- Establishment of the 501(c)(3) entity.

- Financing for the initial capital to be used for charitable causes.

- General working capital for the Foundation

147

The second section of the business plan will further document the initial uses of the grant/sponsorship funds.

1.3 Mission Statement

Unified Charities' mission is to provide donations to institutions that support positive community causes with a focus on providing benefits to children and families in need.

1.4 Management Team

The Company was founded by Jeremy Meadows. Mr. Meadows has more than 10 years of experience in the nonprofit industry. Through his expertise, he will be able to bring the operations of the business to profitability within its first year of operations.

1.5 Sales Forecasts

Mr. Meadows expects a strong rate of growth at the start of operations. Below are the expected financials over the next three years.

Revenues and income statement (yearly)

Year	1	2	3
Sales	$1,046,304	$1,255,565	$1,469,011
Operating costs	$ 585,689	$ 691,309	$ 750,907
EBITDA	$ 174,335	$ 220,719	$ 316,166
Taxes, interest, and depreciation	$ 5,893	$ 5,893	$ 5,893
Net income	$ 168,442	$ 214,826	$ 310,273

Sales, operating costs, and profit forecast

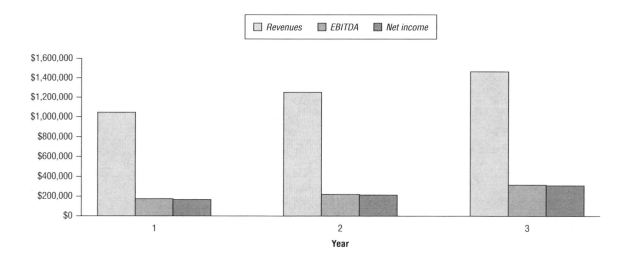

1.6 Expansion Plan

The Founder expects that the business will aggressively expand during the first three years of operation. Mr. Meadows intends to implement marketing campaigns that will effectively target individuals that will donate to the Foundation's operations within the target market. The Foundation will also target corporations that want to use Unified Charities as a conduit for their charitable activities.

2.0 COMPANY AND FINANCING SUMMARY

2.1 Registered Name and Corporate Structure

Unified Charities, Inc. is registered as a 501(3)(c) corporation in the State of New York.

2.2 Required Funds

At this time, Unified Charities requires $250,000 of grant or sponsorship funds. Below is a breakdown of how these funds will be used:

Projected startup costs

Leasehold improvements	$ 35,000
Working capital	$ 65,000
FF&E	$ 15,000
Lease deposits	$ 5,000
501(3)c registration fees and licensure	$ 10,000
Initial marketing budget	$ 15,000
Foundation literature materials	$ 7,500
Initial funds for charitable operations	$ 92,500
Misc. development costs	$ 5,000
Total startup costs	**$250,000**

Use of funds

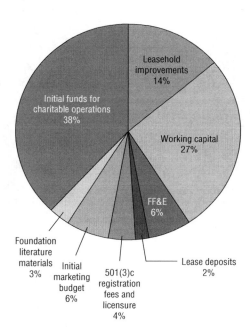

2.3 Investor Equity

As the business is a non-stock corporation, no formal ownership will be held by donors, Management, or corporate sponsors.

2.4 Management Equity

The non-stock corporation exists as its own entity. Management will retain no formal equity interest in the corporation.

2.5 Exit Strategy

In the event that Foundation wishes to cease operations, the Management will file the appropriate articles of dissolution, and the assets of the Foundation will be liquidated and granted to other charitable organizations.

3.0 CHARITABLE SERVICES

As stated in the executive summary, Unified Charities intends to collect sponsorship revenues and donations with the intent to redistribute these funds among other charities, not-for-profit hospitals, children's hospitals, and other groups with a focus on helping needy children and families.

Mr. Meadows is committed to bringing the positive mission of the Foundation to fruition by properly divesting funds to reputable organizations that serve a strong community-based purpose.

4.0 STRATEGIC AND MARKET ANALYSIS

4.1 Economic Outlook

This section of the analysis will detail the economic climate, the nonprofit organization industry, the customer profile, and the competition that the business will face as it progresses through its business operations.

Currently, the economic market condition in the United States is moderate. At this time, the country has completed restructuring after the economic recession that ended three year ago. It should be noted that a downturn in the economy may lead to fewer donations and corporate sponsorships for the Foundation as consumers and corporations will have less discretionary income and profits for distribution to charitable causes, like those offered by Unified Charities.

4.2 Industry Analysis

Total charitable giving to organized charities totaled more than $245 billion dollars. Charitable giving is a luxury for most people and businesses, and as such, during periods of economic decline, Management expects a severe decrease in the amount of donations made to the Foundation. However, there are tremendous tax benefits that allow charitable giving to have benefits regardless of the overall economic market.

Below are some statistics regarding American charitable organizations:

- The majority of that giving came from individuals, $187.9 billion. Giving by individuals grew by 1.4 percent (when adjusted for inflation).

- Giving by bequest was $19.8 billion, foundations gave $28.8 billion, and corporations donated $12 billion.

- Religious organizations received the most support—$88.3 billion. Much of these contributions can be attributed to people giving to their local place of worship. The next largest sector was education ($33.8 billion). When adjusted for inflation, all but two categories of charities saw increases in contributions.

4.3 Donor Profile

Management expects that the average single donor to the Foundation will be a middle aged, upper-middle income earning individual that wants to give back to the community. Management will aggressively seek to create awareness about the Foundation's programs within the northeastern part of the United States. Demographics among individual donors include, but are not limited to:

- Male or Female

- Aged 35+

- Annual household income exceeding $75,000

- Actively supports charitable causes on a regular basis

Additionally, the Foundation expects that it will achieve donations from corporate and large foundation sponsors that are seeking to expand their portfolio of charitable works. One of the keys to achieving the Foundation's goal is to develop strong relationships with corporate benefactors.

4.4 Competition

It is extremely difficult to categorize competition among charities as each organization is competing for the same contributions from corporations, individuals, and grants from government agencies. Among the 10,000 charitable organizations in the United States, all are in competition for the same influx in capital. There are several organizations that serve to help people in need. As such, Management does not feel that Unified Charities is in competition with any other charitable organization that seeks to provide for needy people. All charities are all essentially pursuing the same goal.

5.0 MARKETING PLAN

Unified Charities intends to maintain an extensive marketing campaign that will ensure maximum visibility for the Foundation in its targeted market. Below is an overview of the marketing strategies and objectives of the Foundation.

5.1 Marketing Objectives

- Develop an online presence by developing a website and placing the Foundation's name and contact information with online directories.

- Regularly hold large-scale events that will generate publicity and donation revenue for the Foundation.

- Establish relationships with large grant trusts and corporate benefactors.

5.2 Marketing Strategies

The Foundation will solicit donation revenue from multiple sources. The Foundation intends to engage a large public relations and marketing firm to raise awareness of Unified Charities' charitable services. Management will also seek to gain celebrity support from public personas that want to contribute to growing problems related to needy children and families within in the United States.

The business will conduct mass mailings several times per year in order to gain continual support from the general public.

Timely coverage of the Foundation will be further directed thru ongoing press relations, news releases, and feature stories targeted at key charitable organization communities and other media outlets.

Publicity activities will be designed to generate ongoing coverage about the Foundation in targeted media by providing writers and editors with newsworthy releases, features, stories, briefs, and visual material for their columns and stories. In-depth coverage may also be obtained about the Foundation by hosting in-house interviews to be conducted by the Foundation's spokesperson.

6.0 ORGANIZATIONAL PLAN AND PERSONNEL SUMMARY

6.1 Corporate Organization

6.2 Organizational Budget

Personnel plan—yearly

Year	1	2	3
Senior management	$ 65,000	$ 66,950	$ 68,959
Charitable operations directors	$110,000	$113,300	$116,699
Marketing staff	$ 85,000	$131,325	$135,265
Administrative	$ 84,000	$115,360	$148,526
Accounting	$ 70,000	$ 72,100	$ 74,263
Total	**$414,000**	**$499,035**	**$543,711**

Numbers of personnel

Senior management	1	1	1
Charitable operations directors	2	2	2
Marketing staff	2	3	3
Administrative	3	4	5
Accounting	2	2	2
Totals	**10**	**12**	**13**

Personnel expense breakdown

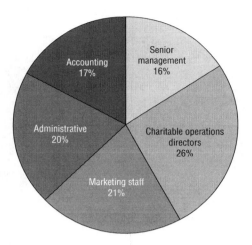

7.0 FINANCIAL PLAN

7.1 Underlying Assumptions

The Company has based its proforma financial statements on the following:

- Unified Charities will have an annual revenue growth rate of 14% per year.

- The Foundation will initially be seeded with $250,000 of grant capital.

7.2 Sensitivity Analysis

The Foundation's revenues are sensitive to the overall condition of the financial markets. Charitable contributions are a luxury, and as such, during times of economic recession, the Foundation expects that its incoming contributions will decrease. Management will enact several procedures to ensure that the Foundation can survive severe decreases in its charitable revenue.

7.3 Source of Funds

Financing

Equity contributions	
Initial grants	$ 250,000.00
Total equity financing	**$250,000.00**
Banks and lenders	
Total debt financing	**$ 0.00**
Total financing	**$250,000.00**

7.4 General Assumptions

General assumptions

Year	1	2	3
Short term interest rate	9.5%	9.5%	9.5%
Long term interest rate	10.0%	10.0%	10.0%
Federal tax rate	0.0%	0.0%	0.0%
State tax rate	0.0%	0.0%	0.0%
Personnel taxes	15.0%	15.0%	15.0%

7.5 Profit and Loss Statements

Revenues and income statement (yearly)

Year	1	2	3
Revenues	**$1,046,304**	**$1,255,565**	**$1,469,011**
Cost of generating revenues	$ 286,280	$ 343,536	$ 401,938
Gross margin	72.64%	72.64%	72.64%
Operating income	**$ 760,024**	**$ 912,028**	**$1,067,073**
Expenses			
Payroll	$ 414,000	$ 499,035	$ 543,711
General and administrative	$ 25,200	$ 26,208	$ 27,256
Marketing expenses	$ 20,000	$ 21,000	$ 22,050
Professional fees and licensure	$ 8,000	$ 8,240	$ 8,487
Insurance costs	$ 11,987	$ 12,586	$ 13,216
Office expenses	$ 17,596	$ 19,356	$ 21,291
Rent and utilities	$ 14,250	$ 14,963	$ 15,711
Miscellaneous costs	$ 12,556	$ 15,067	$ 17,628
Payroll taxes	$ 62,100	$ 74,855	$ 81,557
Total operating costs	**$ 585,689**	**$ 691,309**	**$ 750,907**
EBITDA	**$ 174,335**	**$ 220,719**	**$ 316,166**
Federal income tax	$ 0	$ 0	$ 0
State income tax	$ 0	$ 0	$ 0
Interest expense	$ 0	$ 0	$ 0
Depreciation expenses	$ 5,893	$ 5,893	$ 5,893
Net income	**$ 168,442**	**$ 214,826**	**$ 310,273**
Net income margin	**16.10%**	**17.11%**	**21.12%**

Sales, operating costs, and profit forecast

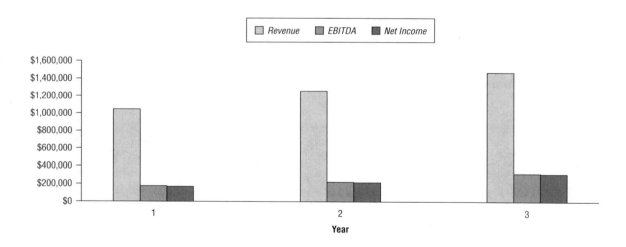

7.6 Cash Flow Analysis

Proforma cash flow analysis – yearly

Year	1	2	3
Cash from operations	$174,335	$220,719	$316,166
Cash from receivables	$ 0	$ 0	$ 0
Operating cash inflow	**$174,335**	**$220,719**	**$316,166**
Other cash inflows			
Equity investment	$250,000	$ 0	$ 0
Increased borrowings	$ 0	$ 0	$ 0
Sales of business assets	$ 0	$ 0	$ 0
A/P increases	$ 37,902	$ 43,587	$ 50,125
Total other cash inflows	**$287,902**	**$ 43,587**	**$ 50,125**
Total cash inflow	**$462,237**	**$264,306**	**$366,291**
Cash outflows			
Repayment of principal	$ 0	$ 0	$ 0
A/P decreases	$ 24,897	$ 29,876	$ 35,852
A/R increases	$ 0	$ 0	$ 0
Asset purchases	$ 82,500	$ 0	$ 0
Charitable disbursements	$132,495	$167,746	$240,286
Total cash outflows	**$239,892**	**$197,623**	**$276,138**
Net cash flow	**$222,345**	**$ 66,683**	**$ 90,154**
Cash balance	**$222,345**	**$289,029**	**$379,182**

Proforma cash flow (yearly)

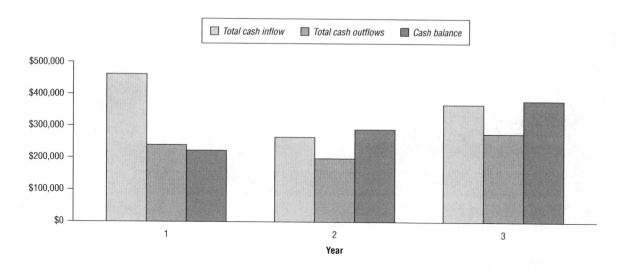

7.7 Balance Sheet

Proforma balance sheet—yearly

Year	1	2	3
Assets			
Cash	$222,345	$289,029	$379,182
Amortized development costs	$ 55,000	$ 55,000	$ 55,000
FF&E	$ 15,000	$ 15,000	$ 15,000
Security deposits	$ 5,000	$ 5,100	$ 5,202
Literature inventory	$ 7,500	$ 7,500	$ 7,500
Accumulated depreciation	($ 5,893)	($ 11,786)	($ 17,679)
Total assets	**$298,953**	**$359,843**	**$444,206**
Liabilities and equity			
Accounts payable	$ 13,005	$ 26,716	$ 40,990
Long term liabilities	$ 0	$ 0	$ 0
Other liabilities	$ 8,200	$ 8,528	$ 8,869
Total liabilities	**$ 21,205**	**$ 35,244**	**$ 49,859**
Net worth	**$277,748**	**$324,599**	**$394,347**
Total liabilities and equity	**$298,953**	**$359,843**	**$444,206**

Proforma balance sheet

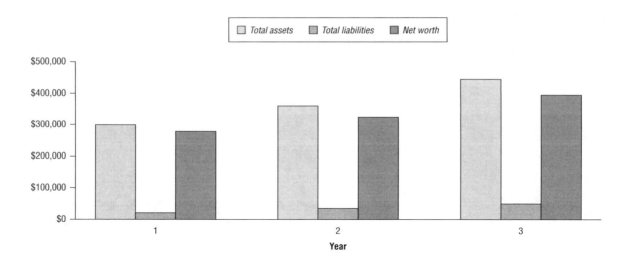

7.8 Breakeven Analysis

Monthly break even analysis

Year	1	2	3
Monthly revenue	$ 67,192	$ 79,309	$ 86,146
Yearly revenue	$806,302	$951,707	$1,033,753

Break even analysis

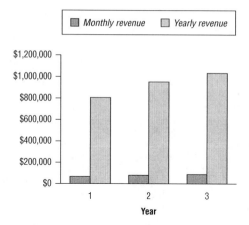

7.9 Business Ratios

Business ratios—yearly

Year	1	2	3
Sales			
Revenue growth	0.00%	20.00%	17.00%
Gross margin	72.60%	72.60%	72.60%
Financials			
Net income margin	16.10%	17.11%	21.12%
Assets to liabilities	14.10	10.21	8.91
Equity to liabilities	13.10	9.21	7.91
Assets to equity	1.08	1.11	1.13
Liquidity			
Acid test	10.49	8.20	7.61
Cash to assets	0.74	0.80	0.85

7.10 Three Year Profit and Loss Statement

Revenues and income statement (first year)

Months	1	2	3	4	5	6	7
Revenues	**$86,400**	**$86,544**	**$86,688**	**$86,832**	**$86,976**	**$87,120**	**$87,264**
Cost of generating revenues	$23,640	$23,679	$23,719	$23,758	$23,798	$23,837	$23,876
Gross margin	72.6%	72.6%	72.6%	72.6%	72.6%	72.6%	72.6%
Operating income	**$62,760**	**$62,865**	**$62,969**	**$63,074**	**$63,178**	**$63,283**	**$63,388**
Expenses							
Payroll	$34,500	$34,500	$34,500	$34,500	$34,500	$34,500	$34,500
General and administrative	$ 2,100	$ 2,100	$ 2,100	$ 2,100	$ 2,100	$ 2,100	$ 2,100
Marketing expenses	$ 1,667	$ 1,667	$ 1,667	$ 1,667	$ 1,667	$ 1,667	$ 1,667
Professional fees and licensure	$ 667	$ 667	$ 667	$ 667	$ 667	$ 667	$ 667
Insurance costs	$ 999	$ 999	$ 999	$ 999	$ 999	$ 999	$ 999
Office expenses	$ 1,466	$ 1,466	$ 1,466	$ 1,466	$ 1,466	$ 1,466	$ 1,466
Rent and utilities	$ 1,188	$ 1,188	$ 1,188	$ 1,188	$ 1,188	$ 1,188	$ 1,188
Miscellaneous costs	$ 1,046	$ 1,046	$ 1,046	$ 1,046	$ 1,046	$ 1,046	$ 1,046
Payroll taxes	$ 5,175	$ 5,175	$ 5,175	$ 5,175	$ 5,175	$ 5,175	$ 5,175
Total operating costs	**$48,807**	**$48,807**	**$48,807**	**$48,807**	**$48,807**	**$48,807**	**$48,807**
EBITDA	**$13,953**	**$14,057**	**$14,162**	**$14,266**	**$14,371**	**$14,476**	**$14,580**
Federal income tax	$ 0	$ 0	$ 0	$ 0	$ 0	$ 0	$ 0
State income tax	$ 0	$ 0	$ 0	$ 0	$ 0	$ 0	$ 0
Interest expense	$ 0	$ 0	$ 0	$ 0	$ 0	$ 0	$ 0
Depreciation expense	$ 491	$ 491	$ 491	$ 491	$ 491	$ 491	$ 491
Net income	**$13,462**	**$13,566**	**$13,671**	**$13,775**	**$13,880**	**$13,985**	**$14,089**

Revenues and income statement (first year cont.)

Month	8	9	10	11	12	1
Revenues	$87,408	$87,552	$87,696	$87,840	$87,984	$1,046,304
Cost of generating revenues	$23,916	$23,955	$23,995	$24,034	$24,073	$ 286,280
Gross margin	72.6%	72.6%	72.6%	72.6%	72.6%	72.6%
Operating income	$63,492	$63,597	$63,701	$63,806	$63,911	$ 760,024
Expenses						
Payroll	$34,500	$34,500	$34,500	$34,500	$34,500	$ 414,000
General and administrative	$ 2,100	$ 2,100	$ 2,100	$ 2,100	$ 2,100	$ 25,200
Marketing expenses	$ 1,667	$ 1,667	$ 1,667	$ 1,667	$ 1,667	$ 20,000
Professional fees and licensure	$ 667	$ 667	$ 667	$ 667	$ 667	$ 8,000
Insurance costs	$ 999	$ 999	$ 999	$ 999	$ 999	$ 11,987
Office expenses	$ 1,466	$ 1,466	$ 1,466	$ 1,466	$ 1,466	$ 17,596
Rent and utilities	$ 1,188	$ 1,188	$ 1,188	$ 1,188	$ 1,188	$ 14,250
Miscellaneous costs	$ 1,046	$ 1,046	$ 1,046	$ 1,046	$ 1,046	$ 12,556
Payroll taxes	$ 5,175	$ 5,175	$ 5,175	$ 5,175	$ 5,175	$ 62,100
Total operating costs	$48,807	$48,807	$48,807	$48,807	$48,807	$ 585,689
EBITDA	$14,685	$14,789	$14,894	$14,999	$15,103	$ 174,335
Federal income tax	$ 0	$ 0	$ 0	$ 0	$ 0	$ 0
State income tax	$ 0	$ 0	$ 0	$ 0	$ 0	$ 0
Interest expense	$ 0	$ 0	$ 0	$ 0	$ 0	$ 0
Depreciation expense	$ 491	$ 491	$ 491	$ 491	$ 491	$ 5,893
Net profit	$14,194	$14,298	$14,403	$14,508	$14,612	$ 168,442

Revenues and income statement (second year)

Quarter	Q1	Q2	Q3	Q4	2
Revenues	$251,113	$313,891	$339,002	$351,558	$1,255,565
Cost of generating revenues	$ 68,707	$ 85,884	$ 92,755	$ 96,190	$ 343,536
Gross margin	72.6%	72.6%	72.6%	72.6%	72.6%
Operating income	$182,406	$228,007	$246,248	$255,368	$ 912,028
Expenses					
Payroll	$ 99,807	$124,759	$134,739	$139,730	$ 499,035
General and administrative	$ 5,242	$ 6,552	$ 7,076	$ 7,338	$ 26,208
Marketing expenses	$ 4,200	$ 5,250	$ 5,670	$ 5,880	$ 21,000
Professional fees and licensure	$ 1,648	$ 2,060	$ 2,225	$ 2,307	$ 8,240
Insurance costs	$ 2,517	$ 3,147	$ 3,398	$ 3,524	$ 12,586
Office expenses	$ 3,871	$ 4,839	$ 5,226	$ 5,420	$ 19,356
Rent and utilities	$ 2,993	$ 3,741	$ 4,040	$ 4,190	$ 14,963
Miscellaneous costs	$ 3,013	$ 3,767	$ 4,068	$ 4,219	$ 15,067
Payroll taxes	$ 14,971	$ 18,714	$ 20,211	$ 20,959	$ 74,855
Total operating costs	$138,262	$172,827	$186,654	$193,567	$ 691,309
EBITDA	$ 44,144	$ 55,180	$ 59,594	$ 61,801	$ 220,719
Federal income tax	$ 0	$ 0	$ 0	$ 0	$ 0
State income tax	$ 0	$ 0	$ 0	$ 0	$ 0
Interest expense	$ 0	$ 0	$ 0	$ 0	$ 0
Depreciation expense	$ 1,473	$ 1,473	$ 1,473	$ 1,473	$ 5,893
Net profit	$ 42,671	$ 53,706	$ 58,121	$ 60,328	$ 214,826

Revenues and income statement (third year)

Quarter	Q1	3 Q2	Q3	Q4	3
Revenues	**$293,802**	**$367,253**	**$396,633**	**$411,323**	**$1,469,011**
Cost of generating revenues	$ 80,388	$100,484	$108,523	$112,543	$ 401,938
Gross margin	72.6%	72.6%	72.6%	72.6%	72.6%
Operating income	**$213,415**	**$266,768**	**$288,110**	**$298,780**	**$1,067,073**
Expenses					
Payroll	$108,742	$135,928	$146,802	$152,239	$ 543,711
General and administrative	$ 5,451	$ 6,814	$ 7,359	$ 7,632	$ 27,256
Marketing expenses	$ 4,410	$ 5,513	$ 5,954	$ 6,174	$ 22,050
Professional fees and licensure	$ 1,697	$ 2,122	$ 2,292	$ 2,376	$ 8,487
Insurance costs	$ 2,643	$ 3,304	$ 3,568	$ 3,700	$ 13,216
Office expenses	$ 4,258	$ 5,323	$ 5,749	$ 5,962	$ 21,291
Rent and utilities	$ 3,142	$ 3,928	$ 4,242	$ 4,399	$ 15,711
Miscellaneous costs	$ 3,526	$ 4,407	$ 4,760	$ 4,936	$ 17,628
Payroll taxes	$ 16,311	$ 20,389	$ 22,020	$ 22,836	$ 81,557
Total operating costs	**$150,181**	**$187,727**	**$202,745**	**$210,254**	**$ 750,907**
EBITDA	**$ 63,233**	**$ 79,042**	**$ 85,365**	**$ 88,527**	**$ 316,166**
Federal income tax	$ 0	$ 0	$ 0	$ 0	$ 0
State income tax	$ 0	$ 0	$ 0	$ 0	$ 0
Interest expense	$ 0	$ 0	$ 0	$ 0	$ 0
Depreciation expense	$ 1,473	$ 1,473	$ 1,473	$ 1,473	$ 5,893
Net profit	**$ 61,760**	**$ 77,568**	**$ 83,892**	**$ 87,053**	**$ 310,273**

7.11 Three Year Cash Flow Analysis

Cash flow analysis (first year)

Month	1	2	3	4	5	6	7
Cash from operations	$ 13,953	$ 14,057	$ 14,162	$ 14,266	$ 14,371	$ 14,476	$ 14,580
Cash from receivables	$ 0	$ 0	$ 0	$ 0	$ 0	$ 0	$ 0
Operating cash inflow	**$ 13,953**	**$ 14,057**	**$ 14,162**	**$ 14,266**	**$ 14,371**	**$ 14,476**	**$ 14,580**
Other cash inflows							
Equity investment	$250,000	$ 0	$ 0	$ 0	$ 0	$ 0	$ 0
Increased borrowings	$ 0	$ 0	$ 0	$ 0	$ 0	$ 0	$ 0
Sales of business assets	$ 0	$ 0	$ 0	$ 0	$ 0	$ 0	$ 0
A/P increases	$ 3,159	$ 3,159	$ 3,159	$ 3,159	$ 3,159	$ 3,159	$ 3,159
Total other cash inflows	**$253,159**	**$ 3,159**	**$ 3,159**	**$ 3,159**	**$ 3,159**	**$ 3,159**	**$ 3,159**
Total cash inflow	**$267,111**	**$ 17,216**	**$ 17,320**	**$ 17,425**	**$ 17,530**	**$ 17,634**	**$ 17,739**
Cash outflows							
Repayment of principal	$ 0	$ 0	$ 0	$ 0	$ 0	$ 0	$ 0
A/P decreases	$ 2,075	$ 2,075	$ 2,075	$ 2,075	$ 2,075	$ 2,075	$ 2,075
A/R increases	$ 0	$ 0	$ 0	$ 0	$ 0	$ 0	$ 0
Asset purchases	$ 82,500	$ 0	$ 0	$ 0	$ 0	$ 0	$ 0
Charitable disbursements	$ 0	$ 0	$ 0	$ 0	$ 0	$ 0	$ 0
Total cash outflows	**$ 84,575**	**$ 2,075**	**$ 2,075**	**$ 2,075**	**$ 2,075**	**$ 2,075**	**$ 2,075**
Net cash flow	**$182,536**	**$ 15,141**	**$ 15,246**	**$ 15,350**	**$ 15,455**	**$ 15,559**	**$ 15,664**
Cash balance	**$182,536**	**$197,677**	**$212,923**	**$228,273**	**$243,728**	**$259,287**	**$274,951**

Cash flow analysis (first year cont.)

Month	8	9	10	11	12	1
Cash from operations	$ 14,685	$ 14,789	$ 14,894	$ 14,999	$ 15,103	$174,335
Cash from receivables	$ 0	$ 0	$ 0	$ 0	$ 0	$ 0
Operating cash inflow	**$ 14,685**	**$ 14,789**	**$ 14,894**	**$ 14,999**	**$ 15,103**	**$174,335**
Other cash inflows						
Equity investment	$ 0	$ 0	$ 0	$ 0	$ 0	$250,000
Increased borrowings	$ 0	$ 0	$ 0	$ 0	$ 0	$ 0
Sales of business assets	$ 0	$ 0	$ 0	$ 0	$ 0	$ 0
A/P increases	$ 3,159	$ 3,159	$ 3,159	$ 3,159	$ 3,159	$ 37,902
Total other cash inflows	**$ 3,159**	**$ 3,159**	**$ 3,159**	**$ 3,159**	**$ 3,159**	**$287,902**
Total cash inflow	**$ 17,843**	**$ 17,948**	**$ 18,053**	**$ 18,157**	**$ 18,262**	**$462,237**
Cash outflows						
Repayment of principal	$ 0	$ 0	$ 0	$ 0	$ 0	$ 0
A/P decreases	$ 2,075	$ 2,075	$ 2,075	$ 2,075	$ 2,075	$ 24,897
A/R increases	$ 0	$ 0	$ 0	$ 0	$ 0	$ 0
Asset purchases	$ 0	$ 0	$ 0	$ 0	$ 0	$ 82,500
Charitable disbursements	$ 0	$ 0	$ 0	$ 0	$132,495	$132,495
Total cash outflows	**$ 2,075**	**$ 2,075**	**$ 2,075**	**$ 2,075**	**$134,570**	**$239,892**
Net cash flow	**$ 15,769**	**$ 15,873**	**$ 15,978**	**$ 16,082**	**−$116,308**	**$222,345**
Cash balance	**$290,720**	**$306,593**	**$322,571**	**$338,653**	**$222,345**	**$222,345**

Cash flow analysis (second year)

Quarter	Q1	2 Q2	Q3	Q4	2
Cash from operations	$ 44,144	$ 55,180	$ 59,594	$ 61,801	$220,719
Cash from receivables	$ 0	$ 0	$ 0	$ 0	$ 0
Operating cash inflow	**$ 44,144**	**$ 55,180**	**$ 59,594**	**$ 61,801**	**$220,719**
Other cash inflows					
Equity investment	$ 0	$ 0	$ 0	$ 0	$ 0
Increased borrowings	$ 0	$ 0	$ 0	$ 0	$ 0
Sales of business assets	$ 0	$ 0	$ 0	$ 0	$ 0
A/P increases	$ 8,717	$ 10,897	$ 11,769	$ 12,204	$ 43,587
Total other cash inflows	**$ 8,717**	**$ 10,897**	**$ 11,769**	**$ 12,204**	**$ 43,587**
Total cash inflow	**$ 52,861**	**$ 66,077**	**$ 71,363**	**$ 74,006**	**$264,306**
Cash outflows					
Repayment of principal	$ 0	$ 0	$ 0	$ 0	$ 0
A/P decreases	$ 5,975	$ 7,469	$ 8,067	$ 8,365	$ 29,876
A/R increases	$ 0	$ 0	$ 0	$ 0	$ 0
Asset purchases	$ 0	$ 0	$ 0	$ 0	$ 0
Charitable disbursements	$ 33,549	$ 41,937	$ 45,292	$ 46,969	$167,746
Total cash outflows	**$ 39,525**	**$ 49,406**	**$ 53,358**	**$ 55,334**	**$197,623**
Net cash flow	**$ 13,337**	**$ 16,671**	**$ 18,005**	**$ 18,671**	**$ 66,683**
Cash balance	**$235,682**	**$252,353**	**$270,357**	**$289,029**	**$289,029**

Cash flow analysis (third year)

Quarter	Q1	3 Q2	Q3	Q4	3
Cash from operations	$ 63,233	$ 79,042	$ 85,365	$ 88,527	$316,166
Cash from receivables	$ 0	$ 0	$ 0	$ 0	$ 0
Operating cash inflow	**$ 63,233**	**$ 79,042**	**$ 85,365**	**$ 88,527**	**$316,166**
Other cash inflows					
Equity investment	$ 0	$ 0	$ 0	$ 0	$ 0
Increased borrowings	$ 0	$ 0	$ 0	$ 0	$ 0
Sales of business assets	$ 0	$ 0	$ 0	$ 0	$ 0
A/P increases	$ 10,025	$ 12,531	$ 13,534	$ 14,035	$ 50,125
Total other cash inflows	**$ 10,025**	**$ 12,531**	**$ 13,534**	**$ 14,035**	**$ 50,125**
Total cash inflow	**$ 73,258**	**$ 91,573**	**$ 98,899**	**$102,562**	**$366,291**
Cash outflows					
Repayment of principal	$ 0	$ 0	$ 0	$ 0	$ 0
A/P decreases	$ 7,170	$ 8,963	$ 9,680	$ 10,038	$ 35,852
A/R increases	$ 0	$ 0	$ 0	$ 0	$ 0
Asset purchases	$ 0	$ 0	$ 0	$ 0	$ 0
Charitable disbursements	$ 48,057	$ 60,072	$ 64,877	$ 67,280	$240,286
Total cash outflows	**$ 55,228**	**$ 69,034**	**$ 74,557**	**$ 77,319**	**$276,138**
Net cash flow	**$ 18,031**	**$ 22,538**	**$ 24,341**	**$ 25,243**	**$ 90,154**
Cash balance	**$307,060**	**$329,598**	**$353,939**	**$379,182**	**$379,182**

Organic Grower and Supplier

Great Lakes Organics

65129 Drake Rd.
Okemos, Michigan 48864

Adam Theurer, Alex Wander, John Benoist, and Gustavo Ramis

We are planning to be the first major organic, hydroponic grower in the Lansing area to target local grocers, markets and restaurants.

*This business plan appeared in a previous volume of **Business Plans Handbook.** It has been updated for this volume.*

EXECUTIVE SUMMARY

If you ask any farmer, chef, or consumer about their personal preferences regarding their foods, they will tell you the importance of organics. Organic foods are grown free from unnecessary additives. They are pure to taste, healthy for the body and an enjoyment for every individual who eats them. This preference for organic foods can be seen across the nation. Markets, chefs, and farmers are realizing the amazing potential of organic produce.

However, over the past several decades, farmers have realized the profitability of growing their foods with high efficiency. This entails applying dangerous chemicals to the soil, practicing hazardous tilling procedures and genetically altering seeds, among many other potentially harmful practices. Over the years, applying these techniques have damaged our soils and have made organic growing a time–consuming venture. Currently, modern farmers that till the soil are agitating natural processes that may have serious consequences.

Tillage practices degrade the fertility of soils, cause air and water pollution, intensify droughts, destroy wildlife habitats, waste energy, and contribute to global warming. These tillage methods are also draining tons of soil into the Gulf of Mexico each year and making America's breadbasket into an arid desert. Other farmers, in warm and tropical climates, have capitalized off of their year–round production and ship their herbs into the Lansing market daily. Importing herbs from warmer climates is an inefficient method. Importing produces excessive water and air pollution. Both of these practices are wearing on an already-fragile environment.

Great Lakes Organics utilizes the concept of hydroponics to grow natural herbs, locally. We are planning to be the first major organic, hydroponic grower in the Lansing area to target local grocers, markets and restaurants. Growing locally will encourage the Lansing community to be involved in the process while encouraging sustainable practices in agriculture. Additionally, Great Lakes Organics will eliminate the high costs associated with shipping by growing locally all year round.

Currently, there are no year-round hydroponic herbal gardens in the Midwest that operate on a commercial scale. There are smaller, seasonal gardens located across the region but none use hydroponic technologies. There are also plenty of seasonal gardens located across the warmer regions of the United

States. In addition to these farms, there are large amounts of imported herbs from warmer climates. These competitors all have high-quality and organic products; however, they are far from our region. This leads to higher shipping costs and lowers efficiency. Great Lakes Organics specializes in supporting the local market, year–round. This local production helps our community, implements new techniques, and promotes efficiency and sustainability.

Creating our greenhouses in the Lansing area will not only help support local markets, grocers, and restaurants, but they will also help educate Midwest farmers about hydroponic technologies. The greenhouses at Great Lakes Organics will also help retail customers support their environmental values.

Greenhouse growing in Michigan:

- Eliminates the need for large shipping infrastructures

- Promotes sustainability

- Grows organic food that is better for our bodies and environment

Customers are becoming increasingly aware about where and how their food is grown. Consumer uncertainty is a large factor when it comes to purchasing foods. Many imported foods are not monitored by USDA growing standards. In addition to where and how their food is grown, consumers like to be certain about quality and care measures associated with their foods. Pesticides, herbicides and insecticides are all potential carcinogens. This creates fear in the customer, and drives them closer to the organic markets.

The greenhouse will not only be supported by a superior staff, but an experienced support network of organic champions will support the greenhouse and operations. Experts from each area of the agriculture industry will provide advice and knowledge. Along the path of Great Lakes Organics origin, many industry alliances have already been made. Sales discussions have already begun with one of Lansing's largest organic grocers. Purchase inquiries have also been noted by two local chefs. Great Lakes Organics will provide the local market with fresh, organic herbs for many years. Our greenhouses are meant to multiply on our current location in Ann Arbor. There are also plans to expand across the Midwest, to support multiple cities with the ability to self–sustain. Many cities located in northern latitudes require greenhouses to grow locally and year–round.

Four critical elements are brought together under the glass roofs at Great Lakes Organics:

- Rich, organic compounds

- Experienced horticulturists

- High quality seeds

- Superior, year–round production

Below is the projected financial summary for Great Lakes Organics for the first four years.

	2014 Totals	2015 Totals	2016 Totals	2017 Totals
Gross sales	82,715	973,847	1,508,042	1,739,997
Total COGS	41,388	389,507	595,565	706,584
Gross margin	41,327	584,340	912,477	1,033,412
Operating expense	111,531	334,011	415,650	455,091
Dividends paid	0	40,118	99,366	115,665
Net income	(76,659)	192,934	382,409	451,608
Year-ending cash balance	56,457	143,702	444,698	852,235

MISSION

Great Lakes Organics provides Lansing with quality organic herbs at a fair price. We provide our customers with healthier options that are grown in an environment that fosters global sustainability.

Great Lakes Organics' mission is to produce the highest quality, locally grown organic herbs. With the utilization of hydroponics and safe, nutrient-rich fertilizers, Great Lakes Organics will grow high quality herbs for the beneficial use of our customers. Only serving locally will allow us to ensure product quality. We will conduct operations prudently and strive to grow steadily, increasing profits, size, and market share. Great Lakes Organics shares the world's obligation to protect the environment and will carry out all operations accordingly.

Great Lakes Organics's Mantra

"Year–Round, Organic Quality"

The 4 Keys to Our Success

1. *Reliable and year–round product delivery.* This enables us to capture peak produce prices in the winter.

2. *Promotion and use of hydroponics.* This allows us to grow organically with scientific accuracy and efficiency.

3. *Community involvement.* By creating a friendly greenhouse environment and sharing our processes with the community, we promote sustainability and educate consumers.

4. *Industry alliances and organizations.* Fraternizing with our vendors, competitors, customers, and affiliations will create an ideal business environment.

OBJECTIVES

As a local grower, Great Lakes Organics strives to provide the Lansing market with locally grown produce. Each year, companies around the world spend unnecessary funds on shipping produce from warmer climates, where the production takes place, to colder climates, where many of the buyers live. In addition to the money spent, energy and resources are wasted by the transfer of these products. Great Lakes Organics' goal is to ease the strain on our environment and on markets by producing food locally.

Local production of these goods will also ensure quality control. Any of our buyers or end–users can visit our grow houses, year–round. This will not only showcase our high quality methods and products, but it will also serve as an education tool for many Lansing families and schools. By educating the end user about our product we can reduce uncertainty factors about the production process of the herbs.

Providing our customers the best organic product is crucial for our success. Not only will we strive to make organic products, but the best. Many organic products lack quality due to prolonged shipping methods, premature harvesting, and too much handling. Our locally grown goods will not be subject to any of their methods and, therefore, none of the repercussions.

Great Lakes Organics will sell high–demand herbs that include basil, mint, and chives, in the Lansing area, where the market for organic produce has not yet reached its full potential. The final system will be composed of five greenhouses, located south of Lansing, that will use modern hydroponics to increase quality control and crop yields. Through automation of the greenhouse and hydroponic systems, the amount of labor required (which is the largest expense in operating a greenhouse) will be reduced (USDA).

Great Lakes Organics will serve the Lansing area with consistent and reliable service. Our products will be recognized as local and organic; this will show our customers that we have higher level of quality control, and give them an opportunity to see it firsthand. We plan to be the first large scale organic greenhouse to serve the Lansing area.

Hydroponics

As mentioned above, we will use a hydroponics system to grow our produce. Hydroponics is the method of growing plants in nutrient rich water, instead of soil. Plants can be grown with their roots directly in this solution or in an inert medium like gravel.

More hydroponics greenhouses in the United States are becoming certified as organic. Aiding this increase are companies like Water Aid that offer hydroponic packages that are certifiable and other certified operations that act as a precedent.

To meet the UDSA standards we will be required to use fertilizer that is not synthetic and contains no refined elements. In other words, the fertilizer will need to be composed of 100 percent organic materials. In the past, these types of fertilizers were difficult to find; however, more companies are producing products that meet these requirements. These companies include Friendly Fertilizer, which makes an organic hydroponic fertilizer, and Hydroponics Inc., which has several products for hydroponics that are 100 percent organic.

The hydroponics system utilized at Great Lakes Organics will make the most of limited greenhouse space. The system used in our greenhouses is the Great Lakes Vertical System. The system is designed so one can stack growing pots on top of each other to obtain the maximum plants per square foot. The stackable pots are manufactured with high density polystyrene foam that will help insulate roots during both hot and cold weather. The stacks of pots are able to be rotated, which allows uniform light absorption for each plant. Rotation also allows for easy harvesting and planting. The Vertical System's direct watering system reduces the amount of water and fertilizers that are required. Vertical System claims that fertilizers and water usage can be reduced by up to 80 percent when compared to other conventional systems. Also, because there is no soil used, there is no chance for soil born diseases. There will be less harm caused by insects and no need for weeding or herbicides. The cost to equip each greenhouse with the hydroponic system will be $9,000.

The Vertical System will increase our growing space within the greenhouse. Because the Vertical System stacks pots vertically, more plants can be grown per square foot than traditional greenhouse growing. "Grow strawberries, lettuce, herbs and many other crops vertically in 80 percent less space." (Vertical System's marketing material).

Growing hydroponically and vertically will help us grow more plants per square foot, conserve energy and water, and control pests.

OPERATIONS

Location

Our location will be in Lansing. The reason this site was chosen is because it is owned by the parents of the owner and will be used rent-free. The tract we will use is in a field on top of a hill. We will have access to a well for water and power lines are less than 100 yards away. Gaining access to this site will be done with ease since there is an existing road that goes to the location. This location also has good access to roads. We are in close proximity to both I-96 and US-23.

Because of our location, we expect to need little security. It is located off the main road in an area where people do not lock their doors. If security does become a problem, a chain link fence will be purchased for an estimated $8,250, and some of the greenhouse lights will be lit at night as a deterrent. Additional precautions may be taken if necessary (i.e. cameras and guards).

Greenhouses

The greenhouses that will be used at Great Lakes Organics will be purchased from York Greenhouse Manufacturing. These greenhouses offer many options that will allow Great Lakes Organics to design a greenhouse that best fits our needs. The model that will be used is the Great Greenhouse because it offers the most square feet per dollar. This greenhouse has a total of 3,264 square feet and will cost around $19,500 for a per square foot cost of $6.

The greenhouses will be equipped with modern equipment that will reduce labor and increase control of the environment. Some of the features include: automatic vents, temperature controls that will be linked to the furnace and cooling fans, and, among other things, insulated wall ends.

The purchase price for each greenhouse will break down as follows:

Frame	9,520
Plastic	Included
Doors	765
Vents	3,775
Wallends	3,225
Gear box	645
Roll up side vents	735
Automated vent control	900
Total	**19,565**

Using a Corn Stove as a Heat Source

In using a corn stove, we will not only be saving money by burning a less expensive fuel, but will also be burning a renewable resource that will add to our image of being green. It was calculated that in the coldest part of winter we will need the ability to produce 2 million BTUs per hour, with a yearly total of 1 billion BTU hours. Our estimated heating expense for using different energy sources is as follows:

		Annual cost
Wood	$150 per cord	$10,300
Corn	$6 per bushel	$17,680
Wood pellets	$260 per ton	$21,630
Electric	11 cents per kilowatt hour	$30,470
Fuel oil	$4.55 per gallon	$40,625
Propane	$3.45 per gallon	$46,980

The reason corn was chosen over wood is because a wood stove requires more around-the-clock attention than a corn stove does. Using corn will allow for more control over the price of fuel. With fuels like electricity and propane, you are limited on who you can purchase from. However, with the numerous farming contacts near the greenhouse location, Great Lakes Organics can likely purchase fuel at a discounted and more consistent rate.

Using an external corn stove will allow for low cost per BTU and will reduce the labor required to feed the stove when compared to a wood stove.

Lighting

In order to maintain consistent production rates, we plan to supplement light in order to maintain a minimum of 12 hours of light a day. On the shortest day of the year, the winter solstice, 3.5 hours of light will be supplemented. Supplemental lighting also gives us more control in the quantity produced. If demand shrinks, we can cut back on the quantity of light to slow growth.

The lamp we chose is a metal halide. Metal halide lamps provide a full light spectrum and are more comfortable to work under than other lamps. They are the best lamp for promoting plant growth. This color of light promotes plant growth and is excellent for green leafy growth. The average lifespan of a bulb is about 10,000 hours so a bulb will last for years.

Lights will be hung 4–6 feet above plants for optimal lighting. Each 1,000 watt bulb will light 140 square feet. A total of 23 lights will be needed per greenhouse at a purchase price of $450 per fixture. Bulb replacement cost will be around $90. The expected electric expense for operating 5 greenhouses, at a kilowatt hour costing $0.15, will be $18,000. The cost for equipping each greenhouse will be $12,000.

Using Metal halide bulbs will encourage plant growth and provide pleasant working conditions for employees.

Propagtion

Through the year some plants will inevitably die. Therefore we will have a propagation system that will allow us to take cuttings from existing plants and grow them into actual plants. Through propagation from plant cuttings instead of from seeds, a plant will be able to be harvested in about half the time. A propagation system can be as simple as a tray of moist sand. Plants can be grown from cuttings instead of seeds which saves time.

Typical Work Day

In going through the day: the day will begin with a 10 minute meeting to discuss any current and potential problems, as well as give praise and feedback for positive items. The meeting will also be used to motivate employees and try to help their job from being monotonous. Employees will have a 15 minute break midmorning, and a half hour lunch. They will be given the option of working through lunch if they desire. This option will not be encouraged because we want to develop community in employees and social times like a lunch break together will help this. Mornings at the greenhouse will consist of harvesting and packaging in order to allow same-day deliveries. Afternoons will be used to propagate plants, and perform any maintenance on the operational systems.

Also, since there is only so much that can be done in a greenhouse, employees will be able to leave early if they accomplish their required jobs. We will not allow this option to be abused, but will allow some leeway because employees will get limited time off during holidays.

Legal Structure

Great Lakes Organics will be structured as a Limited Liability Company. There are several advantages of forming an LLC. First of all, Great Lakes will have limited liability protection. This will not only be good for the company, but also the owners. We will also be a pass-through entity that allows Great Lakes Organics to pass the tax on profits to the owners; this will be helpful, especially during the startup phase. Other advantages of an LLC include flexibility in operations and no ownership restrictions. In Michigan, becoming an LLC is very easy and inexpensive.

ADVERTISING

Packaging

Labels and clamshells will be purchased in bulk in order to reduce the per unit cost. Labels will be purchased online. If we purchase 10,000 at a time, labels will cost 1.7 cents each. Clamshells will be purchased from a company called Jones Specifications. The one ounce packing clamshell we will purchase will cost 11 cents each. Several companies make appropriate packing bags that cost 3 cents each. The yearly total for packaging supplies per greenhouse will be around $22,000. Purchasing packing supplies will reduce the per unit cost.

BUSINESS STRATEGY

There are three unique features of Great Lakes Organics that will aid in becoming an organic competitor in the Lansing market.

The first unique feature of Great Lakes Organics is that the produce will be grown in a greenhouse. This will allow for year–round production that will offer a stable revenue stream as well as provide customers with consistent service and produce. Year round production has a two–fold effect. Not only will we be receiving year round profits, but market price on herbs can increase during the winter months. Additionally, the control of production will increase with the use of a hydroponics system. Further benefits from the greenhouse and hydroponics approach include providing a sanitary environment for product growth, temperature and fertility control, elimination of soil–borne diseases, and availability of technical assistance for the hydroponics system.

The second feature is the locality factor of our business, will provide a competitive advantage over more commercialized, non–local companies. In 2013, 43 percent of consumers typically sought out food grown by local producers whether they were organic or not. Great Lakes Organics will cater to the needs and desires of consumers by promoting our product in the local market, involving the community, and offering the freshest organic produce. Currently, 47 percent of consumers worry that more commercialized, non–local organic companies are not following the production regulations as laid out by the USDA. Concern about the production standards of other companies is a legitimate concern. Several "organic" producers have had pesticides found on their farms (likely being transferred from a nearby farm by the wind). There have also been reports of companies buying nonorganic produce and packaging it as organic. The community–centered nature of Great Lakes Organics could alleviate many of these concerns. By holding greenhouse visitations, other community events, and offering more information for consumers on our production standards and techniques, we can establish a more loyal and committed relationship with the community. Through public awareness we will increase sales of our product and taxable revenue within the community. Being a local grower would also create more job opportunities for the community and, in so doing so, add to the local economy. Another advantage of the locality feature exists in the reduction of transportation costs. Less money is required for shipping since Great Lakes Organics does not ship our products cross–country. The distance a product travels from the farm to its destination and its impact on fuel costs and global warming is a growing concern among consumers.

The third advantage arises from the positive attitudes consumers hold toward organics. For instance, 48 percent of consumers believe organic foods are more nutritious than non–organic, while 30 percent of consumers say that organic food tastes better. Many people are concerned with maintaining a healthy lifestyle. Another benefit for the health–minded consumer is that organic food is not grown using any harmful, potentially cancer–causing chemicals, including pesticides, herbicides, and fungicides. Avoidance of these chemicals is especially important during the pre–natal and early development stages of children. Due to their sensitive systems, small children, pregnant women and consumers with allergies who are especially vulnerable will benefit most from the avoidance of pesticide and chemical use. By switching to organic products, children can lower their pesticide levels in only five days, making for a healthier development process. In addition to growing organics free of chemicals known to be harmful, they also contain no Genetically Modified Organisms, or "GMOs", of which 56 percent of all consumers are concerned about digesting.

Risk Factors

One of the largest threats to the organic food market is the perishable quality of our produce. The inability to sell all of our finished products due to the fact that produce only stays fresh for a short period of time, could lead to lost profits. Organic food is labor intensive and as a result, organic produce costs more than non–organic. This is significant because 67 percent of consumers say they would buy more organics if the cost was less. Therefore, monitoring price and understanding our consumer becomes invaluable as the high price of organics proves to be a barrier for the consumer.

One way around limitation of perishability is value–added activities. These activities can include dehydrating herbs and selling to a packaging company or creating soup or dip packages.

Due to the high margins that can be associated with selling organic food, the USDA published organic regulations in October of 2002 in order to try and regulate the market. Among the most pertinent prohibited materials and practices include the avoidance of genetically engineered seeds and materials, the mandatory waiting period when applying proper composting techniques, and the banning of irradiation and sewage sludge. Complying with these USDA standards can be time consuming and expensive, and claiming to be better than a competitor can be a difficult task with the uniform standards.

We realize that this segment of business can fluctuate and make it difficult to compete. Because of the system Great Lakes Organics will use, there is the option to change what is grown. The existing hydroponics system can be used to grow other products like tomatoes, lettuce and even flowers. Or the hydroponics system can be moved out and replaced with materials that are for growing mushrooms or potted plants.

MARKET ANALYSIS

Popularity of organic foods continues to grow within the continental United States. In fact, the sales of this segment increased nationwide 115 percent at current prices, or 89 percent after adjusting for inflation, from 2007–2012. Sales are expected to continue increasing for future periods, which makes it an ideal opportunity to enter the market.

There is a continuous increase in sales of organic food. The constant increase in growth supports the premise that organic foods are becoming more acceptable—and more in demand by consumers looking for foods they consider to be more healthful. With this trend, the industry continues to grow at a rapid pace, as demand for organically grown food in local markets is also likely to rise, indicating encouraging trends.

Agricultural trends also point to the organic produce market as being one of the fastest growing segments of US agriculture. The organic food industry is in the growth stage. Additionally, there seems to be a trend towards eating healthier in the United States, which includes organic foods. Rising nutritional awareness and a preference for a produce–rich diet across the nation has a positive effect on demand for fruit and vegetables generally, including those grown under cover. A general concern for well–being boosts the market for healthy foods such as organic fruits and vegetables.

In 2000, the organic food industry hit a milestone when traditional supermarkets became the primary venue for organic foods. An organic product reaching the shelves of places such as Schnucks, Dierbergs, Wal–Mart, and other large grocers represents an important step for organics. It signifies that the growth of a product and the demand for the product is still increasing. Large retailers such as Wal–Mart have started to stock organic foods to regain and retain many customers siphoned away by retailers such as Whole Foods. In 2006, retail giant Wal–Mart announced it will increase the variety of organic food in its stores, which is expected to lead to a faster adoption of organic farming.

Through mainstream retailers seeking to stock organic foods, the industry becomes self–promoting. Retailers will respond to a rise in demand by increasing their orders. Therefore, those growers who are able to provide year–round service can reap the benefits of the grocery stores and larger retailers' increasing need for inventory.

Competition

Local competition from large–scale organic greenhouses in Michigan is limited. The current herb industry is located primarily in California, Florida, Colorado, Arizona, Ohio, Texas, Pennsylvania as well as Mexico, Canada, Holland, and Israel. The lack of large regional competitors will reduce the chance of more established companies driving Great Lakes Organics out during our introduction to the market. We will establish a niche market characterized by our locally–grown, year–round products in order to compete with organic growers who may not use a greenhouse but have established themselves in the Michigan market and supply to grocery retailers.

In order to obtain local supply and demand data for the Lansing produce industry, we interviewed the store manager of a prominent grocery store in the area. However, he could not supply exact figures because they were considered confidential. He said that the sales of organic food varied greatly within the city and that consistent suppliers are hard to come by.

Not only is the demand for local produce increasing, produce prices are increasing across the board. This is largely due to the fact that fuel prices have increased substantially over the past decade and that there is a higher demand internationally.

Industry Trends

Currently the organic produce industry is experiencing high growth in all sectors; locally, nationally, and globally. Not only are there higher standards being set by shoppers, but higher standards are also being set by governments. Regulations on USDA organics have been around for a long time; however, new restrictions on pesticide sprays, irrigation practices, and fungicides have been mounting on the industry.

The most important industry trend is driven by our consumers. Each year the demand for organic produce increases. Studies are increasingly showing grocery shoppers the benefits of eating organic foods, and they are willing to pay the premium. Online polls, grocery store surveys and industry reports are all pointing in the same direction. Organic foods are important to consumers and will be in the foreseeable future.

Organic farming is practiced in approximately 100 countries throughout the world, with more than 37.5 million hectares now under organic management. Australia leads with approximately 12 million hectares, followed by Argentina, with approximately 3.6 million hectares; both have extensive grazing lands. Latin America has approximately 6.8 million hectares under organic management, Europe has more than 11.2 million hectares, and the United States has nearly 2.2 million hectares.

Organic is a niche, but a very profitable niche. Give consumers what they truly want/need and they will dig deeply into their pockets. Organic is here to stay, not a fad marching by in the night. Others will likely get involved. Whether you opt in or not, it certainly is a category worth watching. It gives us one more window into the minds of consumers.

CUSTOMERS

Everyone deserves and enjoys high quality produce; however Great Lakes Organics will focus on the early majority and late majority adopters. Our efforts will also be focused on higher-end stores. We are selling our products at local grocery stores which will include Whole Foods, Schnucks, and Dierbergs. We will also focus on smaller, local markets. Most of these grocers buy in smaller increments, fitting for our first year. Many markets and grocers are facing higher demand, due to elevated demand on organic products. This makes it easier for our product to be recognized around the community and our end–user. Placing our products in high–end community supermarkets will facilitate our opportunity to expand quickly. Launching our products to higher–end consumers is vital since they have more disposable income to spend on quality products. As the local community becomes aware of our product, it will be easier for us to expand to other grocery markets that will be attracted in selling our product.

We plan to target areas that have customers who purchase organic food on a regular basis. Many of these areas are easy to find because the stores already exist. Stores like Whole Foods, Trader Joe's, etc. draw in a certain demographic. The main two are income and ethnicity. Middle and upper class people purchase the majority of organic food, likely because of the higher price tag that is associated with it. Also, people of Asian ethnicity purchase the largest amount of organic products per capita.

Each business and individual's adoption processes has an effect on our business. Even though Great Lakes Organics does not sell directly to the retail consumer, their preferences still impact our business. Out of adopters the early majority and innovators are going to be our primary end-users. The early adopters and innovators are consumers who want to buy local products. These are the consumers who desire to eat locally to promote local economic development and reduce the externalities caused by importing goods and shipping goods across the country.

Shoppers who are interested in our products will typically shop at stores that stock organic products. These customers will be interested in locality, organic quality, and price. The main grocers serving these customers are as follows.

- Whole Foods
- Jones and Peters
- Trader Joe's
- Several smaller, local stores

Each of our adopters takes on a different process for perceiving and purchasing new goods. In the case of Great Lakes Organics, we want to know where these adopters are, even though we are not selling directly to them. By understanding the purchasing and adoption habit of the end user, we will be able to better understand the following:

- Where they will go to purchase new/trendy goods
- How much they are looking to spend on organic goods
- And, exactly what kinds of goods they are looking for

Economic Factors

Organic food is one of the fastest growing agricultural markets in the U.S. With a growing presence in supermarkets and satisfied consumer, organic food is an expanding market. Food quality, freshness, and food safety is what makes organic food more demanding.

Each year, the demand for organic foods increases. However, farmers are not increasing their organic production rate at the same rate of the increasing demand. This means a lot for our business. As the demand for organic goods rises, grocers will be struggling to meet demand needs.

We are currently facing a recovering economy, where disposable income is still thin. Our organic produce can be up to ten times the price of normal produce. Knowing that our economy is recovering and budgets are still tight, we will focus on the middle and upper class, and their grocers. We are targeting higher income consumers who are able to spend more on a higher-end product. International consumers spend around 14 percent of their income on quality food, compared to U.S. consumers which spend around 7 percent. Grocery shoppers that are cost consumers will not be our targets. Most of these shoppers purchase goods at Wal-Mart, Costco, and Sam's Club.

One positive aspect of the economic hard times is that it will add protection from foreign competition as the dollar becomes weak. As the dollar weakens, it could become less profitable for foreign companies to export to the United States.

MARKETING & SALES

Our sales and marketing strategy will rely primarily on personal sales abilities as well as market situations. Most of our sales positioning and pricing will be in response to the markets. Our distribution methods will be unique to Great Lakes Organics and our approach to advertising will be a cold call sales tactic, relying on personal selling capabilities.

Informing, Persuasion, and Reminding

The process of *informing* will revolve around defining the technology of hydroponics in simple terms. Most have a general idea of what "organic" entails but we have a responsibility to make sure we educate ourselves as well as our customers when the terminology is vague or unclear. We must also reassure the organic buying customers that our version of hydroponics produce is just as natural, safe, and as organic as soil grown fruits and vegetables. Assuring product quality will also be an important aspect of informing. If our products do not own up to the best organic competitors, they will reject the hydroponics method.

Organic agriculture is an ecological production management system that promotes and enhances biodiversity, biological cycles and soil biological activity. It is based on minimal use of off–farm inputs and on management practices that restore, maintain and enhance ecological harmony.

Not only are we trying to grow a healthy food but also a food that is safer for the consumer and the environment. Although this is a business, we will show that we care about the environment and our production of organic goods will reflect our dedication.

Persuasion of organic products comes naturally, derived from the sale of organic foods, and their continuance to flourish throughout the various lines. The sale of organic foods continues to flourish throughout the various lines. "Products labeled as natural or organic have seen double–digit sales growth in recent years and now represent close to $29.22 billion annually." Currently, in the Lansing market, stores like Whole Foods cannot buy enough produce to stock their shelves.

We will continue to *remind* our customers and the retail buyers about the benefits of organic foods (more nutrients, less harmful to humans and the environment, etc.) We also must remind our customers of the environmental advantages of locally grown produce and hydroponics produce. These characteristics use less energy to distribute and are less harmful to the land. We will also remind them that fruits and vegetables grown organically show significantly higher levels of cancer–fighting anti-oxidants than conventionally grown foods.

Advertising

Our main sources of advertising will come through local newspapers with strong editorial columns pertaining to food (*Sauce Magazine*, Trader Joe's and Whole Foods newspapers/letters, supermarket newspapers) as well as Internet capabilities (online clubs, newsletters, etc).

- *Sauce Magazine*
- Whole Foods' Newsletters
- Lansing newspapers
- Local radio and television shows

Sales Strategy

Positioning

We will position our product against others as being locally produced and of high, organic quality. There are very few distinguishable differences with herbs. Most of our customers will be seeing the same products offered, at similar prices. Great Lakes Organics will sell to grocers and restaurants by positioning ourselves against the competition as a local provider. This characteristic will help us stand out in terms of sustainability. We will also us it to show how shipping our products 30 miles to our customers will give way to better products. Local products will not be subjected to days of unnatural shipping methods, or border crossing. Producing herbs locally, as mentioned, during the winter and colder months will be a competitive advantage.

Another positioning method against wholesale distributors and other sellers is that we will be local and have dependable service. Many of our competitors will depend on distributors to ship their product across the country. This process can be disrupted by weather, infrastructure, and contamination. By providing a local product, Great Lakes Organics will not be at the mercy of conditions around the country. This will let us boast about our unique, dependable service.

Pricing

The price of our product will fluctuate with the supply and demand of the market. In the summer time the market supplied with additional locally produced herbs. Because of this, prices will drop and people will buy more. In the winter, when supply is not as abundant, prices go up. However, if we are able to establish brand recognition, we could likely charge a higher price year round. Selling directly to Michigan chefs and restaurants could pose a lucrative pricing opportunity. Typically, restaurants are much more particular about their products, but they will pay a much higher price. During the winter months, some restaurants will pay up to eight times the summer market price for high quality produce.

Personal Selling

We must make it clear that we are well educated in what we produce and how it is done in order to ensure that our clients and potential clients can confidently purchase our products. We will cold call in order to set up appointments. Setting up appointments, giving free samples, and demonstrating the hydroponic method will be the objective for many of our appointments. Through writing this plan, Great Lakes has made several contacts that could be potential buyers. Between the founders, over fifteen years of sales experience has been accumulated. We will rely on this heavily for our establishment in the organic food markets. Initially we will court our existing contacts. Throughout our research, the founders of Great Lakes Organics have established over ten reputable industry contacts. This will be our base for sales. Our plan will be to establish territories, then split them up and place personal cold calls. Salespersons will earn a base salary of $750 per month plus 7 percent of gross margin.

Indirect Sales/Distribution

We plan to be a selective seller and sell directly to grocers and markets. There is a chance that we could partner with a company like Whole Foods and supply them exclusively. But we may not want to limit ourselves in such a manner. If we grow an excess we could sell to a wholesaler, however they may demand we sell it at a lower price because they become the middle man.

In the winter months we will sell 70 percent of goods to retailers and 30 percent to restaurants. In the summer when there is more local competition, 55 percent will be sold to retailers, 30 percent to restaurants, and 15 percent will be sold wholesale or will participate in value–added activities.

COMPETITION

Great Lakes Organics will only have a handful of competitors in a market seeking an increasing supply. Additionally, our unique advantages will help us stand out amongst this small group of local growers.

Primary Competitors

We currently have a few primary competitors. They are all somewhat local and are producers of organic produce. Several currently have multiple farms and greenhouses all within 150 miles of Lansing. Their ability to produce locally cuts down on their costs, and is more appealing to locavores.

They also operate out of greenhouses in the winter months, allowing them the ability to reap the high profits from winter months.

Secondary Competitors

We have two different types of secondary competitors: Local, but not organic and Organic, but not local. These competitors come from a wide range of locations and operations. Secondary competitors also represent all imports from other countries. Countries such as Poland, Italy, and China have organic farms in place and provide fresh organic goods to their respective regions. Due to their location, lengthy shipping and unknown practices of shipping these goods, international organic goods only represents a small number of producers that will concern our business. Nevertheless, these producers should still be taken into account as we assess the competitive environment surrounding our business.

We will deal with this competition by targeting smaller retail locations during the summer and selling our products as higher quality than those exposed to the unnatural elements found on outdoor farms and nonorganic produce.

Unique Competitors

We will also be dealing with unique competitors. These competitors either grow different products, pose an opportunity to partner, or operate under a different business model. The People's Farm, for instance, is located in the heart of Saginaw, Michigan. They grow organic produce of all sorts, year round, but under the model of a CSA (Community Supported Agriculture). CSAs will collect funds and labor from a neighborhood and provide fresh fruits, vegetables, herbs, and meat for a small community. This CSA will not be seen as a threat to our business, but an opportunity to advertise, give back to the community, and promote Great Lakes Organics.

Competitive Advantages

Great Lakes Organics' competitive advantages can be summarizedin four concise bullets:

- *Greenhouse Growing*—By growing our foods in a greenhouse, we obtain a clear competitive advantage over our competitors. Growing indoors allows us to grow our foods year–round. We will be able to take advantage of higher market prices. Greenhouse growing also allows us to control our environment and therefore our quality. We will not be subject to the elements; floods, high winds, drought, etc. The threat offered by insects and animals can be greatly reduced in using a greenhouse. And lastly, we control our outputs. Conventional farms destroy native environments with water and chemical runoff and organic matter. We will not partake in destructive practices but will focus on sustainability.

- *Organic Produce*—Growing organic produce is the obvious advantage. With prices up to ten times as much as modern produce, organics will increase our profit margins while keeping our customers healthy.

- *Grow System*—Using a hydroponic system allows more control over production. It eliminates the need for pesticides, herbicides and soil borne diseases. It also provides higher production and requires less time required per unit produced. The growing medium, perlite, holds water content and is an excellent vehicle for delivering nutrients to plants. Using automated greenhouses allows for labor savings and year round production reliability.

- *Local*—Being a local provider will cut our costs significantly. We will not have to pay any tariffs or fuel costs for shipping. We will also become more attractive to our customers, more dependable, and environmentally sound.

MANAGEMENT SUMMARY

- *Thomas Graham*—Thomas graduated from Southern Illinois University with honors and a BSBA with a concentration in entrepreneurship. He established his first LLC at the age of 19 and purchased a piece of investment property while a freshmen in college. Thomas has worked in construction since he was 13 and qualified for the advanced placement plumbing apprentice program while still in high school. Much of his family are farmers and he grew up on a plot of land where his chores included maintaining a garden, and tending to small livestock.

- *Alice Wearen*—Alice recently graduated from Central Michigan University. She received a BSBA, with a concentration in entrepreneurship. Alice studied environmental science as well, taking courses focusing on global sustainability and environmental issues. At Central Michigan University, she served as a board member of the Collegiate Entrepreneurs' Organization. For the past 3 years, she has focused on marketing efforts at a local cancer treatment center and office supply company.

- *Erik Clive*—Erik recently graduated from Michigan State University where he received a BSBA with concentrations in Marketing and International Business and a supporting concentration in Entrepreneurship. Erik worked as a Leasing Agent for a local real estate company learning valuable personal selling and interpersonal communication skills.

- *Pilar Christopher*—Pilar recently graduated from Michigan State University where she received a BSBA, with a concentration in entrepreneurship. She gained many interpersonal and human relation skills through her experiences in her previous positions working at local banks. Being naturally from Puerto Rico, her language skills in English as well as in Spanish have helped her excel in the business world. In addition, her strong background in business throughout the years have helped her acquire the experience needed to succeed in this changing and competitive field.

Job Descriptions

The horticulturist's primary job is to monitor the system and make any necessary adjustments to nutrient level, Ph level, lights, and temperature. This portion of his job should become routine because of the automated control systems that will be installed. The horticulturist will also be in charge of ordering materials, such as packing materials, seeds, fertilizers and other regularly needed materials. The horticulturist will also be in charge of supervising the laborers. He/she will need to give laborers direction, make any changes, and keep other employees motivated. The horticulturist will report to the owner and inform about any problems with personnel, production, etc. With the automation of the greenhouse, day–to–day tasks should not have a great deal of variation.

Laborers will have the job of harvesting, packing, and propagating plants, as well as any maintenance on the system the horticulturist sees needed. They will also have the task of record keeping that will be reported to the book keeper and owner. We are looking to have tours (to qualify for educational grants) on Friday afternoons; the laborers will be in charge of conducting the tours and answering any questions.

At the beginning, the owner will make deliveries to restaurants and retailers. Most deliveries will be made in the late morning, and early afternoon. The owner will be at the greenhouse much of the time and will be able to monitor the operation and help things run smoothly.

Strategic Alliances

We have the ability to join groups and organizations throughout the United States. Though joining various organizations we will form a network with those who have similar businesses to ours and offer sound advice in an effort to efficiently run our business.

- *State–Level Organic Association:* Shows our desire to help educate Michiganders on the benefits of organically grown foods.

- *Organic Co–op:* A co–op that offers grants and other funding to help start–up organic growers fund their projects in order to start their businesses.

- *Ecological Farming Association:* Shares concerns about the duties as agriculturalists to protect the earth and provide an economically practical quality product.

- *World Wide Opportunities on Organic Farms (WWOOF–USA):* Started by the EFA in an effort to spread global awareness about the benefits of organically grown foods. Organization places volunteers at organic farms to assist in the daily operations. In return, the volunteers receive education about living the organic lifestyle and its benefits for the world.

- *Organic Trade Association:* Offers free business listings in its group sites and reduced advertisement costs on it website(s) to those who sign up for membership.

- *All Things Organic (Trade Show):* Sponsored by OTA and held in Chicago, IL, this would be an event to consider attending (if held beyond the upcoming show) in order to move our business to a national level and increase brand recognition.

Mentors and Support Network

Through developing this plan we have made several contacts that will aid Great Lakes Organics in the future. Some of these contacts include:

- *Marc Ford:* Marc believes in the benefits of organic food and wants to develop the market of organic food. Marc is working to develop a co–op that will provide people with locally grown and organic food.

- *Gina Spivey:* Gina works at the intellectual property office at the University of Michigan. She previously worked for NASA and has an understanding and interest in hydroponics.

- *York Greenhouses:* York is the company who we are purchasing greenhouses from. They offer a good product with a wide range of options that will allow up to chose the exact options we want for what we are growing. York also offers support information during the construction stage and any maintenance issues that will arise in the future.

- *Henry Wallabee:* Henry is the produce forager for the local Whole Foods Market. He has worked in agricultural business his entire life and has been a valuable mentor for the Great Lakes Organics development team. She has offered her advice for business planning, business development and strategic positioning. She has also helped in networking across Lansing's organic industry.

FINANCIAL ANALYSIS

Additional Revenue Streams

There are several options that will allow for value added activities for any goods that are not able to be sold. We are looking into activities like dehydrating and selling to organic dry herb packagers. We are also considering selling to a salsa or sauce manufacturer or even creating dehydrated soup packages. Value–added activities will protect Great Lakes Organics from lost revenue.

Start–Up Expenses

In order to start business, a first investment will be secured. A total of $270,000 will be needed to cover expenses incurred during that startup phase. Currently there is $97,500 available in the owner's equity provided by the founders. An additional $45,000 has been pledged from the family of one of the owners. A loan of $105,000 will be secured, likely through Whole Foods who has a loan program to help local growers become established. Even though this loan is through a grocer, it does not limit us in who we sell to, but requires us to supply Whole Foods for at least 3 years. The $22,500 difference in funding will come from grants for the promotion and education of sustainable agriculture or a line of credit secured by one of the owners.

Annual income summary

	2014 Totals	2015 Totals	2016 Totals	2017 Totals
Gross sales	82,715	973,847	1,508,042	1,739,997
Total COGS	41,388	389,507	595,565	706,584
Gross margin	41,327	584,340	912,477	1,033,412
Operating expense	111,531	334,011	415,650	455,091
Dividends paid	0	40,118	99,366	115,665
Net income	(76,659)	192,934	382,409	451,608

Income statement

	For the year ending December 31st 2015						
	Jan	Feb	Mar	Apr	May	Jun	Jul
Gross sales	57,144	57,144	57,144	57,144	53,493	80,240	80,240
COGS							
Labor	15,879	15,879	15,879	15,879	15,879	23,819	23,819
Growing material	1,203	1,203	1,203	1,203	1,203	1,727	1,727
Packing material	5,225	5,225	5,225	5,225	5,225	7,838	7,838
Total	22,307	22,307	22,307	22,307	22,307	33,383	33,383
Gross margin	34,838	34,838	34,838	34,838	31,188	46,859	46,859
Operating expenses							
Salaries	15,680	15,680	15,680	15,680	17,886	20,339	20,339
Depreciation	1,316	1,316	1,316	1,316	1,316	1,593	1,593
Other expenses	9,161	7,925	6,962	5,267	3,752	3,767	3,827
Total operating expenses	26,157	24,921	23,958	22,263	22,953	25,698	25,758
Operating income	8,681	9,917	10,880	12,575	8,234	21,159	21,099
Dividends paid	1,736	1,983	2,177	2,516	—	—	—
Interest expense	1,074	1,307	1,286	1,511	1,484	1,457	1,430
Net income	5,871	6,627	7,419	8,550	6,750	19,703	19,670

	Aug	Sep	Oct	Nov	Dec	Totals
Gross sales	78,879	107,828	114,864	114,864	114,864	973,847
COGS						
Labor	23,819	31,757	31,757	31,757	31,757	277,874
Growing material	1,727	2,252	2,252	2,252	2,252	20,202
Packing material	7,838	10,449	10,449	10,449	10,449	91,430
Total	33,383	44,457	44,457	44,457	44,457	389,507
Gross margin	45,497	63,369	70,407	70,407	70,407	584,340
Operating expenses						
Salaries	20,229	22,859	23,426	23,426	23,426	234,645
Depreciation	1,593	1,871	1,871	1,871	1,871	18,843
Other expenses	3,827	5,981	7,805	9,779	11,723	80,523
Total operating expenses	25,649	30,710	33,101	35,075	37,019	334,011
Operating income	19,848	32,660	37,307	35,333	33,389	250,328
Dividends paid	3,969	6,533	7,461	7,067	6,678	40,118
Interest expense	1,403	1,374	1,347	1,319	1,290	16,277
Net income	14,477	24,753	28,499	26,948	25,419	193,934

Cash flow summary

	2014	2015	2016	2017
Beginning cash	270,000	56,457	143,702	444,698
Net income	(76,659)	192,934	382,409	451,608
Depreciation expense	5,831	18,843	23,561	25,781
Cash flow from operations	199,172	269,984	549,671	922,085
Less capital investments	122,327	64,277	32,138	0
Cash flow from investing	165,000	0	0	0
Long term borrowing	105,000	0	0	0
Principal paid	21,138	62,006	72,836	69,849
Year ending cash	56,457	143,702	444,698	852,236

Break even analysis

	2014			2015			2016			2017		
	Basil	Mint	Chives	Basil	Mint	Chives	Basil	Mint	Chives	Basil	Mint	Chives
Total units in ounces	61,866	24,747	24,747	721,769	288,708	288,708	1,072,341	428,937	428,937	1,237,317	494,927	494,927
Unit price	1.35	0.90	1.35	1.35	0.90	1.35	1.35	0.90	1.35	1.35	0.90	1.35
Gross sales	52,740	15,869	14,106	582,803	230,076	160,967	924,038	344,544	239,460	1,065,092	398,790	276,116
COGS	24,833	8,277	8,277	233,705	77,901	77,901	357,339	119,114	119,114	423,951	141,317	141,317
Gross margin	27,908	7,592	5,828	349,098	152,175	83,066	566,699	225,431	120,347	641,141	257,474	134,798
Gross margin/unit	0.68	0.47	0.36	0.72	0.80	0.44	0.80	0.80	0.42	0.78	0.78	0.41
Operating expenses	66,918	22,307	22,307	200,408	66,803	66,803	249,390	83,130	83,130	273,054	91,019	91,019
Break even units needed	148,346	72,719	94,719	414,345	126,738	232,181	471,911	158,175	296,289	526,959	174,959	334,184
Surplus (shortage)	(86,480)	(47,972)	(69,972)	307,424	161,835	56,526	600,432	270,762	132,648	710,358	319,968	160,743

Pet Boarding

Doggie PlayCare

21332 Gratiot Ave.
Columbus, Michigan 48063

Zuzu Enterprises

Doggie PlayCare offers a safe, fun place for dogs to play, socialize, and be trained and groomed when their owners are busy elsewhere.

EXECUTIVE SUMMARY

In 2014, the pet care industry is estimated at $58.51 billion, including food, supplies/medicine, veterinary care, animal purchases, and grooming/boarding. This figure has been steadily rising for the last ten years despite the state of the economy. In fact, according to the 2013-2014 APPA National Pet Owners Survey, 68% of U.S. households own a pet, which equates to 82.5 million homes; this figure is up from 56% of U.S. households in 1988. The most common pet is the dog, with 56.7 million U.S. households having one or more.

A dog, however, is not simply a pet. A dog is a member of our family. We love them as our "children," our "friends," our "companions." What we don't love is the mess they can create, especially when they are bored or untrained. As all dog owners know, a trained and tired dog is a well-behaved dog!

As we need to spend more and more time away from home working, commuting, and taking care of children and elderly family members, however, we have less time to devote to the care and training of our beloved pets. This is where Doggie PlayCare comes in! Doggie PlayCare offers a safe, fun place for your dog to play, socialize, and be trained and groomed when you are busy elsewhere.

Doggie PlayCare offers the following services:

- Dog daycare

- Dog boarding

- Dog grooming

- Dog training

- Pet sitting

- Dog walking/pet visits

- Pooper scooper services

Our facility is located on three acres in the rural community of Columbus, Michigan. Doggie PlayCare features:

- Indoor and outdoor facilities

- Indoor play area with various toys

- Indoor training area with props and obstacles

- ½ acre outdoor, fenced-in area to play and/or train

- Individual and group kennels to serve 30 dogs

- KidsVision video camera system so "parents" can view their pets while they are at Doggie PlayCare

INDUSTRY ANALYSIS

In 2014, the pet care industry is estimated at $58.51 billion, including food, supplies/medicine, veterinary care, animal purchases, and grooming/boarding. This figure has been steadily rising for the last ten years despite the state of the economy and it is predicted that this figure will continue to rise at an annual rate of 4% at least through 2018.

According to the 2013-2014 APPA National Pet Owners Survey, 68% of U.S. households own a pet, which equates to 82.5 million homes; this figure is up from 56% of U.S. households in 1988. The most common pet is the dog, with 56.7 million U.S. households having one or more.

In 2013, it was reported that dog owners spend over $1,500 per year on each dog they own. This includes food, veterinary visits, treat and toys, boarding, and grooming (2013-2014 APPA National Pet Owners Survey). The newest trend in the pet care industry is for specialized services including dog walking, dog training, and full-service boarding.

Doggie PlayCare is well positioned to succeed in this market by catering to pet owners and serving the needs of their canine companions.

SERVICES

Doggie PlayCare is proud to offer a wide variety of services to serve all the needs of the pet owners in the community and surrounding areas. These services include:

Day Camp

Day camp consists of either half- or full-day sessions where dog can come to socialize and play with other dogs as well as staff. It is a great solution for dogs suffering from separation anxiety, young pups with tons of energy, and older dogs that need to go to the bathroom more often. It is also useful when families have long work days, large parties, and family illness or other emergencies. It is nice to drop your dog off knowing they will have fun and be well cared for so that you can fully concentrate on other things.

Day camp consists of a structured day that includes free play time, snack time, rest time, and special play times including bubbles, ice cubes, scent exploration, sprinkler fun, and music time.

Boarding

Overnight boarding is ideal when pet owners are on vacation, business trips, or are hosting allergic houseguests. Dogs that are boarded will attend day camp throughout the day and go to their kennels only at meal time and bedtime. Siblings can share an oversized cabin to make it more like home. Evening treats and soothing music at bedtime are always included in your dog's stay.

Boarding check-in is preferred by 4pm which allows for dinner and play time. You can also bring your dog earlier in the day to enjoy a full day of play. Boarding check-out can occur any time between 7am and 7pm, Monday through Friday or Saturday/Sunday/Holidays from 7am to 11am or 4pm to 7pm.

Cots, fleece blankets, food and water bowls are all included in the boarding package. Food may be brought in from home or dogs may be fed high-quality kibble stocked at the facility.

Requirements

Puppies must be at least 12 weeks old and all adult dogs must be spayed or neutered to attend day camp or be boarded. Dogs must be current with all vaccinations. Dogs must be people-friendly and enjoy other dogs; aggression towards staff, other animals, or customers is grounds for dismissal.

Grooming

Basic grooming services are also offered at Doggie PlayCare. While in our care, dogs may be bathed and have their hair and nails trimmed. Grooming services are not included in Day Camp or Boarding fees, and will be billed separately.

Training

Doggie PlayCare offers several training classes to meet the specific needs of each dog and owner. Classes include:

- Puppy Basic—Basic manners and behavioural issues

- Puppy Socialization—Socialization time

- Adult Basic—Basic manners and behavioural issues

- Adult advanced dog obedience—More advanced behaviours and "tricks"

- Leash walking

Pet Sitting

Pet sitting is ideal for dogs that have extreme anxiety when staying overnight away from home and for those pets that are not easily transported, including fish, hamsters, gerbils, guinea pigs, birds, reptiles, and cats. Our pet sitting service includes travel to your home, giving medications, feeding and refreshing water for pets, potty breaks, litter change, walking your pet, spot cleaning indoor if needed, outdoor waste removal, taking in mail and newspaper, turning lights on/off and security checks.

Dog Walking/Pet Visits

Another service offered by Doggie PlayCare is to come to your home and take care of your pets during the day. When applicable, visits include play time, potty breaks, dog walks or runs, feeding, litter box and/or cage cleaning, and home security checks. In addition to pet care and companionship, we can also provide basic concierge services including mail and newspaper pickup, switching on or off security lights, and anything else that you would like us to do while you are away to ensure your home and pet's safety.

Pooper Scooper

Pet waste removal/pooper scooper services are another convenience offered by Doggie PlayCare. Price varies on number of pets, size of yard, and number of scheduled visits.

PERSONNEL

Owner/Operators

Kelly and Stanley Kyle will own and operate Doggie PlayCare. Kelly is a certified vet technician and has 10 years' experience working with pets in the veterinary and boarding capacity.

Stanley has 12 years' experience operating as a manager of a retail outlet.

The Kyles own three dogs that were rescued and adopted from local shelters. They volunteer countless hours working for the shelter and have made it their mission to be a positive voice for animals everywhere. They feel that Doggie PlayCare will allow them to help dogs in different ways and reach pets and pet owners in a different setting but one that is essential to pets leading a quality life.

Camp Counselors

To start, two camp counselors will be hired on a part-time basis to help cover open hours as well as to care for overnight guests. As business expands, an additional three counselors will be hired.

Home Visitors

One employee will be hired as the designated home visitor to start. He/she must have an impeccable driving record, reliable transportation, and all licenses and insurance. This person will be responsible for all pet sitting, dog walking, and pooper scooper services. Additional home visitors will be hired on an as-needed basis.

OPERATIONS

Doggie PlayCare will be staffed by caring, knowledgeable individuals with a love and dedication to pets. The facilities are spacious and well-appointed to suit our needs and cleanliness will be a priority for the health and well-being of our charges.

Location

Doggie PlayCare is located on three acres of land in the rural area of Columbus, Michigan. Although situated in a rural area, it is easily accessible from I-94, M-19, and M-3, all of which are heavily used by commuters heading north towards the Port Huron area and south towards Detroit and the surrounding suburbs. The location features:

- Indoor and outdoor facilities

- Indoor play area with various toys

- Indoor training area with props and obstacles

- ½ acre outdoor, fenced-in area to play and/or train

- Individual and group kennels to serve 30 dogs

- KidsVision video camera system to "parents" can view their pets while they are at Doggie PlayCare

Hours of Operation

Doggie PlayCare is open 365 days a year to meet the needs of all our customers. Our daily schedule is as follows:

Weekdays:	7am—7pm
Saturday:	7am—7pm
Sunday:	7am—11am and 4pm—7pm
Holidays:	7am—11am and 4pm—7pm

Early drop off and late pickup are available upon request if made in advance.

Pricing

Pricing for each service is outlined below.

Day care

- full day—$24

- half day—$12

Boarding (per night)

- $35 (one dog)

- $65 (two dogs)

Grooming

- Bath—$20-$45, depending on dog size and breed

- Haircut—$20-$45, depending on dog size and breed

- Nail trim—$10

Training

- Puppy Basic—$120

- Puppy Socialization—$25

- Adult Basic—$120

- Adult advanced dog obedience—$120

- Leash walking—$120

Pet Sitting

- Overnight pet care/pet sitting—$70

Dog Walking/Pet Visits

- 30-Minute Visits—$20

- 45- Minute Visits—$25

- 60- Minute Visits—$30

- Vacation Visit (2 visits per day) —$50

Pooper Scooper

- Pooper Scooper Services (Initial Visit) —$30-50

- Once Weekly Poop Scooping Visit—$15/Week

- Bi-Weekly Poop Scooping (once every two weeks) —$20 Bi-Weekly

MARKETING & ADVERTISING

Doggie PlayCare will market its services to potential customers in a variety of ways, including a web site and Facebook page, mailers to be sent to pet owners who have licensed their pets, flyers placed on community bulletin boards, and sponsorship of local "pet walks." Customers will be encouraged to recommend our services to others with a referral reward. Customers who receive exceptional service will be repeat customers, which will be the majority of our clientele.

Pet Services Coordination Business

Parkview Pets LLC

58 James St.
Parkview, MO 64111

Paul Greenland

Parkview Pets LLC is a pet services coordination business, offering a variety of "concierge" services for pet owners, including dog walking, companionship, transportation, and appointment coordination.

EXECUTIVE SUMMARY

Parkview Pets LLC is a pet services coordination business located in Parkview, Missouri, an upscale suburb of Kansas City. The business offers a variety of "concierge" services for pet owners, including dog walking, pet sitting/companionship, transportation, and appointment coordination. Customers have the option of purchasing services individually when needed, or in weekly/monthly packages. Parkview Pets is being established by Jane Irwin. A veterinary technician by training, Jane has decided to start her own business and use her specialized background as a competitive differential in a field with relatively low barriers to entry.

INDUSTRY ANALYSIS

According to data from the American Pet Products Association (APPA), by 2014 pet owners spent an estimated $58.51 billion on their pets each year. Of this total, pet services accounted for $4.73 billion. The association reported that 68 percent of households in the United States (82.5 million homes) owned a pet in 2013-2014. This was an increase from 56 percent of households in 1988. Households with dogs (56.7 million) were by far the largest category, followed by cats at 45.3 million. In terms of the actual number of pets, cats numbered 95.6 million, followed by dogs at 83.3 million, according to the APPA.

MARKET ANALYSIS

Parkview Pets is fortunate to begin operations with a small base of upper-income clients, established through word-of-mouth referrals while owner Jane Irwin was working as a veterinary technician. Because this demographic category has ample disposable income, Jane will concentrate her business' marketing efforts on households with income of $150,000 or more, within a five-mile radius of Parkview.

According to basic demographic data obtained at the Parkview Library, Parkview was home to 6,791 households in 2013. The average household income was $105,131 in 2013. This figure is projected to increase 6.3 percent by 2018. Households with income of more than $150,000 annually represented the largest household income category in 2013 (64.6%, or 4,387 households). Using the APPA's household pet ownership figure of 68 percent, it is reasonable to assume that 2,983 households meeting the business' income threshold have pets, and that this number is somewhat smaller when applied specifically to dog or cat ownership.

PERSONNEL

Jane Irwin (Owner)

A long-time animal lover, Jane Irwin has worked as a veterinary technician since 2004. In that role, she worked alongside veterinarians to provide treatment and diagnose illnesses in a wide range of animals, including dogs and cats. Jane holds an associate's degree in her field, and is licensed as a veterinary technician in the state of Missouri. Although she enjoyed her work at the clinic, the job was demanding, both emotionally and physically. Never married, and without children, she has the flexible schedule needed for success as a pet services provider.

The inspiration to establish Parkview Pets originated at the veterinary clinic where Jane worked. There, she was approached by a long-time, well-to-do customer seeking referrals for dog walking and pet services. The customer explained that trust and reliability were paramount, and eventually asked if Jane would be willing to help. Word-of-mouth referrals ultimately led to two additional customers. Finding it difficult to balance her veterinary assistant position, but not wanting to give up her new side job, Jane began working at the veterinary clinic part-time. Strong word-of-mouth led to increased demand for Jane's pet services, leaving her to formally establish her own business.

Professional & Advisory Support

Parkview Pets has established a commercial checking account with Parkview Bank. Although Jane Irwin will use a popular accounting software program to keep track of her business income and expenses, she received general tax advisement from the local accounting firm of Jackson Spencer LP, which also will prepare and file tax returns for the business.

GROWTH STRATEGY

Based on experience with existing clients, as well as recent service inquiries, Jane Irwin anticipates that she will achieve annual revenues of $85,440 during her first year of business. Furthermore, she anticipates compound annual growth of 25 percent during years two and three. The following table provides a detailed breakdown of revenues by service category:

Service	2015	2016	2017
Dog walking	$ 22,214	$ 27,768	$ 34,710
Transportation	$ 8,544	$ 10,680	$ 13,350
Field trips	$ 5,126	$ 6,408	$ 8,010
Appointment coordination	$ 11,962	$ 14,952	$ 18,690
Pet sitting/companionship	$ 37,594	$ 46,992	$ 58,740
	$ 85,440	$106,800	$133,500

By year three, Parkview Pets will be at full capacity (e.g., it will be difficult or impossible for Jane to take on any additional business without hiring employees or utilizing independent contractors). Midway through 2016, Jane will begin evaluating plans for adding additional staff to the business.

SERVICES

Parkview Pets offers a variety of "concierge" services for pet owners, including dog walking, pet sitting/companionship, transportation, field trips, and appointment coordination. On a percentage basis, Jane Irwin estimates that Parkview Pets' services will break down as follows:

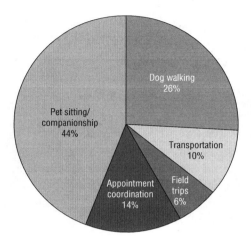

Following is a description of each service:

Dog Walking

Parkview Pets' dog walking services include not only the walk itself, but also a brief summary of the experience (providing assurance that things went well, or to indicate any problems or concerns) for the pet owner via e-mail, phone, or text message. Jane will responsibly pick up and dispose of any waste produced by the pet during the walk. Services also include replenishing or refreshing a pet's food and/or water dish, and administration of basic medication (if needed).

We will take dogs on 15-, 30-, or 45-minute walks in the neighborhood surrounding a client's home at the following price points (rates are for one pet; additional pets $5/each):

*   15 min. ($20)

*   30 min. ($25)

*   45 min. ($30)

*Weekly and monthly packages (which include five walks per week) are available at a discount of 15 percent and 20 percent, respectively.

Doggie Field Trips

For dog owners seeking an experience above and beyond the traditional neighborhood walk, Parkview Pets will take their pet to specific destinations (e.g., local parks, bike paths, forest preserves, and dog parks) for a one-hour walk/hike. This service costs $50 and includes destinations within a five-mile radius of Parkview, transportation, and everything provided during neighborhood walks.

Pet Sitting/Companionship

Parkview Pets' standard pet sitting packages includes spending quality one-on-one time with a customer's pet. Services include replenishing and/or refreshing the pet's food and/or water dish, the administration of basic medication, playing with pet toys, and pet waste cleanup (e.g., backyard and/or litterbox).

- 30 min. visit ($25)
- 60 min. visit ($45)

*The above fees include two dogs or cats. Additional pets can be included for a $5 surcharge.

*Weekly and monthly packages (which include five walks per week) are available at a discount of 15 percent and 20 percent, respectively.

For pet owners seeking overnight companionship arrangements, Parkview Pets will stay at a customer's home for a flat fee of $75.

Pet Transportation

Provided within a five-mile radius of Parkview, transportation services are available in conjunction with, or independent of, appointment coordination. Parkview Pets will transport your dog or cat to a boarding facility, your office (e.g., for a lunchtime visit), to the home of a friend or relative, or any other location. This service is provided at a rate of $45 per hour, billed in 15-minute increments (15-minute minimum).

Appointment Coordination

In addition to transporting your dog or cat to a specific location, Parkview Pets also will coordinate appointments for a variety of services at the owner's specific direction. These include, but are not limited to, grooming, shopping for pet toys and supplies, veterinary care, and boarding. This service is provided at a rate of $45 per hour, billed in 15-minute increments (15-minute minimum).

MARKETING & SALES

Parkview Pets has developed a marketing plan that involves the following primary tactics:

- Printed collateral describing the business and emphasizing Jane Irwin's background as a veterinary technician.

- A magnetic business card featuring the Parkview Pets' name, phone number, e-mail address, and Web site address.

- A word-of-mouth strategy, encouraging existing clients to refer Parkview Pets to their friends and loved ones in exchange for a $25 discount on future services.

- Relationship building with area veterinarians and pet groomers, to generate referrals.

- A Web site with complete details about Parkview Pets and the services it offers, along with testimonials and stories from satisfied customers.

- Flyers distributed via area pet grooming businesses, veterinary clinics, and pet supply stores.

- Highly targeted direct mail campaigns to area pet owners. For this purpose, Jane Irwin will rent the names of subscribers to popular pet-related magazines, as well as the customer files from local pet grooming businesses and supply stores.

- A public relations campaign that involves the submission of periodic stories to local newspapers, demonstrating how Parkview Pets is a perfect solution for busy pet owners.

- Mobile marketing (displaying the Parkview Pets business name, Web site address, and phone number on magnetic graphics applied to the outside of Jane Irwin's vehicle).

OPERATIONS

Location

Parkview Pets will operate as a home-based business at 58 James St. in Parkview. Jane Irwin will use an empty bedroom as home-office space. This space already is equipped with a desk, chair, filing cabinet, desktop computer with productivity and accounting software, and an Internet connection. Jane will communicate with customers via her mobile phone number. She will utilize her personal vehicle for pet transportation services. In addition, Jane has downloaded a mobile app that allows her to track billable hours for clients.

Customer Agreements

Upon receiving a referral, Parkview Pets will provide potential clients with a complementary one-hour consultation at their home, which ideally will include a free "meet-and-greet" session with the owner's pet. Jane Irwin will provide the customer with information about her background, a list of references (if desired), a description of the services provided by Parkview Pets, and information about rates and fees.

Following the consultation, Parkview Pets will prepare a written estimate for the customer. If accepted, customers will be required to sign a basic agreement, outlining the scope of services to be provided. The agreement will specify service fees and payment terms, and will include specific language regarding time frames. In addition, it will include clients' specific instructions regarding the treatment and care of their pets. By establishing an agreement in advance, Parkview Pets will minimize the chance of any potential misunderstandings on the part of the client or service provider.

Legal

Parkview Pets has obtained all of the local permits needed to operate a business in Parkview. The business is bonded and insured (documents and policy available upon request).

Payment

Customers must pay for all of the aforementioned services in advance. Parkview Pets will accept payment via check, or credit/debit card. For the sake of convenience, Jane Irwin will use the payment service, Square, which allows her to accept card payments via her iPhone (in exchange for a 2.75% per-transaction fee).

FINANCIAL ANALYSIS

Jane Irwin anticipates that Parkview Pets essentially will break even during its first year of operations, and then generate net profits during years two and three. In partnership with her accountant, Jane has prepared a complete set of pro forma financial statements for the business, which are available upon request. The following table provides an overview of key projections during Parkview Pets' first three years:

Revenue	2015	2016	2017
Dog walking	$ 22,214	$ 27,768	$ 34,710
Transportation	$ 8,544	$ 10,680	$ 13,350
Field trips	$ 5,126	$ 6,408	$ 8,010
Appointment coordination	$ 11,962	$ 14,952	$ 18,690
Pet sitting/companionship	$ 37,594	$ 46,992	$ 58,740
	$ 85,440	**$106,800**	**$133,500**
Expenses			
Salary	$ 60,000	$ 65,000	$ 70,000
Employment tax	$ 15,600	$ 16,900	$ 18,200
Utilities	$ 350	$ 375	$ 400
Insurance	$ 750	$ 750	$ 750
Office supplies	$ 350	$ 350	$ 350
Equipment	$ 500	$ 1,000	$ 1,000
Marketing & advertising	$ 6,000	$ 7,500	$ 8,500
Telecommunications & internet	$ 1,500	$ 1,500	$ 1,500
Licenses, permits & fees	$ 250	$ 250	$ 250
Total expenses	**$ 85,300**	**$ 93,625**	**$100,950**
Net income/loss	**$ 140**	**$ 13,175**	**$ 32,550**

Shooting Range

R i d g e f i e l d   R a n g e   I n c .

98765 Country Rd. E
Ridgefield, IL 63505

Paul Greenland

Ridgefield Range Inc. is shooting range business located in Ridgefield, Illinois.

EXECUTIVE SUMMARY

Ridgefield Range Inc. is shooting range business located in Ridgefield, Illinois, owned and operated by Tim Stevens and Roy Fisher, who have agreed to acquire Thompson's Shooting Range (an established business with roots dating back nearly 50 years). Bill Thompson, the business' owner, has decided to sell the range, founded by his father in 1965, due to health concerns that have prevented him from investing the time and energy needed for focused growth.

Some of Thompson's facilities are in need of renovation and repair, and new membership options and amenities are needed in order to succeed in an increasingly competitive marketplace. Although Thompson's Shooting Range has many loyal customers, the business has experienced declining membership levels over the past several years, resulting in a downward revenue trend. Tim Stevens and Roy Fisher have a sound strategy for revitalizing and improving the business.

Thompson's Shooting Range is located on 3 acres of land in a rural area of Ridgefield, Illinois. The business includes a 4,000-square-foot building that features a retail store, indoor pistol range, office space, men's and women's restroom facilities, workshop space, locker rooms, a guest lounge, and conference room space. There is room to expand the building to the east. Before agreeing to acquire the business, the owners conducted a detailed evaluation of Thompson's Shooting Range's facilities, operations, and financial position in partnership with a local contractor and accountant.

A sister company named ProtectionStar Inc., which will be located on the grounds of Ridgefield Range, provides both basic and advanced firearm instruction, including "concealed carry" training classes, which equip individuals with the knowledge and skills needed to safely and legally carry a concealed weapon. Roy Fisher is president and majority owner ProtectionStar, while Tim Stevens serves as vice president of operations and has a 19 percent ownership interest.

INDUSTRY ANALYSIS

Operators of shooting ranges and related businesses enjoy support from several leading industry associations. Established in 1871, the Fairfax, Virginia-based National Rifle Association has more than 2.8 million members. Although many of these are individuals, the association also supports businesses, including shooting ranges. In fact, more than 15,000 NRA clubs, associations, and businesses receive services from the association's NRA Clubs & Associations Department, including NRA-endorsed insurance for liability, property & casualty, and health. The NRA's Range Technical Team utilizes a volunteer network to provide assistance in the areas of shooting range development, design, and operations. Training opportunities include courses such as the NRA Club Leadership & Development Course, NRA Range Development and Operations Course, and the NRA Range Safety Officer Course.

Another industry association is the National Shooting Sports Foundation, whose mission is "to promote, protect and preserve hunting and the shooting sports." The foundation's base of approximately 10,000 members includes not only shooting ranges, but also firearms manufacturers, retailers, and distributors.

MARKET ANALYSIS

Interest in gun ownership is on the rise in Illinois, which recently became the very last state in the union to allow concealed carry, following a federal court order in 2013. However, concealed carry is not the only reason for heightened interest. Concerns regarding violent crime within many communities (especially Ridgefield) have led to heightened interest in home defense and security.

An August 2014 report issued by Fenton & Associates, based on national law-enforcement data, attempted to predict the U.S. neighborhoods with the highest rates of violent crime. The report indicated that Illinois was home to five of the 25 most dangerous U.S. neighborhoods, two of which were located in Ridgefield.

Insight regarding the target market for individuals interested in gun ownership, shooting, or concealed carry training can be gained by reviewing reports from states that share demographic data. A report issued on July 31, 2014, by the Florida Department of Agriculture and Consumer Services Division of Licensing provided a profile of concealed weapon or firearm license holders in that state. According to the report, license holders typically are males (78%). In terms of age, the 51-65 category had the highest percentage (31.72%) of active licensees, followed by those aged 36-50 (26.33%), 66+ (23.59%), and 18-35 (18.37%).

Ridgefield Range is open to all customers, regardless of age or gender, but will direct a significant portion of its marketing initiatives toward middle-aged and older males (e.g., those aged 45-74) with higher household income levels (more than $50,000) in the Ridgefield, Illinois metropolitan area. The company also will employ a highly targeted strategy to reach women who have limited or no shooting experience.

Working in partnership with a market research firm, the owners have obtained demographic data on the Ridgefield metropolitan area. In 2014 the area included nearly 345,000 people, 49 percent of which (approximately 169,000) were males. An estimated 60,500 males (35.8% of the total male population) fall within the business' target age range of 45-74. This universe of prospects is further refined to 31,000 after a household income filter of $50,000+ is applied. Although the state does not release gun registration records for marketing purposes, the owners believe that approximately 20 percent of Illinois residents are gun owners. Based on this percentage, it is plausible to believe that about 6,000 of Ridgefield Range's prospects fall within this category.

PERSONNEL

Tim Stevens, President
After retiring as the chief operating officer of a large manufacturing company, Tim Stevens decided to go into business for himself. In conjunction with Roy Fisher, he has plans to significantly improve his

recently acquired shooting range business. In addition, Tim also serves as vice president and part-owner of ProtectionStar, a complementary operation that provides training on the grounds of Ridgefield Range. As majority owner, Tim holds a 60 percent ownership stake in Ridgefield Range.

Roy Fisher, Vice President

Before rising crime rates inspired him to establish Ridgefield Range's sister company, ProtectionStar, entrepreneur Roy Fisher began his business career by developing Fisher's Deli in 1994. Since then, the fast casual restaurant concept has grown to include 13 locations throughout northern Illinois and southern Wisconsin. Roy learned many successful business management principles from his father, Pete, who operated a thriving family-owned hardware store for nearly 40 years. In addition, he holds an undergraduate business administration degree from Northern Illinois University. As vice president, Roy will assist Tim Stevens in the management of the business, and will hold a 40 percent ownership stake.

Support Staff

Ridgefield Range initially will employ two full-time range officers, two part-time range officers, one full-time retail associate, and two part-time retail associates. The range officers' primary goal is to assure the safety of customers and staff by enforcing the Standard Operating Procedure for Range Use. This is accomplished by continuously monitoring shooting lane activity. Additionally, our officers will sell memberships, provide lane and target operation assistance, oversee special events, coordinate training with sister company ProtectionStar, and maintain a member database. Retail associates will manage retail inventory and sell retail items.

Professional & Advisory Support

Ridgefield Range has established a business banking account with Midwestern Regional Bank, including a merchant account for accepting credit card payments. Tax advisement is provided by Leonard Smith Partners LP. The owners worked in partnership with the local law firm, Healy & Brooks, to establish their corporation. The law firm will continue to provide the business with legal counsel on an as-needed basis.

GROWTH STRATEGY

Tim Stevens and Roy Fisher have developed a solid strategy for rebranding and revitalizing Thompson's Shooting Range, with an immediate focus on maximizing the business' customer appeal and profitability. In addition, they have identified a window of opportunity to expand the business after its first three years of operations to accommodate continued growth. Ridgefield Range's growth strategy for its first three years is as follows:

Year one: Rebrand Thompson's Shooting Range as Ridgefield Range. Perform needed facility renovations and repairs. Revamp the business' existing membership program, introducing more membership package options and additional amenities. Achieve annual revenue of $620,970, including retail sales of $151,200.

Year two: Begin offering a video targeting system, providing an exciting option to attract new and retain existing members. Achieve annual revenues of $687,030. Increase retail sales 15 percent, to $173,880.

Year three: Develop a detailed expansion plan and perform a cost-benefit analysis for adding additional indoor shooting lanes, as well as an outdoor trapshooting range (e.g., clay pigeons), to accommodate continued membership and range utilization growth in year four and beyond. Achieve annual revenues of $794,530. Increase retail sales 20%, to $208,656.

SERVICES

Membership

Ridgefield Range will provide a variety of membership options, including monthly, six-month, and annual choices. Family memberships will be available on an annual basis only. In addition, a premium membership option will be available, which gives members priority access for shooting lane reservations, a 10 percent discount on all retail sales (including ammunition), a 20 percent discount on training courses offered by our sister business, ProtectionStar, and five free guest passes annually. Premium memberships are available at the annual level only.

The following table outlines the various membership options at Ridgefield Range and their associated cost:

Membership level	Cost
Individual/monthly	$ 40
Individual/6 months	$210
Individual/annual	$360
Family/annual	$499
Individual/annual (premium)	$510
Family/annual (premium)	$649

*A 15% discount is offered to senior citizens, active military personnel, and members of law enforcement.

Indoor Pistol Range

Ridgefield Range has 10 indoor shooting lanes, with a depth of 30 yards. Our climate controlled facility is equipped with adequate ventilation and sound abatement, to ensure the best environment for customers. Guests are welcome to use handguns up to 44 magnum, along with small-bore rifles. Range fees for non-members are $15 per hour.

Retail

At present, Ridgefield Range's retail space is somewhat limited, mainly providing gun rental and ammunition sales, along with related items such as eye and ear protection. Customers can rent revolvers and semi-automatic handguns in a number of different calibers at a rate of $14 per hour. Ammunition fees are variable. Ridgefield Range also rents eye and ear protection for a nominal charge ($1 per session). Targets are available for purchase for $2/each.

Part of the business' growth strategy focuses on the expansion of retail sales. The owners plan to remodel and expand Ridgefield Range's retail space to include apparel, accessories, knives, as well as a line of Airsoft and paintball products.

Shooting Instruction

All basic and advanced firearm instruction at Ridgefield Range (including concealed carry training) is provided by ProtectionStar Inc., a sister company located on the grounds of Ridgefield Range.

MARKETING & SALES

A marketing plan has been developed for Ridgefield Range that includes these main tactics:

Social Media: Both members and non-members will be able to follow Ridgefield Range on Facebook and Twitter, and take advantage of special offers (designed specifically for both members and non-members).

Web Site: A Web site will be developed that provides essential information about Ridgefield Range, including hours of operation, membership fees, non-member range fees, and rules and regulations. Additionally, the site will include links to the business' social media outlets, including a YouTube channel with video clips. One of the site's primary focal points will be to put inexperienced or non-experienced individuals at ease about shooting, and demonstrate that Ridgefield Range is a welcoming, non-threatening place with friendly staff members who are eager to help others learn and develop their skills.

Mailers: Two four-color, glossy direct-mail pieces will be developed to promote the business. These will include one focused on special events (e.g., bachelor/bachelorette parties, corporate events, scouting troops, church groups, etc.). Another will concentrate on prospective members who meet the criteria listed in the Marketing Analysis section of this plan. In addition to general lists, the business will purchase highly specialized, niche mailing lists from gun shows and gun magazines to ensure that key prospects (e.g., gun enthusiasts and prospective gun owners) are being reached with information about the shooting range and membership opportunities.

Incentives: In conjunction with the aforementioned direct-mail piece, Ridgefield Range will provide individuals with a special incentive (one time only) for considering membership. One hour of range time and handgun rental will be provided at 50 percent off regular cost, along with 20 minutes of free instruction, for individuals who agree to attend a sales consultation with one of our staff and join our mailing list.

Print & Online Advertising: Ridgefield Range will advertise regularly in *Ridgefield Life*, a quarterly lifestyle magazine that reaches the target demographic described in the Market Analysis section of this plan. In addition, the business also will be a regular advertiser in the *Ridgefield Gazette*, a free weekly paper with a loyal readership base.

Exhibition: Ridgefield Range will be a regular exhibitor at regional gun shows, fishing and hunting shows, county fairs, home shows, and related events. The business will exhibit in partnership with our handgun training partner, ProtectionStar.

Radio: In conjunction with ProtectionStar, Ridgefield Range staff also will pursue opportunities to sponsor a handgun-themed radio show on a local AM talk station (this tactic has been successful in other markets nationwide) and will pursue the development of a guest column in a local newspaper.

OPERATIONS

Hours of Operation

Ridgefield Range will maintain the following hours:

Monday—Friday: 10:00 a.m.—8:00 p.m.

Saturday & Sunday: 10:00 a.m.—5:00 p.m.

*Closed on most holidays

Facility Access

Members receive immediate facility access with an ID badge (provided at sign-up, includes name and photo ID), which must be displayed at all times while they are at Ridgefield Range. Access to members-only locker rooms and a member lounge is provided.

Non-members must pay for range time and make appropriate reservations in the retail area (open to the public) before range access is granted.

Standard Operating Procedure for Range Use

1. Customers may reserve shooting lanes by the half-hour or the hour

2. Targets must be purchased from Ridgefield Range (electric/automatic target carrier use provided)

3. Shooters must use only their specific stall (stalls are individually numbered and separated by partitions/single occupancy)

4. All shooting is done at the customer's own risk.

5. Ridgefield Range is not liable for death or injuries resulting from mishandling of any firearms.

6. Customers must adhere to all posted safety rules and regulations, and to range officers' commands, or face ejection from the premises.

7. No loaded firearms are allowed outside of the range area.

8. No food, beverage or tobacco use is allowed at Ridgefield Range.

LEGAL

Ridgefield Range has secured all of the appropriate licenses and permits needed to operate a shooting range in Ridgefield, Illinois. The business adheres to all zoning rules and regulations. In addition, Ridgefield Range is in compliance with all environmental regulations pertaining to air quality and lead abatement. Finally, its owners have received a Federal Firearms License. Specific details regarding the requirements for licensure are available from the Bureau of Alcohol, Tobacco, Firearms and Explosives: https://www.atf.gov/firearms/how-to/become-an-ffl.html.

FINANCIAL ANALYSIS

Prior to becoming Ridgefield Range, Thompson's Shooting Range was an established business with positive cash flow. The owners have agreed to purchase Thompson's for $250,000. Tim Stevens will invest $150,000, while minority partner Roy Fisher will invest $100,000. In addition, Stevens is seeking a $75,000 term loan (36 months, 6% interest), to provide partial funding for renovations and repairs.

The following bar graph provides a snapshot of Ridgefield Range's projected revenue and net income for its first three years of operations:

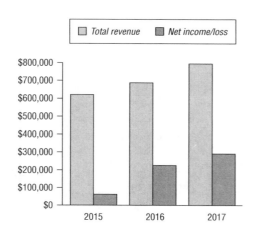

The following pie chart provides a snapshot of anticipated first-year revenues by category:

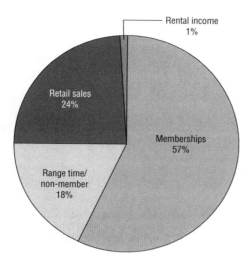

Thompson's Shooting Range's past financial statements are available for review. In addition, Ridgefield Range has prepared a complete set of pro forma financial statements, which are available upon request. The following table provides an overview of key projections during the first three years of operations:

Revenue	2015	2016	2017
Memberships	$352,800	$388,080	$446,292
Range time (non-members)	$108,000	$116,100	$130,612
Retail sales	$151,200	$173,880	$208,656
Rental income (from protection star)	$ 8,970	$ 8,970	$ 8,970
Total revenue	**$620,970**	**$687,030**	**$794,530**
Expenses			
Salaries	$154,520	$162,246	$170,358
Renovations & repairs	$150,000	$ 15,000	$ 15,000
Payroll taxes	$ 23,178	$ 24,337	$ 25,554
Utilities	$ 4,850	$ 5,339	$ 5,872
Insurance	$ 6,500	$ 6,750	$ 7,000
Retail inventory	$105,000	$120,750	$144,900
Range supplies	$ 22,500	$ 24,188	$ 27,211
Office supplies	$ 750	$ 750	$ 750
Equipment	$ 2,000	$ 2,000	$ 2,000
Marketing & advertising	$ 85,000	$ 95,000	$100,000
Telecommunications & internet	$ 1,500	$ 1,500	$ 1,500
Professional development	$ 1,250	$ 1,250	$ 1,250
Travel & entertainment	$ 250	$ 250	$ 250
Licenses, permits & fees	$ 1,500	$ 1,500	$ 1,500
Total expenses	**$558,798**	**$460,860**	**$503,145**
Net income/loss	**$ 62,672**	**$226,170**	**$291,385**

Sports Tournament Organizer

Scramble Sports Tournament Series

31 Stone School Dr.
Muncie, Indiana 47302

Brett Bachelier, Mark Chase, and Justin Renshaw

Our goal is to develop this company into a respected national tournament series encompassing both extreme and traditional sports, and to make this competition open to people of all ages and skill levels.

This business plan provides information relevant to the development of our national tournament series. It describes plans for our events, growth strategies, financial plans, the management team, and an analysis of the industry. It is meant to inform the reader about our company and its operations in years to come.

*This business plan appeared in a previous volume of **Business Plans Handbook.** It has been updated for this volume.*

EXECUTIVE SUMMARY

Objectives

The Scramble Sports Tournament Series is a limited liability company headquartered in Muncie, Indiana. Our goal is to develop this company into a respected national tournament series encompassing both extreme and traditional sports, and to make this competition open to people of all ages and skill levels. We feel that by offering separate divisions for people of various age and skill levels in: Hockey, Soccer, Basketball, Volleyball, Skateboarding, In–Line Skating, and Biking in our first year of operation, with new sports to be added every year, we can tap into a large portion of the massive sports tournament marketplace.

In addition, by offering a vendor tradeshow, live bands, comfortable viewing areas, concessions, merchandise, and a fun family environment, we also hope to encourage spectators to attend our events as well. By enticing both athletes and spectators to attend our events, we will greatly increase our earning potential. We plan not only to charge athletes to compete in our events, but also to charge spectators to view and park at the events, vendors to showcase their merchandise at the events, sponsors to market products at the events, as well as selling concessions, photographs, merchandise, and tournament programs.

We also plan to form strategic partnerships with entities outside of the sporting industry in order to offer other unique competitions and contests which will broaden our customer base. In addition, we will also be partnering with an internet as well as a magazine media outlet so that we may push our content in front of our target market.

In the past our management team was able to start and successfully operate a national hockey tournament series, as well as a regional paintball tournament series. While this is a much larger project, we feel that we have a strong background in the sports tournament industry as well as the contacts and resources at our disposal to help us achieve our goal.

Mission

To become the amateur athletes' hub for knowledge, advancement, and competition.

The mission of the Scramble Sports Tournament Series is to form a respected national tournament series which will allow amateur athletes of various age and skill levels to learn, participate, improve skills, and compete in a variety of both traditional and extreme sports. In addition, contracts with vendors in each sport will provide the amateur athletes with an opportunity to discuss, watch, and learn about different aspects of each sport.

COMPANY HISTORY

The idea behind Scramble spurred from an observation that many athletes are interested in and passionate about a variety of sports; however, the majority of sports tournament series only offer a single sport in one location at a time. The idea behind Scramble is to offer a variety of sports in one single location so that athletes may not only participate in the sport which they are passionate about, but may also have the chance to watch and participate in other sports so that they may develop an understanding and respect for those sports as well.

Our management team observed that in the sports tournament marketplace there are an abundance of tournaments which offer a single sport at a single location, such as a local soccer tournament. In addition, there are a great deal of tournaments which offer a single sport at multiple locations throughout the year, such as a soccer tournament series, and there are a number of tournaments which offer multiple sports at different locations throughout the year, such as a soccer tournament in Muncie and a hockey tournament in Indianapolis.

This leaves a large void in the sports tournament marketplace. It seems that there are relatively few sports tournaments which offer multiple sports at the same location, such as a soccer and hockey tournament at one park. In addition, to take this idea one step further, there are even fewer, if any, sports tournaments which offer both traditional and extreme sports at the same location. This is the void in the sports tournament marketplace which we have identified and intend to fill.

Our design is to offer a multi-sport tournament series, encompassing elements of both extreme and traditional sports, during the summer months when children are not in school and families are more able to travel. In our first year of operation we plan to offer eight regional tournaments taking place in major cities spread across the Midwest, as well as one national championship tournament in Muncie, centrally located in our Midwest region. In addition, during the off season we also plan to offer clinics as well as Sports Highlight tournaments that highlight and showcase each of the sports which we offer: Hockey, Soccer, Basketball, Volleyball, Skateboarding, In–Line Skating, and Biking.

Another big draw for our series will be the extensive vendor showcase. Our goal is to contract with one large vendor in each sport to attend our events and showcase their products as well as answer any questions that athletes may have, provide equipment assistance for athletes, and possibly even bring sponsored athletes to put on demonstrations and explain the intricacies of the various sports to aspiring athletes.

In addition, we also intend to contract with companies outside of the sporting industry so that we may peak other areas of interest at our events as well. While athletes and spectators are at our events we will have a relatively captive audience. Instead of ignoring this audience and forcing them to entertain themselves, or even worse, leave the venue for entertainment, we plan to contract with companies outside of the sporting industry to provide fun family–centered entertainment so that consumers with extra time will desire to remain at the venue and enjoy the atmosphere.

ORGANIZATION

The management team of the Scramble Tournament Series has a strong proven background in the sports tournament industry. One member of the management team, Bobby Risheo, along with his father, Thomas Risheo, was previously involved in starting, owning, and operating a national roller hockey tournament series. In addition, Bobby Risheo was also involved in starting and operating a regional paintball tournament series.

In 2007, the management team of Bobby and Thomas Risheo saw a market opportunity to run hockey tournaments at arenas during the night when the buildings would be otherwise closed and therefore generating no revenue. Due to prior relationships which the management team had with many local hockey rink owners, they were able to convince many local area rink owners to allow them access to the buildings during non–operating nighttime hours on the weekends.

During this time the management team ran a successful "All Night Hockey Tournament Series" at many venues throughout the Muncie area including: Number One Sports Complex located in Hartford City; The Rink located in Indianapolis; Ice Babies located in Muncie; and Wilbur Arena located in Fishers.

As the popularity of the series grew, the demand became too great to simply run the tournaments in the overnight fashion. There was simply not enough time to accommodate all of the teams that wished to participate in the series. Knowing that they had a loyal customer base in the Muncie marketplace, the management team decided to expand their tournaments from nighttime events to weekend–long tournaments and to change the name of the series from "Evening Hockey Tournament Series" to "Weekend Hockey Series."

With the new name and business model the team continued to promote their tournaments and continued to fill them to capacity. While running weekend–long events was much more difficult and time consuming than simply running one night events, the management team found that having consumers at the event for a longer period of time allowed for additional offerings and they were able to expand their revenue streams by offering concessions, merchandise, and even having side competitions when venues had the appropriate space required. These additional revenue streams, along with the additional capacity created by expanding the events from one night to an entire weekend, showed positive results on the company's financials.

With their new business model showing signs of success in the Muncie marketplace, the management team decided that expansion into other areas could be profitable as well. They began by taking the series to a regional level and offering similar events in Lansing, Michigan; Toledo, Ohio; Madison, Wisconsin; and Chicago, Illinois.

Upon success in these areas the management team decided to dream big and expanded the series to a national level by offering sixteen regional qualifying tournaments throughout the United States and a series national championship tournament located at the Number One Sports Complex in Hartford City.

While expanding to a national level continued to make the series even more popular and even more profitable, the management team had never intended to make the series their full–time career. Both members of the team had prior business careers which they wished to return to; therefore, in 2010 the team decided to exit the series via a buyout agreement with another national hockey tournament series whereby the buying series simply dissolved "Weekend Hockey Series" and shifted its clientele into their series.

Late in the year 2010 however Bobby Risheo once again decided to start and operate another tournament series, this time in the paintball industry. While working at a local paintball shop located in Indianapolis, *Total Paintball Madness*, Bobby had developed a close relationship with the owner. When the owner, Josh Doctor, decided to open playing fields in addition to the store, Bobby approached him with the offer to start, operate, and market a regional paintball tournament series at the new fields.

With most of the owner's time being tied up trying to manage the daily business of his store and his new playing fields, he did not have time to worry about a tournament series himself; however, he did think that it was a good idea. Therefore, he allowed Bobby, who had been working at the store for over a year at that point, to run the series. The structure was set up so that the field took a portion of the profits from each tournament and Bobby retained the rest of the profit himself. This worked out well for both parties since Bobby was not required to put up any capital to get the series off the ground, and Mr. Doctor was able to retain ownership and full rights to the series itself.

The buzz generated by the opening of the new fields combined with the marketing efforts of Bobby Risheo created an atmosphere which drew top paintball teams from around the region almost instantaneously. In fact, the first tournament held at the field drew approximately 35 teams, almost 25% more teams than expected and included teams traveling from as far as Knoxville, Tennessee and Chicago, Illinois—cities in which marketing campaigns were not even launched. While Bobby stepped down as tournament director late in 2014, the tournament series is still in operation today and remains one of the top regional paintball tournament series in the area.

BUSINESS STRATEGY

Currently the Scramble Sports Tournament Series is in the start–up phase. The major milestones which we feel we have accomplished towards bringing our business into fruition include:

- Having designed the format which we wish to operate by
- Identifying the sports which we intend to offer in our first season
- Setting a tentative schedule for the 2015–2016 calendar year
- Creating event outlines detailing how each of our various events will operate
- Designing sponsor and vendor packages
- Identifying strategic partnership opportunities
- Performing an analysis of the competition
- Analyzing the industry in which we will be operating
- Identifying various market segments for our tournament series
- Developing a marketing strategy to reach our various market segments
- Outlining the development milestones which we intend to accomplish in the future

Management Summary

Bobby B. Risheo—Owner/CEO

Bobby is a senior majoring in entrepreneurship in the Kelley Business School at Indiana University. Bobby's background in the sports industry is very extensive both as a participant and as a tournament operator. In addition to operating hockey and paintball tournaments, Bobby has participated in a great deal of sports tournaments. Bobby traveled throughout North America playing roller hockey tournaments for four years in addition to traveling around the United States playing paintball tournaments for three years. This extensive tournament knowledge has helped Bobby to understand what features of tournaments help to make them successful, as well as what features tend to lead to failure.

In addition to tournament experience, Bobby has also worked in the life insurance industry at his father's brokerage firm, Family Insurance Solutions. This has provided Bobby with the skills to work with complex database systems, allowed Bobby the opportunity to create and launch various marketing campaigns, as well as allowing Bobby the experience of personal selling.

After having started and operating two separate tournament series in two completely unrelated sports, Bobby came to realize that no matter what the sport may be, the format for running a tournament series remains similar. With this in mind he decided that if he were to create a format for running a national tournament series for a single sport, he might as well expand the idea and apply that same format to a number of different sports in order to create something which has never been done before.

Chad Bloom—Founding Member

Chad is a senior entrepreneurship student at the University of Michigan. In the past Chad has acted as a substitute manager for the Sports Park in Redford, Michigan where daily patron numbers often exceeded 300 people. Also, while working at the Sports Park, Chad helped to organize an annual Goofy Olympics in which nearly 400 children were separated by age groups and competed against one another in an attempt to win their division and be honored at the awards ceremony. Through his past experiences working at Sports Park Chad has gained the managerial and organizational skills necessary to direct and organize large groups of people.

In addition to large group organization, Chad has also dealt first–hand with sales, marketing, and quality control at his internship with Physicstone in 2013. During his time at Physicstone, Chad created accounts for new customers using ACT, which is a Windows–based business organizational tool. Chad also made sales calls to new customers and created Excel databases to organize seasonal mailers for the marketing department. Finally, Chad also called existing customers to ensure customer satisfaction and retention.

Will Reed—Founding Member

Will is a senior at Saint Louis University and is majoring in entrepreneurship. Will's career in leadership and management roles includes acting as a fleet coordinator for the Osage River Barge Company for the last one and a half years. During this time he has organized and deployed tug and barge operations on Lake of the Ozarks. This position also consisted of one on one customer relations that gave him first–hand personal selling experience.

Will has also acted as a boat and watercraft rental manager for The Barge Floating Restaurant where he coordinated all employee activities and contributed to his customers' overall experience with the company, providing an exciting and fulfilling experience for them. Will has been the Internal Vice President for Pi Kappa Alpha fraternity for the past year. His duties as Vice President include the organization of community service and philanthropy events, as well as conducting chapter meetings.

Will is very enthusiastic about, and has a broad range of experience and knowledge in, a wide variety of sports. He acted as captain of both his football and basketball team at Osage High School. Will's experiences in management and athletics have given him the skills necessary to organize people, events, and operations that are necessary to help Scramble reach its goals in the coming years. Furthermore, his leadership roles have given him the knowledge, influence, and charisma to help Scramble become the athlete's hub for knowledge, advancement, and competition.

SERVICES

Tournament Overview

In order to separate ourselves from the competition we plan to offer all seven of our sports in one location at the same time. Not only do we intend to offer all of our sports in one park, but we intend to strategically position our various sports playing surfaces close together (while still leaving room for comfortable viewing areas, vendor booths, sponsor displays and any other such desired space) so that spectators will be able to view a number of different sports without having to travel entirely across the venue.

Our design is to have two divisions in each sport which we intend to offer. The first division will be the competitive division and will consist of top athletes from around the Midwest in each sport. Athletes will be divided by age; however, the only other restriction will be that no professional athletes will be allowed to compete.

In order to entice these top athletes from around the country to participate in our tournament series, we will be working with vendors and sponsors to provide a variety of prizes which will be given to the winners of each division. In addition, we will be creating an atmosphere which will help these top players not only showcase their skills, but also improve them along the way. We will have high quality vendors in each sport on hand to answer any of the athletes' questions and offer advice and tips to help them rise to the top of their game.

The second division will be the recreational division. This division will consist of athletes who simply wish to try out a given sport, or who simply wish to play for fun, not on a competitive level. This division will not have any prizes for the winners, but rather participation prizes and prizes for things such as the 20th point of the day. The goal of this division is to give athletes of all ages a chance to participate in a sport which they have limited knowledge about or limited skill in, but yet wish to get the experience of playing the sport in an exciting venue the same way it is designed to be played by top athletes at a competitive level.

Format

In order to make this series available to more participants and accommodate more teams we have decided not to offer full sports games but rather scaled down versions of the sports. We feel that by offering scaled down versions of the sports with the same basic rules and principals but smaller playing surfaces, shorter game lengths and less participants on the court at a time we can not only accommodate more teams, but will also open the series up to groups of people who do not currently play on an organized team but are interested in becoming involved in a given sport.

In addition to offering full team registration, we will also offer the option to register as an individual and be placed on a team according to age and skill level. We feel that by allowing individuals as well as full teams to register we will greatly increase our draw and will be able to gain access to a great deal of individuals who would have otherwise not participated in the sports tournament marketplace.

In addition to allowing us to cater to a larger market, using a scaled down format also allows us a great deal of additional venue options. Since we will be using scaled down versions of playing surfaces rather than the much larger regulation size surfaces we will be able to purchase and transport our own playing surfaces. Since we will be utilizing our own playing surfaces for each sport we can select venues based on location as opposed to venues which can accommodate all of our sports. By choosing venues located in central areas we will provide participants and spectators easier access and less transportation problems, which should increase attendance.

Finally, using the scaled down format will provide for more exciting competition. Since the playing surface will be smaller than regulation, games should be much faster pace and result in higher scores. Higher scoring games usually result in greater fan interest and involvement and should produce a great deal of excitement. Since many spectators will be viewing new sports for the first time, this more exciting format should help to pique the interest of many new fans and help to generate cross interest among the sports.

Tournament Sports

In order to ensure that each sport receives the attention and publicity that is required to attain the highest possible standards within each individual sport, we have decided to start by offering four traditional team sports and three individual extreme sports. Each year we plan to add an additional traditional sport, as well as one or two additional extreme sports. This idea of starting small and slowly building will allow us to develop personal relationships with the vendors, athletes, and spectators related to each sport, as well as allowing us to expand into sporting events which our patrons are interested in. Our goal is to develop a loyal following that comes to all of our tournaments and to help them expand their horizons by offering events which they are interested in.

Hockey

Due to our management team's previous experience in the hockey tournament industry, hockey was the first sport which we decided to offer. Based on the past success that our management team had in running national hockey tournaments, we feel that this is a logical sport to offer. Due to our previous involvement in the hockey industry we have been able to redevelop many relationships with hockey vendors much more rapidly and with less effort than will be required in other sports.

In addition to our prior experience in the sport of hockey, we also see an opportunity in the street hockey tournament market due to the large void that now exists since the collapse of the NHL's street hockey series. Prior to the recent hockey strike the NHL sponsored a program called NHL Breakout. The NHL Breakout series was a street hockey tournament series that traveled around the country. Due to problems with the NHL, the league decided to stop running outside programs such as the NHL Breakout series. Now that the NHL is back in business, the league has decided not to reopen its Breakout series, but rather to lend its name to NARCH, the largest full scale roller hockey tournament series in North America.

While the NHL has already decided to sponsor another roller hockey league, the style of play between NHL Breakout and NARCH are drastically different. This means that all of the customers of the NHL Breakout series are currently without a league to participate in. We have decided to model many of the features of our league around the NHL Breakout model; however, we have decided to change the format some.

We intend to hold our competition on three small scale hockey rinks as opposed to the street as NHL Breakout did. We feel that holding the competition in an actual rink as opposed to on the street will make the tournament series stand out as something special and out of the ordinary as opposed to something that athletes could simply do at home. We will be purchasing three small scale hockey rinks which will be 60 ft. long x 30 ft. wide x 42 in. high with a full net around the top. We feel that having three small scale rinks setup outdoors will entice athletes and spectators alike to come watch a new version of street hockey come to life.

Our hockey games will consist of two six–minute halves with a continuously running clock. Game play will consist of two three–man teams with one goalie and up to two subs. Normal hockey and soccer fields will be identical and interchangeable street hockey rules will apply (rulebook will be available online as well as provided at registration); the head referee on the rink will have the final ruling on any discrepancies.

Soccer

Soccer has always been a very popular sport with international appeal; however, recent years have seen the popularity of soccer skyrocketing in the United States, especially among children.

Since the glorification of soccer stars such as David Beckham through outlets such as movies and tabloids, the sport has gained amazing popularity. Today pictures of soccer athletes grace the tops of billboards, movies, and even television shows. The trend has gone so far that one cable network recently began airing a series titled, "Soccer Players' Wives." With the popularity of soccer once again on the rise here in America, we feel that offering this world class sport with international appeal is a smart decision.

In addition to the growing popularity of soccer among Americans, the Hispanic population has always had a large involvement in the sport. While the Hispanic population of the Midwest is only roughly 22%, many soccer leagues find that a large portion of their participants are of Hispanic descent. In fact, more than 75% of the players in the Northern Nevada Soccer League are Hispanic, and the Hispanic population in northern Nevada is only roughly 19%. We feel that adding soccer to our mix of sports may generate some cultural diversity in our customer base, and we would like to encourage people from all different backgrounds to participate in our events.

In addition to providing some diversity among our customer base, soccer will prove to be helpful when it comes to expansion on both the west and east coasts as well as in the south. While the Hispanic population in the Midwest may only be 22%, 49% of the Hispanic population of the United States lives in either California or Texas, and 23% of Florida's population is Hispanic as well. In addition, the total Hispanic population in the United States grew 58% between 2000 and 2010. This was an increase of 13 million Hispanics in a period of 10 years. While this high percentage of Hispanics does not guarantee a successful soccer market in these regions, it would seem absurd not to offer soccer and ignore this fast growing market.

Much like hockey, we feel that in order to make the soccer competition stand out and have appeal we must make the soccer field special. We will be purchasing three soccer fields that will have dimensions identical to those of our hockey rinks, 60 ft. long x 30 ft wide x 42 in. high with a net around the top. Also, just like hockey, soccer will consist of two six–minute continuously running clock halves, and game play will consist of two teams with three players, one goalie and two subs. Normal indoor soccer rules will apply (rulebook will be available online as well as provided at registration) and the head referee on the field will have the final say in the event of any discrepancies.

Basketball

Basketball is a sport which offers great diversity. Basketball is enjoyed by people from many different walks of life, from the Ivy League college basketball teams to people playing basketball in the projects; it seems that people from all different backgrounds can find some common ground when it comes to the sport of basketball. Therefore, we feel that basketball is a great sport for us to offer in our first year of operation.

As it is easy to see from our unique mix of extreme and traditional sports, we are not simply trying to cater to one specific social group's taste in our tournament series, but rather trying to diversify our offerings and provide something that everyone can enjoy. By offering basketball as one of our sports in our first year of operation we hope to attract a diverse crowd which will add to the popularity of our tournament series.

Unlike soccer and hockey, we feel that basketball fans would not be attracted to a fancy court. We feel that basketball patrons enjoy the fact that basketball can be played anywhere, anytime, and by anybody. In designing our basketball tournament series we have decided to take an approach similar to that of Hoop It Up and to simply use high quality portable basketball goals placed on pavement. We feel that using street basketball courts will set a certain tone to our basketball tournament series and will help to draw a diverse crowd of players as opposed to intimidating those players not used to playing in big gymnasiums.

Once again modeling ourselves after the Hoop It Up competition, our basketball games will be played in a half court format and will consist of a 30 minute run clock game which ends when either the time expires or one team reaches 20 points. Game play will consist of two teams of three players with two subs. Normal half-court basketball rules will apply (rulebook will be available online as well as provided at registration) and the head referee on the court will have the final say in the event of a discrepancy.

Volleyball

Volleyball is a sport which can be enjoyed by people of all ages and skill levels. One of the main reasons that we decided to offer volleyball in our first year of operation is to illustrate that just because we are not offering separate men's and women's divisions does not mean that men and women cannot compete together. We intend for all of our sports to be coed; however, volleyball is one sport which we feel could easily be dominated by women.

While there are a great deal of talented women hockey, soccer, and basketball players, we feel that the number of skilled female volleyball players is more than likely higher than the number of skilled male players (at an amateur level in the age groups we intend to offer). We feel that the volleyball competition could provide an opportunity for an all women's team to defeat any coed and all male teams. While the idea of a female team winning the competition is not extraordinary, we feel that by offering female dominated sports such as volleyball we may be able to peak the interest of many women who would otherwise not be interested in sports tournaments. Once these women are at our events, perhaps another sport will peak their interest and we can once again generate some cross interest among the sports in a consumer who would have otherwise never put herself in a position to experience such an atmosphere.

In addition, volleyball is also a sport played by many couples. We feel that if parents are going to be taking their children to our tournament series and staying there all weekend with the child anyway, many parents may decide to enter the volleyball competition to provide themselves with something to do while their child is not competing. Since parents will be at the event already, it makes since to offer a sport which will cater to their taste.

Finally, volleyball also allows us a lot of creative venue opportunities. Volleyball can be played on practically any type of surface, and each different surface changes the game slightly Volleyball can be played on grass, sand, pavement, or in a gymnasium. Our goal is to continually switch the format of our volleyball tournaments to keep each one exciting. Some tournaments may involve beach volleyball while some may be played inside of a gymnasium. One of the great things about offering a sport such as volleyball is the diverse venue selections which will allow us to keep the competition interesting.

Our volleyball courts will consist of six high–quality portable volleyball nets. The volleyball game will be played by two teams of four players with up to two subs. Game play will consist of one 30–minute run clock time limit and games will end when either time expires, or one team reaches 11 points. Normal volleyball rules will apply based upon the type of playing surface being utilized at each given venue (rulebook will be available online as well as provided at registration), and the head referee on the court will have the final say regarding any discrepancies.

Skateboarding/In–line/Biking
We choose to offer this mixture of extreme sports in our first year of operation for a number of reasons. To begin, this mix provides a fairly diverse look at some of the different aspects and movements required by extreme sports. These three events were pioneers in the extreme sports category and although they may not receive quite as much press in recent times as some of the other extreme sports which have sprung onto the scene, they still remain staples of the extreme sports industry and should prove to form a great foundation for the extreme sports side of the tournament series.

In addition to the appeal of these sports, all of these sports also allow for the same structures to be used throughout the competition which will help to cut down on costs as well as space requirements. All of these sports utilize the same ramps and rails, meaning one course can be designed for all three sports. Also, all of these sports operate according to the same format so we will have less scheduling issues by running three sports with one format on the same course as opposed to running three separate formats on one course.

We will have three separate competitions in each sport for a total of nine overall extreme sports competitions. The format for the competitions is as follows:

Vert

- An extreme sports vert competition consists of every athlete making two 45–second runs in the qualifying round. In addition, the top ten athletes then qualify for the finals where each athlete makes three 45–second runs.

- An extreme sports vert best trick competition consists of one 45–minute jam session in which every rider performs as many tricks as possible in an attempt to impress the judges.

Street

- An extreme sports street competition consists of every athlete making three 75–second runs.

- An extreme sports street best trick competition consists of one 15–minute jam session in which every rider performs as many tricks as possible in an attempt to impress the judges.

Park

- An extreme sports park competition consists of every athlete making two 3–minute runs.

Each athlete registering to participate in one of the extreme sports will automatically be registered for all three competitions in that sport. Normal rules will apply for each sport (rulebook will be available online as well as provided at registration) and judges scores will be final determinants for all competitions.

Event Schedules and Outlines

Tournament Series Schedule

When developing a schedule for our tournament series we encountered a number of constraints which we had to consider. The following is a list of the constraints which we took into account along with the reasons why we felt it was important to consider these issues.

Desire to operate series tournaments during summer months

- Children are out of school

- Families are more able to travel

- Warm weather allows all sports to be played outside

Seasonal weather

- Need to hold certain sports outside in warm weather

- Ability to hold certain sports indoors

- Varying climates in selected cities

Travel logistics (available upon request)

- Desire to draw maximum amount of patrons to events

- Minimize travel for both tournament staff and patrons

Sports appeal

- Venue availability for showcased sports

- Offer showcased sports in cities with a strong market

Clinic Event Outline

The first events which we intend to offer to kick off our national tournament series are two clinics. These clinics will serve multiple functions including:

- Providing individuals the opportunity to meet other people of their same age and skill level so that they can form teams to enter into our tournaments

- Helping athletes improve their abilities before the start of the series

- Building excitement and generating a buzz about the series

- Qualifying participants for the Officiate & Participate program of the tournament series

Since the clinics will be taking place in April, May and August, when children are still likely to be in school, we will operate the clinics according to the following schedule:

	Start	End	Usable hours
Friday	5:00 PM	10:00 PM	5
Saturday	12:00 PM	5:00 PM	5
Sunday	12:00 PM	5:00 PM	+ 5
			15 hours
			× 60 min.
			900 min.

The clinics will offer professional guidance from top athletes in each sport which will be offered in the tournament series. These clinics will be three day long events whereby on the first day athletes are evaluated as to their skill level and broken down into groups to practice various skills. On the second day athletes will continue training with professional athletes in their chosen sport. In addition, those athletes wishing to participate in the Officiate & Participate program of the tournament series will be given special refereeing classes. Finally, on the third day a small competition will be held whereby athletes are grouped into teams, based upon age and skill level so that teams are fair, and a mini tournament will be held. Athletes participating in the Officiate & Participate program will be observed while they referee games which they are not participating in so that they may be qualified to ref during the national tournament series.

In addition to the two clinics which will be held before the start of the national tournament series, we also intend to offer one clinic immediately following the conclusion of the national tournament series. This clinic also serves multiple functions including:

- Allowing teams that did not place as desired to improve their skills before the start of the next season

- Allowing participants to qualify for the Officiate & Participate program while they are still excited about the tournament series and before something else piques their interest

- Allowing us to kick off any new sports which we intend to offer by demonstrating and teaching them to participants thereby generating interest in the sports and allowing children eight months to practice before competition starts

Based on the amount of playing surfaces which we intend to purchase and the amount of time during which we plan to hold the clinics, we estimate that we will be able to accommodate roughly 100 athletes in each sport. We intend to charge $115 dollars, which is slightly less than the average clinic fees of $120–$150. In addition to charging less for our clinics, we are also providing three days of training from a professional in each sport, as well as allowing our athletes to qualify for the Officiate & Participate program of our national tournament series.

Series Tournament Event Outline

The series tournaments will consist of a full scale tournament being held in each of the sports which we offer. There will be seven individual sports tournaments taking place at one venue for the entire weekend.

Time constraints will be a big issue for our tournaments due to the volume of athletes that we will be trying to accommodate and the limited availability of the playing surfaces. In order to utilize as many hours of game time as possible, we will run our regional events based on the following schedule:

	Start	End	Usable hours
Friday	8:00 AM	10:00 PM	14
Saturday	7:00 AM	10:00 PM	15
Sunday	7:00 AM	8:00 PM	+ 13
			42 hours
			× 60 min.
			2,520 min.

This gives us a total of 42 usable hours, or 2,520 minutes, at any given playing surface assuming that the surface is lighted and continuously available for use. Based on this schedule we have developed the following constraints for each of the sports which we intend to offer in our first year of operation.

	Hockey	Soccer		Basketball	Volleyball
Halves	2	2			
Length of halve	× 6 min.	× 6 min.			
Time of game	12 min.	12 min.			
Warm-up	3 min.	3 min.	Time of game	30 min.	30 min.
Between halves	2 min.	2 min.	Warm-up	3 min.	3 min.
Between games	+ 3 min.	+ 3 min.	Between games	+ 2 min.	+ 2 min.
	20 min.	20 min.		35 min.	35 min.

Based on the above constraints and the number of playing surfaces which we intend to setup for each sport we will be able to accommodate games according to the following schedule:

	Hockey	Soccer	Basketball	Volleyball
Usable hours	2,520 min.	2,520 min.	2,520 min.	2,520 min.
Game length	/ 20 min.	/ 20 min.	/ 35 min.	/ 35 min.
Games accommodated	126	126	72	72
Number of courts	× 3	× 3	× 6	× 6
Games available	378	378	432	432

Based on the above schedule we are hoping to attract teams according to the following table:

Hockey Recreational teams	Age	Competitive teams	Soccer Recreational teams	Age	Competitive teams
12	10	12	12	10	12
12	12	12	12	12	12
12	14	12	12	14	12
12	16	12	12	16	12
6	18	6	6	18	6
6	Junior	6	6	Junior	6
6	Adult	6	6	Adult	6
66	**Total teams**	66	66	**Total teams**	66
	132			132	

Basketball Recreational teams	Age	Competitive teams	Volleyball Recreational teams	Age	Competitive teams
12	10	12	12	10	12
12	12	12	12	12	12
12	14	12	12	14	12
12	16	12	12	16	12
6	18	6	6	18	6
6	Junior	6	6	Junior	6
6	Silver	6	6	Silver	6
6	Gold	6	6	Gold	6
72	**Total teams**	72	72	**Total teams**	72
	144			144	

If each division with 12 teams plays two six–team round robin competitions with the winner of each round robin competition competing in one championship game to determine the winner of the division, each division will require thirty–one games. In addition, if each division with 6 teams plays one round robin competition with the top two teams competing in one championship game to determine the winner of the division, each division will require 16 games. Based on these constraints, the following number of games will be necessary.

Hockey				Soccer		
Recreational teams	Age	Competitive teams		Recreational teams	Age	Competitive teams
31	10	31		31	10	31
31	12	31		31	12	31
31	14	31		31	14	31
31	16	31		31	16	31
16	18	16		16	18	16
16	Junior	16		16	Junior	16
16	Adult	16		16	Adult	16
172	**Total games**	172		172	**Total games**	172
	344				344	

Basketball				Volleyball		
Recreational teams	Age	Competitive teams		Recreational teams	Age	Competitive teams
31	10	31		31	10	31
31	12	31		31	12	31
31	14	31		31	14	31
31	16	31		31	16	31
16	18	16		16	18	16
16	Junior	16		16	Junior	16
16	Silver	16		16	Silver	16
16	Gold	16		16	Gold	16
188	**Total games**	188		188	**Total games**	188
	376				376	

Based on the above information we have comprised the following table to illustrate how much extra court time we will have available in each sport.

	Hockey	Soccer	Basketball	Volleyball
Total games	344	344	376	376
Game length	× 20 min.	× 20 min.	× 35 min.	× 35 min.
Used hours	6,880 min.	6,880 min.	13,160 min.	13,160 min.
Usable hours	2,520 min.	2,520 min.	2,520 min.	2,520 min.
Number of courts	× 3	× 3	× 6	× 6
Total usable hours	7,560 min.	7,560 min.	15,120 min.	15,120 min.
Total usable hours	7,560 min.	7,560 min.	15,120 min.	15,120 min.
Used hours	− 6,880 min.	− 6,880 min.	−13,160 min.	−13,160 min.
Extra hours	680 min.	680 min.	1,960 min.	1,960 min.
	/ 60 min.	/ 60 min.	/ 60 min.	/ 60 min.
Extra hours	11.3 hrs.	11.3 hrs.	32.6 hrs.	32.6 hrs.

This extra time will be used for the skills competitions and awards ceremonies in each sport as well as providing a buffer should we fall behind schedule for any unforeseen reason.

The schedule for our extreme sports in our first year of operation will work a bit differently. Each of our extreme sports has a set amount of fixed time required as well as a certain amount of time that must be allocated to each athlete. The extreme sports will operate according to the following schedule:

	Vert			Street		Park
	Prelims	Finals	Best trick	Competition	Best trick	Competition
Length of run	45 sec.	45 sec.	45 min.	75 sec.	15 min.	180 sec.
Setup	+ 15 sec.	+ 15 sec.		+ 15 sec.		+ 15 sec.
Total time of run	1 min.	1 min.		90 sec.		195 sec.
Number of runs	× 2	× 3		× 3		× 2
Total time per skater	**2 min.**	3 min.		**4.5 min.**		**6.5 min.**
		× 10 athletes				
		30 min.				

Based upon this schedule, the extreme sports will require the following amount of fixed and variable time:

Fixed time		Variable time	
Vert finals	30 min.	Vert prelims	2 min.
Vert best trick	45 min.	Street competition	4.5 min.
Street best trick	15 min.	Park competition	6.5 min.
Total fixed time	90 min.	Time per athlete	13 min.

While the park competition requires the use of the entire skate park, the street and vert competitions may take place within the skate park at the same time. Based on this information the following table illustrates how many athletes can be accommodated in each of our extreme sports.

	Vert	Street
Usable hours	2,520 min.	2,520 min.
Total fixed time	− 75 min.	− 15 min.
Time remaining	2,445 min.	2,505 min.
Variable time	2 min.	4.5 min.
Park competition time	+ 6.5 min.	+ 6.5 min.
Total time	8.5 min.	11 min.
Time remaining	2,445 min.	2,505 min.
Total time	/ 8.5 min.	/ 11 min.
Total athletes accommodated	287	227
Total athletes accommodated	—	227
Number of extreme sports	/ —	/ 3
Total athletes per sport	—	75

National Championship Event Outline

Teams that qualify by placing in the top two at either a series tournament or a Sport Showcase tournament qualify to compete in the national championship. Due to the volume of athletes which we are estimating will be participating in our national championship event, we will need the ability to accommodate more teams in each sport; therefore, our national championship will be a four day event instead of a three day event as the regional tournaments are. The schedule for the national championship is as follows:

	Start	End	Usable hours
Thursday	8:00 AM	10:00 PM	14
Friday	7:00 AM	10:00 PM	15
Saturday	7:00 AM	10:00 PM	15
Sunday	7:00 AM	8:00 PM	+ 13
			57 hours
			× 60 min.
			3,420 min.

This gives us a total of 57 usable hours, or 3,420 minutes, at any given playing surface assuming that the surface is lighted and continuously available for use. We will no longer be limiting each division to a set number of teams but rather we will accommodate any qualifying teams that wish to participate and adjust the schedule accordingly. The following illustrates the maximum number of teams/individuals which could qualify to attend our national championship event:

Hockey			Soccer		
Recreational teams	Age	Competitive teams	Recreational teams	Age	Competitive teams
18	10	18	18	10	18
18	12	18	18	12	18
18	14	18	18	14	18
18	16	18	18	16	18
18	18	18	18	18	18
18	Junior	18	18	Junior	18
18	Adult	18	18	Adult	18
126	Total teams	126	126	Total teams	126
	252			252	

Basketball			Volleyball		
Recreational teams	Age	Competitive teams	Recreational teams	Age	Competitive teams
18	10	18	18	10	18
18	12	18	18	12	18
18	14	18	18	14	18
18	16	18	18	16	18
18	18	18	18	18	18
18	Junior	18	18	Junior	18
18	Silver	18	18	Silver	18
18	Gold	18	18	Gold	18
144	Total teams	144	144	Total teams	144
	288			288	

Skateboarding			In-Line		
Recreational teams	Age	Competitive teams	Recreational teams	Age	Competitive teams
18	10	18	18	10	18
18	12	18	18	12	18
18	14	18	18	14	18
18	16	18	18	16	18
18	18	18	18	18	18
18	Adult	18	18	Adult	18
108	Total teams	108	108	Total teams	108
	216			216	

Biking		
Recreational teams	Age	Competitive teams
18	10	18
18	12	18
18	14	18
18	16	18
18	18	18
18	Adult	18
108	Total teams	108
	216	

The following is a list of constraints on the number of games which we will be able to offer during our national championship.

	Hockey	Soccer	Basketball	Volleyball
Usable hours	3,420 min.	3,420 min.	3,420 min.	3,420 min.
Game length	/ 20 min.	/ 20 min.	/ 35 min.	/ 35 min.
Games accommodated	171	171	97	97
Number of courts	× 3	× 3	× 6	× 6
Games available	513	513	582	582

We will have to adjust the schedule for our national championship event based upon the number of qualifying teams that decide to participate. While we would like to see all of the qualifying teams compete in our national championship, this scenario is not likely. Some teams are likely to miss the event, thereby throwing off any type of schedule which we could develop. For this reason, we do not intend to create a detailed event outline for the national championship event until we have completed the registration process for this event.

Sports Highlight Tournament Outline

Sports Highlight tournaments will provide us with a way to highlight each sport offered in our tournament series. From September thru March we will offer one tournament per month, visiting each city on our series schedule, and showcasing a different sport in each city.

The Sports Highlight tournaments will be centered around a single showcased sport but will still offer a multi-sport format. While all of the sports which we offer in our series may not be offered at every Sports Highlight tournament, every tournament will have a multi-sport format. We will be selecting venues that accentuate the sport being showcased for that event, but will still accommodate other sports as well.

We will offer a combination of either one extreme sport and two traditional sports, or one traditional sport and three extreme sports. This format will allow us to accommodate the maximum number of participants in the sports which we will be showcasing. For example, when we offer soccer we will not offer hockey so that we may use all six of our rinks for the soccer competition. In addition, when we offer basketball and volleyball we will select venues which have extra courts in these sports so that we may accommodate more athletes.

The Sports Highlight tournaments will provide a fast track to the national competition. The tournaments will count as a national qualifier for the showcased sport, but not for any of the additional sports. This means that the top two teams competing in the showcased sport will automatically receive invitations to attend the national championship event.

Due to the fact that children will still be in school during the months when these events will be taking place, we will be forced to once again modify our schedule. For this reason the Sports Highlight tournaments will operate according to the following schedule:

	Start	End	Usable hours
Friday	5:00 AM	10:00 PM	5
Saturday	7:00 AM	10:00 PM	15
Sunday	7:00 AM	8:00 PM	+ 13
			33 hours
			× 60 min.
			1,980 min.

This gives us a total of 33 usable hours, or 1,980 minutes, at any given playing surface assuming that the surface is lighted and continuously available for use. Based on this information, the following is a list of constraints on the number of games which we will be able to offer during our Sports Highlight tournaments.

	Hockey	Soccer	Basketball	Volleyball
Usable hours	1,980 min.	1,980 min.	1,980 min.	1,980 min.
Game length	/ 20 min.	/ 20 min.	/ 35 min.	/ 35 min.
Games accommodated	99	99	56	56
Number of courts	× 6	× 6	× 12	× 12
Games available	594	594	678	678

Based on this information we will be registering teams based on the following schedule:

Hockey				Soccer	
Recreational teams	Age	Competitive teams	Recreational teams	Age	Competitive teams
20	10	20	20	10	20
20	12	20	20	12	20
20	14	20	20	14	20
20	16	20	20	16	20
12	18	12	12	18	12
12	Junior	12	12	Junior	12
12	Adult	12	12	Adult	12
116	Total teams	116	116	Total teams	116
	232			232	

Basketball				Volleyball	
Recreational teams	Age	Competitive teams	Recreational teams	Age	Competitive teams
20	10	20	20	10	20
20	12	20	20	12	20
20	14	20	20	14	20
20	16	20	20	16	20
12	18	12	12	18	12
12	Junior	12	12	Junior	12
12	Silver	12	12	Silver	12
12	Gold	12	12	Gold	12
128	Total teams	128	128	Total teams	128
	256			256	

If each division with 20 teams plays four 5–team round robin competitions with the winner of each round robin competition competing in one championship round robin to determine the winner of the division, each division will require forty six games. In addition, if each division with 12 teams plays two 6–team round robin competitions with the top two teams competing in one championship game to determine the winner of the division, each division will require thirty–one games. Based on these constraints, the following number of games will be necessary.

Hockey				Soccer	
Recreational teams	Age	Competitive teams	Recreational teams	Age	Competitive teams
46	10	46	46	10	46
46	12	46	46	12	46
46	14	46	46	14	46
46	16	46	46	16	46
31	18	31	31	18	31
31	Junior	31	31	Junior	31
31	Adult	31	31	Adult	31
277	Total games	277	277	Total games	277
	554			554	

Basketball				Volleyball	
Recreational teams	Age	Competitive teams	Recreational teams	Age	Competitive teams
46	10	46	46	10	46
46	12	46	46	12	46
46	14	46	46	14	46
46	16	46	46	16	46
31	18	31	31	18	31
31	Junior	31	31	Junior	31
31	Silver	31	31	Silver	31
31	Gold	31	31	Gold	31
308	Total games	308	308	Total games	308
	616			616	

Based on the above information we have comprised the following table to illustrate how much extra court time we will have available in each sport.

	Hockey	Soccer	Basketball	Volleyball
Total games	554	554	616	616
Game length	× 20 min.	× 20 min.	× 35 min.	× 35 min.
Used hours	11,080 min.	11,080 min.	21,560 min.	21,560 min.
Usable hours	1,980 min.	1,980 min.	1,980 min.	1,980 min.
Number of courts	× 6	× 6	× 12	× 12
Total Usable hours	11,880 min.	11,880 min.	23,760 min.	23,760 min.
Total Usable hours	11,880 min.	11,880 min.	23,760 min.	23,760 min.
Used hours	−11,080 min.	−11,080 min.	−21,560 min.	−21,560 min.
Extra hours	800 min.	800 min.	2,200 min.	2,200 min.
	/ 60 min.	/ 60 min.	/ 60 min.	/ 60 min.
Extra hours	13.3 hrs.	13.3 hrs.	36.6 hrs.	36.6 hrs.

As in the series tournaments, extra hours will be used for skills competitions, awards ceremonies, and will provide a buffer should we fall behind schedule for any unforeseen reason.

The following table shows how many athletes we will be able to accommodate in each sport of our extreme sports competition at our Sports Highlight tournaments.

	Vert	Street
Usable hours	1,980 min.	1,980 min.
Total fixed time	− 75 min.	− 15 min.
Time remaining	1,905 min.	1,965 min.
Variable time	2 min.	4.5 min.
Park competition time	+ 6.5 min.	+ 6.5 min.
Total time	8.5 min.	11 min.
Time remaining	1,905 min.	1,965 min.
Total time	/ 8.5 min.	/ 11 min.
Total athletes accommodated	—	178

FINANCIAL ANALYSIS

Revenue Streams

Entry Fees

Our first and most logical revenue stream will come in the form of entry fees paid by the athletes. We plan to collect entry fees based on the following schedule:

	Traditional sports		Extreme sports	
	Recreation	Competitive	Recreation	Competitive
Entry fee	$150	$200	$30	$150

In return for the entry fee, paid athletes will receive a t–shirt/jersey to be worn during the competition as well as prizes provided throughout the competition. In the recreational division, where entry fees are less and the competition is second to the fun of playing the sports, prizes will be awarded on a participation basis as well as creative competitions such as the 20th goal of the day, goalies receiving a shutout, and other such creative competitions.

In the competitive division, where entry fees are higher and the competition is more intense, we will be working with our vendors and sponsors to provide high quality prizes to teams that place in the top three in their division. We intend to offer the winning teams a combination of prizes that will total more than double the original cost of their entry fee.

By offering creative prizes in the recreational division, which allows teams the ability to win a prize even if they have no chance of winning the overall competition, we feel that we can really emphasize the importance of simply playing the sport and having fun. While we would like to see athletes improve and grow as a team, in the recreational division, where people simply sign up to play for fun, we want to keep players from becoming discouraged even if they do not do well in the competition. We want them to understand that just because they did not win the tournament does not mean that they cannot still have fun, win prizes, and come back and do it all over again at the next tournament.

In the competitive division however, we intend to stimulate the competition by offering desirable prizes for the top three teams in each division. In addition, we intend to offer the winning team in each division prizes worth double their entry fee. By doing this we hope to show teams that if they feel they have a chance to win the competitive division of one of our tournaments, not only could they have the fun of participating in the tournament and winning, but they could also benefit financially from the competition. Teams that place in the top three in the competitive division will receive prizes to help compensate them for their entry fees and will therefore essentially be competing in our tournaments for free.

Sponsors

After evaluating the format of our tournaments and clinics, the schedule by which we intend to operate, and our market segment, we have decided to offer the following sponsorship packages:

National			Local		
Number of sponsors	Level of sponsorship	Cost	Number of sponsors	Level of sponsorship	Cost
1	Platinum	$300,000	3	Gold	$10,000
3	Gold	$150,000	5	Silver	$ 5,000
5	Silver	$ 75,000	7	Bronze	$ 2,500

Based on the above table we plan to break our sponsors into two categories, national and local sponsors. National sponsors will sponsor our tournament series for an entire year and will travel with our series to each of our stops. Local sponsors will be sponsors that we pick up in each of the cities our series visits. The cost shown in the local category is the cost of sponsoring one of our events. Since our series will stop in each city multiple times however, sponsors will be encouraged to sponsor our events every time they visit the sponsor's city. In order to encourage this repeat sponsorship, sponsors willing to contract to sponsor each event we offer in their city will be entitled to a 10% discount off of the single tournament sponsor prices. (National sponsorship prices reflect a 20% discount off of the single tournament sponsor prices.)

Based on our evaluation of our tournament series format, the level of contact which we intend to have with our consumers, and numerous other factors, we have identified the following ways in which we can help our sponsors reach our consumers:

- Advertisements on t–shirt/jersey worn during game play

- Advertisements on playing surfaces

- Advertisements on scoreboards

- Advertisements on website

- Distribute sponsor's marketing materials with registration packets

- Provide sponsor's products as prizes

- Allocate space at events for sponsors to setup their own marketing materials

Customers

In order to identify companies which would provide a good fit as sponsors for our tournament series we must first describe the market segment which we intend to target. To begin, we will be offering age brackets in our competition that range from 9 years of age through adult; however, we will have twice as many athletes ranging in age from 9–17 as we will in the 18–adult age range. While this seems to suggest that our market segment will be composed of younger consumers, this is not necessarily true.

We will have twice as many 9–17 year old athletes; however, athletes in the 9–15 year old age range will still need to be accompanied by an adult since they will not be able to drive themselves to the events. In addition, it is our hope that we will entice a substantial amount of the athlete's friends and families to attend our events as well. This means that while it is likely that our mean market age is lower, we also intend to draw adults to our events as well, both in the form of athletes and spectators watching younger athletes compete.

Enticing both younger athletes and their parents to attend our events could have very positive results when it comes to attracting sponsors. As noted later in the market segment section of the business plan, teenagers today have higher disposable incomes than previous generations, bringing in an average of $125 of disposable income per week. While this figure may seem high, we must keep in mind that teenagers do not have the numerous bills incurred by adults, as well as the fact that children today are starting work sooner than previous generations.

While the average teenager in America may have a disposable income of $125 a week, this still does not mean that the teen will be the party responsible for making the purchasing decisions regarding this money, which provides the perfect opportunity for our tournament series. While families are at our tournaments we will have a relatively captive audience. We plan to schedule games far enough apart so that both athletes and spectators have time to enjoy all of our various offerings in between games, yet close enough together that they will not have time to leave the venue to partake in other forms of entertainment.

This provides us with a somewhat unique opportunity. We will have both teenagers, with this relatively high disposable income, as well as their parents, who are most likely in charge of the purchasing allocations of the disposable income, together at a single location with excess time on their hands. This means that a correctly engineered marketing campaign could reach both the end user of the product and the purchaser at the same time, while the two have time to discuss the situation and take action. From a marketing standpoint, this is a powerful statement.

In addition, athletes in the 18–adult age range are also great candidates for marketing campaigns as well. Considering that each of the athletes at one of our events has just spent somewhere around $50 simply to compete in the event, we can assume that these athletes have an above average disposable income. While these athletes may not be extremely wealthy, we can assume from the fact that they can afford to participate in leisurely activities such as sports tournaments that they have some disposable income to spend.

Sponsorship Opportunities
After defining our target market we considered companies which advertise in the sports marketplace. We have identified the following product categories as possible sponsors for our tournament series.

- *Car manufacturer:* (Scion, Chevrolet, Nissan) With twice as many athletes in the 9–17 year old age brackets, who will be accompanied by their parents and families, we feel that we offer the perfect demographic for a car manufacturer. We have a captive audience in a perfect automobile purchasing age range accompanied by their parents and family members, who have a large say in the decision of what car a teenager purchases.

- *Cell phone company:* (AT&T Wireless, Verizon, Sprint, Nextel) While almost everyone uses a cell phone in today's marketplace, the prime market for cell phone companies is teenagers. In addition, cell phone companies are currently pushing the option of family plans. With a captive market of teenagers and their families, our tournament series offers a great demographic to potential cellular company sponsors.

- *Beverages:* (Red Bull, Coca–Cola, Gatorade) With the unique mix of sports which we will be offering in our tournament series we offer the ability for a beverage company to transcend the boundaries and reach both traditional and extreme sports athletes at one venue. In addition to reaching the athletes, reaching the purchaser of the groceries for the household, usually a parent, is also key for obtaining results. With the target market and the purchasers in one venue, beverage companies are presented with a unique opportunity.

- *Gaming:* (IBM, Microsoft, Sony) With a target market which closely mirrors the market for sports tournaments, gaming companies could easily market to our consumers. A gaming company could set up a booth to allow athletes to try out their system and games during the time between sports games. In addition, the company could also get parents of gamers involved and provide information to them regarding some of the benefits of gaming.

- *Hotels:* (Holiday Inn, Days Inn, Marriot) We will be offering our tournament series in eight different cities in our first year of operation before expanding to an even larger area and offering tournaments throughout the entire United States. While traveling from city to city participating in our tournaments our consumers will need to stay at hotels. We can offer the ability to secure a continuous customer base for a national hotel chain, or simply increase bookings for a weekend for a local hotel.

- *Restaurants:* (Applebee's, Cracker Barrel, Subway) Once again, our series will operate in eight different cities in our first year before expanding throughout the United States. Athletes as well as spectators will need nourishment while in these cities and sponsoring our events offers a national restaurant chain the ability to secure a continuous customer base, or a local restaurant the ability to boost its sales for the weekend.

- *Travel:* (Southwest Airlines, Enterprise Rental Car, Travelocity) From airfare to rental cars to ticketing agencies, our consumers will be traveling throughout the Midwest to participate in our tournaments in our first year of operation and throughout the entire United Stated soon thereafter. Sponsoring our tournament series offers travel companies the ability to exclusively market to this group of consumers who is sure to be traveling a great deal.

- *Credit Card Companies:* (MasterCard, Visa, American Express) Credit card companies are constantly trying to sign up new members; however, many people simply throw away applications that arrive in the mail without ever opening them. Our events will provide credit card companies the ability to reach a diverse age group with extra time on their hands to fill out an application. In addition, many families will be attending our events together so the head of the household is likely to be in attendance to make any decisions on the matter.

- *Clothes:* (Nike, Adidas, Reebok) Fashion is important to people of all ages; however, athletes demand fashion with a certain level of functionality. Our tournament series offers the ability for a clothing manufacturer to market its goods to a very diverse crowd spread across seven different sports.

- *Hygiene:* (Oxy, Proactive, Stridex) With a target market of young athletes, our tournament series offers companies in the hygiene industry the ability to reach their key demographic. Young athletes face many challenges when it comes to skin care and a hygiene company could help to educate both athletes and parents about skin care while also providing samples of their products to athletes right when they need them.

Vendors

In addition to our tournament sponsors, we would like to attract one major vendor in each sport to come to our events for a vendor tradeshow. Each vendor will have exclusive rights in their designated sport which could include features such as vendor logos on the playing surface, exclusive sale and use of the vendor's products at the events, as well as many other creative options. We will be looking for a total of seven vendors to accommodate each of our sports and will be charging a fee of $200,000 per vendor, as well as 5% of all vendor sales at the events.

Possible revenue streams which we have identified for vendors at our events include the sale of goods at the events as well as a charge for equipment tech support. In addition to these revenue streams however, vendors will also gain a tremendous amount of exposure and will have the ability to work with us to launch a variety of unique marketing campaigns.

For instance, we would like to work closely with each vendor to provide a number of creative sideshows at the events such as athletic demonstrations. Vendors will be encouraged to have any athletes which they have a relationship with come to the events and simply hang out, talk to aspiring athletes, watch games, provide tips, put on demonstrations, and so on. In addition, we would also encourage vendors to provide prizes at the events thereby further increasing their exposure and also putting their products in the consumers hands themselves.

Additional Revenue Streams

In addition to the revenue which we will generate from entry fees, sponsors and vendors, the following is a list of the additional revenue streams which we have identified for our business.

Tournament Program

We will be developing a tournament program that will be availablebefore each event. This program will provide space for sponsors and vendors to advertise, showcase certain teams/individuals, explain different aspects of our various sports, show pictures of the winning teams from the last event, and so on. One program will be provided to each team in the registration packet and additional programs will be $3 each at the event as well as on our website.

Concessions

We will be subcontracting out concessions at the events to a non–profit group. We will be contacting groups such as the Boy Scouts to organize and manage all concession activity. We plan to collect 5% of the group's sales as another revenue stream. In an attempt to create a wholesome family environment however, no alcoholic beverages will be allowed on the premise. Food such as hamburgers, hotdogs, popcorn, pretzels, chips, soda, water, and sports drinks will be sold at various locations throughout the venue. Our goal for concessions is to keep the menu simple enough that our concessions subcontractors do not require any amenities such as running water or a stove. We plan for them to serve our customers with a barbeque grill and cooler. Our goal is not to serve our customers gourmet meals; we would simply like to provide them with food on the premises so that, should they choose, they will be able to remain at the event for a longer period of time without having to leave to obtain food.

Parking

Parking will be provided free of charge to athletes and coaches. Each athlete and coach will be given a special event parking tag which will allow them to park their vehicle in the lot for the duration of the tournament. Additional spectators without parking passes will however have to pay a small fee of $3 to park their vehicles for the entire event weekend. We feel that people are willing to pay a small amount for parking that is close to the tournament location. Our event–long parking is much cheaper than other tournaments, and offers a safe, close, and convenient location to the tournament.

Admission

Athletes and coaches will be provided with free entry into the venue. In addition, each team will be given five free passes and each individual athlete will be given two free passes. Outside of these, spectators will be charged a fee of $4 to enter the venue for the entire weekend.

Product Sales

T–shirts will be on sale in a number of different sizes, colors, and styles and will be available in pre–printed designs as well as available for personalization on the spot. Consumers will simply be able to choose from the preset templates which we will have loaded into our system, pick the color and size shirt they desire, and within minutes our technician will have their shirt ready for pickup. Some templates will even allow the consumer the ability to put their sport, team, name, and number on the shirt.

In addition, we will also be able to print any of the pictures taken at the event onto a T–shirt within minutes as well. If the athlete has not found a picture he or she likes, we will have a photographer on hand to take a picture which can then be printed onto a shirt within minutes. In addition to T–shirts, our website will offer options such as traditional pictures, coffee mugs, plaques and similar products with pictures printed on them. We will also have player cards available at the end of the series which will be similar to a professional sports card with the athlete's picture on the front and a full list of statistics on back.

Strategic Partnerships

In addition to paying sponsors and vendors, we also hope to form a number of strategic partnerships that will help our tournament series grow while providing a benefit to our partner company as well. The following is a list of the partnerships which we would like to have in place by the start of our first season.

- *Media Partners:* We will be partnering with one or more large media sources in order to get our content broadcast to the public. We would like to partner with one internet company such as America Online or Yahoo as well as one magazine company such as Sports Illustrated, which also has a children's sports magazine. We feel that by having a web presence as well as a hard copy media outlet we can better reach our diverse target market. Media partners such as these could vastly increase the exposure that our tournament series receives and prove to be incredibly helpful, especially during our transition to a national level. These outlets could help us to push our content to the public and could boost not only our athlete registration, but also our spectator turnout, thereby increasing the exposure of our sponsors and vendors and effectively helping us to recruit more companies in these areas. In return for the benefit which we receive we can offer these companies exclusive access to a demographic which closely resembles their target market so that they may market their services. We would effectively be inviting the media companies to all of our events and working with them to generate interest in both our tournament series and their media outlet. By increasing interest in our tournament series and convincing our customers to view our content provided by the media outlets we would effectively be increasing business for the media companies, as well as ourselves.

- *Local Specialty Store Owners:* We will be partnering with local specialty stores in each city we travel to. We will be approaching these local stores with a proposition to recruit teams for our tournament series. We will give each store a supply of registration flyers which will be color coded to allow us to identify which store an athlete was recruited by. Stores will be compensated 5% of the registration dollars generated by their colored registration flyers. Considering that local specialty store owners have: relationships with customers, mailing lists, relationships with sporting facilities, and most likely even have relationships with a number of sports teams, recruiting athletes to compete at our events should not pose a difficult task. We feel that this relationship will be very beneficial to both parties. We gain the local expertise and connections that the store has developed over time, and the store receives a 5% commission on any teams which sign up for our event based on the stores efforts.

- *Photography/Magazine:* Photography poses an interesting opportunity for us to get others involved in our tournament series. Rather than simply hiring photographers to take pictures at our events we plan to hold a competition. We plan on forming a strategic partnership with universities in each city where we are holding an event. We will be talking to these universities' photography and journalism departments. Our plan is to have students from each university come to the event held in their city to be event photographers for us. The photographers will photograph each team/individual before the first round of competition, as well as taking "action" pictures during the games. These pictures will then be for sale at the events themselves as well as on our website. In addition to taking pictures at the event we will also commission each university to create an event magazine. We will give all of the universities a guideline as to what materials are required to be in the magazine; however, we will be giving each university creative control over most aspects of the magazine design. At the end of the series we will have a competition to see which university created the best event magazine, and the winning university will receive a cash prize. We feel that using student photographers is beneficial because not only will it help to reduce our costs, as we will be paying student photographers much less than professional photography companies, but it will also get another group of people interested and hopefully excited about our tournament series. We plan to promote the photography/magazine contest much like another event being held as part of the series. In addition, we hope that it will help to illustrate that we are interested in giving back to the community. We want to give these students valuable experience in working with real life projects under time constraints. Since each magazine will be released at our next event, each university will only have one week to create and ship the magazine.

Officiate & Participate

Seeing as how we are not merely trying to provide a characteristic sports tournament atmosphere, but rather to help broaden athletes' horizons and help educate them on all the different aspects about any given sport, we will be offering a unique option to athletes of the competitive division. Assuming that many of these athletes will be very dedicated and knowledgeable about their sport of choice already, we would like to give them the opportunity to show this knowledge and save some money at the same time.

We will be offering a Officiate & Participate option to athletes of the competitive division. Should any of these athletes be interested in refereeing the recreational division, they may attend one of our three scheduled clinics in order to obtain the certification required to referee in the tournament series. During these clinics each athlete will receive instruction about refereeing, will be observed while refereeing actual games, and will be required to pass a test that will qualify them to referee in the tournament series.

In return for their services, which will include refereeing a set number of games at the tournament, these athletes will receive a $60 discount on their entry fee; however, in order to qualify for this discount, the referee must attend one of the three scheduled clinics and indicate their intent to participate in the program on their teams entry form so that we may clear up any scheduling conflicts which may result.

We feel that this is a very good program because it allows children to broaden their knowledge about sports, helps them feel a connection with the tournament series, and also allows them an opportunity to help with some of the cost, an area that is primarily dominated by parents.

Battle of the Bands

In order to promote the high–energy feel that we envision for our sports tournaments, we plan to host a regional "battle of the bands" contest to keep spectators and athletes pumped up for the tournament. We do not wish to spend a large amount of money on paying performers; however, we developed an idea for a battle of the bands competition.

We plan to bring in local and regional high–energy groups which will compete, based on audience applause, for a cash prize. The battle of the bands will take place in peak tournament hours, ensuring the most possible athletes and spectators.

Smaller bands are constantly trying to find new venues and outlets for their music to be heard, and our summer tournament events provide the perfect venue. We don't plan to drown out all conversation and team communication with music, but rather strategically place the band so that athletes and audience members will have the perfect soundtrack for the weekend. In the downtime between bands we plan to have a DJ play high–energy music over the stage's PA system.

COMPETITION

Amateur Athletic Union of the United States (AAU)

Many other sports tournaments and sports tournament series already exist, targeting many of the same athletes as we plan to. One competitor offering multiple sports competition is the Amateur Athletic Union of the United States (AAU). The AAU offers numerous tournaments and competitions through-out the year, acting as venues where amateur athletes can compete for fun in hopes of qualifying for the final event, the AAU Junior Olympics. The Junior Olympics started in Washington D.C. in 1967, offering two events: swimming and track & field. The Junior Olympics is currently the host of many amateur events including: baseball, baton twirling, beach volleyball, boys' basketball, cheerleading, dance, diving, field hockey, 7 on 7 football, girls' basketball, golf, gymnastics, indoor soccer, jump rope, lacrosse, karate, multi–events, power lifting, softball, swimming, table tennis, teakwood, track & field, trampoline & tumbling, weightlifting, and wrestling.

Hoop it Up

Hoop it Up is a 3 on 3 basketball tournament that runs during the summer months in the United States and Canada. Hoop it Up directly competes with our tournament series as the format for game play is very similar. In addition, the games are played outdoors with portable basketball goals, making for endless venue possibilities. There are 36 divisions consisting of competitive, recreational, adult male, youth male, and youth female. Hoop it Up also hosts camps throughout the year, which will be in direct competition with our sports clinics.

Street Soccer Cup USA

Street Soccer Cup is a 4 on 4 street soccer tournament series currently operating in Wichita, Philadel-phia, Muncie, Detroit, Chicago, Springfield (IL), and Des Moines. The game is played on a street surface with specially designed walls to make game play more exciting. Street Soccer Cup USA is in direct competition with our tournament series, as we plan to offer 4 on 4 soccer games outdoors in small enclosed soccer fields, the same as Street Soccer Cup.

X Games

The X Games is the ESPN owned sports tournament for extreme sports, becoming the first large–scale extreme sports tournament in the world. The X Games started in 1994, and has been hosting a venue for extreme sports in the summer and winter seasons ever since. The X Games is a direct competitor to us because we will be offering three extreme sports in our tournament, with similar rules and judging standards as those used by the X Games. In the past, the X Games has proved a huge success. The attendance at the Winter X Games has grown 91% since 2002, showing that the extreme sports are drawing more and more people. As the market continues to grow, we feel that we can get into this market and expand on it through our tournament series and clinics.

Additional Competition

Since we are offering a variety of sporting events at our tournaments, our primary competition will come from multiple event tournaments, such as the AAU sponsored tournaments and the X Games. Although our primary focus of competition is on multiple event tournaments, we cannot ignore the threat of numerous other sports tournaments taking place almost non–stop throughout the year. Tournaments such as Hoop it Up and Street Soccer Cup USA provide a venue for an exciting, fast–paced version of basketball and soccer, respectively. This type of tournament is a large operation, and they are becoming more and more popular. Athletes are continually looking for a new venue at which they can compete, and new tournaments are offering a little twist to the tournament feel, drawing in new crowds all the time.

Some sports tournaments are organized loosely, such as intramural basketball tournaments, drawing in local amateurs to compete for fun. Other tournaments are strictly structured with multiple sponsors and promotional campaigns, examples being any of the tournaments listed above. Despite the heavy competition in the sports tournament market, we feel that our unique mix of traditional and extreme sports offers a venue unlike any of those offered by the competition, allowing our tournament series to cater to more athletes and become a top sports tournament series in the United States.

Although much of our direct competition comes from sports tournaments, many sporting leagues exist which draw in athletes from all over. Local league competition can be extremely competitive, drawing in loyal athletes who have a strong desire to be the best in the league. These leagues, which exist primarily in the traditional sports, pose a large threat to us, as teams and individual athletes may choose to participate in league play rather than paying even more money to compete in a tournament.

In addition to other sports related events however, we must also consider any form of entertainment that piques the interest of young minds as indirect competition to our tournament series. American children in previous years have become increasingly lethargic and less willing to get outside and partake in any form of physical activity. With the creation of new video game formats that allow children to communicate with their friends through an internet connection as opposed to actually traveling to their homes, previous years have brought many problems with childhood obesity and a sense of complacency among youths in our country.

Recent years however have seen a decrease in this trend as many Americans seem to be on a lasting health craze. Due to national advertising campaigns produced by the government, various news stories, and many shocking health reports, Americans have once again begun to encourage their children to get outside for some activity. While the trend of children staying indoors all day is on a downward spiral, we must still consider any form of entertainment such as video games and movies a form of indirect competition.

Family vacations also act as a competitor to our business. Summer weekends are limited, and many families take advantage of the nice weather to travel. As a result, the Scramble Sports Tournament Series needs to consider the possibility that athletes and spectators may be lost due to vacations, and plan accordingly. Trends in traveling could be changing slightly as gas prices are at an all–time high, and people are traveling less as a result. In addition to gasoline prices rising, plane ticket prices are also rising. This is a threat to us as well, as we encourage athletes to compete in multiple tournaments and clinics in different cities. But, we feel that most people would be willing to drive a shorter distance to our tournaments, whether or not gas prices are higher.

Competitive Advantages

Sports provide an obvious market opportunity because many people like to play sports, and there are many sports that cannot be played alone. Therefore, people need someone to organize and provide them with an opportunity to play these sports. The question is, "Why would people pay the money to play in a sports tournament as opposed to organizing themselves, or paying less money to play in a local sports league?" The idea behind any sports tournament is that tournaments provide a much more exciting venue for people than merely playing locally. There is a certain thrill associated with playing in a sports tournament.

It is true that people could gather themselves to play soccer or basketball, or they could go to a local park to skateboard or bike, but for people who are really passionate about their sport, this is not enough. Some people are so engrossed in their sport of choice that merely playing it with their friends or even playing with others in a local league is not enough. These people want the opportunity to show off their skills and play against other top competitors across the nation. Sports tournaments give these athletes the opportunity to meet and compete against others who share their same love and desire to excel in their chosen sport.

We feel that Scramble is unlike any other sports tournament in the world, offering a unique mix of sports and attracting athletes and sponsors alike in order to successfully run and grow a new sports tournament in the United States. In addition to the unique structure of our tournament, we also have a great source of industry knowledge at our disposal, as well as many close sponsor connections that we will use to grow and promote the Scramble tournament series. The specific competitive advantages which we have identified are explained in detail below.

Unique mix of traditional and extreme sports

As we have stated many times earlier, our tournament offers both traditional and extreme sports for recreational and competitive athletes alike. The Junior Olympics is among our top competition, offering multiple sports, but not including any extreme sports in the mix of events offered. We feel that we are at an advantage by offering extreme sports because they will provide many new opportunities for both athletes and sponsors to pursue new interests. By combining both traditional and extreme sports, interest in each individual sport will increase and potentially inspire and influence many people to broaden their horizons.

The Olympics are starting to add some extreme sports such as snowboarding to their mix of sports and this is broadening their viewing spectrum by drawing in viewers and fans of these sports. However, at an amateur level the Junior Olympics has not caught on by adding any extreme sports into the mix. As a result, we feel that there is a huge opportunity that needs to be seized by combining traditional and extreme sports at both a recreational and competitive level, attracting athletes from all walks and avenues to one major sporting event.

Industry knowledge at our disposal

In addition to our passion and drive for the Scramble tournamentseries, we have an abundance of information and industry knowledge available to us. One advisor and potential investor that we have been meeting extensively with is Thomas Risheo. Thomas, along with the help of his son Bobby Risheo (the Owner/CEO of Scramble) has the experience of starting a successful and profitable national hockey tournament series which brought in sponsors and athletes from all over the United States. He is a great asset to our company, providing us with information for starting a sports tournament, and also acting as a mentor, insuring that we will not commit an obvious mistake or take the Scramble tournament series in a wrong direction.

Close Sponsor Connections

In order to make Scramble a reality we will require contributions from major sponsors and vendors. In order to build the Scramble tournament series to the successful level that we desire, we will not only need local sponsors, but also support from national sponsors and sporting goods vendors across the sports spectrum. Bauer/Nike, a major developer and producer of hockey equipment, has already expressed interest in becoming a vendor and contributing to our tournament series. Thomas Risheo has been in close contact with Bauer/Nike throughout the years and as a result was able to put us in contact with the hockey equipment giant. Bauer/Nike was excited to hear from us and has already sent us high quality equipment and gear as an example of equipment contributions they would be willing to donate for prizes at the Scramble tournament series. We feel that getting a connection with an industry leader such as Bauer/Nike will only help us to secure and land other contracts and deals with industry leaders in other sports. Bauer/Nike is the first potential vendor that we have been in contact with, but a full list of potential sponsors and vendors can be found in the primary revenue streams section of the business plan.

Market Opportunity

Our tournament series hopes not only to attract athletes who are looking for the excitement of competing at the top level in their sport, but also those athletes who simply love the sport in which they compete, even if they are not highly skilled. We intend to provide an atmosphere in which these athletes can learn what separates them from athletes at the top of their sport, and also to provide tips to help close this gap.

Many young athletes are simply interested in watching top athletes compete, and then trying to emulate them. We feel that by offering both a competitive and a recreational division we will give less talented athletes the ability to watch some of their more skilled counterparts and possibly learn a few things before they are scheduled to play.

MARKET ANALYSIS

The sports tournament industry is consistently profitable and always growing over time, as people continue to love sports. The average annual sales (based on over 18 million companies) for a company operating in the amateur sports tournament industry is $2,538,445 (Bizminer.com). As new sports continue to emerge, both children and adults become involved and excited about these new sports. There are constantly new tournaments and venues that host these emerging new sports. Sports such as biking and aggressive inline skating are relatively new and have become popular in the last couple decades. Venues such as The X Games cater to these new sports and provide a successful large–scale tournament.

The Scramble tournament series is combining two separate industries: traditional sports and extreme sports, enabling us to generate a profit in our beginning years of operations, in an industry that already proves to be good for startups. According to Bizmer.com, the average annual sales for a startup company in the amateur sports tournament industry are $242,000, based off of data from seven companies in the first three years of operation.

We plan to grow the Scramble tournament series every year by adding sports to ensure new and larger audiences for future years of operation. Our growth strategy will enable us to attract many different athletes and fans from all sports, traditional or extreme. As our growth continues, we will have to explore new venue opportunities to host so many additional sports. Our growth strategy can be found below in the business plan. As Scramble proves to be a safe, clean, unique and exciting tournament for amateur athletes, we will continue to grow a satisfied customer base that will return for years to come.

The market for the Scramble tournament series is large, and it is somewhat hard to define each and every possible consumer or participant. There are age categories for each amateur sport that we offer, providing a narrowed down group of people. On the other hand, it is much harder to define each and every group of people that may come as spectators to the Scramble tournaments. The diversity of the audience increases even more by combining the traditional and extreme sports into one tournament. The only thing that the overwhelming majority of people attending the tournaments have in common is the fact that they love sports. The various market segments are explained below.

Athletes competing in the tournament

The market for athletes competing in the Scramble tournament series is rather specific, as we provide age groups and requirements to compete. The athletes' age groups range from age 9 to adult, with the 9–17 age range having double the amount of athletes, with a recreational and competitive division offered in most age groups. We picked these age groups strategically, knowing that we can find amateur athletes in each of these age groups to fill up all possible time slots, thereby receiving the highest profit possible. In a recent article explaining teen spending in America, it is said that teens spend $159 billion each year. The article also explains that teens have a high disposable income, bringing in an average of $125 a week. Another article from the Sunday Tribune explains that teens today have a higher disposable income than generations before, buying mobile phones, iPods, clothes, stereos, and CDs. We feel with this recent trend towards more disposable income will only help our tournament series, bringing in athletes that are willing to pay higher amounts for entry fees, and more willing to compete in multiple tournaments or clinics throughout the year. Hoop it Up basketball tournaments offer age divisions ranging from age 8 to adult. Street Soccer Cup USA offers age divisions from under 6 all the way up to adult. The AAU offers age groups ranging from 8 years old to 18 years old at their events. With the amount of time we have allotted for our tournament series, we feel that the age divisions ranging from age 9 and up are appropriate. In addition, we feel that our target age of 9 to 17 is right on track to bring in the athletes with high disposable income.

Friends and Families of Athletes

We expect to see many spectators from the same age groups as outlined for the sports, as people will attend the tournament to watch their friends compete. At younger ages, children tend to be friends with each other, regardless of whether or not they play a sport together, and as a result, we plan to see many friends of athletes attending. In addition to the friends of athletes attending the Scramble tournaments, we also expect to see a great number of families, or family members, attending the tournaments as spectators and coaches. The vast majority of athletes will have family members, which are at the tournament as spectators, to watch their children participate. Families attending sporting events tend to spend money on many different things including: concessions, parking, photographs, magazines, clothing, and equipment. We expect to see much of our revenue coming from the families of the athletes, especially from the younger age divisions where a larger percentage of families will attend the events.

Families and other individuals

Finally, we expect to see many families and individuals that are not associated with athletes or vendors at the Scramble tournaments. We will be advertising in and around the cities where the Scramble tournament will be visiting, ensuring a market of spectators from all different ages. We plan to see a lot of families simply wanting to have something to do on a summer weekend. Also, we expect to see groups of children attending the tournament, again, looking for something to do. The Scramble tournament provides a safe and clean environment for children and adults alike, and we plan to advertise this aspect to parents who are letting their children attend the event as spectators.

Sponsors

Another market segment for our series includes national and local sponsors at each clinic and tournament. A complete sponsor section is described above, which details specific industries and companies within those industries that we would like to contract with. For example, AT&T Wireless is third on the list for the top sports advertisers, and they share a similar target market as us. The Scramble series would be a perfect place for AT&T Wireless to reach new potential cell phone users, while sticking to their sports advertising trend. Local sponsors may include a wide variety of businesses, ranging anywhere from a restaurant to a funeral home. We feel that we can provide local sponsors with a great marketing and advertising opportunity, encouraging the sponsors to pay for sponsorship of multiple events in their city.

Vendors

The Scramble series will generate revenue through vendors operating at the tournaments and clinics, creating another market segment. A significant amount of our income is scheduled to come from vendors, making this a very important segment. We plan to approach big–name, high quality vendors to participate in the Scramble series, as this will draw in more revenue and attract more athletes. The equipment used for game play in each sport will be provided by the vendors, and we hope to associate the Scramble series with quality names in each industry. For example, when a person thinks of quality products in the hockey industry, names such as Bauer/Nike, Easton, and CCM come to mind.

Although some of the market for the Scramble tournaments is unpredictable and variable, we feel that the most important target market is the athletes. If we can fill up all of the individual and team time slots, the Scramble tournament series will be profitable simply from athletes, and the athletes' friends and families. Word-of-mouth is a powerful form of marketing for sports tournaments in general, and we feel that a satisfied group of athletes will be a better marketing device than any advertising or promotional campaign. Satisfied athletes return to tournaments that they enjoy, and therefore, we will try everything within our power to make the Scramble tournament series an exciting, safe, and clean environment for everyone attending, ensuring customer retention for years to come.

MARKETING & SALES

Marketing Strategy

Since we are a startup company, our marketing strategy is set to be a little more intense in the first couple of years of operating as a major sports tournament series. In order to make Scramble a successful tournament series, we will first need to find enough teams to fill all of our competitive and recreational divisions for each sport. This will ensure maximum income and exposure in the first few years of operation. Since the tournament will be running in a variety of different locations and cities, we will need to construct an intensive marketing campaign at each location well in advance of the first tournament date.

Store Owners

We have observed that when children get involved in sports, they tend to surround their entire lives with that sport, constantly hanging out at sporting goods stores or specialty sports stores. As a result, storeowners have knowledge of many teams in their area, as well as a listing of teams in a particular sport. The store may even organize a sports tournament, whether it is on a local or regional level. This information is potentially a great asset to our company, as we plan to utilize a guerilla marketing campaign in each city prior to the start of the tournament series.

Color Coded Forms for Commission

Before the first year of operation, 7 or 8 employees of our tournament series will travel to each city on the tournament schedule, spending 14 days talking with major sports shops in each city that are associated with the sports we intend to offer. Our employees will talk to as many sports shops as the travel time will allow. We will provide each shop with tournament signup forms, which will be color–coded based on the specific store. When a team or individual sings up on a specific form, the store associated with that signup form will be paid a commission. In addition, the employee that gave the forms to the sport shop will be paid a commission. Bobby Risheo and possibly one other founding member will travel around to each city, building strong relationships with shop owners to promote our tournament series. The shop owners will then help us to secure teams for the first annual Scramble tournament series.

Guerilla Marketing

In addition to talking to shop owners, we plan to spend any additional time in each city talking with teams and coaches first hand. We plan to check out local practice areas so that we can establish a personal relationship with teams in an attempt to secure teams for the first year of the series. Most of all, we want to get people in key areas excited about our tournament, and we feel that the best way to do that is to talk with the coaches and teams first hand. If a kid hears one of our employees talk about how much the Scramble tournament series wants their team to compete, that kid is going to be a lot more excited than simply seeing a poster of the tournament hanging up. We feel that by directly speaking and interacting with potential teams and vendors, Scramble can hit the ground running and have a successful inaugural year.

Posters and Flyers

Although we would prefer to reach all potential teams and vendors personally, there is only so much time allocated for each city, resulting in missed opportunities. To counteract this situation, we will hang posters and give out flyers the entire time that we are in a certain city or region. If we can convince sports stores and shops to hang our posters and give out flyers promoting the tournament series, we feel that we can potentially find additional athletes to compete. Also, if we have previously developed a relationship with a shop where the poster is located, the storeowner will potentially be excited about the series and further promote our series to athletes and coaches alike.

Website

Each poster and flyer will also contain a URL address for the Scramble website. Our website will contain information about each event including: times, locations, and requirements for competing in each event. After the first event of our tournament series, the website will also include pictures and highlights from the previous events.

The website will also contain a section that will allow you to register for your events, and pay using a credit or debit card. We will offer a small variety of apparel featuring our tournament logo, which can also be paid for using a credit or debit card. Finally, we will also have any leftover tournament shirts just in case an athlete or spectator didn't get a chance to purchase one at the venue.

In addition, the website will also contain a section about the rules of every sport that we are offering at our tournament. Each rulebook will be in a downloadable PDF file. In addition, the website will have a video section, featuring highlights of current and past tournaments. We will also have a Webcam in the video section, which will feature live footage of the entire summer sports tournament series.

A full sponsor section will be on the website, giving potential sponsors for the national and local level a chance to check out pricing and sponsor benefits. Forms will be linked on the website, letting sponsors register online if desired.

Next, a section on the website will allow anyone to be put on our bi–monthly email list. The people on the email list will receive the latest tournament news and promotions and discounts on various things, such as entry fees and merchandise.

Finally we will have a section on the site about how to get involved with the tournament itself. You can fill out an application online to volunteer or apply for a position with the tournament series. Part time and full time positions will be listed on the website, and allow for us to draw employees and volunteers from all different cities throughout the region.

Word-of-Mouth

Finally, after the first few years of successful tournaments, we plan for a large amount of athletes and coaches contacting us through word–of–mouth marketing. The best advertising for our series will be from happy and satisfied athletes and coaches that competed in the tournament in previous years. Along with limited space for each sport, our tournament has limited time for teams to compete, which restricts the amount of teams that the Scramble tournament series can accommodate. We feel that word–of–mouth advertising, along with strong relationships developed early on, will provide the Scramble tournament series with plenty of potential teams and athletes in future years.

GROWTH STRATEGY

The Scramble tournament series will require a lot of work during the months that we are not in operation, especially in the months preceding the first year of operation. We have devised a series of phases that we will follow in order to prepare for, and to run the company in the first year of operation. Each phase is outlined in detail below.

Phase 1: Prior to First Year of Operation

1. Secure Venues: First, we will secure all of the venues that will be needed to operate the clinics, Sports Highlight tournaments, summer series tournaments, and finally the national championship tournament in Muncie, Indiana. We are currently researching venue opportunities around the country, attempting to find places that will offer accommodations for all of our traditional sports, as well as an area to build courses for the extreme sports.

2. Secure Vendors: In addition to securing sponsors, we must also find one major sports vendor in each sport which we intend to offer. Vendors will provide our series with revenue in the form of the initial vendor fee, as well as a 5% commission on all goods sold at the events. All seven vendors must be identified and contracted before the start of our first season as our extensive vendor showcase is one of the main spectator draws for our tournament series.

3. Secure Sponsors: In order to make our first year of operation a success, we will need sponsors to fill up our requirements for the platinum, gold, silver and bronze sponsor categories. The anticipated number of sponsors which we intend to attract in our first season can be found in the financial section of the business plan. Finding sponsors is a top priority, as they will bring in a great deal of revenue and prizes for the tournament.

Phase 2: Prior to First Year of Operation

1. Purchase/Build Equipment: The next stage of our development cycle will involve purchasing and/or renting all of the equipment for the first year of operation. The biggest pieces of equipment that we will need to provide will be the ramps, rails, and half pipe for the three extreme sports offered in the first year. Also, we will need to purchase materials to build a small wall around the hockey and soccer rinks, to keep flying pucks and balls in play. We plan to buy the raw materials to construct each and every piece of the course, reconstructing the entire course with the help of our volunteers and employees at each location. In addition to the extreme sports course, we will need flood lights for night events. Also, we will need to purchase a large amount of banquet tables and tents for athlete registration, concessions, and parking attendants. In order to travel between events, we plan to purchase trucks to transport our lights, tables, hockey and soccer equipment, and extreme sports course from venue to venue. The purchase of any additional supplies and raw materials, such as extension cords, portable toilets (if necessary) will be made during this stage in the development cycle.

2. Obtain Event/Liability Insurance for Venues: We are currently researching insurance costs for operating at different venues, as some venues have the ability to provide insurance to renters and some do not. Also, we have been in contact with an insurance company that has informed us of the possibility of obtaining outdoor tournament insurance in case of weather delays or cancellations.

Phase 3: First Season of Operation

1. Team Sign Up: The first step before running any clinics or tournaments must be to secure all of our athletes. We cannot expect to fill our age divisions and groups to 100% capacity in the first year; rather, our financial projections for year 1 assume a 70% capacity. Year 2 assumes an 85% capacity, and we predict to be at 100% capacity in year 3. Our primary method for teams to sign up for the tournament is through our website, which features a section allowing teams to register and input all of their information online, including their payment. Teams will be asked on the website to input, if any, the color of the flyer or card from which they heard about the clinic or tournament. This will enable us to pay commission to the employee or volunteer responsible for distributing the flyer or card. Teams may also use the actual flyer, which will have a registration section, and mail the form and payment to our office in Muncie, Indiana.

2. Marketing/Advertising: While actively pursuing teams to participate in our first year of tournaments, we will also be advertising in tournament cities and surrounding areas. In phase 1, we are

planning to secure a media partner, which can provide us with advertising and marketing through different mediums, such as internet, magazine or radio. In addition to the advertising and marketing through the media sponsor, we also plan to invest $40,000 in advertising before the first season of operation.

3. Transportation to Cities: In order to accommodate all of the equipment necessary to run such a large–scale operation, we will purchase 5 trucks with a closed cargo compartments, and 4 flat bed trailers which will be pulled by pickups. Based on weather charts and travel distances, we have devised a yearlong route that we will follow for our first year of operation. The weather charts and a map detailing the travel route which we plan to follow can be found in the appendix of this business plan.

4. Clinic/Tournament Set–Up: The set–up for each clinic and tournament will be rather extensive, as we have 7 sports to prepare for during the summer tournament series. We plan to have 25 employees setting up all necessary equipment for the summer tournaments, under the supervision of 3 high level managers, making sure the set–up runs smoothly. Set–up time will take 500 human hours for the summer series events, bringing the total set–up time to 20 hours.

5. Marketing in Cities of Operation: Although we do not plan to aggressively market our off–season tournaments and clinics during the operation of these events, we do plan to market our summer series in the city of operation, during the weekend of operation. This marketing campaign will require 10 employees who will aggressively travel around the city of operation putting up flyers, and promoting events such as a dunk contest, battle of the bands, and professional athletic demonstrations. We want to try and get the public in each city excited about our event, in hopes of starting a tradition where people look forward to our event each year.

6. Running Clinics/Tournaments: Running the clinics, off–season tournaments, summer series, and championship will all vary from each other in terms of employee numbers. The management and employee duties for each of these events will be basically the same, with the exception of the clinics. Labor costs for the summer series are roughly $50,000, and the off season tournaments demanding $25,000.

7. Equipment Tear Down: The takedown of all equipment used at the clinics or tournaments will require precise coordination between many employees. As with the set–up, we will require 25 employees to help with the tear down, being supervised by 3 managers. The total time for tear down of the summer series events is estimated to take a total of 25 hours. After the completion of phase one and two in the development cycle, the Scramble tournament series will be ready for the first season of operation. Our first event will be a clinic in Bloomington (April), followed by a clinic in Muncie (May) before the summer tournament series kicks off. The actual time allotted for this development cycle is yet to be determined, as we are not sure what the first year of operation will be. If we plan to start the tournament in the summer of 2015, we will have the time available from this current day until the first tournament of the series in the summer of 2015 for phases one and two. We feel that the summer of 2015 is the earliest that we could start the series, ensuring the tournament that we have envisioned. If we were forced to push back the start date to 2016, we will simply have more time for each one of the stages in phase one and two of the development cycle. The three phases described above outline what it takes for us to get through the first year of operation. We plan to have a phase four, which will include growing the tournament to a national level, and adding more sports in the process. As described earlier, the Hispanic population in places such as Florida, Texas, and California provide for much opportunity for the sport of soccer. Depending on the success of our series in the first year, we plan to expand nationally into different regions, slowly taking advantage of new markets. We also plan to add at least one traditional and extreme sport every year, further tapping into new markets, and expanding the size of our tournament series to a new level. We realize that a full–scale national tournament involves many risks, and for this reason, we are starting regionally and expanding based on the successes of our first year of operation.

RISK FACTORS

There are many risks associated with starting a major sporting tournament. The idea of competition and sporting events is not a new concept, and as a result, there are many existing competitors and tournaments already in place for every sport, including those we are offering in our mix. A list of potential risks to the Scramble tournament series, as well as our answers to those risks, follows:

- Not being able to secure enough teams for our first year of the tournament series. If we do not succeed in filling all time slots for every sport, we are losing out on registration money, and losing out on athletes who could potentially visit vendor booths and purchase concessions, photos, and other merchandise. We could also lose money if our city–to–city campaign fails, and we are spending traveling money, while not making the money back on new teams or sponsors. We are however not relying exclusively on our marketing efforts to provide all of the teams. In addition to the marketing campaigns which we are launching on our own, we will also be working with our strategic partners to locate teams. Strategic partnerships with local sporting good and specialty store owners should provide us with a large number of contacts which we can transition into clients.

- Other sporting events taking precedence over the Scramble tournament series. There are constantly sports tournaments occurring, ensuring that the Scramble tournament series will conflict with the schedules of athletes. If we fail to recognize another major tournament going on at the same time, we will lose out on athletes and sponsors for our tournament. In an effort to avoid two tournaments occurring at the same time and preventing athletes from being able to attend one of them, we must conduct extensive market research into the tournament schedules of our competitors and try to avoid scheduling our events opposite our competitors in our first year of operation. We are trying to build a strong tournament that will keep people coming back year after year, and minimizing the overlap of our tournament to others is a key strategy for our future success.

- Offering a mix of traditional and extreme sports. To our knowledge, a major tournament series offering traditional and extreme sports has never been attempted, and this poses a risk as we are attempting a completely new business venture. We feel that our tournament has created a niche market, attracting a mix of athletes which have never previously been brought together, but this mix may not be appealing to the coaches and/or athletes, resulting in a loss of participants. While we are prepared to make every effort to get this mix of sports to work well together and create cross interest between traditional and extreme sports, should this mix not work, we could easily modify our tournament structure and remain in operation. We could simply separate the extreme and traditional sports either at the same venue, or at entirely separate venues. While this would require a small amount of additional work on our part, we do not feel that separating the two sporting types would be out of the question should they fail to work well together.

- Offering seven sports in the first year of the tournament series. Many tournaments provide a venue for only one sport, and still prove to be a challenging event to manage. Starting with seven sports is a big step, one with big potential and also a large amount of risk. We may underestimate the volume of people attending, and the employees and volunteers necessary to make for a successful tournament. While operating a tournament of this magnitude will be a challenge, this is a risk which we have considered in every aspect of the design of our series. We decided to follow a growth strategy similar to that of the AAU Junior Olympics in that we are offering only a limited number of sports in our first year of operation, and we are planning to add between two and three additional sports every year. While this still leaves us offering seven sports in our first year of operation, we have an experienced management team, as well as an experienced mentor, and we feel that if we properly plan, we will be able to handle this difficult task.

FINANCIAL ANALYSIS

The Scramble Sports Tournament Series is tentatively scheduled to be operational in April of 2015, with our first event starting on April 25th in Bloomington, Indiana. One financial goal of the company is to turn a profit after our first season. This is planned and reflected in our financial statements as we plan to have a net income of $800,000 at the end of season one. In order to achieve this goal our most valuable assets will be our relationships with our sponsors/vendors and with our customers. Bringing these two groups of people together in an environment of learning and competition will not only help Scramble accomplish its financial goals, but will also bring athletic knowledge, advancement, and competition to all who participate in our events.

Request for Capital

Scramble is projecting to achieve a positive Net Income at the end of Season 1 while operating at only 70% revenue capacity and we intend to fund the operation with $1.4M in incremental stages. Though the financial statements show that all of Scramble's funding is in the preseason, in reality funding comes in 3 rounds. The current management team will contribute $140,000 in a bootstrap round lasting four months. The second round of funding will be a request for capital of $500,000 in the month of October. The final round of funding will be a request for capital of $1,000,000 in the month of March in order to purchase all fixed assets required for the first season of events.

Scramble offers these funding requests to investors with a passion for increasing the youth of America's athletic knowledge and ability. Potential investors also include vendors and sponsors as they will benefit directly from the success of the Scramble Sports Tournament Series.

Milestone phase 1		Milestone phase 2
Bootstrap June–September 2014 Hard cash establishment: $14,000	**Round 1** October 2014–February 2015 Seed round advertising: $500,000	**Round 2** March 2015–March 2016 Fixed asset purchases: $1,000,000
-Consult with and select venues in different cities where events will be held	-Finalize partnerships/relationships with sponsors/vendors	-Purchase necessary transportation assets
-Consulting with and establishing sponsor/ vendor relationships and strategic partnerships	-Finalize partnerships/relationships with event venues	-Purchase necessary equipment for the events themselves
-Assemble full management team	-Dispatch sales team	-Begin operating and incurring costs associated with events in April.
-Produce and distribute literature	-Establish legal and accounting relationships	
-Assemble sales team		

General Financial Plan Assumptions

- Scramble will have a fiscal season starting at the beginning of April as this is the month of the first event. Upon the month before April, Scramble will have purchased all assets necessary to successfully implement all of the events, whether clinic or tournament, for the first full year's schedule.

- Preseason is established as being from the beginning of June of 2014 to March of 2015. No revenues will be earned in this point and time. The costs and expenditures associated with preseason are not reflected in the financial statements of year one.

- It is assumed, and displayed in the financial statements that during the first season's schedule, Scramble will be able to fill its team/individual slots per event to 70% of their capacity. The second season's events are assumed to be filled to 85% capacity. Events of season three, four, and five are assumed to be filled to their full capacities.

- Fixed assets purchased by Scramble will be transported from event to event with the company's own mode of transportation. Prices for travel/transportation of Scramble's equipment is heavily dependent on prices of fuel and the petroleum industry.

Revenue Assumptions

- There are ten sources of revenue for Scramble that are displayed in the financial statements: Entry Fee, Clinic Signup, Sponsor Revenue, Vendor Revenue, Program Sales, Event General Admission, Concessions, Parking, Magazine Sales and Photograph Sales.

- Entry fees, sponsorships, and vendor revenue comprise close to ninety percent of Scramble's Revenue, therefore, the company's success is heavily dependant on these three revenue streams.

- Concerning the smaller revenue streams, Scramble prescribes that a certain percentage of the population will purchase any one average item from the revenue streams. These percentages and cost of the average items are outlined in the financial statements under Secondary Revenue Streams.

- In projecting the attendance of the different events, several assumptions were made on the number of spectators a participant would draw to the event. It is thought by the management team, conservatively, that on average a participant would draw from 1.5–2.5 spectators per event depending on how close the event is filled to full capacity (whether we have filled all team slots).

- Since the various athletes will likely be present at the event during only the hours of and surrounding his/her own competitions, the management team can safely assume that the full attendance of an event will not be present all at one time, although the company does have the ability to accommodate the full attendance.

Sponsorship and Vendor Assumptions

- The management team concludes and displays in the financial statements that Scramble will have attracted one national Platinum Sponsor, one local and one national Gold Sponsor, one local and one national silver sponsor, and one local Bronze Sponsor to take part in the first season's schedule of events. Over the next four seasons the management team plans to fill all available unit packages for sponsorships.

- The management team assumes that in the first season it is possible to fill all available spaces for vendors. We feel that unlike sponsors, vendors will be readily willing to put their products up for prizes and display as they will have exclusive rights to their designated sport. Other benefits include vendor logos on the playing surface, exclusive sale and use of the vendor's products at the events, as well as many other creative options.

Preseason expenditure operating costs

Preseason expenditure breakdown

Fixed assets	Quantity	
Banquet tables	30	$ 2,000
Skatepark equipment	—	$ 75,000
Flood lights	20	$ 10,000
Tents	10	$ 20,000
Trucks/auto	5	$400,000
Trailers (Flatbed)	4	$ 50,000
Basketball goals	6	$ 3,000
Hockey nets	6	$ 3,000
Volleyball nets	6	$ 3,000
Stage	1	$ 20,000
Grandstands	15	$ 30,000
Soccer nets	6	$ 3,000
Hockey/soccer rinks	6	$120,000
Other equipment	—	$ 20,000
Office furniture & supplies	—	$ 15,000
Total equipment costs		**$774,000**
Business operations		
Advertising	—	$ 40,000
Travel	—	$ 40,000
Accounting	—	$ 10,000
Administrative salaries	—	$ 38,000
Legal fees	—	$ 30,000
Office expenses	—	$ 5,000
Utilities	—	$ 15,000
Literature production	—	$ 20,000
Payroll	—	$ 15,000
Office rent	—	$ 4,000
Office supplies	—	$ 3,000
Total other cost		**$220,000**
Total costs		**$994,000**

Income statement

Preseason—2015 season

Revenue	Preseason	April	May	June	July	Aug	Sept
Entry fee revenue	$ —	$ —	$ 80,000	$400,000	$160,000	$ 135,000	$ 45,000
Clinic revenue	$ —	$ 50,000	$ 55,000	$ —	$ —	$ 50,000	$ —
Sponsor revenue	$ —	$ 75,000	$ 75,000	$ 75,000	$ 75,000	$ 75,000	$ 75,000
Program revenue	$ —	$ 2,008	$ 2,515	$ 10,040	$ 4,016	$ 2,515	$ 2,424
Vendor revenue	$ —	$120,800	$120,800	$120,800	$120,800	$ 120,800	$120,800
Concessions revenue	$ —	$ 869	$ 4,312	$ 17,212	$ 6,885	$ 4,312	$ 2,494
General admission revenue	$ —	$ 518	$ 1,952	$ 7,172	$ 2,869	$ 1,952	$ 1,039
Photography revenue	$ —	$ 1,208	$ 5,989	$ 23,905	$ 9,562	$ 5,989	$ 3,464
Parking revenue	$ —	$ 217	$ 1,078	$ 4,303	$ 1,721	$ 1,484	$ 623
Magazine revenue	$ —	$ 1,546	$ 7,665	$ 30,598	$ 12,239	$ 10,553	$ 4,433
Total revenue	**$ —**	**$252,165**	**$354,310**	**$689,030**	**$393,092**	**$ 407,604**	**$255,277**
Cost of sales							
Payroll	$ 15,000	$ 77,000	$167,000	$450,000	$180,000	$ 167,000	$ 40,000
Office rent	$ 4,000	$ 1,000	$ 1,000	$ 1,000	$ 1,000	$ 1,000	$ 1,000
Venue rent	$ —	$ 15,000	$ 30,000	$ 80,000	$ 30,000	$ 30,000	$ 15,000
Prizes/awards	$ —	$ —	$ 10,000	$ 25,000	$ 10,000	$ 20,000	$ 5,000
Office supplies	$ 3,000	$ 1,000	$ 1,000	$ 3,000	$ 1,500	$ 3,000	$ 1,000
Sales commission	$ —	$ 4,500	$ 12,150	$ 36,000	$ 14,400	$ 16,650	$ 4,050
Total cost of sales	**$ 22,000**	**$ 98,500**	**$221,150**	**$595,000**	**$236,900**	**$ 237,650**	**$ 66,050**
Gross profit	**$ (22,000)**	**$158,165**	**$133,160**	**$ 94,030**	**$156,192**	**$ 169,954**	**$189,227**
Operating expense							
Advertising	$ 40,000	$ 5,000	$ 5,000	$ 5,000	$ 5,000	$ 5,000	$ 5,000
Other rentals	$ —	$ 3,333	$ 3,333	$ 3,333	$ 3,333	$ 3,333	$ 3,333
Travel	$ 40,000	$ 5,000	$ 10,000	$ 25,000	$ 10,000	$ 10,000	$ 5,000
Accounting	$ 10,000	$ 1,000	$ 1,000	$ 1,000	$ 1,000	$ 1,000	$ 1,000
Admin salaries	$ 38,000	$ 12,500	$ 12,500	$ 12,500	$ 12,500	$ 12,500	$ 12,500
Depreciation	$ —	$ 5,000	$ 5,000	$ 5,000	$ 5,000	$ 5,000	$ 5,000
General/event insurance	$ —	$ 15,000	$ 30,000	$ 75,000	$ 30,000	$ 30,000	$ 15,000
Legal fees	$ 30,000	$ 1,000	$ 1,000	$ 5,000	$ 1,000	$ 1,000	$ 1,000
Office expenses	$ 5,000	$ 1,000	$ 1,000	$ 1,000	$ 1,000	$ 1,000	$ 1,000
Utilities	$ 15,000	$ 2,000	$ 2,000	$ 2,000	$ 2,000	$ 2,000	$ 2,000
Literature production	$ 20,000	$ 2,000	$ 2,000	$ 2,000	$ 2,000	$ 2,000	$ 2,000
Total operating expense	**$ 198,000**	**$ 52,833**	**$ 72,833**	**$136,833**	**$ 72,833**	**$ 72,883**	**$ 52,883**
Total costs	**$ 220,000**	**$151,333**	**$293,983**	**$731,833**	**$309,733**	**$ 310,483**	**$118,883**
Operating income	**$(220,000)**	**$ 6,832**	**$ 60,327**	**$ (42,804)**	**$ 83,358**	**$ 97,121**	**$136,394**
Income tax	**$ —**	**$ 2,050**	**$ 18,098**	**$ (12,841)**	**$ 25,008**	**$ 29,136**	**$ 40,918**
Net income	**$(220,000)**	**$ 4,782**	**$ 42,229**	**$ (29,963)**	**$ 58,351**	**$ 67,985**	**$ 95,476**

Income statement [CONTINUED]

Preseason—2015 season

Revenue	Oct	Nov	Dec	Jan	Feb	Mar	Year 1
Entry fee revenue	$ 45,000	$ 45,000	$ 45,000	$ 45,000	$ 45,000	$ 45,000	$1,090,000
Clinic revenue	$ —	$ —	$ —	$ —	$ —	$ —	$ 155,000
Sponsor revenue	$ 75,000	$ 75,000	$ 75,000	$ 75,000	$ 75,000	$ 75,000	$ 900,000
Program revenue	$ 2,424	$ 2,424	$ 2,424	$ 2,424	$ 2,424	$ 2,424	$ 38,066
Vendor revenue	$120,800	$120,800	$120,800	$120,800	$120,800	$120,800	$1,449,600
Concessions revenue	$ 2,494	$ 2,494	$ 2,494	$ 2,494	$ 2,494	$ 2,494	$ 51,045
General admission revenue	$ 1,039	$ 1,039	$ 1,039	$ 1,039	$ 1,039	$ 1,039	$ 21,735
Photography revenue	$ 3,464	$ 3,464	$ 3,464	$ 3,464	$ 3,464	$ 3,464	$ 70,896
Parking revenue	$ 623	$ 623	$ 623	$ 623	$ 623	$ 623	$ 13,167
Magazine revenue	$ 4,433	$ 4,433	$ 4,433	$ 4,433	$ 4,433	$ 4,433	$ 93,635
Total revenue	**$255,277**	**$255,277**	**$255,277**	**$255,277**	**$255,277**	**$255,277**	**$3,883,143**
Cost of sales							
Payroll	$ 40,000	$ 40,000	$ 40,000	$ 40,000	$ 40,000	$ 40,000	$1,321,000
Office rent	$ 1,000	$ 1,000	$ 1,000	$ 1,000	$ 1,000	$ 1,000	$ 12,000
Venue rent	$ 15,000	$ 15,000	$ 15,000	$ 15,000	$ 15,000	$ 15,000	$ 290,000
Prizes/awards	$ 5,000	$ 5,000	$ 5,000	$ 5,000	$ 5,000	$ 5,000	$ 250,000
Office supplies	$ 1,000	$ 1,000	$ 1,000	$ 1,000	$ 1,000	$ 1,000	$ 16,500
Sales commision	$ 4,050	$ 4,050	$ 4,050	$ 4,050	$ 4,050	$ 4,050	$ 112,050
Total cost of sales	$ 66,050	$ 66,050	$ 66,050	$ 66,050	$ 66,050	$ 66,050	$1,851,550
Gross profit	**$189,227**	**$189,227**	**$189,227**	**$189,227**	**$189,227**	**$189,227**	**$2,031,593**
Operating expense							
Advertising	$ 5,000	$ 5,000	$ 5,000	$ 5,000	$ 5,000	$ 5,000	$ 60,000
Other rentals	$ 3,333	$ 3,333	$ 3,333	$ 3,333	$ 3,333	$ 3,333	$ 40,000
Travel	$ 5,000	$ 5,000	$ 5,000	$ 5,000	$ 5,000	$ 5,000	$ 95,000
Accounting	$ 1,000	$ 1,000	$ 1,000	$ 1,000	$ 1,000	$ 1,000	$ 12,000
Admin salaries	$ 12,500	$ 12,500	$ 12,500	$ 12,500	$ 12,500	$ 12,500	$ 150,000
Depreciation	$ 5,000	$ 5,000	$ 5,000	$ 5,000	$ 5,000	$ 5,000	$ 60,000
General/Event insurance	$ 15,000	$ 15,000	$ 15,000	$ 15,000	$ 15,000	$ 28,000	$ 340,000
Legal fees	$ 1,000	$ 1,000	$ 1,000	$ 1,000	$ 1,000	$ 1,000	$ 16,000
Office expenses	$ 1,000	$ 1,000	$ 1,000	$ 1,000	$ 1,000	$ 1,000	$ 12,000
Utilities	$ 2,000	$ 2,000	$ 2,000	$ 2,000	$ 2,000	$ 2,000	$ 24,000
Literature production	$ 2,000	$ 2,000	$ 2,000	$ 2,000	$ 2,000	$ 2,000	$ 24,000
Total operating expense	**$ 52,833**	**$ 52,833**	**$ 52,833**	**$ 52,833**	**$ 52,833**	**$ 65,833**	**$ 791,000**
Total costs	**$118,883**	**$118,883**	**$118,883**	**$118,883**	**$118,883**	**$131,883**	
Operating income	**$136,394**	**$136,394**	**$136,394**	**$136,394**	**$136,394**	**$123,394**	**$1,240,593**
Income tax	**$ 40,918**	**$ 40,918**	**$ 40,918**	**$ 40,918**	**$ 40,918**	**$ 37,018**	**$ 372,178**
Net income	**$ 95,476**	**$ 95,476**	**$ 95,476**	**$ 95,476**	**$ 95,476**	**$ 86,376**	**$ 802,615**

Income statement

Season 1–5

Revenue	Season 1—'15	Season 2—'16	Season 3—'17	Season 4—'18	Season 5—'19
Entry fee revenue	$1,090,000	$1,250,000	$1,470,000	$1,690,500	$1,944,075
Clinic revenue	$ 155,000	$ 203,000	$ 240,000	$ 276,000	$ 317,400
Sponsor revenue	$ 900,000	$1,290,000	$1,880,000	$2,600,000	$3,175,000
Program revenue	$ 38,066	$ 45,679	$ 54,815	$ 65,777	$ 78,933
Vendor revenue	$1,449,600	$1,739,520	$2,087,424	$2,504,909	$3,005,891
Concessions revenue	$ 51,045	$ 30,000	$ 50,000	$ 60,000	$ 72,000
General admission revenue	$ 21,735	$ 16,000	$ 25,000	$ 30,000	$ 36,000
Photography revenue	$ 70,896	$ 38,000	$ 50,000	$ 60,000	$ 72,000
Parking revenue	$ 13,167	$ 18,000	$ 25,000	$ 30,000	$ 36,000
Magazine revenue	$ 93,635	$ 25,000	$ 40,000	$ 48,000	$ 57,600
Total revenue	**$3,883,143**	**$4,655,199**	**$5,922,239**	**$7,365,186**	**$8,794,898**
Cost of sales					
Payroll	$1,321,000	$1,585,200	$1,902,240	$2,282,688	$2,739,226
Office rent	$ 12,000	$ 14,400	$ 17,280	$ 20,736	$ 24,883
Venue rent	$ 290,000	$ 348,000	$ 417,600	$ 501,120	$ 601,344
Prizes/awards	$ 250,000	$ 300,000	$ 360,000	$ 432,000	$ 518,400
Office supplies	$ 16,500	$ 19,800	$ 23,760	$ 28,512	$ 34,214
Total cost of sales	**$1,851,550**	**$2,267,400**	**$2,720,880**	**$3,265,056**	**$3,918,067**
Gross profit	**$2,031,593**	**$2,387,799**	**$3,201,359**	**$4,100,130**	**$4,876,831**
Operating expense					
Advertising	$ 60,000	$ 72,000	$ 86,400	$ 103,680	$ 124,416
Sales commissions	$ 112,050	$ 134,460	$ 161,352	$ 193,622	$ 232,347
Travel	$ 95,000	$ 114,000	$ 136,800	$ 164,160	$ 196,992
Accounting	$ 12,000	$ 14,400	$ 17,280	$ 20,736	$ 24,883
Admin salaries	$ 150,000	$ 180,000	$ 216,000	$ 259,200	$ 311,040
Depreciation	$ 60,000	$ 60,000	$ 60,000	$ 60,000	$ 60,000
General/event insurance	$ 340,000	$ 408,000	$ 489,600	$ 587,520	$ 705,024
Legal fees	$ 16,000	$ 19,200	$ 23,040	$ 27,648	$ 33,178
Office expenses	$ 12,000	$ 14,400	$ 17,280	$ 20,736	$ 24,883
Utilities	$ 24,000	$ 28,800	$ 34,560	$ 41,472	$ 49,766
Literature production	$ 24,000	$ 28,800	$ 34,560	$ 41,472	$ 49,766
Total operating expense	**$ 791,000**	**$1,045,260**	**$1,242,312**	**$1,478,774**	**$1,762,529**
Total costs	**$2,642,550**	**$3,312,660**	**$3,963,192**	**$4,743,830**	**$5,680,596**
Operating income	**$1,240,593**	**$1,342,539**	**$1,959,047**	**$2,621,356**	**$3,114,302**
Income tax	**$ 372,178**	**$ 402,762**	**$ 587,714**	**$ 786,407**	**$ 934,291**
Net income	**$ 802,615**	**$ 939,777**	**$1,371,333**	**$1,834,949**	**$2,180,011**

Balance sheet and cash flows

Preseason and season 1

Balance sheet	Preseason	April	May	June	July	Aug	Sept
Current assets							
Cash	$ 646,000	$ 655,782	$ 703,011	$ 678,049	$ 741,400	$ 814,384	$ 914,860
Total current assets	**$ 646,000**	**$ 655,782**	**$ 703,011**	**$ 678,049**	**$ 741,400**	**$ 814,384**	**$ 914,860**
Long term assets							
Equipment	$ 739,000	$ 739,000	$ 739,000	$ 739,000	$ 739,000	$ 739,000	$ 739,000
Furniture and supplies	$ 35,000	$ 35,000	$ 35,000	$ 35,000	$ 35,000	$ 35,000	$ 35,000
Total long term assets	$ 774,000	$ 774,000	$ 774,000	$ 774,000	$ 774,000	$ 774,000	$ 774,000
Accumulated depreciation	$ —	$ 5,000	$ 10,000	$ 15,000	$ 20,000	$ 25,000	$ 30,000
Net long term assets	$ 774,000	$ 769,000	$ 764,000	$ 759,000	$ 754,000	$ 749,000	$ 744,000
Total assets	**$1,420,000**	**$1,424,782**	**$1,467,011**	**$1,437,049**	**$1,563,384**	**$1,563,384**	**$1,658,860**
Liabilities & owners' equity							
Long term debt	$ —	$ —	$ —	$ —	$ —	$ —	$ —
Total liabilities	**$ —**	**$ —**	**$ —**	**$ —**	**$ —**	**$ —**	**$ —**
Owner/stockholder equity							
Owner's stake in company	$1,640,000	$1,640,000	$1,640,000	$1,640,000	$1,640,000	$1,640,000	$1,640,000
Retained earnings	$ (220,000)	$ 4,782	$ 47,011	$ 17,049	$ 75,400	$ 143,384	$ 238,860
Total owners' equity	**$1,420,000**	**$1,644,782**	**$1,687,011**	**$1,687,049**	**$1,715,400**	**$1,783,384**	**$1,878,860**
Total liabilities & equity	**$1,420,000**	**$1,644,782**	**$1,687,011**	**$1,687,049**	**$1,715,400**	**$1,783,384**	**$1,878,860**
Cash flows							
Operations during the year:							
Net income after taxes	$ (220,000)	$ 4,782	$ 42,229	$ (29,963)	$ 58,351	$ 67,985	$ 95,476
Add deprieciation	$ —	$ 5,000	$ 5,000	$ 5,000	$ 5,000	$ 5,000	$ 5,000
Cash from operations	$ (220,000)	$ 9,782	$ 47,229	$ (24,963)	$ 63,351	$ 72,985	$ 100,476
Paid in capital	$1,640,000	$ —	$ —	$ —	$ —	$ —	$ —
Cash from operations and financing	**$1,420,000**	**$ 9,782**	**$ 47,229**	**$ (24,963)**	**$ 63,351**	**$ 72,985**	**$ 100,476**
Applications of cash:							
Long term assets	$ 774,000	$ —	$ —	$ —	$ —	$ —	$ —
Dividends disbursed							
Increase/(Decrease) in cash	$ 646,000	$ 9,782	$ 47,229	$ (24,963)	$ 63,351	$ 72,985	$ 100,476
Change in cash balance:							
Beginning cash balance	$ —	$ 646,000	$ 655,782	$ 703,011	$ 678,049	$ 741,400	$ 814,384
Increase/(Decrease) in cash	$ 646,000	$ 9,782	$ 47,229	$ (24,963)	$ 63,351	$ 72,985	$ 100,476
Ending cash balance	**$ 646,000**	**$ 655,782**	**$ 703,011**	**$ 678,049**	**$ 741,400**	**$ 814,384**	**$ 914,860**

(continued)

Balance sheet and cash flows [CONTINUED]

Preseason and season 1

Balance sheet	Oct	Nov	Dec	Jan	Feb	Mar	Year 1
Current assets							
Cash	$1,015,336	$1,115,812	$1,216,288	$1,316,764	$1,417,239	$1,508,615	$1,508,615
Total current assets	**$1,015,336**	**$1,115,812**	**$1,216,288**	**$1,316,764**	**$1,417,239**	**$1,508,615**	**$1,508,615**
Long term assets							
Equipment	$ 739,000	$ 739,000	$ 739,000	$ 739,000	$ 739,000	$ 739,000	$ 739,000
Furniture and supplies	$ 35,000	$ 35,000	$ 35,000	$ 35,000	$ 35,000	$ 35,000	$ 35,000
Total long term assets	$ 774,000	$ 774,000	$ 774,000	$ 774,000	$ 774,000	$ 774,000	$ 774,000
Accumulated depreciation	$ 35,000	$ 40,000	$ 45,000	$ 50,000	$ 55,000	$ 60,000	$ 60,000
Net long term assets	$ 739,000	$ 734,000	$ 729,000	$ 724,000	$ 719,000	$ 714,000	$ 714,000
Total assets	**$1,754,336**	**$1,849,812**	**$1,945,288**	**$2,040,764**	**$2,136,239**	**$2,222,615**	**$2,222,615**
Liabilities & owners' equity							
Long term debt	$ —	$ —	$ —	$ —	$ —	$ —	$ —
Total liabilities	**$ —**	**$ —**	**$ —**	**$ —**	**$ —**	**$ —**	**$ —**
Owner/stockholder equity							
Owner's stake in company	$1,640,000	$1,640,000	$1,640,000	$1,640,000	$1,640,000	$1,640,000	$1,640,000
Retained earnings	$ 334,336	$ 429,812	$ 525,288	$ 620,764	$ 716,239	$ 802,615	$ 802,615
Total owners' equity	$1,974,336	$2,069,812	$2,165,288	$2,260,764	$2,356,239	$2,442,615	$2,442,615
Total liabilities & equity	**$1,974,336**	**$2,069,812**	**$2,165,288**	**$2,260,764**	**$2,356,239**	**$2,442,615**	**$2,442,615**
Cash flows							
Operations during the year:							
Net income after taxes	$ 95,476	$ 95,476	$ 95,476	$ 95,476	$ 95,476	$ 86,376	$ 802,615
Add deprieciation	$ 5,000	$ 5,000	$ 5,000	$ 5,000	$ 5,000	$ 5,000	$ 60,000
Cash from operations	$ 100,476	$ 100,476	$ 100,476	$ 100,476	$ 100,476	$ 91,376	$ 862,615
Paid in capital	$ —	$ —	$ —	$ —	$ —	$ —	$1,120,000
Cash from operations and financing	**$ 100,476**	**$ 100,476**	**$ 100,476**	**$ 100,476**	**$ 100,476**	**$ 91,376**	**$1,982,615**
Applications of cash:							
Long term assets	$ —	$ —	$ —	$ —	$ —	$ —	$ —
Dividends disbursed							
Increase/(Decrease) in cash	$ 100,476	$ 100,476	$ 100,476	$ 100,476	$ 100,476	$ 91,376	$1,982,615
Change in cash balance:							
Beginning cash balance	$ 914,860	$1,015,336	$1,115,812	$1,216,288	$1,316,764	$1,417,239	$ —
Increase/(Decrease) in cash	$ 100,476	$ 100,476	$ 100,476	$ 100,476	$ 100,476	$ 91,376	$1,982,615
Ending cash balance	**$1,015,336**	**$1,115,812**	**$1,216,288**	**$1,316,764**	**$1,417,239**	**$1,508,615**	**$1,982,615**

Balance sheet

Assets	Season 1 2015	Season 2 2016	Season 3 2017	Season 4 2018	Season 5 2019
Current assets					
Cash	$1,508,615	$2,982,392	$4,413,725	$6,308,674	$8,548,685
Total current assets	$1,508,615	$2,982,392	$4,413,725	$6,308,674	$8,548,685
Long term assets					
Equipment	$ 739,000	$ 739,000	$ 739,000	$ 739,000	$ 739,000
Furniture and supplies	$ 35,000	$ 35,000	$ 35,000	$ 35,000	$ 35,000
Total long term assets	$ 774,000	$ 774,000	$ 774,000	$ 774,000	$ 774,000
Accumulated depreciation	$ 60,000	$ 120,000	$ 180,000	$ 240,000	$ 300,000
Net long term assets	$ 714,000	$ 654,000	$ 594,000	$ 534,000	$ 474,000
Total assets	**$2,222,615**	**$3,636,392**	**$5,007,725**	**$6,842,674**	**$9,022,685**
Liabilities & owners' equity					
Long term debt	$ —	$ —	$ —	$ —	$ —
Total liabilities	$ —	$ —	$ —	$ —	$ —
Owner/stockholder equity					
Owner's stake in company	$1,400,000	$1,400,000	$1,400,000	$1,400,000	$1,400,000
retained earnings	$ 802,615	$1,742,392	$3,113,725	$4,948,674	$7,128,685
Total owners' equity	$2,202,615	$3,142,392	$4,513,725	$6,348,674	$8,528,685
Total liabilities & equity	**$2,202,615**	**$3,142,392**	**$4,513,725**	**$6,348,674**	**$8,528,685**

Cash flows

	Season 1 2015	Season 2 2016	Season 3 2017	Season 4 2018	Season 5 2019
Operations during the year:					
Net income after taxes	$ 802,615	$ 939,777	$1,371,333	$1,834,949	$2,180,011
Add depreciation	$ 60,000	$ 60,000	$ 60,000	$ 60,000	$ 60,000
Cash from operations	$ 862,615	$ 999,777	$1,431,333	$1,894,949	$2,240,011
Paid in capital	$1,400,000	$ 0	$ 0	$ 0	$ 0
Cash from operations and financing	$2,262,615	$ 999,777	$1,431,333	$1,894,949	$2,240,011
Applications of cash:					
Long term assets	$ —	$ 0	$ 0	$ 0	$ 0
Dividends disbursed					
Increase/(decrease) in cash	$2,262,615	$ 999,777	$1,431,333	$1,894,949	$2,240,011
Change in cash balance	$ —	$ —	$ —	$ —	$ —
Beginning cash balance	$ —	$1,982,615	$2,982,392	$4,413,725	$6,308,674
Increase/(decrease) in cash	$2,262,615	$ 999,777	$1,431,333	$1,894,949	$2,240,011
Ending cash balance	$1,982,615	$2,982,392	$4,413,725	$6,308,674	$8,548,685

Tour Company

SeeDetroit!

PO Box 34543
Detroit, MI 48203

Zuzu Enterprises

Exciting things are happening in Detroit, but many people are unaware of all of the places to see and things to do in the city. See Detroit! is trying to address this discrepancy by offering tours of the city on a daily basis as well as custom tours designed around individual clients' interests and schedule.

EXECUTIVE SUMMARY

Exciting things are happening in Detroit! Detroit is thriving with art and entrepreneurship. The Cobo Hall renovation will be completed soon, plans for a new hockey area are being developed, and downtown Detroit is full of new businesses. The city is safe, easily accessible, and features a 97 percent occupancy rate. More than ever, Detroit is the place to be.

Unfortunately, predominately negative news coverage about the city has left many unaware of the exciting changes happening and all of the places to see and things to do in the city. See Detroit! is trying to address this discrepancy by offering tours of the city on a daily basis as well as custom tours designed around individual clients' interests and schedule.

INDUSTRY/MARKET ANALYSIS

Despite growing competition from online-based travel companies, tour operators are recovery-bound. Improved disposable income levels and a strengthening global economy will encourage more U.S. residents to travel. The growth rate for the travel industry is expected to be at or above 4.2 percent for the next five years.

This, combined with the rich history and current revival of the city, makes Detroit an optimal place to start a tour company.

One entity that actively promotes the city as a destination for conventions and vacations is the Detroit Metro Convention & Visitors Bureau (DMCVB). Some of the highlights that they promote about Detroit include:

- Detroit hosts the largest free jazz festival in the world and is home to Movement: Electronic Music Festival.

- Detroit is among the largest theater districts in the country with over 13,000 theater seats. Major Broadway productions, top headliner entertainers, opera, dance, symphony, and other performing arts light up marquees.

- Detroit is a great sports town with the Detroit Tigers, Detroit Lions and Detroit Red Wings playing downtown, and the Detroit Pistons in Oakland County.

- Home of three major casino complexes in the downtown area: Greektown Casino, MGM Grand Detroit and Motor City Casino.

- Detroit's Corktown, Greektown and Mexicantown districts offer up a menu of authentic foods and spirits.

- Detroit is headquarters for Chrysler, Ford, and General Motors and hundreds of tier one and two auto suppliers.

- It is home of the North American International Auto Show, with more than 500 vehicles on display representing more than 50 world-wide companies.

- The Charles H. Wright Museum of African American History is the largest museum of its kind in the world.

- Detroit's Cultural Center is home to the Detroit Institute of Arts, and its collection is among the top six in the United States.

- The world's first convention and visitors bureau — the Detroit Metro Convention & Visitors Bureau — was founded in 1896.

- The Marriott at the Renaissance Center is the second tallest hotel in North America. When it was opened in 1977, it was the tallest hotel in the world.

- Detroit is home to the world's only floating post office, the J.W. Westcott II, serving international freighters on the Detroit River.

- In 1913 Henry Ford introduced an improved assembly line in Detroit, revolutionizing the auto industry.

- Metro Detroit is home of the auto barons. Historic homes include Fair Lane (Henry and Clara Ford); Fisher Mansion (Lawrence Fisher), Ford House (Edsel & Eleanor Ford); and Meadow Brook Hall (Matilda Dodge Wilson).

- At 987 acres, Belle Isle Park is the largest island park in the United States. First opened to the public in 1884, it is Detroit's first major city park. Designed by Frederick Law Olmstead, the same designer credited with New York City's Central Park.

- Though not the most Northern major U.S. City, Detroit is the only city in the 48 contiguous States where one can gaze south toward Canada.

- Detroit is built over an enormous salt bed. 1,200 feet below the city surface, salt mines spread over 1,400 acres and have more than 50 miles of roads.

- Most people associate Detroit music with the Motown sound. Celebrating its 50th anniversary this year it has earned a well-deserved place in music history. Another sound, however, that is a true Detroit original is Techno. Originating in the 1980s, largely as an underground movement, the increasingly popular new music proved electronics can be used to express both funk and soul. Juan Atkins, Derrick May, and Kevin Saunderson, a Detroit trio who were high school friends, are considered the Godfathers of Techno.

- The Eastern Market, a major commercial food distribution center famous for the quality, freshness and variety of its produce, meat, fish and even flowers, has been in existence since 1892.

In addition to this rich history, Detroit is undergoing improvement and development at break-neck speed. Some current developments include:

- Cobo Hall is being renovated and will be completed soon

- Plans for a new hockey area are being developed

- Downtown Detroit is full of new businesses including Shinola, Autobike, Chalkfly, Detroit Labs, Dr. Sushi, Stik, LevelEleven, UpTo, Are You Human, Motor City 2.0, and Detroit Tread

SERVICES

GENERAL TOURS

SeeDetroit! plans to make Detroit accessible to visitors from near and far by offering daily, general tours. Our two-hour van tours provide a fun overview of Downtown Detroit's highlights and attractions. Knowledgeable local guides provide an insider's perspective and a totally enjoyable Detroit tour experience. General tours will cover the following areas:

- Downtown

- Campus Martius Park

- Stadium & Entertainment District

- Greektown

- Midtown/Cultural Center

- Eastern Market

- RiverWalk/Rivertown

- Heidelberg Project

- Belle Isle Park

- Art and architecture

CUSTOM TOURS

In addition to our daily public tours, we also offer special interest van tours that can easily be tailored to a guest's schedule and individual interests. Examples of special interest custom tours includes:

Art Tour
- Detroit Institute of Arts

- Museum of Contemporary Art Detroit

- Heidleberg Project

- Pewabic Pottery

- People Mover Art in the Stations

- Graffiti art

Sports Tour
- Stadiums—Ford Field, Joe Louis Arena, Comerica Park

- New site for hockey stadium

- Stadium stores and ticket offices

- Old Tiger Stadium site

- Belle Isle race track

Food Tour
- Eastern Market
- Earthworks Urban Farm
- Specialty stops of interest, including such places as Devries Cheese Shop, Slows Bar BQ, Bucharest Grill, Coney Island, Mexican Village, Greektown, Hamtramck (Polish), Dearborn (Middle Eastern), Atwater Block Brewery, Traffic Jam and Snug, etc.

History Tour
- Detroit Historical Museum
- Charles H. Wright Museum of African American History
- Motown Historical Museum
- Michigan Central Station
- Historic neighborhoods and homes
- Historic First Congregational Church of Detroit Underground Railroad Living Museum
- Location of the 1960's riots
- Location of Prohibition sites

Shopping Tour
- Eastern Market
- Park Shelton retail area
- Willis/Canfield Retail Districts
- Specialty stores of interest including Shinola watches and jewelry from Rebel Nell

Casino Tour
- MGM Grand Detroit
- Greektown Casino
- MotorCity Casino
- Caesar's Windsor (passports required)

PICK-UP AND DROP-OFF SERVICES

Hotel Pick-Ups and Drop-Offs
We pick up our tour guests at a number of well-located Downtown hotels. Unless otherwise requested, passengers will be returned to their original starting location.

Downtown and Suburbs Pick-ups and Drop-Offs
Guests living or staying in other places will be picked up in convenient, central locations. We will discuss the best pick-up location for guests when reservations are made. Unless otherwise requested, passengers will be returned to their original starting location.

OTHER SERVICES

Ticket Services
In addition to the sight-seeing tours, SeeDetroit! will also secure admission to local attractions, shows, and events. Cost will be determined by actual cost plus 5-20% finder's fee, depending on availability. This includes bicycle tours, sporting events, concerts, plays and musicals, special museum exhibits, and the like.

Charter Bus Tour Guides
SeeDetroit! also offers a personal guide for a tour operator bringing a motor coach to downtown Detroit as well as larger groups of family, friends, neighbors or business associates. The bus tour will be customized to fit the interests of the group so it is both enjoyable and informative.

PERSONNEL

Owner/Operator
SeeDetroit! is owned and operated by Lisa Pierce. Lisa has lived in the city of Detroit for the past seven years and has been continually amazed at all of the history, art, food, sports, and shopping the city has to offer. When she first moved to the city, finding her way around was daunting. She embraced the city and hopes to share her love of it and all it has to offer with others.

Prior to starting SeeDetroit!, Lisa worked in the tourism industry in such places as Orlando, Florida and Chicago, Illinois. Her experience working with tourists and seeing to their every need will prove essential to the success of SeeDetroit!

Tour Guides
All tour guides live and play in the city. They know their way around and want to share their insider knowledge with others. To begin, one guide will he hired on a part-time, independent basis that specializes in each of the custom tour areas, including art, food, shopping, sports, history, and casinos.

Professional & Advisory Support
SeeDetroit! has established a business banking account with Comerica Bank, including a merchant account for accepting credit card payments. Tax advisement is provided by Baker Tilly. The owner worked in partnership with the local law firm, Goldman & Associates, to establish their corporation. The law firm will continue to provide the business with legal counsel on an as-needed basis.

OPERATIONS

Location
SeeDetroit! will be based out of the owner's home located at 17655 Manderson Rd, Detroit, MI 48203. Correspondence will be done via post office box.

Vehicles
Our tour vans seat five to six passengers comfortably. All vehicles are fully licensed and insured, and all drivers have been vetted for safety. Each van is equipped with a step stool for boarding assistance as well as a first-aid kit and small beverage cooler.

All vehicles will be decorated with a graphic wrap that clearly identifies the company name, logo, phone number, and web address. This wrapping will turn our vehicles into traveling advertisements that will add to our brand recognition as we travel throughout Detroit.

All vehicles will be cleaned daily and free from dirt and debris. Air fresheners will also be used.

We can arrange for larger vehicles to accommodate your group upon request, subject to availability.

Hours of Operation

SeeDetroit! will offer daily tours at 10am and 2pm. Custom tours will be planned and scheduled according to customer interest and availability. No tours will be offered on major holidays including New Year's Day, Easter, Memorial Day, the Fourth of July, Labor Day, Thanksgiving, and Christmas.

Fees

Tour rates for the daily tours are as follows:

- Adults—$59

- Seniors/Students—$49

- 17/Under—$20

Tour rates for custom tours will be determined based on destination and duration.

MARKETING & ADVERTISING

SeeDetroit! will follow several avenues for promoting the business, including internet and social media, common review sites, and curating relationships with concierges of local hotels and casinos. Advertisements will be placed in several local publications.

Internet and Social Media Presence
- Web site

- Facebook

- Instagram

- Tumblr

- Twitter

Review Sites
- tripadvisor

- Google

- Facebook

- Yelp

Marketing
- Hotels

- Casinos

- *Crain's Detroit*

- *Detroit Free Press*

- *MetroTimes*

BUSINESS PLAN TEMPLATE

USING THIS TEMPLATE

A business plan carefully spells out a company's projected course of action over a period of time, usually the first two to three years after the start-up. In addition, banks, lenders, and other investors examine the information and financial documentation before deciding whether or not to finance a new business venture. Therefore, a business plan is an essential tool in obtaining financing and should describe the business itself in detail as well as all important factors influencing the company, including the market, industry, competition, operations and management policies, problem solving strategies, financial resources and needs, and other vital information. The plan enables the business owner to anticipate costs, plan for difficulties, and take advantage of opportunities, as well as design and implement strategies that keep the company running as smoothly as possible.

This template has been provided as a model to help you construct your own business plan. Please keep in mind that there is no single acceptable format for a business plan, and that this template is in no way comprehensive, but serves as an example.

The business plans provided in this section are fictional and have been used by small business agencies as models for clients to use in compiling their own business plans.

GENERIC BUSINESS PLAN

Main headings included below are topics that should be covered in a comprehensive business plan. They include:

Business Summary

Purpose
Provides a brief overview of your business, succinctly highlighting the main ideas of your plan.

Includes

- Name and Type of Business
- Description of Product/Service
- Business History and Development
- Location
- Market

- Competition
- Management
- Financial Information
- Business Strengths and Weaknesses
- Business Growth

Table of Contents

Purpose
Organized in an Outline Format, the Table of Contents illustrates the selection and arrangement of information contained in your plan.

Includes

- Topic Headings and Subheadings
- Page Number References

Business History and Industry Outlook

Purpose

Examines the conception and subsequent development of your business within an industry specific context.

Includes

- Start-up Information
- Owner/Key Personnel Experience
- Location
- Development Problems and Solutions
- Investment/Funding Information
- Future Plans and Goals
- Market Trends and Statistics
- Major Competitors
- Product/Service Advantages
- National, Regional, and Local Economic Impact

Product/Service

Purpose

Introduces, defines, and details the product and/or service that inspired the information of your business.

Includes

- Unique Features
- Niche Served
- Market Comparison
- Stage of Product/Service Development
- Production
- Facilities, Equipment, and Labor
- Financial Requirements
- Product/Service Life Cycle
- Future Growth

Market Examination

Purpose

Assessment of product/service applications in relation to consumer buying cycles.

Includes

- Target Market
- Consumer Buying Habits
- Product/Service Applications
- Consumer Reactions
- Market Factors and Trends
- Penetration of the Market
- Market Share
- Research and Studies
- Cost
- Sales Volume and Goals

Competition

Purpose

Analysis of Competitors in the Marketplace.

Includes

- Competitor Information
- Product/Service Comparison
- Market Niche
- Product/Service Strengths and Weaknesses
- Future Product/Service Development

Marketing

Purpose

Identifies promotion and sales strategies for your product/service.

Includes

- Product/Service Sales Appeal
- Special and Unique Features
- Identification of Customers
- Sales and Marketing Staff
- Sales Cycles
- Type of Advertising/ Promotion
- Pricing
- Competition
- Customer Services

Operations

Purpose

Traces product/service development from production/inception to the market environment.

Includes

- Cost Effective Production Methods
- Facility
- Location
- Equipment
- Labor
- Future Expansion

Administration and Management

Purpose

Offers a statement of your management philosophy with an in-depth focus on processes and procedures.

Includes

- Management Philosophy
- Structure of Organization
- Reporting System
- Methods of Communication
- Employee Skills and Training
- Employee Needs and Compensation
- Work Environment
- Management Policies and Procedures
- Roles and Responsibilities

Key Personnel

Purpose

Describes the unique backgrounds of principle employees involved in business.

Includes

- Owner(s)/Employee Education and Experience
- Positions and Roles
- Benefits and Salary
- Duties and Responsibilities
- Objectives and Goals

Potential Problems and Solutions

Purpose

Discussion of problem solving strategies that change issues into opportunities.

Includes

- Risks
- Litigation
- Future Competition
- Economic Impact
- Problem Solving Skills

Financial Information

Purpose

Secures needed funding and assistance through worksheets and projections detailing financial plans, methods of repayment, and future growth opportunities.

Includes

- Financial Statements
- Bank Loans
- Methods of Repayment
- Tax Returns
- Start-up Costs
- Projected Income (3 years)
- Projected Cash Flow (3 Years)
- Projected Balance Statements (3 years)

Appendices

Purpose

Supporting documents used to enhance your business proposal.

Includes

- Photographs of product, equipment, facilities, etc.
- Copyright/Trademark Documents
- Legal Agreements
- Marketing Materials
- Research and or Studies
- Operation Schedules
- Organizational Charts
- Job Descriptions
- Resumes
- Additional Financial Documentation

Fictional Food Distributor

Commercial Foods, Inc.

3003 Avondale Ave.
Knoxville, TN 37920

This plan demonstrates how a partnership can have a positive impact on a new business. It demonstrates how two individuals can carve a niche in the specialty foods market by offering gourmet foods to upscale restaurants and fine hotels. This plan is fictional and has not been used to gain funding from a bank or other lending institution.

STATEMENT OF PURPOSE

Commercial Foods, Inc. seeks a loan of $75,000 to establish a new business. This sum, together with $5,000 equity investment by the principals, will be used as follows:

- Merchandise inventory $25,000
- Office fixture/equipment $12,000
- Warehouse equipment $14,000
- One delivery truck $10,000
- Working capital $39,000
- Total $100,000

DESCRIPTION OF THE BUSINESS

Commercial Foods, Inc. will be a distributor of specialty food service products to hotels and upscale restaurants in the geographical area of a 50 mile radius of Knoxville. Richard Roberts will direct the sales effort and John Williams will manage the warehouse operation and the office. One delivery truck will be used initially with a second truck added in the third year. We expect to begin operation of the business within 30 days after securing the requested financing.

MANAGEMENT

A. Richard Roberts is a native of Memphis, Tennessee. He is a graduate of Memphis State University with a Bachelor's degree from the School of Business. After graduation, he worked for a major manufacturer of specialty food service products as a detail sales person for five years, and, for the past three years, he has served as a product sales manager for this firm.

B. John Williams is a native of Nashville, Tennessee. He holds a B.S. Degree in Food Technology from the University of Tennessee. His career includes five years as a product development chemist in gourmet food products and five years as operations manager for a food service distributor.

Both men are healthy and energetic. Their backgrounds complement each other, which will ensure the success of Commercial Foods, Inc. They will set policies together and personnel decisions will be made jointly. Initial salaries for the owners will be $1,000 per month for the first few years. The spouses of both principals are successful in the business world and earn enough to support the families.

They have engaged the services of Foster Jones, CPA, and William Hale, Attorney, to assist them in an advisory capacity.

PERSONNEL

The firm will employ one delivery truck driver at a wage of $8.00 per hour. One office worker will be employed at $7.50 per hour. One part-time employee will be used in the office at $5.00 per hour. The driver will load and unload his own trucks. Mr. Williams will assist in the warehouse operation as needed to assist one stock person at $7.00 per hour. An additional delivery truck and driver will be added the third year.

LOCATION

The firm will lease a 20,000 square foot building at 3003 Avondale Ave., in Knoxville, which contains warehouse and office areas equipped with two-door truck docks. The annual rental is $9,000. The building was previously used as a food service warehouse and very little modification to the building will be required.

PRODUCTS AND SERVICES

The firm will offer specialty food service products such as soup bases, dessert mixes, sauce bases, pastry mixes, spices, and flavors, normally used by upscale restaurants and nice hotels. We are going after a niche in the market with high quality gourmet products. There is much less competition in this market than in standard run of the mill food service products. Through their work experiences, the principals have contacts with supply sources and with local chefs.

THE MARKET

We know from our market survey that there are over 200 hotels and upscale restaurants in the area we plan to serve. Customers will be attracted by a direct sales approach. We will offer samples of our products and product application data on use of our products in the finished prepared foods. We will cultivate the chefs in these establishments. The technical background of John Williams will be especially useful here.

COMPETITION

We find that we will be only distributor in the area offering a full line of gourmet food service products. Other foodservice distributors offer only a few such items in conjunction with their standard product line. Our survey shows that many of the chefs are ordering products from Atlanta and Memphis because of a lack of adequate local supply.

SUMMARY

Commercial Foods, Inc. will be established as a foodservice distributor of specialty food in Knoxville. The principals, with excellent experience in the industry, are seeking a $75,000 loan to establish the business. The principals are investing $25,000 as equity capital.

The business will be set up as an S Corporation with each principal owning 50% of the common stock in the corporation.

FICTIONAL HARDWARE STORE

OSHKOSH HARDWARE, INC.

123 Main St.
Oshkosh, WI 54901

The following plan outlines how a small hardware store can survive competition from large discount chains by offering products and providing expert advice in the use of any product it sells. This plan is fictional and has not been used to gain funding from a bank or other lending institution.

EXECUTIVE SUMMARY

Oshkosh Hardware, Inc. is a new corporation that is going to establish a retail hardware store in a strip mall in Oshkosh, Wisconsin. The store will sell hardware of all kinds, quality tools, paint, and housewares. The business will make revenue and a profit by servicing its customers not only with needed hardware but also with expert advice in the use of any product it sells.

Oshkosh Hardware, Inc. will be operated by its sole shareholder, James Smith. The company will have a total of four employees. It will sell its products in the local market. Customers will buy our products because we will provide free advice on the use of all of our products and will also furnish a full refund warranty.

Oshkosh Hardware, Inc. will sell its products in the Oshkosh store staffed by three sales representatives. No additional employees will be needed to achieve its short and long range goals. The primary short range goal is to open the store by October 1, 1994. In order to achieve this goal a lease must be signed by July 1, 1994 and the complete inventory ordered by August 1, 1994.

Mr. James Smith will invest $30,000 in the business. In addition, the company will have to borrow $150,000 during the first year to cover the investment in inventory, accounts receivable, and furniture and equipment. The company will be profitable after six months of operation and should be able to start repayment of the loan in the second year.

THE BUSINESS

The business will sell hardware of all kinds, quality tools, paint, and housewares. We will purchase our products from three large wholesale buying groups.

In general our customers are homeowners who do their own repair and maintenance, hobbyists, and housewives. Our business is unique in that we will have a complete line of all hardware items and will be able to get special orders by overnight delivery. The business makes revenue and profits by servicing our customers not only with needed hardware but also with expert advice in the use of any product we sell. Our major costs for bringing our products to market are cost of merchandise of 36%, salaries of $45,000, and occupancy costs of $60,000.

Oshkosh Hardware, Inc.'s retail outlet will be located at 1524 Frontage Road, which is in a newly developed retail center of Oshkosh. Our location helps facilitate accessibility from all parts of town and reduces our delivery costs. The store will occupy 7500 square feet of space. The major equipment involved in our business is counters and shelving, a computer, a paint mixing machine, and a truck.

THE MARKET

Oshkosh Hardware, Inc. will operate in the local market. There are 15,000 potential customers in this market area. We have three competitors who control approximately 98% of the market at present. We feel we can capture 25% of the market within the next four years. Our major reason for believing this is that our staff is technically competent to advise our customers in the correct use of all products we sell.

After a careful market analysis, we have determined that approximately 60% of our customers are men and 40% are women. The percentage of customers that fall into the following age categories are:

Under 16: 0%
17-21: 5%
22-30: 30%
31-40: 30%
41-50: 20%
51-60: 10%
61-70: 5%
Over 70: 0%

The reasons our customers prefer our products is our complete knowledge of their use and our full refund warranty.

We get our information about what products our customers want by talking to existing customers. There seems to be an increasing demand for our product. The demand for our product is increasing in size based on the change in population characteristics.

SALES

At Oshkosh Hardware, Inc. we will employ three sales people and will not need any additional personnel to achieve our sales goals. These salespeople will need several years experience in home repair and power tool usage. We expect to attract 30% of our customers from newspaper ads, 5% of our customers from local directories, 5% of our customers from the yellow pages, 10% of our customers from family and friends, and 50% of our customers from current customers. The most cost effect source will be current customers. In general our industry is growing.

MANAGEMENT

We would evaluate the quality of our management staff as being excellent. Our manager is experienced and very motivated to achieve the various sales and quality assurance objectives we have set. We will use a management information system that produces key inventory, quality assurance, and sales data on a weekly basis. All data is compared to previously established goals for that week, and deviations are the primary focus of the management staff.

GOALS IMPLEMENTATION

The short term goals of our business are:

1. Open the store by October 1, 1994
2. Reach our breakeven point in two months
3. Have sales of $100,000 in the first six months

In order to achieve our first short term goal we must:

1. Sign the lease by July 1, 1994
2. Order a complete inventory by August 1, 1994

In order to achieve our second short term goal we must:

1. Advertise extensively in Sept. and Oct.
2. Keep expenses to a minimum

In order to achieve our third short term goal we must:

1. Promote power tool sales for the Christmas season
2. Keep good customer traffic in Jan. and Feb.

The long term goals for our business are:

1. Obtain sales volume of $600,000 in three years
2. Become the largest hardware dealer in the city
3. Open a second store in Fond du Lac

The most important thing we must do in order to achieve the long term goals for our business is to develop a highly profitable business with excellent cash flow.

FINANCE

Oshkosh Hardware, Inc. Faces some potential threats or risks to our business. They are discount house competition. We believe we can avoid or compensate for this by providing quality products complimented by quality advice on the use of every product we sell. The financial projections we have prepared are located at the end of this document.

JOB DESCRIPTION-GENERAL MANAGER

The General Manager of the business of the corporation will be the president of the corporation. He will be responsible for the complete operation of the retail hardware store which is owned by the corporation. A detailed description of his duties and responsibilities is as follows.

Sales

Train and supervise the three sales people. Develop programs to motivate and compensate these employees. Coordinate advertising and sales promotion effects to achieve sales totals as outlined in budget. Oversee purchasing function and inventory control procedures to insure adequate merchandise at all times at a reasonable cost.

Finance

Prepare monthly and annual budgets. Secure adequate line of credit from local banks. Supervise office personnel to insure timely preparation of records, statements, all government reports, control of receivables and payables, and monthly financial statements.

Administration

Perform duties as required in the areas of personnel, building leasing and maintenance, licenses and permits, and public relations.

Organizations, Agencies, & Consultants

A listing of Associations and Consultants of interest to entrepreneurs, followed by the ten Small Business Administration Regional Offices, Small Business Development Centers, Service Corps of Retired Executives offices, and Venture Capital and Finance Companies.

Associations

This section contains a listing of associations and other agencies of interest to the small business owner. Entries are listed alphabetically by organization name.

American Business Women's Association
9100 Ward Pkwy.
PO Box 8728
Kansas City, MO 64114-0728
(800)228-0007
E-mail: abwa@abwa.org
Website: http://www.abwa.org
Jeanne Banks, National President

American Franchisee Association
53 W Jackson Blvd., Ste. 1157
Chicago, IL 60604
(312)431-0545
E-mail: info@franchisee.org
Website: http://www.franchisee.org
Susan P. Kezios, President

American Independent Business Alliance
222 S Black Ave.
Bozeman, MT 59715
(406)582-1255
E-mail: info@amiba.net
Website: http://www.amiba.net
Jennifer Rockne, Director

American Small Businesses Association
206 E College St., Ste. 201
Grapevine, TX 76051
800-942-2722
E-mail: info@asbaonline.org
Website: http://www.asbaonline.org/

American Women's Economic Development Corporation
216 East 45th St., 10th Floor
New York, NY 10017
(917)368-6100

Fax: (212)986-7114
E-mail: info@awed.org
Website: http://www.awed.org
Roseanne Antonucci, Exec. Dir.

Association for Enterprise Opportunity
1601 N Kent St., Ste. 1101
Arlington, VA 22209
(703)841-7760
Fax: (703)841-7748
E-mail: aeo@assoceo.org
Website: http://www.micro enterpriseworks.org
Bill Edwards, Exec.Dir.

Association of Small Business Development Centers
c/o Don Wilson
8990 Burke Lake Rd.
Burke, VA 22015
(703)764-9850
Fax: (703)764-1234
E-mail: info@asbdc-us.org
Website: http://www.asbdc-us.org
Don Wilson, Pres./CEO

BEST Employers Association
2505 McCabe Way
Irvine, CA 92614
(949)253-4080
800-433-0088
Fax: (714)553-0883
E-mail: info@bestlife.com
Website: http://www.bestlife.com
Donald R. Lawrenz, CEO

Center for Family Business
PO Box 24219
Cleveland, OH 44124
(440)460-5409
E-mail: grummi@aol.com
Dr. Leon A. Danco, Chm.

Coalition for Government Procurement
1990 M St. NW, Ste. 400
Washington, DC 20036
(202)331-0975
E-mail: info@thecgp.org
Website: http://www.coalgovpro.org
Paul Caggiano, Pres.

Employers of America
PO Box 1874
Mason City, IA 50402-1874
(641)424-3187
800-728-3187
Fax: (641)424-1673
E-mail: employer@employerhelp.org
Website: http://www.employerhelp.org
Jim Collison, Pres.

Family Firm Institute
200 Lincoln St., Ste. 201
Boston, MA 02111
(617)482-3045
Fax: (617)482-3049
E-mail: ffi@ffi.org
Website: http://www.ffi.org
Judy L. Green, Ph.D., Exec.Dir.

Independent Visually Impaired Enterprisers
500 S 3rd St., Apt. H
Burbank, CA 91502
(818)238-9321
E-mail: abazyn@bazyn communications.com
http://www.acb.org/affiliates
Adris Bazyn, Pres.

International Association for Business Organizations
3 Woodthorn Ct., Ste. 12
Owings Mills, MD 21117
(410)581-1373
E-mail: nahbb@msn.com
Rudolph Lewis, Exec. Officer

263

International Council for Small Business
The George Washington University School of Business and Public Management
2115 G St. NW, Ste. 403
Washington, DC 20052
(202)994-0704
Fax: (202)994-4930
E-mail: icsb@gwu.edu
Website: http://www.icsb.org
Susan G. Duffy. Admin.

International Small Business Consortium
3309 Windjammer St.
Norman, OK 73072
E-mail: sb@isbc.com
Website: http://www.isbc.com

Kauffman Center for Entrepreneurial Leadership
4801 Rockhill Rd.
Kansas City, MO 64110-2046
(816)932-1000
E-mail: info@kauffman.org
Website: http://www.entreworld.org

National Alliance for Fair Competition
3 Bethesda Metro Center, Ste. 1100
Bethesda, MD 20814
(410)235-7116
Fax: (410)235-7116
E-mail: ampesq@aol.com
Tony Ponticelli, Exec.Dir.

National Association for the Self-Employed
PO Box 612067
DFW Airport
Dallas, TX 75261-2067
(800)232-6273
E-mail: mpetron@nase.org
Website: http://www.nase.org
Robert Hughes, Pres.

National Association of Business Leaders
4132 Shoreline Dr., Ste. J & H
Earth City, MO 63045
Fax: (314)298-9110
E-mail: nabl@nabl.com
Website: http://www.nabl.com/
Gene Blumenthal, Contact

National Association of Private Enterprise
PO Box 15550
Long Beach, CA 90815
888-224-0953

Fax: (714)844-4942
Website: http://www.napeonline.net
Laura Squiers, Exec.Dir.

National Association of Small Business Investment Companies
666 11th St. NW, Ste. 750
Washington, DC 20001
(202)628-5055
Fax: (202)628-5080
E-mail: nasbic@nasbic.org
Website: http://www.nasbic.org
Lee W. Mercer, Pres.

National Business Association
PO Box 700728
5151 Beltline Rd., Ste. 1150
Dallas, TX 75370
(972)458-0900
800-456-0440
Fax: (972)960-9149
E-mail: info@nationalbusiness.org
Website: http://www.national business.org
Raj Nisankarao, Pres.

National Business Owners Association
PO Box 111
Stuart, VA 24171
(276)251-7500
(866)251-7505
Fax: (276)251-2217
E-mail: membershipservices@nboa.org
Website: http://www.rvmdb.com.nboa
Paul LaBarr, Pres.

National Center for Fair Competition
PO Box 220
Annandale, VA 22003
(703)280-4622
Fax: (703)280-0942
E-mail: kentonp1@aol.com
Kenton Pattie, Pres.

National Family Business Council
1640 W. Kennedy Rd.
Lake Forest, IL 60045
(847)295-1040
Fax: (847)295-1898
E-mail: lmsnfbc@email.msn.com
Jogn E. Messervey, Pres.

National Federation of Independent Business
53 Century Blvd., Ste. 250
Nashville, TN 37214
(615)872-5800
800-NFIBNOW
Fax: (615)872-5353
Website: http://www.nfib.org
Jack Faris, Pres. and CEO

National Small Business Association
1156 15th St. NW, Ste. 1100
Washington, DC 20005
(202)293-8830
800-345-6728
Fax: (202)872-8543
E-mail: press@nsba.biz
Website: http://www.nsba.biz
Rob Yunich, Dir. of Communications

PUSH Commercial Division
930 E 50th St.
Chicago, IL 60615-2702
(773)373-3366
Fax: (773)373-3571
E-mail: info@rainbowpush.org
Website: http://www.rainbowpush.org
Rev. Willie T. Barrow, Co-Chm.

Research Institute for Small and Emerging Business
722 12th St. NW
Washington, DC 20005
(202)628-8382
Fax: (202)628-8392
E-mail: info@riseb.org
Website: http://www.riseb.org
Allan Neece, Jr., Chm.

Sales Professionals USA
PO Box 149
Arvada, CO 80001
(303)534-4937
888-736-7767
E-mail: salespro@salesprofessionals-usa.com
Website: http://www.salesprofessionals-usa.com
Sharon Herbert, Natl. Pres.

Score Association - Service Corps of Retired Executives
409 3rd St. SW, 6th Fl.
Washington, DC 20024
(202)205-6762
800-634-0245
Fax: (202)205-7636
E-mail: media@score.org
Website: http://www.score.org
W. Kenneth Yancey, Jr., CEO

Small Business and Entrepreneurship Council
1920 L St. NW, Ste. 200
Washington, DC 20036
(202)785-0238
Fax: (202)822-8118
E-mail: membership@sbec.org
Website: http://www.sbecouncil.org
Karen Kerrigan, Pres./CEO

Small Business in Telecommunications
1331 H St. NW, Ste. 500
Washington, DC 20005
(202)347-4511
Fax: (202)347-8607
E-mail: sbt@sbthome.org
Website: http://www.sbthome.org
Lonnie Danchik, Chm.

Small Business Legislative Council
1010 Massachusetts Ave. NW, Ste. 540
Washington, DC 20005
(202)639-8500
Fax: (202)296-5333
E-mail: email@sblc.org
Website: http://www.sblc.org
John Satagaj, Pres.

Small Business Service Bureau
554 Main St.
PO Box 15014
Worcester, MA 01615-0014
(508)756-3513
800-343-0939
Fax: (508)770-0528
E-mail: membership@sbsb.com
Website: http://www.sbsb.com
Francis R. Carroll, Pres.

Small Publishers Association of North America
1618 W Colorado Ave.
Colorado Springs, CO 80904
(719)475-1726
Fax: (719)471-2182
E-mail: span@spannet.org
Website: http://www.spannet.org
Scott Flora, Exec. Dir.

SOHO America
PO Box 941
Hurst, TX 76053-0941
800-495-SOHO
E-mail: soho@1sas.com
Website: http://www.soho.org

Structured Employment Economic Development Corporation
915 Broadway, 17th Fl.
New York, NY 10010
(212)473-0255
Fax: (212)473-0357
E-mail: info@seedco.org
Website: http://www.seedco.org
William Grinker, CEO

Support Services Alliance
107 Prospect St.
Schoharie, NY 12157
800-836-4772

E-mail: info@ssamembers.com
Website: http://www.ssainfo.com
Steve COle, Pres.

United States Association for Small Business and Entrepreneurship
975 University Ave., No. 3260
Madison, WI 53706
(608)262-9982
Fax: (608)263-0818
E-mail: jgillman@wisc.edu
Website: http://www.ususbe.org
Joan Gillman, Exec. Dir.

Consultants

This section contains a listing of consultants specializing in small business development. It is arranged alphabetically by country, then by state or province, then by city, then by firm name.

Canada

Alberta

Common Sense Solutions
3405 16A Ave.
Edmonton, AB, Canada
(403)465-7330
Fax: (403)465-7380
E-mail: gcoulson@comsense solutions.com
Website: http://www.comsense solutions.com

Varsity Consulting Group
School of Business
University of Alberta
Edmonton, AB, Canada T6G 2R6
(780)492-2994
Fax: (780)492-5400
Website: http://www.bus.ualberta.ca/vcg

Viro Hospital Consulting
42 Commonwealth Bldg., 9912-106 St. NW
Edmonton, AB, Canada T5K 1C5
(403)425-3871
Fax: (403)425-3871
E-mail: rpb@freenet.edmonton.ab.ca

British Columbia

SRI Strategic Resources Inc.
4330 Kingsway, Ste. 1600
Burnaby, BC, Canada V5H 4G7
(604)435-0627
Fax: (604)435-2782

E-mail: inquiry@sri.bc.ca
Website: http://www.sri.com

Andrew R. De Boda Consulting
1523 Milford Ave.
Coquitlam, BC, Canada V3J 2V9
(604)936-4527
Fax: (604)936-4527
E-mail: deboda@intergate.bc.ca
Website: http://www.ourworld.
compuserve.com/homepages/deboda

The Sage Group Ltd.
980 - 355 Burrard St.
744 W Haistings, Ste. 410
Vancouver, BC, Canada V6C 1A5
(604)669-9269
Fax: (604)669-6622

Tikkanen-Bradley
1345 Nelson St., Ste. 202
Vancouver, BC, Canada V6E 1J8
(604)669-0583
E-mail: webmaster@tikkanen bradley.com
Website: http://www.tikkanenbradley.com

Ontario

The Cynton Co.
17 Massey St.
Brampton, ON, Canada L6S 2V6
(905)792-7769
Fax: (905)792-8116
E-mail: cynton@home.com
Website: http://www.cynton.com

Begley & Associates
RR 6
Cambridge, ON, Canada N1R 5S7
(519)740-3629
Fax: (519)740-3629
E-mail: begley@in.on.ca
Website: http://www.in.on.ca/~begley/index.htm

CRO Engineering Ltd.
1895 William Hodgins Ln.
Carp, ON, Canada K0A 1L0
(613)839-1108
Fax: (613)839-1406
E-mail: J.Grefford@ieee.ca
Website: http://www.geocities.com/WallStreet/District/7401/

Task Enterprises
Box 69, RR 2 Hamilton
Flamborough, ON, Canada L8N 2Z7
(905)659-0153
Fax: (905)659-0861

HST Group Ltd.
430 Gilmour St.
Ottawa, ON, Canada K2P 0R8
(613)236-7303
Fax: (613)236-9893

Harrison Associates
BCE Pl.
181 Bay St., Ste. 3740
PO Box 798
Toronto, ON, Canada M5J 2T3
(416)364-5441
Fax: (416)364-2875

TCI Convergence Ltd. Management Consultants
99 Crown's Ln.
Toronto, ON, Canada M5R 3P4
(416)515-4146
Fax: (416)515-2097
E-mail: tci@inforamp.net
Website: http://tciconverge.com/index.1.html

Ken Wyman & Associates Inc.
64B Shuter St., Ste. 200
Toronto, ON, Canada M5B 1B1
(416)362-2926
Fax: (416)362-3039
E-mail: kenwyman@compuserve.com

JPL Business Consultants
82705 Metter Rd.
Wellandport, ON, Canada L0R 2J0
(905)386-7450
Fax: (905)386-7450
E-mail: plamarch@freenet.npiec.on.ca

Quebec

The Zimmar Consulting Partnership Inc.
Westmount
PO Box 98
Montreal, QC, Canada H3Z 2T1
(514)484-1459
Fax: (514)484-3063

Saskatchewan

Trimension Group
No. 104-110 Research Dr.
Innovation Place, SK, Canada S7N 3R3
(306)668-2560
Fax: (306)975-1156
E-mail: trimension@trimension.ca
Website: http://www.trimension.ca

Corporate Management Consultants
40 Government Road - PO Box 185
Prud Homme, SK, Canada, SOK 3K0
(306)654-4569
Fax: (650)618-2742

E-mail: cmccorporatemanagement@shaw.ca
Website: http://www.Corporate managementconsultants.com
Gerald Rekve

United States

Alabama

Business Planning Inc.
300 Office Park Dr.
Birmingham, AL 35223-2474
(205)870-7090
Fax: (205)870-7103

Tradebank of Eastern Alabama
546 Broad St., Ste. 3
Gadsden, AL 35901
(205)547-8700
Fax: (205)547-8718
E-mail: mansion@webex.com
Website: http://www.webex.com/~tea

Alaska

AK Business Development Center
3335 Arctic Blvd., Ste. 203
Anchorage, AK 99503
(907)562-0335
Free: 800-478-3474
Fax: (907)562-6988
E-mail: abdc@gci.net
Website: http://www.abdc.org

Business Matters
PO Box 287
Fairbanks, AK 99707
(907)452-5650

Arizona

Carefree Direct Marketing Corp.
8001 E Serene St.
PO Box 3737
Carefree, AZ 85377-3737
(480)488-4227
Fax: (480)488-2841

Trans Energy Corp.
1739 W 7th Ave.
Mesa, AZ 85202
(480)827-7915
Fax: (480)967-6601
E-mail: aha@clean-air.org
Website: http://www.clean-air.org

CMAS
5125 N 16th St.
Phoenix, AZ 85016

(602)395-1001
Fax: (602)604-8180

Comgate Telemanagement Ltd.
706 E Bell Rd., Ste. 105
Phoenix, AZ 85022
(602)485-5708
Fax: (602)485-5709
E-mail: comgate@netzone.com
Website: http://www.comgate.com

Moneysoft Inc.
1 E Camelback Rd. #550
Phoenix, AZ 85012
Free: 800-966-7797
E-mail: mbray@moneysoft.com

Harvey C. Skoog
PO Box 26439
Prescott Valley, AZ 86312
(520)772-1714
Fax: (520)772-2814

LMC Services
8711 E Pinnacle Peak Rd., No. 340
Scottsdale, AZ 85255-3555
(602)585-7177
Fax: (602)585-5880
E-mail: louws@earthlink.com

Sauerbrun Technology Group Ltd.
7979 E Princess Dr., Ste. 5
Scottsdale, AZ 85255-5878
(602)502-4950
Fax: (602)502-4292
E-mail: info@sauerbrun.com
Website: http://www.sauerbrun.com

Gary L. McLeod
PO Box 230
Sonoita, AZ 85637
Fax: (602)455-5661

Van Cleve Associates
6932 E 2nd St.
Tucson, AZ 85710
(520)296-2587
Fax: (520)296-3358

California

Acumen Group Inc.
(650)949-9349
Fax: (650)949-4845
E-mail: acumen-g@ix.netcom.com
Website: http://pw2.netcom.com/~janed/acumen.html

On-line Career and Management Consulting
420 Central Ave., No. 314
Alameda, CA 94501

(510)864-0336
Fax: (510)864-0336
E-mail: career@dnai.com
Website: http://www.dnai.com/~career

Career Paths-Thomas E. Church & Associates Inc.
PO Box 2439
Aptos, CA 95001
(408)662-7950
Fax: (408)662-7955
E-mail: church@ix.netcom.com
Website: http://www.careerpaths-tom.com

Keck & Co. Business Consultants
410 Walsh Rd.
Atherton, CA 94027
(650)854-9588
Fax: (650)854-7240
E-mail: info@keckco.com
Website: http://www.keckco.com

Ben W. Laverty III, PhD, REA, CEI
4909 Stockdale Hwy., Ste. 132
Bakersfield, CA 93309
(661)283-8300
Free: 800-833-0373
Fax: (661)283-8313
E-mail: cstc@cstcsafety.com
Website: http://www.cstcsafety.com/cstc

Lindquist Consultants-Venture Planning
225 Arlington Ave.
Berkeley, CA 94707
(510)524-6685
Fax: (510)527-6604

Larson Associates
PO Box 9005
Brea, CA 92822
(714)529-4121
Fax: (714)572-3606
E-mail: ray@consultlarson.com
Website: http://www.consultlarson.com

Kremer Management Consulting
PO Box 500
Carmel, CA 93921
(408)626-8311
Fax: (408)624-2663
E-mail: ddkremer@aol.com

W and J PARTNERSHIP
PO Box 2499
18876 Edwin Markham Dr.
Castro Valley, CA 94546
(510)583-7751
Fax: (510)583-7645
E-mail: wamorgan@wjpartnership.com
Website: http://www.wjpartnership.com

JB Associates
21118 Gardena Dr.
Cupertino, CA 95014
(408)257-0214
Fax: (408)257-0216
E-mail: semarang@sirius.com

House Agricultural Consultants
PO Box 1615
Davis, CA 95617-1615
(916)753-3361
Fax: (916)753-0464
E-mail: infoag@houseag.com
Website: http://www.houseag.com/

3C Systems Co.
16161 Ventura Blvd., Ste. 815
Encino, CA 91436
(818)907-1302
Fax: (818)907-1357
E-mail: mark@3CSysCo.com
Website: http://www.3CSysCo.com

Technical Management Consultants
3624 Westfall Dr.
Encino, CA 91436-4154
(818)784-0626
Fax: (818)501-5575
E-mail: tmcrs@aol.com

RAINWATER-GISH & Associates, Business Finance & Development
317 3rd St., Ste. 3
Eureka, CA 95501
(707)443-0030
Fax: (707)443-5683

Global Tradelinks
451 Pebble Beach Pl.
Fullerton, CA 92835
(714)441-2280
Fax: (714)441-2281
E-mail: info@globaltradelinks.com
Website: http://www.globaltradelinks.com

Strategic Business Group
800 Cienaga Dr.
Fullerton, CA 92835-1248
(714)449-1040
Fax: (714)525-1631

Burnes Consulting
20537 Wolf Creek Rd.
Grass Valley, CA 95949
(530)346-8188
Free: 800-949-9021
Fax: (530)346-7704
E-mail: kent@burnesconsulting.com
Website: http://www.burnesconsulting.com

Pioneer Business Consultants
9042 Garfield Ave., Ste. 312
Huntington Beach, CA 92646
(714)964-7600

Beblie, Brandt & Jacobs Inc.
16 Technology, Ste. 164
Irvine, CA 92618
(714)450-8790
Fax: (714)450-8799
E-mail: darcy@bbjinc.com
Website: http://198.147.90.26

Fluor Daniel Inc.
3353 Michelson Dr.
Irvine, CA 92612-0650
(949)975-2000
Fax: (949)975-5271
E-mail: sales.consulting@fluordaniel.com
Website: http://www.fluordaniel
consulting.com

MCS Associates
18300 Von Karman, Ste. 710
Irvine, CA 92612
(949)263-8700
Fax: (949)263-0770
E-mail: info@mcsassociates.com
Website: http://www.mcsassociates.com

Inspired Arts Inc.
4225 Executive Sq., Ste. 1160
La Jolla, CA 92037
(619)623-3525
Free: 800-851-4394
Fax: (619)623-3534
E-mail: info@inspiredarts.com
Website: http://www.inspiredarts.com

The Laresis Companies
PO Box 3284
La Jolla, CA 92038
(619)452-2720
Fax: (619)452-8744

RCL & Co.
PO Box 1143
737 Pearl St., Ste. 201
La Jolla, CA 92038
(619)454-8883
Fax: (619)454-8880

Comprehensive Business Services
3201 Lucas Cir.
Lafayette, CA 94549
(925)283-8272
Fax: (925)283-8272

The Ribble Group
27601 Forbes Rd., Ste. 52
Laguna Niguel, CA 92677

(714)582-1085
Fax: (714)582-6420
E-mail: ribble@deltanet.com

Norris Bernstein, CMC
9309 Marina Pacifica Dr. N
Long Beach, CA 90803
(562)493-5458
Fax: (562)493-5459
E-mail: norris@ctecomputer.com
Website: http://foodconsultants.com/
bernstein/

Horizon Consulting Services
1315 Garthwick Dr.
Los Altos, CA 94024
(415)967-0906
Fax: (415)967-0906

Brincko Associates Inc.
1801 Avenue of the Stars, Ste. 1054
Los Angeles, CA 90067
(310)553-4523
Fax: (310)553-6782

Rubenstein/Justman Management Consultants
2049 Century Park E, 24th Fl.
Los Angeles, CA 90067
(310)282-0800
Fax: (310)282-0400
E-mail: info@rjmc.net
Website: http://www.rjmc.net

F.J. Schroeder & Associates
1926 Westholme Ave.
Los Angeles, CA 90025
(310)470-2655
Fax: (310)470-6378
E-mail: fjsacons@aol.com
Website: http://www.mcninet.com/
GlobalLook/Fjschroe.html

Western Management Associates
5959 W Century Blvd., Ste. 565
Los Angeles, CA 90045-6506
(310)645-1091
Free: (888)788-6534
Fax: (310)645-1092
E-mail: gene@cfoforrent.com
Website: http://www.cfoforrent.com

Darrell Sell and Associates
Los Gatos, CA 95030
(408)354-7794
E-mail: darrell@netcom.com

Leslie J. Zambo
3355 Michael Dr.
Marina, CA 93933
(408)384-7086

Fax: (408)647-4199
E-mail: 104776.1552@compuserve.com

Marketing Services Management
PO Box 1377
Martinez, CA 94553
(510)370-8527
Fax: (510)370-8527
E-mail: markserve@biotechnet.com

William M. Shine Consulting Service
PO Box 127
Moraga, CA 94556-0127
(510)376-6516

Palo Alto Management Group Inc.
2672 Bayshore Pky., Ste. 701
Mountain View, CA 94043
(415)968-4374
Fax: (415)968-4245
E-mail: mburwen@pamg.com

BizplanSource
1048 Irvine Ave., Ste. 621
Newport Beach, CA 92660
Free: 888-253-0974
Fax: 800-859-8254
E-mail: info@bizplansource.com
Website: http://www.bizplansource.com
Adam Greengrass, President

The Market Connection
4020 Birch St., Ste. 203
Newport Beach, CA 92660
(714)731-6273
Fax: (714)833-0253

Muller Associates
PO Box 7264
Newport Beach, CA 92658
(714)646-1169
Fax: (714)646-1169

International Health Resources
PO Box 329
North San Juan, CA 95960-0329
(530)292-1266
Fax: (530)292-1243
Website: http://www.futureof
healthcare.com

NEXUS - Consultants to Management
PO Box 1531
Novato, CA 94948
(415)897-4400
Fax: (415)898-2252
E-mail: jimnexus@aol.com

Aerospcace.Org
PO Box 28831
Oakland, CA 94604-8831

(510)530-9169
Fax: (510)530-3411
Website: http://www.aerospace.org

Intelequest Corp.
722 Gailen Ave.
Palo Alto, CA 94303
(415)968-3443
Fax: (415)493-6954
E-mail: frits@iqix.com

McLaughlin & Associates
66 San Marino Cir.
Rancho Mirage, CA 92270
(760)321-2932
Fax: (760)328-2474
E-mail: jackmcla@msn.com

Carrera Consulting Group, a division of Maximus
2110 21st St., Ste. 400
Sacramento, CA 95818
(916)456-3300
Fax: (916)456-3306
E-mail: central@carreraconsulting.com
Website: http://www.carreraconsulting.com

Bay Area Tax Consultants and Bayhill Financial Consultants
1150 Bayhill Dr., Ste. 1150
San Bruno, CA 94066-3004
(415)952-8786
Fax: (415)588-4524
E-mail: baytax@compuserve.com
Website: http://www.baytax.com/

AdCon Services, LLC
8871 Hillery Dr.
Dan Diego, CA 92126
(858)433-1411
E-mail: adam@adconservices.com
Website: http://www.adconservices.com
Adam Greengrass

California Business Incubation Network
101 W Broadway, No. 480
San Diego, CA 92101
(619)237-0559
Fax: (619)237-0521

G.R. Gordetsky Consultants Inc.
11414 Windy Summit Pl.
San Diego, CA 92127
(619)487-4939
Fax: (619)487-5587
E-mail: gordet@pacbell.net

Freeman, Sullivan & Co.
131 Steuart St., Ste. 500
San Francisco, CA 94105
(415)777-0707

Free: 800-777-0737
Fax: (415)777-2420
Website: http://www.fsc-research.com

Ideas Unlimited
2151 California St., Ste. 7
San Francisco, CA 94115
(415)931-0641
Fax: (415)931-0880

Russell Miller Inc.
300 Montgomery St., Ste. 900
San Francisco, CA 94104
(415)956-7474
Fax: (415)398-0620
E-mail: rmi@pacbell.net
Website: http://www.rmisf.com

PKF Consulting
425 California St., Ste. 1650
San Francisco, CA 94104
(415)421-5378
Fax: (415)956-7708
E-mail: callahan@pkfc.com
Website: http://www.pkfonline.com

Welling & Woodard Inc.
1067 Broadway
San Francisco, CA 94133
(415)776-4500
Fax: (415)776-5067

Highland Associates
16174 Highland Dr.
San Jose, CA 95127
(408)272-7008
Fax: (408)272-4040

ORDIS Inc.
6815 Trinidad Dr.
San Jose, CA 95120-2056
(408)268-3321
Free: 800-446-7347
Fax: (408)268-3582
E-mail: ordis@ordis.com
Website: http://www.ordis.com

Stanford Resources Inc.
20 Great Oaks Blvd., Ste. 200
San Jose, CA 95119
(408)360-8400
Fax: (408)360-8410
E-mail: sales@stanfordsources.com
Website: http://www.stanfordresources.com

Technology Properties Ltd. Inc.
PO Box 20250
San Jose, CA 95160
(408)243-9898
Fax: (408)296-6637
E-mail: sanjose@tplnet.com

Helfert Associates
1777 Borel Pl., Ste. 508
San Mateo, CA 94402-3514
(650)377-0540
Fax: (650)377-0472

Mykytyn Consulting Group Inc.
185 N Redwood Dr., Ste. 200
San Rafael, CA 94903
(415)491-1770
Fax: (415)491-1251
E-mail: info@mcgi.com
Website: http://www.mcgi.com

Omega Management Systems Inc.
3 Mount Darwin Ct.
San Rafael, CA 94903-1109
(415)499-1300
Fax: (415)492-9490
E-mail: omegamgt@ix.netcom.com

The Information Group Inc.
4675 Stevens Creek Blvd., Ste. 100
Santa Clara, CA 95051
(408)985-7877
Fax: (408)985-2945
E-mail: dvincent@tig-usa.com
Website: http://www.tig-usa.com

Cast Management Consultants
1620 26th St., Ste. 2040N
Santa Monica, CA 90404
(310)828-7511
Fax: (310)453-6831

Cuma Consulting Management
Box 724
Santa Rosa, CA 95402
(707)785-2477
Fax: (707)785-2478

The E-Myth Academy
131B Stony Cir., Ste. 2000
Santa Rosa, CA 95401
(707)569-5600
Free: 800-221-0266
Fax: (707)569-5700
E-mail: info@e-myth.com
Website: http://www.e-myth.com

Reilly, Connors & Ray
1743 Canyon Rd.
Spring Valley, CA 91977
(619)698-4808
Fax: (619)460-3892
E-mail: davidray@adnc.com

Management Consultants
Sunnyvale, CA 94087-4700
(408)773-0321

RJR Associates
1639 Lewiston Dr.
Sunnyvale, CA 94087
(408)737-7720
E-mail: bobroy@rjrassoc.com
Website: http://www.rjrassoc.com

Schwafel Associates
333 Cobalt Way, Ste. 21
Sunnyvale, CA 94085
(408)720-0649
Fax: (408)720-1796
E-mail: schwafel@ricochet.net
Website: http://www.patca.org

Staubs Business Services
23320 S Vermont Ave.
Torrance, CA 90502-2940
(310)830-9128
Fax: (310)830-9128
E-mail: Harry_L_Staubs@Lamg.com

Out of Your Mind...and Into the Marketplace
13381 White Sands Dr.
Tustin, CA 92780-4565
(714)544-0248
Free: 800-419-1513
Fax: (714)730-1414
E-mail: lpinson@aol.com
Website: http://www.business-plan.com

Independent Research Services
PO Box 2426
Van Nuys, CA 91404-2426
(818)993-3622

Ingman Company Inc.
7949 Woodley Ave., Ste. 120
Van Nuys, CA 91406-1232
(818)375-5027
Fax: (818)894-5001

Innovative Technology Associates
3639 E Harbor Blvd., Ste. 203E
Ventura, CA 93001
(805)650-9353

Grid Technology Associates
20404 Tufts Cir.
Walnut, CA 91789
(909)444-0922
Fax: (909)444-0922
E-mail: grid_technology@msn.com

Ridge Consultants Inc.
100 Pringle Ave., Ste. 580
Walnut Creek, CA 94596
(925)274-1990
Fax: (510)274-1956
E-mail: info@ridgecon.com
Website: http://www.ridgecon.com

Bell Springs Publishing
PO Box 1240
Willits, CA 95490
(707)459-6372
E-mail: bellsprings@sabernet
Website: http://www.bellsprings.com

Hutchinson Consulting and Appraisal
23245 Sylvan St., Ste. 103
Woodland Hills, CA 91367
(818)888-8175
Free: 800-977-7548
Fax: (818)888-8220
E-mail: r.f.hutchinson-cpa@worldnet.
att.net

Colorado

Sam Boyer & Associates
4255 S Buckley Rd., No. 136
Aurora, CO 80013
Free: 800-785-0485
Fax: (303)766-8740
E-mail: samboyer@samboyer.com
Website: http://www.samboyer.com/

Ameriwest Business Consultants Inc.
PO Box 26266
Colorado Springs, CO 80936
(719)380-7096
Fax: (719)380-7096
E-mail: email@abchelp.com
Website: http://www.abchelp.com

GVNW Consulting Inc.
2270 La Montana Way
Colorado Springs, CO 80936
(719)594-5800
Fax: (719)594-5803
Website: http://www.gvnw.com

M-Squared Inc.
755 San Gabriel Pl.
Colorado Springs, CO 80906
(719)576-2554
Fax: (719)576-2554

Thornton Financial FNIC
1024 Centre Ave., Bldg. E
Fort Collins, CO 80526-1849
(970)221-2089
Fax: (970)484-5206

TenEyck Associates
1760 Cherryville Rd.
Greenwood Village, CO 80121-1503
(303)758-6129
Fax: (303)761-8286

Associated Enterprises Ltd.
13050 W Ceder Dr., Unit 11
Lakewood, CO 80228

(303)988-6695
Fax: (303)988-6739
E-mail: ael1@classic.msn.com

The Vincent Company Inc.
200 Union Blvd., Ste. 210
Lakewood, CO 80228
(303)989-7271
Free: 800-274-0733
Fax: (303)989-7570
E-mail: vincent@vincentco.com
Website: http://www.vincentco.com

Johnson & West Management Consultants Inc.
7612 S Logan Dr.
Littleton, CO 80122
(303)730-2810
Fax: (303)730-3219

Western Capital Holdings Inc.
10050 E Applwood Dr.
Parker, CO 80138
(303)841-1022
Fax: (303)770-1945

Connecticut

Stratman Group Inc.
40 Tower Ln.
Avon, CT 06001-4222
(860)677-2898
Free: 800-551-0499
Fax: (860)677-8210

Cowherd Consulting Group Inc.
106 Stephen Mather Rd.
Darien, CT 06820
(203)655-2150
Fax: (203)655-6427

Greenwich Associates
8 Greenwich Office Park
Greenwich, CT 06831-5149
(203)629-1200
Fax: (203)629-1229
E-mail: lisa@greenwich.com
Website: http://www.greenwich.com

Follow-up News
185 Pine St., Ste. 818
Manchester, CT 06040
(860)647-7542
Free: 800-708-0696
Fax: (860)646-6544
E-mail: Followupnews@aol.com

Lovins & Associates Consulting
309 Edwards St.
New Haven, CT 06511
(203)787-3367

Fax: (203)624-7599
E-mail: Alovinsphd@aol.com
Website: http://www.lovinsgroup.com

JC Ventures Inc.
4 Arnold St.
Old Greenwich, CT 06870-1203
(203)698-1990
Free: 800-698-1997
Fax: (203)698-2638

Charles L. Hornung Associates
52 Ned's Mountain Rd.
Ridgefield, CT 06877
(203)431-0297

Manus
100 Prospect St., S Tower
Stamford, CT 06901
(203)326-3880
Free: 800-445-0942
Fax: (203)326-3890
E-mail: manus1@aol.com
Website: http://www.RightManus.com

RealBusinessPlans.com
156 Westport Rd.
Wilton, CT 06897
(914)837-2886
E-mail: ct@realbusinessplans.com
Website: http://www.RealBusinessPlans.com
Tony Tecce

Delaware

Focus Marketing
61-7 Habor Dr.
Claymont, DE 19703
(302)793-3064

Daedalus Ventures Ltd.
PO Box 1474
Hockessin, DE 19707
(302)239-6758
Fax: (302)239-9991
E-mail: daedalus@mail.del.net

The Formula Group
PO Box 866
Hockessin, DE 19707
(302)456-0952
Fax: (302)456-1354
E-mail: formula@netaxs.com

Selden Enterprises Inc.
2502 Silverside Rd., Ste. 1
Wilmington, DE 19810-3740
(302)529-7113
Fax: (302)529-7442
E-mail: selden2@bellatlantic.net
Website: http://www.seldenenterprises.com

District of Columbia

Bruce W. McGee and Associates
7826 Eastern Ave. NW, Ste. 30
Washington, DC 20012
(202)726-7272
Fax: (202)726-2946

McManis Associates Inc.
1900 K St. NW, Ste. 700
Washington, DC 20006
(202)466-7680
Fax: (202)872-1898
Website: http://www.mcmanis-mmi.com

Smith, Dawson & Andrews Inc.
1000 Connecticut Ave., Ste. 302
Washington, DC 20036
(202)835-0740
Fax: (202)775-8526
E-mail: webmaster@sda-inc.com
Website: http://www.sda-inc.com

Florida

BackBone, Inc.
20404 Hacienda Court
Boca Raton, FL 33498
(561)470-0965
Fax: 516-908-4038
E-mail: BPlans@backboneinc.com
Website: http://www.backboneinc.com
Charles Epstein, President

Whalen & Associates Inc.
4255 Northwest 26 Ct.
Boca Raton, FL 33434
(561)241-5950
Fax: (561)241-7414
E-mail: drwhalen@ix.netcom.com

E.N. Rysso & Associates
180 Bermuda Petrel Ct.
Daytona Beach, FL 32119
(386)760-3028
E-mail: erysso@aol.com

Virtual Technocrats LLC
560 Lavers Circle, #146
Delray Beach, FL 33444
(561)265-3509
E-mail: josh@virtualtechnocrats.com;
info@virtualtechnocrats.com
Website: http://www.virtualtechno
crats.com
Josh Eikov, Managing Director

Eric Sands Consulting Services
6193 Rock Island Rd., Ste. 412
Fort Lauderdale, FL 33319
(954)721-4767

Fax: (954)720-2815
E-mail: easands@aol.com
Website: http://www.ericsandsconsultig.com

Professional Planning Associates, Inc.
1975 E. Sunrise Blvd. Suite 607
Fort Lauderdale, FL 33304
(954)764-5204
Fax: 954-463-4172
E-mail: Mgoldstein@proplana.com
Website: http://proplana.com
Michael Goldstein, President

Host Media Corp.
3948 S 3rd St., Ste. 191
Jacksonville Beach, FL 32250
(904)285-3239
Fax: (904)285-5618
E-mail: msconsulting@compuserve.com
Website: http://www.media
servicesgroup.com

William V. Hall
1925 Brickell, Ste. D-701
Miami, FL 33129
(305)856-9622
Fax: (305)856-4113
E-mail: williamvhall@compuserve.com

F.A. McGee Inc.
800 Claughton Island Dr., Ste. 401
Miami, FL 33131
(305)377-9123

Taxplan Inc.
Mirasol International Ctr.
2699 Collins Ave.
Miami Beach, FL 33140
(305)538-3303

T.C. Brown & Associates
8415 Excalibur Cir., Apt. B1
Naples, FL 34108
(941)594-1949
Fax: (941)594-0611
E-mail: tcater@naples.net.com

RLA International Consulting
713 Lagoon Dr.
North Palm Beach, FL 33408
(407)626-4258
Fax: (407)626-5772

Comprehensive Franchising Inc.
2465 Ridgecrest Ave.
Orange Park, FL 32065
(904)272-6567
Free: 800-321-6567
Fax: (904)272-6750
E-mail: theimp@cris.com
Website: http://www.franchise411.com

Hunter G. Jackson Jr. - Consulting Environmental Physicist
PO Box 618272
Orlando, FL 32861-8272
(407)295-4188
E-mail: hunterjackson@juno.com

F. Newton Parks
210 El Brillo Way
Palm Beach, FL 33480
(561)833-1727
Fax: (561)833-4541

Avery Business Development Services
2506 St. Michel Ct.
Ponte Vedra Beach, FL 32082
(904)285-6033
Fax: (904)285-6033

Strategic Business Planning Co.
PO Box 821006
South Florida, FL 33082-1006
(954)704-9100
Fax: (954)438-7333
E-mail: info@bizplan.com
Website: http://www.bizplan.com

Dufresne Consulting Group Inc.
10014 N Dale Mabry, Ste. 101
Tampa, FL 33618-4426
(813)264-4775
Fax: (813)264-9300
Website: http://www.dcgconsult.com

Agrippa Enterprises Inc.
PO Box 175
Venice, FL 34284-0175
(941)355-7876
E-mail: webservices@agrippa.com
Website: http://www.agrippa.com

Center for Simplified Strategic Planning Inc.
PO Box 3324
Vero Beach, FL 32964-3324
(561)231-3636
Fax: (561)231-1099
Website: http://www.cssp.com

Georgia

Marketing Spectrum Inc.
115 Perimeter Pl., Ste. 440
Atlanta, GA 30346
(770)395-7244
Fax: (770)393-4071

Business Ventures Corp.
1650 Oakbrook Dr., Ste. 405
Norcross, GA 30093
(770)729-8000
Fax: (770)729-8028

Informed Decisions Inc.
100 Falling Cheek
Sautee Nacoochee, GA 30571
(706)878-1905
Fax: (706)878-1802
E-mail: skylake@compuserve.com

Tom C. Davis & Associates, P.C.
3189 Perimeter Rd.
Valdosta, GA 31602
(912)247-9801
Fax: (912)244-7704
E-mail: mail@tcdcpa.com
Website: http://www.tcdcpa.com/

Illinois

TWD and Associates
431 S Patton
Arlington Heights, IL 60005
(847)398-6410
Fax: (847)255-5095
E-mail: tdoo@aol.com

Management Planning Associates Inc.
2275 Half Day Rd., Ste. 350
Bannockburn, IL 60015-1277
(847)945-2421
Fax: (847)945-2425

Phil Faris Associates
86 Old Mill Ct.
Barrington, IL 60010
(847)382-4888
Fax: (847)382-4890
E-mail: pfaris@meginsnet.net

Seven Continents Technology
787 Stonebridge
Buffalo Grove, IL 60089
(708)577-9653
Fax: (708)870-1220

Grubb & Blue Inc.
2404 Windsor Pl.
Champaign, IL 61820
(217)366-0052
Fax: (217)356-0117

ACE Accounting Service Inc.
3128 N Bernard St.
Chicago, IL 60618
(773)463-7854
Fax: (773)463-7854

AON Consulting Worldwide
200 E Randolph St., 10th Fl.
Chicago, IL 60601
(312)381-4800
Free: 800-438-6487
Fax: (312)381-0240
Website: http://www.aon.com

FMS Consultants
5801 N Sheridan Rd., Ste. 3D
Chicago, IL 60660
(773)561-7362
Fax: (773)561-6274

Grant Thornton
800 1 Prudential Plz.
130 E Randolph St.
Chicago, IL 60601
(312)856-0001
Fax: (312)861-1340
E-mail: gtinfo@gt.com
Website: http://www.grantthornton.com

Kingsbury International Ltd.
5341 N Glenwood Ave.
Chicago, IL 60640
(773)271-3030
Fax: (773)728-7080
E-mail: jetlag@mcs.com
Website: http://www.kingbiz.com

MacDougall & Blake Inc.
1414 N Wells St., Ste. 311
Chicago, IL 60610-1306
(312)587-3330
Fax: (312)587-3699
E-mail: jblake@compuserve.com

James C. Osburn Ltd.
6445 N. Western Ave., Ste. 304
Chicago, IL 60645
(773)262-4428
Fax: (773)262-6755
E-mail: osburnltd@aol.com

Tarifero & Tazewell Inc.
211 S Clark
Chicago, IL 60690
(312)665-9714
Fax: (312)665-9716

Human Energy Design Systems
620 Roosevelt Dr.
Edwardsville, IL 62025
(618)692-0258
Fax: (618)692-0819

China Business Consultants Group
931 Dakota Cir.
Naperville, IL 60563
(630)778-7992
Fax: (630)778-7915
E-mail: cbcq@aol.com

Center for Workforce Effectiveness
500 Skokie Blvd., Ste. 222
Northbrook, IL 60062
(847)559-8777
Fax: (847)559-8778

E-mail: office@cwelink.com
Website: http://www.cwelink.com

Smith Associates
1320 White Mountain Dr.
Northbrook, IL 60062
(847)480-7200
Fax: (847)480-9828

Francorp Inc.
20200 Governors Dr.
Olympia Fields, IL 60461
(708)481-2900
Free: 800-372-6244
Fax: (708)481-5885
E-mail: francorp@aol.com
Website: http://www.francorpinc.com

Camber Business Strategy Consultants
1010 S Plum Tree Ct
Palatine, IL 60078-0986
(847)202-0101
Fax: (847)705-7510
E-mail: camber@ameritech.net

Partec Enterprise Group
5202 Keith Dr.
Richton Park, IL 60471
(708)503-4047
Fax: (708)503-9468

Rockford Consulting Group Ltd.
Century Plz., Ste. 206
7210 E State St.
Rockford, IL 61108
(815)229-2900
Free: 800-667-7495
Fax: (815)229-2612
E-mail: rligus@RockfordConsulting.com
Website: http://www.Rockford
Consulting.com

RSM McGladrey Inc.
1699 E Woodfield Rd., Ste. 300
Schaumburg, IL 60173-4969
(847)413-6900
Fax: (847)517-7067
Website: http://www.rsmmcgladrey.com

A.D. Star Consulting
320 Euclid
Winnetka, IL 60093
(847)446-7827
Fax: (847)446-7827
E-mail: startwo@worldnet.att.net

Indiana

Modular Consultants Inc.
3109 Crabtree Ln.
Elkhart, IN 46514

(219)264-5761
Fax: (219)264-5761
E-mail: sasabo5313@aol.com

Midwest Marketing Research
PO Box 1077
Goshen, IN 46527
(219)533-0548
Fax: (219)533-0540
E-mail: 103365.654@compuserve

Ketchum Consulting Group
8021 Knue Rd., Ste. 112
Indianapolis, IN 46250
(317)845-5411
Fax: (317)842-9941

**MDI Management
Consulting**
1519 Park Dr.
Munster, IN 46321
(219)838-7909
Fax: (219)838-7909

Iowa

McCord Consulting Group Inc.
4533 Pine View Dr. NE
PO Box 11024
Cedar Rapids, IA 52410
(319)378-0077
Fax: (319)378-1577
E-mail: smmccord@hom.com
Website: http://www.mccordgroup.com

Management Solutions L.C.
3815 Lincoln Pl. Dr.
Des Moines, IA 50312
(515)277-6408
Fax: (515)277-3506
E-mail: wasunimers@uswest.net

Grandview Marketing
15 Red Bridge Dr.
Sioux City, IA 51104
(712)239-3122
Fax: (712)258-7578
E-mail: eandrews@pionet.net

Kansas

Assessments in Action
513A N Mur-Len
Olathe, KS 66062
(913)764-6270
Free: (888)548-1504
Fax: (913)764-6495
E-mail: lowdene@qni.com
Website: http://www.assessments-
in-action.com

Maine

Edgemont Enterprises
PO Box 8354
Portland, ME 04104
(207)871-8964
Fax: (207)871-8964

Pan Atlantic Consultants
5 Milk St.
Portland, ME 04101
(207)871-8622
Fax: (207)772-4842
E-mail: pmurphy@maine.rr.com
Website: http://www.panatlantic.net

Maryland

Clemons & Associates Inc.
5024-R Campbell Blvd.
Baltimore, MD 21236
(410)931-8100
Fax: (410)931-8111
E-mail: info@clemonsmgmt.com
Website: http://www.clemonsmgmt.com

Imperial Group Ltd.
305 Washington Ave., Ste. 204
Baltimore, MD 21204-6009
(410)337-8500
Fax: (410)337-7641

Leadership Institute
3831 Yolando Rd.
Baltimore, MD 21218
(410)366-9111
Fax: (410)243-8478
E-mail: behconsult@aol.com

Burdeshaw Associates Ltd.
4701 Sangamore Rd.
Bethesda, MD 20816-2508
(301)229-5800
Fax: (301)229-5045
E-mail: jstacy@burdeshaw.com
Website: http://www.burdeshaw.com

Michael E. Cohen
5225 Pooks Hill Rd., Ste. 1119 S
Bethesda, MD 20814
(301)530-5738
Fax: (301)530-2988
E-mail: mecohen@crosslink.net

World Development Group Inc.
5272 River Rd., Ste. 650
Bethesda, MD 20816-1405
(301)652-1818
Fax: (301)652-1250
E-mail: wdg@has.com
Website: http://www.worlddg.com

Swartz Consulting
PO Box 4301
Crofton, MD 21114-4301
(301)262-6728

Software Solutions International Inc.
9633 Duffer Way
Gaithersburg, MD 20886
(301)330-4136
Fax: (301)330-4136

Strategies Inc.
8 Park Center Ct., Ste. 200
Owings Mills, MD 21117
(410)363-6669
Fax: (410)363-1231
E-mail: strategies@strat1.com
Website: http://www.strat1.com

Hammer Marketing Resources
179 Inverness Rd.
Severna Park, MD 21146
(410)544-9191
Fax: (305)675-3277
E-mail: info@gohammer.com
Website: http://www.gohammer.com

Andrew Sussman & Associates
13731 Kretsinger
Smithsburg, MD 21783
(301)824-2943
Fax: (301)824-2943

Massachusetts

Geibel Marketing and Public Relations
PO Box 611
Belmont, MA 02478-0005
(617)484-8285
Fax: (617)489-3567
E-mail: jgeibel@geibelpr.com
Website: http://www.geibelpr.com

Bain & Co.
2 Copley Pl.
Boston, MA 02116
(617)572-2000
Fax: (617)572-2427
E-mail: corporate.inquiries@bain.com
Website: http://www.bain.com

Mehr & Co.
62 Kinnaird St.
Cambridge, MA 02139
(617)876-3311
Fax: (617)876-3023
E-mail: mehrco@aol.com

Monitor Company Inc.
2 Canal Park
Cambridge, MA 02141

(617)252-2000
Fax: (617)252-2100
Website: http://www.monitor.com

Information & Research Associates
PO Box 3121
Framingham, MA 01701
(508)788-0784

Walden Consultants Ltd.
252 Pond St.
Hopkinton, MA 01748
(508)435-4882
Fax: (508)435-3971
Website: http://www.waldencon
sultants.com

Jeffrey D. Marshall
102 Mitchell Rd.
Ipswich, MA 01938-1219
(508)356-1113
Fax: (508)356-2989

Consulting Resources Corp.
6 Northbrook Park
Lexington, MA 02420
(781)863-1222
Fax: (781)863-1441
E-mail: res@consultingresources.net
Website: http://www.consulting
resources.net

Planning Technologies Group L.L.C.
92 Hayden Ave.
Lexington, MA 02421
(781)778-4678
Fax: (781)861-1099
E-mail: ptg@plantech.com
Website: http://www.plantech.com

Kalba International Inc.
23 Sandy Pond Rd.
Lincoln, MA 01773
(781)259-9589
Fax: (781)259-1460
E-mail: info@kalbainternational.com
Website: http://www.kalbainter
national.com

VMB Associates Inc.
115 Ashland St.
Melrose, MA 02176
(781)665-0623
Fax: (425)732-7142
E-mail: vmbinc@aol.com

The Company Doctor
14 Pudding Stone Ln.
Mendon, MA 01756
(508)478-1747
Fax: (508)478-0520

Data and Strategies Group Inc.
190 N Main St.
Natick, MA 01760
(508)653-9990
Fax: (508)653-7799
E-mail: dsginc@dsggroup.com
Website: http://www.dsggroup.com

The Enterprise Group
73 Parker Rd.
Needham, MA 02494
(617)444-6631
Fax: (617)433-9991
E-mail: lsacco@world.std.com
Website: http://www.enterprise-group.com

PSMJ Resources Inc.
10 Midland Ave.
Newton, MA 02458
(617)965-0055
Free: 800-537-7765
Fax: (617)965-5152
E-mail: psmj@tiac.net
Website: http://www.psmj.com

Scheur Management Group Inc.
255 Washington St., Ste. 100
Newton, MA 02458-1611
(617)969-7500
Fax: (617)969-7508
E-mail: smgnow@scheur.com
Website: http://www.scheur.com

I.E.E.E., Boston Section
240 Bear Hill Rd., 202B
Waltham, MA 02451-1017
(781)890-5294
Fax: (781)890-5290

Business Planning and Consulting Services
20 Beechwood Ter.
Wellesley, MA 02482
(617)237-9151
Fax: (617)237-9151

Michigan

Walter Frederick Consulting
1719 South Blvd.
Ann Arbor, MI 48104
(313)662-4336
Fax: (313)769-7505

Fox Enterprises
6220 W Freeland Rd.
Freeland, MI 48623
(517)695-9170
Fax: (517)695-9174
E-mail: foxjw@concentric.net
Website: http://www.cris.com/~foxjw

G.G.W. and Associates
1213 Hampton
Jackson, MI 49203
(517)782-2255
Fax: (517)782-2255

Altamar Group Ltd.
6810 S Cedar, Ste. 2-B
Lansing, MI 48911
(517)694-0910
Free: 800-443-2627
Fax: (517)694-1377

Sheffieck Consultants Inc.
23610 Greening Dr.
Novi, MI 48375-3130
(248)347-3545
Fax: (248)347-3530
E-mail: cfsheff@concentric.net

Rehmann, Robson PC
5800 Gratiot
Saginaw, MI 48605
(517)799-9580
Fax: (517)799-0227
Website: http://www.rrpc.com

Francis & Co.
17200 W 10 Mile Rd., Ste. 207
Southfield, MI 48075
(248)559-7600
Fax: (248)559-5249

Private Ventures Inc.
16000 W 9 Mile Rd., Ste. 504
Southfield, MI 48075
(248)569-1977
Free: 800-448-7614
Fax: (248)569-1838
E-mail: pventuresi@aol.com

JGK Associates
14464 Kerner Dr.
Sterling Heights, MI 48313
(810)247-9055
Fax: (248)822-4977
E-mail: kozlowski@home.com

Minnesota

Health Fitness Corp.
3500 W 80th St., Ste. 130
Bloomington, MN 55431
(612)831-6830
Fax: (612)831-7264

Consatech Inc.
PO Box 1047
Burnsville, MN 55337
(612)953-1088
Fax: (612)435-2966

Robert F. Knotek
14960 Ironwood Ct.
Eden Prairie, MN 55346
(612)949-2875

DRI Consulting
7715 Stonewood Ct.
Edina, MN 55439
(612)941-9656
Fax: (612)941-2693
E-mail: dric@dric.com
Website: http://www.dric.com

Markin Consulting
12072 87th Pl. N
Maple Grove, MN 55369
(612)493-3568
Fax: (612)493-5744
E-mail: markin@markinconsulting.com
Website: http://www.markin
consulting.com

**Minnesota Cooperation Office for
Small Business & Job Creation Inc.**
5001 W 80th St., Ste. 825
Minneapolis, MN 55437
(612)830-1230
Fax: (612)830-1232
E-mail: mncoop@msn.com
Website: http://www.mnco.org

Enterprise Consulting Inc.
PO Box 1111
Minnetonka, MN 55345
(612)949-5909
Fax: (612)906-3965

Amdahl International
724 1st Ave. SW
Rochester, MN 55902
(507)252-0402
Fax: (507)252-0402
E-mail: amdahl@best-service.com
Website: http://www.wp.com/amdahl_int

Power Systems Research
1365 Corporate Center Curve, 2nd Fl.
St. Paul, MN 55121
(612)905-8400
Free: (888)625-8612
Fax: (612)454-0760
E-mail: Barb@Powersys.com
Website: http://www.powersys.com

Missouri

**Business Planning and Development
Corp.**
4030 Charlotte St.
Kansas City, MO 64110
(816)753-0495

E-mail: humph@bpdev.demon.co.uk
Website: http://www.bpdev.demon.co.uk

CFO Service
10336 Donoho
St. Louis, MO 63131
(314)750-2940
E-mail: jskae@cfoservice.com
Website: http://www.cfoservice.com

Nebraska

**International Management Consulting
Group Inc.**
1309 Harlan Dr., Ste. 205
Bellevue, NE 68005
(402)291-4545
Free: 800-665-IMCG
Fax: (402)291-4343
E-mail: imcg@neonramp.com
Website: http://www.mgtcon
sulting.com

**Heartland Management Consulting
Group**
1904 Barrington Pky.
Papillion, NE 68046
(402)339-2387
Fax: (402)339-1319

Nevada

The DuBois Group
865 Tahoe Blvd., Ste. 108
Incline Village, NV 89451
(775)832-0550
Free: 800-375-2935
Fax: (775)832-0556
E-mail: DuBoisGrp@aol.com

New Hampshire

Wolff Consultants
10 Buck Rd.
Hanover, NH 03755
(603)643-6015

BPT Consulting Associates Ltd.
12 Parmenter Rd., Ste. B-6
Londonderry, NH 03053
(603)437-8484
Free: (888)278-0030
Fax: (603)434-5388
E-mail: bptcons@tiac.net
Website: http://www.bptconsulting.com

New Jersey

Bedminster Group Inc.
1170 Rte. 22 E
Bridgewater, NJ 08807

(908)500-4155
Fax: (908)766-0780
E-mail: info@bedminstergroup.com
Website: http://www.bedminster
group.com
Fax: (202)806-1777
Terry Strong, Acting Regional Dir.

Delta Planning Inc.
PO Box 425
Denville, NJ 07834
(913)625-1742
Free: 800-672-0762
Fax: (973)625-3531
E-mail: DeltaP@worldnet.att.net
Website: http://deltaplanning.com

Kumar Associates Inc.
1004 Cumbermeade Rd.
Fort Lee, NJ 07024
(201)224-9480
Fax: (201)585-2343
E-mail: mail@kumarassociates.com
Website: http://kumarassociates.com

John Hall & Company Inc.
PO Box 187
Glen Ridge, NJ 07028
(973)680-4449
Fax: (973)680-4581
E-mail: jhcompany@aol.com

Market Focus
PO Box 402
Maplewood, NJ 07040
(973)378-2470
Fax: (973)378-2470
E-mail: mcss66@marketfocus.com

Vanguard Communications Corp.
100 American Rd.
Morris Plains, NJ 07950
(973)605-8000
Fax: (973)605-8329
Website: http://www.vanguard.net/

ConMar International Ltd.
1901 US Hwy. 130
North Brunswick, NJ 08902
(732)940-8347
Fax: (732)274-1199

KLW New Products
156 Cedar Dr.
Old Tappan, NJ 07675
(201)358-1300
Fax: (201)664-2594
E-mail: lrlarsen@usa.net
Website: http://www.klwnew
products.com

PA Consulting Group
315A Enterprise Dr.
Plainsboro, NJ 08536
(609)936-8300
Fax: (609)936-8811
E-mail: info@paconsulting.com
Website: http://www.pa-consulting.com

Aurora Marketing Management Inc.
66 Witherspoon St., Ste. 600
Princeton, NJ 08542
(908)904-1125
Fax: (908)359-1108
E-mail: aurora2@voicenet.com
Website: http://www.auroramarketing.net

Smart Business Supersite
88 Orchard Rd., CN-5219
Princeton, NJ 08543
(908)321-1924
Fax: (908)321-5156
E-mail: irv@smartbiz.com
Website: http://www.smartbiz.com

Tracelin Associates
1171 Main St., Ste. 6K
Rahway, NJ 07065
(732)381-3288

Schkeeper Inc.
130-6 Bodman Pl.
Red Bank, NJ 07701
(732)219-1965
Fax: (732)530-3703

Henry Branch Associates
2502 Harmon Cove Twr.
Secaucus, NJ 07094
(201)866-2008
Fax: (201)601-0101
E-mail: hbranch161@home.com

Robert Gibbons & Company Inc.
46 Knoll Rd.
Tenafly, NJ 07670-1050
(201)871-3933
Fax: (201)871-2173
E-mail: crisisbob@aol.com

PMC Management Consultants Inc.
6 Thistle Ln.
Three Bridges, NJ 08887-0332
(908)788-1014
Free: 800-PMC-0250
Fax: (908)806-7287
E-mail: int@pmc-management.com
Website: http://www.pmc-management.com

R.W. Bankart & Associates
20 Valley Ave., Ste. D-2

Westwood, NJ 07675-3607
(201)664-7672

New Mexico

Vondle & Associates Inc.
4926 Calle de Tierra, NE
Albuquerque, NM 87111
(505)292-8961
Fax: (505)296-2790
E-mail: vondle@aol.com

InfoNewMexico
2207 Black Hills Rd., NE
Rio Rancho, NM 87124
(505)891-2462
Fax: (505)896-8971

New York

Powers Research and Training Institute
PO Box 78
Bayville, NY 11709
(516)628-2250
Fax: (516)628-2252
E-mail: powercocch@compuserve.com
Website: http://www.nancypowers.com

Consortium House
296 Wittenberg Rd.
Bearsville, NY 12409
(845)679-8867
Fax: (845)679-9248
E-mail: eugenegs@aol.com
Website: http://www.chpub.com

Progressive Finance Corp.
3549 Tiemann Ave.
Bronx, NY 10469
(718)405-9029
Free: 800-225-8381
Fax: (718)405-1170

Wave Hill Associates Inc.
2621 Palisade Ave., Ste. 15-C
Bronx, NY 10463
(718)549-7368
Fax: (718)601-9670
E-mail: pepper@compuserve.com

Management Insight
96 Arlington Rd.
Buffalo, NY 14221
(716)631-3319
Fax: (716)631-0203
E-mail: michalski@foodservice
insight.com
Website: http://www.foodservice
insight.com

Samani International Enterprises, Marions Panyaught Consultancy
2028 Parsons
Flushing, NY 11357-3436
(917)287-8087
Fax: 800-873-8939
E-mail: vjp2@biostrategist.com
Website: http://www.biostrategist.com

Marketing Resources Group
71-58 Austin St.
Forest Hills, NY 11375
(718)261-8882

Mangabay Business Plans & Development Subsidiary of Innis Asset Allocation
125-10 Queens Blvd., Ste. 2202
Kew Gardens, NY 11415
(905)527-1947
Fax: 509-472-1935
E-mail: mangabay@mangabay.com
Website: http://www.mangabay.com
Lee Toh, Managing Partner

ComputerEase Co.
1301 Monmouth Ave.
Lakewood, NY 08701
(212)406-9464
Fax: (914)277-5317
E-mail: crawfordc@juno.com

Boice Dunham Group
30 W 13th St.
New York, NY 10011
(212)924-2200
Fax: (212)924-1108

Elizabeth Capen
27 E 95th St.
New York, NY 10128
(212)427-7654
Fax: (212)876-3190

Haver Analytics
60 E 42nd St., Ste. 2424
New York, NY 10017
(212)986-9300
Fax: (212)986-5857
E-mail: data@haver.com
Website: http://www.haver.com

The Jordan, Edmiston Group Inc.
150 E 52nd Ave., 18th Fl.
New York, NY 10022
(212)754-0710
Fax: (212)754-0337

KPMG International
345 Park Ave.
New York, NY 10154-0102
(212)758-9700

Fax: (212)758-9819
Website: http://www.kpmg.com

Mahoney Cohen Consulting Corp.
111 W 40th St., 12th Fl.
New York, NY 10018
(212)490-8000
Fax: (212)790-5913

Management Practice Inc.
342 Madison Ave.
New York, NY 10173-1230
(212)867-7948
Fax: (212)972-5188
Website: http://www.mpiweb.com

Moseley Associates Inc.
342 Madison Ave., Ste. 1414
New York, NY 10016
(212)213-6673
Fax: (212)687-1520

Practice Development Counsel
60 Sutton Pl. S
New York, NY 10022
(212)593-1549
Fax: (212)980-7940
E-mail: pwhaserot@pdcounsel.com
Website: http://www.pdcounsel.com

Unique Value International Inc.
575 Madison Ave., 10th Fl.
New York, NY 10022-1304
(212)605-0590
Fax: (212)605-0589

The Van Tulleken Co.
126 E 56th St.
New York, NY 10022
(212)355-1390
Fax: (212)755-3061
E-mail: newyork@vantulleken.com

Vencon Management Inc.
301 W 53rd St.
New York, NY 10019
(212)581-8787
Fax: (212)397-4126
Website: http://www.venconinc.com

Werner International Inc.
55 E 52nd, 29th Fl.
New York, NY 10055
(212)909-1260
Fax: (212)909-1273
E-mail: richard.downing@rgh.com
Website: http://www.wernertex.com

Zimmerman Business Consulting Inc.
44 E 92nd St., Ste. 5-B
New York, NY 10128

(212)860-3107
Fax: (212)860-7730
E-mail: ljzzbci@aol.com
Website: http://www.zbcinc.com

Overton Financial
7 Allen Rd.
Peekskill, NY 10566
(914)737-4649
Fax: (914)737-4696

Stromberg Consulting
2500 Westchester Ave.
Purchase, NY 10577
(914)251-1515
Fax: (914)251-1562
E-mail: strategy@stromberg_consul
ting.com
Website: http://www.stromberg_
consulting.com

Innovation Management Consulting Inc.
209 Dewitt Rd.
Syracuse, NY 13214-2006
(315)425-5144
Fax: (315)445-8989
E-mail: missonneb@axess.net

M. Clifford Agress
891 Fulton St.
Valley Stream, NY 11580
(516)825-8955
Fax: (516)825-8955

Destiny Kinal Marketing Consultancy
105 Chemung St.
Waverly, NY 14892
(607)565-8317
Fax: (607)565-4083

Valutis Consulting Inc.
5350 Main St., Ste. 7
Williamsville, NY 14221-5338
(716)634-2553
Fax: (716)634-2554
E-mail: valutis@localnet.com
Website: http://www.valutisconsulting.com

North Carolina

Best Practices L.L.C.
6320 Quadrangle Dr., Ste. 200
Chapel Hill, NC 27514
(919)403-0251
Fax: (919)403-0144
E-mail: best@best:in/class
Website: http://www.best-in-class.com

Norelli & Co.
Bank of America Corporate Ctr.
100 N Tyron St., Ste. 5160

Charlotte, NC 28202-4000
(704)376-5484
Fax: (704)376-5485
E-mail: consult@norelli.com
Website: http://www.norelli.com

North Dakota

Center for Innovation
4300 Dartmouth Dr.
PO Box 8372
Grand Forks, ND 58202
(701)777-3132
Fax: (701)777-2339
E-mail: bruce@innovators.net
Website: http://www.innovators.net

Ohio

Transportation Technology Services
208 Harmon Rd.
Aurora, OH 44202
(330)562-3596

Empro Systems Inc.
4777 Red Bank Expy., Ste. 1
Cincinnati, OH 45227-1542
(513)271-2042
Fax: (513)271-2042

Alliance Management International Ltd.
1440 Windrow Ln.
Cleveland, OH 44147-3200
(440)838-1922
Fax: (440)838-0979
E-mail: bgruss@amiltd.com
Website: http://www.amiltd.com

Bozell Kamstra Public Relations
1301 E 9th St., Ste. 3400
Cleveland, OH 44114
(216)623-1511
Fax: (216)623-1501
E-mail: jfeniger@cleveland.bozellk
amstra.com
Website: http://www.bozellk
amstra.com

Cory Dillon Associates
111 Schreyer Pl. E
Columbus, OH 43214
(614)262-8211
Fax: (614)262-3806

Holcomb Gallagher Adams
300 Marconi, Ste. 303
Columbus, OH 43215
(614)221-3343
Fax: (614)221-3367
E-mail: riadams@acme.freenet.oh.us

Young & Associates
PO Box 711
Kent, OH 44240
(330)678-0524
Free: 800-525-9775
Fax: (330)678-6219
E-mail: online@younginc.com
Website: http://www.younginc.com

Robert A. Westman & Associates
8981 Inversary Dr. SE
Warren, OH 44484-2551
(330)856-4149
Fax: (330)856-2564

Oklahoma

Innovative Partners L.L.C.
4900 Richmond Sq., Ste. 100
Oklahoma City, OK 73118
(405)840-0033
Fax: (405)843-8359
E-mail: ipartners@juno.com

Oregon

INTERCON - The International Converting Institute
5200 Badger Rd.
Crooked River Ranch, OR 97760
(541)548-1447
Fax: (541)548-1618
E-mail: johnbowler@
crookedriverranch.com

Talbott ARM
HC 60, Box 5620
Lakeview, OR 97630
(541)635-8587
Fax: (503)947-3482

Management Technology Associates Ltd.
2768 SW Sherwood Dr, Ste. 105
Portland, OR 97201-2251
(503)224-5220
Fax: (503)224-5334
E-mail: lcuster@mta-ltd.com
Website: http://www.mgmt-tech.com

Pennsylvania

Healthscope Inc.
400 Lancaster Ave.
Devon, PA 19333
(610)687-6199
Fax: (610)687-6376
E-mail: health@voicenet.com
Website: http://www.healthscope.net/

Elayne Howard & Associates Inc.
3501 Masons Mill Rd., Ste. 501

Huntingdon Valley, PA 19006-3509
(215)657-9550

GRA Inc.
115 West Ave., Ste. 201
Jenkintown, PA 19046
(215)884-7500
Fax: (215)884-1385
E-mail: gramail@gra-inc.com
Website: http://www.gra-inc.com

Mifflin County Industrial Development Corp.
Mifflin County Industrial Plz.
6395 SR 103 N
Bldg. 50
Lewistown, PA 17044
(717)242-0393
Fax: (717)242-1842
E-mail: mcide@acsworld.net

Autech Products
1289 Revere Rd.
Morrisville, PA 19067
(215)493-3759
Fax: (215)493-9791
E-mail: autech4@yahoo.com

Advantage Associates
434 Avon Dr.
Pittsburgh, PA 15228
(412)343-1558
Fax: (412)362-1684
E-mail: ecocba1@aol.com

Regis J. Sheehan & Associates
Pittsburgh, PA 15220
(412)279-1207

James W. Davidson Company Inc.
23 Forest View Rd.
Wallingford, PA 19086
(610)566-1462

Puerto Rico

Diego Chevere & Co.
Metro Parque 7, Ste. 204
Metro Office
Caparra Heights, PR 00920
(787)774-9595
Fax: (787)774-9566
E-mail: dcco@coqui.net

Manuel L. Porrata and Associates
898 Munoz Rivera Ave., Ste. 201
San Juan, PR 00927
(787)765-2140
Fax: (787)754-3285
E-mail: m_porrata@manuelporrata.com
Website: http://manualporrata.com

South Carolina

Aquafood Business Associates
PO Box 13267
Charleston, SC 29422
(843)795-9506
Fax: (843)795-9477
E-mail: rraba@aol.com

Profit Associates Inc.
PO Box 38026
Charleston, SC 29414
(803)763-5718
Fax: (803)763-5719
E-mail: bobrog@awod.com
Website: http://www.awod.com/gallery/
business/proasc

Strategic Innovations International
12 Executive Ct.
Lake Wylie, SC 29710
(803)831-1225
Fax: (803)831-1177
E-mail: stratinnov@aol.com
Website: http://www.
strategicinnovations.com

Minus Stage
Box 4436
Rock Hill, SC 29731
(803)328-0705
Fax: (803)329-9948

Tennessee

Daniel Petchers & Associates
8820 Fernwood CV
Germantown, TN 38138
(901)755-9896

Business Choices
1114 Forest Harbor, Ste. 300
Hendersonville, TN 37075-9646
(615)822-8692
Free: 800-737-8382
Fax: (615)822-8692
E-mail: bz-ch@juno.com

RCFA Healthcare Management Services L.L.C.
9648 Kingston Pke., Ste. 8
Knoxville, TN 37922
(865)531-0176
Free: 800-635-4040
Fax: (865)531-0722
E-mail: info@rcfa.com
Website: http://www.rcfa.com

Growth Consultants of America
3917 Trimble Rd.
Nashville, TN 37215

(615)383-0550
Fax: (615)269-8940
E-mail: 70244.451@compuserve.com

Texas

Integrated Cost Management Systems Inc.
2261 Brookhollow Plz. Dr., Ste. 104
Arlington, TX 76006
(817)633-2873
Fax: (817)633-3781
E-mail: abm@icms.net
Website: http://www.icms.net

Lori Williams
1000 Leslie Ct.
Arlington, TX 76012
(817)459-3934
Fax: (817)459-3934

Business Resource Software Inc.
2013 Wells Branch Pky., Ste. 305
Austin, TX 78728
Free: 800-423-1228
Fax: (512)251-4401
E-mail: info@brs-inc.com
Website: http://www.brs-inc.com

Erisa Adminstrative Services Inc.
12325 Hymeadow Dr., Bldg. 4
Austin, TX 78750-1847
(512)250-9020
Fax: (512)250-9487
Website: http://www.cserisa.com

R. Miller Hicks & Co.
1011 W 11th St.
Austin, TX 78703
(512)477-7000
Fax: (512)477-9697
E-mail: millerhicks@rmhicks.com
Website: http://www.rmhicks.com

Pragmatic Tactics Inc.
3303 Westchester Ave.
College Station, TX 77845
(409)696-5294
Free: 800-570-5294
Fax: (409)696-4994
E-mail: ptactics@aol.com
Website: http://www.ptatics.com

Perot Systems
12404 Park Central Dr.
Dallas, TX 75251
(972)340-5000
Free: 800-688-4333
Fax: (972)455-4100
E-mail: corp.comm@ps.net
Website: http://www.perotsystems.com

ReGENERATION Partners
3838 Oak Lawn Ave.
Dallas, TX 75219
(214)559-3999
Free: 800-406-1112
E-mail: info@regeneration-partner.com
Website: http://www.regeneration-partners.com

High Technology Associates - Division of Global Technologies Inc.
1775 St. James Pl., Ste. 105
Houston, TX 77056
(713)963-9300
Fax: (713)963-8341
E-mail: hta@infohwy.com

MasterCOM
103 Thunder Rd.
Kerrville, TX 78028
(830)895-7990
Fax: (830)443-3428
E-mail: jmstubblefield@mastertraining.com
Website: http://www.mastertraining.com

PROTEC
4607 Linden Pl.
Pearland, TX 77584
(281)997-9872
Fax: (281)997-9895
E-mail: p.oman@ix.netcom.com

Alpha Quadrant Inc.
10618 Auldine
San Antonio, TX 78230
(210)344-3330
Fax: (210)344-8151
E-mail: mbussone@sbcglobal.net
Website:http://www.a-quadrant.com
Michele Bussone

Bastian Public Relations
614 San Dizier
San Antonio, TX 78232
(210)404-1839
E-mail: lisa@bastianpr.com
Website: http://www.bastianpr.com
Lisa Bastian CBC

Business Strategy Development Consultants
PO Box 690365
San Antonio, TX 78269
(210)696-8000
Free: 800-927-BSDC
Fax: (210)696-8000

Tom Welch, CPC
6900 San Pedro Ave., Ste. 147
San Antonio, TX 78216-6207

(210)737-7022
Fax: (210)737-7022
E-mail: bplan@iamerica.net
Website: http://www.moneywords.com

Utah

Business Management Resource
PO Box 521125
Salt Lake City, UT 84152-1125
(801)272-4668
Fax: (801)277-3290
E-mail: pingfong@worldnet.att.net

Virginia

Tindell Associates
209 Oxford Ave.
Alexandria, VA 22301
(703)683-0109
Fax: 703-783-0219
E-mail: scott@tindell.net
Website: http://www.tindell.net
Scott Lockett, President

Elliott B. Jaffa
2530-B S Walter Reed Dr.
Arlington, VA 22206
(703)931-0040
E-mail: thetrainingdoctor@excite.com
Website: http://www.tregistry.com/jaffa.htm

Koach Enterprises - USA
5529 N 18th St.
Arlington, VA 22205
(703)241-8361
Fax: (703)241-8623

Federal Market Development
5650 Chapel Run Ct.
Centreville, VA 20120-3601
(703)502-8930
Free: 800-821-5003
Fax: (703)502-8929

Huff, Stuart & Carlton
2107 Graves Mills Rd., Ste. C
Forest, VA 24551
(804)316-9356
Free: (888)316-9356
Fax: (804)316-9357
Website: http://www.wealthmgt.net

AMX International Inc.
1420 Spring Hill Rd. , Ste. 600
McLean, VA 22102-3006
(703)690-4100
Fax: (703)643-1279
E-mail: amxmail@amxi.com
Website: http://www.amxi.com

Charles Scott Pugh (Investor)
4101 Pittaway Dr.
Richmond, VA 23235-1022
(804)560-0979
Fax: (804)560-4670

John C. Randall and Associates Inc.
PO Box 15127
Richmond, VA 23227
(804)746-4450
Fax: (804)730-8933
E-mail: randalljcx@aol.com
Website: http://www.johncrandall.com

McLeod & Co.
410 1st St.
Roanoke, VA 24011
(540)342-6911
Fax: (540)344-6367
Website: http://www.mcleodco.com/

Salzinger & Company Inc.
8000 Towers Crescent Dr., Ste. 1350
Vienna, VA 22182
(703)442-5200
Fax: (703)442-5205
E-mail: info@salzinger.com
Website: http://www.salzinger.com

The Small Business Counselor
12423 Hedges Run Dr., Ste. 153
Woodbridge, VA 22192
(703)490-6755
Fax: (703)490-1356

Washington

Burlington Consultants
10900 NE 8th St., Ste. 900
Bellevue, WA 98004
(425)688-3060
Fax: (425)454-4383
E-mail: partners@burlington
consultants.com
Website: http://www.burlington
consultants.com

Perry L. Smith Consulting
800 Bellevue Way NE, Ste. 400
Bellevue, WA 98004-4208
(425)462-2072
Fax: (425)462-5638

St. Charles Consulting Group
1420 NW Gilman Blvd.
Issaquah, WA 98027
(425)557-8708
Fax: (425)557-8731
E-mail: info@stcharlesconsulting.com
Website: http://www.stcharlescon
sulting.com

Independent Automotive Training Services
PO Box 334
Kirkland, WA 98083
(425)822-5715
E-mail: ltunney@autosvccon.com
Website: http://www.autosvccon.com

Kahle Associate Inc.
6203 204th Dr. NE
Redmond, WA 98053
(425)836-8763
Fax: (425)868-3770
E-mail: randykahle@kahleassociates.com
Website: http://www.kahleassociates.com

Dan Collin
3419 Wallingord Ave N, No. 2
Seattle, WA 98103
(206)634-9469
E-mail: dc@dancollin.com
Website: http://members.home.net/
dcollin/

ECG Management Consultants Inc.
1111 3rd Ave., Ste. 2700
Seattle, WA 98101-3201
(206)689-2200
Fax: (206)689-2209
E-mail: ecg@ecgmc.com
Website: http://www.ecgmc.com

Northwest Trade Adjustment Assistance Center
900 4th Ave., Ste. 2430
Seattle, WA 98164-1001
(206)622-2730
Free: 800-667-8087
Fax: (206)622-1105
E-mail: matchingfunds@nwtaac.org
Website: http://www.taacenters.org

Business Planning Consultants
S 3510 Ridgeview Dr.
Spokane, WA 99206
(509)928-0332
Fax: (509)921-0842
E-mail: bpci@nextdim.com

West Virginia

**Stanley & Associates Inc./
BusinessandMarketingPlans.com**
1687 Robert C. Byrd Dr.
Beckley, WV 25801
(304)252-0324
Free: 888-752-6720
Fax: (304)252-0470
E-mail: cclay@charterinternet.com

Website: http://www.Businessand
MarketingPlans.com
Christopher Clay

Wisconsin

White & Associates Inc.
5349 Somerset Ln. S
Greenfield, WI 53221
(414)281-7373
Fax: (414)281-7006
E-mail: wnaconsult@aol.com

Small business administration regional offices

This section contains a listing of Small Business Administration offices arranged numerically by region. Service areas are provided. Contact the appropriate office for a referral to the nearest field office, or visit the Small Business Administration online at www.sba.gov.

Region 1

U.S. Small Business Administration
Region I Office
10 Causeway St., Ste. 812
Boston, MA 02222-1093
Phone: (617)565-8415
Fax: (617)565-8420
Serves Connecticut, Maine, Massachusetts, New Hampshire, Rhode Island, and Vermont.

Region 2

U.S. Small Business Administration
Region II Office
26 Federal Plaza, Ste. 3108
New York, NY 10278
Phone: (212)264-1450
Fax: (212)264-0038
Serves New Jersey, New York, Puerto Rico, and the Virgin Islands.

Region 3

U.S. Small Business Administration
Region III Office
Robert N C Nix Sr. Federal Building
900 Market St., 5th Fl.
Philadelphia, PA 19107
(215)580-2807
Serves Delaware, the District of Columbia, Maryland, Pennsylvania, Virginia, and West Virginia.

Region 4

U.S. Small Business Administration
Region IV Office
233 Peachtree St. NE
Harris Tower 1800
Atlanta, GA 30303
Phone: (404)331-4999
Fax: (404)331-2354
Serves Alabama, Florida, Georgia, Kentucky, Mississippi, North Carolina, South Carolina, and Tennessee.

Region 5

U.S. Small Business Administration
Region V Office
500 W. Madison St.
Citicorp Center, Ste. 1240
Chicago, IL 60661-2511
Phone: (312)353-0357
Fax: (312)353-3426
Serves Illinois, Indiana, Michigan, Minnesota, Ohio, and Wisconsin.

Region 6

U.S. Small Business Administration
Region VI Office
4300 Amon Carter Blvd., Ste. 108
Fort Worth, TX 76155
Phone: (817)684-5581
Fax: (817)684-5588
Serves Arkansas, Louisiana, New Mexico, Oklahoma, and Texas.

Region 7

U.S. Small Business Administration
Region VII Office
323 W. 8th St., Ste. 307
Kansas City, MO 64105-1500
Phone: (816)374-6380
Fax: (816)374-6339
Serves Iowa, Kansas, Missouri, and Nebraska.

Region 8

U.S. Small Business Administration
Region VIII Office
721 19th St., Ste. 400
Denver, CO 80202
Phone: (303)844-0500
Fax: (303)844-0506
Serves Colorado, Montana, North Dakota, South Dakota, Utah, and Wyoming.

Region 9

U.S. Small Business Administration
Region IX Office
330 N Brand Blvd., Ste. 1270
Glendale, CA 91203-2304
Phone: (818)552-3434
Fax: (818)552-3440
Serves American Samoa, Arizona, California, Guam, Hawaii, Nevada, and the Trust Territory of the Pacific Islands.

Region 10

U.S. Small Business Administration
Region X Office
2401 Fourth Ave., Ste. 400
Seattle, WA 98121
Phone: (206)553-5676
Fax: (206)553-4155
Serves Alaska, Idaho, Oregon, and Washington.

Small business development centers

This section contains a listing of all Small Business Development Centers, organized alphabetically by state/U.S. territory, then by city, then by agency name.

Alabama

Alabama SBDC
UNIVERSITY OF ALABAMA
2800 Milan Court Suite 124
Birmingham, AL 35211-6908
Phone: 205-943-6750
Fax: 205-943-6752
E-Mail: wcampbell@provost.uab.edu
Website: http://www.asbdc.org
Mr. William Campbell Jr, State Director

Alaska

Alaska SBDC
UNIVERSITY OF ALASKA - ANCHORAGE
430 West Seventh Avenue, Suite 110
Anchorage, AK 99501
Phone: 907-274 -7232
Fax: 907-274-9524
E-Mail: anerw@uaa.alaska.edu
Website: http://www.aksbdc.org
Ms. Jean R. Wall, State Director

American Samoa

American Samoa SBDC
AMERICAN SAMOA COMMUNITY COLLEGE
P.O. Box 2609
Pago Pago, American Samoa 96799
Phone: 011-684-699-4830
Fax: 011-684-699-6132
E-Mail: htalex@att.net
Mr. Herbert Thweatt, Director

Arizona

Arizona SBDC
MARICOPA COUNTY COMMUNITY COLLEGE
2411 West 14th Street, Suite 132
Tempe, AZ 85281
Phone: 480-731-8720
Fax: 480-731-8729
E-Mail: mike.york@domail.maricopa.edu
Website: http://www.dist.maricopa.edu.sbdc
Mr. Michael York, State Director

Arkansas

Arkansas SBDC
UNIVERSITY OF ARKANSAS
2801 South University Avenue
Little Rock, AR 72204
Phone: 501-324-9043
Fax: 501-324-9049
E-Mail: jmroderick@ualr.edu
Website: http://asbdc.ualr.edu
Ms. Janet M. Roderick, State Director

California

California - San Francisco SBDC
Northern California SBDC Lead Center
HUMBOLDT STATE UNIVERSITY
Office of Economic Development
1 Harpst Street 2006A, Siemens Hall
Arcata, CA, 95521
Phone: 707-826-3922
Fax: 707-826-3206
E-Mail: gainer@humboldt.edu
Ms. Margaret A. Gainer, Regional Director

California - Sacramento SBDC
CALIFORNIA STATE UNIVERSITY - CHICO
Chico, CA 95929-0765
Phone: 530-898-4598
Fax: 530-898-4734

E-Mail: dripke@csuchico.edu
Website: http://gsbdc.csuchico.edu
Mr. Dan Ripke, Interim Regional Director

California - San Diego SBDC
SOUTHWESTERN COMMUNITY
COLLEGE DISTRICT
900 Otey Lakes Road
Chula Vista, CA 91910
Phone: 619-482-6388
Fax: 619-482-6402
E-Mail: dtrujillo@swc.cc.ca.us
Website: http://www.sbditc.org
Ms. Debbie P. Trujillo, Regional Director

California - Fresno SBDC
UC Merced Lead Center
UNIVERSITY OF CALIFORNIA -
MERCED
550 East Shaw, Suite 105A
Fresno, CA 93710
Phone: 559-241-6590
Fax: 559-241-7422
E-Mail: crosander@ucmerced.edu
Website: http://sbdc.ucmerced.edu
Mr. Chris Rosander, State Director

California - Santa Ana SBDC
Tri-County Lead SBDC
CALIFORNIA STATE UNIVERSITY -
FULLERTON
800 North State College Boulevard, LH640
Fullerton, CA 92834
Phone: 714-278-2719
Fax: 714-278-7858
E-Mail: vpham@fullerton.edu
Website: http://www.leadsbdc.org
Ms. Vi Pham, Lead Center Director

California - Los Angeles Region SBDC
LONG BEACH COMMUNITY
COLLEGE DISTRICT
3950 Paramount Boulevard, Ste 101
Lakewood, CA 90712
Phone: 562-938-5004
Fax: 562-938-5030
E-Mail: ssloan@lbcc.edu
Ms. Sheneui Sloan, Interim Lead Center
Director

Colorado

Colorado SBDC
OFFICE OF ECONOMIC
DEVELOPMENT
1625 Broadway, Suite 170
Denver, CO 80202
Phone: 303-892-3864
Fax: 303-892-3848
E-Mail: Kelly.Manning@state.co.us

Website: http://www.state.co.us/oed/sbdc
Ms. Kelly Manning, State Director

Connecticut

Connecticut SBDC
UNIVERSITY OF CONNECTICUT
1376 Storrs Road, Unit 4094
Storrs, CT 06269-1094
Phone: 860-870-6370
Fax: 860-870-6374
E-Mail: richard.cheney@uconn.edu
Website: http://www.sbdc.uconn.edu
Mr. Richard Cheney, Interim State Director

Delaware

Delaware SBDC
DELAWARE TECHNOLOGY PARK
1 Innovation Way, Suite 301
Newark, DE 19711
Phone: 302-831-2747
Fax: 302-831-1423
E-Mail: Clinton.tymes@mvs.udel.edu
Website: http://www.delawaresbdc.org
Mr. Clinton Tymes, State Director

District of Columbia

District of Columbia SBDC
HOWARD UNIVERSITY
2600 6th Street, NW Room 128
Washington, DC 20059
Phone: 202-806-1550
Fax: 202-806-1777
E-Mail: hturner@howard.edu
Website: http://www.dcsbdc.com/
Mr. Henry Turner, Executive Director

Florida

Florida SBDC
UNIVERSITY OF WEST FLORIDA
401 East Chase Street, Suite 100
Pensacola, FL 32502
Phone: 850-473-7800
Fax: 850-473-7813
E-Mail: jcartwri@uwf.edu
Website: http://www.floridasbdc.com
Mr. Jerry Cartwright, State Director

Georgia

Georgia SBDC
UNIVERSITY OF GEORGIA
1180 East Broad Street
Athens, GA 30602
Phone: 706-542-6762
Fax: 706-542-6776
E-mail: aadams@sbdc.uga.edu

Website: http://www.sbdc.uga.edu
Mr. Allan Adams, Interim State Director

Guam

Guam Small Business Development
Center
UNIVERSITY OF GUAM
Pacific Islands SBDC
P.O. Box 5014 - U.O.G. Station
Mangilao, GU 96923
Phone: 671-735-2590
Fax: 671-734-2002
E-mail: casey@pacificsbdc.com
Website: http://www.uog.edu/sbdc
Mr. Casey Jeszenka, Director

Hawaii

Hawaii SBDC
UNIVERSITY OF HAWAII - HILO
308 Kamehameha Avenue, Suite 201
Hilo, HI 96720
Phone: 808-974-7515
Fax: 808-974-7683
E-Mail: darrylm@interpac.net
Website: http://www.hawaii-sbdc.org
Mr. Darryl Mleynek, State Director

Idaho

Idaho SBDC
BOISE STATE UNIVERSITY
1910 University Drive
Boise, ID 83725
Phone: 208-426-3799
Fax: 208-426-3877
E-mail: jhogge@boisestate.edu
Website: http://www.idahosbdc.org
Mr. Jim Hogge, State Director

Illinois

Illinois SBDC
DEPARTMENT OF COMMERCE
AND ECONOMIC OPPORTUNITY
620 E. Adams, S-4
Springfield, IL 62701
Phone: 217-524-5700
Fax: 217-524-0171
E-mail: mpatrilli@ildceo.net
Website: http://www.ilsbdc.biz
Mr. Mark Petrilli, State Director

Indiana

Indiana SBDC
INDIANA ECONOMIC
DEVELOPMENT CORPORATION
One North Capitol, Suite 900
Indianapolis, IN 46204

Phone: 317-234-8872
Fax: 317-232-8874
E-mail: dtrocha@isbdc.org
Website: http://www.isbdc.org
Ms. Debbie Bishop Trocha, State Director

Iowa

Iowa SBDC
IOWA STATE UNIVERSITY
340 Gerdin Business Bldg.
Ames, IA 50011-1350
Phone: 515-294-2037
Fax: 515-294-6522
E-mail: jonryan@iastate.edu
Website: http://www.iabusnet.org
Mr. Jon Ryan, State Director

Kansas

Kansas SBDC
FORT HAYS STATE UNIVERSITY
214 SW Sixth Street, Suite 301
Topeka, KS 66603
Phone: 785-296-6514
Fax: 785-291-3261
E-mail: ksbdc.wkearns@fhsu.edu
Website: http://www.fhsu.edu/ksbdc
Mr. Wally Kearns, State Director

Kentucky

Kentucky SBDC
UNIVERSITY OF KENTUCKY
225 Gatton College of Business
Economics Building
Lexington, KY 40506-0034
Phone: 859-257-7668
Fax: 859-323-1907
E-mail: lrnaug0@pop.uky.edu
Website: http://www.ksbdc.org
Ms. Becky Naugle, State Director

Louisiana

Louisiana SBDC
UNIVERSITY OF LOUISIANA - MONROE
College of Business Administration
700 University Avenue
Monroe, LA 71209
Phone: 318-342-5506
Fax: 318-342-5510
E-mail: wilkerson@ulm.edu
Website: http://www.lsbdc.org
Ms. Mary Lynn Wilkerson, State Director

Maine

Maine SBDC
UNIVERSITY OF SOUTHERN MAINE
96 Falmouth Street P.O. Box 9300
Portland, ME 04103
Phone: 207-780-4420
Fax: 207-780-4810
E-mail: jrmassaua@maine.edu
Website: http://www.mainesbdc.org
Mr. John Massaua, State Director

Maryland

Maryland SBDC
UNIVERSITY OF MARYLAND
7100 Baltimore Avenue, Suite 401
College Park, MD 20742
Phone: 301-403-8300
Fax: 301-403-8303
E-mail: rsprow@mdsbdc.umd.edu
Website: http://www.mdsbdc.umd.edu
Ms. Renee Sprow, State Director

Massachusetts

Massachusetts SBDC
UNIVERSITY OF MASSACHUSETTS
School of Management, Room 205
Amherst, MA 01003-4935
Phone: 413-545-6301
Fax: 413-545-1273
E-mail: gep@msbdc.umass.edu
Website: http://msbdc.som.umass.edu
Ms. Georgianna Parkin, State Director

Michigan

Michigan SBTDC
GRAND VALLEY STATE UNIVERSITY
510 West Fulton Avenue
Grand Rapids, MI 49504
Phone: 616-331-7485
Fax: 616-331-7389
E-mail: lopuckic@gvsu.edu
Website: http://www.misbtdc.org
Ms. Carol Lopucki, State Director

Minnesota

Minnesota SBDC
MINNESOTA SMALL BUSINESS DEVELOPMENT CENTER
1st National Bank Building
332 Minnesota Street, Suite E200
St. Paul, MN 55101-1351
Phone: 651-297-5773
Fax: 651-296-5287

E-mail: michael.myhre@state.mn.us
Website: http://www.mnsbdc.com
Mr. Michael Myhre, State Director

Mississippi

Mississippi SBDC
UNIVERSITY OF MISSISSIPPI
B-19 Jeanette Phillips Drive
P.O. Box 1848
University, MS 38677
Phone: 662-915-5001
Fax: 662-915-5650
E-mail: wgurley@olemiss.edu
Website: http://www.olemiss.edu/depts/mssbdc
Mr. Doug Gurley, Jr., State Director

Missouri

Missouri SBDC
UNIVERSITY OF MISSOURI
1205 University Avenue, Suite 300
Columbia, MO 65211
Phone: 573-882-1348
Fax: 573-884-4297
E-mail: summersm@missouri.edu
Website: http://www.mo-sbdc.org/index.shtml
Mr. Max Summers, State Director

Montana

Montana SBDC
DEPARTMENT OF COMMERCE
301 South Park Avenue, Room 114 / P.O. Box 200505
Helena, MT 59620
Phone: 406-841-2746
Fax: 406-444-1872
E-mail: adesch@state.mt.us
Website: http://commerce.state.mt.us/brd/BRD_SBDC.html
Ms. Ann Desch, State Director

Nebraska

Nebraska SBDC
UNIVERSITY OF NEBRASKA - OMAHA
60th & Dodge Street, CBA Room 407
Omaha, NE 68182
Phone: 402-554-2521
Fax: 402-554-3473
E-mail: rbernier@unomaha.edu
Website: http://nbdc.unomaha.edu
Mr. Robert Bernier, State Director

Nevada

Nevada SBDC
UNIVERSITY OF NEVADA - RENO
Reno College of Business
Administration, Room 411
Reno, NV 89557-0100
Phone: 775-784-1717
Fax: 775-784-4337
E-mail: males@unr.edu
Website: http://www.nsbdc.org
Mr. Sam Males, State Director

New Hampshire

New Hampshire SBDC
UNIVERSITY OF NEW HAMPSHIRE
108 McConnell Hall
Durham, NH 03824-3593
Phone: 603-862-4879
Fax: 603-862-4876
E-mail: Mary.Collins@unh.edu
Website: http://www.nhsbdc.org
Ms. Mary Collins, State Director

New Jersey

New Jersey SBDC
RUTGERS UNIVERSITY
49 Bleeker Street
Newark, NJ 07102-1993
Phone: 973-353-5950
Fax: 973-353-1110
E-mail: bhopper@njsbdc.com
Website: http://www.njsbdc.com/home
Ms. Brenda Hopper, State Director

New Mexico

New Mexico SBDC
SANTA FE COMMUNITY COLLEGE
6401 Richards Avenue
Santa Fe, NM 87505
Phone: 505-428-1362
Fax: 505-471-9469
E-mail: rmiller@santa-fe.cc.nm.us
Website: http://www.nmsbdc.org
Mr. Roy Miller, State Director

New York

New York SBDC
STATE UNIVERSITY OF NEW YORK
SUNY Plaza, S-523
Albany, NY 12246
Phone: 518-443-5398
Fax: 518-443-5275
E-mail: j.king@nyssbdc.org
Website: http://www.nyssbdc.org
Mr. Jim King, State Director

North Carolina

North Carolina SBDTC
UNIVERSITY OF NORTH CAROLINA
5 West Hargett Street, Suite 600
Raleigh, NC 27601
Phone: 919-715-7272
Fax: 919-715-7777
E-mail: sdaugherty@sbtdc.org
Website: http://www.sbtdc.org
Mr. Scott Daugherty, State Director

North Dakota

North Dakota SBDC
UNIVERSITY OF NORTH DAKOTA
1600 E. Century Avenue, Suite 2
Bismarck, ND 58503
Phone: 701-328-5375
Fax: 701-328-5320
E-mail: christine.martin@und.nodak.edu
Website: http://www.ndsbdc.org
Ms. Christine Martin-Goldman, State
Director

Ohio

Ohio SBDC
OHIO DEPARTMENT
OF DEVELOPMENT
77 South High Street
Columbus, OH 43216
Phone: 614-466-5102
Fax: 614-466-0829
E-mail: mabraham@odod.state.oh.us
Website: http://www.ohiosbdc.org
Ms. Michele Abraham, State Director

Oklahoma

Oklahoma SBDC
SOUTHEAST OKLAHOMA STATE
UNIVERSITY
517 University, Box 2584, Station A
Durant, OK 74701
Phone: 580-745-7577
Fax: 580-745-7471
E-mail: gpennington@sosu.edu
Website: http://www.osbdc.org
Mr. Grady Pennington, State Director

Oregon

Oregon SBDC
LANE COMMUNITY COLLEGE
99 West Tenth Avenue, Suite 390
Eugene, OR 97401-3021
Phone: 541-463-5250
Fax: 541-345-6006
E-mail: carterb@lanecc.edu

Website: http://www.bizcenter.org
Mr. William Carter, State Director

Pennsylvania

Pennsylvania SBDC
UNIVERSITY OF PENNSYLVANIA
The Wharton School
3733 Spruce Street
Philadelphia, PA 19104-6374
Phone: 215-898-1219
Fax: 215-573-2135
E-mail: ghiggins@wharton.upenn.edu
Website: http://pasbdc.org
Mr. Gregory Higgins, State Director

Puerto Rico

Puerto Rico SBDC
INTER-AMERICAN UNIVERSITY
OF PUERTO RICO
416 Ponce de Leon Avenue, Union Plaza,
Seventh Floor
Hato Rey, PR 00918
Phone: 787-763-6811
Fax: 787-763-4629
E-mail: cmarti@prsbdc.org
Website: http://www.prsbdc.org
Ms. Carmen Marti, Executive Director

Rhode Island

Rhode Island SBDC
BRYANT UNIVERSITY
1150 Douglas Pike
Smithfield, RI 02917
Phone: 401-232-6923
Fax: 401-232-6933
E-mail: adawson@bryant.edu
Website: http://www.risbdc.org
Ms. Diane Fournaris, Interim State Director

South Carolina

South Carolina SBDC
UNIVERSITY OF SOUTH CAROLINA
College of Business Administration
1710 College Street
Columbia, SC 29208
Phone: 803-777-4907
Fax: 803-777-4403
E-mail: lenti@moore.sc.edu
Website: http://scsbdc.moore.sc.edu
Mr. John Lenti, State Director

South Dakota

South Dakota SBDC
UNIVERSITY OF SOUTH DAKOTA
414 East Clark Street, Patterson Hall
Vermillion, SD 57069

Phone: 605-677-6256
Fax: 605-677-5427
E-mail: jshemmin@usd.edu
Website: http://www.sdsbdc.org
Mr. John S. Hemmingstad, State
Director

Tennessee

Tennessee SBDC
TENNESSEE BOARD OF REGENTS
1415 Murfressboro Road, Suite 540
Nashville, TN 37217-2833
Phone: 615-898-2745
Fax: 615-893-7089
E-mail: pgeho@mail.tsbdc.org
Website: http://www.tsbdc.org
Mr. Patrick Geho, State Director

Texas

Texas-North SBDC
**DALLAS COUNTY COMMUNITY
COLLEGE**
1402 Corinth Street
Dallas, TX 75215
Phone: 214-860-5835
Fax: 214-860-5813
E-mail: emk9402@dcccd.edu
Website: http://www.ntsbdc.org
Ms. Liz Klimback, Region Director

Texas-Houston SBDC
UNIVERSITY OF HOUSTON
2302 Fannin, Suite 200
Houston, TX 77002
Phone: 713-752-8425
Fax: 713-756-1500
E-mail: fyoung@uh.edu
Website: http://sbdcnetwork.uh.edu
Mr. Mike Young, Executive Director

Texas-NW SBDC
TEXAS TECH UNIVERSITY
2579 South Loop 289, Suite 114
Lubbock, TX 79423
Phone: 806-745-3973
Fax: 806-745-6207
E-mail: c.bean@nwtsbdc.org
Website: http://www.nwtsbdc.org
Mr. Craig Bean, Executive Director

**Texas-South-West Texas Border
Region SBDC**
**UNIVERSITY OF TEXAS -
SAN ANTONIO**
501 West Durango Boulevard
San Antonio, TX 78207-4415
Phone: 210-458-2742
Fax: 210-458-2464

E-mail: albert.salgado@utsa.edu
Website: http://www.iedtexas.org
Mr. Alberto Salgado, Region Director

Utah

Utah SBDC
SALT LAKE COMMUNITY COLLEGE
9750 South 300 West
Sandy, UT 84070
Phone: 801-957-3493
Fax: 801-957-3488
E-mail: Greg.Panichello@slcc.edu
Website: http://www.slcc.edu/sbdc
Mr. Greg Panichello, State Director

Vermont

Vermont SBDC
VERMONT TECHNICAL COLLEGE
PO Box 188, 1 Main Street
Randolph Center, VT 05061-0188
Phone: 802-728-9101
Fax: 802-728-3026
E-mail: lquillen@vtc.edu
Website: http://www.vtsbdc.org
Ms. Lenae Quillen-Blume, State Director

Virgin Islands

Virgin Islands SBDC
**UNIVERSITY OF THE VIRGIN
ISLANDS**
8000 Nisky Center, Suite 720
St. Thomas, VI 00802-5804
Phone: 340-776-3206
Fax: 340-775-3756
E-mail: wbush@webmail.uvi.edu
Website: http://rps.uvi.edu/SBDC
Mr. Warren Bush, State Director

Virginia

Virginia SBDC
GEORGE MASON UNIVERSITY
4031 University Drive, Suite 200
Fairfax, VA 22030-3409
Phone: 703-277-7727
Fax: 703-352-8515
E-mail: jkeenan@gmu.edu
Website: http://www.virginiasbdc.org
Ms. Jody Keenan, Director

Washington

Washington SBDC
WASHINGTON STATE UNIVERSITY
534 E. Trent Avenue
P.O. Box 1495
Spokane, WA 99210-1495

Phone: 509-358-7765
Fax: 509-358-7764
E-mail: barogers@wsu.edu
Website: http://www.wsbdc.org
Mr. Brett Rogers, State Director

West Virginia

West Virginia SBDC
**WEST VIRGINIA DEVELOPMENT
OFFICE**
Capital Complex, Building 6, Room 652
Charleston, WV 25301
Phone: 304-558-2960
Fax: 304-558-0127
E-mail: csalyer@wvsbdc.org
Website: http://www.wvsbdc.org
Mr. Conley Salyor, State Director

Wisconsin

Wisconsin SBDC
UNIVERSITY OF WISCONSIN
432 North Lake Street, Room 423
Madison, WI 53706
Phone: 608-263-7794
Fax: 608-263-7830
E-mail: erica.kauten@uwex.edu
Website: http://www.wisconsinsbdc.org
Ms. Erica Kauten, State Director

Wyoming

Wyoming SBDC
UNIVERSITY OF WYOMING
P.O. Box 3922
Laramie, WY 82071-3922
Phone: 307-766-3505
Fax: 307-766-3406
E-mail: DDW@uwyo.edu
Website: http://www.uwyo.edu/sbdc
Ms. Debbie Popp, Acting State Director

Service corps of retired executives (score) offices

*This section contains a listing of all
SCORE offices organized alphabetically by
state/U.S. territory, then by city, then by
agency name.*

Alabama

SCORE Office (Northeast Alabama)
1330 Quintard Ave.
Anniston, AL 36202
(256)237-3536

SCORE Office (North Alabama)
901 South 15th St, Rm. 201
Birmingham, AL 35294-2060
(205)934-6868
Fax: (205)934-0538

SCORE Office (Baldwin County)
29750 Larry Dee Cawyer Dr.
Daphne, AL 36526
(334)928-5838

SCORE Office (Shoals)
612 S. COurt
Florence, AL 35630
(256)764-4661
Fax: (256)766-9017
E-mail: shoals@shoalschamber.com

SCORE Office (Mobile)
600 S Court St.
Mobile, AL 36104
(334)240-6868
Fax: (334)240-6869

SCORE Office (Alabama Capitol City)
600 S. Court St.
Montgomery, AL 36104
(334)240-6868
Fax: (334)240-6869

SCORE Office (East Alabama)
601 Ave. A
Opelika, AL 36801
(334)745-4861
E-mail: score636@hotmail.com
Website: http://www.angelfire.com/sc/
score636/

SCORE Office (Tuscaloosa)
2200 University Blvd.
Tuscaloosa, AL 35402
(205)758-7588

Alaska

SCORE Office (Anchorage)
510 L St., Ste. 310
Anchorage, AK 99501
(907)271-4022
Fax: (907)271-4545

Arizona

SCORE Office (Lake Havasu)
10 S. Acoma Blvd.
Lake Havasu City, AZ 86403
(520)453-5951
E-mail: SCORE@ctaz.com
Website: http://www.scorearizona.org/
lake_havasu/

SCORE Office (East Valley)
Federal Bldg., Rm. 104
26 N. MacDonald St.
Mesa, AZ 85201
(602)379-3100
Fax: (602)379-3143
E-mail: 402@aol.com
Website: http://www.scorearizona.
org/mesa/

SCORE Office (Phoenix)
2828 N. Central Ave., Ste. 800
Central & One Thomas
Phoenix, AZ 85004
(602)640-2329
Fax: (602)640-2360
E-mail: e-mail@SCORE-phoenix.org
Website: http://www.score-phoenix.org/

SCORE Office (Prescott Arizona)
1228 Willow Creek Rd., Ste. 2
Prescott, AZ 86301
(520)778-7438
Fax: (520)778-0812
E-mail: score@northlink.com
Website: http://www.scorearizona.org/
prescott/

SCORE Office (Tucson)
110 E. Pennington St.
Tucson, AZ 85702
(520)670-5008
Fax: (520)670-5011
E-mail: score@azstarnet.com
Website: http://www.scorearizona.org/
tucson/

SCORE Office (Yuma)
281 W. 24th St., Ste. 116
Yuma, AZ 85364
(520)314-0480
E-mail: score@C2i2.com
Website: http://www.scorearizona.org/
yuma

Arkansas

SCORE Office (South Central)
201 N. Jackson Ave.
El Dorado, AR 71730-5803
(870)863-6113
Fax: (870)863-6115

SCORE Office (Ozark)
Fayetteville, AR 72701
(501)442-7619

SCORE Office (Northwest Arkansas)
Glenn Haven Dr., No. 4
Ft. Smith, AR 72901
(501)783-3556

SCORE Office (Garland County)
Grand & Ouachita
PO Box 6012
Hot Springs Village, AR 71902
(501)321-1700

SCORE Office (Little Rock)
2120 Riverfront Dr., Rm. 100
Little Rock, AR 72202-1747
(501)324-5893
Fax: (501)324-5199

SCORE Office (Southeast Arkansas)
121 W. 6th
Pine Bluff, AR 71601
(870)535-7189
Fax: (870)535-1643

California

SCORE Office (Golden Empire)
1706 Chester Ave., No. 200
Bakersfield, CA 93301
(805)322-5881
Fax: (805)322-5663

SCORE Office (Greater Chico Area)
1324 Mangrove St., Ste. 114
Chico, CA 95926
(916)342-8932
Fax: (916)342-8932

SCORE Office (Concord)
2151-A Salvio St., Ste. B
Concord, CA 94520
(510)685-1181
Fax: (510)685-5623

SCORE Office (Covina)
935 W. Badillo St.
Covina, CA 91723
(818)967-4191
Fax: (818)966-9660

SCORE Office (Rancho Cucamonga)
8280 Utica, Ste. 160
Cucamonga, CA 91730
(909)987-1012
Fax: (909)987-5917

SCORE Office (Culver City)
PO Box 707
Culver City, CA 90232-0707
(310)287-3850
Fax: (310)287-1350

SCORE Office (Danville)
380 Diablo Rd., Ste. 103
Danville, CA 94526
(510)837-4400

SCORE Office (Downey)
11131 Brookshire Ave.
Downey, CA 90241
(310)923-2191
Fax: (310)864-0461

SCORE Office (El Cajon)
109 Rea Ave.
El Cajon, CA 92020
(619)444-1327
Fax: (619)440-6164

SCORE Office (El Centro)
1100 Main St.
El Centro, CA 92243
(619)352-3681
Fax: (619)352-3246

SCORE Office (Escondido)
720 N. Broadway
Escondido, CA 92025
(619)745-2125
Fax: (619)745-1183

SCORE Office (Fairfield)
1111 Webster St.
Fairfield, CA 94533
(707)425-4625
Fax: (707)425-0826

SCORE Office (Fontana)
17009 Valley Blvd., Ste. B
Fontana, CA 92335
(909)822-4433
Fax: (909)822-6238

SCORE Office (Foster City)
1125 E. Hillsdale Blvd.
Foster City, CA 94404
(415)573-7600
Fax: (415)573-5201

SCORE Office (Fremont)
2201 Walnut Ave., Ste. 110
Fremont, CA 94538
(510)795-2244
Fax: (510)795-2240

SCORE Office (Central California)
2719 N. Air Fresno Dr., Ste. 200
Fresno, CA 93727-1547
(559)487-5605
Fax: (559)487-5636

SCORE Office (Gardena)
1204 W. Gardena Blvd.
Gardena, CA 90247
(310)532-9905
Fax: (310)515-4893

SCORE Office (Lompoc)
330 N. Brand Blvd., Ste. 190
Glendale, CA 91203-2304

(818)552-3206
Fax: (818)552-3323

SCORE Office (Los Angeles)
330 N. Brand Blvd., Ste. 190
Glendale, CA 91203-2304
(818)552-3206
Fax: (818)552-3323

SCORE Office (Glendora)
131 E. Foothill Blvd.
Glendora, CA 91740
(818)963-4128
Fax: (818)914-4822

SCORE Office (Grover Beach)
177 S. 8th St.
Grover Beach, CA 93433
(805)489-9091
Fax: (805)489-9091

SCORE Office (Hawthorne)
12477 Hawthorne Blvd.
Hawthorne, CA 90250
(310)676-1163
Fax: (310)676-7661

SCORE Office (Hayward)
22300 Foothill Blvd., Ste. 303
Hayward, CA 94541
(510)537-2424

SCORE Office (Hemet)
1700 E. Florida Ave.
Hemet, CA 92544-4679
(909)652-4390
Fax: (909)929-8543

SCORE Office (Hesperia)
16367 Main St.
PO Box 403656
Hesperia, CA 92340
(619)244-2135

SCORE Office (Holloster)
321 San Felipe Rd., No. 11
Hollister, CA 95023

SCORE Office (Hollywood)
7018 Hollywood Blvd.
Hollywood, CA 90028
(213)469-8311
Fax: (213)469-2805

SCORE Office (Indio)
82503 Hwy. 111
PO Drawer TTT
Indio, CA 92202
(619)347-0676

SCORE Office (Inglewood)
330 Queen St.

Inglewood, CA 90301
(818)552-3206

SCORE Office (La Puente)
218 N. Grendanda St. D.
La Puente, CA 91744
(818)330-3216
Fax: (818)330-9524

SCORE Office (La Verne)
2078 Bonita Ave.
La Verne, CA 91750
(909)593-5265
Fax: (714)929-8475

SCORE Office (Lake Elsinore)
132 W. Graham Ave.
Lake Elsinore, CA 92530
(909)674-2577

SCORE Office (Lakeport)
PO Box 295
Lakeport, CA 95453
(707)263-5092

SCORE Office (Lakewood)
5445 E. Del Amo Blvd., Ste. 2
Lakewood, CA 90714
(213)920-7737

SCORE Office (Long Beach)
1 World Trade Center
Long Beach, CA 90831

SCORE Office (Los Alamitos)
901 W. Civic Center Dr., Ste. 160
Los Alamitos, CA 90720

SCORE Office (Los Altos)
321 University Ave.
Los Altos, CA 94022
(415)948-1455

SCORE Office (Manhattan Beach)
PO Box 3007
Manhattan Beach, CA 90266
(310)545-5313
Fax: (310)545-7203

SCORE Office (Merced)
1632 N. St.
Merced, CA 95340
(209)725-3800
Fax: (209)383-4959

SCORE Office (Milpitas)
75 S. Milpitas Blvd., Ste. 205
Milpitas, CA 95035
(408)262-2613
Fax: (408)262-2823

SCORE Office (Yosemite)
1012 11th St., Ste. 300
Modesto, CA 95354
(209)521-9333

SCORE Office (Montclair)
5220 Benito Ave.
Montclair, CA 91763

SCORE Office (Monterey Bay)
380 Alvarado St.
PO Box 1770
Monterey, CA 93940-1770
(408)649-1770

SCORE Office (Moreno Valley)
25480 Alessandro
Moreno Valley, CA 92553

SCORE Office (Morgan Hill)
25 W. 1st St.
PO Box 786
Morgan Hill, CA 95038
(408)779-9444
Fax: (408)778-1786

SCORE Office (Morro Bay)
880 Main St.
Morro Bay, CA 93442
(805)772-4467

SCORE Office (Mountain View)
580 Castro St.
Mountain View, CA 94041
(415)968-8378
Fax: (415)968-5668

SCORE Office (Napa)
1556 1st St.
Napa, CA 94559
(707)226-7455
Fax: (707)226-1171

SCORE Office (North Hollywood)
5019 Lankershim Blvd.
North Hollywood, CA 91601
(818)552-3206

SCORE Office (Northridge)
8801 Reseda Blvd.
Northridge, CA 91324
(818)349-5676

SCORE Office (Novato)
807 De Long Ave.
Novato, CA 94945
(415)897-1164
Fax: (415)898-9097

SCORE Office (East Bay)
519 17th St.
Oakland, CA 94612

(510)273-6611
Fax: (510)273-6015
E-mail: webmaster@eastbayscore.org
Website: http://www.eastbayscore.org

SCORE Office (Oceanside)
928 N. Coast Hwy.
Oceanside, CA 92054
(619)722-1534

SCORE Office (Ontario)
121 West B. St.
Ontario, CA 91762
Fax: (714)984-6439

SCORE Office (Oxnard)
PO Box 867
Oxnard, CA 93032
(805)385-8860
Fax: (805)487-1763

SCORE Office (Pacifica)
450 Dundee Way, Ste. 2
Pacifica, CA 94044
(415)355-4122

SCORE Office (Palm Desert)
72990 Hwy. 111
Palm Desert, CA 92260
(619)346-6111
Fax: (619)346-3463

SCORE Office (Palm Springs)
650 E. Tahquitz Canyon Way Ste. D
Palm Springs, CA 92262-6706
(760)320-6682
Fax: (760)323-9426

SCORE Office (Lakeside)
2150 Low Tree
Palmdale, CA 93551
(805)948-4518
Fax: (805)949-1212

SCORE Office (Palo Alto)
325 Forest Ave.
Palo Alto, CA 94301
(415)324-3121
Fax: (415)324-1215

SCORE Office (Pasadena)
117 E. Colorado Blvd., Ste. 100
Pasadena, CA 91105
(818)795-3355
Fax: (818)795-5663

SCORE Office (Paso Robles)
1225 Park St.
Paso Robles, CA 93446-2234
(805)238-0506
Fax: (805)238-0527

SCORE Office (Petaluma)
799 Baywood Dr., Ste. 3
Petaluma, CA 94954
(707)762-2785
Fax: (707)762-4721

SCORE Office (Pico Rivera)
9122 E. Washington Blvd.
Pico Rivera, CA 90660

SCORE Office (Pittsburg)
2700 E. Leland Rd.
Pittsburg, CA 94565
(510)439-2181
Fax: (510)427-1599

SCORE Office (Pleasanton)
777 Peters Ave.
Pleasanton, CA 94566
(510)846-9697

SCORE Office (Monterey Park)
485 N. Garey
Pomona, CA 91769

SCORE Office (Pomona)
485 N. Garey Ave.
Pomona, CA 91766
(909)622-1256

SCORE Office (Antelope Valley)
4511 West Ave. M-4
Quartz Hill, CA 93536
(805)272-0087
E-mail: avscore@ptw.com
Website: http://www.score.av.org/

SCORE Office (Shasta)
737 Auditorium Dr.
Redding, CA 96099
(916)225-2770

SCORE Office (Redwood City)
1675 Broadway
Redwood City, CA 94063
(415)364-1722
Fax: (415)364-1729

SCORE Office (Richmond)
3925 MacDonald Ave.
Richmond, CA 94805

SCORE Office (Ridgecrest)
PO Box 771
Ridgecrest, CA 93555
(619)375-8331
Fax: (619)375-0365

SCORE Office (Riverside)
3685 Main St., Ste. 350
Riverside, CA 92501
(909)683-7100

SCORE Office (Sacramento)
9845 Horn Rd., 260-B
Sacramento, CA 95827
(916)361-2322
Fax: (916)361-2164
E-mail: sacchapter@directcon.net

SCORE Office (Salinas)
PO Box 1170
Salinas, CA 93902
(408)424-7611
Fax: (408)424-8639

SCORE Office (Inland Empire)
777 E. Rialto Ave.
Purchasing
San Bernardino, CA 92415-0760
(909)386-8278

SCORE Office (San Carlos)
San Carlos Chamber of Commerce
PO Box 1086
San Carlos, CA 94070
(415)593-1068
Fax: (415)593-9108

SCORE Office (Encinitas)
550 W. C St., Ste. 550
San Diego, CA 92101-3540
(619)557-7272
Fax: (619)557-5894

SCORE Office (San Diego)
550 West C. St., Ste. 550
San Diego, CA 92101-3540
(619)557-7272
Fax: (619)557-5894
Website: http://www.score-sandiego.org

SCORE Office (Menlo Park)
1100 Merrill St.
San Francisco, CA 94105
(415)325-2818
Fax: (415)325-0920

SCORE Office (San Francisco)
455 Market St., 6th Fl.
San Francisco, CA 94105
(415)744-6827
Fax: (415)744-6750
E-mail: sfscore@sfscore.
Website: http://www.sfscore.com

SCORE Office (San Gabriel)
401 W. Las Tunas Dr.
San Gabriel, CA 91776
(818)576-2525
Fax: (818)289-2901

SCORE Office (San Jose)
Deanza College
208 S. 1st. St., Ste. 137
San Jose, CA 95113
(408)288-8479
Fax: (408)535-5541

SCORE Office (Silicon Valley)
84 W. Santa Clara St., Ste. 100
San Jose, CA 95113
(408)288-8479
Fax: (408)535-5541
E-mail: info@svscore.org
Website: http://www.svscore.org

SCORE Office (San Luis Obispo)
3566 S. Hiquera, No. 104
San Luis Obispo, CA 93401
(805)547-0779

SCORE Office (San Mateo)
1021 S. El Camino, 2nd Fl.
San Mateo, CA 94402
(415)341-5679

SCORE Office (San Pedro)
390 W. 7th St.
San Pedro, CA 90731
(310)832-7272

SCORE Office (Orange County)
200 W. Santa Anna Blvd., Ste. 700
Santa Ana, CA 92701
(714)550-7369
Fax: (714)550-0191
Website: http://www.score114.org

SCORE Office (Santa Barbara)
3227 State St.
Santa Barbara, CA 93130
(805)563-0084

SCORE Office (Central Coast)
509 W. Morrison Ave.
Santa Maria, CA 93454
(805)347-7755

SCORE Office (Santa Maria)
614 S. Broadway
Santa Maria, CA 93454-5111
(805)925-2403
Fax: (805)928-7559

SCORE Office (Santa Monica)
501 Colorado, Ste. 150
Santa Monica, CA 90401
(310)393-9825
Fax: (310)394-1868

SCORE Office (Santa Rosa)
777 Sonoma Ave., Rm. 115E
Santa Rosa, CA 95404

(707)571-8342
Fax: (707)541-0331
Website: http://www.pressdemo.com/community/score/score.html

SCORE Office (Scotts Valley)
4 Camp Evers Ln.
Scotts Valley, CA 95066
(408)438-1010
Fax: (408)438-6544

SCORE Office (Simi Valley)
40 W. Cochran St., Ste. 100
Simi Valley, CA 93065
(805)526-3900
Fax: (805)526-6234

SCORE Office (Sonoma)
453 1st St. E
Sonoma, CA 95476
(707)996-1033

SCORE Office (Los Banos)
222 S. Shepard St.
Sonora, CA 95370
(209)532-4212

SCORE Office (Tuolumne County)
39 North Washington St.
Sonora, CA 95370
(209)588-0128
E-mail: score@mlode.com

SCORE Office (South San Francisco)
445 Market St., Ste. 6th Fl.
South San Francisco, CA 94105
(415)744-6827
Fax: (415)744-6812

SCORE Office (Stockton)
401 N. San Joaquin St., Rm. 215
Stockton, CA 95202
(209)946-6293

SCORE Office (Taft)
314 4th St.
Taft, CA 93268
(805)765-2165
Fax: (805)765-6639

SCORE Office (Conejo Valley)
625 W. Hillcrest Dr.
Thousand Oaks, CA 91360
(805)499-1993
Fax: (805)498-7264

SCORE Office (Torrance)
3400 Torrance Blvd., Ste. 100
Torrance, CA 90503
(310)540-5858
Fax: (310)540-7662

SCORE Office (Truckee)
PO Box 2757
Truckee, CA 96160
(916)587-2757
Fax: (916)587-2439

SCORE Office (Visalia)
113 S. M St,
Tulare, CA 93274
(209)627-0766
Fax: (209)627-8149

SCORE Office (Upland)
433 N. 2nd Ave.
Upland, CA 91786
(909)931-4108

SCORE Office (Vallejo)
2 Florida St.
Vallejo, CA 94590
(707)644-5551
Fax: (707)644-5590

SCORE Office (Van Nuys)
14540 Victory Blvd.
Van Nuys, CA 91411
(818)989-0300
Fax: (818)989-3836

SCORE Office (Ventura)
5700 Ralston St., Ste. 310
Ventura, CA 93001
(805)658-2688
Fax: (805)658-2252
E-mail: scoreven@jps.net
Website: http://www.jps.net/scoreven

SCORE Office (Vista)
201 E. Washington St.
Vista, CA 92084
(619)726-1122
Fax: (619)226-8654

SCORE Office (Watsonville)
PO Box 1748
Watsonville, CA 95077
(408)724-3849
Fax: (408)728-5300

SCORE Office (West Covina)
811 S. Sunset Ave.
West Covina, CA 91790
(818)338-8496
Fax: (818)960-0511

SCORE Office (Westlake)
30893 Thousand Oaks Blvd.
Westlake Village, CA 91362
(805)496-5630
Fax: (818)991-1754

Colorado

SCORE Office (Colorado Springs)
2 N. Cascade Ave., Ste. 110
Colorado Springs, CO 80903
(719)636-3074
Website: http://www.cscc.org/score02/
index.html

SCORE Office (Denver)
US Custom's House, 4th Fl.
721 19th St.
Denver, CO 80201-0660
(303)844-3985
Fax: (303)844-6490
E-mail: score62@csn.net
Website: http://www.sni.net/score62

SCORE Office (Tri-River)
1102 Grand Ave.
Glenwood Springs, CO 81601
(970)945-6589

SCORE Office (Grand Junction)
2591 B & 3/4 Rd.
Grand Junction, CO 81503
(970)243-5242

SCORE Office (Gunnison)
608 N. 11th
Gunnison, CO 81230
(303)641-4422

SCORE Office (Montrose)
1214 Peppertree Dr.
Montrose, CO 81401
(970)249-6080

SCORE Office (Pagosa Springs)
PO Box 4381
Pagosa Springs, CO 81157
(970)731-4890

SCORE Office (Rifle)
0854 W. Battlement Pky., Apt. C106
Parachute, CO 81635
(970)285-9390

SCORE Office (Pueblo)
302 N. Santa Fe
Pueblo, CO 81003
(719)542-1704
Fax: (719)542-1624
E-mail: mackey@iex.net
Website: http://www.pueblo.org/score

SCORE Office (Ridgway)
143 Poplar Pl.
Ridgway, CO 81432

SCORE Office (Silverton)
PO Box 480

Silverton, CO 81433
(303)387-5430

SCORE Office (Minturn)
PO Box 2066
Vail, CO 81658
(970)476-1224

Connecticut

SCORE Office (Greater Bridgeport)
230 Park Ave.
Bridgeport, CT 06601-0999
(203)576-4369
Fax: (203)576-4388

SCORE Office (Bristol)
10 Main St. 1st. Fl.
Bristol, CT 06010
(203)584-4718
Fax: (203)584-4722

SCORE office (Greater Danbury)
246 Federal Rd.
Unit LL2, Ste. 7
Brookfield, CT 06804
(203)775-1151

SCORE Office (Greater Danbury)
246 Federal Rd., Unit LL2, Ste. 7
Brookfield, CT 06804
(203)775-1151

SCORE Office (Eastern Connecticut)
Administration Bldg., Rm. 313
PO 625
61 Main St. (Chapter 579)
Groton, CT 06475
(203)388-9508

SCORE Office (Greater Hartford County)
330 Main St.
Hartford, CT 06106
(860)548-1749
Fax: (860)240-4659
Website: http://www.score56.org

SCORE Office (Manchester)
20 Hartford Rd.
Manchester, CT 06040
(203)646-2223
Fax: (203)646-5871

SCORE Office (New Britain)
185 Main St., Ste. 431
New Britain, CT 06051
(203)827-4492
Fax: (203)827-4480

SCORE Office (New Haven)
25 Science Pk., Bldg. 25, Rm. 366

New Haven, CT 06511
(203)865-7645

SCORE Office (Fairfield County)
24 Beldon Ave., 5th Fl.
Norwalk, CT 06850
(203)847-7348
Fax: (203)849-9308

SCORE Office (Old Saybrook)
146 Main St.
Old Saybrook, CT 06475
(860)388-9508

SCORE Office (Simsbury)
Box 244
Simsbury, CT 06070
(203)651-7307
Fax: (203)651-1933

SCORE Office (Torrington)
23 North Rd.
Torrington, CT 06791
(203)482-6586

Delaware

SCORE Office (Dover)
Treadway Towers
PO Box 576
Dover, DE 19903
(302)678-0892
Fax: (302)678-0189

SCORE Office (Lewes)
PO Box 1
Lewes, DE 19958
(302)645-8073
Fax: (302)645-8412

SCORE Office (Milford)
204 NE Front St.
Milford, DE 19963
(302)422-3301

SCORE Office (Wilmington)
824 Market St., Ste. 610
Wilmington, DE 19801
(302)573-6652
Fax: (302)573-6092
Website: http://www.scoredelaware.com

District of Columbia

SCORE Office (George Mason University)
409 3rd St. SW, 4th Fl.
Washington, DC 20024
800-634-0245

SCORE Office (Washington DC)
1110 Vermont Ave. NW, 9th Fl.

Washington, DC 20043
(202)606-4000
Fax: (202)606-4225
E-mail: dcscore@hotmail.com
Website: http://www.scoredc.org/

Florida

SCORE Office (Desota County Chamber of Commerce)
16 South Velucia Ave.
Arcadia, FL 34266
(941)494-4033

SCORE Office (Suncoast/Pinellas)
Airport Business Ctr.
4707 - 140th Ave. N, No. 311
Clearwater, FL 33755
(813)532-6800
Fax: (813)532-6800

SCORE Office (DeLand)
336 N. Woodland Blvd.
DeLand, FL 32720
(904)734-4331
Fax: (904)734-4333

SCORE Office (South Palm Beach)
1050 S. Federal Hwy., Ste. 132
Delray Beach, FL 33483
(561)278-7752
Fax: (561)278-0288

SCORE Office (Ft. Lauderdale)
Federal Bldg., Ste. 123
299 E. Broward Blvd.
Ft. Lauderdale, FL 33301
(954)356-7263
Fax: (954)356-7145

SCORE Office (Southwest Florida)
The Renaissance
8695 College Pky., Ste. 345 & 346
Ft. Myers, FL 33919
(941)489-2935
Fax: (941)489-1170

SCORE Office (Treasure Coast)
Professional Center, Ste. 2
3220 S. US, No. 1
Ft. Pierce, FL 34982
(561)489-0548

SCORE Office (Gainesville)
101 SE 2nd Pl., Ste. 104
Gainesville, FL 32601
(904)375-8278

SCORE Office (Hialeah Dade Chamber)
59 W. 5th St.
Hialeah, FL 33010

(305)887-1515
Fax: (305)887-2453

SCORE Office (Daytona Beach)
921 Nova Rd., Ste. A
Holly Hills, FL 32117
(904)255-6889
Fax: (904)255-0229
E-mail: score87@dbeach.com

SCORE Office (South Broward)
3475 Sheridian St., Ste. 203
Hollywood, FL 33021
(305)966-8415

SCORE Office (Citrus County)
5 Poplar Ct.
Homosassa, FL 34446
(352)382-1037

SCORE Office (Jacksonville)
7825 Baymeadows Way, Ste. 100-B
Jacksonville, FL 32256
(904)443-1911
Fax: (904)443-1980
E-mail: scorejax@juno.com
Website: http://www.scorejax.org/

SCORE Office (Jacksonville Satellite)
3 Independent Dr.
Jacksonville, FL 32256
(904)366-6600
Fax: (904)632-0617

SCORE Office (Central Florida)
5410 S. Florida Ave., No. 3
Lakeland, FL 33801
(941)687-5783
Fax: (941)687-6225

SCORE Office (Lakeland)
100 Lake Morton Dr.
Lakeland, FL 33801
(941)686-2168

SCORE Office (St. Petersburg)
800 W. Bay Dr., Ste. 505
Largo, FL 33712
(813)585-4571

SCORE Office (Leesburg)
9501 US Hwy. 441
Leesburg, FL 34788-8751
(352)365-3556
Fax: (352)365-3501

SCORE Office (Cocoa)
1600 Farno Rd., Unit 205
Melbourne, FL 32935
(407)254-2288

ORGANIZATIONS, AGENCIES, & CONSULTANTS

SCORE Office (Melbourne)
Melbourne Professional Complex
1600 Sarno, Ste. 205
Melbourne, FL 32935
(407)254-2288
Fax: (407)245-2288

SCORE Office (Merritt Island)
1600 Sarno Rd., Ste. 205
Melbourne, FL 32935
(407)254-2288
Fax: (407)254-2288

SCORE Office (Space Coast)
Melbourn Professional Complex
1600 Sarno, Ste. 205
Melbourne, FL 32935
(407)254-2288
Fax: (407)254-2288

SCORE Office (Dade)
49 NW 5th St.
Miami, FL 33128
(305)371-6889
Fax: (305)374-1882
E-mail: score@netrox.net
Website: http://www.netrox.net/~score/

SCORE Office (Naples of Collier)
International College
2654 Tamiami Trl. E
Naples, FL 34112
(941)417-1280
Fax: (941)417-1281
E-mail: score@naples.net
Website: http://www.naples.net/clubs/score/index.htm

SCORE Office (Pasco County)
6014 US Hwy. 19, Ste. 302
New Port Richey, FL 34652
(813)842-4638

SCORE Office (Southeast Volusia)
115 Canal St.
New Smyrna Beach, FL 32168
(904)428-2449
Fax: (904)423-3512

SCORE Office (Ocala)
110 E. Silver Springs Blvd.
Ocala, FL 34470
(352)629-5959

Clay County SCORE Office
Clay County Chamber of Commerce
1734 Kingsdey Ave.
PO Box 1441
Orange Park, FL 32073
(904)264-2651
Fax: (904)269-0363

SCORE Office (Orlando)
80 N. Hughey Ave.
Rm. 445 Federal Bldg.
Orlando, FL 32801
(407)648-6476
Fax: (407)648-6425

SCORE Office (Emerald Coast)
19 W. Garden St., No. 325
Pensacola, FL 32501
(904)444-2060
Fax: (904)444-2070

SCORE Office (Charlotte County)
201 W. Marion Ave., Ste. 211
Punta Gorda, FL 33950
(941)575-1818
E-mail: score@gls3c.com
Website: http://www.charlotte-florida.com/business/scorepg01.htm

SCORE Office (St. Augustine)
1 Riberia St.
St. Augustine, FL 32084
(904)829-5681
Fax: (904)829-6477

SCORE Office (Bradenton)
2801 Fruitville, Ste. 280
Sarasota, FL 34237
(813)955-1029

SCORE Office (Manasota)
2801 Fruitville Rd., Ste. 280
Sarasota, FL 34237
(941)955-1029
Fax: (941)955-5581
E-mail: score116@gte.net
Website: http://www.score-suncoast.org/

SCORE Office (Tallahassee)
200 W. Park Ave.
Tallahassee, FL 32302
(850)487-2665

SCORE Office (Hillsborough)
4732 Dale Mabry Hwy. N, Ste. 400
Tampa, FL 33614-6509
(813)870-0125

SCORE Office (Lake Sumter)
122 E. Main St.
Tavares, FL 32778-3810
(352)365-3556

SCORE Office (Titusville)
2000 S. Washington Ave.
Titusville, FL 32780
(407)267-3036
Fax: (407)264-0127

SCORE Office (Venice)
257 N. Tamiami Trl.
Venice, FL 34285
(941)488-2236
Fax: (941)484-5903

SCORE Office (Palm Beach)
500 Australian Ave. S, Ste. 100
West Palm Beach, FL 33401
(561)833-1672
Fax: (561)833-1712

SCORE Office (Wildwood)
103 N. Webster St.
Wildwood, FL 34785

Georgia

SCORE Office (Atlanta)
Harris Tower, Suite 1900
233 Peachtree Rd., NE
Atlanta, GA 30309
(404)347-2442
Fax: (404)347-1227

SCORE Office (Augusta)
3126 Oxford Rd.
Augusta, GA 30909
(706)869-9100

SCORE Office (Columbus)
School Bldg.
PO Box 40
Columbus, GA 31901
(706)327-3654

SCORE Office (Dalton-Whitfield)
305 S. Thorton Ave.
Dalton, GA 30720
(706)279-3383

SCORE Office (Gainesville)
PO Box 374
Gainesville, GA 30503
(770)532-6206
Fax: (770)535-8419

SCORE Office (Macon)
711 Grand Bldg.
Macon, GA 31201
(912)751-6160

SCORE Office (Brunswick)
4 Glen Ave.
St. Simons Island, GA 31520
(912)265-0620
Fax: (912)265-0629

SCORE Office (Savannah)
111 E. Liberty St., Ste. 103
Savannah, GA 31401
(912)652-4335

Fax: (912)652-4184
E-mail: info@scoresav.org
Website: http://www.coastalempire.com/
score/index.htm

Guam

SCORE Office (Guam)
Pacific News Bldg., Rm. 103
238 Archbishop Flores St.
Agana, GU 96910-5100
(671)472-7308

Hawaii

SCORE Office (Hawaii, Inc.)
1111 Bishop St., Ste. 204
PO Box 50207
Honolulu, HI 96813
(808)522-8132
Fax: (808)522-8135
E-mail: hnlscore@juno.com

SCORE Office (Kahului)
250 Alamaha, Unit N16A
Kahului, HI 96732
(808)871-7711

SCORE Office (Maui, Inc.)
590 E. Lipoa Pkwy., Ste. 227
Kihei, HI 96753
(808)875-2380

Idaho

SCORE Office (Treasure Valley)
1020 Main St., No. 290
Boise, ID 83702
(208)334-1696
Fax: (208)334-9353

SCORE Office (Eastern Idaho)
2300 N. Yellowstone, Ste. 119
Idaho Falls, ID 83401
(208)523-1022
Fax: (208)528-7127

Illinois

SCORE Office (Fox Valley)
40 W. Downer Pl.
PO Box 277
Aurora, IL 60506
(630)897-9214
Fax: (630)897-7002

SCORE Office (Greater Belvidere)
419 S. State St.
Belvidere, IL 61008
(815)544-4357
Fax: (815)547-7654

SCORE Office (Bensenville)
1050 Busse Hwy. Suite 100
Bensenville, IL 60106
(708)350-2944
Fax: (708)350-2979

SCORE Office (Central Illinois)
402 N. Hershey Rd.
Bloomington, IL 61704
(309)644-0549
Fax: (309)663-8270
E-mail: webmaster@central-illinois-
score.org
Website: http://www.central-illinois-
score.org/

SCORE Office (Southern Illinois)
150 E. Pleasant Hill Rd.
Box 1
Carbondale, IL 62901
(618)453-6654
Fax: (618)453-5040

SCORE Office (Chicago)
Northwest Atrium Ctr.
500 W. Madison St., No. 1250
Chicago, IL 60661
(312)353-7724
Fax: (312)886-5688
Website: http://www.mcs.net/~bic/

SCORE Office (Chicago–Oliver Harvey College)
Pullman Bldg.
1000 E. 11th St., 7th Fl.
Chicago, IL 60628
Fax: (312)468-8086

SCORE Office (Danville)
28 W. N. Street
Danville, IL 61832
(217)442-7232
Fax: (217)442-6228

SCORE Office (Decatur)
Milliken University
1184 W. Main St.
Decatur, IL 62522
(217)424-6297
Fax: (217)424-3993
E-mail: charding@mail.millikin.edu
Website: http://www.millikin.edu/
academics/Tabor/score.html

SCORE Office (Downers Grove)
925 Curtis
Downers Grove, IL 60515
(708)968-4050
Fax: (708)968-8368

SCORE Office (Elgin)
24 E. Chicago, 3rd Fl.
PO Box 648
Elgin, IL 60120
(847)741-5660
Fax: (847)741-5677

SCORE Office (Freeport Area)
26 S. Galena Ave.
Freeport, IL 61032
(815)233-1350
Fax: (815)235-4038

SCORE Office (Galesburg)
292 E. Simmons St.
PO Box 749
Galesburg, IL 61401
(309)343-1194
Fax: (309)343-1195

SCORE Office (Glen Ellyn)
500 Pennsylvania
Glen Ellyn, IL 60137
(708)469-0907
Fax: (708)469-0426

SCORE Office (Greater Alton)
Alden Hall
5800 Godfrey Rd.
Godfrey, IL 62035-2466
(618)467-2280
Fax: (618)466-8289
Website: http://www.altonweb.com/
score/

SCORE Office (Grayslake)
19351 W. Washington St.
Grayslake, IL 60030
(708)223-3633
Fax: (708)223-9371

SCORE Office (Harrisburg)
303 S. Commercial
Harrisburg, IL 62946-1528
(618)252-8528
Fax: (618)252-0210

SCORE Office (Joliet)
100 N. Chicago
Joliet, IL 60432
(815)727-5371
Fax: (815)727-5374

SCORE Office (Kankakee)
101 S. Schuyler Ave.
Kankakee, IL 60901
(815)933-0376
Fax: (815)933-0380

SCORE Office (Macomb)
216 Seal Hall, Rm. 214

Macomb, IL 61455
(309)298-1128
Fax: (309)298-2520

SCORE Office (Matteson)
210 Lincoln Mall
Matteson, IL 60443
(708)709-3750
Fax: (708)503-9322

SCORE Office (Mattoon)
1701 Wabash Ave.
Mattoon, IL 61938
(217)235-5661
Fax: (217)234-6544

SCORE Office (Quad Cities)
622 19th St.
Moline, IL 61265
(309)797-0082
Fax: (309)757-5435
E-mail: score@qconline.com
Website: http://www.qconline.com/
business/score/

SCORE Office (Naperville)
131 W. Jefferson Ave.
Naperville, IL 60540
(708)355-4141
Fax: (708)355-8355

SCORE Office (Northbrook)
2002 Walters Ave.
Northbrook, IL 60062
(847)498-5555
Fax: (847)498-5510

SCORE Office (Palos Hills)
10900 S. 88th Ave.
Palos Hills, IL 60465
(847)974-5468
Fax: (847)974-0078

SCORE Office (Peoria)
124 SW Adams, Ste. 300
Peoria, IL 61602
(309)676-0755
Fax: (309)676-7534

SCORE Office (Prospect Heights)
1375 Wolf Rd.
Prospect Heights, IL 60070
(847)537-8660
Fax: (847)537-7138

SCORE Office (Quincy Tri-State)
300 Civic Center Plz., Ste. 245
Quincy, IL 62301
(217)222-8093
Fax: (217)222-3033

SCORE Office (River Grove)
2000 5th Ave.
River Grove, IL 60171
(708)456-0300
Fax: (708)583-3121

SCORE Office (Northern Illinois)
515 N. Court St.
Rockford, IL 61103
(815)962-0122
Fax: (815)962-0122

SCORE Office (St. Charles)
103 N. 1st Ave.
St. Charles, IL 60174-1982
(847)584-8384
Fax: (847)584-6065

SCORE Office (Springfield)
511 W. Capitol Ave., Ste. 302
Springfield, IL 62704
(217)492-4416
Fax: (217)492-4867

SCORE Office (Sycamore)
112 Somunak St.
Sycamore, IL 60178
(815)895-3456
Fax: (815)895-0125

SCORE Office (University)
Hwy. 50 & Stuenkel Rd. Ste. C3305
University Park, IL 60466
(708)534-5000
Fax: (708)534-8457

Indiana

SCORE Office (Anderson)
205 W. 11th St.
Anderson, IN 46015
(317)642-0264

SCORE Office (Bloomington)
Star Center
216 W. Allen
Bloomington, IN 47403
(812)335-7334
E-mail: wtfische@indiana.edu
Website: http://www.brainfreezemedia.
com/score527/

SCORE Office (South East Indiana)
500 Franklin St.
Box 29
Columbus, IN 47201
(812)379-4457

SCORE Office (Corydon)
310 N. Elm St.
Corydon, IN 47112

(812)738-2137
Fax: (812)738-6438

SCORE Office (Crown Point)
Old Courthouse Sq. Ste. 206
PO Box 43
Crown Point, IN 46307
(219)663-1800

SCORE Office (Elkhart)
418 S. Main St.
Elkhart, IN 46515
(219)293-1531
Fax: (219)294-1859

SCORE Office (Evansville)
1100 W. Lloyd Expy., Ste. 105
Evansville, IN 47708
(812)426-6144

SCORE Office (Fort Wayne)
1300 S. Harrison St.
Ft. Wayne, IN 46802
(219)422-2601
Fax: (219)422-2601

SCORE Office (Gary)
973 W. 6th Ave., Rm. 326
Gary, IN 46402
(219)882-3918

SCORE Office (Hammond)
7034 Indianapolis Blvd.
Hammond, IN 46324
(219)931-1000
Fax: (219)845-9548

SCORE Office (Indianapolis)
429 N. Pennsylvania St., Ste. 100
Indianapolis, IN 46204-1873
(317)226-7264
Fax: (317)226-7259
E-mail: inscore@indy.net
Website: http://www.score-
indianapolis.org/

SCORE Office (Jasper)
PO Box 307
Jasper, IN 47547-0307
(812)482-6866

SCORE Office (Kokomo/Howard Counties)
106 N. Washington St.
Kokomo, IN 46901
(765)457-5301
Fax: (765)452-4564

SCORE Office (Logansport)
300 E. Broadway, Ste. 103
Logansport, IN 46947
(219)753-6388

SCORE Office (Madison)
301 E. Main St.
Madison, IN 47250
(812)265-3135
Fax: (812)265-2923

SCORE Office (Marengo)
Rt. 1 Box 224D
Marengo, IN 47140
Fax: (812)365-2793

SCORE Office (Marion/Grant Counties)
215 S. Adams
Marion, IN 46952
(765)664-5107

SCORE Office (Merrillville)
255 W. 80th Pl.
Merrillville, IN 46410
(219)769-8180
Fax: (219)736-6223

SCORE Office (Michigan City)
200 E. Michigan Blvd.
Michigan City, IN 46360
(219)874-6221
Fax: (219)873-1204

SCORE Office (South Central Indiana)
4100 Charleston Rd.
New Albany, IN 47150-9538
(812)945-0066

SCORE Office (Rensselaer)
104 W. Washington
Rensselaer, IN 47978

SCORE Office (Salem)
210 N. Main St.
Salem, IN 47167
(812)883-4303
Fax: (812)883-1467

SCORE Office (South Bend)
300 N. Michigan St.
South Bend, IN 46601
(219)282-4350
E-mail: chair@southbend-score.org
Website: http://www.southbend-score.org/

SCORE Office (Valparaiso)
150 Lincolnway
Valparaiso, IN 46383
(219)462-1105
Fax: (219)469-5710

SCORE Office (Vincennes)
27 N. 3rd
PO Box 553
Vincennes, IN 47591
(812)882-6440
Fax: (812)882-6441

SCORE Office (Wabash)
PO Box 371
Wabash, IN 46992
(219)563-1168
Fax: (219)563-6920

Iowa

SCORE Office (Burlington)
Federal Bldg.
300 N. Main St.
Burlington, IA 52601
(319)752-2967

SCORE Office (Cedar Rapids)
2750 1st Ave. NE, Ste 350
Cedar Rapids, IA 52401-1806
(319)362-6405
Fax: (319)362-7861
E:mail: score@scorecr.org
Website: http://www.scorecr.org

SCORE Office (Illowa)
333 4th Ave. S
Clinton, IA 52732
(319)242-5702

SCORE Office (Council Bluffs)
7 N. 6th St.
Council Bluffs, IA 51502
(712)325-1000

SCORE Office (Northeast Iowa)
3404 285th St.
Cresco, IA 52136
(319)547-3377

SCORE Office (Des Moines)
Federal Bldg., Rm. 749
210 Walnut St.
Des Moines, IA 50309-2186
(515)284-4760

SCORE Office (Ft. Dodge)
Federal Bldg., Rm. 436
205 S. 8th St.
Ft. Dodge, IA 50501
(515)955-2622

SCORE Office (Independence)
110 1st. St. east
Independence, IA 50644
(319)334-7178
Fax: (319)334-7179

SCORE Office (Iowa City)
210 Federal Bldg.
PO Box 1853
Iowa City, IA 52240-1853
(319)338-1662

SCORE Office (Keokuk)
401 Main St.
Pierce Bldg., No. 1
Keokuk, IA 52632
(319)524-5055

SCORE Office (Central Iowa)
Fisher Community College
709 S. Center
Marshalltown, IA 50158
(515)753-6645

SCORE Office (River City)
15 West State St.
Mason City, IA 50401
(515)423-5724

SCORE Office (South Central)
SBDC, Indian Hills Community College
525 Grandview Ave.
Ottumwa, IA 52501
(515)683-5127
Fax: (515)683-5263

SCORE Office (Dubuque)
10250 Sundown Rd.
Peosta, IA 52068
(319)556-5110

SCORE Office (Southwest Iowa)
614 W. Sheridan
Shenandoah, IA 51601
(712)246-3260

SCORE Office (Sioux City)
Federal Bldg.
320 6th St.
Sioux City, IA 51101
(712)277-2324
Fax: (712)277-2325

SCORE Office (Iowa Lakes)
122 W. 5th St.
Spencer, IA 51301
(712)262-3059

SCORE Office (Vista)
119 W. 6th St.
Storm Lake, IA 50588
(712)732-3780

SCORE Office (Waterloo)
215 E. 4th
Waterloo, IA 50703
(319)233-8431

Kansas

SCORE Office (Southwest Kansas)
501 W. Spruce
Dodge City, KS 67801
(316)227-3119

SCORE Office (Emporia)
811 Homewood
Emporia, KS 66801
(316)342-1600

SCORE Office (Golden Belt)
1307 Williams
Great Bend, KS 67530
(316)792-2401

SCORE Office (Hays)
PO Box 400
Hays, KS 67601
(913)625-6595

SCORE Office (Hutchinson)
1 E. 9th St.
Hutchinson, KS 67501
(316)665-8468
Fax: (316)665-7619

SCORE Office (Southeast Kansas)
404 Westminster Pl.
PO Box 886
Independence, KS 67301
(316)331-4741

SCORE Office (McPherson)
306 N. Main
PO Box 616
McPherson, KS 67460
(316)241-3303

SCORE Office (Salina)
120 Ash St.
Salina, KS 67401
(785)243-4290
Fax: (785)243-1833

SCORE Office (Topeka)
1700 College
Topeka, KS 66621
(785)231-1010

SCORE Office (Wichita)
100 E. English, Ste. 510
Wichita, KS 67202
(316)269-6273
Fax: (316)269-6499

SCORE Office (Ark Valley)
205 E. 9th St.
Winfield, KS 67156
(316)221-1617

Kentucky

SCORE Office (Ashland)
PO Box 830
Ashland, KY 41105
(606)329-8011
Fax: (606)325-4607

SCORE Office (Bowling Green)
812 State St.
PO Box 51
Bowling Green, KY 42101
(502)781-3200
Fax: (502)843-0458

SCORE Office (Tri-Lakes)
508 Barbee Way
Danville, KY 40422-1548
(606)231-9902

SCORE Office (Glasgow)
301 W. Main St.
Glasgow, KY 42141
(502)651-3161
Fax: (502)651-3122

SCORE Office (Hazard)
B & I Technical Center
100 Airport Gardens Rd.
Hazard, KY 41701
(606)439-5856
Fax: (606)439-1808

SCORE Office (Lexington)
410 W. Vine St., Ste. 290, Civic C
Lexington, KY 40507
(606)231-9902
Fax: (606)253-3190
E-mail: scorelex@uky.campus.mci.net

SCORE Office (Louisville)
188 Federal Office Bldg.
600 Dr. Martin L. King Jr. Pl.
Louisville, KY 40202
(502)582-5976

SCORE Office (Madisonville)
257 N. Main
Madisonville, KY 42431
(502)825-1399
Fax: (502)825-1396

SCORE Office (Paducah)
Federal Office Bldg.
501 Broadway, Rm. B-36
Paducah, KY 42001
(502)442-5685

Louisiana

SCORE Office (Central Louisiana)
802 3rd St.
Alexandria, LA 71309
(318)442-6671

SCORE Office (Baton Rouge)
564 Laurel St.
PO Box 3217
Baton Rouge, LA 70801

(504)381-7130
Fax: (504)336-4306

SCORE Office (North Shore)
2 W. Thomas
Hammond, LA 70401
(504)345-4457
Fax: (504)345-4749

SCORE Office (Lafayette)
804 St. Mary Blvd.
Lafayette, LA 70505-1307
(318)233-2705
Fax: (318)234-8671
E-mail: score302@aol.com

SCORE Office (Lake Charles)
120 W. Pujo St.
Lake Charles, LA 70601
(318)433-3632

SCORE Office (New Orleans)
365 Canal St., Ste. 3100
New Orleans, LA 70130
(504)589-2356
Fax: (504)589-2339

SCORE Office (Shreveport)
400 Edwards St.
Shreveport, LA 71101
(318)677-2536
Fax: (318)677-2541

Maine

SCORE Office (Augusta)
40 Western Ave.
Augusta, ME 04330
(207)622-8509

SCORE Office (Bangor)
Peabody Hall, Rm. 229
One College Cir.
Bangor, ME 04401
(207)941-9707

SCORE Office (Central & Northern Arroostock)
111 High St.
Caribou, ME 04736
(207)492-8010
Fax: (207)492-8010

SCORE Office (Penquis)
South St.
Dover Foxcroft, ME 04426
(207)564-7021

SCORE Office (Maine Coastal)
Mill Mall
Box 1105
Ellsworth, ME 04605-1105

(207)667-5800
E-mail: score@arcadia.net

SCORE Office (Lewiston-Auburn)
BIC of Maine-Bates Mill Complex
35 Canal St.
Lewiston, ME 04240-7764
(207)782-3708
Fax: (207)783-7745

SCORE Office (Portland)
66 Pearl St., Rm. 210
Portland, ME 04101
(207)772-1147
Fax: (207)772-5581
E-mail: Score53@score.maine.org
Website: http://www.score.maine.org/
chapter53/

SCORE Office (Western Mountains)
255 River St.
PO Box 252
Rumford, ME 04257-0252
(207)369-9976

SCORE Office (Oxford Hills)
166 Main St.
South Paris, ME 04281
(207)743-0499

Maryland

SCORE Office (Southern Maryland)
2525 Riva Rd., Ste. 110
Annapolis, MD 21401
(410)266-9553
Fax: (410)573-0981
E-mail: score390@aol.com
Website: http://members.aol.com/
score390/index.htm

SCORE Office (Baltimore)
The City Crescent Bldg., 6th Fl.
10 S. Howard St.
Baltimore, MD 21201
(410)962-2233
Fax: (410)962-1805

SCORE Office (Bel Air)
108 S. Bond St.
Bel Air, MD 21014
(410)838-2020
Fax: (410)893-4715

SCORE Office (Bethesda)
7910 Woodmont Ave., Ste. 1204
Bethesda, MD 20814
(301)652-4900
Fax: (301)657-1973

SCORE Office (Bowie)
6670 Race Track Rd.
Bowie, MD 20715
(301)262-0920
Fax: (301)262-0921

SCORE Office (Dorchester County)
203 Sunburst Hwy.
Cambridge, MD 21613
(410)228-3575

SCORE Office (Upper Shore)
210 Marlboro Ave.
Easton, MD 21601
(410)822-4606
Fax: (410)822-7922

SCORE Office (Frederick County)
43A S. Market St.
Frederick, MD 21701
(301)662-8723
Fax: (301)846-4427

SCORE Office (Gaithersburg)
9 Park Ave.
Gaithersburg, MD 20877
(301)840-1400
Fax: (301)963-3918

SCORE Office (Glen Burnie)
103 Crain Hwy. SE
Glen Burnie, MD 21061
(410)766-8282
Fax: (410)766-9722

SCORE Office (Hagerstown)
111 W. Washington St.
Hagerstown, MD 21740
(301)739-2015
Fax: (301)739-1278

SCORE Office (Laurel)
7901 Sandy Spring Rd. Ste. 501
Laurel, MD 20707
(301)725-4000
Fax: (301)725-0776

SCORE Office (Salisbury)
300 E. Main St.
Salisbury, MD 21801
(410)749-0185
Fax: (410)860-9925

Massachusetts

SCORE Office (NE Massachusetts)
100 Cummings Ctr., Ste. 101 K
Beverly, MA 01923
(978)922-9441
Website: http://www1.shore.net/~score/

SCORE Office (Boston)
10 Causeway St., Rm. 265
Boston, MA 02222-1093
(617)565-5591
Fax: (617)565-5598
E-mail: boston-score-20@worldnet.att.net
Website: http://www.scoreboston.org/

SCORE office (Bristol/Plymouth County)
53 N. 6th St., Federal Bldg.
Bristol, MA 02740
(508)994-5093

SCORE Office (SE Massachusetts)
60 School St.
Brockton, MA 02401
(508)587-2673
Fax: (508)587-1340
Website: http://www.metrosouth
chamber.com/score.html

SCORE Office (North Adams)
820 N. State Rd.
Cheshire, MA 01225
(413)743-5100

SCORE Office (Clinton Satellite)
1 Green St.
Clinton, MA 01510
Fax: (508)368-7689

SCORE Office (Greenfield)
PO Box 898
Greenfield, MA 01302
(413)773-5463
Fax: (413)773-7008

SCORE Office (Haverhill)
87 Winter St.
Haverhill, MA 01830
(508)373-5663
Fax: (508)373-8060

SCORE Office (Hudson Satellite)
PO Box 578
Hudson, MA 01749
(508)568-0360
Fax: (508)568-0360

SCORE Office (Cape Cod)
Independence Pk., Ste. 5B
270 Communications Way
Hyannis, MA 02601
(508)775-4884
Fax: (508)790-2540

SCORE Office (Lawrence)
264 Essex St.
Lawrence, MA 01840
(508)686-0900
Fax: (508)794-9953

SCORE Office (Leominster Satellite)
110 Erdman Way
Leominster, MA 01453
(508)840-4300
Fax: (508)840-4896

SCORE Office (Bristol/Plymouth Counties)
53 N. 6th St., Federal Bldg.
New Bedford, MA 02740
(508)994-5093

SCORE Office (Newburyport)
29 State St.
Newburyport, MA 01950
(617)462-6680

SCORE Office (Pittsfield)
66 West St.
Pittsfield, MA 01201
(413)499-2485

SCORE Office (Haverhill-Salem)
32 Derby Sq.
Salem, MA 01970
(508)745-0330
Fax: (508)745-3855

SCORE Office (Springfield)
1350 Main St.
Federal Bldg.
Springfield, MA 01103
(413)785-0314

SCORE Office (Carver)
12 Taunton Green, Ste. 201
Taunton, MA 02780
(508)824-4068
Fax: (508)824-4069

SCORE Office (Worcester)
33 Waldo St.
Worcester, MA 01608
(508)753-2929
Fax: (508)754-8560

Michigan

SCORE Office (Allegan)
PO Box 338
Allegan, MI 49010
(616)673-2479

SCORE Office (Ann Arbor)
425 S. Main St., Ste. 103
Ann Arbor, MI 48104
(313)665-4433

SCORE Office (Battle Creek)
34 W. Jackson Ste. 4A
Battle Creek, MI 49017-3505

(616)962-4076
Fax: (616)962-6309

SCORE Office (Cadillac)
222 Lake St.
Cadillac, MI 49601
(616)775-9776
Fax: (616)768-4255

SCORE Office (Detroit)
477 Michigan Ave., Rm. 515
Detroit, MI 48226
(313)226-7947
Fax: (313)226-3448

SCORE Office (Flint)
708 Root Rd., Rm. 308
Flint, MI 48503
(810)233-6846

SCORE Office (Grand Rapids)
111 Pearl St. NW
Grand Rapids, MI 49503-2831
(616)771-0305
Fax: (616)771-0328
E-mail: scoreone@iserv.net
Website: http://www.iserv.net/
~scoreone/

SCORE Office (Holland)
480 State St.
Holland, MI 49423
(616)396-9472

SCORE Office (Jackson)
209 East Washington
PO Box 80
Jackson, MI 49204
(517)782-8221
Fax: (517)782-0061

SCORE Office (Kalamazoo)
345 W. Michigan Ave.
Kalamazoo, MI 49007
(616)381-5382
Fax: (616)384-0096
E-mail: score@nucleus.net

SCORE Office (Lansing)
117 E. Allegan
PO Box 14030
Lansing, MI 48901
(517)487-6340
Fax: (517)484-6910

SCORE Office (Livonia)
15401 Farmington Rd.
Livonia, MI 48154
(313)427-2122
Fax: (313)427-6055

SCORE Office (Madison Heights)
26345 John R
Madison Heights, MI 48071
(810)542-5010
Fax: (810)542-6821

SCORE Office (Monroe)
111 E. 1st
Monroe, MI 48161
(313)242-3366
Fax: (313)242-7253

SCORE Office (Mt. Clemens)
58 S/B Gratiot
Mt. Clemens, MI 48043
(810)463-1528
Fax: (810)463-6541

SCORE Office (Muskegon)
PO Box 1087
230 Terrace Plz.
Muskegon, MI 49443
(616)722-3751
Fax: (616)728-7251

SCORE Office (Petoskey)
401 E. Mitchell St.
Petoskey, MI 49770
(616)347-4150

SCORE Office (Pontiac)
Executive Office Bldg.
1200 N. Telegraph Rd.
Pontiac, MI 48341
(810)975-9555

SCORE Office (Pontiac)
PO Box 430025
Pontiac, MI 48343
(810)335-9600

SCORE Office (Port Huron)
920 Pinegrove Ave.
Port Huron, MI 48060
(810)985-7101

SCORE Office (Rochester)
71 Walnut Ste. 110
Rochester, MI 48307
(810)651-6700
Fax: (810)651-5270

SCORE Office (Saginaw)
901 S. Washington Ave.
Saginaw, MI 48601
(517)752-7161
Fax: (517)752-9055

SCORE Office (Upper Peninsula)
2581 I-75 Business Spur
Sault Ste. Marie, MI 49783
(906)632-3301

SCORE Office (Southfield)
21000 W. 10 Mile Rd.
Southfield, MI 48075
(810)204-3050
Fax: (810)204-3099

SCORE Office (Traverse City)
202 E. Grandview Pkwy.
PO Box 387
Traverse City, MI 49685
(616)947-5075
Fax: (616)946-2565

SCORE Office (Warren)
30500 Van Dyke, Ste. 118
Warren, MI 48093
(810)751-3939

Minnesota

SCORE Office (Aitkin)
Aitkin, MN 56431
(218)741-3906

SCORE Office (Albert Lea)
202 N. Broadway Ave.
Albert Lea, MN 56007
(507)373-7487

SCORE Office (Austin)
PO Box 864
Austin, MN 55912
(507)437-4561
Fax: (507)437-4869

SCORE Office (South Metro)
Ames Business Ctr.
2500 W. County Rd., No. 42
Burnsville, MN 55337
(612)898-5645
Fax: (612)435-6972
E-mail: southmetro@scoreminn.org
Website: http://www.scoreminn.org/
southmetro/

SCORE Office (Duluth)
1717 Minnesota Ave.
Duluth, MN 55802
(218)727-8286
Fax: (218)727-3113
E-mail: duluth@scoreminn.org
Website: http://www.scoreminn.org

SCORE Office (Fairmont)
PO Box 826
Fairmont, MN 56031
(507)235-5547
Fax: (507)235-8411

SCORE Office (Southwest Minnesota)
112 Riverfront St.

Box 999
Mankato, MN 56001
(507)345-4519
Fax: (507)345-4451
Website: http://www.scoreminn.org/

SCORE Office (Minneapolis)
North Plaza Bldg., Ste. 51
5217 Wayzata Blvd.
Minneapolis, MN 55416
(612)591-0539
Fax: (612)544-0436
Website: http://www.scoreminn.org/

SCORE Office (Owatonna)
PO Box 331
Owatonna, MN 55060
(507)451-7970
Fax: (507)451-7972

SCORE Office (Red Wing)
2000 W. Main St., Ste. 324
Red Wing, MN 55066
(612)388-4079

SCORE Office (Southeastern Minnesota)
220 S. Broadway, Ste. 100
Rochester, MN 55901
(507)288-1122
Fax: (507)282-8960
Website: http://www.scoreminn.org/

SCORE Office (Brainerd)
St. Cloud, MN 56301

SCORE Office (Central Area)
1527 Northway Dr.
St. Cloud, MN 56301
(320)240-1332
Fax: (320)255-9050
Website: http://www.scoreminn.org/

SCORE Office (St. Paul)
350 St. Peter St., No. 295
Lowry Professional Bldg.
St. Paul, MN 55102
(651)223-5010
Fax: (651)223-5048
Website: http://www.scoreminn.org/

SCORE Office (Winona)
Box 870
Winona, MN 55987
(507)452-2272
Fax: (507)454-8814

SCORE Office (Worthington)
1121 3rd Ave.
Worthington, MN 56187
(507)372-2919
Fax: (507)372-2827

Mississippi

SCORE Office (Delta)
915 Washington Ave.
PO Box 933
Greenville, MS 38701
(601)378-3141

SCORE Office (Gulfcoast)
1 Government Plaza
2909 13th St., Ste. 203
Gulfport, MS 39501
(228)863-0054

SCORE Office (Jackson)
1st Jackson Center, Ste. 400
101 W. Capitol St.
Jackson, MS 39201
(601)965-5533

SCORE Office (Meridian)
5220 16th Ave.
Meridian, MS 39305
(601)482-4412

Missouri

SCORE Office (Lake of the Ozark)
University Extension
113 Kansas St.
PO Box 1405
Camdenton, MO 65020
(573)346-2644
Fax: (573)346-2694
E-mail: score@cdoc.net
Website: http://sites.cdoc.net/score/

Chamber of Commerce (Cape Girardeau)
PO Box 98
Cape Girardeau, MO 63702-0098
(314)335-3312

SCORE Office (Mid-Missouri)
1705 Halstead Ct.
Columbia, MO 65203
(573)874-1132

SCORE Office (Ozark-Gateway)
1486 Glassy Rd.
Cuba, MO 65453-1640
(573)885-4954

SCORE Office (Kansas City)
323 W. 8th St., Ste. 104
Kansas City, MO 64105
(816)374-6675
Fax: (816)374-6692
E-mail: SCOREBIC@AOL.COM
Website: http://www.crn.org/score/

SCORE Office (Sedalia)
Lucas Place
323 W. 8th St., Ste.104
Kansas City, MO 64105
(816)374-6675

SCORE office (Tri-Lakes)
PO Box 1148
Kimberling, MO 65686
(417)739-3041

SCORE Office (Tri-Lakes)
HCRI Box 85
Lampe, MO 65681
(417)858-6798

SCORE Office (Mexico)
111 N. Washington St.
Mexico, MO 65265
(314)581-2765

SCORE Office (Southeast Missouri)
Rte. 1, Box 280
Neelyville, MO 63954
(573)989-3577

SCORE office (Poplar Bluff Area)
806 Emma St.
Poplar Bluff, MO 63901
(573)686-8892

SCORE Office (St. Joseph)
3003 Frederick Ave.
St. Joseph, MO 64506
(816)232-4461

SCORE Office (St. Louis)
815 Olive St., Rm. 242
St. Louis, MO 63101-1569
(314)539-6970
Fax: (314)539-3785
E-mail: info@stlscore.org
Website: http://www.stlscore.org/

SCORE Office (Lewis & Clark)
425 Spencer Rd.
St. Peters, MO 63376
(314)928-2900
Fax: (314)928-2900
E-mail: score01@mail.win.org

SCORE Office (Springfield)
620 S. Glenstone, Ste. 110
Springfield, MO 65802-3200
(417)864-7670
Fax: (417)864-4108

SCORE office (Southeast Kansas)
1206 W. First St.
Webb City, MO 64870
(417)673-3984

Montana

SCORE Office (Billings)
815 S. 27th St.
Billings, MT 59101
(406)245-4111

SCORE Office (Bozeman)
1205 E. Main St.
Bozeman, MT 59715
(406)586-5421

SCORE Office (Butte)
1000 George St.
Butte, MT 59701
(406)723-3177

SCORE Office (Great Falls)
710 First Ave. N
Great Falls, MT 59401
(406)761-4434
E-mail: scoregtf@in.tch.com

SCORE Office (Havre, Montana)
518 First St.
Havre, MT 59501
(406)265-4383

SCORE Office (Helena)
Federal Bldg.
301 S. Park
Helena, MT 59626-0054
(406)441-1081

SCORE Office (Kalispell)
2 Main St.
Kalispell, MT 59901
(406)756-5271
Fax: (406)752-6665

SCORE Office (Missoula)
723 Ronan
Missoula, MT 59806
(406)327-8806
E-mail: score@safeshop.com
Website: http://missoula.bigsky.net/score/

Nebraska

SCORE Office (Columbus)
Columbus, NE 68601
(402)564-2769

SCORE Office (Fremont)
92 W. 5th St.
Fremont, NE 68025
(402)721-2641

SCORE Office (Hastings)
Hastings, NE 68901
(402)463-3447

SCORE Office (Lincoln)
8800 O St.
Lincoln, NE 68520
(402)437-2409

SCORE Office (Panhandle)
150549 CR 30
Minatare, NE 69356
(308)632-2133
Website: http://www.tandt.com/SCORE

SCORE Office (Norfolk)
3209 S. 48th Ave.
Norfolk, NE 68106
(402)564-2769

SCORE Office (North Platte)
3301 W. 2nd St.
North Platte, NE 69101
(308)532-4466

SCORE Office (Omaha)
11145 Mill Valley Rd.
Omaha, NE 68154
(402)221-3606
Fax: (402)221-3680
E-mail: infoctr@ne.uswest.net
Website: http://www.tandt.com/score/

Nevada

SCORE Office (Incline Village)
969 Tahoe Blvd.
Incline Village, NV 89451
(702)831-7327
Fax: (702)832-1605

SCORE Office (Carson City)
301 E. Stewart
PO Box 7527
Las Vegas, NV 89125
(702)388-6104

SCORE Office (Las Vegas)
300 Las Vegas Blvd. S, Ste. 1100
Las Vegas, NV 89101
(702)388-6104

SCORE Office (Northern Nevada)
SBDC, College of Business
Administration
Univ. of Nevada
Reno, NV 89557-0100
(702)784-4436
Fax: (702)784-4337

New Hampshire

SCORE Office (North Country)
PO Box 34

Berlin, NH 03570
(603)752-1090

SCORE Office (Concord)
143 N. Main St., Rm. 202A
PO Box 1258
Concord, NH 03301
(603)225-1400
Fax: (603)225-1409

SCORE Office (Dover)
299 Central Ave.
Dover, NH 03820
(603)742-2218
Fax: (603)749-6317

SCORE Office (Monadnock)
34 Mechanic St.
Keene, NH 03431-3421
(603)352-0320

SCORE Office (Lakes Region)
67 Water St., Ste. 105
Laconia, NH 03246
(603)524-9168

SCORE Office (Upper Valley)
Citizens Bank Bldg., Rm. 310
20 W. Park St.
Lebanon, NH 03766
(603)448-3491
Fax: (603)448-1908
E-mail: billt@valley.net
Website: http://www.valley.net/~score/

SCORE Office (Merrimack Valley)
275 Chestnut St., Rm. 618
Manchester, NH 03103
(603)666-7561
Fax: (603)666-7925

SCORE Office (Mt. Washington Valley)
PO Box 1066
North Conway, NH 03818
(603)383-0800

SCORE Office (Seacoast)
195 Commerce Way, Unit-A
Portsmouth, NH 03801-3251
(603)433-0575

New Jersey

SCORE Office (Somerset)
Paritan Valley Community College,
Rte. 28
Branchburg, NJ 08807
(908)218-8874
E-mail: nj-score@grizbiz.com.
Website: http://www.nj-score.org/

SCORE Office (Chester)
5 Old Mill Rd.
Chester, NJ 07930
(908)879-7080

**SCORE Office
(Greater Princeton)**
4 A George Washington Dr.
Cranbury, NJ 08512
(609)520-1776

SCORE Office (Freehold)
36 W. Main St.
Freehold, NJ 07728
(908)462-3030
Fax: (908)462-2123

SCORE Office (North West)
Picantinny Innovation Ctr.
3159 Schrader Rd.
Hamburg, NJ 07419
(973)209-8525
Fax: (973)209-7252
E-mail: nj-score@grizbiz.com
Website: http://www.nj-score.org/

SCORE Office (Monmouth)
765 Newman Springs Rd.
Lincroft, NJ 07738
(908)224-2573
E-mail: nj-score@grizbiz.com
Website: http://www.nj-score.org/

SCORE Office (Manalapan)
125 Symmes Dr.
Manalapan, NJ 07726
(908)431-7220

SCORE Office (Jersey City)
2 Gateway Ctr., 4th Fl.
Newark, NJ 07102
(973)645-3982
Fax: (973)645-2375

SCORE Office (Newark)
2 Gateway Center, 15th Fl.
Newark, NJ 07102-5553
(973)645-3982
Fax: (973)645-2375
E-mail: nj-score@grizbiz.com
Website: http://www.nj-score.org

SCORE Office (Bergen County)
327 E. Ridgewood Ave.
Paramus, NJ 07652
(201)599-6090
E-mail: nj-score@grizbiz.com
Website: http://www.nj-score.org/

SCORE Office (Pennsauken)
4900 Rte. 70

Pennsauken, NJ 08109
(609)486-3421

SCORE Office (Southern New Jersey)
4900 Rte. 70
Pennsauken, NJ 08109
(609)486-3421
E-mail: nj-score@grizbiz.com
Website: http://www.nj-score.org/

SCORE Office (Greater Princeton)
216 Rockingham Row
Princeton Forrestal Village
Princeton, NJ 08540
(609)520-1776
Fax: (609)520-9107
E-mail: nj-score@grizbiz.com
Website: http://www.nj-score.org/

SCORE Office (Shrewsbury)
Hwy. 35
Shrewsbury, NJ 07702
(908)842-5995
Fax: (908)219-6140

SCORE Office (Ocean County)
33 Washington St.
Toms River, NJ 08754
(732)505-6033
E-mail: nj-score@grizbiz.com
Website: http://www.nj-score.org/

SCORE Office (Wall)
2700 Allaire Rd.
Wall, NJ 07719
(908)449-8877

SCORE Office (Wayne)
2055 Hamburg Tpke.
Wayne, NJ 07470
(201)831-7788
Fax: (201)831-9112

New Mexico

SCORE Office (Albuquerque)
525 Buena Vista, SE
Albuquerque, NM 87106
(505)272-7999
Fax: (505)272-7963

SCORE Office (Las Cruces)
Loretto Towne Center
505 S. Main St., Ste. 125
Las Cruces, NM 88001
(505)523-5627
Fax: (505)524-2101
E-mail: score.397@zianet.com

SCORE Office (Roswell)
Federal Bldg., Rm. 237

Roswell, NM 88201
(505)625-2112
Fax: (505)623-2545

SCORE Office (Santa Fe)
Montoya Federal Bldg.
120 Federal Place, Rm. 307
Santa Fe, NM 87501
(505)988-6302
Fax: (505)988-6300

New York

SCORE Office (Northeast)
1 Computer Dr. S
Albany, NY 12205
(518)446-1118
Fax: (518)446-1228

SCORE Office (Auburn)
30 South St.
PO Box 675
Auburn, NY 13021
(315)252-7291

SCORE Office (South Tier Binghamton)
Metro Center, 2nd Fl.
49 Court St.
PO Box 995
Binghamton, NY 13902
(607)772-8860

SCORE Office (Queens County City)
12055 Queens Blvd., Rm. 333
Borough Hall, NY 11424
(718)263-8961

SCORE Office (Buffalo)
Federal Bldg., Rm. 1311
111 W. Huron St.
Buffalo, NY 14202
(716)551-4301
Website: http://www2.pcom.net/score/
buf45.html

SCORE Office (Canandaigua)
Chamber of Commerce Bldg.
113 S. Main St.
Canandaigua, NY 14424
(716)394-4400
Fax: (716)394-4546

SCORE Office (Chemung)
333 E. Water St., 4th Fl.
Elmira, NY 14901
(607)734-3358

SCORE Office (Geneva)
Chamber of Commerce Bldg.
PO Box 587

Geneva, NY 14456
(315)789-1776
Fax: (315)789-3993

SCORE Office (Glens Falls)
84 Broad St.
Glens Falls, NY 12801
(518)798-8463
Fax: (518)745-1433

SCORE Office (Orange County)
40 Matthews St.
Goshen, NY 10924
(914)294-8080
Fax: (914)294-6121

SCORE Office (Huntington Area)
151 W. Carver St.
Huntington, NY 11743
(516)423-6100

SCORE Office (Tompkins County)
904 E. Shore Dr.
Ithaca, NY 14850
(607)273-7080

SCORE Office (Long Island City)
120-55 Queens Blvd.
Jamaica, NY 11424
(718)263-8961
Fax: (718)263-9032

SCORE Office (Chatauqua)
101 W. 5th St.
Jamestown, NY 14701
(716)484-1103

SCORE Office (Westchester)
2 Caradon Ln.
Katonah, NY 10536
(914)948-3907
Fax: (914)948-4645
E-mail: score@w-w-w.com
Website: http://w-w-w.com/score/

SCORE Office (Queens County)
Queens Borough Hall
120-55 Queens Blvd. Rm. 333
Kew Gardens, NY 11424
(718)263-8961
Fax: (718)263-9032

SCORE Office (Brookhaven)
3233 Rte. 112
Medford, NY 11763
(516)451-6563
Fax: (516)451-6925

SCORE Office (Melville)
35 Pinelawn Rd., Rm. 207-W
Melville, NY 11747
(516)454-0771

SCORE Office (Nassau County)
400 County Seat Dr., No. 140
Mineola, NY 11501
(516)571-3303
E-mail: Counse1998@aol.com
Website: http://members.aol.com/
Counse1998/Default.htm

SCORE Office (Mt. Vernon)
4 N. 7th Ave.
Mt. Vernon, NY 10550
(914)667-7500

SCORE Office (New York)
26 Federal Plz., Rm. 3100
New York, NY 10278
(212)264-4507
Fax: (212)264-4963
E-mail: score1000@erols.com
Website: http://users.erols.com/
score-nyc/

SCORE Office (Newburgh)
47 Grand St.
Newburgh, NY 12550
(914)562-5100

SCORE Office (Owego)
188 Front St.
Owego, NY 13827
(607)687-2020

SCORE Office (Peekskill)
1 S. Division St.
Peekskill, NY 10566
(914)737-3600
Fax: (914)737-0541

SCORE Office (Penn Yan)
2375 Rte. 14A
Penn Yan, NY 14527
(315)536-3111

SCORE Office (Dutchess)
110 Main St.
Poughkeepsie, NY 12601
(914)454-1700

SCORE Office (Rochester)
601 Keating Federal Bldg., Rm. 410
100 State St.
Rochester, NY 14614
(716)263-6473
Fax: (716)263-3146
Website: http://www.ggw.org/score/

SCORE Office (Saranac Lake)
30 Main St.
Saranac Lake, NY 12983
(315)448-0415

SCORE Office (Suffolk)
286 Main St.
Setauket, NY 11733
(516)751-3886

SCORE Office (Staten Island)
130 Bay St.
Staten Island, NY 10301
(718)727-1221

SCORE Office (Ulster)
Clinton Bldg., Rm. 107
Stone Ridge, NY 12484
(914)687-5035
Fax: (914)687-5015
Website: http://www.scoreulster.org/

SCORE Office (Syracuse)
401 S. Salina, 5th Fl.
Syracuse, NY 13202
(315)471-9393

SCORE Office (Utica)
SUNY Institute of Technology, Route 12
Utica, NY 13504-3050
(315)792-7553

SCORE Office (Watertown)
518 Davidson St.
Watertown, NY 13601
(315)788-1200
Fax: (315)788-8251

North Carolina

SCORE office (Asheboro)
317 E. Dixie Dr.
Asheboro, NC 27203
(336)626-2626
Fax: (336)626-7077

SCORE Office (Asheville)
Federal Bldg., Rm. 259
151 Patton
Asheville, NC 28801-5770
(828)271-4786
Fax: (828)271-4009

SCORE Office (Chapel Hill)
104 S. Estes Dr.
PO Box 2897
Chapel Hill, NC 27514
(919)967-7075

SCORE Office (Coastal Plains)
PO Box 2897
Chapel Hill, NC 27515
(919)967-7075
Fax: (919)968-6874

SCORE Office (Charlotte)
200 N. College St., Ste. A-2015

Charlotte, NC 28202
(704)344-6576
Fax: (704)344-6769
E-mail: CharlotteSCORE47@AOL.com
Website: http://www.charweb.org/
business/score/

SCORE Office (Durham)
411 W. Chapel Hill St.
Durham, NC 27707
(919)541-2171

SCORE Office (Gastonia)
PO Box 2168
Gastonia, NC 28053
(704)864-2621
Fax: (704)854-8723

SCORE Office (Greensboro)
400 W. Market St., Ste. 103
Greensboro, NC 27401-2241
(910)333-5399

SCORE Office (Henderson)
PO Box 917
Henderson, NC 27536
(919)492-2061
Fax: (919)430-0460

SCORE Office (Hendersonville)
Federal Bldg., Rm. 108
W. 4th Ave. & Church St.
Hendersonville, NC 28792
(828)693-8702
E-mail: score@circle.net
Website: http://www.wncguide.com/
score/Welcome.html

SCORE Office (Unifour)
PO Box 1828
Hickory, NC 28603
(704)328-6111

SCORE Office (High Point)
1101 N. Main St.
High Point, NC 27262
(336)882-8625
Fax: (336)889-9499

SCORE Office (Outer Banks)
Collington Rd. and Mustain
Kill Devil Hills, NC 27948
(252)441-8144

SCORE Office (Down East)
312 S. Front St., Ste. 6
New Bern, NC 28560
(252)633-6688
Fax: (252)633-9608

SCORE Office (Kinston)
PO Box 95

New Bern, NC 28561
(919)633-6688

SCORE Office (Raleigh)
Century Post Office Bldg., Ste. 306
300 Federal St. Mall
Raleigh, NC 27601
(919)856-4739
E-mail: jendres@ibm.net
Website: http://www.intrex.net/score96/
score96.htm

SCORE Office (Sanford)
1801 Nash St.
Sanford, NC 27330
(919)774-6442
Fax: (919)776-8739

SCORE Office (Sandhills Area)
1480 Hwy. 15-501
PO Box 458
Southern Pines, NC 28387
(910)692-3926

SCORE Office (Wilmington)
Corps of Engineers Bldg.
96 Darlington Ave., Ste. 207
Wilmington, NC 28403
(910)815-4576
Fax: (910)815-4658

North Dakota

SCORE Office
(Bismarck-Mandan)
700 E. Main Ave., 2nd Fl.
PO Box 5509
Bismarck, ND 58506-5509
(701)250-4303

SCORE Office (Fargo)
657 2nd Ave., Rm. 225
Fargo, ND 58108-3083
(701)239-5677

SCORE Office (Upper Red River)
4275 Technology Dr., Rm. 156
Grand Forks, ND 58202-8372
(701)777-3051

SCORE Office (Minot)
100 1st St. SW
Minot, ND 58701-3846
(701)852-6883
Fax: (701)852-6905

Ohio

SCORE Office (Akron)
1 Cascade Plz., 7th Fl.
Akron, OH 44308

Organizations, Agencies, & Consultants

(330)379-3163
Fax: (330)379-3164

SCORE Office (Ashland)
Gill Center
47 W. Main St.
Ashland, OH 44805
(419)281-4584

SCORE Office (Canton)
116 Cleveland Ave. NW, Ste. 601
Canton, OH 44702-1720
(330)453-6047

SCORE Office (Chillicothe)
165 S. Paint St.
Chillicothe, OH 45601
(614)772-4530

SCORE Office (Cincinnati)
Ameritrust Bldg., Rm. 850
525 Vine St.
Cincinnati, OH 45202
(513)684-2812
Fax: (513)684-3251
Website: http://www.score.
chapter34.org/

SCORE Office (Cleveland)
Eaton Center, Ste. 620
1100 Superior Ave.
Cleveland, OH 44114-2507
(216)522-4194
Fax: (216)522-4844

SCORE Office (Columbus)
2 Nationwide Plz., Ste. 1400
Columbus, OH 43215-2542
(614)469-2357
Fax: (614)469-2391
E-mail: info@scorecolumbus.org
Website: http://www.scorecolumbus.org/

SCORE Office (Dayton)
Dayton Federal Bldg., Rm. 505
200 W. Second St.
Dayton, OH 45402-1430
(513)225-2887
Fax: (513)225-7667

SCORE Office (Defiance)
615 W. 3rd St.
PO Box 130
Defiance, OH 43512
(419)782-7946

SCORE Office (Findlay)
123 E. Main Cross St.
PO Box 923
Findlay, OH 45840
(419)422-3314

SCORE Office (Lima)
147 N. Main St.
Lima, OH 45801
(419)222-6045
Fax: (419)229-0266

SCORE Office (Mansfield)
55 N. Mulberry St.
Mansfield, OH 44902
(419)522-3211

SCORE Office (Marietta)
Thomas Hall
Marietta, OH 45750
(614)373-0268

SCORE Office (Medina)
County Administrative Bldg.
144 N. Broadway
Medina, OH 44256
(216)764-8650

SCORE Office (Licking County)
50 W. Locust St.
Newark, OH 43055
(614)345-7458

SCORE Office (Salem)
2491 State Rte. 45 S
Salem, OH 44460
(216)332-0361

SCORE Office (Tiffin)
62 S. Washington St.
Tiffin, OH 44883
(419)447-4141
Fax: (419)447-5141

SCORE Office (Toledo)
608 Madison Ave, Ste. 910
Toledo, OH 43624
(419)259-7598
Fax: (419)259-6460

SCORE Office (Heart of Ohio)
377 W. Liberty St.
Wooster, OH 44691
(330)262-5735
Fax: (330)262-5745

SCORE Office (Youngstown)
306 Williamson Hall
Youngstown, OH 44555
(330)746-2687

Oklahoma

SCORE Office (Anadarko)
PO Box 366
Anadarko, OK 73005
(405)247-6651

SCORE Office (Ardmore)
410 W. Main
Ardmore, OK 73401
(580)226-2620

SCORE Office (Northeast Oklahoma)
210 S. Main
Grove, OK 74344
(918)787-2796
Fax: (918)787-2796
E-mail: Score595@greencis.net

SCORE Office (Lawton)
4500 W. Lee Blvd., Bldg. 100, Ste. 107
Lawton, OK 73505
(580)353-8727
Fax: (580)250-5677

SCORE Office (Oklahoma City)
210 Park Ave., No. 1300
Oklahoma City, OK 73102
(405)231-5163
Fax: (405)231-4876
E-mail: score212@usa.net

SCORE Office (Stillwater)
439 S. Main
Stillwater, OK 74074
(405)372-5573
Fax: (405)372-4316

SCORE Office (Tulsa)
616 S. Boston, Ste. 406
Tulsa, OK 74119
(918)581-7462
Fax: (918)581-6908
Website: http://www.ionet.net/~tulscore/

Oregon

SCORE Office (Bend)
63085 N. Hwy. 97
Bend, OR 97701
(541)923-2849
Fax: (541)330-6900

SCORE Office (Willamette)
1401 Willamette St.
PO Box 1107
Eugene, OR 97401-4003
(541)465-6600
Fax: (541)484-4942

SCORE Office (Florence)
3149 Oak St.
Florence, OR 97439
(503)997-8444
Fax: (503)997-8448

SCORE Office (Southern Oregon)
33 N. Central Ave., Ste. 216

Medford, OR 97501
(541)776-4220
E-mail: pgr134f@prodigy.com

SCORE Office (Portland)
1515 SW 5th Ave., Ste. 1050
Portland, OR 97201
(503)326-3441
Fax: (503)326-2808
E-mail: gr134@prodigy.com

SCORE Office (Salem)
416 State St. (corner of Liberty)
Salem, OR 97301
(503)370-2896

Pennsylvania

SCORE Office (Altoona-Blair)
1212 12th Ave.
Altoona, PA 16601-3493
(814)943-8151

SCORE Office (Lehigh Valley)
Rauch Bldg. 37
Lehigh University
621 Taylor St.
Bethlehem, PA 18015
(610)758-4496
Fax: (610)758-5205

SCORE Office (Butler County)
100 N. Main St.
PO Box 1082
Butler, PA 16003
(412)283-2222
Fax: (412)283-0224

SCORE Office (Harrisburg)
4211 Trindle Rd.
Camp Hill, PA 17011
(717)761-4304
Fax: (717)761-4315

SCORE Office (Cumberland Valley)
75 S. 2nd St.
Chambersburg, PA 17201
(717)264-2935

SCORE Office (Monroe County-Stroudsburg)
556 Main St.
East Stroudsburg, PA 18301
(717)421-4433

SCORE Office (Erie)
120 W. 9th St.
Erie, PA 16501
(814)871-5650
Fax: (814)871-7530

SCORE Office (Bucks County)
409 Hood Blvd.
Fairless Hills, PA 19030
(215)943-8850
Fax: (215)943-7404

SCORE Office (Hanover)
146 Broadway
Hanover, PA 17331
(717)637-6130
Fax: (717)637-9127

SCORE Office (Harrisburg)
100 Chestnut, Ste. 309
Harrisburg, PA 17101
(717)782-3874

SCORE Office (East Montgomery County)
Baederwood Shopping Center
1653 The Fairways, Ste. 204
Jenkintown, PA 19046
(215)885-3027

SCORE Office (Kittanning)
2 Butler Rd.
Kittanning, PA 16201
(412)543-1305
Fax: (412)543-6206

SCORE Office (Lancaster)
118 W. Chestnut St.
Lancaster, PA 17603
(717)397-3092

SCORE Office (Westmoreland County)
300 Fraser Purchase Rd.
Latrobe, PA 15650-2690
(412)539-7505
Fax: (412)539-1850

SCORE Office (Lebanon)
252 N. 8th St.
PO Box 899
Lebanon, PA 17042-0899
(717)273-3727
Fax: (717)273-7940

SCORE Office (Lewistown)
3 W. Monument Sq., Ste. 204
Lewistown, PA 17044
(717)248-6713
Fax: (717)248-6714

SCORE Office (Delaware County)
602 E. Baltimore Pike
Media, PA 19063
(610)565-3677
Fax: (610)565-1606

SCORE Office (Milton Area)
112 S. Front St.
Milton, PA 17847

(717)742-7341
Fax: (717)792-2008

SCORE Office (Mon-Valley)
435 Donner Ave.
Monessen, PA 15062
(412)684-4277
Fax: (412)684-7688

SCORE Office (Monroeville)
William Penn Plaza
2790 Mosside Blvd., Ste. 295
Monroeville, PA 15146
(412)856-0622
Fax: (412)856-1030

SCORE Office (Airport Area)
986 Brodhead Rd.
Moon Township, PA 15108-2398
(412)264-6270
Fax: (412)264-1575

SCORE Office (Northeast)
8601 E. Roosevelt Blvd.
Philadelphia, PA 19152
(215)332-3400
Fax: (215)332-6050

SCORE Office (Philadelphia)
1315 Walnut St., Ste. 500
Philadelphia, PA 19107
(215)790-5050
Fax: (215)790-5057
E-mail: score46@bellatlantic.net
Website: http://www.pgweb.net/score46/

SCORE Office (Pittsburgh)
1000 Liberty Ave., Rm. 1122
Pittsburgh, PA 15222
(412)395-6560
Fax: (412)395-6562

SCORE Office (Tri-County)
801 N. Charlotte St.
Pottstown, PA 19464
(610)327-2673

SCORE Office (Reading)
601 Penn St.
Reading, PA 19601
(610)376-3497

SCORE Office (Scranton)
Oppenheim Bldg.
116 N. Washington Ave., Ste. 650
Scranton, PA 18503
(717)347-4611
Fax: (717)347-4611

SCORE Office (Central Pennsylvania)
200 Innovation Blvd., Ste. 242-B
State College, PA 16803

(814)234-9415
Fax: (814)238-9686
Website: http://countrystore.org/
business/score.htm

SCORE Office (Monroe-Stroudsburg)
556 Main St.
Stroudsburg, PA 18360
(717)421-4433

SCORE Office (Uniontown)
Federal Bldg.
Pittsburg St.
PO Box 2065 DTS
Uniontown, PA 15401
(412)437-4222
E-mail: uniontownscore@lcsys.net

SCORE Office (Warren County)
315 2nd Ave.
Warren, PA 16365
(814)723-9017

SCORE Office (Waynesboro)
323 E. Main St.
Waynesboro, PA 17268
(717)762-7123
Fax: (717)962-7124

SCORE Office (Chester County)
Government Service Center, Ste. 281
601 Westtown Rd.
West Chester, PA 19382-4538
(610)344-6910
Fax: (610)344-6919
E-mail: score@locke.ccil.org

SCORE Office (Wilkes-Barre)
7 N. Wilkes-Barre Blvd.
Wilkes Barre, PA 18702-5241
(717)826-6502
Fax: (717)826-6287

SCORE Office (North Central Pennsylvania)
240 W. 3rd St., Rm. 227
PO Box 725
Williamsport, PA 17703
(717)322-3720
Fax: (717)322-1607
E-mail: score234@mail.csrlink.net
Website: http://www.lycoming.org/
score/

SCORE Office (York)
Cyber Center
2101 Pennsylvania Ave.
York, PA 17404
(717)845-8830
Fax: (717)854-9333

Puerto Rico

SCORE Office (Puerto Rico & Virgin Islands)
PO Box 12383-96
San Juan, PR 00914-0383
(787)726-8040
Fax: (787)726-8135

Rhode Island

SCORE Office (Barrington)
281 County Rd.
Barrington, RI 02806
(401)247-1920
Fax: (401)247-3763

SCORE Office (Woonsocket)
640 Washington Hwy.
Lincoln, RI 02865
(401)334-1000
Fax: (401)334-1009

SCORE Office (Wickford)
8045 Post Rd.
North Kingstown, RI 02852
(401)295-5566
Fax: (401)295-8987

SCORE Office (J.G.E. Knight)
380 Westminster St.
Providence, RI 02903
(401)528-4571
Fax: (401)528-4539
Website: http://www.riscore.org

SCORE Office (Warwick)
3288 Post Rd.
Warwick, RI 02886
(401)732-1100
Fax: (401)732-1101

SCORE Office (Westerly)
74 Post Rd.
Westerly, RI 02891
(401)596-7761
800-732-7636
Fax: (401)596-2190

South Carolina

SCORE Office (Aiken)
PO Box 892
Aiken, SC 29802
(803)641-1111
800-542-4536
Fax: (803)641-4174

SCORE Office (Anderson)
Anderson Mall
3130 N. Main St.

Anderson, SC 29621
(864)224-0453

SCORE Office (Coastal)
284 King St.
Charleston, SC 29401
(803)727-4778
Fax: (803)853-2529

SCORE Office (Midlands)
Strom Thurmond Bldg., Rm. 358
1835 Assembly St., Rm 358
Columbia, SC 29201
(803)765-5131
Fax: (803)765-5962
Website: http://www.scoremid
lands.org/

SCORE Office (Piedmont)
Federal Bldg., Rm. B-02
300 E. Washington St.
Greenville, SC 29601
(864)271-3638

SCORE Office (Greenwood)
PO Drawer 1467
Greenwood, SC 29648
(864)223-8357

SCORE Office (Hilton Head Island)
52 Savannah Trail
Hilton Head, SC 29926
(803)785-7107
Fax: (803)785-7110

SCORE Office (Grand Strand)
937 Broadway
Myrtle Beach, SC 29577
(803)918-1079
Fax: (803)918-1083
E-mail: score381@aol.com

SCORE Office (Spartanburg)
PO Box 1636
Spartanburg, SC 29304
(864)594-5000
Fax: (864)594-5055

South Dakota

SCORE Office (West River)
Rushmore Plz. Civic Ctr.
444 Mount Rushmore Rd., No. 209
Rapid City, SD 57701
(605)394-5311
E-mail: score@gwtc.net

SCORE Office (Sioux Falls)
First Financial Center
110 S. Phillips Ave., Ste. 200
Sioux Falls, SD 57104-6727

(605)330-4231
Fax: (605)330-4231

Tennessee

SCORE Office (Chattanooga)
Federal Bldg., Rm. 26
900 Georgia Ave.
Chattanooga, TN 37402
(423)752-5190
Fax: (423)752-5335

SCORE Office (Cleveland)
PO Box 2275
Cleveland, TN 37320
(423)472-6587
Fax: (423)472-2019

SCORE Office (Upper Cumberland Center)
1225 S. Willow Ave.
Cookeville, TN 38501
(615)432-4111
Fax: (615)432-6010

SCORE Office (Unicoi County)
PO Box 713
Erwin, TN 37650
(423)743-3000
Fax: (423)743-0942

SCORE Office (Greeneville)
115 Academy St.
Greeneville, TN 37743
(423)638-4111
Fax: (423)638-5345

SCORE Office (Jackson)
194 Auditorium St.
Jackson, TN 38301
(901)423-2200

SCORE Office (Northeast Tennessee)
1st Tennessee Bank Bldg.
2710 S. Roan St., Ste. 584
Johnson City, TN 37601
(423)929-7686
Fax: (423)461-8052

SCORE Office (Kingsport)
151 E. Main St.
Kingsport, TN 37662
(423)392-8805

SCORE Office (Greater Knoxville)
Farragot Bldg., Ste. 224
530 S. Gay St.
Knoxville, TN 37902
(423)545-4203
E-mail: scoreknox@ntown.com
Website: http://www.scoreknox.org/

SCORE Office (Maryville)
201 S. Washington St.
Maryville, TN 37804-5728
(423)983-2241
800-525-6834
Fax: (423)984-1386

SCORE Office (Memphis)
Federal Bldg., Ste. 390
167 N. Main St.
Memphis, TN 38103
(901)544-3588

SCORE Office (Nashville)
50 Vantage Way, Ste. 201
Nashville, TN 37228-1500
(615)736-7621

Texas

SCORE Office (Abilene)
2106 Federal Post Office and Court Bldg.
Abilene, TX 79601
(915)677-1857

SCORE Office (Austin)
2501 S. Congress
Austin, TX 78701
(512)442-7235
Fax: (512)442-7528

SCORE Office (Golden Triangle)
450 Boyd St.
Beaumont, TX 77704
(409)838-6581
Fax: (409)833-6718

SCORE Office (Brownsville)
3505 Boca Chica Blvd., Ste. 305
Brownsville, TX 78521
(210)541-4508

SCORE Office (Brazos Valley)
3000 Briarcrest, Ste. 302
Bryan, TX 77802
(409)776-8876
E-mail: 102633.2612@compuserve.com

SCORE Office (Cleburne)
Watergarden Pl., 9th Fl., Ste. 400
Cleburne, TX 76031
(817)871-6002

SCORE Office (Corpus Christi)
651 Upper North Broadway, Ste. 654
Corpus Christi, TX 78477
(512)888-4322
Fax: (512)888-3418

SCORE Office (Dallas)
6260 E. Mockingbird
Dallas, TX 75214-2619

(214)828-2471
Fax: (214)821-8033

SCORE Office (El Paso)
10 Civic Center Plaza
El Paso, TX 79901
(915)534-0541
Fax: (915)534-0513

SCORE Office (Bedford)
100 E. 15th St., Ste. 400
Ft. Worth, TX 76102
(817)871-6002

SCORE Office (Ft. Worth)
100 E. 15th St., No. 24
Ft. Worth, TX 76102
(817)871-6002
Fax: (817)871-6031
E-mail: fwbac@onramp.net

SCORE Office (Garland)
2734 W. Kingsley Rd.
Garland, TX 75041
(214)271-9224

SCORE Office (Granbury Chamber of Commerce)
416 S. Morgan
Granbury, TX 76048
(817)573-1622
Fax: (817)573-0805

SCORE Office (Lower Rio Grande Valley)
222 E. Van Buren, Ste. 500
Harlingen, TX 78550
(956)427-8533
Fax: (956)427-8537

SCORE Office (Houston)
9301 Southwest Fwy., Ste. 550
Houston, TX 77074
(713)773-6565
Fax: (713)773-6550

SCORE Office (Irving)
3333 N. MacArthur Blvd., Ste. 100
Irving, TX 75062
(214)252-8484
Fax: (214)252-6710

SCORE Office (Lubbock)
1205 Texas Ave., Rm. 411D
Lubbock, TX 79401
(806)472-7462
Fax: (806)472-7487

SCORE Office (Midland)
Post Office Annex
200 E. Wall St., Rm. P121
Midland, TX 79701
(915)687-2649

SCORE Office (Orange)
1012 Green Ave.
Orange, TX 77630-5620
(409)883-3536
800-528-4906
Fax: (409)886-3247

SCORE Office (Plano)
1200 E. 15th St.
PO Drawer 940287
Plano, TX 75094-0287
(214)424-7547
Fax: (214)422-5182

SCORE Office (Port Arthur)
4749 Twin City Hwy., Ste. 300
Port Arthur, TX 77642
(409)963-1107
Fax: (409)963-3322

SCORE Office (Richardson)
411 Belle Grove
Richardson, TX 75080
(214)234-4141
800-777-8001
Fax: (214)680-9103

SCORE Office (San Antonio)
Federal Bldg., Rm. A527
727 E. Durango
San Antonio, TX 78206
(210)472-5931
Fax: (210)472-5935

SCORE Office (Texarkana State College)
819 State Line Ave.
Texarkana, TX 75501
(903)792-7191
Fax: (903)793-4304

SCORE Office (East Texas)
RTDC
1530 SSW Loop 323, Ste. 100
Tyler, TX 75701
(903)510-2975
Fax: (903)510-2978

SCORE Office (Waco)
401 Franklin Ave.
Waco, TX 76701
(817)754-8898
Fax: (817)756-0776
Website: http://www.brc-waco.com/

SCORE Office (Wichita Falls)
Hamilton Bldg.
900 8th St.
Wichita Falls, TX 76307
(940)723-2741
Fax: (940)723-8773

Utah

SCORE Office (Northern Utah)
160 N. Main
Logan, UT 84321
(435)746-2269

SCORE Office (Ogden)
1701 E. Windsor Dr.
Ogden, UT 84604
(801)629-8613
E-mail: score158@netscape.net

SCORE Office (Central Utah)
1071 E. Windsor Dr.
Provo, UT 84604
(801)373-8660

SCORE Office (Southern Utah)
225 South 700 East
St. George, UT 84770
(435)652-7751

SCORE Office (Salt Lake)
310 S Main St.
Salt Lake City, UT 84101
(801)746-2269
Fax: (801)746-2273

Vermont

SCORE Office (Champlain Valley)
Winston Prouty Federal Bldg.
11 Lincoln St., Rm. 106
Essex Junction, VT 05452
(802)951-6762

SCORE Office (Montpelier)
87 State St., Rm. 205
PO Box 605
Montpelier, VT 05601
(802)828-4422
Fax: (802)828-4485

SCORE Office (Marble Valley)
256 N. Main St.
Rutland, VT 05701-2413
(802)773-9147

SCORE Office (Northeast Kingdom)
20 Main St.
PO Box 904
St. Johnsbury, VT 05819
(802)748-5101

Virgin Islands

SCORE Office (St. Croix)
United Plaza Shopping Center
PO Box 4010, Christiansted
St. Croix, VI 00822
(809)778-5380

SCORE Office (St. Thomas-St. John)
Federal Bldg., Rm. 21
Veterans Dr.
St. Thomas, VI 00801
(809)774-8530

Virginia

SCORE Office (Arlington)
2009 N. 14th St., Ste. 111
Arlington, VA 22201
(703)525-2400

SCORE Office (Blacksburg)
141 Jackson St.
Blacksburg, VA 24060
(540)552-4061

SCORE Office (Bristol)
20 Volunteer Pkwy.
Bristol, VA 24203
(540)989-4850

SCORE Office (Central Virginia)
1001 E. Market St., Ste. 101
Charlottesville, VA 22902
(804)295-6712
Fax: (804)295-7066

SCORE Office (Alleghany Satellite)
241 W. Main St.
Covington, VA 24426
(540)962-2178
Fax: (540)962-2179

SCORE Office (Central Fairfax)
3975 University Dr., Ste. 350
Fairfax, VA 22030
(703)591-2450

SCORE Office (Falls Church)
PO Box 491
Falls Church, VA 22040
(703)532-1050
Fax: (703)237-7904

SCORE Office (Glenns)
Glenns Campus
Box 287
Glenns, VA 23149
(804)693-9650

SCORE Office (Peninsula)
6 Manhattan Sq.
PO Box 7269
Hampton, VA 23666
(757)766-2000
Fax: (757)865-0339
E-mail: score100@seva.net

SCORE Office (Tri-Cities)
108 N. Main St.

Hopewell, VA 23860
(804)458-5536

SCORE Office (Lynchburg)
Federal Bldg.
1100 Main St.
Lynchburg, VA 24504-1714
(804)846-3235

SCORE Office (Greater Prince William)
8963 Center St
Manassas, VA 20110
(703)368-4813
Fax: (703)368-4733

SCORE Office (Martinsvile)
115 Broad St.
Martinsville, VA 24112-0709
(540)632-6401
Fax: (540)632-5059

SCORE Office (Hampton Roads)
Federal Bldg., Rm. 737
200 Grandby St.
Norfolk, VA 23510
(757)441-3733
Fax: (757)441-3733
E-mail: scorehr60@juno.com

SCORE Office (Norfolk)
Federal Bldg., Rm. 737
200 Granby St.
Norfolk, VA 23510
(757)441-3733
Fax: (757)441-3733

SCORE Office (Virginia Beach)
Chamber of Commerce
200 Grandby St., Rm 737
Norfolk, VA 23510
(804)441-3733

SCORE Office (Radford)
1126 Norwood St.
Radford, VA 24141
(540)639-2202

SCORE Office (Richmond)
Federal Bldg.
400 N. 8th St., Ste. 1150
PO Box 10126
Richmond, VA 23240-0126
(804)771-2400
Fax: (804)771-8018
E-mail: scorechapter12@yahoo.com
Website: http://www.cvco.org/score/

SCORE Office (Roanoke)
Federal Bldg., Rm. 716
250 Franklin Rd.
Roanoke, VA 24011

(540)857-2834
Fax: (540)857-2043
E-mail: scorerva@juno.com
Website: http://hometown.aol.com/
scorerv/Index.html

SCORE Office (Fairfax)
8391 Old Courthouse Rd., Ste. 300
Vienna, VA 22182
(703)749-0400

SCORE Office (Greater Vienna)
513 Maple Ave. West
Vienna, VA 22180
(703)281-1333
Fax: (703)242-1482

SCORE Office (Shenandoah Valley)
301 W. Main St.
Waynesboro, VA 22980
(540)949-8203
Fax: (540)949-7740
E-mail: score427@intelos.net

SCORE Office (Williamsburg)
201 Penniman Rd.
Williamsburg, VA 23185
(757)229-6511
E-mail: wacc@williamsburgcc.com

SCORE Office (Northern Virginia)
1360 S. Pleasant Valley Rd.
Winchester, VA 22601
(540)662-4118

Washington

SCORE Office (Gray's Harbor)
506 Duffy St.
Aberdeen, WA 98520
(360)532-1924
Fax: (360)533-7945

SCORE Office (Bellingham)
101 E. Holly St.
Bellingham, WA 98225
(360)676-3307

SCORE Office (Everett)
2702 Hoyt Ave.
Everett, WA 98201-3556
(206)259-8000

SCORE Office (Gig Harbor)
3125 Judson St.
Gig Harbor, WA 98335
(206)851-6865

SCORE Office (Kennewick)
PO Box 6986
Kennewick, WA 99336
(509)736-0510

SCORE Office (Puyallup)
322 2nd St. SW
PO Box 1298
Puyallup, WA 98371
(206)845-6755
Fax: (206)848-6164

SCORE Office (Seattle)
1200 6th Ave., Ste. 1700
Seattle, WA 98101
(206)553-7320
Fax: (206)553-7044
E-mail: score55@aol.com
Website: http://www.scn.org/civic/score-
online/index55.html

SCORE Office (Spokane)
801 W. Riverside Ave., No. 240
Spokane, WA 99201
(509)353-2820
Fax: (509)353-2600
E-mail: score@dmi.net
Website: http://www.dmi.net/score/

SCORE Office (Clover Park)
PO Box 1933
Tacoma, WA 98401-1933
(206)627-2175

SCORE Office (Tacoma)
1101 Pacific Ave.
Tacoma, WA 98402
(253)274-1288
Fax: (253)274-1289

SCORE Office (Fort Vancouver)
1701 Broadway, S-1
Vancouver, WA 98663
(360)699-1079

SCORE Office (Walla Walla)
500 Tausick Way
Walla Walla, WA 99362
(509)527-4681

SCORE Office (Mid-Columbia)
1113 S. 14th Ave.
Yakima, WA 98907
(509)574-4944
Fax: (509)574-2943
Website: http://www.ellensburg.com/
~score/

West Virginia

SCORE Office (Charleston)
1116 Smith St.
Charleston, WV 25301
(304)347-5463
E-mail: score256@juno.com

SCORE Office (Virginia Street)
1116 Smith St., Ste. 302
Charleston, WV 25301
(304)347-5463

SCORE Office (Marion County)
PO Box 208
Fairmont, WV 26555-0208
(304)363-0486

SCORE Office (Upper Monongahela Valley)
1000 Technology Dr., Ste. 1111
Fairmont, WV 26555
(304)363-0486
E-mail: score537@hotmail.com

SCORE Office (Huntington)
1101 6th Ave., Ste. 220
Huntington, WV 25701-2309
(304)523-4092

SCORE Office (Wheeling)
1310 Market St.
Wheeling, WV 26003
(304)233-2575
Fax: (304)233-1320

Wisconsin

SCORE Office (Fox Cities)
227 S. Walnut St.
Appleton, WI 54913
(920)734-7101
Fax: (920)734-7161

SCORE Office (Beloit)
136 W. Grand Ave., Ste. 100
PO Box 717
Beloit, WI 53511
(608)365-8835
Fax: (608)365-9170

SCORE Office (Eau Claire)
Federal Bldg., Rm. B11
510 S. Barstow St.
Eau Claire, WI 54701
(715)834-1573
E-mail: score@ecol.net
Website: http://www.ecol.net/~score/

SCORE Office (Fond du Lac)
207 N. Main St.
Fond du Lac, WI 54935
(414)921-9500
Fax: (414)921-9559

SCORE Office (Green Bay)
835 Potts Ave.
Green Bay, WI 54304
(414)496-8930
Fax: (414)496-6009

SCORE Office (Janesville)
20 S. Main St., Ste. 11
PO Box 8008
Janesville, WI 53547
(608)757-3160
Fax: (608)757-3170

SCORE Office (La Crosse)
712 Main St.
La Crosse, WI 54602-0219
(608)784-4880

SCORE Office (Madison)
505 S. Rosa Rd.
Madison, WI 53719
(608)441-2820

SCORE Office (Manitowoc)
1515 Memorial Dr.
PO Box 903
Manitowoc, WI 54221-0903
(414)684-5575
Fax: (414)684-1915

SCORE Office (Milwaukee)
310 W. Wisconsin Ave., Ste. 425
Milwaukee, WI 53203
(414)297-3942
Fax: (414)297-1377

SCORE Office (Central Wisconsin)
1224 Lindbergh Ave.
Stevens Point, WI 54481
(715)344-7729

SCORE Office (Superior)
Superior Business Center Inc.
1423 N. 8th St.
Superior, WI 54880
(715)394-7388
Fax: (715)393-7414

SCORE Office (Waukesha)
223 Wisconsin Ave.
Waukesha, WI 53186-4926
(414)542-4249

SCORE Office (Wausau)
300 3rd St., Ste. 200
Wausau, WI 54402-6190
(715)845-6231

SCORE Office (Wisconsin Rapids)
2240 Kingston Rd.
Wisconsin Rapids, WI 54494
(715)423-1830

Wyoming

SCORE Office (Casper)
Federal Bldg., No. 2215
100 East B St.

Casper, WY 82602
(307)261-6529
Fax: (307)261-6530

Venture capital & financing companies

This section contains a listing of financing and loan companies in the United States and Canada. These listing are arranged alphabetically by country, then by state or province, then by city, then by organization name.

Canada

Alberta

Launchworks Inc.
1902J 11th St., S.E.
Calgary, AB, Canada T2G 3G2
(403)269-1119
Fax: (403)269-1141
Website: http://www.launchworks.com

Native Venture Capital Company, Inc.
21 Artist View Point, Box 7
Site 25, RR 12
Calgary, AB, Canada T3E 6W3
(903)208-5380

Miralta Capital Inc.
4445 Calgary Trail South
888 Terrace Plaza Alberta
Edmonton, AB, Canada T6H 5R7
(780)438-3535
Fax: (780)438-3129

Vencap Equities Alberta Ltd.
10180-101st St., Ste. 1980
Edmonton, AB, Canada T5J 3S4
(403)420-1171
Fax: (403)429-2541

British Columbia

Discovery Capital
5th Fl., 1199 West Hastings
Vancouver, BC, Canada V6E 3T5
(604)683-3000
Fax: (604)662-3457
E-mail: info@discoverycapital.com
Website: http://www.discoverycapital.com

Greenstone Venture Partners
1177 West Hastings St.
Ste. 400
Vancouver, BC, Canada V6E 2K3
(604)717-1977
Fax: (604)717-1976
Website: http://www.greenstonevc.com

Growthworks Capital
2600-1055 West Georgia St.
Box 11170 Royal Centre
Vancouver, BC, Canada V6E 3R5
(604)895-7259
Fax: (604)669-7605
Website: http://www.wofund.com

MDS Discovery Venture Management, Inc.
555 W. Eighth Ave., Ste. 305
Vancouver, BC, Canada V5Z 1C6
(604)872-8464
Fax: (604)872-2977
E-mail: info@mds-ventures.com

Ventures West Management Inc.
1285 W. Pender St., Ste. 280
Vancouver, BC, Canada V6E 4B1
(604)688-9495
Fax: (604)687-2145
Website: http://www.ventureswest.com

Nova Scotia

ACF Equity Atlantic Inc.
Purdy's Wharf Tower II
Ste. 2106
Halifax, NS, Canada B3J 3R7
(902)421-1965
Fax: (902)421-1808

Montgomerie, Huck & Co.
146 Bluenose Dr.
PO Box 538
Lunenburg, NS, Canada B0J 2C0
(902)634-7125
Fax: (902)634-7130

Ontario

IPS Industrial Promotion Services Ltd.
60 Columbia Way, Ste. 720
Markham, ON, Canada L3R 0C9
(905)475-9400
Fax: (905)475-5003

Betwin Investments Inc.
Box 23110
Sault Ste. Marie, ON, Canada P6A 6W6
(705)253-0744
Fax: (705)253-0744

Bailey & Company, Inc.
594 Spadina Ave.
Toronto, ON, Canada M5S 2H4
(416)921-6930
Fax: (416)925-4670

BCE Capital
200 Bay St.

South Tower, Ste. 3120
Toronto, ON, Canada M5J 2J2
(416)815-0078
Fax: (416)941-1073
Website: http://www.bcecapital.com

Castlehill Ventures
55 University Ave., Ste. 500
Toronto, ON, Canada M5J 2H7
(416)862-8574
Fax: (416)862-8875

CCFL Mezzanine Partners of Canada
70 University Ave.
Ste. 1450
Toronto, ON, Canada M5J 2M4
(416)977-1450
Fax: (416)977-6764
E-mail: info@ccfl.com
Website: http://www.ccfl.com

Celtic House International
100 Simcoe St., Ste. 100
Toronto, ON, Canada M5H 3G2
(416)542-2436
Fax: (416)542-2435
Website: http://www.celtic-house.com

Clairvest Group Inc.
22 St. Clair Ave. East
Ste. 1700
Toronto, ON, Canada M4T 2S3
(416)925-9270
Fax: (416)925-5753

Crosbie & Co., Inc.
One First Canadian Place
9th Fl.
PO Box 116
Toronto, ON, Canada M5X 1A4
(416)362-7726
Fax: (416)362-3447
E-mail: info@crosbieco.com
Website: http://www.crosbieco.com

Drug Royalty Corp.
Eight King St. East
Ste. 202
Toronto, ON, Canada M5C 1B5
(416)863-1865
Fax: (416)863-5161

Grieve, Horner, Brown & Asculai
8 King St. E, Ste. 1704
Toronto, ON, Canada M5C 1B5
(416)362-7668
Fax: (416)362-7660

Jefferson Partners
77 King St. West
Ste. 4010

PO Box 136
Toronto, ON, Canada M5K 1H1
(416)367-1533
Fax: (416)367-5827
Website: http://www.jefferson.com

J.L. Albright Venture Partners
Canada Trust Tower, 161 Bay St.
Ste. 4440
PO Box 215
Toronto, ON, Canada M5J 2S1
(416)367-2440
Fax: (416)367-4604
Website: http://www.jlaventures.com

McLean Watson Capital Inc.
One First Canadian Place
Ste. 1410
PO Box 129
Toronto, ON, Canada M5X 1A4
(416)363-2000
Fax: (416)363-2010
Website: http://www.mcleanwatson.com

Middlefield Capital Fund
One First Canadian Place
85th Fl.
PO Box 192
Toronto, ON, Canada M5X 1A6
(416)362-0714
Fax: (416)362-7925
Website: http://www.middlefield.com

Mosaic Venture Partners
24 Duncan St.
Ste. 300
Toronto, ON, Canada M5V 3M6
(416)597-8889
Fax: (416)597-2345

Onex Corp.
161 Bay St.
PO Box 700
Toronto, ON, Canada M5J 2S1
(416)362-7711
Fax: (416)362-5765

Penfund Partners Inc.
145 King St. West
Ste. 1920
Toronto, ON, Canada M5H 1J8
(416)865-0300
Fax: (416)364-6912
Website: http://www.penfund.com

Primaxis Technology Ventures Inc.
1 Richmond St. West, 8th Fl.
Toronto, ON, Canada M5H 3W4
(416)313-5210
Fax: (416)313-5218
Website: http://www.primaxis.com

Priveq Capital Funds
240 Duncan Mill Rd., Ste. 602
Toronto, ON, Canada M3B 3P1
(416)447-3330
Fax: (416)447-3331
E-mail: priveq@sympatico.ca

Roynat Ventures
40 King St. West, 26th Fl.
Toronto, ON, Canada M5H 1H1
(416)933-2667
Fax: (416)933-2783
Website: http://www.roynatcapital.com

Tera Capital Corp.
366 Adelaide St. East, Ste. 337
Toronto, ON, Canada M5A 3X9
(416)368-1024
Fax: (416)368-1427

Working Ventures Canadian Fund Inc.
250 Bloor St. East, Ste. 1600
Toronto, ON, Canada M4W 1E6
(416)934-7718
Fax: (416)929-0901
Website: http://www.workingventures.ca

Quebec

Altamira Capital Corp.
202 University
Niveau de Maisoneuve, Bur. 201
Montreal, QC, Canada H3A 2A5
(514)499-1656
Fax: (514)499-9570

Federal Business Development Bank
Venture Capital Division
Five Place Ville Marie, Ste. 600
Montreal, QC, Canada H3B 5E7
(514)283-1896
Fax: (514)283-5455

Hydro-Quebec Capitech Inc.
75 Boul, Rene Levesque Quest
Montreal, QC, Canada H2Z 1A4
(514)289-4783
Fax: (514)289-5420
Website: http://www.hqcapitech.com

Investissement Desjardins
2 complexe Desjardins
C.P. 760
Montreal, QC, Canada H5B 1B8
(514)281-7131
Fax: (514)281-7808
Website: http://www.desjardins.com/id

Marleau Lemire Inc.
One Place Ville-Marie, Ste. 3601
Montreal, QC, Canada H3B 3P2

(514)877-3800
Fax: (514)875-6415

Speirs Consultants Inc.
365 Stanstead
Montreal, QC, Canada H3R 1X5
(514)342-3858
Fax: (514)342-1977

Tecnocap Inc.
4028 Marlowe
Montreal, QC, Canada H4A 3M2
(514)483-6009
Fax: (514)483-6045
Website: http://www.technocap.com

Telsoft Ventures
1000, Rue de la Gauchetiere
Quest, 25eme Etage
Montreal, QC, Canada H3B 4W5
(514)397-8450
Fax: (514)397-8451

Saskatchewan

Saskatchewan Government Growth Fund
1801 Hamilton St., Ste. 1210
Canada Trust Tower
Regina, SK, Canada S4P 4B4
(306)787-2994
Fax: (306)787-2086

United states

Alabama

FHL Capital Corp.
600 20th Street North
Suite 350
Birmingham, AL 35203
(205)328-3098
Fax: (205)323-0001

Harbert Management Corp.
One Riverchase Pkwy. South
Birmingham, AL 35244
(205)987-5500
Fax: (205)987-5707
Website: http://www.harbert.net

Jefferson Capital Fund
PO Box 13129
Birmingham, AL 35213
(205)324-7709

Private Capital Corp.
100 Brookwood Pl., 4th Fl.
Birmingham, AL 35209
(205)879-2722
Fax: (205)879-5121

21st Century Health Ventures
One Health South Pkwy.
Birmingham, AL 35243
(256)268-6250
Fax: (256)970-8928

FJC Growth Capital Corp.
200 W. Side Sq., Ste. 340
Huntsville, AL 35801
(256)922-2918
Fax: (256)922-2909

Hickory Venture Capital Corp.
301 Washington St. NW
Suite 301
Huntsville, AL 35801
(256)539-1931
Fax: (256)539-5130
E-mail: hvcc@hvcc.com
Website: http://www.hvcc.com

Southeastern Technology Fund
7910 South Memorial Pkwy., Ste. F
Huntsville, AL 35802
(256)883-8711
Fax: (256)883-8558

Cordova Ventures
4121 Carmichael Rd., Ste. 301
Montgomery, AL 36106
(334)271-6011
Fax: (334)260-0120
Website: http://www.cordova
ventures.com

**Small Business Clinic of Alabama/AG
Bartholomew & Associates**
PO Box 231074
Montgomery, AL 36123-1074
(334)284-3640

Arizona

Miller Capital Corp.
4909 E. McDowell Rd.
Phoenix, AZ 85008
(602)225-0504
Fax: (602)225-9024
Website: http://www.themiller
group.com

The Columbine Venture Funds
9449 North 90th St., Ste. 200
Scottsdale, AZ 85258
(602)661-9222
Fax: (602)661-6262

Koch Ventures
17767 N. Perimeter Dr., Ste. 101
Scottsdale, AZ 85255
(480)419-3600

Fax: (480)419-3606
Website: http://www.kochventures.com

McKee & Co.
7702 E. Doubletree Ranch Rd.
Suite 230
Scottsdale, AZ 85258
(480)368-0333
Fax: (480)607-7446

Merita Capital Ltd.
7350 E. Stetson Dr., Ste. 108-A
Scottsdale, AZ 85251
(480)947-8700
Fax: (480)947-8766

Valley Ventures / Arizona Growth Partners L.P.
6720 N. Scottsdale Rd., Ste. 208
Scottsdale, AZ 85253
(480)661-6600
Fax: (480)661-6262

Estreetcapital.com
660 South Mill Ave., Ste. 315
Tempe, AZ 85281
(480)968-8400
Fax: (480)968-8480
Website: http://www.estreetcapital.com

Coronado Venture Fund
PO Box 65420
Tucson, AZ 85728-5420
(520)577-3764
Fax: (520)299-8491

Arkansas

Arkansas Capital Corp.
225 South Pulaski St.
Little Rock, AR 72201
(501)374-9247
Fax: (501)374-9425
Website: http://www.arcapital.com

California

Sundance Venture Partners, L.P.
100 Clocktower Place, Ste. 130
Carmel, CA 93923
(831)625-6500
Fax: (831)625-6590

Westar Capital (Costa Mesa)
949 South Coast Dr., Ste. 650
Costa Mesa, CA 92626
(714)481-5160
Fax: (714)481-5166
E-mail: mailbox@westarcapital.com
Website: http://www.westarcapital.com

Alpine Technology Ventures
20300 Stevens Creek Boulevard, Ste. 495
Cupertino, CA 95014
(408)725-1810
Fax: (408)725-1207
Website: http://www.alpineventures.com

Bay Partners
10600 N. De Anza Blvd.
Cupertino, CA 95014-2031
(408)725-2444
Fax: (408)446-4502
Website: http://www.baypartners.com

Novus Ventures
20111 Stevens Creek Blvd., Ste. 130
Cupertino, CA 95014
(408)252-3900
Fax: (408)252-1713
Website: http://www.novusventures.com

Triune Capital
19925 Stevens Creek Blvd., Ste. 200
Cupertino, CA 95014
(310)284-6800
Fax: (310)284-3290

Acorn Ventures
268 Bush St., Ste. 2829
Daly City, CA 94014
(650)994-7801
Fax: (650)994-3305
Website: http://www.acornventures.com

Digital Media Campus
2221 Park Place
El Segundo, CA 90245
(310)426-8000
Fax: (310)426-8010
E-mail: info@thecampus.com
Website: http://www.digital
mediacampus.com

BankAmerica Ventures / BA Venture Partners
950 Tower Ln., Ste. 700
Foster City, CA 94404
(650)378-6000
Fax: (650)378-6040
Website: http://
www.baventurepartners.com

Starting Point Partners
666 Portofino Lane
Foster City, CA 94404
(650)722-1035
Website: http://www.startingpoint
partners.com

Opportunity Capital Partners
2201 Walnut Ave., Ste. 210

Fremont, CA 94538
(510)795-7000
Fax: (510)494-5439
Website: http://www.ocpcapital.com

Imperial Ventures Inc.
9920 S. La Cienega Boulevar, 14th Fl.
Inglewood, CA 90301
(310)417-5409
Fax: (310)338-6115

Ventana Global (Irvine)
18881 Von Karman Ave., Ste. 1150
Irvine, CA 92612
(949)476-2204
Fax: (949)752-0223
Website: http://www.ventanaglobal.com

Integrated Consortium Inc.
50 Ridgecrest Rd.
Kentfield, CA 94904
(415)925-0386
Fax: (415)461-2726

Enterprise Partners
979 Ivanhoe Ave., Ste. 550
La Jolla, CA 92037
(858)454-8833
Fax: (858)454-2489
Website: http://www.epvc.com

Domain Associates
28202 Cabot Rd., Ste. 200
Laguna Niguel, CA 92677
(949)347-2446
Fax: (949)347-9720
Website: http://www.domainvc.com

Cascade Communications Ventures
60 E. Sir Francis Drake Blvd., Ste. 300
Larkspur, CA 94939
(415)925-6500
Fax: (415)925-6501

Allegis Capital
One First St., Ste. Two
Los Altos, CA 94022
(650)917-5900
Fax: (650)917-5901
Website: http://www.allegiscapital.com

Aspen Ventures
1000 Fremont Ave., Ste. 200
Los Altos, CA 94024
(650)917-5670
Fax: (650)917-5677
Website: http://www.aspenventures.com

AVI Capital L.P.
1 First St., Ste. 2
Los Altos, CA 94022

(650)949-9862
Fax: (650)949-8510
Website: http://www.avicapital.com

Bastion Capital Corp.
1999 Avenue of the Stars, Ste. 2960
Los Angeles, CA 90067
(310)788-5700
Fax: (310)277-7582
E-mail: ga@bastioncapital.com
Website: http://www.bastioncapital.com

Davis Group
PO Box 69953
Los Angeles, CA 90069-0953
(310)659-6327
Fax: (310)659-6337

Developers Equity Corp.
1880 Century Park East, Ste. 211
Los Angeles, CA 90067
(213)277-0300

Far East Capital Corp.
350 S. Grand Ave., Ste. 4100
Los Angeles, CA 90071
(213)687-1361
Fax: (213)617-7939
E-mail: free@fareastnationalbank.com

Kline Hawkes & Co.
11726 San Vicente Blvd., Ste. 300
Los Angeles, CA 90049
(310)442-4700
Fax: (310)442-4707
Website: http://www.klinehawkes.com

Lawrence Financial Group
701 Teakwood
PO Box 491773
Los Angeles, CA 90049
(310)471-4060
Fax: (310)472-3155

Riordan Lewis & Haden
300 S. Grand Ave., 29th Fl.
Los Angeles, CA 90071
(213)229-8500
Fax: (213)229-8597

Union Venture Corp.
445 S. Figueroa St., 9th Fl.
Los Angeles, CA 90071
(213)236-4092
Fax: (213)236-6329

Wedbush Capital Partners
1000 Wilshire Blvd.
Los Angeles, CA 90017
(213)688-4545
Fax: (213)688-6642
Website: http://www.wedbush.com

Advent International Corp.
2180 Sand Hill Rd., Ste. 420
Menlo Park, CA 94025
(650)233-7500
Fax: (650)233-7515
Website: http://www.adventinter
national.com

Altos Ventures
2882 Sand Hill Rd., Ste. 100
Menlo Park, CA 94025
(650)234-9771
Fax: (650)233-9821
Website: http://www.altosvc.com

Applied Technology
1010 El Camino Real, Ste. 300
Menlo Park, CA 94025
(415)326-8622
Fax: (415)326-8163

APV Technology Partners
535 Middlefield, Ste. 150
Menlo Park, CA 94025
(650)327-7871
Fax: (650)327-7631
Website: http://www.apvtp.com

August Capital Management
2480 Sand Hill Rd., Ste. 101
Menlo Park, CA 94025
(650)234-9900
Fax: (650)234-9910
Website: http://www.augustcap.com

Baccharis Capital Inc.
2420 Sand Hill Rd., Ste. 100
Menlo Park, CA 94025
(650)324-6844
Fax: (650)854-3025

Benchmark Capital
2480 Sand Hill Rd., Ste. 200
Menlo Park, CA 94025
(650)854-8180
Fax: (650)854-8183
E-mail: info@benchmark.com
Website: http://www.benchmark.com

Bessemer Venture Partners (Menlo Park)
535 Middlefield Rd., Ste. 245
Menlo Park, CA 94025
(650)853-7000
Fax: (650)853-7001
Website: http://www.bvp.com

The Cambria Group
1600 El Camino Real Rd., Ste. 155
Menlo Park, CA 94025
(650)329-8600

Fax: (650)329-8601
Website: http://www.cambriagroup.com

Canaan Partners
2884 Sand Hill Rd., Ste. 115
Menlo Park, CA 94025
(650)854-8092
Fax: (650)854-8127
Website: http://www.canaan.com

Capstone Ventures
3000 Sand Hill Rd., Bldg. One, Ste. 290
Menlo Park, CA 94025
(650)854-2523
Fax: (650)854-9010
Website: http://www.capstonevc.com

Comdisco Venture Group (Silicon Valley)
3000 Sand Hill Rd., Bldg. 1, Ste. 155
Menlo Park, CA 94025
(650)854-9484
Fax: (650)854-4026

Commtech International
535 Middlefield Rd., Ste. 200
Menlo Park, CA 94025
(650)328-0190
Fax: (650)328-6442

Compass Technology Partners
1550 El Camino Real, Ste. 275
Menlo Park, CA 94025-4111
(650)322-7595
Fax: (650)322-0588
Website: http://www.compass
techpartners.com

Convergence Partners
3000 Sand Hill Rd., Ste. 235
Menlo Park, CA 94025
(650)854-3010
Fax: (650)854-3015
Website: http://www.conver
gencepartners.com

The Dakota Group
PO Box 1025
Menlo Park, CA 94025
(650)853-0600
Fax: (650)851-4899
E-mail: info@dakota.com

Delphi Ventures
3000 Sand Hill Rd.
Bldg. One, Ste. 135
Menlo Park, CA 94025
(650)854-9650
Fax: (650)854-2961
Website: http://www.delphiventures.com

El Dorado Ventures
2884 Sand Hill Rd., Ste. 121
Menlo Park, CA 94025
(650)854-1200
Fax: (650)854-1202
Website: http://www.eldorado
ventures.com

Glynn Ventures
3000 Sand Hill Rd., Bldg. 4, Ste. 235
Menlo Park, CA 94025
(650)854-2215

Indosuez Ventures
2180 Sand Hill Rd., Ste. 450
Menlo Park, CA 94025
(650)854-0587
Fax: (650)323-5561
Website: http://www.indosuez
ventures.com

Institutional Venture Partners
3000 Sand Hill Rd., Bldg. 2, Ste. 290
Menlo Park, CA 94025
(650)854-0132
Fax: (650)854-5762
Website: http://www.ivp.com

Interwest Partners (Menlo Park)
3000 Sand Hill Rd., Bldg. 3, Ste. 255
Menlo Park, CA 94025-7112
(650)854-8585
Fax: (650)854-4706
Website: http://www.interwest.com

Kleiner Perkins Caufield & Byers (Menlo Park)
2750 Sand Hill Rd.
Menlo Park, CA 94025
(650)233-2750
Fax: (650)233-0300
Website: http://www.kpcb.com

Magic Venture Capital LLC
1010 El Camino Real, Ste. 300
Menlo Park, CA 94025
(650)325-4149

Matrix Partners
2500 Sand Hill Rd., Ste. 113
Menlo Park, CA 94025
(650)854-3131
Fax: (650)854-3296
Website: http://www.matrixpartners.com

Mayfield Fund
2800 Sand Hill Rd.
Menlo Park, CA 94025
(650)854-5560
Fax: (650)854-5712
Website: http://www.mayfield.com

McCown De Leeuw and Co. (Menlo Park)
3000 Sand Hill Rd., Bldg. 3, Ste. 290
Menlo Park, CA 94025-7111
(650)854-6000
Fax: (650)854-0853
Website: http://www.mdcpartners.com

Menlo Ventures
3000 Sand Hill Rd., Bldg. 4, Ste. 100
Menlo Park, CA 94025
(650)854-8540
Fax: (650)854-7059
Website: http://www.menloventures.com

Merrill Pickard Anderson & Eyre
2480 Sand Hill Rd., Ste. 200
Menlo Park, CA 94025
(650)854-8600
Fax: (650)854-0345

New Enterprise Associates (Menlo Park)
2490 Sand Hill Rd.
Menlo Park, CA 94025
(650)854-9499
Fax: (650)854-9397
Website: http://www.nea.com

Onset Ventures
2400 Sand Hill Rd., Ste. 150
Menlo Park, CA 94025
(650)529-0700
Fax: (650)529-0777
Website: http://www.onset.com

Paragon Venture Partners
3000 Sand Hill Rd., Bldg. 1, Ste. 275
Menlo Park, CA 94025
(650)854-8000
Fax: (650)854-7260

Pathfinder Venture Capital Funds (Menlo Park)
3000 Sand Hill Rd., Bldg. 3, Ste. 255
Menlo Park, CA 94025
(650)854-0650
Fax: (650)854-4706

Rocket Ventures
3000 Sandhill Rd., Bldg. 1, Ste. 170
Menlo Park, CA 94025
(650)561-9100
Fax: (650)561-9183
Website: http://www.rocketventures.com

Sequoia Capital
3000 Sand Hill Rd., Bldg. 4, Ste. 280
Menlo Park, CA 94025
(650)854-3927
Fax: (650)854-2977

E-mail: sequoia@sequoiacap.com
Website: http://www.sequoiacap.com

Sierra Ventures
3000 Sand Hill Rd., Bldg. 4, Ste. 210
Menlo Park, CA 94025
(650)854-1000
Fax: (650)854-5593
Website: http://www.sierraventures.com

Sigma Partners
2884 Sand Hill Rd., Ste. 121
Menlo Park, CA 94025-7022
(650)853-1700
Fax: (650)853-1717
E-mail: info@sigmapartners.com
Website: http://www.sigmapartners.com

Sprout Group (Menlo Park)
3000 Sand Hill Rd.
Bldg. 3, Ste. 170
Menlo Park, CA 94025
(650)234-2700
Fax: (650)234-2779
Website: http://www.sproutgroup.com

TA Associates (Menlo Park)
70 Willow Rd., Ste. 100
Menlo Park, CA 94025
(650)328-1210
Fax: (650)326-4933
Website: http://www.ta.com

Thompson Clive & Partners Ltd.
3000 Sand Hill Rd., Bldg. 1, Ste. 185
Menlo Park, CA 94025-7102
(650)854-0314
Fax: (650)854-0670
E-mail: mail@tcvc.com
Website: http://www.tcvc.com

Trinity Ventures Ltd.
3000 Sand Hill Rd., Bldg. 1, Ste. 240
Menlo Park, CA 94025
(650)854-9500
Fax: (650)854-9501
Website: http://www.trinityventures.com

U.S. Venture Partners
2180 Sand Hill Rd., Ste. 300
Menlo Park, CA 94025
(650)854-9080
Fax: (650)854-3018
Website: http://www.usvp.com

USVP-Schlein Marketing Fund
2180 Sand Hill Rd., Ste. 300
Menlo Park, CA 94025
(415)854-9080
Fax: (415)854-3018
Website: http://www.usvp.com

Venrock Associates
2494 Sand Hill Rd., Ste. 200
Menlo Park, CA 94025
(650)561-9580
Fax: (650)561-9180
Website: http://www.venrock.com

Brad Peery Capital Inc.
145 Chapel Pkwy.
Mill Valley, CA 94941
(415)389-0625
Fax: (415)389-1336

Dot Edu Ventures
650 Castro St., Ste. 270
Mountain View, CA 94041
(650)575-5638
Fax: (650)325-5247
Website: http://www.dotedu
ventures.com

Forrest, Binkley & Brown
840 Newport Ctr. Dr., Ste. 480
Newport Beach, CA 92660
(949)729-3222
Fax: (949)729-3226
Website: http://www.fbbvc.com

Marwit Capital LLC
180 Newport Center Dr., Ste. 200
Newport Beach, CA 92660
(949)640-6234
Fax: (949)720-8077
Website: http://www.marwit.com

Kaiser Permanente / National Venture Development
1800 Harrison St., 22nd Fl.
Oakland, CA 94612
(510)267-4010
Fax: (510)267-4036
Website: http://www.kpventures.com

Nu Capital Access Group, Ltd.
7677 Oakport St., Ste. 105
Oakland, CA 94621
(510)635-7345
Fax: (510)635-7068

Inman and Bowman
4 Orinda Way, Bldg. D, Ste. 150
Orinda, CA 94563
(510)253-1611
Fax: (510)253-9037

Accel Partners (San Francisco)
428 University Ave.
Palo Alto, CA 94301
(650)614-4800
Fax: (650)614-4880
Website: http://www.accel.com

Advanced Technology Ventures
485 Ramona St., Ste. 200
Palo Alto, CA 94301
(650)321-8601
Fax: (650)321-0934
Website: http://www.atvcapital.com

Anila Fund
400 Channing Ave.
Palo Alto, CA 94301
(650)833-5790
Fax: (650)833-0590
Website: http://www.anila.com

Asset Management Company Venture Capital
2275 E. Bayshore, Ste. 150
Palo Alto, CA 94303
(650)494-7400
Fax: (650)856-1826
E-mail: postmaster@assetman.com
Website: http://www.assetman.com

BancBoston Capital / BancBoston Ventures
435 Tasso St., Ste. 250
Palo Alto, CA 94305
(650)470-4100
Fax: (650)853-1425
Website: http://www.bancboston
capital.com

Charter Ventures
525 University Ave., Ste. 1400
Palo Alto, CA 94301
(650)325-6953
Fax: (650)325-4762
Website: http://www.charterventures.com

Communications Ventures
505 Hamilton Avenue, Ste. 305
Palo Alto, CA 94301
(650)325-9600
Fax: (650)325-9608
Website: http://www.comven.com

HMS Group
2468 Embarcadero Way
Palo Alto, CA 94303-3313
(650)856-9862
Fax: (650)856-9864

Jafco America Ventures, Inc.
505 Hamilton Ste. 310
Palto Alto, CA 94301
(650)463-8800
Fax: (650)463-8801
Website: http://www.jafco.com

New Vista Capital
540 Cowper St., Ste. 200

Palo Alto, CA 94301
(650)329-9333
Fax: (650)328-9434
E-mail: fgreene@nvcap.com
Website: http://www.nvcap.com

Norwest Equity Partners (Palo Alto)
245 Lytton Ave., Ste. 250
Palo Alto, CA 94301-1426
(650)321-8000
Fax: (650)321-8010
Website: http://www.norwestvp.com

Oak Investment Partners
525 University Ave., Ste. 1300
Palo Alto, CA 94301
(650)614-3700
Fax: (650)328-6345
Website: http://www.oakinv.com

Patricof & Co. Ventures, Inc. (Palo Alto)
2100 Geng Rd., Ste. 150
Palo Alto, CA 94303
(650)494-9944
Fax: (650)494-6751
Website: http://www.patricof.com

RWI Group
835 Page Mill Rd.
Palo Alto, CA 94304
(650)251-1800
Fax: (650)213-8660
Website: http://www.rwigroup.com

Summit Partners (Palo Alto)
499 Hamilton Ave., Ste. 200
Palo Alto, CA 94301
(650)321-1166
Fax: (650)321-1188
Website: http://www.summit
partners.com

Sutter Hill Ventures
755 Page Mill Rd., Ste. A-200
Palo Alto, CA 94304
(650)493-5600
Fax: (650)858-1854
E-mail: shv@shv.com

Vanguard Venture Partners
525 University Ave., Ste. 600
Palo Alto, CA 94301
(650)321-2900
Fax: (650)321-2902
Website: http://www.vanguard
ventures.com

Venture Growth Associates
2479 East Bayshore St., Ste. 710
Palo Alto, CA 94303

(650)855-9100
Fax: (650)855-9104

Worldview Technology Partners
435 Tasso St., Ste. 120
Palo Alto, CA 94301
(650)322-3800
Fax: (650)322-3880
Website: http://www.worldview.com

Draper, Fisher, Jurvetson / Draper Associates
400 Seaport Ct., Ste.250
Redwood City, CA 94063
(415)599-9000
Fax: (415)599-9726
Website: http://www.dfj.com

Gabriel Venture Partners
350 Marine Pkwy., Ste. 200
Redwood Shores, CA 94065
(650)551-5000
Fax: (650)551-5001
Website: http://www.gabrielvp.com

Hallador Venture Partners, L.L.C.
740 University Ave., Ste. 110
Sacramento, CA 95825-6710
(916)920-0191
Fax: (916)920-5188
E-mail: chris@hallador.com

Emerald Venture Group
12396 World Trade Dr., Ste. 116
San Diego, CA 92128
(858)451-1001
Fax: (858)451-1003
Website: http://www.emerald
venture.com

Forward Ventures
9255 Towne Centre Dr.
San Diego, CA 92121
(858)677-6077
Fax: (858)452-8799
E-mail: info@forwardventure.com
Website: http://www.forward
venture.com

Idanta Partners Ltd.
4660 La Jolla Village Dr., Ste. 850
San Diego, CA 92122
(619)452-9690
Fax: (619)452-2013
Website: http://www.idanta.com

Kingsbury Associates
3655 Nobel Dr., Ste. 490
San Diego, CA 92122
(858)677-0600
Fax: (858)677-0800

Kyocera International Inc.
Corporate Development
8611 Balboa Ave.
San Diego, CA 92123
(858)576-2600
Fax: (858)492-1456

Sorrento Associates, Inc.
4370 LaJolla Village Dr., Ste. 1040
San Diego, CA 92122
(619)452-3100
Fax: (619)452-7607
Website: http://www.sorrento
ventures.com

Western States Investment Group
9191 Towne Ctr. Dr., Ste. 310
San Diego, CA 92122
(619)678-0800
Fax: (619)678-0900

Aberdare Ventures
One Embarcadero Center, Ste. 4000
San Francisco, CA 94111
(415)392-7442
Fax: (415)392-4264
Website: http://www.aberdare.com

Acacia Venture Partners
101 California St., Ste. 3160
San Francisco, CA 94111
(415)433-4200
Fax: (415)433-4250
Website: http://www.acaciavp.com

Access Venture Partners
319 Laidley St.
San Francisco, CA 94131
(415)586-0132
Fax: (415)392-6310
Website: http://www.access
venturepartners.com

Alta Partners
One Embarcadero Center, Ste. 4050
San Francisco, CA 94111
(415)362-4022
Fax: (415)362-6178
E-mail: alta@altapartners.com
Website: http://www.altapartners.com

Bangert Dawes Reade Davis & Thom
220 Montgomery St., Ste. 424
San Francisco, CA 94104
(415)954-9900
Fax: (415)954-9901
E-mail: bdrdt@pacbell.net

Berkeley International Capital Corp.
650 California St., Ste. 2800
San Francisco, CA 94108-2609

(415)249-0450
Fax: (415)392-3929
Website: http://www.berkeleyvc.com

Blueprint Ventures LLC
456 Montgomery St., 22nd Fl.
San Francisco, CA 94104
(415)901-4000
Fax: (415)901-4035
Website: http://www.blue
printventures.com

Blumberg Capital Ventures
580 Howard St., Ste. 401
San Francisco, CA 94105
(415)905-5007
Fax: (415)357-5027
Website: http://www.blumberg-
capital.com

Burr, Egan, Deleage, and Co. (San Francisco)
1 Embarcadero Center, Ste. 4050
San Francisco, CA 94111
(415)362-4022
Fax: (415)362-6178

Burrill & Company
120 Montgomery St., Ste. 1370
San Francisco, CA 94104
(415)743-3160
Fax: (415)743-3161
Website: http://www.burrillandco.com

CMEA Ventures
235 Montgomery St., Ste. 920
San Francisco, CA 94401
(415)352-1520
Fax: (415)352-1524
Website: http://www.cmeaventures.com

Crocker Capital
1 Post St., Ste. 2500
San Francisco, CA 94101
(415)956-5250
Fax: (415)959-5710

Dominion Ventures, Inc.
44 Montgomery St., Ste. 4200
San Francisco, CA 94104
(415)362-4890
Fax: (415)394-9245

Dorset Capital
Pier 1
Bay 2
San Francisco, CA 94111
(415)398-7101
Fax: (415)398-7141
Website: http://www.dorsetcapital.com

Gatx Capital
Four Embarcadero Center, Ste. 2200
San Francisco, CA 94904
(415)955-3200
Fax: (415)955-3449

IMinds
135 Main St., Ste. 1350
San Francisco, CA 94105
(415)547-0000
Fax: (415)227-0300
Website: http://www.iminds.com

LF International Inc.
360 Post St., Ste. 705
San Francisco, CA 94108
(415)399-0110
Fax: (415)399-9222
Website: http://www.lfvc.com

Newbury Ventures
535 Pacific Ave., 2nd Fl.
San Francisco, CA 94133
(415)296-7408
Fax: (415)296-7416
Website: http://www.newburyven.com

Quest Ventures (San Francisco)
333 Bush St., Ste. 1750
San Francisco, CA 94104
(415)782-1414
Fax: (415)782-1415

Robertson-Stephens Co.
555 California St., Ste. 2600
San Francisco, CA 94104
(415)781-9700
Fax: (415)781-2556
Website: http://www.omegaad
ventures.com

Rosewood Capital, L.P.
One Maritime Plaza, Ste. 1330
San Francisco, CA 94111-3503
(415)362-5526
Fax: (415)362-1192
Website: http://www.rosewoodvc.com

Ticonderoga Capital Inc.
555 California St., No. 4950
San Francisco, CA 94104
(415)296-7900
Fax: (415)296-8956

21st Century Internet Venture Partners
Two South Park
2nd Floor
San Francisco, CA 94107
(415)512-1221
Fax: (415)512-2650
Website: http://www.21vc.com

VK Ventures
600 California St., Ste.1700
San Francisco, CA 94111
(415)391-5600
Fax: (415)397-2744

Walden Group of Venture Capital Funds
750 Battery St., Seventh Floor
San Francisco, CA 94111
(415)391-7225
Fax: (415)391-7262

Acer Technology Ventures
2641 Orchard Pkwy.
San Jose, CA 95134
(408)433-4945
Fax: (408)433-5230

Authosis
226 Airport Pkwy., Ste. 405
San Jose, CA 95110
(650)814-3603
Website: http://www.authosis.com

Western Technology Investment
2010 N. First St., Ste. 310
San Jose, CA 95131
(408)436-8577
Fax: (408)436-8625
E-mail: mktg@westerntech.com

Drysdale Enterprises
177 Bovet Rd., Ste. 600
San Mateo, CA 94402
(650)341-6336
Fax: (650)341-1329
E-mail: drysdale@aol.com

Greylock
2929 Campus Dr., Ste. 400
San Mateo, CA 94401
(650)493-5525
Fax: (650)493-5575
Website: http://www.greylock.com

Technology Funding
2000 Alameda de las Pulgas, Ste. 250
San Mateo, CA 94403
(415)345-2200
Fax: (415)345-1797

2M Invest Inc.
1875 S. Grant St.
Suite 750
San Mateo, CA 94402
(650)655-3765
Fax: (650)372-9107
E-mail: 2minfo@2minvest.com
Website: http://www.2minvest.com

Phoenix Growth Capital Corp.
2401 Kerner Blvd.
San Rafael, CA 94901
(415)485-4569
Fax: (415)485-4663

NextGen Partners LLC
1705 East Valley Rd.
Santa Barbara, CA 93108
(805)969-8540
Fax: (805)969-8542
Website: http://www.nextgen
partners.com

Denali Venture Capital
1925 Woodland Ave.
Santa Clara, CA 95050
(408)690-4838
Fax: (408)247-6979
E-mail: wael@denaliventurecapital.com
Website: http://www.denali
venturecapital.com

Dotcom Ventures LP
3945 Freedom Circle, Ste. 740
Santa Clara, CA 95045
(408)919-9855
Fax: (408)919-9857
Website: http://www.dotcom
venturesatl.com

Silicon Valley Bank
3003 Tasman
Santa Clara, CA 95054
(408)654-7400
Fax: (408)727-8728

Al Shugart International
920 41st Ave.
Santa Cruz, CA 95062
(831)479-7852
Fax: (831)479-7852
Website: http://www.alshugart.com

Leonard Mautner Associates
1434 Sixth St.
Santa Monica, CA 90401
(213)393-9788
Fax: (310)459-9918

Palomar Ventures
100 Wilshire Blvd., Ste. 450
Santa Monica, CA 90401
(310)260-6050
Fax: (310)656-4150
Website: http://www.palomar
ventures.com

Medicus Venture Partners
12930 Saratoga Ave., Ste. D8
Saratoga, CA 95070

(408)447-8600
Fax: (408)447-8599
Website: http://www.medicusvc.com

Redleaf Venture Management
14395 Saratoga Ave., Ste. 130
Saratoga, CA 95070
(408)868-0800
Fax: (408)868-0810
E-mail: nancy@redleaf.com
Website: http://www.redleaf.com

Artemis Ventures
207 Second St., Ste. E
3rd Fl.
Sausalito, CA 94965
(415)289-2500
Fax: (415)289-1789
Website: http://www.artemisventures.com

Deucalion Venture Partners
19501 Brooklime
Sonoma, CA 95476
(707)938-4974
Fax: (707)938-8921

Windward Ventures
PO Box 7688
Thousand Oaks, CA 91359-7688
(805)497-3332
Fax: (805)497-9331

National Investment Management, Inc.
2601 Airport Dr., Ste.210
Torrance, CA 90505
(310)784-7600
Fax: (310)784-7605

Southern California Ventures
406 Amapola Ave. Ste. 125
Torrance, CA 90501
(310)787-4381
Fax: (310)787-4382

Sandton Financial Group
21550 Oxnard St., Ste. 300
Woodland Hills, CA 91367
(818)702-9283

Woodside Fund
850 Woodside Dr.
Woodside, CA 94062
(650)368-5545
Fax: (650)368-2416
Website: http://www.woodsidefund.com

Colorado

Colorado Venture Management
Ste. 300
Boulder, CO 80301

(303)440-4055
Fax: (303)440-4636

Dean & Associates
4362 Apple Way
Boulder, CO 80301
Fax: (303)473-9900

Roser Ventures LLC
1105 Spruce St.
Boulder, CO 80302
(303)443-6436
Fax: (303)443-1885
Website: http://www.roserventures.com

Sequel Venture Partners
4430 Arapahoe Ave., Ste. 220
Boulder, CO 80303
(303)546-0400
Fax: (303)546-9728
E-mail: tom@sequelvc.com
Website: http://www.sequelvc.com

New Venture Resources
445C E. Cheyenne Mtn. Blvd.
Colorado Springs, CO 80906-4570
(719)598-9272
Fax: (719)598-9272

The Centennial Funds
1428 15th St.
Denver, CO 80202-1318
(303)405-7500
Fax: (303)405-7575
Website: http://www.centennial.com

Rocky Mountain Capital Partners
1125 17th St., Ste. 2260
Denver, CO 80202
(303)291-5200
Fax: (303)291-5327

Sandlot Capital LLC
600 South Cherry St., Ste. 525
Denver, CO 80246
(303)893-3400
Fax: (303)893-3403
Website: http://www.sandlotcapital.com

Wolf Ventures
50 South Steele St., Ste. 777
Denver, CO 80209
(303)321-4800
Fax: (303)321-4848
E-mail: businessplan@wolf
ventures.com
Website: http://www.wolfventures.com

The Columbine Venture Funds
5460 S. Quebec St., Ste. 270
Englewood, CO 80111

(303)694-3222
Fax: (303)694-9007

Investment Securities of Colorado, Inc.
4605 Denice Dr.
Englewood, CO 80111
(303)796-9192

Kinship Partners
6300 S. Syracuse Way, Ste. 484
Englewood, CO 80111
(303)694-0268
Fax: (303)694-1707
E-mail: block@vailsys.com

Boranco Management, L.L.C.
1528 Hillside Dr.
Fort Collins, CO 80524-1969
(970)221-2297
Fax: (970)221-4787

Aweida Ventures
890 West Cherry St., Ste. 220
Louisville, CO 80027
(303)664-9520
Fax: (303)664-9530
Website: http://www.aweida.com

Access Venture Partners
8787 Turnpike Dr., Ste. 260
Westminster, CO 80030
(303)426-8899
Fax: (303)426-8828

Medmax Ventures LP
1 Northwestern Dr., Ste. 203
Bloomfield, CT 06002
(860)286-2960
Fax: (860)286-9960

James B. Kobak & Co.
Four Mansfield Place
Darien, CT 06820
(203)656-3471
Fax: (203)655-2905

Orien Ventures
1 Post Rd.
Fairfield, CT 06430
(203)259-9933
Fax: (203)259-5288

ABP Acquisition Corporation
115 Maple Ave.
Greenwich, CT 06830
(203)625-8287
Fax: (203)447-6187

Catterton Partners
9 Greenwich Office Park
Greenwich, CT 06830
(203)629-4901

Organizations, Agencies, & Consultants

Fax: (203)629-4903
Website: http://www.cpequity.com

Consumer Venture Partners
3 Pickwick Plz.
Greenwich, CT 06830
(203)629-8800
Fax: (203)629-2019

Insurance Venture Partners
31 Brookside Dr., Ste. 211
Greenwich, CT 06830
(203)861-0030
Fax: (203)861-2745

The NTC Group
Three Pickwick Plaza
Ste. 200
Greenwich, CT 06830
(203)862-2800
Fax: (203)622-6538

Regulus International Capital Co., Inc.
140 Greenwich Ave.
Greenwich, CT 06830
(203)625-9700
Fax: (203)625-9706

Axiom Venture Partners
City Place II
185 Asylum St., 17th Fl.
Hartford, CT 06103
(860)548-7799
Fax: (860)548-7797
Website: http://www.axiomventures.com

Conning Capital Partners
City Place II
185 Asylum St.
Hartford, CT 06103-4105
(860)520-1289
Fax: (860)520-1299
E-mail: pe@conning.com
Website: http://www.conning.com

First New England Capital L.P.
100 Pearl St.
Hartford, CT 06103
(860)293-3333
Fax: (860)293-3338
E-mail: info@firstnewenglandcapital.com
Website: http://www.firstnewengland
capital.com

Northeast Ventures
One State St., Ste. 1720
Hartford, CT 06103
(860)547-1414
Fax: (860)246-8755

Windward Holdings
38 Sylvan Rd.
Madison, CT 06443
(203)245-6870
Fax: (203)245-6865

Advanced Materials Partners, Inc.
45 Pine St.
PO Box 1022
New Canaan, CT 06840
(203)966-6415
Fax: (203)966-8448
E-mail: wkb@amplink.com

RFE Investment Partners
36 Grove St.
New Canaan, CT 06840
(203)966-2800
Fax: (203)966-3109
Website: http://www.rfeip.com

Connecticut Innovations, Inc.
999 West St.
Rocky Hill, CT 06067
(860)563-5851
Fax: (860)563-4877
E-mail: pamela.hartley@ctin
novations.com
Website: http://www.ctinnovations.com

Canaan Partners
105 Rowayton Ave.
Rowayton, CT 06853
(203)855-0400
Fax: (203)854-9117
Website: http://www.canaan.com

Landmark Partners, Inc.
10 Mill Pond Ln.
Simsbury, CT 06070
(860)651-9760
Fax: (860)651-8890
Website: http://
www.landmarkpartners.com

Sweeney & Company
PO Box 567
Southport, CT 06490
(203)255-0220
Fax: (203)255-0220
E-mail: sweeney@connix.com

Baxter Associates, Inc.
PO Box 1333
Stamford, CT 06904
(203)323-3143
Fax: (203)348-0622

Beacon Partners Inc.
6 Landmark Sq., 4th Fl.
Stamford, CT 06901-2792

(203)359-5776
Fax: (203)359-5876

Collinson, Howe, and Lennox, LLC
1055 Washington Blvd., 5th Fl.
Stamford, CT 06901
(203)324-7700
Fax: (203)324-3636
E-mail: info@chlmedical.com
Website: http://www.chlmedical.com

Prime Capital Management Co.
550 West Ave.
Stamford, CT 06902
(203)964-0642
Fax: (203)964-0862

Saugatuck Capital Co.
1 Canterbury Green
Stamford, CT 06901
(203)348-6669
Fax: (203)324-6995
Website: http://www.sauga
tuckcapital.com

Soundview Financial Group Inc.
22 Gatehouse Rd.
Stamford, CT 06902
(203)462-7200
Fax: (203)462-7350
Website: http://www.sndv.com

TSG Ventures, L.L.C.
177 Broad St., 12th Fl.
Stamford, CT 06901
(203)406-1500
Fax: (203)406-1590

Whitney & Company
177 Broad St.
Stamford, CT 06901
(203)973-1400
Fax: (203)973-1422
Website: http://www.jhwhitney.com

Cullinane & Donnelly Venture Partners L.P.
970 Farmington Ave.
West Hartford, CT 06107
(860)521-7811

The Crestview Investment and Financial Group
431 Post Rd. E, Ste. 1
Westport, CT 06880-4403
(203)222-0333
Fax: (203)222-0000

Marketcorp Venture Associates, L.P. (MCV)
274 Riverside Ave.
Westport, CT 06880

(203)222-3030
Fax: (203)222-3033

Oak Investment Partners (Westport)
1 Gorham Island
Westport, CT 06880
(203)226-8346
Fax: (203)227-0372
Website: http://www.oakinv.com

Oxford Bioscience Partners
315 Post Rd. W
Westport, CT 06880-5200
(203)341-3300
Fax: (203)341-3309
Website: http://www.oxbio.com

Prince Ventures (Westport)
25 Ford Rd.
Westport, CT 06880
(203)227-8332
Fax: (203)226-5302

LTI Venture Leasing Corp.
221 Danbury Rd.
Wilton, CT 06897
(203)563-1100
Fax: (203)563-1111
Website: http://www.ltileasing.com

Delaware

Blue Rock Capital
5803 Kennett Pike, Ste. A
Wilmington, DE 19807
(302)426-0981
Fax: (302)426-0982
Website: http://www.bluerockcapital.com

District of Columbia

Allied Capital Corp.
1919 Pennsylvania Ave. NW
Washington, DC 20006-3434
(202)331-2444
Fax: (202)659-2053
Website: http://www.alliedcapital.com

Atlantic Coastal Ventures, L.P.
3101 South St. NW
Washington, DC 20007
(202)293-1166
Fax: (202)293-1181
Website: http://www.atlanticcv.com

Columbia Capital Group, Inc.
1660 L St. NW, Ste. 308
Washington, DC 20036
(202)775-8815
Fax: (202)223-0544

Core Capital Partners
901 15th St., NW
9th Fl.
Washington, DC 20005
(202)589-0090
Fax: (202)589-0091
Website: http://www.core-capital.com

Next Point Partners
701 Pennsylvania Ave. NW, Ste. 900
Washington, DC 20004
(202)661-8703
Fax: (202)434-7400
E-mail: mf@nextpoint.vc
Website: http://www.nextpointvc.com

Telecommunications Development Fund
2020 K. St. NW
Ste. 375
Washington, DC 20006
(202)293-8840
Fax: (202)293-8850
Website: http://www.tdfund.com

Wachtel & Co., Inc.
1101 4th St. NW
Washington, DC 20005-5680
(202)898-1144

Winslow Partners LLC
1300 Connecticut Ave. NW
Washington, DC 20036-1703
(202)530-5000
Fax: (202)530-5010
E-mail: winslow@winslowpartners.com

Women's Growth Capital Fund
1054 31st St., NW
Ste. 110
Washington, DC 20007
(202)342-1431
Fax: (202)341-1203
Website: http://www.wgcf.com

Sigma Capital Corp.
22668 Caravelle Circle
Boca Raton, FL 33433
(561)368-9783

North American Business Development Co., L.L.C.
111 East Las Olas Blvd.
Ft. Lauderdale, FL 33301
(305)463-0681
Fax: (305)527-0904
Website: http://
www.northamericanfund.com

Chartwell Capital Management Co. Inc.
1 Independent Dr., Ste. 3120

Jacksonville, FL 32202
(904)355-3519
Fax: (904)353-5833
E-mail: info@chartwellcap.com

CEO Advisors
1061 Maitland Center Commons
Ste. 209
Maitland, FL 32751
(407)660-9327
Fax: (407)660-2109

Henry & Co.
8201 Peters Rd., Ste. 1000
Plantation, FL 33324
(954)797-7400

Avery Business Development Services
2506 St. Michel Ct.
Ponte Vedra, FL 32082
(904)285-6033

New South Ventures
5053 Ocean Blvd.
Sarasota, FL 34242
(941)358-6000
Fax: (941)358-6078
Website: http://www.newsouth
ventures.com

Venture Capital Management Corp.
PO Box 2626
Satellite Beach, FL 32937
(407)777-1969

Florida Capital Venture Ltd.
325 Florida Bank Plaza
100 W. Kennedy Blvd.
Tampa, FL 33602
(813)229-2294
Fax: (813)229-2028

Quantum Capital Partners
339 South Plant Ave.
Tampa, FL 33606
(813)250-1999
Fax: (813)250-1998
Website: http://www.quantum
capitalpartners.com

South Atlantic Venture Fund
614 W. Bay St.
Tampa, FL 33606-2704
(813)253-2500
Fax: (813)253-2360
E-mail: venture@southatlantic.com
Website: http://www.southatlantic.com

LM Capital Corp.
120 S. Olive, Ste. 400
West Palm Beach, FL 33401

(561)833-9700
Fax: (561)655-6587
Website: http://www.lmcapital
securities.com

Georgia

Venture First Associates
4811 Thornwood Dr.
Acworth, GA 30102
(770)928-3733
Fax: (770)928-6455

Alliance Technology Ventures
8995 Westside Pkwy., Ste. 200
Alpharetta, GA 30004
(678)336-2000
Fax: (678)336-2001
E-mail: info@atv.com
Website: http://www.atv.com

Cordova Ventures
2500 North Winds Pkwy., Ste. 475
Alpharetta, GA 30004
(678)942-0300
Fax: (678)942-0301
Website: http://www.cordovaventures.
com

Advanced Technology Development Fund
1000 Abernathy, Ste. 1420
Atlanta, GA 30328-5614
(404)668-2333
Fax: (404)668-2333

CGW Southeast Partners
12 Piedmont Center, Ste. 210
Atlanta, GA 30305
(404)816-3255
Fax: (404)816-3258
Website: http://www.cgwlp.com

Cyberstarts
1900 Emery St., NW
3rd Fl.
Atlanta, GA 30318
(404)267-5000
Fax: (404)267-5200
Website: http://www.cyberstarts.com

EGL Holdings, Inc.
10 Piedmont Center, Ste. 412
Atlanta, GA 30305
(404)949-8300
Fax: (404)949-8311

Equity South
1790 The Lenox Bldg.
3399 Peachtree Rd. NE
Atlanta, GA 30326

(404)237-6222
Fax: (404)261-1578

Five Paces
3400 Peachtree Rd., Ste. 200
Atlanta, GA 30326
(404)439-8300
Fax: (404)439-8301
Website: http://www.fivepaces.com

Frontline Capital, Inc.
3475 Lenox Rd., Ste. 400
Atlanta, GA 30326
(404)240-7280
Fax: (404)240-7281

Fuqua Ventures LLC
1201 W. Peachtree St. NW, Ste. 5000
Atlanta, GA 30309
(404)815-4500
Fax: (404)815-4528
Website: http://www.fuquaventures.com

Noro-Moseley Partners
4200 Northside Pkwy., Bldg. 9
Atlanta, GA 30327
(404)233-1966
Fax: (404)239-9280
Website: http://www.noro-moseley.com

Renaissance Capital Corp.
34 Peachtree St. NW, Ste. 2230
Atlanta, GA 30303
(404)658-9061
Fax: (404)658-9064

River Capital, Inc.
Two Midtown Plaza
1360 Peachtree St. NE, Ste. 1430
Atlanta, GA 30309
(404)873-2166
Fax: (404)873-2158

State Street Bank & Trust Co.
3414 Peachtree Rd. NE, Ste. 1010
Atlanta, GA 30326
(404)364-9500
Fax: (404)261-4469

UPS Strategic Enterprise Fund
55 Glenlake Pkwy. NE
Atlanta, GA 30328
(404)828-8814
Fax: (404)828-8088
E-mail: jcacyce@ups.com
Website: http://www.ups.com/sef/
sef_home

Wachovia
191 Peachtree St. NE, 26th Fl.
Atlanta, GA 30303

(404)332-1000
Fax: (404)332-1392
Website: http://www.wachovia.com/wca

Brainworks Ventures
4243 Dunwoody Club Dr.
Chamblee, GA 30341
(770)239-7447

First Growth Capital Inc.
Best Western Plaza, Ste. 105
PO Box 815
Forsyth, GA 31029
(912)781-7131

Financial Capital Resources, Inc.
21 Eastbrook Bend, Ste. 116
Peachtree City, GA 30269
(404)487-6650

Hawaii

HMS Hawaii Management Partners
Davies Pacific Center
841 Bishop St., Ste. 860
Honolulu, HI 96813
(808)545-3755
Fax: (808)531-2611

Idaho

Sun Valley Ventures
160 Second St.
Ketchum, ID 83340
(208)726-5005
Fax: (208)726-5094

Illinois

Open Prairie Ventures
115 N. Neil St., Ste. 209
Champaign, IL 61820
(217)351-7000
Fax: (217)351-7051
E-mail: inquire@openprairie.com
Website: http://www.openprairie.com

ABN AMRO Private Equity
208 S. La Salle St., 10th Fl.
Chicago, IL 60604
(312)855-7079
Fax: (312)553-6648
Website: http://www.abnequity.com

Alpha Capital Partners, Ltd.
122 S. Michigan Ave., Ste. 1700
Chicago, IL 60603
(312)322-9800
Fax: (312)322-9808
E-mail: acp@alphacapital.com

Ameritech Development Corp.
30 S. Wacker Dr., 37th Fl.
Chicago, IL 60606
(312)750-5083
Fax: (312)609-0244

Apex Investment Partners
225 W. Washington, Ste. 1450
Chicago, IL 60606
(312)857-2800
Fax: (312)857-1800
E-mail: apex@apexvc.com
Website: http://www.apexvc.com

Arch Venture Partners
8725 W. Higgins Rd., Ste. 290
Chicago, IL 60631
(773)380-6600
Fax: (773)380-6606
Website: http://www.archventure.com

The Bank Funds
208 South LaSalle St., Ste. 1680
Chicago, IL 60604
(312)855-6020
Fax: (312)855-8910

Batterson Venture Partners
303 W. Madison St., Ste. 1110
Chicago, IL 60606-3309
(312)269-0300
Fax: (312)269-0021
Website: http://www.battersonvp.com

William Blair Capital Partners, L.L.C.
222 W. Adams St., Ste. 1300
Chicago, IL 60606
(312)364-8250
Fax: (312)236-1042
E-mail: privateequity@wmblair.com
Website: http://www.wmblair.com

Bluestar Ventures
208 South LaSalle St., Ste. 1020
Chicago, IL 60604
(312)384-5000
Fax: (312)384-5005
Website: http://www.bluestarventures.com

The Capital Strategy Management Co.
233 S. Wacker Dr.
Box 06334
Chicago, IL 60606
(312)444-1170

DN Partners
77 West Wacker Dr., Ste. 4550
Chicago, IL 60601
(312)332-7960
Fax: (312)332-7979

Dresner Capital Inc.
29 South LaSalle St., Ste. 310
Chicago, IL 60603
(312)726-3600
Fax: (312)726-7448

Eblast Ventures LLC
11 South LaSalle St., 5th Fl.
Chicago, IL 60603
(312)372-2600
Fax: (312)372-5621
Website: http://www.eblastventures.com

Essex Woodlands Health Ventures, L.P.
190 S. LaSalle St., Ste. 2800
Chicago, IL 60603
(312)444-6040
Fax: (312)444-6034
Website: http://www.essexwoodlands.com

First Analysis Venture Capital
233 S. Wacker Dr., Ste. 9500
Chicago, IL 60606
(312)258-1400
Fax: (312)258-0334
Website: http://www.firstanalysis.com

Frontenac Co.
135 S. LaSalle St., Ste.3800
Chicago, IL 60603
(312)368-0044
Fax: (312)368-9520
Website: http://www.frontenac.com

GTCR Golder Rauner, LLC
6100 Sears Tower
Chicago, IL 60606
(312)382-2200
Fax: (312)382-2201
Website: http://www.gtcr.com

High Street Capital LLC
311 South Wacker Dr., Ste. 4550
Chicago, IL 60606
(312)697-4990
Fax: (312)697-4994
Website: http://www.highstr.com

IEG Venture Management, Inc.
70 West Madison
Chicago, IL 60602
(312)644-0890
Fax: (312)454-0369
Website: http://www.iegventure.com

JK&B Capital
180 North Stetson, Ste. 4500
Chicago, IL 60601
(312)946-1200
Fax: (312)946-1103

E-mail: gspencer@jkbcapital.com
Website: http://www.jkbcapital.com

Kettle Partners L.P.
350 W. Hubbard, Ste. 350
Chicago, IL 60610
(312)329-9300
Fax: (312)527-4519
Website: http://www.kettlevc.com

Lake Shore Capital Partners
20 N. Wacker Dr., Ste. 2807
Chicago, IL 60606
(312)803-3536
Fax: (312)803-3534

LaSalle Capital Group Inc.
70 W. Madison St., Ste. 5710
Chicago, IL 60602
(312)236-7041
Fax: (312)236-0720

Linc Capital, Inc.
303 E. Wacker Pkwy., Ste. 1000
Chicago, IL 60601
(312)946-2670
Fax: (312)938-4290
E-mail: bdemars@linccap.com

Madison Dearborn Partners, Inc.
3 First National Plz., Ste. 3800
Chicago, IL 60602
(312)895-1000
Fax: (312)895-1001
E-mail: invest@mdcp.com
Website: http://www.mdcp.com

Mesirow Private Equity Investments Inc.
350 N. Clark St.
Chicago, IL 60610
(312)595-6950
Fax: (312)595-6211
Website: http://www.meisrowfinancial.com

Mosaix Ventures LLC
1822 North Mohawk
Chicago, IL 60614
(312)274-0988
Fax: (312)274-0989
Website: http://www.mosaixventures.com

Nesbitt Burns
111 West Monroe St.
Chicago, IL 60603
(312)416-3855
Fax: (312)765-8000
Website: http://www.harrisbank.com

Polestar Capital, Inc.
180 N. Michigan Ave., Ste. 1905
Chicago, IL 60601
(312)984-9090
Fax: (312)984-9877
E-mail: wl@polestarvc.com
Website: http://www.polestarvc.com

Prince Ventures (Chicago)
10 S. Wacker Dr., Ste. 2575
Chicago, IL 60606-7407
(312)454-1408
Fax: (312)454-9125

Prism Capital
444 N. Michigan Ave.
Chicago, IL 60611
(312)464-7900
Fax: (312)464-7915
Website: http://www.prismfund.com

Third Coast Capital
900 N. Franklin St., Ste. 700
Chicago, IL 60610
(312)337-3303
Fax: (312)337-2567
E-mail: manic@earthlink.com
Website: http://www.third
coastcapital.com

Thoma Cressey Equity Partners
4460 Sears Tower, 92nd Fl.
233 S. Wacker Dr.
Chicago, IL 60606
(312)777-4444
Fax: (312)777-4445
Website: http://www.thomacressey.com

Tribune Ventures
435 N. Michigan Ave., Ste. 600
Chicago, IL 60611
(312)527-8797
Fax: (312)222-5993
Website: http://www.tribuneventures.com

Wind Point Partners (Chicago)
676 N. Michigan Ave., Ste. 330
Chicago, IL 60611
(312)649-4000
Website: http://www.wppartners.com

Marquette Venture Partners
520 Lake Cook Rd., Ste. 450
Deerfield, IL 60015
(847)940-1700
Fax: (847)940-1724
Website: http://www.marquette
ventures.com

Duchossois Investments Limited, LLC
845 Larch Ave.
Elmhurst, IL 60126

(630)530-6105
Fax: (630)993-8644
Website: http://www.duchtec.com

Evanston Business Investment Corp.
1840 Oak Ave.
Evanston, IL 60201
(847)866-1840
Fax: (847)866-1808
E-mail: t-parkinson@nwu.com
Website: http://www.ebic.com

Inroads Capital Partners L.P.
1603 Orrington Ave., Ste. 2050
Evanston, IL 60201-3841
(847)864-2000
Fax: (847)864-9692

The Cerulean Fund/WGC Enterprises
1701 E. Lake Ave., Ste. 170
Glenview, IL 60025
(847)657-8002
Fax: (847)657-8168

Ventana Financial Resources, Inc.
249 Market Sq.
Lake Forest, IL 60045
(847)234-3434

Beecken, Petty & Co.
901 Warrenville Rd., Ste. 205
Lisle, IL 60532
(630)435-0300
Fax: (630)435-0370
E-mail: hep@bpcompany.com
Website: http://www.bpcompany.com

Allstate Private Equity
3075 Sanders Rd., Ste. G5D
Northbrook, IL 60062-7127
(847)402-8247
Fax: (847)402-0880

KB Partners
1101 Skokie Blvd., Ste. 260
Northbrook, IL 60062-2856
(847)714-0444
Fax: (847)714-0445
E-mail: keith@kbpartners.com
Website: http://www.kbpartners.com

Transcap Associates Inc.
900 Skokie Blvd., Ste. 210
Northbrook, IL 60062
(847)753-9600
Fax: (847)753-9090

**Graystone Venture Partners, L.L.C. /
Portage Venture Partners**
One Northfield Plaza, Ste. 530
Northfield, IL 60093

(847)446-9460
Fax: (847)446-9470
Website: http://www.portage
ventures.com

Motorola Inc.
1303 E. Algonquin Rd.
Schaumburg, IL 60196-1065
(847)576-4929
Fax: (847)538-2250
Website: http://www.mot.com/mne

Indiana

Irwin Ventures LLC
500 Washington St.
Columbus, IN 47202
(812)373-1434
Fax: (812)376-1709
Website: http://www.irwinventures.com

Cambridge Venture Partners
4181 East 96th St., Ste. 200
Indianapolis, IN 46240
(317)814-6192
Fax: (317)944-9815

CID Equity Partners
One American Square, Ste. 2850
Box 82074
Indianapolis, IN 46282
(317)269-2350
Fax: (317)269-2355
Website: http://www.cidequity.com

Gazelle Techventures
6325 Digital Way, Ste. 460
Indianapolis, IN 46278
(317)275-6800
Fax: (317)275-1101
Website: http://www.gazellevc.com

Monument Advisors Inc.
Bank One Center/Circle
111 Monument Circle, Ste. 600
Indianapolis, IN 46204-5172
(317)656-5065
Fax: (317)656-5060
Website: http://www.monumentadv.com

MWV Capital Partners
201 N. Illinois St., Ste. 300
Indianapolis, IN 46204
(317)237-2323
Fax: (317)237-2325
Website: http://www.mwvcapital.com

First Source Capital Corp.
100 North Michigan St.
PO Box 1602
South Bend, IN 46601

(219)235-2180
Fax: (219)235-2227

Iowa

Allsop Venture Partners
118 Third Ave. SE, Ste. 837
Cedar Rapids, IA 52401
(319)368-6675
Fax: (319)363-9515

InvestAmerica Investment Advisors, Inc.
101 2nd St. SE, Ste. 800
Cedar Rapids, IA 52401
(319)363-8249
Fax: (319)363-9683

Pappajohn Capital Resources
2116 Financial Center
Des Moines, IA 50309
(515)244-5746
Fax: (515)244-2346
Website: http://www.pappajohn.com

Berthel Fisher & Company Planning Inc.
701 Tama St.
PO Box 609
Marion, IA 52302
(319)497-5700
Fax: (319)497-4244

Kansas

Enterprise Merchant Bank
7400 West 110th St., Ste. 560
Overland Park, KS 66210
(913)327-8500
Fax: (913)327-8505

Kansas Venture Capital, Inc. (Overland Park)
6700 Antioch Plz., Ste. 460
Overland Park, KS 66204
(913)262-7117
Fax: (913)262-3509
E-mail: jdalton@kvci.com

Child Health Investment Corp.
6803 W. 64th St., Ste. 208
Shawnee Mission, KS 66202
(913)262-1436
Fax: (913)262-1575
Website: http://www.chca.com

Kansas Technology Enterprise Corp.
214 SW 6th, 1st Fl.
Topeka, KS 66603-3719
(785)296-5272
Fax: (785)296-1160

E-mail: ktec@ktec.com
Website: http://www.ktec.com

Kentucky

Kentucky Highlands Investment Corp.
362 Old Whitley Rd.
London, KY 40741
(606)864-5175
Fax: (606)864-5194
Website: http://www.khic.org

Chrysalis Ventures, L.L.C.
1850 National City Tower
Louisville, KY 40202
(502)583-7644
Fax: (502)583-7648
E-mail: bobsany@chrysalisventures.com
Website: http://www.chrysalis
ventures.com

Humana Venture Capital
500 West Main St.
Louisville, KY 40202
(502)580-3922
Fax: (502)580-2051
E-mail: gemont@humana.com
George Emont, Director

Summit Capital Group, Inc.
6510 Glenridge Park Pl., Ste. 8
Louisville, KY 40222
(502)332-2700

Louisiana

Bank One Equity Investors, Inc.
451 Florida St.
Baton Rouge, LA 70801
(504)332-4421
Fax: (504)332-7377

Advantage Capital Partners
LLE Tower
909 Poydras St., Ste. 2230
New Orleans, LA 70112
(504)522-4850
Fax: (504)522-4950
Website: http://www.advantagecap.com

Maine

CEI Ventures / Coastal Ventures LP
2 Portland Fish Pier, Ste. 201
Portland, ME 04101
(207)772-5356
Fax: (207)772-5503
Website: http://www.ceiventures.com

Commwealth Bioventures, Inc.
4 Milk St.
Portland, ME 04101

(207)780-0904
Fax: (207)780-0913

Maryland

Annapolis Ventures LLC
151 West St., Ste. 302
Annapolis, MD 21401
(443)482-9555
Fax: (443)482-9565
Website: http://www.annapolis
ventures.com

Delmag Ventures
220 Wardour Dr.
Annapolis, MD 21401
(410)267-8196
Fax: (410)267-8017
Website: http://www.delmag
ventures.com

Abell Venture Fund
111 S. Calvert St., Ste. 2300
Baltimore, MD 21202
(410)547-1300
Fax: (410)539-6579
Website: http://www.abell.org

ABS Ventures (Baltimore)
1 South St., Ste. 2150
Baltimore, MD 21202
(410)895-3895
Fax: (410)895-3899
Website: http://www.absventures.com

Anthem Capital, L.P.
16 S. Calvert St., Ste. 800
Baltimore, MD 21202-1305
(410)625-1510
Fax: (410)625-1735
Website: http://www.anthemcapital.com

Catalyst Ventures
1119 St. Paul St.
Baltimore, MD 21202
(410)244-0123
Fax: (410)752-7721

Maryland Venture Capital Trust
217 E. Redwood St., Ste. 2200
Baltimore, MD 21202
(410)767-6361
Fax: (410)333-6931

New Enterprise Associates (Baltimore)
1119 St. Paul St.
Baltimore, MD 21202
(410)244-0115
Fax: (410)752-7721
Website: http://www.nea.com

T. Rowe Price Threshold Partnerships
100 E. Pratt St., 8th Fl.
Baltimore, MD 21202
(410)345-2000
Fax: (410)345-2800

Spring Capital Partners
16 W. Madison St.
Baltimore, MD 21201
(410)685-8000
Fax: (410)727-1436
E-mail: mailbox@springcap.com

Arete Corporation
3 Bethesda Metro Ctr., Ste. 770
Bethesda, MD 20814
(301)657-6268
Fax: (301)657-6254
Website: http://www.arete-microgen.com

Embryon Capital
7903 Sleaford Place
Bethesda, MD 20814
(301)656-6837
Fax: (301)656-8056

Potomac Ventures
7920 Norfolk Ave., Ste. 1100
Bethesda, MD 20814
(301)215-9240
Website: http://www.potomac
ventures.com

Toucan Capital Corp.
3 Bethesda Metro Center, Ste. 700
Bethesda, MD 20814
(301)961-1970
Fax: (301)961-1969
Website: http://www.toucancapital.com

Kinetic Ventures LLC
2 Wisconsin Cir., Ste. 620
Chevy Chase, MD 20815
(301)652-8066
Fax: (301)652-8310
Website: http://www.kineticventures.com

Boulder Ventures Ltd.
4750 Owings Mills Blvd.
Owings Mills, MD 21117
(410)998-3114
Fax: (410)356-5492
Website: http://www.boulderventures.com

Grotech Capital Group
9690 Deereco Rd., Ste. 800
Timonium, MD 21093
(410)560-2000
Fax: (410)560-1910
Website: http://www.grotech.com

Massachusetts

Adams, Harkness & Hill, Inc.
60 State St.
Boston, MA 02109
(617)371-3900

Advent International
75 State St., 29th Fl.
Boston, MA 02109
(617)951-9400
Fax: (617)951-0566
Website: http://www.adventinter
national.com

American Research and Development
30 Federal St.
Boston, MA 02110-2508
(617)423-7500
Fax: (617)423-9655

Ascent Venture Partners
255 State St., 5th Fl.
Boston, MA 02109
(617)270-9400
Fax: (617)270-9401
E-mail: info@ascentvp.com
Website: http://www.ascentvp.com

Atlas Venture
222 Berkeley St.
Boston, MA 02116
(617)488-2200
Fax: (617)859-9292
Website: http://www.atlasventure.com

Axxon Capital
28 State St., 37th Fl.
Boston, MA 02109
(617)722-0980
Fax: (617)557-6014
Website: http://www.axxoncapital.com

BancBoston Capital/BancBoston Ventures
175 Federal St., 10th Fl.
Boston, MA 02110
(617)434-2509
Fax: (617)434-6175
Website: http://
www.bancbostoncapital.com

Boston Capital Ventures
Old City Hall
45 School St.
Boston, MA 02108
(617)227-6550
Fax: (617)227-3847
E-mail: info@bcv.com
Website: http://www.bcv.com

Boston Financial & Equity Corp.
20 Overland St.
PO Box 15071
Boston, MA 02215
(617)267-2900
Fax: (617)437-7601
E-mail: debbie@bfec.com

Boston Millennia Partners
30 Rowes Wharf
Boston, MA 02110
(617)428-5150
Fax: (617)428-5160
Website: http://www.millennia
partners.com

Bristol Investment Trust
842A Beacon St.
Boston, MA 02215-3199
(617)566-5212
Fax: (617)267-0932

Brook Venture Management LLC
50 Federal St., 5th Fl.
Boston, MA 02110
(617)451-8989
Fax: (617)451-2369
Website: http://www.brookventure.com

Burr, Egan, Deleage, and Co. (Boston)
200 Clarendon St., Ste. 3800
Boston, MA 02116
(617)262-7770
Fax: (617)262-9779

Cambridge/Samsung Partners
One Exeter Plaza
Ninth Fl.
Boston, MA 02116
(617)262-4440
Fax: (617)262-5562

Chestnut Street Partners, Inc.
75 State St., Ste. 2500
Boston, MA 02109
(617)345-7220
Fax: (617)345-7201
E-mail: chestnut@chestnutp.com

Claflin Capital Management, Inc.
10 Liberty Sq., Ste. 300
Boston, MA 02109
(617)426-6505
Fax: (617)482-0016
Website: http://www.claflincapital.com

Copley Venture Partners
99 Summer St., Ste. 1720
Boston, MA 02110
(617)737-1253
Fax: (617)439-0699

Corning Capital / Corning Technology Ventures
121 High Street, Ste. 400
Boston, MA 02110
(617)338-2656
Fax: (617)261-3864
Website: http://www.corningventures.com

Downer & Co.
211 Congress St.
Boston, MA 02110
(617)482-6200
Fax: (617)482-6201
E-mail: cdowner@downer.com
Website: http://www.downer.com

Fidelity Ventures
82 Devonshire St.
Boston, MA 02109
(617)563-6370
Fax: (617)476-9023
Website: http://www.fidelityventures.com

Greylock Management Corp. (Boston)
1 Federal St.
Boston, MA 02110-2065
(617)423-5525
Fax: (617)482-0059

Gryphon Ventures
222 Berkeley St., Ste.1600
Boston, MA 02116
(617)267-9191
Fax: (617)267-4293
E-mail: all@gryphoninc.com

Halpern, Denny & Co.
500 Boylston St.
Boston, MA 02116
(617)536-6602
Fax: (617)536-8535

Harbourvest Partners, LLC
1 Financial Center, 44th Fl.
Boston, MA 02111
(617)348-3707
Fax: (617)350-0305
Website: http://www.hvpllc.com

Highland Capital Partners
2 International Pl.
Boston, MA 02110
(617)981-1500
Fax: (617)531-1550
E-mail: info@hcp.com
Website: http://www.hcp.com

Lee Munder Venture Partners
John Hancock Tower T-53
200 Clarendon St.
Boston, MA 02103

(617)380-5600
Fax: (617)380-5601
Website: http://www.leemunder.com

M/C Venture Partners
75 State St., Ste. 2500
Boston, MA 02109
(617)345-7200
Fax: (617)345-7201
Website: http://www.mcventure
partners.com

Massachusetts Capital Resources Co.
420 Boylston St.
Boston, MA 02116
(617)536-3900
Fax: (617)536-7930

Massachusetts Technology Development Corp. (MTDC)
148 State St.
Boston, MA 02109
(617)723-4920
Fax: (617)723-5983
E-mail: jhodgman@mtdc.com
Website: http://www.mtdc.com

New England Partners
One Boston Place, Ste. 2100
Boston, MA 02108
(617)624-8400
Fax: (617)624-8999
Website: http://www.nepartners.com

North Hill Ventures
Ten Post Office Square
11th Fl.
Boston, MA 02109
(617)788-2112
Fax: (617)788-2152
Website: http://www.northhill
ventures.com

OneLiberty Ventures
150 Cambridge Park Dr.
Boston, MA 02140
(617)492-7280
Fax: (617)492-7290
Website: http://www.oneliberty.com

Schroder Ventures
Life Sciences
60 State St., Ste. 3650
Boston, MA 02109
(617)367-8100
Fax: (617)367-1590
Website: http://www.shroderventures.com

Shawmut Capital Partners
75 Federal St., 18th Fl.
Boston, MA 02110

(617)368-4900
Fax: (617)368-4910
Website: http://www.shawmutcapital.com

Solstice Capital LLC
15 Broad St., 3rd Fl.
Boston, MA 02109
(617)523-7733
Fax: (617)523-5827
E-mail: solticecapital@solcap.com

Spectrum Equity Investors
One International Pl., 29th Fl.
Boston, MA 02110
(617)464-4600
Fax: (617)464-4601
Website: http://www.spectrumequity.com

Spray Venture Partners
One Walnut St.
Boston, MA 02108
(617)305-4140
Fax: (617)305-4144
Website: http://www.sprayventure.com

The Still River Fund
100 Federal St., 29th Fl.
Boston, MA 02110
(617)348-2327
Fax: (617)348-2371
Website: http://www.stillriverfund.com

Summit Partners
600 Atlantic Ave., Ste. 2800
Boston, MA 02210-2227
(617)824-1000
Fax: (617)824-1159
Website: http://www.summitpartners.com

TA Associates, Inc. (Boston)
High Street Tower
125 High St., Ste. 2500
Boston, MA 02110
(617)574-6700
Fax: (617)574-6728
Website: http://www.ta.com

TVM Techno Venture Management
101 Arch St., Ste. 1950
Boston, MA 02110
(617)345-9320
Fax: (617)345-9377
E-mail: info@tvmvc.com
Website: http://www.tvmvc.com

UNC Ventures
64 Burough St.
Boston, MA 02130-4017
(617)482-7070
Fax: (617)522-2176

Venture Investment Management Company (VIMAC)
177 Milk St.
Boston, MA 02190-3410
(617)292-3300
Fax: (617)292-7979
E-mail: bzeisig@vimac.com
Website: http://www.vimac.com

MDT Advisers, Inc.
125 Cambridge Park Dr.
Cambridge, MA 02140-2314
(617)234-2200
Fax: (617)234-2210
Website: http://www.mdtai.com

TTC Ventures
One Main St., 6th Fl.
Cambridge, MA 02142
(617)528-3137
Fax: (617)577-1715
E-mail: info@ttcventures.com

Zero Stage Capital Co. Inc.
101 Main St., 17th Fl.
Cambridge, MA 02142
(617)876-5355
Fax: (617)876-1248
Website: http://www.zerostage.com

Atlantic Capital
164 Cushing Hwy.
Cohasset, MA 02025
(617)383-9449
Fax: (617)383-6040
E-mail: info@atlanticcap.com
Website: http://www.atlanticcap.com

Seacoast Capital Partners
55 Ferncroft Rd.
Danvers, MA 01923
(978)750-1300
Fax: (978)750-1301
E-mail: gdeli@seacoastcapital.com
Website: http://www.seacoast
capital.com

Sage Management Group
44 South Street
PO Box 2026
East Dennis, MA 02641
(508)385-7172
Fax: (508)385-7272
E-mail: sagemgt@capecod.net

Applied Technology
1 Cranberry Hill
Lexington, MA 02421-7397
(617)862-8622
Fax: (617)862-8367

Royalty Capital Management
5 Downing Rd.
Lexington, MA 02421-6918
(781)861-8490

Argo Global Capital
210 Broadway, Ste. 101
Lynnfield, MA 01940
(781)592-5250
Fax: (781)592-5230
Website: http://www.gsmcapital.com

Industry Ventures
6 Bayne Lane
Newburyport, MA 01950
(978)499-7606
Fax: (978)499-0686
Website: http://
www.industryventures.com

Softbank Capital Partners
10 Langley Rd., Ste. 202
Newton Center, MA 02459
(617)928-9300
Fax: (617)928-9305
E-mail: clax@bvc.com

Advanced Technology Ventures (Boston)
281 Winter St., Ste. 350
Waltham, MA 02451
(781)290-0707
Fax: (781)684-0045
E-mail: info@atvcapital.com
Website: http://www.atvcapital.com

Castile Ventures
890 Winter St., Ste. 140
Waltham, MA 02451
(781)890-0060
Fax: (781)890-0065
Website: http://www.castileventures.com

Charles River Ventures
1000 Winter St., Ste. 3300
Waltham, MA 02451
(781)487-7060
Fax: (781)487-7065
Website: http://www.crv.com

Comdisco Venture Group (Waltham)
Totton Pond Office Center
400-1 Totten Pond Rd.
Waltham, MA 02451
(617)672-0250
Fax: (617)398-8099

Marconi Ventures
890 Winter St., Ste. 310
Waltham, MA 02451
(781)839-7177

Fax: (781)522-7477
Website: http://www.marconi.com

Matrix Partners
Bay Colony Corporate Center
1000 Winter St., Ste.4500
Waltham, MA 02451
(781)890-2244
Fax: (781)890-2288
Website: http://www.matrix
partners.com

North Bridge Venture Partners
950 Winter St. Ste. 4600
Waltham, MA 02451
(781)290-0004
Fax: (781)290-0999
E-mail: eta@nbvp.com

Polaris Venture Partners
Bay Colony Corporate Ctr.
1000 Winter St., Ste. 3500
Waltham, MA 02451
(781)290-0770
Fax: (781)290-0880
E-mail: partners@polarisventures.com
Website: http://www.polar
isventures.com

Seaflower Ventures
Bay Colony Corporate Ctr.
1000 Winter St. Ste. 1000
Waltham, MA 02451
(781)466-9552
Fax: (781)466-9553
E-mail: moot@seaflower.com
Website: http://www.seaflower.com

Ampersand Ventures
55 William St., Ste. 240
Wellesley, MA 02481
(617)239-0700
Fax: (617)239-0824
E-mail: info@ampersandventures.com
Website: http://www.ampersand
ventures.com

Battery Ventures (Boston)
20 William St., Ste. 200
Wellesley, MA 02481
(781)577-1000
Fax: (781)577-1001
Website: http://www.battery.com

Commonwealth Capital Ventures, L.P.
20 William St., Ste.225
Wellesley, MA 02481
(781)237-7373
Fax: (781)235-8627
Website: http://www.ccvlp.com

Fowler, Anthony & Company
20 Walnut St.
Wellesley, MA 02481
(781)237-4201
Fax: (781)237-7718

Gemini Investors
20 William St.
Wellesley, MA 02481
(781)237-7001
Fax: (781)237-7233

Grove Street Advisors Inc.
20 William St., Ste. 230
Wellesley, MA 02481
(781)263-6100
Fax: (781)263-6101
Website: http://www.groves
treetadvisors.com

Mees Pierson Investeringsmaat B.V.
20 William St., Ste. 210
Wellesley, MA 02482
(781)239-7600
Fax: (781)239-0377

Norwest Equity Partners
40 William St., Ste. 305
Wellesley, MA 02481-3902
(781)237-5870
Fax: (781)237-6270
Website: http://www.norwestvp.com

Bessemer Venture Partners (Wellesley Hills)
83 Walnut St.
Wellesley Hills, MA 02481
(781)237-6050
Fax: (781)235-7576
E-mail: travis@bvpny.com
Website: http://www.bvp.com

Venture Capital Fund of New England
20 Walnut St., Ste. 120
Wellesley Hills, MA 02481-2175
(781)239-8262
Fax: (781)239-8263

Prism Venture Partners
100 Lowder Brook Dr., Ste. 2500
Westwood, MA 02090
(781)302-4000
Fax: (781)302-4040
E-mail: dwbaum@prismventure.com

Palmer Partners LP
200 Unicorn Park Dr.
Woburn, MA 01801
(781)933-5445
Fax: (781)933-0698

Michigan

Arbor Partners, L.L.C.
130 South First St.
Ann Arbor, MI 48104
(734)668-9000
Fax: (734)669-4195
Website: http://www.arborpartners.com

EDF Ventures
425 N. Main St.
Ann Arbor, MI 48104
(734)663-3213
Fax: (734)663-7358
E-mail: edf@edfvc.com
Website: http://www.edfvc.com

White Pines Management, L.L.C.
2401 Plymouth Rd., Ste. B
Ann Arbor, MI 48105
(734)747-9401
Fax: (734)747-9704
E-mail: ibund@whitepines.com
Website: http://www.whitepines.com

Wellmax, Inc.
3541 Bendway Blvd., Ste. 100
Bloomfield Hills, MI 48301
(248)646-3554
Fax: (248)646-6220

Venture Funding, Ltd.
Fisher Bldg.
3011 West Grand Blvd., Ste. 321
Detroit, MI 48202
(313)871-3606
Fax: (313)873-4935

Investcare Partners L.P. / GMA Capital LLC
32330 W. Twelve Mile Rd.
Farmington Hills, MI 48334
(248)489-9000
Fax: (248)489-8819
E-mail: gma@gmacapital.com
Website: http://www.gmacapital.com

Liberty Bidco Investment Corp.
30833 Northwestern Highway, Ste. 211
Farmington Hills, MI 48334
(248)626-6070
Fax: (248)626-6072

Seaflower Ventures
5170 Nicholson Rd.
PO Box 474
Fowlerville, MI 48836
(517)223-3335
Fax: (517)223-3337
E-mail: gibbons@seaflower.com
Website: http://www.seaflower.com

Ralph Wilson Equity Fund LLC
15400 E. Jefferson Ave.
Gross Pointe Park, MI 48230
(313)821-9122
Fax: (313)821-9101
Website: http://www.Ralph
WilsonEquityFund.com
J. Skip Simms, President

Minnesota

Development Corp. of Austin
1900 Eighth Ave., NW
Austin, MN 55912
(507)433-0346
Fax: (507)433-0361
E-mail: dca@smig.net
Website: http://www.spamtownusa.com

Northeast Ventures Corp.
802 Alworth Bldg.
Duluth, MN 55802
(218)722-9915
Fax: (218)722-9871

Medical Innovation Partners, Inc.
6450 City West Pkwy.
Eden Prairie, MN 55344-3245
(612)828-9616
Fax: (612)828-9596

St. Paul Venture Capital, Inc.
10400 Vicking Dr., Ste. 550
Eden Prairie, MN 55344
(612)995-7474
Fax: (612)995-7475
Website: http://www.stpaulvc.com

Cherry Tree Investments, Inc.
7601 France Ave. S, Ste. 150
Edina, MN 55435
(612)893-9012
Fax: (612)893-9036
Website: http://www.cherrytree.com

Shared Ventures, Inc.
6550 York Ave. S
Edina, MN 55435
(612)925-3411

Sherpa Partners LLC
5050 Lincoln Dr., Ste. 490
Edina, MN 55436
(952)942-1070
Fax: (952)942-1071
Website: http://www.sherpapartners.com

Affinity Capital Management
901 Marquette Ave., Ste. 1810
Minneapolis, MN 55402
(612)252-9900

Fax: (612)252-9911
Website: http://www.affinitycapital.com

Artesian Capital
1700 Foshay Tower
821 Marquette Ave.
Minneapolis, MN 55402
(612)334-5600
Fax: (612)334-5601
E-mail: artesian@artesian.com

Coral Ventures
60 S. 6th St., Ste. 3510
Minneapolis, MN 55402
(612)335-8666
Fax: (612)335-8668
Website: http://www.coralventures.com

Crescendo Venture Management, L.L.C.
800 LaSalle Ave., Ste. 2250
Minneapolis, MN 55402
(612)607-2800
Fax: (612)607-2801
Website: http://www.crescendo
ventures.com

Gideon Hixon Venture
1900 Foshay Tower
821 Marquette Ave.
Minneapolis, MN 55402
(612)904-2314
Fax: (612)204-0913

Norwest Equity Partners
3600 IDS Center
80 S. 8th St.
Minneapolis, MN 55402
(612)215-1600
Fax: (612)215-1601
Website: http://www.norwestvp.com

Oak Investment Partners (Minneapolis)
4550 Norwest Center
90 S. 7th St.
Minneapolis, MN 55402
(612)339-9322
Fax: (612)337-8017
Website: http://www.oakinv.com

Pathfinder Venture Capital Funds (Minneapolis)
7300 Metro Blvd., Ste. 585
Minneapolis, MN 55439
(612)835-1121
Fax: (612)835-8389
E-mail: jahrens620@aol.com

U.S. Bancorp Piper Jaffray Ventures, Inc.
800 Nicollet Mall, Ste. 800
Minneapolis, MN 55402

(612)303-5686
Fax: (612)303-1350
Website: http://www.paperjaffrey
ventures.com

The Food Fund, Ltd. Partnership
5720 Smatana Dr., Ste. 300
Minnetonka, MN 55343
(612)939-3950
Fax: (612)939-8106

Mayo Medical Ventures
200 First St. SW
Rochester, MN 55905
(507)266-4586
Fax: (507)284-5410
Website: http://www.mayo.edu

Missouri

Bankers Capital Corp.
3100 Gillham Rd.
Kansas City, MO 64109
(816)531-1600
Fax: (816)531-1334

Capital for Business, Inc. (Kansas City)
1000 Walnut St., 18th Fl.
Kansas City, MO 64106
(816)234-2357
Fax: (816)234-2952
Website: http://
www.capitalforbusiness.com

De Vries & Co. Inc.
800 West 47th St.
Kansas City, MO 64112
(816)756-0055
Fax: (816)756-0061

InvestAmerica Venture Group Inc. (Kansas City)
Commerce Tower
911 Main St., Ste. 2424
Kansas City, MO 64105
(816)842-0114
Fax: (816)471-7339

Kansas City Equity Partners
233 W. 47th St.
Kansas City, MO 64112
(816)960-1771
Fax: (816)960-1777
Website: http://www.kcep.com

Bome Investors, Inc.
8000 Maryland Ave., Ste. 1190
St. Louis, MO 63105
(314)721-5707
Fax: (314)721-5135

Website: http://www.gateway
ventures.com

Capital for Business, Inc. (St. Louis)
11 S. Meramac St., Ste. 1430
St. Louis, MO 63105
(314)746-7427
Fax: (314)746-8739
Website: http://www.capitalfor
business.com

Crown Capital Corp.
540 Maryville Centre Dr., Ste. 120
Saint Louis, MO 63141
(314)576-1201
Fax: (314)576-1525
Website: http://www.crown-
cap.com

Gateway Associates L.P.
8000 Maryland Ave., Ste. 1190
St. Louis, MO 63105
(314)721-5707
Fax: (314)721-5135

Harbison Corp.
8112 Maryland Ave., Ste. 250
Saint Louis, MO 63105
(314)727-8200
Fax: (314)727-0249

Heartland Capital Fund, Ltd.
PO Box 642117
Omaha, NE 68154
(402)778-5124
Fax: (402)445-2370
Website: http://www.heartland
capitalfund.com

Odin Capital Group
1625 Farnam St., Ste. 700
Omaha, NE 68102
(402)346-6200
Fax: (402)342-9311
Website: http://www.odincapital.com

Nevada

Edge Capital Investment Co. LLC
1350 E. Flamingo Rd., Ste. 3000
Las Vegas, NV 89119
(702)438-3343
E-mail: info@edgecapital.net
Website: http://www.edgecapital.net

The Benefit Capital Companies Inc.
PO Box 542
Logandale, NV 89021
(702)398-3222
Fax: (702)398-3700

Millennium Three Venture Group LLC
6880 South McCarran Blvd., Ste. A-11
Reno, NV 89509
(775)954-2020
Fax: (775)954-2023
Website: http://www.m3vg.com

New Jersey

Alan I. Goldman & Associates
497 Ridgewood Ave.
Glen Ridge, NJ 07028
(973)857-5680
Fax: (973)509-8856

CS Capital Partners LLC
328 Second St., Ste. 200
Lakewood, NJ 08701
(732)901-1111
Fax: (212)202-5071
Website: http://www.cs-capital.com

Edison Venture Fund
1009 Lenox Dr., Ste. 4
Lawrenceville, NJ 08648
(609)896-1900
Fax: (609)896-0066
E-mail: info@edisonventure.com
Website: http://www.edisonventure.com

Tappan Zee Capital Corp. (New Jersey)
201 Lower Notch Rd.
PO Box 416
Little Falls, NJ 07424
(973)256-8280
Fax: (973)256-2841

The CIT Group/Venture Capital, Inc.
650 CIT Dr.
Livingston, NJ 07039
(973)740-5429
Fax: (973)740-5555
Website: http://www.cit.com

Capital Express, L.L.C.
1100 Valleybrook Ave.
Lyndhurst, NJ 07071
(201)438-8228
Fax: (201)438-5131
E-mail: niles@capitalexpress.com
Website: http://www.capitalexpress.com

Westford Technology Ventures, L.P.
17 Academy St.
Newark, NJ 07102
(973)624-2131
Fax: (973)624-2008

Accel Partners
1 Palmer Sq.
Princeton, NJ 08542

(609)683-4500
Fax: (609)683-4880
Website: http://www.accel.com

Cardinal Partners
221 Nassau St.
Princeton, NJ 08542
(609)924-6452
Fax: (609)683-0174
Website: http://www.cardinal
healthpartners.com

Domain Associates L.L.C.
One Palmer Sq., Ste. 515
Princeton, NJ 08542
(609)683-5656
Fax: (609)683-9789
Website: http://www.domainvc.com

Johnston Associates, Inc.
181 Cherry Valley Rd.
Princeton, NJ 08540
(609)924-3131
Fax: (609)683-7524
E-mail: jaincorp@aol.com

Kemper Ventures
Princeton Forrestal Village
155 Village Blvd.
Princeton, NJ 08540
(609)936-3035
Fax: (609)936-3051

Penny Lane Parnters
One Palmer Sq., Ste. 309
Princeton, NJ 08542
(609)497-4646
Fax: (609)497-0611

Early Stage Enterprises L.P.
995 Route 518
Skillman, NJ 08558
(609)921-8896
Fax: (609)921-8703
Website: http://www.esevc.com

MBW Management Inc.
1 Springfield Ave.
Summit, NJ 07901
(908)273-4060
Fax: (908)273-4430

BCI Advisors, Inc.
Glenpointe Center W.
Teaneck, NJ 07666
(201)836-3900
Fax: (201)836-6368
E-mail: info@bciadvisors.com
Website: http://www.bci
partners.com

Demuth, Folger & Wetherill / DFW Capital Partners
Glenpointe Center E., 5th Fl.
300 Frank W. Burr Blvd.
Teaneck, NJ 07666
(201)836-2233
Fax: (201)836-5666
Website: http://www.dfwcapital.com

First Princeton Capital Corp.
189 Berdan Ave., No. 131
Wayne, NJ 07470-3233
(973)278-3233
Fax: (973)278-4290
Website: http://www.lytellcatt.net

Edelson Technology Partners
300 Tice Blvd.
Woodcliff Lake, NJ 07675
(201)930-9898
Fax: (201)930-8899
Website: http://www.edelsontech.com

New Mexico

Bruce F. Glaspell & Associates
10400 Academy Rd. NE, Ste. 313
Albuquerque, NM 87111
(505)292-4505
Fax: (505)292-4258

High Desert Ventures, Inc.
6101 Imparata St. NE, Ste. 1721
Albuquerque, NM 87111
(505)797-3330
Fax: (505)338-5147

New Business Capital Fund, Ltd.
5805 Torreon NE
Albuquerque, NM 87109
(505)822-8445

SBC Ventures
10400 Academy Rd. NE, Ste. 313
Albuquerque, NM 87111
(505)292-4505
Fax: (505)292-4528

Technology Ventures Corp.
1155 University Blvd. SE
Albuquerque, NM 87106
(505)246-2882
Fax: (505)246-2891

New York

New York State Science & Technology Foundation
Small Business Technology Investment Fund
99 Washington Ave., Ste. 1731
Albany, NY 12210

(518)473-9741
Fax: (518)473-6876

Rand Capital Corp.
2200 Rand Bldg.
Buffalo, NY 14203
(716)853-0802
Fax: (716)854-8480
Website: http://www.randcapital.com

Seed Capital Partners
620 Main St.
Buffalo, NY 14202
(716)845-7520
Fax: (716)845-7539
Website: http://www.seedcp.com

Coleman Venture Group
5909 Northern Blvd.
PO Box 224
East Norwich, NY 11732
(516)626-3642
Fax: (516)626-9722

Vega Capital Corp.
45 Knollwood Rd.
Elmsford, NY 10523
(914)345-9500
Fax: (914)345-9505

Herbert Young Securities, Inc.
98 Cuttermill Rd.
Great Neck, NY 11021
(516)487-8300
Fax: (516)487-8319

Sterling/Carl Marks Capital, Inc.
175 Great Neck Rd., Ste. 408
Great Neck, NY 11021
(516)482-7374
Fax: (516)487-0781
E-mail: stercrlmar@aol.com
Website: http://www.serling
carlmarks.com

Impex Venture Management Co.
PO Box 1570
Green Island, NY 12183
(518)271-8008
Fax: (518)271-9101

Corporate Venture Partners L.P.
200 Sunset Park
Ithaca, NY 14850
(607)257-6323
Fax: (607)257-6128

Arthur P. Gould & Co.
One Wilshire Dr.
Lake Success, NY 11020
(516)773-3000
Fax: (516)773-3289

Dauphin Capital Partners
108 Forest Ave.
Locust Valley, NY 11560
(516)759-3339
Fax: (516)759-3322
Website: http://www.dauphincapital.com

550 Digital Media Ventures
555 Madison Ave., 10th Fl.
New York, NY 10022
Website: http://www.550dmv.com

Aberlyn Capital Management Co., Inc.
500 Fifth Ave.
New York, NY 10110
(212)391-7750
Fax: (212)391-7762

Adler & Company
342 Madison Ave., Ste. 807
New York, NY 10173
(212)599-2535
Fax: (212)599-2526

Alimansky Capital Group, Inc.
605 Madison Ave., Ste. 300
New York, NY 10022-1901
(212)832-7300
Fax: (212)832-7338

Allegra Partners
515 Madison Ave., 29th Fl.
New York, NY 10022
(212)826-9080
Fax: (212)759-2561

The Argentum Group
The Chyrsler Bldg.
405 Lexington Ave.
New York, NY 10174
(212)949-6262
Fax: (212)949-8294
Website: http://www.argentum
group.com

Axavision Inc.
14 Wall St., 26th Fl.
New York, NY 10005
(212)619-4000
Fax: (212)619-7202

Bedford Capital Corp.
18 East 48th St., Ste. 1800
New York, NY 10017
(212)688-5700
Fax: (212)754-4699
E-mail: info@bedfordnyc.com
Website: http://www.bedfordnyc.com

Bloom & Co.
950 Third Ave.

New York, NY 10022
(212)838-1858
Fax: (212)838-1843

Bristol Capital Management
300 Park Ave., 17th Fl.
New York, NY 10022
(212)572-6306
Fax: (212)705-4292

**Citicorp Venture Capital Ltd.
(New York City)**
399 Park Ave., 14th Fl.
Zone 4
New York, NY 10043
(212)559-1127
Fax: (212)888-2940

CM Equity Partners
135 E. 57th St.
New York, NY 10022
(212)909-8428
Fax: (212)980-2630

Cohen & Co., L.L.C.
800 Third Ave.
New York, NY 10022
(212)317-2250
Fax: (212)317-2255
E-mail: nlcohen@aol.com

Cornerstone Equity Investors, L.L.C.
717 5th Ave., Ste. 1100
New York, NY 10022
(212)753-0901
Fax: (212)826-6798
Website: http://www.cornerstone-
equity.com

CW Group, Inc.
1041 3rd Ave., 2nd fl.
New York, NY 10021
(212)308-5266
Fax: (212)644-0354
Website: http://www.cwventures.com

DH Blair Investment Banking Corp.
44 Wall St., 2nd Fl.
New York, NY 10005
(212)495-5000
Fax: (212)269-1438

Dresdner Kleinwort Capital
75 Wall St.
New York, NY 10005
(212)429-3131
Fax: (212)429-3139
Website: http://www.dresdnerkb.com

East River Ventures, L.P.
645 Madison Ave., 22nd Fl.

New York, NY 10022
(212)644-2322
Fax: (212)644-5498

Easton Hunt Capital Partners
641 Lexington Ave., 21st Fl.
New York, NY 10017
(212)702-0950
Fax: (212)702-0952
Website: http://www.eastoncapital.com

Elk Associates Funding Corp.
747 3rd Ave., Ste. 4C
New York, NY 10017
(212)355-2449
Fax: (212)759-3338

EOS Partners, L.P.
320 Park Ave., 22nd Fl.
New York, NY 10022
(212)832-5800
Fax: (212)832-5815
E-mail: mfirst@eospartners.com
Website: http://www.eospartners.com

Euclid Partners
45 Rockefeller Plaza, Ste. 3240
New York, NY 10111
(212)218-6880
Fax: (212)218-6877
E-mail: graham@euclidpartners.com
Website: http://www.euclidpartners.com

Evergreen Capital Partners, Inc.
150 East 58th St.
New York, NY 10155
(212)813-0758
Fax: (212)813-0754

Exeter Capital L.P.
10 E. 53rd St.
New York, NY 10022
(212)872-1172
Fax: (212)872-1198
E-mail: exeter@usa.net

Financial Technology Research Corp.
518 Broadway
Penthouse
New York, NY 10012
(212)625-9100
Fax: (212)431-0300
E-mail: fintek@financier.com

4C Ventures
237 Park Ave., Ste. 801
New York, NY 10017
(212)692-3680
Fax: (212)692-3685
Website: http://www.4cventures.com

Fusient Ventures
99 Park Ave., 20th Fl.
New York, NY 10016
(212)972-8999
Fax: (212)972-9876
E-mail: info@fusient.com
Website: http://www.fusient.com

Generation Capital Partners
551 Fifth Ave., Ste. 3100
New York, NY 10176
(212)450-8507
Fax: (212)450-8550
Website: http://www.genpartners.com

Golub Associates, Inc.
555 Madison Ave.
New York, NY 10022
(212)750-6060
Fax: (212)750-5505

Hambro America Biosciences Inc.
650 Madison Ave., 21st Floor
New York, NY 10022
(212)223-7400
Fax: (212)223-0305

Hanover Capital Corp.
505 Park Ave., 15th Fl.
New York, NY 10022
(212)755-1222
Fax: (212)935-1787

Harvest Partners, Inc.
280 Park Ave, 33rd Fl.
New York, NY 10017
(212)559-6300
Fax: (212)812-0100
Website: http://www.harvpart.com

Holding Capital Group, Inc.
10 E. 53rd St., 30th Fl.
New York, NY 10022
(212)486-6670
Fax: (212)486-0843

Hudson Venture Partners
660 Madison Ave., 14th Fl.
New York, NY 10021-8405
(212)644-9797
Fax: (212)644-7430
Website: http://www.hudsonptr.com

IBJS Capital Corp.
1 State St., 9th Fl.
New York, NY 10004
(212)858-2018
Fax: (212)858-2768

InterEquity Capital Partners, L.P.
220 5th Ave.
New York, NY 10001

(212)779-2022
Fax: (212)779-2103
Website: http://www.interequity-capital.com

The Jordan Edmiston Group Inc.
150 East 52nd St., 18th Fl.
New York, NY 10022
(212)754-0710
Fax: (212)754-0337

Josephberg, Grosz and Co., Inc.
633 3rd Ave., 13th Fl.
New York, NY 10017
(212)974-9926
Fax: (212)397-5832

J.P. Morgan Capital Corp.
60 Wall St.
New York, NY 10260-0060
(212)648-9000
Fax: (212)648-5002
Website: http://www.jpmorgan.com

The Lambda Funds
380 Lexington Ave., 54th Fl.
New York, NY 10168
(212)682-3454
Fax: (212)682-9231

Lepercq Capital Management Inc.
1675 Broadway
New York, NY 10019
(212)698-0795
Fax: (212)262-0155

Loeb Partners Corp.
61 Broadway, Ste. 2400
New York, NY 10006
(212)483-7000
Fax: (212)574-2001

Madison Investment Partners
660 Madison Ave.
New York, NY 10021
(212)223-2600
Fax: (212)223-8208

MC Capital Inc.
520 Madison Ave., 16th Fl.
New York, NY 10022
(212)644-0841
Fax: (212)644-2926

McCown, De Leeuw and Co. (New York)
65 E. 55th St., 36th Fl.
New York, NY 10022
(212)355-5500
Fax: (212)355-6283
Website: http://www.mdcpartners.com

Morgan Stanley Venture Partners
1221 Avenue of the Americas, 33rd Fl.
New York, NY 10020
(212)762-7900
Fax: (212)762-8424
E-mail: msventures@ms.com
Website: http://www.msvp.com

Nazem and Co.
645 Madison Ave., 12th Fl.
New York, NY 10022
(212)371-7900
Fax: (212)371-2150

Needham Capital Management, L.L.C.
445 Park Ave.
New York, NY 10022
(212)371-8300
Fax: (212)705-0299
Website: http://www.needhamco.com

Norwood Venture Corp.
1430 Broadway, Ste. 1607
New York, NY 10018
(212)869-5075
Fax: (212)869-5331
E-mail: nvc@mail.idt.net
Website: http://www.norven.com

Noveltek Venture Corp.
521 Fifth Ave., Ste. 1700
New York, NY 10175
(212)286-1963

Paribas Principal, Inc.
787 7th Ave.
New York, NY 10019
(212)841-2005
Fax: (212)841-3558

**Patricof & Co. Ventures, Inc.
(New York)**
445 Park Ave.
New York, NY 10022
(212)753-6300
Fax: (212)319-6155
Website: http://www.patricof.com

The Platinum Group, Inc.
350 Fifth Ave, Ste. 7113
New York, NY 10118
(212)736-4300
Fax: (212)736-6086
Website: http://www.platinumgroup.com

Pomona Capital
780 Third Ave., 28th Fl.
New York, NY 10017
(212)593-3639
Fax: (212)593-3987
Website: http://www.pomonacapital.com

Prospect Street Ventures
10 East 40th St., 44th Fl.
New York, NY 10016
(212)448-0702
Fax: (212)448-9652
E-mail: wkohler@prospectstreet.com
Website: http://www.prospectstreet.com

Regent Capital Management
505 Park Ave., Ste. 1700
New York, NY 10022
(212)735-9900
Fax: (212)735-9908

Rothschild Ventures, Inc.
1251 Avenue of the Americas, 51st Fl.
New York, NY 10020
(212)403-3500
Fax: (212)403-3652
Website: http://www.nmrothschild.com

Sandler Capital Management
767 Fifth Ave., 45th Fl.
New York, NY 10153
(212)754-8100
Fax: (212)826-0280

Siguler Guff & Company
630 Fifth Ave., 16th Fl.
New York, NY 10111
(212)332-5100
Fax: (212)332-5120

Spencer Trask Ventures Inc.
535 Madison Ave.
New York, NY 10022
(212)355-5565
Fax: (212)751-3362
Website: http://www.spencertrask.com

Sprout Group (New York City)
277 Park Ave.
New York, NY 10172
(212)892-3600
Fax: (212)892-3444
E-mail: info@sproutgroup.com
Website: http://www.sproutgroup.com

US Trust Private Equity
114 W.47th St.
New York, NY 10036
(212)852-3949
Fax: (212)852-3759
Website: http://www.ustrust.com/
privateequity

Vencon Management Inc.
301 West 53rd St., Ste. 10F
New York, NY 10019
(212)581-8787
Fax: (212)397-4126
Website: http://www.venconinc.com

Venrock Associates
30 Rockefeller Plaza, Ste. 5508
New York, NY 10112
(212)649-5600
Fax: (212)649-5788
Website: http://www.venrock.com

Venture Capital Fund of America, Inc.
509 Madison Ave., Ste. 812
New York, NY 10022
(212)838-5577
Fax: (212)838-7614
E-mail: mail@vcfa.com
Website: http://www.vcfa.com

Venture Opportunities Corp.
150 E. 58th St.
New York, NY 10155
(212)832-3737
Fax: (212)980-6603

Warburg Pincus Ventures, Inc.
466 Lexington Ave., 11th Fl.
New York, NY 10017
(212)878-9309
Fax: (212)878-9200
Website: http://www.warburgpincus.com

Wasserstein, Perella & Co. Inc.
31 W. 52nd St., 27th Fl.
New York, NY 10019
(212)702-5691
Fax: (212)969-7879

Welsh, Carson, Anderson, & Stowe
320 Park Ave., Ste. 2500
New York, NY 10022-6815
(212)893-9500
Fax: (212)893-9575

Whitney and Co. (New York)
630 Fifth Ave. Ste. 3225
New York, NY 10111
(212)332-2400
Fax: (212)332-2422
Website: http://www.jhwitney.com

Winthrop Ventures
74 Trinity Place, Ste. 600
New York, NY 10006
(212)422-0100

The Pittsford Group
8 Lodge Pole Rd.
Pittsford, NY 14534
(716)223-3523

Genesee Funding
70 Linden Oaks, 3rd Fl.
Rochester, NY 14625
(716)383-5550
Fax: (716)383-5305

Gabelli Multimedia Partners
One Corporate Center
Rye, NY 10580
(914)921-5395
Fax: (914)921-5031

Stamford Financial
108 Main St.
Stamford, NY 12167
(607)652-3311
Fax: (607)652-6301
Website: http://www.stamford
financial.com

Northwood Ventures LLC
485 Underhill Blvd., Ste. 205
Syosset, NY 11791
(516)364-5544
Fax: (516)364-0879
E-mail: northwood@northwood.com
Website: http://www.north
woodventures.com

Exponential Business Development Co.
216 Walton St.
Syracuse, NY 13202-1227
(315)474-4500
Fax: (315)474-4682
E-mail: dirksonn@aol.com
Website: http://www.exponential-ny.com

Onondaga Venture Capital Fund Inc.
714 State Tower Bldg.
Syracuse, NY 13202
(315)478-0157
Fax: (315)478-0158

Bessemer Venture Partners (Westbury)
1400 Old Country Rd., Ste. 109
Westbury, NY 11590
(516)997-2300
Fax: (516)997-2371
E-mail: bob@bvpny.com
Website: http://www.bvp.com

Ovation Capital Partners
120 Bloomingdale Rd., 4th Fl.
White Plains, NY 10605
(914)258-0011
Fax: (914)684-0848
Website: http://www.ovation
capital.com

North Carolina

Carolinas Capital Investment Corp.
1408 Biltmore Dr.
Charlotte, NC 28207
(704)375-3888
Fax: (704)375-6226

First Union Capital Partners
1st Union Center, 12th Fl.
301 S. College St.
Charlotte, NC 28288-0732
(704)383-0000
Fax: (704)374-6711
Website: http://www.fucp.com

Frontier Capital LLC
525 North Tryon St., Ste. 1700
Charlotte, NC 28202
(704)414-2880
Fax: (704)414-2881
Website: http://www.frontierfunds.com

Kitty Hawk Capital
2700 Coltsgate Rd., Ste. 202
Charlotte, NC 28211
(704)362-3909
Fax: (704)362-2774
Website: http://www.kittyhawk
capital.com

Piedmont Venture Partners
One Morrocroft Centre
6805 Morisson Blvd., Ste. 380
Charlotte, NC 28211
(704)731-5200
Fax: (704)365-9733
Website: http://www.piedmontvp.com

Ruddick Investment Co.
1800 Two First Union Center
Charlotte, NC 28282
(704)372-5404
Fax: (704)372-6409

The Shelton Companies Inc.
3600 One First Union Center
301 S. College St.
Charlotte, NC 28202
(704)348-2200
Fax: (704)348-2260

Wakefield Group
1110 E. Morehead St.
PO Box 36329
Charlotte, NC 28236
(704)372-0355
Fax: (704)372-8216
Website: http://www.wakefield
group.com

Aurora Funds, Inc.
2525 Meridian Pkwy., Ste. 220
Durham, NC 27713
(919)484-0400
Fax: (919)484-0444
Website: http://www.aurora
funds.com

Intersouth Partners
3211 Shannon Rd., Ste. 610
Durham, NC 27707
(919)493-6640
Fax: (919)493-6649
E-mail: info@intersouth.com
Website: http://www.intersouth.com

Geneva Merchant Banking Partners
PO Box 21962
Greensboro, NC 27420
(336)275-7002
Fax: (336)275-9155
Website: http://www.geneva
merchantbank.com

The North Carolina Enterprise Fund, L.P.
3600 Glenwood Ave., Ste. 107
Raleigh, NC 27612
(919)781-2691
Fax: (919)783-9195
Website: http://www.ncef.com

Ohio

Senmend Medical Ventures
4445 Lake Forest Dr., Ste. 600
Cincinnati, OH 45242
(513)563-3264
Fax: (513)563-3261

The Walnut Group
312 Walnut St., Ste. 1151
Cincinnati, OH 45202
(513)651-3300
Fax: (513)929-4441
Website: http://www.thewal
nutgroup.com

Brantley Venture Partners
20600 Chagrin Blvd., Ste. 1150
Cleveland, OH 44122
(216)283-4800
Fax: (216)283-5324

Clarion Capital Corp.
1801 E. 9th St., Ste. 1120
Cleveland, OH 44114
(216)687-1096
Fax: (216)694-3545

Crystal Internet Venture Fund, L.P.
1120 Chester Ave., Ste. 418
Cleveland, OH 44114
(216)263-5515
Fax: (216)263-5518
E-mail: jf@crystalventure.com
Website: http://www.crystal
venture.com

Key Equity Capital Corp.
127 Public Sq., 28th Fl.
Cleveland, OH 44114
(216)689-3000
Fax: (216)689-3204
Website: http://www.keybank.com

Morgenthaler Ventures
Terminal Tower
50 Public Square, Ste. 2700
Cleveland, OH 44113
(216)416-7500
Fax: (216)416-7501
Website: http://www.morgenthaler.com

National City Equity Partners Inc.
1965 E. 6th St.
Cleveland, OH 44114
(216)575-2491
Fax: (216)575-9965
E-mail: nccap@aol.com
Website: http://www.nccapital.com

Primus Venture Partners, Inc.
5900 LanderBrook Dr., Ste. 2000
Cleveland, OH 44124-4020
(440)684-7300
Fax: (440)684-7342
E-mail: info@primusventure.com
Website: http://www.primusventure.com

Banc One Capital Partners (Columbus)
150 East Gay St., 24th Fl.
Columbus, OH 43215
(614)217-1100
Fax: (614)217-1217

Battelle Venture Partners
505 King Ave.
Columbus, OH 43201
(614)424-7005
Fax: (614)424-4874

Ohio Partners
62 E. Board St., 3rd Fl.
Columbus, OH 43215
(614)621-1210
Fax: (614)621-1240

Capital Technology Group, L.L.C.
400 Metro Place North, Ste. 300
Dublin, OH 43017
(614)792-6066
Fax: (614)792-6036
E-mail: info@capitaltech.com
Website: http://www.capitaltech.com

Northwest Ohio Venture Fund
4159 Holland-Sylvania R., Ste. 202
Toledo, OH 43623
(419)824-8144

Fax: (419)882-2035
E-mail: bwalsh@novf.com

Oklahoma

Moore & Associates
1000 W. Wilshire Blvd., Ste. 370
Oklahoma City, OK 73116
(405)842-3660
Fax: (405)842-3763

Chisholm Private Capital Partners
100 West 5th St., Ste. 805
Tulsa, OK 74103
(918)584-0440
Fax: (918)584-0441
Website: http://www.chisholmvc.com

Davis, Tuttle Venture Partners (Tulsa)
320 S. Boston, Ste. 1000
Tulsa, OK 74103-3703
(918)584-7272
Fax: (918)582-3404
Website: http://www.davistuttle.com

RBC Ventures
2627 E. 21st St.
Tulsa, OK 74114
(918)744-5607
Fax: (918)743-8630

Oregon

Utah Ventures II LP
10700 SW Beaverton-Hillsdale Hwy.,
Ste. 548
Beaverton, OR 97005
(503)574-4125
E-mail: adishlip@uven.com
Website: http://www.uven.com

Orien Ventures
14523 SW Westlake Dr.
Lake Oswego, OR 97035
(503)699-1680
Fax: (503)699-1681

OVP Venture Partners (Lake Oswego)
340 Oswego Pointe Dr., Ste. 200
Lake Oswego, OR 97034
(503)697-8766
Fax: (503)697-8863
E-mail: info@ovp.com
Website: http://www.ovp.com

Oregon Resource and Technology Development Fund
4370 NE Halsey St., Ste. 233
Portland, OR 97213-1566
(503)282-4462
Fax: (503)282-2976

Shaw Venture Partners
400 SW 6th Ave., Ste. 1100
Portland, OR 97204-1636
(503)228-4884
Fax: (503)227-2471
Website: http://www.shawventures.com

Pennsylvania

Mid-Atlantic Venture Funds
125 Goodman Dr.
Bethlehem, PA 18015
(610)865-6550
Fax: (610)865-6427
Website: http://www.mavf.com

Newspring Ventures
100 W. Elm St., Ste. 101
Conshohocken, PA 19428
(610)567-2380
Fax: (610)567-2388
Website: http://www.news
printventures.com

Patricof & Co. Ventures, Inc.
455 S. Gulph Rd., Ste. 410
King of Prussia, PA 19406
(610)265-0286
Fax: (610)265-4959
Website: http://www.patricof.com

Loyalhanna Venture Fund
527 Cedar Way, Ste. 104
Oakmont, PA 15139
(412)820-7035
Fax: (412)820-7036

Innovest Group Inc.
2000 Market St., Ste. 1400
Philadelphia, PA 19103
(215)564-3960
Fax: (215)569-3272

Keystone Venture Capital Management Co.
1601 Market St., Ste. 2500
Philadelphia, PA 19103
(215)241-1200
Fax: (215)241-1211
Website: http://www.keystonevc.com

Liberty Venture Partners
2005 Market St., Ste. 200
Philadelphia, PA 19103
(215)282-4484
Fax: (215)282-4485
E-mail: info@libertyvp.com
Website: http://www.libertyvp.com

Penn Janney Fund, Inc.
1801 Market St., 11th Fl.
Philadelphia, PA 19103

(215)665-4447
Fax: (215)557-0820

Philadelphia Ventures, Inc.
The Bellevue
200 S. Broad St.
Philadelphia, PA 19102
(215)732-4445
Fax: (215)732-4644

Birchmere Ventures Inc.
2000 Technology Dr.
Pittsburgh, PA 15219-3109
(412)803-8000
Fax: (412)687-8139
Website: http://www.birchmerevc.com

CEO Venture Fund
2000 Technology Dr., Ste. 160
Pittsburgh, PA 15219-3109
(412)687-3451
Fax: (412)687-8139
E-mail: ceofund@aol.com
Website: http://www.ceoventure
fund.com

Innovation Works Inc.
2000 Technology Dr., Ste. 250
Pittsburgh, PA 15219
(412)681-1520
Fax: (412)681-2625
Website: http://www.innovation
works.org

Keystone Minority Capital Fund L.P.
1801 Centre Ave., Ste. 201
Williams Sq.
Pittsburgh, PA 15219
(412)338-2230
Fax: (412)338-2224

Mellon Ventures, Inc.
One Mellon Bank Ctr., Rm. 3500
Pittsburgh, PA 15258
(412)236-3594
Fax: (412)236-3593
Website: http://www.mellon
ventures.com

Pennsylvania Growth Fund
5850 Ellsworth Ave., Ste. 303
Pittsburgh, PA 15232
(412)661-1000
Fax: (412)361-0676

Point Venture Partners
The Century Bldg.
130 Seventh St., 7th Fl.
Pittsburgh, PA 15222
(412)261-1966
Fax: (412)261-1718

Cross Atlantic Capital Partners
5 Radnor Corporate Center, Ste. 555
Radnor, PA 19087
(610)995-2650
Fax: (610)971-2062
Website: http://www.xacp.com

Meridian Venture Partners (Radnor)
The Radnor Court Bldg., Ste. 140
259 Radnor-Chester Rd.
Radnor, PA 19087
(610)254-2999
Fax: (610)254-2996
E-mail: mvpart@ix.netcom.com

TDH
919 Conestoga Rd., Bldg. 1, Ste. 301
Rosemont, PA 19010
(610)526-9970
Fax: (610)526-9971

Adams Capital Management
500 Blackburn Ave.
Sewickley, PA 15143
(412)749-9454
Fax: (412)749-9459
Website: http://www.acm.com

S.R. One, Ltd.
Four Tower Bridge
200 Barr Harbor Dr., Ste. 250
W. Conshohocken, PA 19428
(610)567-1000
Fax: (610)567-1039

Greater Philadelphia Venture Capital Corp.
351 East Conestoga Rd.
Wayne, PA 19087
(610)688-6829
Fax: (610)254-8958

PA Early Stage
435 Devon Park Dr., Bldg. 500, Ste. 510
Wayne, PA 19087
(610)293-4075
Fax: (610)254-4240
Website: http://www.paearlystage.com

The Sandhurst Venture Fund, L.P.
351 E. Constoga Rd.
Wayne, PA 19087
(610)254-8900
Fax: (610)254-8958

TL Ventures
700 Bldg.
435 Devon Park Dr.
Wayne, PA 19087-1990
(610)975-3765
Fax: (610)254-4210
Website: http://www.tlventures.com

Rockhill Ventures, Inc.
100 Front St., Ste. 1350
West Conshohocken, PA 19428
(610)940-0300
Fax: (610)940-0301

Puerto Rico

Advent-Morro Equity Partners
Banco Popular Bldg.
206 Tetuan St., Ste. 903
San Juan, PR 00902
(787)725-5285
Fax: (787)721-1735

North America Investment Corp.
Mercantil Plaza, Ste. 813
PO Box 191831
San Juan, PR 00919
(787)754-6178
Fax: (787)754-6181

Rhode Island

Manchester Humphreys, Inc.
40 Westminster St., Ste. 900
Providence, RI 02903
(401)454-0400
Fax: (401)454-0403

Navis Partners
50 Kennedy Plaza, 12th Fl.
Providence, RI 02903
(401)278-6770
Fax: (401)278-6387
Website: http://www.navis
partners.com

South Carolina

Capital Insights, L.L.C.
PO Box 27162
Greenville, SC 29616-2162
(864)242-6832
Fax: (864)242-6755
E-mail: jwarner@capitalinsights.com
Website: http://www.capitalin
sights.com

Transamerica Mezzanine Financing
7 N. Laurens St., Ste. 603
Greenville, SC 29601
(864)232-6198
Fax: (864)241-4444

Tennessee

Valley Capital Corp.
Krystal Bldg.
100 W. Martin Luther King Blvd.,
Ste. 212

Chattanooga, TN 37402
(423)265-1557
Fax: (423)265-1588

Coleman Swenson Booth Inc.
237 2nd Ave. S
Franklin, TN 37064-2649
(615)791-9462
Fax: (615)791-9636
Website: http://
www.colemanswenson.com

Capital Services & Resources, Inc.
5159 Wheelis Dr., Ste. 106
Memphis, TN 38117
(901)761-2156
Fax: (907)767-0060

Paradigm Capital Partners LLC
6410 Poplar Ave., Ste. 395
Memphis, TN 38119
(901)682-6060
Fax: (901)328-3061

SSM Ventures
845 Crossover Ln., Ste. 140
Memphis, TN 38117
(901)767-1131
Fax: (901)767-1135
Website: http://www.ssm
ventures.com

Capital Across America L.P.
501 Union St., Ste. 201
Nashville, TN 37219
(615)254-1414
Fax: (615)254-1856
Website: http://
www.capitalacrossamerica.com

Equitas L.P.
2000 Glen Echo Rd., Ste. 101
PO Box 158838
Nashville, TN 37215-8838
(615)383-8673
Fax: (615)383-8693

Massey Burch Capital Corp.
One Burton Hills Blvd., Ste. 350
Nashville, TN 37215
(615)665-3221
Fax: (615)665-3240
E-mail: tcalton@masseyburch.com
Website: http://www.masseyburch.com

Nelson Capital Corp.
3401 West End Ave., Ste. 300
Nashville, TN 37203
(615)292-8787
Fax: (615)385-3150

Texas

Phillips-Smith Specialty Retail Group
5080 Spectrum Dr., Ste. 805 W
Addison, TX 75001
(972)387-0725
Fax: (972)458-2560
E-mail: pssrg@aol.com
Website: http://www.phillips-smith.com

Austin Ventures, L.P.
701 Brazos St., Ste. 1400
Austin, TX 78701
(512)485-1900
Fax: (512)476-3952
E-mail: info@ausven.com
Website: http://www.austinventures.com

The Capital Network
3925 West Braker Lane, Ste. 406
Austin, TX 78759-5321
(512)305-0826
Fax: (512)305-0836

Techxas Ventures LLC
5000 Plaza on the Lake
Austin, TX 78746
(512)343-0118
Fax: (512)343-1879
E-mail: bruce@techxas.com
Website: http://www.techxas.com

Alliance Financial of Houston
218 Heather Ln.
Conroe, TX 77385-9013
(936)447-3300
Fax: (936)447-4222

Amerimark Capital Corp.
1111 W. Mockingbird, Ste. 1111
Dallas, TX 75247
(214)638-7878
Fax: (214)638-7612
E-mail: amerimark@amcapital.com
Website: http://www.amcapital.com

AMT Venture Partners / AMT Capital Ltd.
5220 Spring Valley Rd., Ste. 600
Dallas, TX 75240
(214)905-9757
Fax: (214)905-9761
Website: http://www.amtcapital.com

Arkoma Venture Partners
5950 Berkshire Lane, Ste. 1400
Dallas, TX 75225
(214)739-3515
Fax: (214)739-3572
E-mail: joelf@arkomavp.com

Capital Southwest Corp.
12900 Preston Rd., Ste. 700
Dallas, TX 75230
(972)233-8242
Fax: (972)233-7362
Website: http://
www.capitalsouthwest.com

Dali, Hook Partners
One Lincoln Center, Ste. 1550
5400 LBJ Freeway
Dallas, TX 75240
(972)991-5457
Fax: (972)991-5458
E-mail: dhook@hookpartners.com
Website: http://www.hookpartners.com

HO2 Partners
Two Galleria Tower
13455 Noel Rd., Ste. 1670
Dallas, TX 75240
(972)702-1144
Fax: (972)702-8234
Website: http://www.ho2.com

Interwest Partners (Dallas)
2 Galleria Tower
13455 Noel Rd., Ste. 1670
Dallas, TX 75240
(972)392-7279
Fax: (972)490-6348
Website: http://www.interwest.com

Kahala Investments, Inc.
8214 Westchester Dr., Ste. 715
Dallas, TX 75225
(214)987-0077
Fax: (214)987-2332

MESBIC Ventures Holding Co.
2435 North Central Expressway, Ste. 200
Dallas, TX 75080
(972)991-1597
Fax: (972)991-4770
Website: http://www.mvhc.com

North Texas MESBIC, Inc.
9500 Forest Lane, Ste. 430
Dallas, TX 75243
(214)221-3565
Fax: (214)221-3566

Richard Jaffe & Company, Inc,
7318 Royal Cir.
Dallas, TX 75230
(214)265-9397
Fax: (214)739-1845

Sevin Rosen Management Co.
13455 Noel Rd., Ste. 1670
Dallas, TX 75240

(972)702-1100
Fax: (972)702-1103
E-mail: info@srfunds.com
Website: http://www.srfunds.com

Stratford Capital Partners, L.P.
300 Crescent Ct., Ste. 500
Dallas, TX 75201
(214)740-7377
Fax: (214)720-7393
E-mail: stratcap@hmtf.com

Sunwestern Investment Group
12221 Merit Dr., Ste. 935
Dallas, TX 75251
(972)239-5650
Fax: (972)701-0024

Wingate Partners
750 N. St. Paul St., Ste. 1200
Dallas, TX 75201
(214)720-1313
Fax: (214)871-8799

Buena Venture Associates
201 Main St., 32nd Fl.
Fort Worth, TX 76102
(817)339-7400
Fax: (817)390-8408
Website: http://www.buenaventure.com

The Catalyst Group
3 Riverway, Ste. 770
Houston, TX 77056
(713)623-8133
Fax: (713)623-0473
E-mail: herman@thecatalystgroup.net
Website: http://www.thecatalyst
group.net

Cureton & Co., Inc.
1100 Louisiana, Ste. 3250
Houston, TX 77002
(713)658-9806
Fax: (713)658-0476

Davis, Tuttle Venture Partners (Dallas)
8 Greenway Plaza, Ste. 1020
Houston, TX 77046
(713)993-0440
Fax: (713)621-2297
Website: http://www.davistuttle.com

Houston Partners
401 Louisiana, 8th Fl.
Houston, TX 77002
(713)222-8600
Fax: (713)222-8932

Southwest Venture Group
10878 Westheimer, Ste. 178

Houston, TX 77042
(713)827-8947
(713)461-1470

AM Fund
4600 Post Oak Place, Ste. 100
Houston, TX 77027
(713)627-9111
Fax: (713)627-9119

Ventex Management, Inc.
3417 Milam St.
Houston, TX 77002-9531
(713)659-7870
Fax: (713)659-7855

MBA Venture Group
1004 Olde Town Rd., Ste. 102
Irving, TX 75061
(972)986-6703

First Capital Group Management Co.
750 East Mulberry St., Ste. 305
PO Box 15616
San Antonio, TX 78212
(210)736-4233
Fax: (210)736-5449

The Southwest Venture Partnerships
16414 San Pedro, Ste. 345
San Antonio, TX 78232
(210)402-1200
Fax: (210)402-1221
E-mail: swvp@aol.com

Medtech International Inc.
1742 Carriageway
Sugarland, TX 77478
(713)980-8474
Fax: (713)980-6343

Utah

First Security Business Investment Corp.
15 East 100 South, Ste. 100
Salt Lake City, UT 84111
(801)246-5737
Fax: (801)246-5740

Utah Ventures II, L.P.
423 Wakara Way, Ste. 206
Salt Lake City, UT 84108
(801)583-5922
Fax: (801)583-4105
Website: http://www.uven.com

Wasatch Venture Corp.
1 S. Main St., Ste. 1400
Salt Lake City, UT 84133
(801)524-8939

Fax: (801)524-8941
E-mail: mail@wasatchvc.com

Vermont

North Atlantic Capital Corp.
76 Saint Paul St., Ste. 600
Burlington, VT 05401
(802)658-7820
Fax: (802)658-5757
Website: http://www.north
atlanticcapital.com

Green Mountain Advisors Inc.
PO Box 1230
Quechee, VT 05059
(802)296-7800
Fax: (802)296-6012
Website: http://www.gmtcap.com

Virginia

Oxford Financial Services Corp.
Alexandria, VA 22314
(703)519-4900
Fax: (703)519-4910
E-mail: oxford133@aol.com

Continental SBIC
4141 N. Henderson Rd.
Arlington, VA 22203
(703)527-5200
Fax: (703)527-3700

Novak Biddle Venture Partners
1750 Tysons Blvd., Ste. 1190
McLean, VA 22102
(703)847-3770
Fax: (703)847-3771
E-mail: roger@novakbiddle.com
Website: http://www.novakbiddle.com

Spacevest
11911 Freedom Dr., Ste. 500
Reston, VA 20190
(703)904-9800
Fax: (703)904-0571
E-mail: spacevest@spacevest.com
Website: http://www.spacevest.com

Virginia Capital
1801 Libbie Ave., Ste. 201
Richmond, VA 23226
(804)648-4802
Fax: (804)648-4809
E-mail: webmaster@vacapital.com
Website: http://www.vacapital.com

Calvert Social Venture Partners
402 Maple Ave. W
Vienna, VA 22180

Organizations, Agencies, & Consultants

(703)255-4930
Fax: (703)255-4931
E-mail: calven2000@aol.com

Fairfax Partners
8000 Towers Crescent Dr., Ste. 940
Vienna, VA 22182
(703)847-9486
Fax: (703)847-0911

Global Internet Ventures
8150 Leesburg Pike, Ste. 1210
Vienna, VA 22182
(703)442-3300
Fax: (703)442-3388
Website: http://www.givinc.com

Walnut Capital Corp. (Vienna)
8000 Towers Crescent Dr., Ste. 1070
Vienna, VA 22182
(703)448-3771
Fax: (703)448-7751

Washington

Encompass Ventures
777 108th Ave. NE, Ste. 2300
Bellevue, WA 98004
(425)486-3900
Fax: (425)486-3901
E-mail: info@evpartners.com
Website: http://www.encom
passventures.com

Fluke Venture Partners
11400 SE Sixth St., Ste. 230
Bellevue, WA 98004
(425)453-4590
Fax: (425)453-4675
E-mail: gabelein@flukeventures.com
Website: http://www.flukeventures.com

Pacific Northwest Partners SBIC, L.P.
15352 SE 53rd St.
Bellevue, WA 98006
(425)455-9967
Fax: (425)455-9404

Materia Venture Associates, L.P.
3435 Carillon Pointe
Kirkland, WA 98033-7354
(425)822-4100
Fax: (425)827-4086

OVP Venture Partners (Kirkland)
2420 Carillon Pt.
Kirkland, WA 98033
(425)889-9192
Fax: (425)889-0152
E-mail: info@ovp.com
Website: http://www.ovp.com

Digital Partners
999 3rd Ave., Ste. 1610
Seattle, WA 98104
(206)405-3607
Fax: (206)405-3617
Website: http://www.digitalpartners.com

Frazier & Company
601 Union St., Ste. 3300
Seattle, WA 98101
(206)621-7200
Fax: (206)621-1848
E-mail: jon@frazierco.com

Kirlan Venture Capital, Inc.
221 First Ave. W, Ste. 108
Seattle, WA 98119-4223
(206)281-8610
Fax: (206)285-3451
Website: http://www.kirlanventure.com

Phoenix Partners
1000 2nd Ave., Ste. 3600
Seattle, WA 98104
(206)624-8968
Fax: (206)624-1907

Voyager Capital
800 5th St., Ste. 4100
Seattle, WA 98103
(206)470-1180
Fax: (206)470-1185
E-mail: info@voyagercap.com
Website: http://www.voyagercap.com

Northwest Venture Associates
221 N. Wall St., Ste. 628
Spokane, WA 99201
(509)747-0728
Fax: (509)747-0758
Website: http://www.nwva.com

Wisconsin

Venture Investors Management, L.L.C.
University Research Park
505 S. Rosa Rd.
Madison, WI 53719
(608)441-2700
Fax: (608)441-2727
E-mail: roger@ventureinvestors.com
Website: http://www.venture
investers.com

Capital Investments, Inc.
1009 West Glen Oaks Lane, Ste. 103
Mequon, WI 53092
(414)241-0303
Fax: (414)241-8451
Website: http://
www.capitalinvestmentsinc.com

Future Value Venture, Inc.
2745 N. Martin Luther King
Dr., Ste. 204
Milwaukee, WI 53212-2300
(414)264-2252
Fax: (414)264-2253
E-mail: fvvventures@aol.com
William Beckett, President

Lubar and Co., Inc.
700 N. Water St., Ste. 1200
Milwaukee, WI 53202
(414)291-9000
Fax: (414)291-9061

GCI
20875 Crossroads Cir., Ste. 100
Waukesha, WI 53186
(262)798-5080
Fax: (262)798-5087

Glossary of Small Business Terms

Absolute liability
Liability that is incurred due to product defects or negligent actions. Manufacturers or retail establishments are held responsible, even though the defect or action may not have been intentional or negligent.

ACE
See Active Corps of Executives

Accident and health benefits
Benefits offered to employees and their families in order to offset the costs associated with accidental death, accidental injury, or sickness.

Account statement
A record of transactions, including payments, new debt, and deposits, incurred during a defined period of time.

Accounting system
System capturing the costs of all employees and/or machinery included in business expenses.

Accounts payable
See Trade credit

Accounts receivable
Unpaid accounts which arise from unsettled claims and transactions from the sale of a company's products or services to its customers.

Active Corps of Executives (ACE)
A group of volunteers for a management assistance program of the U.S. Small Business Administration; volunteers provide one-on-one counseling and teach workshops and seminars for small firms.

ADA
See Americans with Disabilities Act

Adaptation
The process whereby an invention is modified to meet the needs of users.

Adaptive engineering
The process whereby an invention is modified to meet the manufacturing and commercial requirements of a targeted market.

Adverse selection
The tendency for higher-risk individuals to purchase health care and more comprehensive plans, resulting in increased costs.

Advertising
A marketing tool used to capture public attention and influence purchasing decisions for a product or service. Utilizes various forms of media to generate consumer response, such as flyers, magazines, newspapers, radio, and television.

Age discrimination
The denial of the rights and privileges of employment based solely on the age of an individual.

Agency costs
Costs incurred to insure that the lender or investor maintains control over assets while allowing the borrower or entrepreneur to use them. Monitoring and information costs are the two major types of agency costs.

Agribusiness
The production and sale of commodities and products from the commercial farming industry.

America Online
An online service which is accessible by computer modem. The service features Internet access, bulletin boards, online periodicals, electronic mail, and other services for subscribers.

Americans with Disabilities Act (ADA)
Law designed to ensure equal access and opportunity to handicapped persons.

Annual report
Yearly financial report prepared by a business that adheres to the requirements set forth by the Securities and Exchange Commission (SEC).

Antitrust immunity
Exemption from prosecution under antitrust laws. In the transportation industry, firms with antitrust immunity are permitted under certain conditions to set schedules and sometimes prices for the public benefit.

Applied research
Scientific study targeted for use in a product or process.

Asians
A minority category used by the U.S. Bureau of the Census to represent a diverse group that includes Aleuts, Eskimos, American Indians, Asian Indians, Chinese, Japanese, Koreans, Vietnamese, Filipinos, Hawaiians, and other Pacific Islanders.

Assets
Anything of value owned by a company.

Audit
The verification of accounting records and business procedures conducted by an outside accounting service.

Average cost
Total production costs divided by the quantity produced.

Balance Sheet
A financial statement listing the total assets and liabilities of a company at a given time.

Bankruptcy
The condition in which a business cannot meet its debt obligations and petitions a federal district court either for reorganization of its debts (Chapter 11) or for liquidation of its assets (Chapter 7).

Basic research
Theoretical scientific exploration not targeted to application.

Basket clause
A provision specifying the amount of public pension funds that may be placed in investments not included on a state's legal list (see separate citation).

BBS
See Bulletin Board Service

BDC
See Business development corporation

Benefit
Various services, such as health care, flextime, day care, insurance, and vacation, offered to employees as part of a hiring package. Typically subsidized in whole or in part by the business.

BIDCO
See Business and industrial development company

Billing cycle
A system designed to evenly distribute customer billing throughout the month, preventing clerical backlogs.

Birth
See Business birth

Blue chip security
A low-risk, low-yield security representing an interest in a very stable company.

Blue sky laws
A general term that denotes various states' laws regulating securities.

Bond
A written instrument executed by a bidder or contractor (the principal) and a second party (the surety or sureties) to assure fulfillment of the principal's obligations to a third party (the obligee or government) identified in the bond. If the principal's obligations are not met, the bond assures payment to the extent stipulated of any loss sustained by the obligee.

Bonding requirements
Terms contained in a bond (see separate citation).

Bonus
An amount of money paid to an employee as a reward for achieving certain business goals or objectives.

Brainstorming
A group session where employees contribute their ideas for solving a problem or meeting a company objective without fear of retribution or ridicule.

Brand name
The part of a brand, trademark, or service mark that can be spoken. It can be a word, letter, or group of words or letters.

Bridge financing
A short-term loan made in expectation of intermediateterm or long-term financing. Can be used when a company plans to go public in the near future.

Broker
One who matches resources available for innovation with those who need them.

Budget
An estimate of the spending necessary to complete a project or offer a service in comparison to cash-on-hand and expected earnings for the coming year, with an emphasis on cost control.

Bulletin Board Service (BBS)
An online service enabling users to communicate with each other about specific topics.

Business and industrial development company (BIDCO)
A private, for-profit financing corporation chartered by the state to provide both equity and long-term debt capital to small business owners (see separate citations for equity and debt capital).

Business birth
The formation of a new establishment or enterprise. The appearance of a new establishment or enterprise in the Small Business Data Base (see separate citation).

Business conditions
Outside factors that can affect the financial performance of a business.

Business contractions
The number of establishments that have decreased in employment during a specified time.

Business cycle
A period of economic recession and recovery. These cycles vary in duration.

Business death
The voluntary or involuntary closure of a firm or establishment. The disappearance of an establishment or enterprise from the Small Business Data Base (see separate citation).

Business development corporation (BDC)
A business financing agency, usually composed of the financial institutions in an area or state, organized to assist in financing businesses unable to obtain assistance through normal channels; the risk is spread among various members of the business development corporation, and interest rates may vary somewhat from those charged by member institutions. A venture capital firm in which shares of ownership are publicly held and to which the Investment Act of 1940 applies.

Business dissolution
For enumeration purposes, the absence of a business that was present in the prior time period from any current record.

Business entry
See Business birth

Business ethics
Moral values and principles espoused by members of the business community as a guide to fair and honest business practices.

Business exit
See Business death

Business expansions
The number of establishments that added employees during a specified time.

Business failure
Closure of a business causing a loss to at least one creditor.

Business format franchising
The purchase of the name, trademark, and an ongoing business plan of the parent corporation or franchisor by the franchisee.

Business license
A legal authorization issued by municipal and state governments and required for business operations.

Business name
Enterprises must register their business names with local governments usually on a "doing business as" (DBA) form. (This name is sometimes referred to as a

Glossary

"fictional name.") The procedure is part of the business licensing process and prevents any other business from using that same name for a similar business in the same locality.

Business norms
See Financial ratios

Business permit
See Business license

Business plan
A document that spells out a company's expected course of action for a specified period, usually including a detailed listing and analysis of risks and uncertainties. For the small business, it should examine the proposed products, the market, the industry, the management policies, the marketing policies, production needs, and financial needs. Frequently, it is used as a prospectus for potential investors and lenders.

Business proposal
See Business plan

Business service firm
An establishment primarily engaged in rendering services to other business organizations on a fee or contract basis.

Business start
For enumeration purposes, a business with a name or similar designation that did not exist in a prior time period.

Cafeteria plan
See Flexible benefit plan

Capacity
Level of a firm's, industry's, or nation's output corresponding to full practical utilization of available resources.

Capital
Assets less liabilities, representing the ownership interest in a business. A stock of accumulated goods, especially at a specified time and in contrast to income received during a specified time period. Accumulated goods devoted to production. Accumulated possessions calculated to bring income.

Capital expenditure
Expenses incurred by a business for improvements that will depreciate over time.

Capital gain
The monetary difference between the purchase price and the selling price of capital. Capital gains are taxed at a rate of 28% by the federal government.

Capital intensity
The relative importance of capital in the production process, usually expressed as the ratio of capital to labor but also sometimes as the ratio of capital to output.

Capital resource
The equipment, facilities and labor used to create products and services.

Caribbean Basin Initiative
An interdisciplinary program to support commerce among the businesses in the nations of the Caribbean Basin and the United States. Agencies involved include: the Agency for International Development, the U.S. Small Business Administration, the International Trade Administration of the U.S. Department of Commerce, and various private sector groups.

Catastrophic care
Medical and other services for acute and long-term illnesses that cost more than insurance coverage limits or that cost the amount most families may be expected to pay with their own resources.

CDC
See Certified development corporation

CD-ROM
Compact disc with read-only memory used to store large amounts of digitized data.

Certified development corporation (CDC)
A local area or statewide corporation or authority (for profit or nonprofit) that packages U.S. Small Business Administration (SBA), bank, state, and/or private money into financial assistance for existing business capital improvements. The SBA holds the second lien on its maximum share of 40 percent involvement. Each state has at least one certified development corporation. This program is called the SBA 504 Program.

Certified lenders
Banks that participate in the SBA guaranteed loan program (see separate citation). Such banks must have a good track record with the U.S. Small Business Administration (SBA) and must agree to certain conditions set forth by the agency. In return, the SBA agrees to process any guaranteed loan application within three business days.

Champion
An advocate for the development of an innovation.

Channel of distribution
The means used to transport merchandise from the manufacturer to the consumer.

Chapter 7 of the 1978 Bankruptcy Act
Provides for a court-appointed trustee who is responsible for liquidating a company's assets in order to settle outstanding debts.

Chapter 11 of the 1978 Bankruptcy Act
Allows the business owners to retain control of the company while working with their creditors to reorganize their finances and establish better business practices to prevent liquidation of assets.

Closely held corporation
A corporation in which the shares are held by a few persons, usually officers, employees, or others close to the management; these shares are rarely offered to the public.

Code of Federal Regulations
Codification of general and permanent rules of the federal government published in the Federal Register.

Code sharing
See Computer code sharing

Coinsurance
Upon meeting the deductible payment, health insurance participants may be required to make additional health care cost-sharing payments. Coinsurance is a payment of a fixed percentage of the cost of each service; copayment is usually a fixed amount to be paid with each service.

Collateral
Securities, evidence of deposit, or other property pledged by a borrower to secure repayment of a loan.

Collective ratemaking
The establishment of uniform charges for services by a group of businesses in the same industry.

Commercial insurance plan
See Underwriting

Commercial loans
Short-term renewable loans used to finance specific capital needs of a business.

Commercialization
The final stage of the innovation process, including production and distribution.

Common stock
The most frequently used instrument for purchasing ownership in private or public companies. Common stock generally carries the right to vote on certain corporate actions and may pay dividends, although it rarely does in venture investments. In liquidation, common stockholders are the last to share in the proceeds from the sale of a corporation's assets; bondholders and preferred shareholders have priority. Common stock is often used in firstround start-up financing.

Community development corporation
A corporation established to develop economic programs for a community and, in most cases, to provide financial support for such development.

Competitor
A business whose product or service is marketed for the same purpose/use and to the same consumer group as the product or service of another.

Computer code sharing
An arrangement whereby flights of a regional airline are identified by the two-letter code of a major carrier in the computer reservation system to help direct passengers to new regional carriers.

Consignment
A merchandising agreement, usually referring to secondhand shops, where the dealer pays the owner of an item a percentage of the profit when the item is sold.

Consortium
A coalition of organizations such as banks and corporations for ventures requiring large capital resources.

Consultant
An individual that is paid by a business to provide advice and expertise in a particular area.

Consumer price index
A measure of the fluctuation in prices between two points in time.

Consumer research
Research conducted by a business to obtain information about existing or potential consumer markets.

Continuation coverage
Health coverage offered for a specified period of time to employees who leave their jobs and to their widows, divorced spouses, or dependents.

Contractions
See Business contractions

Convertible preferred stock
A class of stock that pays a reasonable dividend and is convertible into common stock (see separate citation). Generally the convertible feature may only be exercised after being held for a stated period of time. This arrangement is usually considered second-round financing when a company needs equity to maintain its cash flow.

Convertible securities
A feature of certain bonds, debentures, or preferred stocks that allows them to be exchanged by the owner for another class of securities at a future date and in accordance with any other terms of the issue.

Copayment
See Coinsurance

Copyright
A legal form of protection available to creators and authors to safeguard their works from unlawful use or claim of ownership by others. Copyrights may be acquired for works of art, sculpture, music, and published or unpublished manuscripts. All copyrights should be registered at the Copyright Office of the Library of Congress.

Corporate financial ratios
The relationship between key figures found in a company's financial statement expressed as a numeric value. Used to evaluate risk and company performance. Also known as Financial averages, Operating ratios, and Business ratios.

Corporation
A legal entity, chartered by a state or the federal government, recognized as a separate entity having its own rights, privileges, and liabilities distinct from those of its members.

Cost containment
Actions taken by employers and insurers to curtail rising health care costs; for example, increasing employee cost sharing (see separate citation), requiring second opinions, or preadmission screening.

Cost sharing
The requirement that health care consumers contribute to their own medical care costs through deductibles and coinsurance (see separate citations). Cost sharing does not include the amounts paid in premiums. It is used to control utilization of services; for example, requiring a fixed amount to be paid with each health care service.

Cottage industry
Businesses based in the home in which the family members are the labor force and family-owned equipment is used to process the goods.

Credit Rating
A letter or number calculated by an organization (such as Dun & Bradstreet) to represent the ability and disposition of a business to meet its financial obligations.

Customer service
Various techniques used to ensure the satisfaction of a customer.

Cyclical peak
The upper turning point in a business cycle.

Cyclical trough
The lower turning point in a business cycle.

DBA
See Business name

Death
See Business death

Debenture
A certificate given as acknowledgment of a debt (see separate citation) secured by the general credit of the issuing corporation. A bond, usually without security, issued by a corporation and sometimes convertible to common stock.

Debt
Something owed by one person to another. Financing in which a company receives capital that must be repaid; no ownership is transferred.

Debt capital
Business financing that normally requires periodic interest payments and repayment of the principal within a specified time.

Debt financing
See Debt capital

Debt securities
Loans such as bonds and notes that provide a specified rate of return for a specified period of time.

Deductible
A set amount that an individual must pay before any benefits are received.

Demand shock absorbers
A term used to describe the role that some small firms play by expanding their output levels to accommodate a transient surge in demand.

Demographics
Statistics on various markets, including age, income, and education, used to target specific products or services to appropriate consumer groups.

Demonstration
Showing that a product or process has been modified sufficiently to meet the needs of users.

Deregulation
The lifting of government restrictions; for example, the lifting of government restrictions on the entry of

new businesses, the expansion of services, and the setting of prices in particular industries.

Desktop Publishing
Using personal computers and specialized software to produce camera-ready copy for publications.

Disaster loans
Various types of physical and economic assistance available to individuals and businesses through the U.S. Small Business Administration (SBA). This is the only SBA loan program available for residential purposes.

Discrimination
The denial of the rights and privileges of employment based on factors such as age, race, religion, or gender.

Diseconomies of scale
The condition in which the costs of production increase faster than the volume of production.

Dissolution
See Business dissolution

Distribution
Delivering a product or process to the user.

Distributor
One who delivers merchandise to the user.

Diversified company
A company whose products and services are used by several different markets.

Doing business as (DBA)
See Business name

Dow Jones
An information services company that publishes the Wall Street Journal and other sources of financial information.

Dow Jones Industrial Average
An indicator of stock market performance.

Earned income
A tax term that refers to wages and salaries earned by the recipient, as opposed to monies earned through interest and dividends.

Economic efficiency
The use of productive resources to the fullest practical extent in the provision of the set of goods

and services that is most preferred by purchasers in the economy.

Economic indicators
Statistics used to express the state of the economy. These include the length of the average work week, the rate of unemployment, and stock prices.

Economically disadvantaged
See Socially and economically disadvantaged

Economies of scale
See Scale economies

EEOC
See Equal Employment Opportunity Commission

8(a) Program
A program authorized by the Small Business Act that directs federal contracts to small businesses owned and operated by socially and economically disadvantaged individuals.

Electronic mail (e-mail)
The electronic transmission of mail via phone lines.

E-mail
See Electronic mail

Employee leasing
A contract by which employers arrange to have their workers hired by a leasing company and then leased back to them for a management fee. The leasing company typically assumes the administrative burden of payroll and provides a benefit package to the workers.

Employee tenure
The length of time an employee works for a particular employer.

Employer identification number
The business equivalent of a social security number. Assigned by the U.S. Internal Revenue Service.

Enterprise
An aggregation of all establishments owned by a parent company. An enterprise may consist of a single, independent establishment or include subsidiaries and other branches under the same ownership and control.

Enterprise zone
A designated area, usually found in inner cities and other areas with significant unemployment, where businesses receive tax credits and other incentives to entice them to establish operations there.

Entrepreneur
A person who takes the risk of organizing and operating a new business venture.

Entry
See Business entry

Equal Employment Opportunity Commission (EEOC)
A federal agency that ensures nondiscrimination in the hiring and firing practices of a business.

Equal opportunity employer
An employer who adheres to the standards set by the Equal Employment Opportunity Commission (see separate citation).

Equity
The ownership interest. Financing in which partial or total ownership of a company is surrendered in exchange for capital. An investor's financial return comes from dividend payments and from growth in the net worth of the business.

Equity capital
See Equity; Equity midrisk venture capital

Equity financing
See Equity; Equity midrisk venture capital

Equity midrisk venture capital
An unsecured investment in a company. Usually a purchase of ownership interest in a company that occurs in the later stages of a company's development.

Equity partnership
A limited partnership arrangement for providing start-up and seed capital to businesses.

Equity securities
See Equity

Equity-type
Debt financing subordinated to conventional debt.

Establishment
A single-location business unit that may be independent (a single-establishment enterprise) or owned by a parent enterprise.

Establishment and Enterprise Microdata File
See U.S. Establishment and Enterprise Microdata File

Establishment birth
See Business birth

Establishment Longitudinal Microdata File
See U.S. Establishment Longitudinal Microdata File

Ethics
See Business ethics

Evaluation
Determining the potential success of translating an invention into a product or process.

Exit
See Business exit

Experience rating
See Underwriting

Export
A product sold outside of the country.

Export license
A general or specific license granted by the U.S. Department of Commerce required of anyone wishing to export goods. Some restricted articles need approval from the U.S. Departments of State, Defense, or Energy.

Failure
See Business failure

Fair share agreement
An agreement reached between a franchisor and a minority business organization to extend business ownership to minorities by either reducing the amount of capital required or by setting aside certain marketing areas for minority business owners.

Feasibility study
A study to determine the likelihood that a proposed product or development will fulfill the objectives of a particular investor.

Federal Trade Commission (FTC)
Federal agency that promotes free enterprise and competition within the U.S.

Federal Trade Mark Act of 1946
See Lanham Act

Fictional name
See Business name

Fiduciary
An individual or group that hold assets in trust for a beneficiary.

Financial analysis
The techniques used to determine money needs in a business. Techniques include ratio analysis, calculation of return on investment, guides for measuring profitability, and break-even analysis to determine ultimate success.

Financial intermediary
A financial institution that acts as the intermediary between borrowers and lenders. Banks, savings and loan associations, finance companies, and venture capital companies are major financial intermediaries in the United States.

Financial ratios
See Corporate financial ratios; Industry financial ratios

Financial statement
A written record of business finances, including balance sheets and profit and loss statements.

Financing
See First-stage financing; Second-stage financing; Thirdstage financing

First-stage financing
Financing provided to companies that have expended their initial capital, and require funds to start full-scale manufacturing and sales. Also known as First-round financing.

Fiscal year
Any twelve-month period used by businesses for accounting purposes.

504 Program
See Certified development corporation

Flexible benefit plan
A plan that offers a choice among cash and/or qualified benefits such as group term life insurance,

accident and health insurance, group legal services, dependent care assistance, and vacations.

FOB
See Free on board

Format franchising
See Business format franchising; Franchising

401(k) plan
A financial plan where employees contribute a percentage of their earnings to a fund that is invested in stocks, bonds, or money markets for the purpose of saving money for retirement.

Four Ps
Marketing terms referring to Product, Price, Place, and Promotion.

Franchising
A form of licensing by which the owner-the franchisor- distributes or markets a product, method, or service through affiliated dealers called franchisees. The product, method, or service being marketed is identified by a brand name, and the franchisor maintains control over the marketing methods employed. The franchisee is often given exclusive access to a defined geographic area.

Free on board (FOB)
A pricing term indicating that the quoted price includes the cost of loading goods into transport vessels at a specified place.

Frictional unemployment
See Unemployment

FTC
See Federal Trade Commission

Fulfillment
The systems necessary for accurate delivery of an ordered item, including subscriptions and direct marketing.

Full-time workers
Generally, those who work a regular schedule of more than 35 hours per week.

Garment registration number
A number that must appear on every garment sold in the U.S. to indicate the manufacturer of the garment,

which may or may not be the same as the label under which the garment is sold. The U.S. Federal Trade Commission assigns and regulates garment registration numbers.

Gatekeeper
A key contact point for entry into a network.

GDP
See Gross domestic product

General obligation bond
A municipal bond secured by the taxing power of the municipality. The Tax Reform Act of 1986 limits the purposes for which such bonds may be issued and establishes volume limits on the extent of their issuance.

GNP
See Gross national product

Good Housekeeping Seal
Seal appearing on products that signifies the fulfillment of the standards set by the Good Housekeeping Institute to protect consumer interests.

Goods sector
All businesses producing tangible goods, including agriculture, mining, construction, and manufacturing businesses.

GPO
See Gross product originating

Gross domestic product (GDP)
The part of the nation's gross national product (see separate citation) generated by private business using resources from within the country.

Gross national product (GNP)
The most comprehensive single measure of aggregate economic output. Represents the market value of the total output of goods and services produced by a nation's economy.

Gross product originating (GPO)
A measure of business output estimated from the income or production side using employee compensation, profit income, net interest, capital consumption, and indirect business taxes.

HAL
See Handicapped assistance loan program

Handicapped assistance loan program (HAL)
Low-interest direct loan program through the U.S. Small Business Administration (SBA) for handicapped persons. The SBA requires that these persons demonstrate that their disability is such that it is impossible for them to secure employment, thus making it necessary to go into their own business to make a living.

Health maintenance organization (HMO)
Organization of physicians and other health care professionals that provides health services to subscribers and their dependents on a prepaid basis.

Health provider
An individual or institution that gives medical care. Under Medicare, an institutional provider is a hospital, skilled nursing facility, home health agency, or provider of certain physical therapy services.

Hispanic
A person of Cuban, Mexican, Puerto Rican, Latin American (Central or South American), European Spanish, or other Spanish-speaking origin or ancestry.

HMO
See Health maintenance organization

Home-based business
A business with an operating address that is also a residential address (usually the residential address of the proprietor).

Hub-and-spoke system
A system in which flights of an airline from many different cities (the spokes) converge at a single airport (the hub). After allowing passengers sufficient time to make connections, planes then depart for different cities.

Human Resources Management
A business program designed to oversee recruiting, pay, benefits, and other issues related to the company's work force, including planning to determine the optimal use of labor to increase production, thereby increasing profit.

Idea
An original concept for a new product or process.

Import
Products produced outside the country in which they are consumed.

Income
Money or its equivalent, earned or accrued, resulting from the sale of goods and services.

Income statement
A financial statement that lists the profits and losses of a company at a given time.

Incorporation
The filing of a certificate of incorporation with a state's secretary of state, thereby limiting the business owner's liability.

Incubator
A facility designed to encourage entrepreneurship and minimize obstacles to new business formation and growth, particularly for high-technology firms, by housing a number of fledgling enterprises that share an array of services, such as meeting areas, secretarial services, accounting, research library, on-site financial and management counseling, and word processing facilities.

Independent contractor
An individual considered self-employed (see separate citation) and responsible for paying Social Security taxes and income taxes on earnings.

Indirect health coverage
Health insurance obtained through another individual's health care plan; for example, a spouse's employersponsored plan.

Industrial development authority
The financial arm of a state or other political subdivision established for the purpose of financing economic development in an area, usually through loans to nonprofit organizations, which in turn provide facilities for manufacturing and other industrial operations.

Industry financial ratios
Corporate financial ratios averaged for a specified industry. These are used for comparison purposes and reveal industry trends and identify differences between

Glossary

the performance of a specific company and the performance of its industry. Also known as Industrial averages, Industry ratios, Financial averages, and Business or Industrial norms.

Inflation
Increases in volume of currency and credit, generally resulting in a sharp and continuing rise in price levels.

Informal capital
Financing from informal, unorganized sources; includes informal debt capital such as trade credit or loans from friends and relatives and equity capital from informal investors.

Initial public offering (IPO)
A corporation's first offering of stock to the public.

Innovation
The introduction of a new idea into the marketplace in the form of a new product or service or an improvement in organization or process.

Intellectual property
Any idea or work that can be considered proprietary in nature and is thus protected from infringement by others.

Internal capital
Debt or equity financing obtained from the owner or through retained business earnings.

Internet
A government-designed computer network that contains large amounts of information and is accessible through various vendors for a fee.

Intrapreneurship
The state of employing entrepreneurial principles to nonentrepreneurial situations.

Invention
The tangible form of a technological idea, which could include a laboratory prototype, drawings, formulas, etc.

IPO
See Initial public offering

Job description
The duties and responsibilities required in a particular position.

Job tenure
A period of time during which an individual is continuously employed in the same job.

Joint marketing agreements
Agreements between regional and major airlines, often involving the coordination of flight schedules, fares, and baggage transfer. These agreements help regional carriers operate at lower cost.

Joint venture
Venture in which two or more people combine efforts in a particular business enterprise, usually a single transaction or a limited activity, and agree to share the profits and losses jointly or in proportion to their contributions.

Keogh plan
Designed for self-employed persons and unincorporated businesses as a tax-deferred pension account.

Labor force
Civilians considered eligible for employment who are also willing and able to work.

Labor force participation rate
The civilian labor force as a percentage of the civilian population.

Labor intensity
The relative importance of labor in the production process, usually measured as the capital-labor ratio; i.e., the ratio of units of capital (typically, dollars of tangible assets) to the number of employees. The higher the capital-labor ratio exhibited by a firm or industry, the lower the capital intensity of that firm or industry is said to be.

Labor surplus area
An area in which there exists a high unemployment rate. In procurement (see separate citation), extra points are given to firms in counties that are designated a labor surplus area; this information is requested on procurement bid sheets.

Labor union
An organization of similarly-skilled workers who collectively bargain with management over the conditions of employment.

Laboratory prototype
See Prototype

LAN
See Local Area Network

Lanham Act
Refers to the Federal Trade Mark Act of 1946. Protects registered trademarks, trade names, and other service marks used in commerce.

Large business-dominated industry
Industry in which a minimum of 60 percent of employment or sales is in firms with more than 500 workers.

LBO
See Leveraged buy-out

Leader pricing
A reduction in the price of a good or service in order to generate more sales of that good or service.

Legal list
A list of securities selected by a state in which certain institutions and fiduciaries (such as pension funds, insurance companies, and banks) may invest. Securities not on the list are not eligible for investment. Legal lists typically restrict investments to high quality securities meeting certain specifications. Generally, investment is limited to U.S. securities and investment-grade blue chip securities (see separate citation).

Leveraged buy-out (LBO)
The purchase of a business or a division of a corporation through a highly leveraged financing package.

Liability
An obligation or duty to perform a service or an act. Also defined as money owed.

License
A legal agreement granting to another the right to use a technological innovation.

Limited partnerships
See Venture capital limited partnerships

Liquidity
The ability to convert a security into cash promptly.

Loans
See Commercial loans; Disaster loans; SBA direct loans; SBA guaranteed loans; SBA special lending institution categories Local Area Network (LAN) Computer networks contained within a single building or small area; used to facilitate the sharing of information.

Local development corporation
An organization, usually made up of local citizens of a community, designed to improve the economy of the area by inducing business and industry to locate and expand there. A local development corporation establishes a capability to finance local growth.

Long-haul rates
Rates charged by a transporter in which the distance traveled is more than 800 miles.

Long-term debt
An obligation that matures in a period that exceeds five years.

Low-grade bond
A corporate bond that is rated below investment grade by the major rating agencies (Standard and Poor's, Moody's).

Macro-efficiency
Efficiency as it pertains to the operation of markets and market systems.

Managed care
A cost-effective health care program initiated by employers whereby low-cost health care is made available to the employees in return for exclusive patronage to program doctors.

Management Assistance Programs
See SBA Management Assistance Programs

Management and technical assistance
A term used by many programs to mean business (as opposed to technological) assistance.

Mandated benefits
Specific treatments, providers, or individuals required by law to be included in commercial health plans.

Market evaluation
The use of market information to determine the sales potential of a specific product or process.

Market failure
The situation in which the workings of a competitive market do not produce the best results from the point of view of the entire society.

Market information
Data of any type that can be used for market evaluation, which could include demographic data, technology forecasting, regulatory changes, etc.

Market research
A systematic collection, analysis, and reporting of data about the market and its preferences, opinions, trends, and plans; used for corporate decision-making.

Market share
In a particular market, the percentage of sales of a specific product.

Marketing
Promotion of goods or services through various media.

Master Establishment List (MEL)
A list of firms in the United States developed by the U.S. Small Business Administration; firms can be selected by industry, region, state, standard metropolitan statistical area (see separate citation), county, and zip code.

Maturity
The date upon which the principal or stated value of a bond or other indebtedness becomes due and payable.

Medicaid (Title XIX)
A federally aided, state-operated and administered program that provides medical benefits for certain low income persons in need of health and medical care who are eligible for one of the government's welfare cash payment programs, including the aged, the blind, the disabled, and members of families with dependent children where one parent is absent, incapacitated, or unemployed.

Medicare (Title XVIII)
A nationwide health insurance program for disabled and aged persons. Health insurance is available to insured persons without regard to income. Monies from payroll taxes cover hospital insurance and monies from general revenues and beneficiary premiums pay for supplementary medical insurance.

MEL
See Master Establishment List

MESBIC
See Minority enterprise small business investment corporation

MET
See Multiple employer trust

Metropolitan statistical area (MSA)
A means used by the government to define large population centers that may transverse different governmental jurisdictions. For example, the Washington, D.C. MSA includes the District of Columbia and contiguous parts of Maryland and Virginia because all of these geopolitical areas comprise one population and economic operating unit.

Mezzanine financing
See Third-stage financing

Micro-efficiency
Efficiency as it pertains to the operation of individual firms.

Microdata
Information on the characteristics of an individual business firm.

Mid-term debt
An obligation that matures within one to five years.

Midrisk venture capital
See Equity midrisk venture capital

Minimum premium plan
A combination approach to funding an insurance plan aimed primarily at premium tax savings. The employer self-funds a fixed percentage of estimated monthly claims and the insurance company insures the excess.

Minimum wage
The lowest hourly wage allowed by the federal government.

Minority Business Development Agency
Contracts with private firms throughout the nation to sponsor Minority Business Development Centers which provide minority firms with advice and technical assistance on a fee basis.

Minority Enterprise Small Business Investment Corporation (MESBIC)
A federally funded private venture capital firm licensed by the U.S. Small Business Administration to provide capital to minority-owned businesses (see separate citation).

Minority-owned business
Businesses owned by those who are socially or economically disadvantaged (see separate citation).

Mom and Pop business
A small store or enterprise having limited capital, principally employing family members.

Moonlighter
A wage-and-salary worker with a side business.

MSA
See Metropolitan statistical area

Multi-employer plan
A health plan to which more than one employer is required to contribute and that may be maintained through a collective bargaining agreement and required to meet standards prescribed by the U.S. Department of Labor.

Multi-level marketing
A system of selling in which you sign up other people to assist you and they, in turn, recruit others to help them. Some entrepreneurs have built successful companies on this concept because the main focus of their activities is their product and product sales.

Multimedia
The use of several types of media to promote a product or service. Also, refers to the use of several different types of media (sight, sound, pictures, text) in a CD-ROM (see separate citation) product.

Multiple employer trust (MET)
A self-funded benefit plan generally geared toward small employers sharing a common interest.

NAFTA
See North American Free Trade Agreement

NASDAQ
See National Association of Securities Dealers Automated Quotations

National Association of Securities Dealers Automated Quotations
Provides price quotes on over-the-counter securities as well as securities listed on the New York Stock Exchange.

National income
Aggregate earnings of labor and property arising from the production of goods and services in a nation's economy.

Net assets
See Net worth

Net income
The amount remaining from earnings and profits after all expenses and costs have been met or deducted. Also known as Net earnings.

Net profit
Money earned after production and overhead expenses (see separate citations) have been deducted.

Net worth
The difference between a company's total assets and its total liabilities.

Network
A chain of interconnected individuals or organizations sharing information and/or services.

New York Stock Exchange (NYSE)
The oldest stock exchange in the U.S. Allows for trading in stocks, bonds, warrants, options, and rights that meet listing requirements.

Niche
A career or business for which a person is well-suited. Also, a product which fulfills one need of a particular market segment, often with little or no competition.

Nodes
One workstation in a network, either local area or wide area (see separate citations).

Nonbank bank
A bank that either accepts deposits or makes loans, but not both. Used to create many new branch banks.

Noncompetitive awards
A method of contracting whereby the federal government negotiates with only one contractor to supply a product or service.

Nonmember bank
A state-regulated bank that does not belong to the federal bank system.

Nonprofit
An organization that has no shareholders, does not distribute profits, and is without federal and state tax liabilities.

Norms
See Financial ratios

North American Free Trade Agreement (NAFTA)
Passed in 1993, NAFTA eliminates trade barriers among businesses in the U.S., Canada, and Mexico.

NYSE
See New York Stock Exchange

Occupational Safety & Health Administration (OSHA)
Federal agency that regulates health and safety standards within the workplace.

Optimal firm size
The business size at which the production cost per unit of output (average cost) is, in the long run, at its minimum.

Organizational chart
A hierarchical chart tracking the chain of command within an organization.

OSHA
See Occupational Safety & Health Administration

Overhead
Expenses, such as employee benefits and building utilities, incurred by a business that are unrelated to the actual product or service sold.

Owner's capital
Debt or equity funds provided by the owner(s) of a business; sources of owner's capital are personal savings, sales of assets, or loans from financial institutions.

P & L
See Profit and loss statement

Part-time workers
Normally, those who work less than 35 hours per week. The Tax Reform Act indicated that part-time workers who work less than 17.5 hours per week may

be excluded from health plans for purposes of complying with federal nondiscrimination rules.

Part-year workers
Those who work less than 50 weeks per year.

Partnership
Two or more parties who enter into a legal relationship to conduct business for profit. Defined by the U.S. Internal Revenue Code as joint ventures, syndicates, groups, pools, and other associations of two or more persons organized for profit that are not specifically classified in the IRS code as corporations or proprietorships.

Patent
A grant made by the government assuring an inventor the sole right to make, use, and sell an invention for a period of 17 years.

PC
See Professional corporation

Peak
See Cyclical peak

Pension
A series of payments made monthly, semiannually, annually, or at other specified intervals during the lifetime of the pensioner for distribution upon retirement. The term is sometimes used to denote the portion of the retirement allowance financed by the employer's contributions.

Pension fund
A fund established to provide for the payment of pension benefits; the collective contributions made by all of the parties to the pension plan.

Performance appraisal
An established set of objective criteria, based on job description and requirements, that is used to evaluate the performance of an employee in a specific job.

Permit
See Business license

Plan
See Business plan

Pooling
An arrangement for employers to achieve efficiencies and lower health costs by joining together to purchase group health insurance or self-insurance.

PPO
See Preferred provider organization

Preferred lenders program
See SBA special lending institution categories

Preferred provider organization (PPO)
A contractual arrangement with a health care services organization that agrees to discount its health care rates in return for faster payment and/or a patient base.

Premiums
The amount of money paid to an insurer for health insurance under a policy. The premium is generally paid periodically (e.g., monthly), and often is split between the employer and the employee. Unlike deductibles and coinsurance or copayments, premiums are paid for coverage whether or not benefits are actually used.

Prime-age workers
Employees 25 to 54 years of age.

Prime contract
A contract awarded directly by the U.S. Federal Government.

Private company
See Closely held corporation

Private placement
A method of raising capital by offering for sale an investment or business to a small group of investors (generally avoiding registration with the Securities and Exchange Commission or state securities registration agencies). Also known as Private financing or Private offering.

Pro forma
The use of hypothetical figures in financial statements to represent future expenditures, debts, and other potential financial expenses.

Proactive
Taking the initiative to solve problems and anticipate future events before they happen, instead of reacting to an already existing problem or waiting for a difficult situation to occur.

Procurement
A contract from an agency of the federal government for goods or services from a small business.

Prodigy
An online service which is accessible by computer modem. The service features Internet access, bulletin boards, online periodicals, electronic mail, and other services for subscribers.

Product development
The stage of the innovation process where research is translated into a product or process through evaluation, adaptation, and demonstration.

Product franchising
An arrangement for a franchisee to use the name and to produce the product line of the franchisor or parent corporation.

Production
The manufacture of a product.

Production prototype
See Prototype

Productivity
A measurement of the number of goods produced during a specific amount of time.

Professional corporation (PC)
Organized by members of a profession such as medicine, dentistry, or law for the purpose of conducting their professional activities as a corporation. Liability of a member or shareholder is limited in the same manner as in a business corporation.

Profit and loss statement (P & L)
The summary of the incomes (total revenues) and costs of a company's operation during a specific period of time. Also known as Income and expense statement.

Proposal
See Business plan

Proprietorship
The most common legal form of business ownership; about 85 percent of all small businesses are proprietorships. The liability of the owner is unlimited in this form of ownership.

Prospective payment system
A cost-containment measure included in the Social Security Amendments of 1983 whereby Medicare payments to hospitals are based on established prices, rather than on cost reimbursement.

Prototype
A model that demonstrates the validity of the concept of an invention (laboratory prototype); a model that meets the needs of the manufacturing process and the user (production prototype).

Prudent investor rule or standard
A legal doctrine that requires fiduciaries to make investments using the prudence, diligence, and intelligence that would be used by a prudent person in making similar investments. Because fiduciaries make investments on behalf of third-party beneficiaries, the standard results in very conservative investments. Until recently, most state regulations required the fiduciary to apply this standard to each investment. Newer, more progressive regulations permit fiduciaries to apply this standard to the portfolio taken as a whole, thereby allowing a fiduciary to balance a portfolio with higher-yield, higher-risk investments. In states with more progressive regulations, practically every type of security is eligible for inclusion in the portfolio of investments made by a fiduciary, provided that the portfolio investments, in their totality, are those of a prudent person.

Public equity markets
Organized markets for trading in equity shares such as common stocks, preferred stocks, and warrants. Includes markets for both regularly traded and nonregularly traded securities.

Public offering
General solicitation for participation in an investment opportunity. Interstate public offerings are supervised by the U.S. Securities and Exchange Commission (see separate citation).

Quality control
The process by which a product is checked and tested to ensure consistent standards of high quality.

Rate of return
The yield obtained on a security or other investment based on its purchase price or its current market price. The total rate of return is current income plus or minus capital appreciation or depreciation.

Real property
Includes the land and all that is contained on it.

Realignment
See Resource realignment

Recession
Contraction of economic activity occurring between the peak and trough (see separate citations) of a business cycle.

Regulated market
A market in which the government controls the forces of supply and demand, such as who may enter and what price may be charged.

Regulation D
A vehicle by which small businesses make small offerings and private placements of securities with limited disclosure requirements. It was designed to ease the burdens imposed on small businesses utilizing this method of capital formation.

Regulatory Flexibility Act
An act requiring federal agencies to evaluate the impact of their regulations on small businesses before the regulations are issued and to consider less burdensome alternatives.

Research
The initial stage of the innovation process, which includes idea generation and invention.

Research and development financing
A tax-advantaged partnership set up to finance product development for start-ups as well as more mature companies.

Resource mobility
The ease with which labor and capital move from firm to firm or from industry to industry.

Resource realignment
The adjustment of productive resources to interindustry changes in demand.

Resources
The sources of support or help in the innovation process, including sources of financing, technical evaluation, market evaluation, management and business assistance, etc.

Retained business earnings
Business profits that are retained by the business rather than being distributed to the shareholders as dividends.

Revolving credit
An agreement with a lending institution for an amount of money, which cannot exceed a set maximum, over a specified period of time. Each time the borrower repays a portion of the loan, the amount of the repayment may be borrowed yet again.

Risk capital
See Venture capital

Risk management
The act of identifying potential sources of financial loss and taking action to minimize their negative impact.

Routing
The sequence of steps necessary to complete a product during production.

S corporations
See Sub chapter S corporations

SBA
See Small Business Administration

SBA direct loans
Loans made directly by the U.S. Small Business Administration (SBA); monies come from funds appropriated specifically for this purpose. In general, SBA direct loans carry interest rates slightly lower than those in the private financial markets and are available only to applicants unable to secure private financing or an SBA guaranteed loan.

SBA 504 Program
See Certified development corporation

SBA guaranteed loans
Loans made by lending institutions in which the U.S. Small Business Administration (SBA) will pay a prior agreed-upon percentage of the outstanding principal in the event the borrower of the loan defaults. The terms of the loan and the interest rate are negotiated between theborrower and the lending institution, within set parameters.

SBA loans
See Disaster loans; SBA direct loans; SBA guaranteed loans; SBA special lending institution categories

SBA Management Assistance Programs
Classes, workshops, counseling, and publications offered by the U.S. Small Business Administration.

SBA special lending institution categories
U.S. Small Business Administration (SBA) loan program in which the SBA promises certified banks a 72-hour turnaround period in giving its approval for a loan, and in which preferred lenders in a pilot program are allowed to write SBA loans without seeking prior SBA approval.

SBDB
See Small Business Data Base

SBDC
See Small business development centers

SBI
See Small business institutes program

SBIC
See Small business investment corporation

SBIR Program
See Small Business Innovation Development Act of 1982

Scale economies
The decline of the production cost per unit of output (average cost) as the volume of output increases.

Scale efficiency
The reduction in unit cost available to a firm when producing at a higher output volume.

SCORE
See Service Corps of Retired Executives

SEC
See Securities and Exchange Commission

SECA
See Self-Employment Contributions Act

Second-stage financing
Working capital for the initial expansion of a company that is producing, shipping, and has growing accounts receivable and inventories. Also known as Second-round financing.

Glossary

Secondary market
A market established for the purchase and sale of outstanding securities following their initial distribution.

Secondary worker
Any worker in a family other than the person who is the primary source of income for the family.

Secondhand capital
Previously used and subsequently resold capital equipment (e.g., buildings and machinery).

Securities and Exchange Commission (SEC)
Federal agency charged with regulating the trade of securities to prevent unethical practices in the investor market.

Securitized debt
A marketing technique that converts long-term loans to marketable securities.

Seed capital
Venture financing provided in the early stages of the innovation process, usually during product development.

Self-employed person
One who works for a profit or fees in his or her own business, profession, or trade, or who operates a farm.

Self-Employment Contributions Act (SECA)
Federal law that governs the self-employment tax (see separate citation).

Self-employment income
Income covered by Social Security if a business earns a net income of at least $400.00 during the year. Taxes are paid on earnings that exceed $400.00.

Self-employment retirement plan
See Keogh plan

Self-employment tax
Required tax imposed on self-employed individuals for the provision of Social Security and Medicare. The tax must be paid quarterly with estimated income tax statements.

Self-funding
A health benefit plan in which a firm uses its own funds to pay claims, rather than transferring the financial risks of paying claims to an outside insurer in exchange for premium payments.

Service Corps of Retired Executives (SCORE)
Volunteers for the SBA Management Assistance Program who provide one-on-one counseling and teach workshops and seminars for small firms.

Service firm
See Business service firm

Service sector
Broadly defined, all U.S. industries that produce intangibles, including the five major industry divisions of transportation, communications, and utilities; wholesale trade; retail trade; finance, insurance, and real estate; and services.

Set asides
See Small business set asides

Short-haul service
A type of transportation service in which the transporter supplies service between cities where the maximum distance is no more than 200 miles.

Short-term debt
An obligation that matures in one year.

SIC codes
See Standard Industrial Classification codes

Single-establishment enterprise
See Establishment

Small business
An enterprise that is independently owned and operated, is not dominant in its field, and employs fewer than 500 people. For SBA purposes, the U.S. Small Business Administration (SBA) considers various other factors (such as gross annual sales) in determining size of a business.

Small Business Administration (SBA)
An independent federal agency that provides assistance with loans, management, and advocating interests before other federal agencies.

Small Business Data Base
A collection of microdata (see separate citation) files on individual firms developed and maintained by the U.S. Small Business Administration.

Small business development centers (SBDC)
Centers that provide support services to small businesses, such as individual counseling, SBA advice, seminars and conferences, and other learning center activities. Most services are free of charge, or available at minimal cost.

Small business development corporation
See Certified development corporation

Small business-dominated industry
Industry in which a minimum of 60 percent of employment or sales is in firms with fewer than 500 employees.

Small Business Innovation Development Act of 1982
Federal statute requiring federal agencies with large extramural research and development budgets to allocate a certain percentage of these funds to small research and development firms. The program, called the Small Business Innovation Research (SBIR) Program, is designed to stimulate technological innovation and make greater use of small businesses in meeting national innovation needs.

Small business institutes (SBI) program
Cooperative arrangements made by U.S. Small Business Administration district offices and local colleges and universities to provide small business firms with graduate students to counsel them without charge.

Small business investment corporation (SBIC)
A privately owned company licensed and funded through the U.S. Small Business Administration and private sector sources to provide equity or debt capital to small businesses.

Small business set asides
Procurement (see separate citation) opportunities required by law to be on all contracts under $10,000 or a certain percentage of an agency's total procurement expenditure.

Smaller firms
For U.S. Department of Commerce purposes, those firms not included in the Fortune 1000.

SMSA
See Metropolitan statistical area

Socially and economically disadvantaged
Individuals who have been subjected to racial or ethnic prejudice or cultural bias without regard to their qualities as individuals, and whose abilities to compete are impaired because of diminished opportunities to obtain capital and credit.

Sole proprietorship
An unincorporated, one-owner business, farm, or professional practice.

Special lending institution categories
See SBA special lending institution categories

Standard Industrial Classification (SIC) codes
Four-digit codes established by the U.S. Federal Government to categorize businesses by type of economic activity; the first two digits correspond to major groups such as construction and manufacturing, while the last two digits correspond to subgroups such as home construction or highway construction.

Standard metropolitan statistical area (SMSA)
See Metropolitan statistical area

Start-up
A new business, at the earliest stages of development and financing.

Start-up costs
Costs incurred before a business can commence operations.

Start-up financing
Financing provided to companies that have either completed product development and initial marketing or have been in business for less than one year but have not yet sold their product commercially.

Stock
A certificate of equity ownership in a business.

Stop-loss coverage
Insurance for a self-insured plan that reimburses the company for any losses it might incur in its health claims beyond a specified amount.

Strategic planning
Projected growth and development of a business to establish a guiding direction for the future. Also used to determine which market segments to explore for optimal sales of products or services.

Glossary

Structural unemployment
See Unemployment

Sub chapter S corporations
Corporations that are considered noncorporate for tax purposes but legally remain corporations.

Subcontract
A contract between a prime contractor and a subcontractor, or between subcontractors, to furnish supplies or services for performance of a prime contract (see separate citation) or a subcontract.

Surety bonds
Bonds providing reimbursement to an individual, company, or the government if a firm fails to complete a contract. The U.S. Small Business Administration guarantees surety bonds in a program much like the SBA guaranteed loan program (see separate citation).

Swing loan
See Bridge financing

Target market
The clients or customers sought for a business' product or service.

Targeted Jobs Tax Credit
Federal legislation enacted in 1978 that provides a tax credit to an employer who hires structurally unemployed individuals.

Tax number
A number assigned to a business by a state revenue department that enables the business to buy goods without paying sales tax.

Taxable bonds
An interest-bearing certificate of public or private indebtedness. Bonds are issued by public agencies to finance economic development.

Technical assistance
See Management and technical assistance

Technical evaluation
Assessment of technological feasibility.

Technology
The method in which a firm combines and utilizes labor and capital resources to produce goods or services; the application of science for commercial or industrial purposes.

Technology transfer
The movement of information about a technology or intellectual property from one party to another for use.

Tenure
See Employee tenure

Term
The length of time for which a loan is made.

Terms of a note
The conditions or limits of a note; includes the interest rate per annum, the due date, and transferability and convertibility features, if any.

Third-party administrator
An outside company responsible for handling claims and performing administrative tasks associated with health insurance plan maintenance.

Third-stage financing
Financing provided for the major expansion of a company whose sales volume is increasing and that is breaking even or profitable. These funds are used for further plant expansion, marketing, working capital, or development of an improved product. Also known as Third-round or Mezzanine financing.

Time deposit
A bank deposit that cannot be withdrawn before a specified future time.

Time management
Skills and scheduling techniques used to maximize productivity.

Trade credit
Credit extended by suppliers of raw materials or finished products. In an accounting statement, trade credit is referred to as "accounts payable."

Trade name
The name under which a company conducts business, or by which its business, goods, or services are identified. It may or may not be registered as a trademark.

Trade periodical
A publication with a specific focus on one or more aspects of business and industry.

Trade secret
Competitive advantage gained by a business through the use of a unique manufacturing process or formula.

Trade show
An exhibition of goods or services used in a particular industry. Typically held in exhibition centers where exhibitors rent space to display their merchandise.

Trademark
A graphic symbol, device, or slogan that identifies a business. A business has property rights to its trademark from the inception of its use, but it is still prudent to register all trademarks with the Trademark Office of the U.S. Department of Commerce.

Translation
See Product development

Treasury bills
Investment tender issued by the Federal Reserve Bank in amounts of $10,000 that mature in 91 to 182 days.

Treasury bonds
Long-term notes with maturity dates of not less than seven and not more than twenty-five years.

Treasury notes
Short-term notes maturing in less than seven years.

Trend
A statistical measurement used to track changes that occur over time.

Trough
See Cyclical trough

UCC
See Uniform Commercial Code

UL
See Underwriters Laboratories

Underwriters Laboratories (UL)
One of several private firms that tests products and processes to determine their safety. Although various firms can provide this kind of testing service, many local and insurance codes specify UL certification.

Underwriting
A process by which an insurer determines whether or not and on what basis it will accept an application for insurance. In an experience-rated plan, premiums are based on a firm's or group's past claims; factors other than prior claims are used for community-rated or manually rated plans.

Unfair competition
Refers to business practices, usually unethical, such as using unlicensed products, pirating merchandise, or misleading the public through false advertising, which give the offending business an unequitable advantage over others.

Unfunded accrued liability
The excess of total liabilities, both present and prospective, over present and prospective assets.

Unemployment
The joblessness of individuals who are willing to work, who are legally and physically able to work, and who are seeking work. Unemployment may represent the temporary joblessness of a worker between jobs (frictional unemployment) or the joblessness of a worker whose skills are not suitable for jobs available in the labor market (structural unemployment).

Uniform Commercial Code (UCC)
A code of laws governing commercial transactions across the U.S., except Louisiana. Their purpose is to bring uniformity to financial transactions.

Uniform product code (UPC symbol)
A computer-readable label comprised of ten digits and stripes that encodes what a product is and how much it costs. The first five digits are assigned by the Uniform Product Code Council, and the last five digits by the individual manufacturer.

Unit cost
See Average cost

UPC symbol
See Uniform product code

U.S. Establishment and Enterprise Microdata (USEEM) File
A cross-sectional database containing information on employment, sales, and location for individual enterprises and establishments with employees that have a Dun & Bradstreet credit rating.

U.S. Establishment Longitudinal Microdata (USELM) File
A database containing longitudinally linked sample microdata on establishments drawn from the U.S. Establishment and Enterprise Microdata file (see separate citation).

U.S. Small Business Administration 504 Program
See Certified development corporation

USEEM
See U.S. Establishment and Enterprise Microdata File

USELM
See U.S. Establishment Longitudinal Microdata File

VCN
See Venture capital network

Venture capital
Money used to support new or unusual business ventures that exhibit above-average growth rates, significant potential for market expansion, and are in need of additional financing to sustain growth or further research and development; equity or equity-type financing traditionally provided at the commercialization stage, increasingly available prior to commercialization.

Venture capital company
A company organized to provide seed capital to a business in its formation stage, or in its first or second stage of expansion. Funding is obtained through public or private pension funds, commercial banks and bank holding companies, small business investment corporations licensed by the U.S. Small Business Administration, private venture capital firms, insurance companies, investment management companies, bank trust departments, industrial companies seeking to diversify their investment, and investment bankers acting as intermediaries for other investors or directly investing on their own behalf.

Venture capital limited partnerships
Designed for business development, these partnerships are an institutional mechanism for providing capital for young, technology-oriented businesses. The investors' money is pooled and invested in money market assets until venture investments have been selected. The general partners are experienced investment managers who select and invest the equity and debt securities of firms with high growth potential and the ability to go public in the near future.

Venture capital network (VCN)
A computer database that matches investors with entrepreneurs.

WAN
See Wide Area Network

Wide Area Network (WAN)
Computer networks linking systems throughout a state or around the world in order to facilitate the sharing of information.

Withholding
Federal, state, social security, and unemployment taxes withheld by the employer from employees' wages; employers are liable for these taxes and the corporate umbrella and bankruptcy will not exonerate an employer from paying back payroll withholding. Employers should escrow these funds in a separate account and disperse them quarterly to withholding authorities.

Workers' compensation
A state-mandated form of insurance covering workers injured in job-related accidents. In some states, the state is the insurer; in other states, insurance must be acquired from commercial insurance firms. Insurance rates are based on a number of factors, including salaries, firm history, and risk of occupation.

Working capital
Refers to a firm's short-term investment of current assets, including cash, short-term securities, accounts receivable, and inventories.

Yield
The rate of income returned on an investment, expressed as a percentage. Income yield is obtained by dividing the current dollar income by the current market price of the security. Net yield or yield to maturity is the current income yield minus any premium above par or plus any discount from par in purchase price, with the adjustment spread over the period from the date of purchase to the date of maturity.

Index

Listings in this index are arranged alphabetically by business plan type, then alphabetically by business plan name. Users are provided with the volume number in which the plan appears.

Index

Index

Index